Abnormal and Clinical Psychology

SECOND EDITION

Abnormal and Clinical Psychology

AN INTRODUCTORY TEXTBOOK

SECOND EDITION

Paul Bennett

Open University Press

Open University Press
McGraw-Hill Education
McGraw-Hill House
Shoppenhangers Road
Maidenhead
Berkshire
England
SL6 2QL

email: enquiries@openup.co.uk
world wide web: www.openup.co.uk

and Two Penn Plaza, New York, NY 10121–2289, USA

First published 2005
Reprinted 2006, 2007, 2008

Copyright © Paul Bennett 2006

A catalogue record of this book is available from the British Library

ISBN10: 0 335 21943 8 (pb)
ISBN13: 978 0 335 21943 8 (pb)

Library of Congress Cataloging-in-Publication Data
CIP data applied for

Typeset by RefineCatch Limited, Bungay, Suffolk
Printed in the UK by Bell & Bain Ltd., Glasgow
www.bell-bain.com

Contents

Illustrations

Boxes

Acknowledgements

This second edition would not have been possible without the invaluable help of Rachel and Emma. I am incredibly grateful to both of them for all the help and support they have given me.

I am grateful to the following people for their help, feedback and encouragement in writing the first edition of the book, in particular: Mandy Iles, Ceri Phelps, John Baird, Lucy Johnstone, Graham Turpin, Peter Kinderman, Stu Brooke, Lucie Byrne, Ian Sutherland, Mary Birchall, and of course the unknown people who have kindly allowed me to tell their stories.

PART I

Background and methods

1

Introduction

This chapter introduces a number of issues relevant to abnormal psychology, many of which are returned to in more detail later in the book. It starts by considering what is meant by abnormal psychology and how this relates to mental health. It looks at how these ideas have changed over time, before considering ways in which mental health problems are now conceptualized. The chapter then examines a number of factors that contribute to the development and differing presentation of mental health disorders, focusing on genetic, biological, psychological, social, cultural and familial explanations. Finally, it introduces the biopsychosocial approach, which attempts to integrate these various factors into one holistic model. By the end of the chapter, you should have an understanding of:

- Modern concepts of abnormality
- Historical concepts and treatments of abnormality
- Issues of diagnosis: the key diagnostic classification systems and their alternatives
- Models of the **aetiology** of mental health problems: genetic, biological, psychological, socio-cultural and systemic or familial
- The biopsychosocial approach.

Modern concepts of abnormality

This book focuses on factors that contribute to mental health problems and their treatment. Despite its title, it actually excludes many individuals who would be considered 'abnormal', if one were to define abnormal as 'to differ from the norm'. Indeed, a number of simple definitions of abnormality may be proposed, none of which captures the essence of what is generally meant by the term abnormal in the context of mental health problems:

- *Statistical abnormality* implies that people who are statistically different from the norm are 'abnormal': the further from the norm one is, the greater the abnormality. While this may be true, it does not necessarily imply the presence of a mental disorder. People who are rich or highly attractive, those who engage in dangerous sports or who significantly achieve in their career, all differ markedly from the norm. But none of these would be seen as having a mental health problem.

- *Psychometric abnormality* implicates abnormality as a deviation from a statistically determined norm, such as the population average IQ of 100. In this case, an IQ score less than about 70–75 may define someone as having a learning disability and suggests they will have some difficulties coping with life. However, the problems associated with a low IQ differ widely across individuals depending on their life circumstances. So, even when an individual is defined as psychometrically 'abnormal', this tells us little about their actual condition or problems. Furthermore, if one takes the other end of the IQ spectrum, a deviation of 30 points above the mean is generally not considered to be abnormal or to indicate the presence of mental health problems.

- *The Utopian model* suggests that only those who achieve their maximum potential within their lives are free of mental health problems. However, even those who propose this model (e.g. Rogers 1961: see Chapter 2) accept that only relatively few people truly achieve their maximum potential. Accordingly, this model assumes that the majority of the population deviate from their optimal mental state and experience some degree of mental health problems. Poor mental health may be considered the norm, not the exception.

- *The presence of abnormal or deviant behaviour* is perhaps the closest of the simple models to provide an understanding of abnormality as it relates to mental health problems, because it implies a deviation from normal behaviour in some 'negative' way. But as a single criterion it is inadequate. Not all people with mental health problems engage in deviant behaviour, and not all deviant behaviours are a sign of mental health problems: stealing a car and 'joy riding', which places many people in danger, may be considered deviant, abnormal, behaviour by many people, but it is not a sign of a mental health problem.

More complex models of abnormality in the context of mental health consider abnormal behaviour to be a sign of a mental health problem when

- it is the result of distorted psychological processes
- it causes or is the result of distress and/or is dysfunctional
- it is an out-of-the-ordinary response to particular circumstances.

A fourth criterion is that the individual may place themself in danger as a result of a distorted view of the world, although this is relatively infrequent even among those who may be thought of as having a mental health problem. These criteria can perhaps be summarized as the 'four Ds':

- deviance (from the norm)
- distress
- dysfunctional
- dangerous.

These generally hold true, but there are important exceptions. Paedophilia, for example, is not necessarily associated with personal distress, nor do people who engage in psychopathic behaviour experience remorse as a result of their actions.

Despite these criteria, which suggest some universality about what is and what is not a mental disorder, such judgements differ across social groups, societies and time. Definitions of mental disorders, deviance or abnormality are societally defined, not absolute. In some societies, people who see visions and speak to themselves are considered wise and to have special powers. In others, they are considered to have a **psychotic** illness and to require treatment. In Puerto Rico, for example, a belief that one is surrounded by spirits is common; in the UK, such beliefs would probably result in an individual being treated for schizophrenia. It is noteworthy that the activity of joy riding provided earlier as an example of abnormal behaviour will be considered so only by some groups in society; others may consider this to be acceptable, even admirable, behaviour.

In some cases, odd behaviour may result in an individual being labelled eccentric – a more benign label than 'mad' or 'mentally ill'. What label is assigned may vary according to the degree to which the individual differs from the norm, how many of their behaviours are abnormal, and the implications of these behaviours for others. However, the nature of the label assigned has powerful implications for the individual. Perhaps the most extreme example of this can be found in a classic study reported by Rosenhan (1973). In it, he taught a number of students to act as if they were psychotic – by stating that they heard one-word **hallucinations** – in an attempt to study the processes of diagnosis and hospitalization. As Rosenhan predicted, most students were admitted into the hospital and assigned a diagnosis of schizophrenia. What was perhaps more surprising was that when the students dropped their disguise and admitted to the hoax, many of their psychiatrists took this to be further evidence of their 'illness'. It took some weeks before some students were discharged from hospital, some with a diagnosis of 'schizophrenia in remission'.

Historical overview

Explanations of 'madness' have existed for much of our history, and have varied markedly over time. Early Chinese, Hebrew and Egyptian writings ascribed bizarre behaviours to demonic possession. By the first century BC, biological explanations were predominant. Hippocrates, for example, considered abnormal behaviour to result from an imbalance between four fluids, or humours, within the body: yellow and black bile, blood, and phlegm. Excess yellow bile, for example, resulted in mania; excess black bile resulted in melancholia. Treatment involved reducing levels of the relevant fluids through a variety of means. Levels of black bile, for example, could be reduced by a quiet life, a vegetarian diet, temperance, exercise and celibacy. Although radical treatment approaches such as bleeding or restraint by mechanical devices were evident at this time, the first-line treatment of both ancient Greeks and Romans was generally humane, and included providing comfort and a supportive atmosphere.

By the Middle Ages, the dominance of religious thinking and the clergy resulted in abnormal behaviour once more being considered the result of demonic possession. Treatment was provided by priests and involved attempts to rid the individual of the demon through prayer, chanting and administration of holy water or bitter drinks. More radical approaches included insulting the devil, starving, whipping or stretching the affected individual. Perhaps the most dramatic treatment of people supposedly possessed by demons was the Catholic Church's *Malleus Malforum* (witches' hammer) which provided a guide to the identification and treatment of witches, who were considered to blame for any ills that occurred within society. The manual stated that a sudden loss of reason was the result of demonic possession, and that burning was the one way to expel the devil.

Towards the end of the Middle Ages, power again shifted to the secular authorities and, as a result, biological theories of mental health problems once more became dominant. Institutions for the humane care of people with mental health problems were established. However, the initial success of these asylums led to them becoming overcrowded. As a result, the quality of care they provided gradually deteriorated and became increasingly inhumane. One of the most famous of these institutions was Bethlem Hospital in London. Here, patients were bound by chains and, in certain phases of the moon, some were chained and whipped to prevent violence. Restraints were cruel and inhumane. The hospital became one of the most popular tourist attractions in London, with people paying to see the crazed inmates: hence the term, Bedlam.

The care of mentally disturbed people changed once more in the eighteenth century. William Tuke in Britain and Phillipe Pinel in France re-established more humane treatments; although asylums remained, their inmates were able to move around them freely. Treatments included working closely with inmates, reading and talking to them and taking them on regular walks. Many people were released from hospital as a result of their improved condition. This 'moral approach' to the treatment of the insane was based on the assumption that if all those with mental health problems were treated with care, they would improve sufficiently not to need further care. However, as success rates did not achieve this optimistic level and it became clear that not all those treated in this way would be cured, prejudice against people with mental health problems increased. Long-term incarceration once more became the norm.

Somatogenic and psychogenic perspectives

In the early twentieth century, theories and treatments of mental disorders diverged into two approaches: the somatogenic and psychogenic perspectives. The *somatogenic approach* considered mental abnormalities to result from biological disorders of the brain. A highly influential advocate of this approach, Emil Kraepelin, constructed the first modern typology of abnormal behaviour (Kraepelin [1883] 1981). He identified various clusters of symptoms, gave them a diagnostic label and reported on their course. In addition, he measured the effects of various drugs on abnormal behaviour. Despite the rapid adoption of this approach, many of the interventions it led to, including remedies as diverse as tonsillectomy and **lobotomy** (see Chapter 3), proved ineffective. More recently, the biological approach has led to the development of powerful drugs used in the treatment of conditions as varied as depression, schizophrenia and anxiety disorders.

The *psychogenic approach* considered the primary causes of mental disorders to be psychological. It was initially led by an Austrian physician, Friedrich Mesmer. In 1778, he established a clinic in Paris to treat people with **hysterical disorders**. The treatment he provided, called mesmerism, involved the patient sitting in a darkened room filled with music. Mesmer then appeared dressed in a flamboyant costume and touched the troubled area of the individual's body with a special rod, a treatment that proved effective in a number of cases. Despite this, he was considered a charlatan and eventually banned from holding his clinics in Paris. Other leading advocates of the psychogenic approach, Jean Charcot and then Sigmund Freud, used hypnotism in the treatment of hysterical disorders. Treatment typically involved hypnotizing the patient before encouraging them to identify the factors precipitating the onset of their symptoms and to re-experience their emotions at this time, a process known as **catharsis**. Freud later rejected this method in favour of free association and the use of **psychoanalysis**.

The latter part of the twentieth century saw a revolution in the treatment of mental health problems and a strengthening of both the biological and psychological approaches. Humanistic therapies advocated by Carl Rogers added to those of Freud and the analysts, as did the behavioural and cognitive behavioural approaches led by theorists and clinicians such as Hans Eysenck and Stanley Rachman in the UK, and Aaron Beck and Donald Meichenbaum in the USA and Canada (see Chapter 2). Psychological therapies now provide effective treatment for conditions as diverse as schizophrenia, depression and anxiety disorders.

Care in the community

Modern treatments have allowed thousands of individuals with chronic mental health conditions, who would have required hospital care in the first half of the twentieth century, to be treated in the community. The change from hospital to community care began in the UK in the 1950s, and reached its peak in the 1970s. Over this time, many people who had spent years, perhaps decades, in hospital were gradually moved back into the communities from which they came. This was not an easy process, as by the time these changes in care were enacted, many of these people had become totally institutionalized. Their behaviour was determined by the rules of the hospital, which were generally more accepting of deviance than the general population. They had limited self-care skills, as they had not been responsible for cooking, cleaning and other elements of self-care for many years. Often the impact of living in an institution was more disabling than the condition for which they had originally been hospitalized, which could have been as non-problematic as vagrancy or being an unmarried mother. As a result of these factors, people discharged into the community had to be taught how to survive outside the hospital environment. Without this, many struggled after discharge, ending up as 'rotating door' cases; that is, as quickly as they were discharged into the community, they were readmitted to the hospital.

To avoid these difficulties, modern treatment seeks to minimize the use of hospital facilities and to maintain people within the community in which they live. People with relatively minor mental health problems, including most people with anxiety or mild–moderate depression, are treated by their general practitioner in a **primary care** setting. Even relatively serious mental health problems are usually treated through outpatient appointments or through visits to the individual's home by members of multidisciplinary teams of health care workers. Admission to hospital occurs only at times of crisis or exacerbation of problems, with discharge back to the community as quickly as is reasonably possible.

Multidisciplinary teams are often led by a consultant psychiatrist who has medical responsibility for the care of their patients. They and the more junior doctors are medical graduates who have specialized in the care of the 'mentally ill'. At the time of writing, they are the only members of the team who can prescribe medication, although many adopt other clinical interests and may be involved in the provision of other therapies. Nurses within the team have a specialized training in the care of people with mental health problems. They have a multifaceted role involving, among other things, monitoring an individual's progress, recommending changes in medication, providing basic psychological therapies and acting as advocate for the patient. More specialized professions may also be involved in the provision of care. Occupational therapists can help the individual develop or maintain life skills such as cooking or strategies for coping with stress. Clinical psychologists provide therapy for people with complex problems, and support others in their therapeutic work with **clients**, through **clinical supervision** and training in therapy skills. Finally, social workers help the individual deal with social problems such as lack of money or unemployment that may contribute to their problems.

Issues of diagnosis

The medical model

This book is generally organized around a set of diagnostic labels that can be ascribed to people with common mental experiences or who behave in similar ways – schizophrenia, depression, and so on. The approach is rooted in the 'medical model', which assumes that mental health problems are the result of physiological abnormalities, generally involving brain systems. The disorder is considered as an illness, much as other medical problems are, and is therefore treated with physical treatments that modify the underlying biological disorder, the most common of which involves drug therapy. The type of treatment given is determined by a diagnosis, which is itself determined by the presence or absence of various signs or symptoms. This assumes that people with mental health problems are experiencing a state divorced from that of 'normal' individuals: a mental illness.

Classification systems

The historical roots of this approach lie in the work of Kraepelin in the late nineteenth century. He described a number of syndromes, each of which had a common set of symptoms which differed from those of other syndromes, in a classification system of mental health disorders which later formed the basis of the World Health Organization's (WHO) International Classification of Diseases (ICD: WHO 1992). Indicating how such systems have struggled to accurately identify and classify mental health conditions, this is currently in its tenth revision. The American Psychiatric

Association (APA) devised its own classification system, known as the *Diagnostic and Statistical Manual* (DSM), which although having much in common with the ICD system, differs in a number of details. Like the ICD, it has changed over the years and, having first been published in 1952, is now in its fifth revision (**DSM-IV-TR**: APA 2000).

The DSM system is 'multi-axial'. That is, it allows an individual's mental state to be evaluated on five different axes:

- *Axis 1:* the presence or absence of most clinical syndromes, including schizophrenia, mood, anxiety, sexual and eating disorders.
- *Axis 2:* the presence or absence of stable long-term conditions, including personality disorders and learning disabilities.
- *Axis 3:* relevant information on the individual's physical health.
- *Axis 4:* psychosocial and environmental problems.
- *Axis 5:* rating of an individual's global level of functioning: from a score of 1 for persistent violence, suicidal behaviour or inability to maintain personal hygiene to 100, symptom-free.

These classification systems provide a number of benefits, not the least of which is an apparent simplicity – many would say an oversimplification – of definitions of mental health problems. In addition, they provide doctors and others using the system with a dichotomous outcome that fits the medical model of treatment. Whether an individual has an 'illness' or not will determine whether or not they are treated, admitted to hospital, and so on. Proponents of the medical model have argued that a reliable diagnosis that is consistent both within and between countries ensures that:

- any individual presenting with a set of problems will receive the same diagnosis across the world
- they will therefore receive the same treatment wherever they are in the world
- research that informs treatment focuses on the same condition wherever it is conducted.

Diagnoses are particularly important in relation to drug therapies where a diagnosis will determine which class of drugs is used to treat the presenting problem: antidepressants for depression, **major tranquillizers** for schizophrenia, and so on. An incorrect diagnosis will mean that incorrect medication is prescribed. In the case of research, incorrect diagnosis will result in unreliable results from any treatment trial and confuse rather than help the development of new treatments.

Before considering how well the present diagnostic systems have achieved these goals, it is important to indicate some fundamental scientific and philosophical implications to this approach:

- The model implies a dichotomy between normal and abnormal mental states. An individual either is mentally ill or is not. This dichotomy is becoming increasingly difficult to sustain. Many 'abnormal' states ascribed to the 'mentally ill' have now been found to occur to large numbers of the 'normal' population; many people who live normal lives and who have never been considered in any way 'abnormal', for example, report having heard voices in their head – almost a defining characteristic of schizophrenia.

- The model implies that when an individual is ill, they behave or experience mental events that are in some way abnormal and different from those of 'normal' people – an argument rejected by the findings of cognitive psychology. There is increasing evidence that while the thought content and behaviour of people with and without mental health problems may differ from the norm, the cognitive processes underlying them are essentially the same. This issue will be returned to on many occasions later in the book.

- The approach fails to recognize the experience of the individual; they are assigned a diagnosis and the diagnosis is treated, not the individual.

- The model implies that biological factors are primary in the development of mental health problems and that, therefore, biological treatments are also primary. This ignores findings that social and psychological factors appear to be critical in the development of mental health problems and that biological factors involved in mental health problems change as a result of changes in these factors (see Chapter 4). This also distracts from findings that pharmacological therapies may prove only partially effective in the treatment of a number of apparently biologically mediated conditions (such as schizophrenia, depression) and that psychological therapies have proved more effective than pharmacological interventions in the treatment of many conditions.

Diagnostic consistency

Despite the development of clear criteria for each disorder, making a diagnosis is not a clear-cut process. Even within countries, levels of agreement on diagnoses may be low. In the 1960s, Beck et al. (1962) reported only a 54 per cent agreement between four psychiatrists on the diagnoses assigned to 154 patients based on their own interviews. By the mid-1980s, things had not changed. Lipton and Simon (1985), for example, compared the diagnoses made by hospital doctors with those made by an inspection team in one psychiatric hospital. While 89 patients were assigned a diagnosis of schizophrenia by the hospital doctors, the review team assigned only 16 such diagnoses. Originally 15 patients were assigned a diagnosis of depression; 50 received this on review. The goal of DSM is to minimize the possibility of such errors, and each new edition strives to make the criteria for each diagnosis more clear-cut. Its latest version, DSM-IV-TR (APA 2000), has been tested by a number of clinicians to ensure consistency of diagnosis, although its reliability still has to be formally assessed.

What even a clear diagnostic system may have difficulty in dealing with are the biases that clinicians bring to the diagnostic process. Clinicians may reach varying diagnostic decisions as a result of the different information they obtain either as a result of their consultative style or the biases they bring to the assessment. Diagnoses may also be influenced by clinicians' knowledge of the disorder or any previous

diagnoses made by other doctors, the frequency with which the doctor has encountered the condition, and the costs and benefits of giving a diagnosis. Under conditions
of uncertainty, for example, clinicians may diagnose a condition that they feel is likely
to benefit the patient most and harm them least, even if it is wrong.

Diagnostic validity: schizophrenia

Validity of classification labels can also be difficult to achieve. Perhaps the most controversy lies with the diagnosis of schizophrenia. One of the important criteria for the
diagnosis of schizophrenia when first identified by Kraepelin was that it was a progressive and deteriorating condition with no return to levels of functioning achieved
before its onset. Bleuler (1908) later identified four fundamental symptoms of what
he termed the group of schizophrenias: ambivalence, disturbance of association,
disturbance of affect, and a preference of fantasy over reality.

Subsequent diagnostic systems have, until recently, adapted Kraepelin and
Bleuler's diagnostic categories, and attempted to develop increasingly clear and
unambivalent diagnostic criteria for various sub-types of the disorder. Until the
mid-1990s, DSM-III (APA 1987) identified four types of schizophrenia:

- *Simple:* progressive development of 'oddities of conduct', an inability to meet
  the demands of society, and withdrawal from everyday life.
- *Paranoid:* stable, paranoid **delusions**, frequently accompanied by auditory
  hallucinations that support these delusional beliefs.
- *Catatonic:* marked **psychomotor** disturbances, switching between extreme
  excitement, stupor and **waxy flexibility** in which the individual may be placed in
  a position and maintain it for several hours.
- *Hebephrenic*: changes in mood and irresponsible and unpredictable behaviour,
  accompanied by disorganized thought processes and speech that is frequently
  rambling and incoherent.

Unfortunately, this categorization disregarded any form of causal theory of linkages
between the various symptom clusters, and may have actually inhibited our developing
understanding of the nature and treatment of schizophrenia. A more useful classification system has now been derived from consideration of the causes of the symptoms
of schizophrenia.

Factor analysis of the signs and symptoms of the various sub-types of schizophrenia has identified three clusters of symptoms, known as **disorganized symptoms, positive symptoms** and **negative symptoms** (Liddle et al. 1994) that tend
to co-occur. The positive cluster includes hallucinations, delusions, disorganized
speech or positive thought disorder. Negative symptoms denote an absence of activation, and include apathy, lack of motivation or poverty of speech. Disorganized
symptoms include disorganized speech and behaviour, and flat or inappropriate
mood. These may have differing biological and neuropsychological foundations, and
prove a more useful way of categorizing the various schizophrenic-type disorders
(see Chapter 6).

Even if diagnostic criteria have both high reliability and validity, they carry some
negatives. Perhaps the most important is that the process of diagnosis implies the

individual has an 'abnormal' medical condition. They 'medicalize' individuals and place them within the remit of the mental health profession, sometimes quite inappropriately. Until 1973, homosexuality was listed as a sexual disorder within DSM, legitimizing attempts at treatment and legislation against homosexuals. Now, the criteria for personality disorder include within them a number of characteristics that many would argue should be considered as personality styles, not mental disorders (Widiger and Costa 1994: see Chapter 11).

Cultural relativity

One important goal of DSM is to identify and diagnose mental health problems in a similar way across cultures. The approach assumes that medical illnesses will present in a universal way throughout the world. Whether this is actually the case is questionable. Work by the World Health Organization (1979), for example, suggested that people who develop schizophrenia presented in the same way in nine different countries. Their study was, however, compromised by their use of the same set of criteria to determine whether people had or had not schizophrenia in each country, and their exclusion from this diagnosis of those who presented with differing symptoms. Accordingly, while these data suggested that some people do present with similar problems across the world, they could not exclude the possibility that other people with the same underlying problems may have presented in quite different ways.

One way in which people from different cultures have been found to present quite differently is through the reporting of negative emotions in terms of psychological or physical factors. Somatization involves the presentation or experience of physical problems rather than emotional ones: 'My heart is burning', for example, may imply depression or anxiety. This type of reporting is relatively rare in western cultures, and very common in Asian cultures and countries such as Turkey, possibly because such cultures disapprove of the strong expression of emotions, particularly negative ones (Chen 1995). Seeking help for physical problems therefore becomes an acceptable route for help with psychological ones. This cultural relativism indicates that it may be inappropriate to assume that a set of diagnostic symptoms may be appropriate for all cultures and at all times. This issue is considered in more detail in Chapter 4.

A social critique

In addition to the scientific critique, a number of social commentators have raised strong ethical objections to the medical model. Farber (1990), for example, argued that the medical model underestimates the individual's capacity for change, and consequently inhibits this capacity. At its most stark, the model assumes that unchangeable biological factors lead to psychological states that are distinct from the mental processes of 'normal' individuals. These may remit, either as a result of treatment or through natural recovery, but the individual is still prone to further episodes of the disorder.

Farber identified two types of medical models: one that assumes that mental disorders are the result of genetic and biological factors and the psychoanalytic model that assumes the adult disorders are the result of psychological, but biologically driven, mental structures that are set down in childhood and are unchangeable over the life course. He saw the ethical danger of the medical model in its legitimization of the health care professions', and therefore the state's, control of people considered as disordered. Perhaps the most extreme example of this has been various extreme left- and right-wing governments' use of psychiatry to control its dissenters. According to Farber, the medical treatment that people with mental health disorders receive prevents them from self-change and serves to reinforce assumptions that they are not capable of self-development and change. He also contended that such treatment is coercive, and that any attempt at self-change is viewed negatively and resisted: the patient who wishes to discontinue medical treatment, for example, is told that this is a sign that they are resisting treatment, and that they do not want to get 'well'. Only the experts know when people who are mentally ill are well enough to make authentic choices.

Having provided such a critique of the medical model, the astute reader may now be asking why the book is organized around a set of diagnoses which may be so seriously questioned. Their use here perhaps reflects both a dilemma and one of the reasons for their continued use by psychologists and others that reject the medical model. They provide a shorthand means of orienting the reader to the content of each chapter. However, their use does not imply an acceptance of the medical model – even the 'reality' of the conditions described within them is occasionally questioned – and while biological explanations for each disorder are provided, this certainly does not indicate that these are considered their primary cause.

Alternatives to the medical model

Any alternative to the medical model needs necessarily to differ from it on some important dimensions. In particular, it needs to do the following:

- consider there to be no dichotomy between abnormal and normal mental states
- consider the social and psychological processes that lead to and accompany any mental health problems
- make the affected individual (and not their diagnosis) the focus of any assessment and treatment
- at least consider non-pharmacologically based interventions as primary.

Two alternative approaches that address these issues, at least to some degree, are the dimensional approach and psychological formulation.

Dimensional approaches

While accepting the benefits of some form of diagnostic system, a number of commentators (e.g. Widiger and Costa 1994; Clark et al. 1995) have challenged the categorical approach adopted by the DSM. In DSM, diagnoses are based on the presence of a number of symptoms, such as poor sleep, feeling depressed, and so on. It provides a categorical classification: the individual either has the symptoms, and therefore a disorder, or does not. A dimensional approach rejects this all-or-nothing approach and the assumption that the mental states of people with a mental health problem are distinctly different from those of the 'normal' population. Proponents of the dimensional approach argue that categorical models of psychopathology are challenged by a number of problems, including:

- co-morbidity, in which a single person might satisfy criteria for more than one diagnosis, such as schizophrenia and affective disorder
- heterogcneity, in which two people with the same diagnosis can present with entirely different patterns of symptoms (see, for example, the discussion of diagnoses of schizophrenia in Chapter 6)
- the provision in DSM of a subcategory of 'not otherwise specified', which seems to be a mechanism for assigning diagnoses that do not really 'fit'.

The dimensional approach suggests that people who are now diagnosed as having a mental disorder may better be considered to be at the extreme end of a distribution of normality, not categorically different from others. Many of us have been anxious or depressed at one time or another, felt like not engaging with the world, or slept poorly. These experiences are not unique to people with a depressive disorder. Whether or not we consider them to be problematic is dependent on their frequency and the intensity to which they are experienced. Dimensional approaches adopt this approach, and suggest it is the degree to which problems are experienced, not merely their presence or absence, that determines whether or not an individual has a mental health problem. This approach fits well with increasing findings that some 'symptoms' of mental health disorders, such as hearing voices, are relatively common within the general population, and may never lead an individual to seek help or impair their everyday living (see Chapter 6). As a compromise with the diagnostic approach, proponents of the dimensional system suggest that if an individual scores above a threshold score, based on the severity and frequency of their experiences, they may be given some form of diagnosis.

The dimensional approach has a number of strengths. In particular it highlights which aspects of a person's life are problematic and for which they may require some form of help, and avoids 'forcing' the presenting problems into a diagnostic category into which they do not easily fit. What it does not address is the processes through which an individual developed their problems or an understanding of the factors that maintain them. This level of assessment is provided by the psychological formulation.

Research box 1

Hankin, B.L., Fraley, R.C., Lahey, B.B. et al. (2005) Is depression best viewed as a continuum or discrete category? A taxometric analysis of childhood and adolescent depression in a population-based sample, *Journal of Abnormal Psychology*, 114: 96–110.

The authors note that the 'types versus dimensions' issue – whether mental health problems are 'a matter of degree or kind' – is of considerable importance in developing and evaluating a diagnostic system such as DSM. They note that current psychiatric diagnostic structures consider depression to be a qualitatively distinct disorder; that is, the experience of depression is categorically different from any other mental state. By contrast, a number of researchers have argued that depression may best be viewed as a deviation from 'normal' affective experience – the dimensional view. The goal of the reported research was to evaluate the extent to which major depression among young people, as defined by DSM-IV, is categorical or dimensional by using a form of statistical analysis developed by Meehl which allows the validity of these differing models of psychopathology to be assessed.

Method

The study sample comprised 845 young people aged between 9 and 17 years from Atlanta, USA. The age distribution of the sample was uniform across the age range. Part of the sample was drawn from a larger study known as the Georgia Health and Behavior Study. A second sample taken specifically for this study was also obtained. For both studies, a stratified random sample of households was selected from the population of addresses in Georgia. Researchers then visited each house to screen for the presence of eligible individuals. If a young person lived in the house, they and a carer were asked to participate in the study. If they agreed, they were paid a small sum and interviewed in the family home. The overall response rate was about 74 per cent.

Clinical interview

The young people and carer (who were asked about their child) were interviewed using the investigational version of the Child and Adolescent Psychopathology Scale (I-CAPS), which assessed all of the symptoms of major depression as defined by DSM-IV. Respondents rated the I-CAPS items on a 4-point response scale that ranged from 1 (not at all) to 4 (very much). They rated each symptom according to how well it described their (or their child's) emotion or behaviour, how often such symptoms occurred, and how serious the symptom was over the past 12 months. Several questions tapped each symptom. For example, for the symptom of fatigue or loss of energy, the authors averaged the following I-CAPS items: (a) sluggish and tired; (b) tired out by little things; (c) sluggish and not energetic; and (d) had less energy than usual.

Statistical procedures

One way in which the authors addressed the dimension versus category issue was by analysing the interview data using tan analysis known as Maximum Covariance-Hitmax (MAXCOV or MAXCOV-HITMAX). This analyses the covariance between two variables as a function of a third variable. The function characterizing these conditional covariances is called a MAXCOV function and its shape depends on the status of the latent variable (in this case each symptom of depression) under study. If the latent variable is categorical (i.e. depressed individuals had the symptom, non-depressed individuals did not), the MAXCOV curves tend to have a mountain-like peak. If the latent variable is continuous (i.e. if the symptoms were present to a lesser or greater degree in both depressed and non-depressed individuals), the MAXCOV curves tend to resemble a flat line.

Results

MAXCOV analyses were conducted on the nine symptoms of DSM-IV major depression. Overall, the derived MAXCOV curves were more similar to those expected under a dimensional model than a categorical one. Figure 1.1 illustrates the average MAXCOV curves for data based on youth (a) and parent reports (b). The shaded regions of the graphs show the range of MAXCOV functions that should be observed under if the various symptoms were dimensional in nature. The spiked line represents the type of graph that would imply the symptoms were categorical. The data (marked with dots) clearly follow the pattern expected in a dimensional patterning of symptoms.

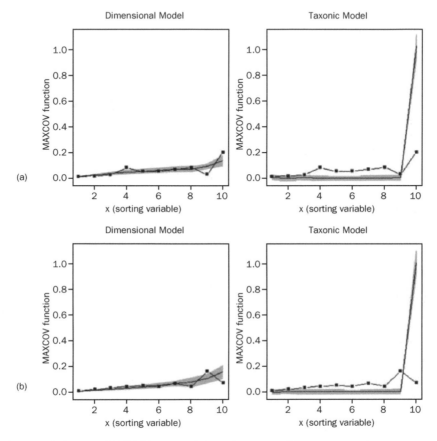

Figure 1.1 Average MAXCOV curves, (a) youth reports, (b) parent reports

Discussion

The findings of this study suggest that depression in young people is continuously, not categorically, distributed. This finding held for both youth and parent reports, and for all DSM-IV depressive symptoms, and across gender. The current diagnostic system and nomenclature, used by DSM-IV and all other diagnostic systems, assume that disorders, such as depression, are categorical. The authors' findings, as well as other studies, argue against DSM's categorical emphasis for depression in children, adolescents and adults. The authors therefore concluded that dimensional approaches may be valuable for studying and assessing depression. Indeed, if individual differences in depression really are continuous, but researchers continue to use categorical measurement models, the empirical study of depression may suffer.

Psychological formulation

Diagnostic criteria are helpful in determining the pharmacological treatment that may benefit an individual. They are of less benefit to therapists using other treatment approaches. Here, any diagnostic label simplifies and reduces the information it carries to a degree beyond that which is useful. At its most basic, a clinician adopting a biological model of mental health disorders would aim to give a diagnostic label to a cluster of symptoms, and then provide the drug treatment related to that condition. The exact nature of the problems an individual faces or how they are expressed will be of only secondary interest. A person with schizophrenia who is hallucinating will be treated with drugs that stop hallucinations; the nature of the hallucinations will not influence the drug treatment given. A depressed individual will receive antidepressants regardless of the nature and causes of their condition.

A quite different view is taken by **psychotherapists**. From their perspective, the nature of the hallucinations or conditions that led to a period of depression are of paramount importance, and are the focus of any intervention. The diagnostic label assigned has little impact on the type of treatment given. A psychotherapist working with someone who is experiencing hallucinations, for example, would want to know their exact nature and content so they can apply specific techniques tailored to the specific needs of the individual to help them cope or respond to them more appropriately.

Psychological formulations attempt to identify the processes that led to and maintain the problems an individual is facing. These may be external: negative life-events, rape, bereavement, and so on. They may be internal: distorted interpretations of the world, **hyperventilation** leading to panic disorder, and so on. They may be short-term or longer-term sequelae to childhood events such as sexual abuse or poor parental relationships. The goal of the therapist is to identify the specific factors that have led to and are maintaining the problem for the particular individual they are working with at the time. These factors then become the target for future interventions.

A formulation is an explanatory hypothesis about the nature of the clinical problem. This usually reflects the theoretical orientation of the therapist. For a cognitive therapist, it will address the nature of faulty cognitions or maladaptive behaviours, how they were established, what maintains them, and so on. A Freudian analyst would be concerned with how an individual's behaviour is linked to unconscious processes and their developmental history. It includes a number of 'best guesses' and the causes of the problem, what is maintaining it, and how it may be resolved. The formulation has two main functions: first, to guide the therapist in what to do, and second, to help establish criteria for evaluating the intervention: to determine what the goals of therapy are and how success or failure in achieving these goals is measured. Formulations are not static. They may well change in the light of new evidence gained over time, as will the focus and form of any intervention.

Formulations are guided by theory. These guide the questions asked by a therapist and the formulation of the problem they establish. This, of course, is both a strength and a weakness. A strength because they allow the therapist to select, in a relatively parsimonious way, from the myriad of potential contributors to a problem those most likely to be relevant. A weakness because they may focus the therapist too exclusively on what they deem to be important aspects of a client's experience and too little on what may actually be important, but seem irrelevant to the therapist as a result of their theoretical 'blinkers'. On this basis, some have argued that good therapists are aware of several aetiological models and can either integrate them into a meaningful synthesis or identify which are relevant to particular clients.

The aetiology of mental health problems

There are a number of diverse literatures focusing on risk factors for mental health problems. These do not act independently, but combine in some way to influence the risk an individual has for developing a disorder. The rest of this chapter provides an introduction to each type of explanation. The following chapters examine the issues in more detail in relation to specific disorders.

- *Genetic models* consider how genetic factors influence an individual's risk of developing a mental health disorder. Genetic factors have been implicated in conditions as varied as schizophrenia, **Alzheimer's disease** and depression.

- *Biological models* focus on biochemical processes, usually involving chemicals known as **neurotransmitters**, which mediate mood and behaviour. They also consider how damage to the brain can result in a number of mental health disorders.

- *Psychological models* focus on the internal mental processes that influence mood and behaviour. Unlike the genetic or biochemical models, there is no single explanatory paradigm. Instead, there are a number of psychological explanations of mental health disorders, the best known being psychoanalytic, humanistic, behavioural and cognitive behavioural.

- *The socio-cultural approach* focuses on the role of social and cultural factors in mental health disorders.

- *Systemic models* focus on the role of smaller social systems, frequently the family, in which the individual is situated. Disorders are considered to be the consequence of stressful or disordered interactions with families.

- *The biopsychosocial approach* attempts to integrate these various factors into a holistic causal model. This approach suggests that genetic or other biological factors may increase an individual's risk of developing a mental health disorder. However, whether the disorder will actually develop depends on whether the 'at risk' individual encounters factors such as social or family stress and/or whether they have the coping resources to help them cope with such stresses.

Genetic models

With the exception of egg, sperm and red blood cells, each of the approximately 100 trillion cells of the body contains two complete sets of the human genome: one set from the individual's father, the other from their mother. Each genome comprises 23 pairs of **chromosomes**. Each set of chromosomes carries the 60,000–80,000 genes that contribute to both the physical and psychological characteristics of the individual.

Each gene in a set of matched genes affecting the same processes is known as an allele. The instructions in the sets of genes from each parent may be the same or quite different, for example, blue versus brown eyes. Where the alleles are the same, the individual is described as homozygotic. Where they differ, they are termed hetero-zygotic. The expression of these 'competing' genes is determined by whether the genes are dominant or recessive. Some genes, such as those determining the eye colour brown, are described as dominant. When linked to a gene with other instruc-tions they are expressed. Recessive genes are expressed only when matched with other recessive genes with the same instructions. The development of most mental health disorders is associated with recessive genes. If they were the result of dominant genes, their expression in each generation would be virtually guaranteed, resulting in continuing disadvantage and limited chances of reproduction.

Genetic studies of the aetiology of mental health problems have done so using several methods. Family studies measure whether those with genotypes that are more or less similar to the affected individual are at different risk for the disorder. If there is a genetic linkage in a disorder, one would expect someone with an identical genetic make-up (a **monozygotic (MZ) twin**), to be more likely to develop the disorder than a non-identical or **dyzygotic (DZ) twin**, who has roughly 50 per cent of genes in common, who in turn would be more at risk than a cousin or aunt with even less genetic similarity. Many family studies focus on the degree to which both MZ and DZ twins develop the same disorder. Where more MZ than DZ twins are concordant for the disorder, this is taken to imply some level of genetic risk. This approach has a number of limitations. Critically, not only do closer family members share more genes, they also share a more common environment. MZ twins, for example, tend to be treated more similarly than DZ twins. Any concordance for a condition may therefore be attributable to a shared environment rather than shared genes.

In an attempt to separate out environment from genetic factors, a number of studies have examined concordance rates in twins brought up in differing environ-ments, usually as a result of adoption. This method typically identifies MZ twins separated close to birth and examines whether they are or are not concordant for the condition under examination. It is assumed that because the separated twins have a common genetic make-up and different environments, any concordance for the condition under examination is the result of genetic factors. However, there are a number of reasons why any **heritability coefficient** determined by this method may not prove totally accurate. First, even twins that are separated have factors other than their genes in common. If nothing else, they have shared the same prenatal experiences that may determine risk for various disorders.

Another factor that can result in overestimation of genetic risk involves any gen-etic influence on the behaviour of a child, particularly where they are 'difficult' or 'problematic', instigating similar reactions from those caring for them. As a result, separated children may experience both a common genetic heritage and a common family background, despite their separation. Where the family reaction is one that itself contributes to risk for emotional or behavioural problems, this may result in high levels of concordance between twins being attributed solely to genetic factors using traditional analytical methods.

This kind of interpretive problem has resulted in new methodologies in this type of study. Rather than assume the nature of the environment in which the person lives, they have now begun to measure genetic, environmental, social and other life stresses. These data are then subject to statistical modelling techniques that allow the investigators to determine the degree to which both genetic and environmental factors contribute to the development of the disorder under investigation.

This type of research is able to identify the strength of any genetic linkage, but not isolate the nature or location of the gene or genes involved. Work on the human genome now permits this more fundamental research. Most disorders are likely to result from a number of genes (that is, they are **polygenic**), and in some cases problems may arise from the absence of a gene, rather than its presence. There is evidence, for example, of a gene locus on chromosome 4 that may be protective against alcohol problems. Whatever the genetic linkages found, there is a general consensus that genes, at most, influence risk for a particular mental health disorder. It is also important to note that while risk for a particular disorder may be increased as a result of genetic factors, many if not most people with the disorder will not carry the relevant gene. Eighty-nine per cent of individuals diagnosed with schizophrenia, for example, have no known relative with the disorder. Not carrying the gene that increases risk for a disorder does not mean that you are immune to that disorder.

Despite this lack of absolute determinism, genetic technologies carry a number of social consequences. At its most extreme, social and political groups such as the Eugenics movement in the late nineteenth and early twentieth centuries advocated the use of selective birth control and sterilization to rid the nation of 'national and racial degeneracy' that was thought to result in mental illness, feeble-mindedness, criminality, alcoholism and sexual promiscuity. Ideas such as this gained widespread political support in the mid-twentieth century, and were used by Hitler to justify the mass extermination of people with mental health problems or learning difficulties.

The potential for testing for genes that confer risk of both physical and mental health problems also carries a number of challenges to modern society. At present, screening programmes for genetic risk of disorders such as cystic fibrosis, Huntington's disease, and breast, ovarian or colo-rectal cancer are now being widely instituted. These testing programmes bring with them a whole series of ethical dilemmas. The UK testing programme for genetic risk of breast cancer, for example, rates people as being at low (population), moderate or high risk of developing breast cancer. We are now learning how a generation of men and women cope with knowledge of their risk of this disease. So far, it seems that it is not easy, and testing seems to evoke high levels of health anxiety among vulnerable individuals in both the short and the long term (Brain et al. 2002). At a societal level, the likelihood of genetic screening for medical insurance and even job selection is increasing. Will genetic testing result in an underclass that will find it difficult or impossible to get insurance, buy a house, or even hold a job? Time will tell.

Biological models

Biochemical explanations of mental health problems focus on the biological processes underlying mood and behaviour. Both are regulated by brain systems, whose actions are mediated by neurotransmitters. These systems allow us to perceive information, integrate that information with past memories and other salient factors, and then respond emotionally and behaviourally. Disruption of these systems as a result of inappropriate neurotransmitter actions results in inappropriate perception, mood and behaviour. The exact nature of the systems and the neurotransmitters involved in different mental health problems are considered in more detail in Chapter 3 and in each of the chapters in Part II of the book.

Other biochemical processes have been implicated in some conditions. Hormones such as melatonin appear to be involved in the aetiology of seasonal affective disorder, a type of depression considered in Chapter 8. Other disorders may be the result of problems in the architecture of the brain. Some of the symptoms of schizophrenia, for example, may arise from degeneration or failures of brain development that lead to fundamental errors in information processing, and disordered thoughts and behaviour. Alzheimer's disease results from progressive neuronal damage evident through the deterioration of cognitive functioning in later life.

Biochemical models are often considered to be in opposition to psychological explanations: mental health problems are seen as either psychological in nature or to have a biological cause. A more appropriate way of thinking about the two approaches is that they provide different *levels* of explanation, somewhat analogous to the levels of explanation provided by physics and chemistry. Biochemical processes underpin all our behaviour at all times. The act of writing this sentence is activating numerous sensory, motor and neuronal processes, all of which are mediated by chemical transmissions. But understanding these fundamental processes explains only part of the behaviour: it does not easily account for the motivation for writing the sentence, the process of mental construction of the sentence, or, indeed, my mood as it was written. To understand these, one needs to address the psychological processes driving the behaviour. In this way, both biochemical and psychological explanations of the behaviour are 'correct'.

Psychological models

In contrast to the biochemical and genetic models where most scientists and practitioners believe in a common process through which mental health disorders arise, there are many psychological models. There are many 'fringe' therapies, most of which have little or no theoretical rationale and whose practice may be somewhat dubious. There are also a number of 'mainstream' theories of mental health disorders and related treatments which largely reflect the development of more general psychological theories over the past century. The first psychological therapy to be practised was psychoanalysis in the beginning of the twentieth century, with Freud and his followers being the leaders of this movement. This was the dominant therapy for a number of years and is still practised, albeit with some modifications, over 100 years after its inception.

Psychoanalytic principles were rejected by two therapies, both of which began in the 1950s and 1960s. **Behaviour therapy** (e.g. Wolpe 1982) rejected the notion of psychic processes influencing mood and behaviour and the unscientific nature of psychoanalysis. Its practitioners argued that behaviour is largely controlled by external events, and based its principles on the 'hard' science of classical and **operant conditioning**. At a similar time, humanistic therapies (Rogers 1961) rejected psycho-analysis, not because of its psychic nature, but because of the *nature* of its psychic phenomena. In contrast to psychoanalysis which assumes that behaviour and mood are influenced by past traumas, humanistic therapies are based on the assumption that behaviour is driven by aspirations towards the future, with the potential of **self-actualization** available to all. Therapy was designed to help the individual achieve their potential, not to resolve the traumas of the past.

The most widely practised therapy is a derivative of behaviour therapy, known as cognitive or cognitive behavioural therapy (Beck 1977). It considers our thought processes, or cognitions, as the prime determinant of behaviour and mood. It makes no assumptions of past trauma or future aspirations and is not based on a model of personality as are psychoanalysis and humanistic therapies. Instead, it focuses on how the thoughts we have at any one time influence mood and behaviour. It assumes that the cognitions that result in mental health problems are somehow 'faulty' and dysfunctional. Therapy focuses on changing them to more functional and less inappropriate ones through a number of educational and therapeutic strategies. It also retains a strong behavioural focus: distorted cognitions, for example, may be challenged by behavioural experiments designed to illustrate errors of thinking. Each of these models is described and discussed in more detail in Chapter 2 and the chapters in Part II.

Psychotherapy versus pharmacotherapy

It is possible to argue that, because biochemical processes underpin behaviour at a fundamental level, altering the levels of neurotransmitters that influence mood through pharmacological processes provides the most direct and effective form of treatment of mental health disorders. While there is some logic in this argument, it certainly does not hold for all cases and it implicitly assumes that psychological therapy does not influence the fundamental biological processes underpinning mental health disorders. This is not the case: there is a powerful reciprocity between the two forms of treat-ment. Psychological treatments cause changes at the biochemical level: otherwise they would not alter mood. Similarly, **pharmacotherapy** alters cognitions and behaviour, the primary targets of most psychological interventions.

One argument favouring the use of psychological therapy is that many of the drugs prescribed are effective only while they are being taken. Once a course of drugs has finished, their action stops and the individual's biochemical status, and hence mood and behaviour, may revert to the state it was in before the treatment was commenced. To prevent this, many people are now being prescribed drugs such as antidepressants for much longer than was initially considered to be necessary. In contrast, some have argued that psychological therapy prepares the individual to cope with the stresses they face now and in the future, making them at significantly less risk of relapse once therapy is terminated.

Both arguments may be overstating the case. There is good evidence that many people maintain good mental health following cessation of pharmacological treatments, although the reasons for this may be more psychological than pharmacological. A depressed individual who has withdrawn from family and social life, for example, may benefit from a drug treatment that helps them re-engage with people and enjoy life more. The pleasure gained from this may, itself, increase levels of the neurotransmitters that prevent depression (serotonin and norepinephrine: see Chapter 3) and maintain them in a healthy state once drug therapy is stopped. If they had not re-engaged so positively, the risk of relapse may have been much greater.

It is also true that some individuals do not benefit from psychological therapies, or they relapse following successful psychological treatments. They may find it difficult to adopt a psychological approach to reducing their problems. They may forget, be unable to use the new skills they have learned, or feel so overwhelmed by circumstances that they once more experience a deterioration in their mental health. For this reason, some advocates of psychological therapy suggest the need for 'booster' sessions some months after the completion of therapy to help maintain a positive mental state.

Both pharmacological and psychological therapies are effective in treating most mental health conditions. Psychological therapies seem to be more effective than drug treatments in treating conditions such as anorexia, panic disorder and some sexual problems. In contrast, although psychological treatments are increasingly being used in the treatment of schizophrenia, the mainstay of treatment remains drug therapy. The relative effectiveness of the two forms of treatment for some conditions such as depression is still hotly debated (see Chapter 8). This debate is returned to in more detail in Chapter 3 and in each of the chapters in Part II of the book.

Socio-cultural models

All the models so far discussed assume that mental disorders arise as a result of problems within the individual, be they genetic, biochemical or psychological. By contrast, the socio-cultural approach assumes that external, social factors contribute to their development. Socio-cultural factors include a wide range of influences, from the family to wider socio-economic factors, some of which were identified in the British Psychiatric Morbidity Survey (Jenkins et al. 1998). This revealed increased rates of depression or anxiety among women, those living in urban settings, unemployed people, and those who are separated, divorced or widowed. Psychoses were more prevalent among urban than rural dwellers. Alcohol dependence was nearly twice as common among people who were unemployed than among those who were employed: drug dependence was five times greater among those who were unemployed than those in jobs. People who are members of ethnic minorities or in the lower socio-economic groups are also more likely to experience depression, non-specific distress, schizophrenia or substance abuse problems than those in other sectors of society (Ulbrich et al. 1989). A number of, sometimes competing, theories to explain these differences have been proposed, each of which is discussed in more detail in Chapter 4.

Socio-economic status differences

- *Social drift:* this approach suggests that high levels of mental health problems among the lower socio-economic groups are the result of affected individuals developing a mental health problem, which renders them less economically viable. They may be unable to maintain a job or the levels of overtime required to maintain their standard of living, and drift down the socio-economic scale. That is, mental health problems precede a decline in socio-economic status.

- *Social stress:* this approach assumes that living in different socio-economic conditions results in differing levels of stress: the lower the socio-economic group, the higher the stress. That is, the stresses associated with social deprivation result in mental health problems.

- *Lack of resource model:* similar to the social stress model, this model assumes that those who are economically deprived have fewer resources to help them cope with any life demands they face. These resources may be economic, psychological, social or environmental. Poor mental health is thought to be a direct consequence of a lack of resources.

Gender differences

- *Willingness to express distress:* one theory is that gender differences in the **prevalence** of mental health problems are more apparent than real, and result from women's willingness to visit their doctor and complain of mental health problems. This theory has not been substantiated (Weich et al. 1998).

- *Role strain:* an alternative hypothesis suggests that women encounter more role strain and **spillover** between the demands of work and home than men. The resultant stress places them at increased risk for stress and mental health problems.

Minority status

- *Confound with social class:* this model suggests that the apparent relationship between minority status and mental health problems is spurious. It suggests that people in ethnic minorities largely occupy the lower socio-economic groups. That they also have higher levels of mental health problems is a result of this association, not of being a member of an ethnic minority *per se.*

- *The effects of prejudice:* this suggests a more direct link between ethnic minority status and mental health. Mental health problems may result from the additional stresses, including overt and covert prejudice, experienced by the members of minority ethnic groups.

- *Cultural transitions:* a further source of stress may be the tension experienced as individuals adopt or reject some of the norms of their own or other cultures. Both may result in feelings of alienation, rejection by members of differing cultures, and consequent mental health problems.

Social and cultural factors may also influence the type of problems people report, and how acceptable, or unacceptable, they are within a society. Some cultures positively affirm what might be considered hallucinations and signs of mental disturbance in others. People from different cultures may also report what we define as mental health problems in many different ways – and seek different treatments for them. Asian people, for example, often report mental distress framed as physical symptoms and their first line of treatment may involve herbs or other natural physical treatments. These issues are considered in more detail in Chapter 4.

Thinking about . . .

Most strategies for reducing the burden of mental health disorders have focused on treatment once they have developed. The importance of social and cultural factors points to another way of addressing the issue: to reduce the social, economic and cultural factors that may contribute to poor mental health. This could be done in a number of ways – anti-bullying campaigns in schools, providing cheap or free crèches so that young single mothers can access recreational facilities or have a break from child care, ensuring economic security for people in old age – that on the surface have little to do with mental health, but may actually have a significant impact on it.

So, if you had carte blanche, how would you change the society in which we live to maximize the mental health of the general population?

Systemic models

A more enclosed system that impacts on mental health is the family. Family system theorists consider the individuals within a family to form an interacting system. Each has a reciprocal influence on those around them. The behaviour of individuals within these systems, and the communication between them, can lead to individual members behaving in ways that seems 'abnormal'. Perhaps the most extreme form of family dysfunction occurs when a member of a family sexually abuses a child within it. Levels of sexual abuse are very high among women who seek psychological therapy for conditions as varied as depression, anxiety and anorexia (Jaffe et al. 2002).

One of the first models of family interactions in relation to mental health focused on people with schizophrenia. Brown and colleagues (e.g. Brown et al. 1972) were the first to identify a family characteristic, now termed high negative expressed emotion (NEE), in which individuals who were prone to episodes of schizophrenia fared particularly badly. Individuals in families who were particularly critical, hostile or overinvolved had a higher rate of relapse than those who did not experience this environment. Reducing levels of NEE resulted in a dramatic reduction in relapse rates. A second, more complex, family system is thought by family therapists to contribute to the development of anorexia in young women (Minuchin 1974). These and other family models of pathology are considered in more detail in Chapter 4 and other chapters in Part II of the book.

Biopsychosocial models

Evidence reviewed so far in this chapter has shown that living in a stressful environment, however defined, does not inevitably lead to mental health disorders, nor does carrying the gene for a particular disorder. Both sets of factors place an individual at increased *risk* for the disorder. Whether or not this potential is realized is the result of an interaction between these, and other, factors. An individual who has some genetic risk for depression, for example, is more likely to develop the disorder if they live in a stressful environment than if they never encounter such conditions. Someone without genetic risk for the disorder is less likely to become depressed, but they are not invulnerable. If they encounter certain environmental conditions or adverse life-events, they may still become depressed. The same factors may work by protecting an individual against risk of mental health problems. Some genes may protect against disorders. Similarly, some social environments may help an individual to develop resilience and to cope effectively with stress.

For most mental health problems, vulnerability to, or resilience against, mental health disorders is determined by a number of factors, some of which include

- *biological factors:* genetic make-up, viral infections, injuries
- *psychological factors:* childhood trauma, maladaptive cognitive responses to environmental events
- *social/environmental factors:* socio-economic stress, the quality of personal relationships, the availability and quality of social support.

It is noteworthy that the boundaries between each of these dimensions of risk is somewhat fuzzy, and even this simple categorization fails to take account of the interaction between them. People in the lower socio-economic groups, for example, may be more prone to viral infections or injury. People with more or less adaptive coping styles, as a result of previous family experiences, may respond to potentially stressful events in differing ways. Nevertheless, they indicate the key risk dimensions involved in the aetiology of mental health problems.

Diathesis-stress model

The risk factors have been placed into a simple biopsychosocial model known as the diathesis-stress model. In it, diathesis refers to the biological vulnerability an individual carries: stress involves any event or condition that interacts with this vulnerability to influence risk for the expression of the disorder. The lower the individual's biological vulnerability for a particular disorder, the greater the stress needed to trigger that disorder: the higher their biological vulnerability, the less stress is needed. The nature of both the biological vulnerability and the type of stress that triggers the problems is likely to differ across disorders. In the chapters in Part II of the book, each of the various factors that contribute separately to risk of mental health problems is identified and discussed. Note that in most cases, these risk factors can be combined into this diathesis-stress/biopsychosocial model, even when this is not explicitly stated in the chapter.

Some commentators (e.g. Johnstone 2000) have argued that while the diathesis-stress model acknowledges the role of stress in the aetiology of mental health problems, it still adopts an essentially medical model of mental disorders, as it suggests that stress acts as a trigger to provoke an underlying biologically determined disease process. In other words, the role of stress is relatively minor, and the role of biological factors remains primary. It does not accept that mental health problems can result from the experience of stress or negative events alone, without there being a biological propensity to respond to stress in a way that leads to mental health problems. As such, it maintains the medicalization of what is an essentially psychological phenomenon. Despite these reservations, the diathesis-stress model remains the pre-eminent overarching model of the development of mental health problems.

Chapter summary

1 Defining 'abnormality' in relation to mental health disorders usually involves distorted cognitive processes, distress or dysfunction, and an unusual response to particular circumstances. It may also involve the individual being a danger to themselves, but this is relatively infrequent.

2 Diagnosis of mental health conditions, such as those within DSM and ICD classifications, largely follows the biological or disease/medical model of mental health established by Kraepelin in the late nineteenth century.

3 According to this model, accurate diagnosis is important to ensure consistent treatment and research in relation to mental health disorders.

4 Diagnosis is typically based on the presence of a number of symptoms, including hallucinations, poor sleep, low mood, and so on. This categorical approach leads to a dichotomous diagnosis process in which the individual either has or does not have a disorder.

5 Dimensional approaches state that the experiences of individuals with mental health disorders differ in degree from those of the 'normal' population but are not categorically different.

6 Psychotherapists generally find diagnostic labels to be unhelpful. Instead, they focus on the nature of the factors that contribute to and maintain the individual's problems. These become the focus of therapy.

7 A number of factors may contribute to the development of mental health disorders: genetic and biological factors, socio-cultural and family factors, and individual psychological factors. No one approach is able to explain the development of any one disorder, and most result from a combination of factors: the biopsychosocial approach.

For discussion

1 Should we limit the types of people with mental health disorders who are treated in the community? Should people such as psychopaths or so-called 'predatory' paedophiles thought to be at risk of reoffending be permitted to live or be treated outside hospital or prison?

2 What would you think if told an individual is 'schizophrenic'? How might this alter your interpretation of their behaviour or your responses to them?

3 Some severe psychiatric conditions such as Huntington's disease in which the individual develops increasing muscular spasticity and mental deterioration leading to death in middle age can be predicted by genetic testing. It cannot be prevented, but those who have the gene for the condition may choose not to have children and pass the gene on to them. Would you want to know as a young person whether you carry the gene?

4 If offered the choice of medication or psychological therapy for a mental health problem, which would you choose – and why?

Further reading

Bentall, R. (2004) *Madness Explained: Psychosis and Human Nature*. Harmondsworth: Penguin.

Johnstone, L. (2000) *Users and Abusers of Psychiatry: A Critical Look at Psychiatric Practice*. London: Routledge.

Schaler, J. (ed.) (2004) *Szasz under Fire*. Chicago: Open Court Publishers.

2

The psychological perspective

There have been four major schools of psychological therapy since the late nineteenth century, each based on very different theories of the aetiology of mental health problems:

- *Psychoanalytic:* views childhood trauma and the unconscious as the causes of problems in adulthood.
- *Behavioural:* considers psychopathology to arise from conditioning processes.
- *Cognitive or cognitive behavioural:* assumes that the critical element of psychopathology is inappropriate, dysfunctional, cognitions. This approach to understanding and treatment can be considered to have gone through two distinct generations. Examples of both are considered in the chapter.
- *Humanistic:* considers psychopathology to be the consequence of deviation from the drive towards **self-actualization**.

To understand the rationale behind the therapies, it is necessary to understand the theories of aetiology upon which they are based. This chapter therefore provides both an overview of the theory relating to the development of mental health problems that underpins each therapeutic approach and some of the strategies they use to achieve change. By the end of the chapter you should have an understanding of:

- Key psychological models of the aetiology of mental health disorders: psychoanalytic, behavioural, cognitive and humanistic
- Some of the widely used interventions based on these models.

The psychoanalytic approach

Freud

Sigmund Freud (e.g. Freud 1900) was one of the first clinicians to explore the role of childhood factors and the unconscious in explaining problems of adulthood. His work, conducted in the late nineteenth and early twentieth centuries, was highly innovative and based on his formulation of the unconscious. These insights were largely derived from cases he saw in his practice in Vienna.

Freud considered personality to have three basic components: the **id**, **ego** and **superego**:

- The *id* is driven by the basic instincts of sex and aggression, which Freud considered the basic motivating forces of human behaviour. It operates under the pleasure principle. That is, it seeks to maximize immediate gratification. It is greedy, demanding and has no natural self-control.

- The *ego* is the realistic component of personality. It operates under what Freud termed the reality principle and also works to maximize gratification, but within the constraints of the real world.

- The *superego* contains the individual's morals and societal values. It acts as the conscience, creating feelings of guilt if social norms are violated.

These basic personality components are in a continuous struggle to control the individual. Sexual desire, for example, is rooted in the id. However, its immediate urge for sexual gratification is tempered by the superego's moralistic statements that such urges are a sin, and the ego's realistic consideration of the costs and benefits of various actions. The outcome of these competing processes is usually some form of socially acceptable sexual behaviour. However, should the id gain control, the likely outcome is rape or some other violent act.

Five stages of psychosexual development

According to Freud, the development of personality occurs through a five-stage sequence of psychosexual development. The first stage, known as the *oral stage*, is characterized by receiving gratification through oral means: sucking, crying or exploring objects with the mouth. The oral stage occurs between the ages of 18 and 24 months. At this time, children have only the id. Accordingly, the stage is characterized by an inability to delay gratification, and selfish and demanding behaviour. Immediately following this is the *anal stage*, which continues until the child is between 42 and 48 months old. At this time, children achieve gratification through anal means. Freud argued that the process of toilet training is the first time the child becomes aware of their actions on other people, and learns to modify their behaviour to gain gratification from them. If the child satisfies parental demands, it receives praise and approval. If not, it experiences disapproval. Realistic expectation of these outcomes is the beginning of the ego development.

The third stage of psychosexual development is the *phallic stage*. This continues through to the age of about 5 or 6 years. In this stage, the superego begins to develop as a result of the child's experiences of sexual conflicts and the means by which they are resolved. According to Freud, boys in the phallic stage develop incestuous wishes towards their mother, driven by the urges of the id. These desires are known as the oedipal complex. By this stage, the ego is able to judge the realistic consequences of these actions and recognizes that they would meet the disapproval of their rival, their father. The boy also recognizes that if he were to enter into open rivalry with his father, he would be defeated. He begins to fear that his father will castrate him to prevent him from becoming a future rival for his mother – a phenomenon known as castration anxiety. The boy resolves this dilemma by identifying with his father. This permits him, at least symbolically, to make love to his mother as does his father. As part of this identification process, he begins to adopt the father's beliefs and values. He begins to develop a superego.

The young girl develops her superego in a similar way. Freud suggested that when a girl enters the phallic stage she begins to recognize that she is different from boys. She experiences penis envy: she feels incomplete or inadequate as a result of her lack of a penis. She also believes that if she makes love with her father she will 'possess' her father's penis, at least temporarily. In addition, if she is made pregnant, she may bring a penis into the world by giving birth to a boy. In this way, the girl's basic sense of inferiority leads her to develop incestuous desires for her father. These feelings are resolved by the girl identifying with her mother, allowing her to symbolically make love to her father when her mother does so, and leading her to adopt her mother's moral values: her superego.

The fourth stage of development is the *latency stage*. It continues until puberty. During this stage, the individual channels their sexual and aggressive urges through age-appropriate interests and activities such as sports and hobbies. The final stage is the *genital stage*. This begins in puberty and continues throughout life. In it, the individual is driven by the two basic motivating forces: sex and aggression. Our bodies generate both sexual (libido) and aggressive energy. Healthy individuals discharge this energy through socially appropriate channels: sexual intercourse with age-appropriate adults, sports, career progression, and so on. Where people fail to find such outlets, energy builds until it can no longer be contained and is released in an uncontrolled fashion, guided by unconscious influences. To prevent the inappropriate discharge of these forces, the individual diverts or blocks them through a variety of unconscious mechanisms.

Defence mechanisms

According to Freud, mental health problems are the result of either ego anxieties or the defence mechanisms it sets up to prevent these anxieties becoming conscious. Ego anxieties frequently relate to troubling experiences experienced in early childhood. These can lead the individual to become fixated at a particular developmental stage, and to behave in ways appropriate to that stage during adulthood. Such behaviour forms an unconscious defence against anxiety caused by the experience and its memories. Its function is to prevent recognition of the hurt that was experienced at the time. Individuals may also regress to previous levels of psychosexual functioning through which they have successfully passed as a result of stresses in adulthood. The stage to which they regress is influenced by the severity of the stress, the similarity of the current stressor to problems experienced in previous stages, and the success with which each stage was passed through. Some of the repressed or fixated personality types in adulthood are summarized in Table 2.1.

A number of other defence mechanisms that do not involve regression may also be used to counter ego anxieties. The most basic Freudian defence mechanism is repression. In this, threatening material is unconsciously and actively blocked from awareness to prevent it from entering consciousness. Some other defence mechanisms are outlined in Table 2.2.

A classic case involving ego defence mechanisms was that of Little Hans. This young boy had an extreme fear of horses, which Freud suggested indicated a fear of

Table 2.1 Some adult personality characteristics associated with a failure to progress through Freud's development stages

Stage	Associated problems
Oral	Depression, narcissism, dependence
Anal	Obstinacy, obsessive-compulsive disorder, sadomasochism
Phallic	Gender identity problems, antisocial personality
Latent	Inadequate or excessive self-control
Genital	Identity diffusion

Table 2.2 Some Freudian defence mechanisms

Defence	Definition	Example
Repression	Blocking threatening material from consciousness	An adult who cannot recall being abused as a child
Denial	Preventing threatening material from entering consciousness	A parent who cannot accept the death of their child
Projection	Attributing one's own unacceptable impulse or action to another	Someone who denies their homosexuality, and considers that homosexuals are constantly making sexual approaches
Displacement	Changing the target of an unacceptable impulse	'Kicking the cat' instead of whoever caused anger or upset
Reaction formation	Expressing the exact opposite of an unacceptable desire	A person who is considering ending a relationship, but continues to show strong affection for their partner
Sublimation	Expressing an unacceptable impulse in a symbolic manner	An individual with a strong drive for unattainable sexual relationships focuses their attention on achieving in their career or sport
Conversion	Expressing painful psychic material through symbolic physiological symptoms	A soldier who finds it unacceptable to shoot others, develops paralysis in his hands
Undoing	A repetitive action that symbolically atones for an unacceptable impulse or behaviour	Repeated washing of hands following an extramarital affair

his father: that is, castration anxiety. Hans's defence mechanism was to displace the fear of his father to more acceptable objects, horses, which were large and strong like his father, and acted as symbolic representations of him. Another condition which Freud identified as a defence mechanism was bed wetting, which he considered a symbolic form of masturbation. Its perpetrators expressed their underlying sexual urges by converting them to a more acceptable physical symptom.

Criticisms of Freudian theory

Freud broke new ground to develop a complex model of human development. His contribution to the development of theories of personality and psychopathology is without question. However, his theories are beset with the problems of any theory, particularly one so encompassing, developed before our present rigour of science and its empirical process ware established. Even though a number of researchers (e.g. Dollard and Miller 1950) have developed experimental studies to assess Freud's theory, it is beset with such fundamental interpretive problems that whatever the results of such studies, they provide little evidence to support or disprove Freud's theories. Because processes such as id drives, ego defences and fixation are abstract and supposedly operate at an unconscious level, there is no way of knowing for certain whether or not they are occurring. In addition, the theory provides few, if any, testable hypotheses. If an individual engages in a set of behaviours predicted by the theory, it may be considered supported. However, if they do not, the theory is not challenged or falsified, as it could be hypothesized that they did not do so as a consequence of the individual's defence mechanisms.

Some other criticisms of Freudian theory include the following:

- Freud's theories were based on interpretation of information gleaned from a relatively small and specific group of patients, in particular, middle-class Viennese women. The ability to generalize from these cases to the wider population is questionable.
- Freud's views on women were misogynistic and based on cultural attitudes of his time, rather than a true scientific perspective.
- Freud's theory changed over time, sometimes without clear rejection of previous versions. It is therefore difficult to know which theory should be tested.

Freud's contemporaries and descendants

Jung

Psychoanalysis now encompasses a diverse set of theories, all of which see childhood experiences or the unconscious as the driving forces of behaviour, but differ considerably from Freud's original theory. Carl Jung ([1912] 1956), for example, was seen by Freud as the 'Crown Prince' of psychoanalysis. However, his beliefs became less and less congruent with those of Freud, and he broke away to develop his own analytical psychology. Jung considered Freud's emphasis on sex as the major motivator of human behaviour to be simplistic and reductionist. By contrast, Jung emphasized the psychological and spiritual influences on behaviour. He also disagreed with Freud's notion that personality and adult neurosis are established in early childhood. He suggested that people are motivated by future goals rather than by past events. While Jung believed that our unconscious was developed through individual experiences, he also considered part of it to reflect universal themes and ideas. He considered this 'collective unconscious' to be biologically based and evident through symbols and myths common to all races and times – a sort of race memory that influences our reactions to the present world. Jung considered that the goal of personal development is to expand conscious awareness through the ego making contact with the unconscious. The ultimate end of this process is union between the conscious and the unconscious, although this is rarely completely achieved. In this, Jung was close to the humanistic school, considered later in the chapter.

Klein

A generation later, Melanie Klein (1927) focused on the psychological processes of young children, placing emphasis on the relationship between mother and child in the first few months of life. She considered psychic structures to evolve from human interactions rather than biologically derived tensions. She also considered people to be driven by a need for human contact, and that conflicts and anxieties experienced by children arose from their relationships with adults rather than from sexual impulses. According to Klein, the mother is initially represented by the child as 'part-object' of the breast, and is experienced as either a 'good object' or a 'bad object'. She is good when the needs of the baby are met through feeding, bad when these needs are not met. The baby responds to the bad object with feelings of terror, insecurity and destructive rage.

Over time, the baby begins to see his or her mother as a more realistic 'whole object' rather than the part object of the breast, and to understand that good and bad can coexist in the same person. This revelation leads to a deep sense of disappointment and anger that a loved person can be bad as well as good. There is a primitive sense of loss and separation now the possibility of complete fusion with the 'good mother' is no longer possible. There may also be a sense of guilt that the child may be responsible for the end of this relationship. Klein did not suggest that this formed a coherent and conscious set of beliefs. Rather, she considered the awareness of the child to be fragmented and dreamlike. According to Klein, at times of stress or distress, adults may revert to this childhood understanding of the world or people as either good or bad – a process known as splitting. This is more likely to occur if the individual has been traumatized as a child, and may adversely influence adult relationships.

The practice of psychoanalysis

Despite the differences between the various psychoanalytic theories, they all share a number of therapeutic goals, including gaining insight into the nature of the original trauma and bringing troubling material to consciousness so the individual can cope with it without the use of ego defence mechanisms. By removing the need for the ego to engage its defence mechanisms, the symptoms may be 'cured'.

Freudian psychoanalysis

Freud experimented with a number of therapeutic techniques, including hypnosis and a form of suggestion in which he sat behind the patient, held their head in his hands, exerted mild pressure, and suggested that the troubling material would be 'released' when he released the physical pressure. He then stopped using these methods because he came to believe that the patient–therapist relationship was critical to good psychotherapy. Instead, he used the process of free association. This involved the client speaking aloud whatever came to mind, with the therapist making no conscious effort to monitor or censor their speech. To facilitate the process, the client lay down so they were unable to see the therapist's face and not be guided by any facial expressions resulting from their flow of thoughts.

Through free association, clients may remember actual childhood events. However, given the ego's use of defence mechanisms, such revelations are unlikely. Instead, the therapist is guided more by what the client does *not* say than what they do. Absences, where the client is unable to think of a word or finish a sentence, or abrupt changes in topic may indicate the proximity of sensitive issues. Errors, in which a client may mean to say one thing and actually say something different (the so-called 'Freudian slip') may also be indicative of sensitive issues that the therapist would then explore more deeply

Another technique used by Freud involved the interpretation of dreams, which he considered 'the Royal Road to the unconscious'. An example can be found in Freud's (1900) interpretation of the dream of one woman which included images of flowers as table decorations for a party. When asked to freely associate to the elements in her dream, she associated *violet* with *violate*, a word carrying both sexual and aggressive connotations. Freud interpreted the flowers as symbols of fertility and the birthday as a symbol of an impending birth or pregnancy. Accordingly, her dreams symbolized her desire to become impregnated by her fiancé.

A third source of information about childhood experiences can be found through examination of the client's relationship with their therapist. Freud suggested that a client may develop strong positive or negative feelings towards their therapist, a process known as **transference**. Positive transference may result in the client becoming dependent on the therapist or even falling in love with them. Negative transference includes resentment and anger. According to Freud, these feelings reflect those held for significant others earlier in the client's life. If they fall in love with their therapist, for example, this may mean they have failed to resolve an earlier oedipal conflict. Freud used the transference process in two ways: first, as a diagnostic process, and second, for resolving earlier conflicts by 'working through' the transference process. Freud contended that once having achieved insight, the individual may still need to work through the issues raised by an understanding of the trauma. In a process known as catharsis, the individual is encouraged to expresses the emotions previously damped down by the defence mechanisms.

Contemporary psychoanalysis

Classical psychoanalysis was extremely lengthy. Freud preferred to see clients six times a week, and even 'mild' cases were seen for three sessions a week. In addition, because psychoanalysis used free association to bring insight into the clients'

problems, and there may be weeks or even months between sessions in which significant insights were attained, analysis took many months or even years. More recent
versions of psychoanalysis tend to be shorter, typically lasting fewer than 25 sessions.
They have three distinct phases: beginning, an active phase, and termination. Beginning involves assessment, developing a therapeutic alliance and preparing the client
for therapy. In the active phase, the therapist determines the direction of therapy and
the issues addressed within it. Strategies may involve the use of interpretation of
current feelings in terms of past experiences, and the elicitation of emotions experienced at the time of any trauma. Issues of transference are deliberately minimized, for
example, by discouraging client dependence. The end of therapy is a negotiated
process, in which issues of loss and separation are considered and dealt with.

Most people who take part in psychoanalysis in Britain do so by seeking private
therapy. Not surprisingly, most find it a useful experience:

> I found the process remarkably useful. No one to judge you, no one to comment –
> you don't even have to talk to anyone. It provides a space for me without pressure
> to explore issues that are important to me that I cannot speak – quite literally – to
> anyone else about. I feel my unhappiness stems from my poor relationship with
> my parents – and this has provided me with a means to explore this, and
> disentangle some of the issues that confuse me about this time.

Behavioural approaches

The roots of behaviour therapy lie in the theories of classical and operant conditioning
developed in the early to mid-twentieth century by Pavlov ([1927] 1960) and Skinner
(1953). Although differing considerably in their explanations of behaviour, both
theories held that:

- behaviour is determined by external events
- past learning experiences drive present behaviour
- behavioural change can be achieved through direct manipulation of external
  events; there is no need to explore or change the individual's 'psyche' or 'inner
  world'
- the principles of learning are subject to scientific exploration and hold across all
  species: studies in rats and mice inform our understanding of human behaviour.

Classical conditioning

Classical conditioning was initially explored by Pavlov's work on the salivatory
response of dogs. During his experiments he noticed that, on occasion, his dogs would
salivate *before* being given food, a response he termed 'psychic salivation'. Exploration
of the process through which this occurred led to the discovery of what is now termed
classical conditioning. Pavlov considered salivation to be a basic reflex to the presence
of food that required no learning: an unconditioned response to an unconditioned
stimulus. The novel element of Pavlov's work was that he noted that other salient

stimuli present at the time of the elicitation of the unconditioned response sub-sequently come to elicit the same behaviours: in learning theory jargon, an initially neutral stimulus became a conditioned stimulus and elicited a conditioned response, identical to the unconditioned one. Learning the association between the neutral stimulus and unconditioned stimulus may take several pairings. Repeated presenta-tion of the conditioned stimulus in the absence of the unconditioned stimulus will result in a gradual fading of response to it, a process known as extinction.

The link between these processes and emotional disorders was made when it became clear that conditioning experiences may influence emotional as well as behavioural responses to stimuli. Behavioural explanations of phobias, for example, assume that they result from a conditioning experience in which the inappropriately feared object or situation was associated with the experience of fear or anxiety at some time in the past. The conditioned stimulus subsequently evokes a conditioned fear response. The conditioning process can be so powerful when acute fear is experi-enced, that it may require only one conditioning experience to result in a long-term fear response that is difficult to extinguish. Being in a car crash, for example, may result in a phobic reaction to being in a car, and subsequent avoidance of being in a car or driving. This response has three components: a *behavioural element* involving avoidance or escape from the feared object, a high state of *physiological arousal* evident through a variety of symptoms including physical tension, increased startle response, tremor or sweating, and the *emotion* of anxiety and fear.

The most famous early example of the conditioning of a phobic response was Watson and Rayner's (1920) conditioning of 'Little Albert'. Eleven-month-old Albert was a hospitalized child who had a fear of furry animals induced through the experi-mental association of loud noises at the same time as being given a rabbit to play with. Over time, he developed a conditioned fear (phobic reaction) to the presence of furry animals, a fear which generalized to similar-looking stimuli including balls of cotton, white fur and a Santa Claus mask. Sadly, although Albert was subsequently allowed to play with the toys in the absence of the loud noises, he was discharged from hospital with his phobia intact – an outcome now deemed ethically unacceptable.

Operant conditioning

In contrast to the reflexive behaviour associated with classical conditioning, operant conditioning attempts to explain behaviours that are voluntary and purposive. Skin-ner's basic premise was that behaviour that is rewarded (reinforced) will increase in frequency or be repeated; that which is not rewarded or is punished will decrease in frequency or not be repeated. His definition of a reinforcer was behavioural: that which is observed to increase the frequency or strength of a behaviour. He made no assumptions about internal mediating processes such as liking, pleasure or enjoyment.

Skinner distinguished between two types of reinforcer: *primary reinforcers*, such as food and water that have innate biological significance, and *conditioned reinforcers*, that have become associated with these primary reinforcers through a complex pro-cess of classical conditioning. In this way, reinforcers such as attention and social interaction, which are associated with the primary reinforcer of food and drink for young children, take on reinforcing properties in themselves.

Operant processes have been implicated in the development of a number of mental disorders. Lewinsohn et al. (1979), for example, considered depression to be the result of an individual being removed from a reward system they had previously occupied. Conversely, Seligman (1975) considered depression to arise from a failure to avoid negative stimuli within the environment. His theory stemmed from a series of studies in which animals received electric shocks they were either able or unable to avoid. Animals that could avoid the shocks seemed to experience no ill-effects. Those that could not, exhibited what Seligman termed learned helplessness. They were apathetic and, even when they were in conditions where they could avoid shocks, made no attempt to do so. This was seen as analogous to some elements of depression.

Combining classical and operant conditioning

The classical conditioning model of phobias so far considered is adequate in its description of the process of acquisition of anxiety and phobias. However, it is less able to explain why they are maintained over long periods, as repeated exposure to the feared object or situation in the absence of any negative consequences should lead to a reduction of anxiety through the process of extinction. Mowrer's (1947) two-factor theory combined both classical and operant process to provide an explanation of this phenomenon. He noted that once a phobic response is established through classical conditioning processes, the affected individual tends to avoid the feared stimulus. This has two consequences. First, it prevents the classical conditioning process of extinction, as the individual does not experience the conditioned stimulus under conditions of safety. Second, because avoidance itself produces feelings of relief (it is reinforcing), the avoidance response is strengthened by operant conditioning processes. In this way, anxiety is potentially maintained over long periods.

Behaviour therapy

Behaviour therapy assumes behaviour to be governed by the laws of learning: disorders arise as a consequence of specific learning experiences and can be treated using the same principles. The type of therapy it engendered differed fundamentally from psychoanalytic therapies:

- It is directive: the therapist actively treats the client using methods based on learning principles.
- The goal of therapy is behavioural change, not personality reconstruction.
- Behaviour therapy is generally shorter than other forms of therapy.
- Interventions are condition-specific: there is no common therapeutic goal such as 'insight' or catharsis.

Classical conditioning-based interventions

Classical conditioning-based interventions have primarily been developed for the treatment of anxiety disorders including phobias. Techniques include systematic desensitization and flooding. The primary goal of both methods is to weaken and eliminate the conditioned fear response and to condition less aversive emotional associations to the previously feared object.

Systematic desensitization

Systematic desensitization involves the client being repeatedly exposed to a series of stimuli, initially somewhat distant from, and then increasingly like, the feared stimulus, while in a state of relaxation. At the beginning of the intervention, the individual is taught to relax using standardized relaxation procedures. At the same time, they construct a hierarchy of stimuli that progressively resemble the feared object or situation.

Therapy proceeds through a series of stages. In each stage, the client first relaxes and is then exposed to a stimulus within the hierarchy, starting with the most distant stimulus from the feared object or situation. On each occasion, they remain in the presence of the stimulus until they feel fully relaxed. This process is repeated several times until the stimulus no longer elicits an anxiety response. They then progress along the hierarchy, repeating the same procedures until they are able to cope in the presence of their feared stimulus or situation. These procedures are thought to have a number of conditioning effects. First, they extinguish the fear response to the stimulus. Second, by being relaxed in the presence of the feared stimulus, a process of counter-conditioning is established which conditions a state of relaxation to the previously feared stimulus (see Box 2.1).

Box 2.1 Ruth's spider phobia: an example of systematic desensitization

The image of an individual with a spider phobia is a person who, when they see a spider, becomes anxious and jittery, and usually asks for someone to remove it from their presence. But for Ruth, the problem was much greater. From spring to autumn her fear of spiders was so strong that she would not enter a room without someone first checking that there were no spiders in it. Similarly, she would not go into the hall or stairs of her house without a family member making checks. As a consequence, she remained restricted to one room in her house, unless there was someone in the house to check 'safety'. If she saw a spider, she hyperventilated, panicked, and would run as far away as possible from it.

Ruth entered a programme of systematic desensitization in the spring. She was taught to relax using a programme of deep muscle relaxation. At the same time, she developed a hierarchy of stimuli to be used in a desensitization programme. She also determined her desired end-point of the programme, which was to be able to enter a room where there may be a spider without undue anxiety and to be able to kill any spiders she noticed in the room. The initial hierarchy she and her therapist constructed included the following stimuli:

1 A pencil drawn line, resembling the leg of a spider.
2 A pencil oval, resembling the body of a spider.
3 A pencil-drawn sketch of a spider.
4 A picture of an actual spider.
5 A dead spider in a jar.
6 A dead spider on a nearby table.
7 A live spider in a jar.
8 A live spider constrained by the therapist.
9 A live, unconstrained spider.

Ruth worked through this hierarchy over a period of weekly meetings. On each occasion, she used the relaxation techniques and was exposed to the relevant stimulus within the hierarchy on several occasions. Each time, she remained in the presence of the stimulus until she was fully relaxed and calm. The stimulus was removed and then re-presented, and the procedure repeated, until there was good evidence that she was fully relaxed at that stage in the hierarchy and she felt confident to move to the next stage.

Once she was able to be relaxed in the presence of a live spider, Ruth began a second hierarchy:

1 Walking into a room with a constrained spider in it.
2 Walking into a room with the possibility of an unconstrained spider in it, remaining by the door.
3 Walking into a room in which she knew there was a spider and killing it with a heavy object.
4 Walking into a room with the possibility of an unconstrained spider in it, and being able to sit down in the room for several minutes.

Not all people with a phobia of spiders would require such a gradual or extended treatment programme. Nevertheless, this programme provides an example of the use of systematic desensitization.

Flooding

Systematic desensitization provides a gradual approach to the treatment of phobias and is user friendly, but relatively slow. Flooding involves a diametrically opposite approach. In it, clients are exposed directly to their most feared stimulus and encouraged to remain with it until they no longer experience any fear, a process that may take an hour or more. The therapy is based on the principles of *habituation*. We cannot sustain a fear response for prolonged periods of time – physical exhaustion results in a diminution of a fear response even under circumstances that initially provoke high levels of fear. Accordingly, even though initial levels of anxiety or fear may be extremely high, if the client remains in the feared situation sufficiently long, they will experience a reduction in anxiety to normal levels. This low level of fear is then associated with the previously feared stimulus. Repeated flooding is usually necessary to fully extinguish some fear responses. Flooding can be an effective form of therapy

(Wolpe 1982). However, many therapists prefer to use desensitization methods as they do not provoke the high levels of client distress associated with flooding. Nor do they run the risk of the recipient leaving before extinction of the fear is achieved, something that may actually add to their problems as avoidance of the feared stimulus is once more reinforced.

Emerging problems

While behavioural therapies achieved (and still do achieve) some notable successes, by the 1970s, conditioning theories of the acquisition of fear and other emotional responses were finding it increasingly difficult to account for emerging experimental and clinical findings (Davey 1997):

- Many people with a phobia were unable to identify any traumatic conditioning incident.
- Many common phobias were to relatively benign stimuli (such as spiders).
- Many common phobias were to stimuli rarely if ever directly encountered by most individuals (for example, snakes).
- By contrast, rates of phobias to many frequently encountered and potentially frightening stimuli (such as traffic) were relatively low.
- Phobias tend to 'run' in families.

Seligman (1970) provided one explanation of these findings. He suggested that some basic anxieties may be biologically 'hardwired'. This has survival advantages, in that avoidance of small, quick and possibly dangerous animals is likely to be of enormous benefit to individuals who live in a dangerous and wild environment. These instinctual reactions become problematic when we no longer live in these conditions, but because they are hardwired, we find it difficult to stop responding in this basic way.

While Seligman's theory gave some support to the behavioural model, other findings made it increasingly difficult to maintain purely behavioural models of fear acquisition. One of the most problematic findings stemmed from cases such as the individual whose initial fear of beetles generalized to a number of other stimuli including Volkswagen cars and the Beatles pop group (Carr 1974). While behavioural theory acknowledged the potential for the generalization of a fear response to stimuli that were similar to the phobic stimulus, this was based on the physical characteristics of the related stimuli. What was clear from cases such as this was that the associations between feared stimuli were of a semantic nature: the development of fear was based on cognitive processes.

Social learning theory

At the same time as these problems in explaining clinical phenomena became evident, other theorists were beginning to explore the role of cognitive processes in directing behaviour. One influential theory to stem from this period was social learning theory (Bandura 1977). This suggested that we can learn fear responses without having direct experience of the feared object ourselves. Instead, fear is learned from observation of other people's responses, through a process known as **vicarious learning**.

People with a fear of flying, for example, may develop this fear as a result of seeing air crashes on the television or hearing accounts of people describing their fear experienced during turbulence. Social learning theory also provided a cognitive explanation of why phobias run in families. Again, this involves learning fear from observation of other family members: children may learn a fear of spiders, for example, from observation of their parents' responses to them. Bandura also provided a cognitive explanation of the therapeutic mechanisms of systematic desensitization and flooding: reductions in anxiety were the result of the individual's increasing confidence – or self-efficacy as Bandura termed it – in their ability to cope with the presence of the feared object.

Cognitive approaches

Further pressure to integrate cognitive elements into behavioural interventions stemmed from the emerging cognitive therapies of Aaron Beck (1977) and Albert Ellis (1977). Both clinicians assumed that our cognitive response to events – not the events themselves – determines our mood, and that mental health problems are a consequence of 'faulty' or 'irrational' thinking. Emotional disorders result from *misinterpretations* of environmental events. These thoughts impact directly on our mood, our behaviour and our physiological state. Ellis referred to this process as the *A-B-C theory* of personality functioning, where:

- A refers to an activating event: something that triggers off an emotional response.
- C is the emotional or behavioural reaction to that event.
- B refers to the intervening cognitive processing, the individual's beliefs about the event that always occur between A and C.

Beck referred to the thoughts that drive negative emotions as automatic negative assumptions. They come to mind automatically as the individual's first response to a particular situation and without logic or grounding in reality. Despite this, their very automaticity means they are unchallenged and taken as true. He identified two levels of cognitions:

- *Surface cognitions:* thoughts we are aware of – the automatic negative assumptions. We can access them and report them relatively easily. They are thought to influence emotions, behaviour and levels of physiological arousal.
- **Cognitive schema** (plural *schemata*): underlying our surface cognitions is a set of unconscious beliefs about ourselves and the world that influence our surface cognitions.

Beck hypothesized that our cognitive schemata develop in childhood. Some may affect an individual in their day-to-day life. Beck suggested, for example, that people with an avoidant personality hold the fundamental belief that 'If people get close to me, they will discover the real me and would reject me – that would be intolerable.' As a consequence, they continually avoid others to prevent this catastrophe occurring.

Other schemata, such as those underlying depression, may impact only at certain times in their life.

To explain why people with some negative self-schemata are not in a permanent state of emotional distress or sadness, Beck suggested that some vulnerable individuals are able to override negative schemata for much of the time. However, when they encounter stressful circumstances in adulthood, in particular those that echo previous childhood experiences (divorce or separation, for example, reflecting earlier experiences of parental rejection), underlying negative schemata are activated, influence their surface cognitions, and lead to depression or other emotional disorders.

Evidence of the activation of underlying schemata at times of low mood can be found in experimental work reported by, for example, Miranda and Gross (1997). They studied the different reactions of people with and without a history of depression when asked to rate themselves on a series of self-descriptive adjectives either before or after listening to sad music designed to lower mood. They found no differences in self-ratings on measures taken before listening to the music. However, after listening to the sad music, participants who had previously experienced a period of depression endorsed more negative attributes than those who had not been depressed, a finding they interpreted as indicating the presence of underlying negative cognitive schemata that were activated by the induction of low mood (see Chapter 8, for more discussion of this issue).

A network model of emotions

Beck and theorists like him provide a rich clinical view of the types of thoughts associated with a variety of mental health problems – many of which are considered later in the book. At a more fundamental level, a number of psychologists have considered the cognitive architecture in which factual and emotional memories are stored and are recalled under various circumstances. One key early approach was developed by Collins and Loftus (1975). Their theory of semantic recognition suggested that we store bits of information (concepts) within a network. Associations between concepts are formed through their co-occurrence in time. The concept 'car', for example, may be associated with semantic nodes of 'fast', 'exciting', 'sporty', and so on. Such associations would result in a positive attitudes towards cars and their use. Associations between car and concepts such as 'dirty', 'polluting', 'expensive', or 'gas-guzzling' may be associated with a more negative attitude towards cars.

The relevance of this type of network to psychopathology occurred when Bower (1981) suggested that such networks may not only involve semantic information but also include emotional associations. Accordingly, emotions such as excitement, love, and so on (depending on the use the car had been put to!) may be associated with the concept of 'car'. Bower suggested that these emotional concepts are established at the same time as other encoding takes place. In this way, they form a key element of any network. Being in a car going at speed and having fun would begin to build a network involving car–fast–fun. Such a network would encourage the use of cars – and using them as a means of enjoyment as well as simply travelling from A to B. By contrast, the network of associations that may occur following a car crash may result in associations between the following nodes: car–fear–injury. Such a network, which could be established very quickly, may be typical of that held by someone who feels anxious when in a car, following a car accident.

Once networks are established, activation of any nodes within the network will activate related nodes, including those with emotional content. This means that, for the person with a phobia of cars described above, seeing a car may trigger emotions of fear and memories of pain and fear of death. However, things are not that simple because most people who develop this type of network will have a pre-existing network of more positive associations with cars and car travel. Accordingly, there may be competition between the activation of established networks when the person sees a car: car–anxiety–injury, etc. versus car–fun–fast. The mood state of the individual at the time of the activation determines to a large extent which of these networks is activated. The network that is congruent with the mood at the time of recall will most likely be activated. If the person is feeling anxious when they get into a car, the fear network will be activated. If they are feeling happy and confident, the pre-existing more positive network is more likely to be activated. Most theorists suggest that some of the details of Bower's network model may not be perfect. However, this type of network provides a basic architecture to explain the linkages between various thoughts and life-events that theorists such as Beck explain in a richer clinical detail.

This type of network also provides a cognitive model of what may be occurring during some behavioural programmes – the strength of associations between a particular stimulus and fear-related concepts may gradually weaken over time, while linkages between the stimulus and more neutral or positive concepts may be developed or strengthened. Such linkages may also be developed using cognitive techniques, which are considered in the next section.

Cognitive behavioural therapy

Acceptance of the role of cognitions in mental health disorders has not led to the wholesale rejection of behavioural techniques. There has been a therapeutic evolution rather than revolution, and behavioural and cognitive techniques are now frequently used together under the rubric of cognitive or cognitive behavioural therapy. That said, the goal of cognitive behavioural therapy is now primarily one of cognitive change, albeit through the use of both behavioural and cognitive techniques. Cognitive behavioural therapy has a number of elements:

- Its primary goal is to change cognitive distortions.
- It is usually short term.
- It maintains a large behavioural component.
- Therapy focuses on the here-and-now, although exploration of cognitive schemata may require some investigation of past events.
- It is directive: the therapist is active in identifying cognitive errors and helping the client change them.

- It focuses on skills (cognitive, behavioural) taught to the individual to help them cope better with their emotional problem. Meichenbaum (1985) referred to the therapist as 'educator'.

Beck, Ellis and other early cognitive therapists argued that cognitions did not follow the laws of learning – Ellis (1977) described faulty cognitions as 'magical', Beck (1977) described them as automatic assumptions. This meant that they required a different type of intervention from those aimed at behavioural change, which did follow the laws of conditioning. This involved direct attempts to change both surface cognitions and more fundamental schemata through logical disputation: people with phobias could dispute the rationality of their fears, depressed people could dispute the reality of their negative expectations, and so on. In doing so, their fear or depression would dissipate. Beidel and Turner (1986) disputed this assumption and provided evidence of the operant conditioning of, at least, the reporting of cognitions and other 'internal experiences'. If cognitions could be changed by environmental contingencies, they argued, there is no need to use these cognitive methods to change them.

This view gained some support from a British cognitive therapist. Teasdale (e g 1993) argued that changes in cognitions made within the therapy session were only short term in nature. They led the individual to engage in behaviours that tested the old and new assumptions developed within the therapy session: the person with a phobia may approach their feared object with less expectation of their being harmed, the depressed person may try out a new, more active, way of dealing with their problems with greater expectations of success. However, longer-term cognitive, emotional or behavioural change occurred only *after* these new assumptions were tested and confirmed. Incidentally, this view is fully consistent with the network models outlined above.

This model suggests that the role of cognitive therapy is essentially one of encouraging the individual to engage in some form of behavioural intervention. According to Beidel and Turner (1986), an alternative, behavioural intervention in which the client is directly encouraged to test their assumptions without the cognitive preparation should prove equally effective in engendering emotional change. Because cognitive therapy has a significant behavioural component, tests of this hypothesis have been lacking, as any relevant comparisons have been between behaviour therapy and a combination of behavioural and cognitive therapy. However, since the early 1990s, a number of studies have been conducted in which 'pure' cognitive therapies have been compared with 'pure' behavioural therapies. These have frequently (e.g Clark et al. 1998), but by no means always (e.g. Burke et al. 2003), shown cognitive interventions to be more effective than behavioural therapies. More consistent evidence has shown the combination of cognitive and behavioural interventions to be more effective than those that utilize just one intervention type. Together, these data suggest that the cognitive element of cognitive behavioural therapy frequently can do more than simply encourage people to change their behaviour – it can have a direct influence on both short- and long-term emotional and behavioural outcomes (see Figure 2.1).

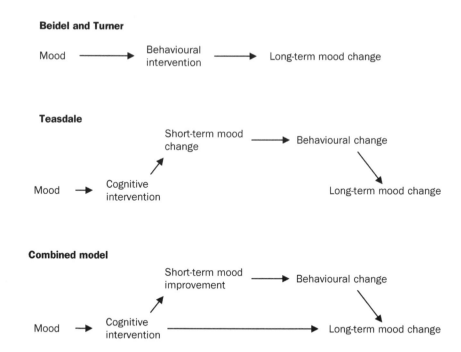

Beidel and Turner

Mood ⟶ Behavioural intervention ⟶ Long-term mood change

Teasdale

Short-term mood change ⟶ Behavioural change

Mood ⟶ Cognitive intervention ⟶ Long-term mood change

Combined model

Short-term mood improvement ⟶ Behavioural change

Mood ⟶ Cognitive intervention ⟶ Long-term mood change

Figure 2.1 Schematic view of the simple behavioural model of emotional change, the Teasdale model, and a synthesis of both

Research box 2

Burke, M., Drummond, L.M., Johnston, D.W. et al. (1997) Treatment choice for agoraphobic women: exposure or cognitive-behaviour therapy? *British Journal of Clinical Psychology*, 36: 409–20.

This study addressed the issue of whether cognitive therapy adds to the effectiveness of behavioural therapy in the treatment of agoraphobia, by comparing the effects of a 'pure' behavioural exposure programme with one that involved exposure combined with a cognitive intervention designed to encourage participants to challenge negative automatic thoughts and dysfunctional assumptions.

Method

Thirty-nine women were referred to the study either by their family doctor or a **Community Mental Health Team**. All had a primary diagnosis of agoraphobia; 23 had a diagnosis of agoraphobia and panic disorder. Participants were randomly assigned to receive either an exposure programme or cognitive behavioural therapy:

- The exposure programme involved 10 weekly sessions in the participant's home. Each session involved two hours of graded exposure to increasingly difficult situations away from the home. This was augmented by discussions about their progress and setting homework to be followed between sessions.

- The cognitive behavioural therapy involved the same 10 weekly sessions and homework assignments. However, in addition, time was spent with the therapist identifying and challenging negative thoughts, and this challenge was incorporated into the daily homework assignments.

Therapists providing the interventions included clinical psychologists, nurses and occupational therapists. All were supervised by an expert consultant clinical psychologist and received 14 hours of specialist training before the trial. The quality of their intervention was monitored by taping and reviewing sessions with participants.

Assessments

Assessments were taken before and after treatment, and at six-month follow-up. They included self-reported measures of agoraphobia using the Fear Scale Agoraphobia Sub-scale (FSAS), the Spielberger Trait Anxiety Inventory (STAI) and Beck Depression Inventory (BDI). In addition, a behavioural measure of agoraphobia involved travelling alone on a standardized route, including a walk, bus ride, ride on the London Tube, and shopping. The test was scored according to how many stages participants completed.

Results

Analysis by ANOVA revealed significant gains on all measures over time, but no significant between-group differences at any time. However, there was a significant time × group interaction on one measure. Participants in the exposure programme achieved a significantly greater increase in the number of completed stages on the behavioural test at the end of the therapy period. However, by the end of the follow-up period, the cognitive behavioural group performed best on this test – although the between-group differences were not significant at any time. Table 2.3 shows the mean scores on some of the key outcomes at each stage of the study.

Discussion

The authors noted that the study showed exposure therapy to be as effective as cognitive therapy. They suggested a few cautions to this interpretation. First, therapist

Table 2.3 Mean scores on different measures

Measure	Pre-test	Post-test	Follow-up
FSAS			
Exposure	29.38	20.21	18.66
CBT	29.25	15.16	15.00
STAI			
Exposure	54.28	51.21	48.00
CBT	58.08	53.00	54.09
BDI			
Exposure	20.50	17.21	13.55
CBT	20.41	12.58	12.81
Behavioural test			
Exposure	4.07	9.16	6.50
CBT	6.08	7.81	10.00

rating showed that the quality of the CBT was not good. It was rated as mechanistic and non-collaborative. It is possible that the intervention would have been more effective if it had been better implemented. Another reason for the lack of statistical differences between the groups could have been the low number of participants in the study. A quick scan of the data suggests the CBT group achieved larger gains on the measures central to the agoraphobia than the exposure-only group on (e.g. 10.72 versus 14.25 drop in the FSAS at follow-up; 2.43 versus 3.92 gain at follow-up). The small numbers of participants may have prevented these differences being statistically different. Larger studies are necessary to confirm this finding before the study's conclusions can be fully supported.

Cognitive techniques

Perhaps the simplest method of directly changing cognitions is known as **self-instruction training** (Meichenbaum 1985). This involves interrupting the flow of stress or negative-emotion-provoking thoughts by replacing them with pre-prepared realistic or 'coping' ones. These typically fall into one of two categories: reminders to use any stress-coping techniques the person has practised, and reminders that the individual can cope effectively with the situation ('You can cope with this . . . you have before . . . remember to relax . . .').

A more complex approach, known as **cognitive challenge**, involves identifying and challenging the reality of the negative assumptions an individual is experiencing. In this, the person is taught to 'catch' their thoughts and identify the association between thoughts, emotions and behaviour. They then learn to treat their immediate negative cognitive response to particular situations as hypotheses or guesses, not reality; to challenge their veracity, and to replace them with more appropriate and less emotionally disturbing thoughts ('I'm feeling faint. I'm going to pass out and make a fool of myself' versus 'Well, I've felt this way before and nothing bad happened – It won't happen this time . . .'). This skill can be practised within the therapy session, before being used in the 'real world'.

Ways of identifying and changing negative assumptions can be taught through the Socratic method or *guided discovery* (Beck 1977). This involves the therapist helping the client to identify distorted patterns of thinking that are contributing to their problems by directly challenging their assumptions. It encourages them to consider and evaluate different sources of information that provide evidence of the reality or unreality of the beliefs they hold. One technique that has been developed specifically to help identify and challenge core beliefs is known as the *downward arrow technique* (Beck et al. 1979). When clients express what seem to be inappropriate thoughts or reactions to events, the downward arrow technique can be used to identify distortions in core beliefs that are contributing to their problems. Key questions include:

- What is your concern about . . .?
- What would the implications be . . .?
- What would the consequences be . . .?
- What would the ultimate consequences be . . .?

One example of their use is provided by this extract from a session with a problem drinker adapted from Beck et al. (1993):

Therapist: You feel quite strongly that you need to be 'relaxed' by alcohol when you go to a party. What is your concern about being sober?

Client: I wouldn't enjoy myself and I wouldn't be much fun to be with.

T: What would be the implications of that?

C: Well, people wouldn't talk to me.

T: And what would be the consequence of that?

C: I need to have people like me. My job depends on it. If I can't entertain people at a party, them I'm no good at my job . . .

T: So, what happens if that is the case?

C: Well, I guess I lose my job!

T: So, you lose your job because you didn't get drunk at a party?

C: Well, put like that, I think I may have not had it in the right perspective.

Here, the downward arrow technique has been used both to identify some of the client's core beliefs and to get them to reconsider the accuracy of those beliefs

Behavioural strategies

Behavioural interventions form an important element of many interventions. Two commonly used strategies in depression, for example, are behavioural activation and behavioural challenge. The first is usually targeted at people who are significantly depressed, and involves increasing levels of activity in a planned progressive manner: this may involve planning times to get out of bed, go to the shops, and so on. For those who are less depressed, it may involve engaging in more social or 'pleasant' activities. Behavioural challenge involves setting up behavioural experiments within the therapy session or as homework that directly test the cognitive beliefs that clients may hold, in the expectation that negative beliefs are disconfirmed and more positive ones affirmed. In the above case, for example, the individual may be encouraged to go to a party and try not to drink, to see whether or not this has the disastrous consequences they originally hypothesized. Success in these tasks is thought to bring about long-term cognitive, behavioural and emotional changes (see the discussion earlier in the chapter). One interesting behavioural challenge used by a colleague, Helen Barker, in the treatment of two people with schizophrenia involved simultaneously testing their assumptions about their unusual abilities. One felt that their thoughts were being 'broadcast' and heard by other people: the other believed that they could hear what other people were thinking. As a test of both their beliefs, both people were put in a room. One was asked to look at cards often used to test extrasensory perception (ESP), and asked to broadcast an image of the each of the cards he looked at. The other was asked to write down the images that he was 'receiving'. Of course, the received images bore no relationship to the images that were actually being 'broadcast': so both sets of beliefs were challenged by this particular behavioural experiment.

Relaxation techniques
Some emotional disorders, such as anxiety and pathological anger, have a large physiological component varying from high levels of physical tension to **hyperventilation** (see Chapter 3). Chronic stress may also be associated with high levels of physical tension, which may not be so noticeable but nevertheless result in chronic tiredness, poor sleep and an increase in an individual's vulnerability to a variety of health problems. Relaxation provides a mechanism for moderating this drive. Relaxation skills enable the individual to relax as much as is possible at times of both acute and chronic stress. This moderates the unpleasant symptoms experienced at such times as well as increases actual or perceived control over the stress response – a valuable outcome in itself.

The relaxation process most commonly taught is a derivative of Jacobson's deep muscle relaxation technique. This involves alternately tensing and relaxing muscle groups throughout the body in an ordered sequence. As the individual becomes more skilled, the emphasis of practice shifts towards relaxation without prior tension, or relaxing specific muscle groups while using others, in order to mimic the circumstances in which relaxation will be used in 'real life'. The order in which the muscles are relaxed varies, but a typical exercise may involve the following stages (the tensing procedure is described in parentheses):

- hands and forearms (making a fist)
- upper arms (touching fingers to shoulder)
- shoulders and lower neck (pulling up shoulders)
- back of neck (touching chin to chest)
- lips (pushing them together)
- forehead (frowning)
- abdomen/chest (holding deep breath)
- abdomen (tensing stomach muscles)
- legs and feet (push heel away, pull toes to point at head: not lifting leg).

Monitoring physical tension   Where high levels of tension are clearly associated with specific stimuli, an individual may quickly learn to use relaxation techniques to help them relax at such times. Where people are more chronically stressed and perhaps less aware of any excess tension, learning to relax effectively may involve a more structured approach. This may begin by the individual learning to monitor their levels of physical tension throughout the day. Initially, this provides an educative effect, helping them identify how tense they are during the day and what triggers their tension. As they move through the practice stage, monitoring may help identify further triggers and provide clues as to when the use of relaxation procedures may be particularly useful. This phase may entail the use of a 'Tension diary' in which the individual typically records their level of tension on some form of numerical scale (0 = no tension, 10 = very high levels of tension) at regular intervals through the day.

In vivo relaxation   After a period of monitoring tension and learning relaxation techniques, individuals can begin to integrate them into their daily lives. At this stage, relaxation involves the individual in monitoring and reducing tension to appropriate levels while engaging in their everyday activities or at times of acute stress. Relaxation is best used initially at times of relatively low levels of excess tension. The consistent use of relaxation techniques at these times can prepare the person to cope with times of greater tension. An alternative strategy that many find useful involves relaxing at regular intervals (such as coffee breaks) throughout the day.

Stress inoculation training

The exact nature of any cognitive behavioural intervention will differ according to the nature of the presenting problem and resources of the individual in therapy. A number of these differing approaches are considered in the chapters in Part II of the book. However, one simple approach combining the various therapy components was developed by Meichenbaum (1985) in his approach to treating general stress. He suggested that the various strands of cognitive behavioural therapy could be combined into a simple iterative learning process. He combined these strands in two ways. First, he suggested that when an individual is facing a stressor, they need to keep three processes under review: (1) check that their behaviour is appropriate to the circumstances; (2) maintain relaxation; and (3) give themselves appropriate self-talk. Second, he suggested that where a particular stressor can be anticipated, the opportunity should be taken to rehearse these actions before the event itself. Once in the situation, the planned strategies should be enacted. Finally, after the situation has occurred, time should be given to review what occurred and the successes or failures to be learned from this.

Experiencing cognitive behavioural therapy

Here are some views about the experience of cognitive behavioural therapy:

> I found it really helpful – but it was difficult. The therapist asked me to, like, question my thoughts. I found that really difficult. I couldn't really work out what I was thinking . . . let alone try to question them! But I remember one appointment when we talked through how I felt when I went on holiday, and I felt really sad at the beginning of the session. By the end I felt really good about myself! And I began to see how thinking about things differently could help me feel better. In the end I found this part of therapy really useful.

> I found the relaxation really good . . . I really enjoyed it. Yeah, it worked well – the rest wasn't easy. But I really valued the support of my therapist. I actually think that that was the most important thing I got out of therapy.

> I found it good to take a gradual approach to dealing with my panics. The therapist was very good as they listened to my concerns, and gave me advice about what to do to stop me panicking. I don't think I would have liked just talking – and telling her about my childhood and so on – I can't see the point in that.

These comments reflect some of the problems that people face in cognitive behavioural therapy and the importance of the relationship between client and therapist, even in the relatively structured use of cognitive behavioural techniques.

Emerging cognitive therapies

The cognitive therapies of Beck and Meichenbaum may now be considered 'first-generation cognitive therapies'. More recently, a number of differing and condition-specific understandings of psychopathology and related interventions have been developed (see Chapter 5 onwards). The fundamental core of these theories and therapies remains the belief that distorted cognitions lie at the heart of psychopathology. However, they have taken their therapeutic approach a step further than that of Beck and Ellis.

One increasingly popular approach, certainly in the UK where it was initially developed, is known as Cognitive Analytic Therapy (CAT: Ryle 1975), and has been used particularly for the treatment of personality disorders (see Chapter 11). As its name suggests, CAT is an integrative therapy, drawing on psychodynamic and cognitive therapies.

The central tenet of CAT is that our beliefs about ourselves and the world develop through social interaction with important others. According to Ryle, long-term mental health is dependent on a strong attachment between a parent (usually the mother) and child. As the baby develops, they learn to be self-aware and self-reflective: they start to think about themselves and the world. A good parent/mother facilitates this process by helping the child reflect on their thoughts, feelings and consequence of their actions. This encourages the development of a moral framework which is added to and further developed through subsequent relationships with friends, peers and other important people as the child grows older and moves into adulthood. Secondary sources of information such as books or television also shape our beliefs about the world. A good childhood, with close relationships, allows the individual to develop good and meaningful relationships as an adult. A poor relationship leads to a re-enactment of this poor relationship with others and low self-esteem.

Psychological health and ill-health

According to Ryle, the nature of our early relationships establishes our response to people we encounter later in life. That is, we develop a standard response to people we meet, which takes little account of their individual characteristics. This response, in turn, elicits a response which is repeated over many encounters: suspicion and withdrawal are met with avoidance; open-hearted conversation is met by engagement and a developing relationship; and so on. Ryle suggested that such responses are driven by processes he termed procedural sequences. These involve:

- reflection on our own thoughts and feelings, and expectations about the intentions of others
- linking these to past memories and belief systems
- planning a response based on these processes
- executing the plan and appraising any response to our actions.

Problems arise when the individual expects negative consequences from any social encounter, and then behaves in a way that encourages or elicits them from those around them. In this way, their thoughts become a self-fulfilling prophecy. A socially anxious person, for example, may experience the following type of procedural sequence:

- See someone they would like to make friends with.

- Think back to previous occasions where this has happened, and where attempts at developing friendships have gone wrong.

- Avoid conversation with the individual, or, if they talk, try to disengage as quickly as possible.

This procedural sequence is driven by what Beck would term a negative schema, a belief that one is incapable of establishing a good relationship, which is then maintained over the long term and in many similar interactions by the actions in which the individual engages.

Ryle described three categories of disturbed parent–child relationships that may establish inappropriate procedural sequences:

- *Neurotic parenting:* includes being critical and bullying or under-demanding and 'spoiling'.

- *Abusive parenting:* includes rejection or repeated abandonment and physical or emotional deprivation.

- *Narcissistic parenting:* involves receiving too much or too little attention and praise.

Cognitive analytic therapy (CAT)

The main goal of CAT is to help individuals identify the pattern of repetitive procedural sequences that has resulted in low mood or personal problems and then to develop alternative sequences to avoid these problems. Therapy typically has four phases:

1 *Information gathering:* involves gaining information about the individual, their procedural sequences and coping strategies.

2 *Reformulation:* here, the therapist provides the client with a written account of their understanding of the information given – a formulation of the problem. This acknowledges the emotional difficulties they have experienced and provides a historical perspective of the procedural sequences throughout their life.

3 *Recognition and revision of procedural sequences:* this typically identifies two or three target problems, which form the initial focus of therapy. The strategies used can be very similar to the cognitive behavioural strategies outlined earlier in the chapter. However, more emphasis is placed on the identification of the origins of faulty procedural sequences and situations in which they occur. Then the client is encouraged to consider alternative ways of thinking and acting at such times, recording progress in a diary.

4 *Ending therapy:* this is seen as an important part of the process of therapy, and is prepared for from the first therapy session, as it involves ending a relationship with the therapist, which may echo previous difficult or distressing relationship endings. The last few sessions are spent working on a positive end of therapy. This involves the therapist writing a summary of the progress the individual has made, what needs further work, comments on progress, and a comment on the therapeutic process. The client is also invited to provide a written view of their therapy. These can then form the focus of a discussion between client and therapist.

Humanistic approaches

The humanistic school of psychology began in the 1950s in the USA. Its major figures include Carl Rogers (1961) and Abraham Maslow (1970). It developed largely as a reaction against both psychoanalysis and behaviourism, and formed a 'Third Force' countering both approaches. Humanists considered psychoanalysis to be too pessimistic as it emphasized the pathological, irrational, unconscious fragmentation of personality. Behaviourism was rejected because of its mechanistic approach to understanding the human condition. By contrast, humanistic psychologists wanted a psychology that focused on healthy, rational, higher motivations.

There are two common elements to the humanist approach:

- Behaviour is understood in terms of the subjective experience of the individual: the phenomenological perspective. This accepts the subjective experience of the individual as a valid source of information about their values, motives and the meaning of their behaviour.
- Behaviour is not constrained by either past experiences or current circumstances. The individual has 'free will' and makes behavioural choices independent of past learning history or the unconscious influence of innate drives.

Models of the individual and neurosis

Rogers
Carl Rogers (1961) was one of the leading humanists. His theory of the individual has been termed a *self-theory*, in that it focuses on the individual's self-concept and their subjective experience of the world. His basic premise was that all individuals have an innate drive to grow, develop and enhance their abilities in ways they choose: a process he called self-actualization. This 'actualizing tendency' stimulates creativity and leads us to seek new challenges and skills that motivate healthy growth. When the individual is in touch with their actualizing tendency, their behaviour is directed in ways that foster positive growth and happiness. When they are not, the result is sadness, anxiety or depression.

Rogers also noted that we live in subjective worlds of our own creation, formed by a process of perception: the *phenomenal field*. In many ways, this maps onto reality, but it may also be distorted and inaccurate. Nevertheless, our reaction to events, be they emotional or behavioural, is based on our perception of the world, not 'objective' reality. Within this framework, the most significant element is the sense of self, our understanding of 'who we are'. Rogers considered the self to be constantly in a process of forming and reforming. We experience it as unchanging only as a result of biases and selectivity in attending those elements of our phenomenal field that are consistent with our prior experience. Our sense of self is influenced by past experiences, our present situation and expectations of the future. However, unlike the psychoanalysts, he argued that the past is only as important as the individual chooses to make it, through conscious choice. Free will allows us to break away from the past, and for our behaviour and emotions to be related more to the present, and perhaps the future.

Although the individual acknowledges their *actual self*, our actualizing tendency drives us towards another version of the self: the *ideal self*. This reflects who we would like to be: the goals and aspirations of our lives. Like the self, this is a changing and evolving concept. The degree to which the actual and ideal selves match each other has a profound effect on our emotions and behaviour. When the two are relatively similar (what Rogers termed congruent), we experience positive emotions. When the two are incongruent, we experience sadness and other negative emotions, and the actualizing process is inhibited.

For many, the beginnings of incongruence lie in childhood. Rogers argued that the way parental love and approval are given has a strong impact on the developing person. Subtle elements of parent–child interactions contribute to the development of pathology. One important process, known as *conditional positive regard*, occurs when parents simultaneously show their disapproval both of bad behaviour and of the child ('Your behaviour is bad, and I don't love you when you behave in this way'). Love and approval are granted only if the child behaves in a way that their parents want them to. As a result, children adopt their parents' 'conditions of worth'. That is, the child comes to associate their self-worth with their behaviour, and begins to adopt behaviours that are valued by their parents. The child begins to internalize the goals of his or her parents into its ideal self, and work towards achieving them rather than his or her own goals and aspirations. As a result, the child fails to progress towards self-actualization.

According to Rogers, three elements of the individual's interactions with others can facilitate their move towards self-actualization:

- *Unconditional positive regard:* acceptance and love that are not contingent upon the individual behaving in required manner: 'I do not approve of your behaviour . . . but I love you nonetheless'.

- *Genuineness:* an environment in which the individual is able to freely express their own sense of self, rather than playing a role or hiding behind a façade.

- *Empathy:* an environment in which the individual is involved with people who can understand the world from their viewpoint – who share their phenomenal field.

Maslow
Rogers's work and beliefs about the development of the individual largely stemmed from his therapeutic work, which is considered later in the chapter. Others, such as

Abraham Maslow, contributed to humanistic theory but not to the development of therapy. Like Rogers, he believed that the individual strives throughout their life to achieve their human potential: to achieve *self-actualization.*

Maslow (1970) believed that we are motivated to fulfil a variety of needs, which are hierarchically structured, starting with basic biological imperatives such as obtaining warmth and food. Self-actualization, he argued, can be achieved only by obtaining the needs of the highest tier of the hierarchy. In addition, the individual can progress up the hierarchy only if all the needs of each subordinate level are achieved. As a result, the individual is motivated to meet the needs within the different levels of the hierarchy and to progress upwards towards self-actualization. The hierarchy of needs described by Maslow had the following levels:

- *Physiological:* including food, air, sleep, sex, and so on.
- *Safety:* including both physical and psychological safety – stability, social order, and so on.
- *Love and belongingness:* giving and receiving acceptance and affection.
- *Esteem:* feelings of self-respect, competence, and receiving the regard of others.

Once the basic needs of biological and physical security are met, the individual can engage in behaviours that allow them to express their potential for growth and to use their capacities to the fullest. Maslow referred to the needs at this level as *meta-needs:* those which are based on a desire to grow. The hierarchy is not rigid, and may differ across individuals or time, but holds for most people, most of the time.

Maslow considered a number of experiences to be related to self-actualization. He termed the most profound and vibrant level of being a *peak experience*, a period of intense emotion when we really feel what it is to be alive. Other, longer-term experiences of heightened awareness can also exist. In what Maslow termed a *plateau experience*, the individual may feel a sustained heightened appreciation of life over months or even years. These two factors are related to self-actualization but are not synonymous with it. According to Maslow, it is possible to have both these experiences without integrating them into the process of self-actualization. Conversely, some individuals who live productive, self-actualized lives may never experience the shift of awareness associated with the peak or plateau experiences. Self-actualization results from a balance of needs being met and the individual achieving the 'full use' of their abilities, not just a transcendent episode.

Maslow considered self-actualizing to be something the individual actively works towards, but is achieved only by a small minority. It is not an inevitable outcome, and the individual may have to overcome obstacles or make choices that progress them towards self-actualization. A significant source of deviation from this process may be the culture the individual is situated within. Maslow contended that the western culture places great emphasis on material sources of gratification, which satisfy physiological and safety needs, but not the higher ones of love, affection and esteem.

Humanistic therapy

There are several schools of humanistic therapy, with the *client-centred therapy* of Rogers being pre-eminent. Rogers considered pathology to be the result of a deviation from the self-actualizing process, usually as a consequence of experiencing conditional positive regard. Therapy involves the individual realigning with their own actualizing tendency.

Early in the history of Rogers's therapy, he described his approach as non-directive. The role of the therapist was to help the individual explore issues relevant to them and their development, with an equal relationship between therapist and client giving the client control over the issues explored. However, careful analysis of therapy transcripts by Truax (1966) indicated that rather than act as a neutral facilitator, the therapist (in this case Rogers himself) unconsciously reinforced statements that indicated progress on the client's part, and ignored those that were less positive. Acknowledging the impossibility of total neutrality by the therapist, Rogers abandoned the term non-directive, but still emphasized that therapy should focus on the development of the individual, not the interpretations or actions of the therapist. The name 'client-centred therapy' (later charged to person-centred) was deliberately chosen by Rogers to contrast with the medicalization and power structure implied by use of the term 'patient' by the psychoanalysts.

The goal of person-centred therapy is to provide an environment in which the individual can identify their own life goals and how they wish to determine them: to place them on the pathway to self-actualization. Rogers stated that therapy does not rely on techniques or doing things *to* the client. Rather, the quality of the interpersonal encounter is the most significant element in determining effectiveness. The goal of the therapist is to provide a setting in which the individual is not judged but can be free to explore new ways of being. That is, therapy provides the conditions necessary for growth identified earlier. To achieve this, the therapist must have three characteristics:

- they are integrated and genuine in their relationship with the client
- they gain an empathic understanding of the client's perspective and communicate this to them
- they provide unconditional positive regard.

Being genuine means that the therapist shares feeling or gives feedback about how they feel as a consequence of what the client is telling them. Such feedback may be positive or negative, and shows that the therapist is human with human feelings. It may involve expressions of sadness or even anger in response to individual's stories. Empathy involves the therapist gaining an understanding of the individual's situation, problems, feelings and concerns, from *their* perspective and showing the client that they have achieved this level of understanding. The most frequent method by which this is achieved is through a process of reflecting back the therapist's understanding of the client's perspective. The final component of the therapeutic relationship is that the therapist is not judgemental, and does not repeat the past experiences of conditional positive regard.

Rogers suggested that these three therapist characteristics can facilitate a shift from the externally imposed standards of others to the identification and shift to the pathway towards self-actualization. This is thought to be achieved through a series of seven stages (Rogers 1961), in which the client:

1   fails to acknowledge feelings, and considers personal relationships as dangerous
2   is able to describe their behaviour, but rarely their feelings, which are not 'owned'
3   can begin to describe their emotional reactions to past events, and recognize contradictions in their experience
4   develops an awareness of their current feelings, but finds it difficult to cope with them
5   begins to explore their inner life in a more meaningful and emotional way
6   is able to fully experience feelings while talking of past events
7   develops a basic trust in their own inner processes: feelings experienced with immediacy and intensity.

The therapist's actions facilitate each of these processes. Empathic feedback encourages and validates the exploration and expression of personal feelings and meanings of statements made in therapy. Acceptance and genuineness encourage the growth of trust in the self and increased risk-taking in the expression of previously withheld thoughts or emotions.

Experiencing person-centred therapy
Here are some reactions to this type of approach:

> I found it really quite disconcerting. All my therapist seemed to do was to repeat back to me things that I'd said to him. I wanted someone to suggest things and advise me what to do to help me cope with my problems. But all he seemed to do was to avoid this and say it was up to me!

> I really liked the space to sit and think – without someone on my back or things to deal with. Just thinking things through can help you change your perspective or think how to do things different. Just unloading some of the shit I'd had during the week really helped.

> I found it really useful – it gave me time to think and develop my plans for the future. Sometimes you need this sort of space, with someone you can trust and who does not sit in judgement on you – even if some of the things you say may not always put you in the best light.

These comments reflect some of the benefits that many people get from humanistic therapy. They also hint that different people may benefit from different types of therapeutic approach. The first person here, for example, may have benefited from a more structured form of therapy. Finally, they also draw attention to the non-specific benefits of therapy, which may just involve expressing negative emotions that cannot be expressed elsewhere.

How effective are the therapies?

The therapeutic approaches outlined in this chapter developed from different historical roots and at different times. Nevertheless, they are all still practised in one form or other, although the dominant method is now the cognitive behavioural approach. The reasons for this can be attributed to a number of factors, including the dominance of cognitive psychology within the broader discipline of psychology and the accessibility of the approach to both practitioner and client. However, the strongest argument for its use is the evidence of its effectiveness relative to the other therapeutic approaches.

Meta-analyses

As the number of studies of interventions in specific conditions proliferate, comparisons between the various approaches have increasingly become condition-specific. However, a number of **meta-analyses** have drawn together evidence of the relative effectiveness of each of the therapeutic approaches over a broad spectrum of disorders. These have consistently shown cognitive behavioural approaches to be superior to both psychoanalytic and humanistic approaches. One of the most stringent meta-analyses was reported by Shapiro and Shapiro (1983), who identified 143 studies that compared different therapies both to one another and to a control condition. They found the following **effect sizes**: psychoanalytic therapy, 0.40; behavioural therapy, 1.06; cognitive behavioural therapy, 1.42. These compared with an effect size for **placebo** interventions of 0.71. These data both emphasized the relative strength of cognitive behavioural interventions and showed the analytic therapies to be marginally less effective than placebo. M. Smith et al. (1980) had previously found a mean effect size of 0.63 for client-centred therapy, suggesting a modest benefit. However, they also found that this did not differ markedly from that achieved by placebo treatment and was significantly less than that achieved by cognitive or behavioural treatments. In a more specific meta-analysis, Butler et al. (2006) synthesized data from 16 meta-analyses, and found large effect sizes for cognitive behavioural interventions in the treatment of depression, generalized anxiety disorder, panic disorder with or without agoraphobia, social phobia, post-traumatic stress disorder, childhood depression, schizophrenia and bulimia nervosa. They found moderate effect sizes for the treatment of marital distress, anger, childhood somatic disorders and chronic pain.

Chapter summary

1 Different psychoanalytic models of psychopathology place differing emphases on sexual and developmental issues. They are central to Freud's theory, but not those of Jung and Klein. All, however, place childhood experiences and trauma at the centre of later psychopathology.

2 Psychoanalytic therapy is aimed at gaining insight into the traumas that lay the foundations for future emotional problems. Insight may lead to catharsis, the expression of emotions previously withheld from consciousness by ego defence mechanisms. Therapy also focuses on within-therapy issues such as transference.

3 Behavioural models of psychopathology have focused mainly on various types of anxiety. Phobias, for example, are considered a conditioned response to a particular stimulus, with the fear maintained through operant conditioning processes.

4 Behavioural therapies are based on classical and operant conditioning paradigms. Key approaches involve flooding and systematic desensitization. These are thought to result in counter-conditioning or habituation of the fear response.

5 Cognitive understandings of psychopathology place cognitions as central to psychopathology. Network models can provide an understanding of the building blocks of emotional disorders, while therapists such as Beck have provided insight into the thought content associated with a variety of disorders

6 Cognitive behavioural interventions target changing inappropriate cognitions, which leads to changes in mood and behaviour.

7 Some approaches to understanding and treating psychopathology have focused on longer-term factors. Ryle combined the psychoanalytical insights of the role of early experiences and the emerging understanding of the role of cognitions in guiding behaviour and mood to develop a form of treatment combining both elements, known as cognitive analytic therapy.

8 Humanistic therapies aim to provide the individual with the emotional space to reorient them towards the path to self-actualization.

9 The key factor within humanistic therapy is the relationship between therapist and client, which removes conditions of worth imposed by parents and others, and allows the individual to move towards self-actualization.

10 Cognitive behavioural therapy has proven the most effective of the therapeutic approaches. However, many of the characteristics of the therapist–client relationship identified by Rogers have also proven important in the therapeutic process.

For discussion

1 Some clinical psychology training courses encourage their trainees to undertake a course of psychotherapy during their training. How might this be useful to their practice as clinicians? Should all clinicians receive some form of psychotherapy while practising?

2 One of the claims of the early behaviour therapists was that therapy could be delivered without the need of a therapist. Written and now computer-driven programmes could provide the skills and structure to treat mental health problems. Was this a realistic claim?

3 How accessible are the thoughts that influence mood, and how easy is it to change them?

4 What commonalities and differences are there between the various schools of therapy?

5 'It's not who you are, but what you do . . .' Discuss this statement in the context of the treatment of mental health disorders.

Further reading

Beck, A. (1991) *Cognitive Therapy and the Emotional Disorders*. Harmondsworth: Penguin.

Berry, R. (2000) *Freud: A Beginner's Guide*. London: Headway.

Dryden, W. (ed.) (2002) *Handbook of Individual Therapy*, 4th edn. London: Sage.

Rogers, C.R. (1961) *On Becoming a Person*. Boston, MA: Houghton Mifflin.

Ryle, A. and Kerr, B. (2002). *Introducing Cognitive Analytic Therapy: Principles and Practice*. Chichester: Wiley.

3

Biological explanations and treatments

The basis of biological explanations and treatments of mental disorders is that behaviour and mood are regulated by brain systems. These allow us to perceive information, integrate that information with past memories and other salient factors, and then respond emotionally and behaviourally. Their disruption results in inappropriate perception, mood and behaviour. This may occur as a result of structural damage, or disruption of chemicals, known as neuro-transmitters, responsible for activating different areas of the brain. By the end of the chapter, you should have an understanding of:

- Basic neuro-anatomy as it relates to mental health disorders
- The neurotransmitter systems and the key neurotransmitters that influence mood and behaviour
- The drug treatments that are used to alter neurotransmitter levels and, hence, mood and behaviour
- Three physical interventions used to treat mental health problems: transcranial magnetic stimulation (TMS), **electroconvulsive therapy (ECT)** and psychosurgery.

The behavioural anatomy of the brain

The brain is an intricately patterned complex of nerve cell bodies. It is divided into four anatomical areas: the hindbrain, midbrain, forebrain and cerebrum.

Hindbrain, midbrain and forebrain

The hindbrain contains the parts of the brain necessary for life: the *medulla oblongata*, which controls respiration, blood pressure and heart beat, the *reticular formation*, which controls wakefulness and alertness, and the *pons* and *cerebellum*, which correlate muscular and positional information.

Above these lies the midbrain, which also contains part of the reticular system and both sensory and motor correlation centres which integrate reflex and automatic responses involving the visual and auditory systems and are involved in the integration of muscle movements.

Many of the key structures that influence mood and behaviour are situated in the forebrain. These include the following:

- *Thalamus:* links the basic functions of the hindbrain and midbrain with the higher centres of processing, the cerebral cortex. Regulates attention and contributes to memory functions. The portion that enters the limbic system is involved in the experience of emotions.
- *Hypothalamus:* regulates appetite, sexual arousal and thirst. Also appears to have some control over emotions.
- *Limbic system:* a series of structures including a linked group of brain areas known as the Circuit of Papez: hippocampus–fornix–mammillary bodies–thalamus–cingulated cortex–hippocampus. The hippocampus–fornix–mammillary bodies circuit is also involved in memory. The hippocampus is one site of interaction between the perceptual and memory systems. A further part of the system, known as the amygdala, links sensory information to emotionally relevant behaviours, particularly responses to fear and anger. It has been called the 'emotional computer' because of its role in coordinating the process that begins with the evaluation of sensory information for significance (such as threat) and then controls the resulting behavioural and autonomic responses.
- The *ventral tegmental area* (VTA) is an important nerve tract in the limbic system. Activation of the VTA sends messages to clusters of nerve cells in the nucleus accumbens and the frontal cortex. This linkage, known as the mesolimbic dopamine system, forms the brain's primary reward pathway.

Cerebrum

Above these three sets of structures lies the cerebrum. This is the part of the brain we are most familiar with, and is the most recently evolved part. It contains a number of structures:

- *Basal ganglia:* a dense mass of neurons at its core. It includes the corpus striatum responsible for complex motor coordination.
- *Cortex:* the convoluted outer layer of grey matter comprising nerve cell bodies and their synaptic connections. It is the most highly organized centre of the brain. Most cortical areas are involved to some degree in the mediation of any complex behaviour, although there are centres of functional control within it. It is divided into two functional hemispheres, linked by the *corpus callosum,* a series of interconnecting neural fibres, at its base. It is divided into four lobes: frontal, temporal, occipital and parietal (see Figures 3.1 and 3.2). As these are involved in the aetiology of a number of mental health and neurological disorders, the function of each will now be considered in more detail.

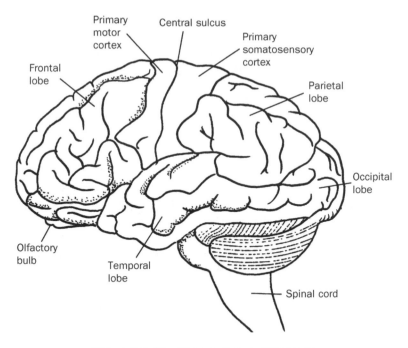

Figure 3.1 The gross anatomy of the brain

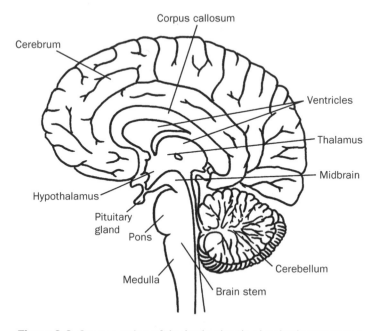

Figure 3.2 Cross-section of the brain showing key brain structures

Frontal lobes

The frontal lobes make up about one-third of the mass of the brain. The frontal cortex has an **executive function**, in that it coordinates a number of complex processes, including speech, motor coordination and behavioural planning. Loss of this executive function, as a consequence of damage, can result in a number of outcomes, including diminished anxiety and concern for the future, impulsiveness, lack of initiative and spontaneity, impairments in recent memory, loss of capacity to think in abstract terms, and an inability to plan and follow through a course of action or to take account of the outcome of actions. Individuals with frontal damage become inflexible and rigid. They have difficulty in shifting from one concept or task to another and changing from one established habit or behaviour to another. This can result in **perseveration**, where a particular behaviour is continued even in the face of clear instructions to change. The frontal lobes also seem to influence motivation levels. Damage to them can lead to a condition known as adynamia, evident through a complete or relative lack of verbal or overt behaviour. The prefrontal lobes are connected to the limbic system via the thalamus and motor system within the cortex. Links between the prefrontal cortex and the limbic system are activated during rewarding behaviours.

Temporal lobes

Although their functions are distributed, there are clear functional centres within the temporal lobes. The location of these centres differs according to handedness. In those who are right-handed, the main language centre is located in the left hemisphere, and visuo-spatial processing is located in the right hemisphere. In left-handed individuals, there is less localization within hemispheres. The temporal lobes are also intimately involved in the sense systems of smell and hearing. They are responsible for the integration of visual experience with those of the other senses to make meaningful wholes. Disruption within the temporal lobes, for example, as a consequence of temporal lobe epilepsy, can result in visual illusions or hallucinations. Olfactory (smell) hallucinations have also been reported, although less commonly. Reflecting the multifaceted functioning of the temporal lobes, these illusions or hallucinations may be accompanied by strong emotions, in particular, fear (Hermann and Chabria 1980). The temporal lobes have an important role in memory and contain systems which preserve the record of conscious experience. Damage to one of the temporal lobes results in relatively minor memory difficulties, some of which may be evident on psychometric testing, but may not cause problems to the individual. Damage to both can result in profound memory deficits. Finally, they have an intimate connection with the limbic system and link emotions to events and memories.

Occipital and parietal lobes

These lobes are primarily involved in the integration of sensory information. Their functions are distributed and there are no clear functional centres. The occipital lobe is primarily involved in visual perception. Links to the cortex permit interpretation of visual stimuli.

The synapse

Each of the millions of interconnecting nerves within the brain is known as a neuron. Activation of systems within the brain is the result of small electrical currents progressing along many different neurons. Critical to the flow of this current are the small gaps between neurons, known as synapses. Here, chemicals known as neurotransmitters are responsible for activation of the system.

Each neuron has a number of fine branches known as axons at its terminal. At the end of these is an area known as the presynaptic terminal which, in turn, is in close proximity to the postsynaptic terminal within the axon of another neuron. Between them is an enclosed area known as the synaptic cleft (see Figure 3.3). Neurotransmitter chemicals are stored within the axon in small pockets known as synaptic vesicles. Electrical stimulation of the nerve results in release of the vesicles' contents into the synaptic cleft. Once the transmitter has been released into the synaptic cleft, it moves across the gap between the two axons, where it is taken up by specialist cells within the postsynaptic membrane, known as receptor molecules. Once in the receiving neuron, chemicals known as second messengers are released and trigger the firing of the neuron, continuing the activity of the activated neurological system. If not all the transmitter is taken up by the postsynaptic receptor, further activation may be inhibited either by re-uptake of the unused molecules back into vesicles in the initiating neuron or by degradation by other chemicals, such as monoamine oxidase released into the synaptic cleft.

Neuronal activity itself is mediated by small electrical impulses that travel down the nerve axon towards the nerve ending. When a neuron is at rest, the outside of the cell wall is lined with sodium ions, and the inside wall is lined with potassium ions. Nerve transmission is mediated by an electrical pulse moving through the nerve axon.

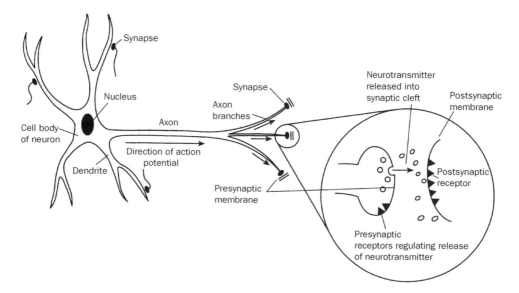

Figure 3.3 A neuron and close-up of the synaptic cleft

When the neuron is stimulated by an incoming message at its receptor site, the sodium ions move from the outer side of the cell membrane to its inside. This starts a wave of electrochemical activity that continues down the length of the axon and results in it 'firing'. Immediately following this, the potassium ions shift from the inside to the outside of the neuron, returning it to its original resting state.

The neurotransmitters

A relatively small number of neurotransmitters have been implicated in the aetiology of the most common mental disorders. The effects of those considered in this chapter are summarized in Table 3.1, and are considered in more detail in the relevant chapters later in the book.

Serotonin

First identified in the 1950s, serotonin is an amino acid, and is synthesized from its precursor L-tryptophan. It is found in the striatum, mesolimbic system, forebrain, cortex, hippocampus, thalamus and hypothalamus. It is thought to be involved in moderating mood, with low levels leading to conditions including depression and obsessive-compulsive disorder.

Norepinephrine

Norepinephrine is a second neurotransmitter involved in depression as well as a number of anxiety disorders. Among other areas, it is found in the hypothalamus, cerebellum and hippocampus. It belongs to a family of chemicals known as catecholamines.

Table 3.1 The key neurotransmitters, the drugs that affect them and their role in mental health disorders

Neurotransmitter	Primary disorder	Treatment*	Mode of action
Monoamine			
Serotonin	↓ in depression	Tricyclics	Prevent re-uptake
	↓ in obsessive-compulsive disorder	SSRIs	Prevent re-uptake
Catecholamines			
Dopamine	↓ in schizophrenia	Phenothiazines	Block receptor sites
		Reserpine	Block vesicular storage
Norepinephrine	↓ in depression	MAOIs	Prevent degradation
		Tricyclics	Prevent re-uptake
Amino acids			
GABA	↓ in anxiety	Benzodiazepines	Enhance GABA

* See pp. 69–77.

Dopamine

Dopamine is one of the key neurotransmitters involved in schizophrenia. Neurons mediated by dopamine are found in the mesolimbic system, in a brain area known as A10, with links to the thalamus, hippocampus, frontal cortex and the substantia nigra. High levels of dopamine activity are associated with schizophrenia. Dopaminergic dysregulation has also been associated with autism and attentional deficit/hyperactivity disorders.

GABA

A group of drugs known as benzodiazepines were found to be an effective treatment of anxiety before their mode of action was understood. It is now known that they enhance the action of a neurotransmitter known as gamma-aminobutyric acid (GABA). GABA carries inhibitory messages: when it is received at the postsynaptic receptor site it prevents the neuron from firing. Sites of GABA include the brain stem, cerebellum and limbic system.

The autonomic nervous system

Although most explanations of mental health problems focus on neurotransmitters and neurological processes, another system, known as the autonomic nervous system, is also involved in some conditions, particularly those involving stress or anxiety. The autonomic nervous system links the brain to many of the body organs, including the heart, gut and smooth muscles. Its job is to control the activity of these organs in response to the various demands being placed on them, for example, by increasing heart rate, blood pressure and breathing rate during exercise. Overall control of the autonomic nervous system is provided by the hypothalamus. It receives blood-borne and nervous system inputs concerning the state of the body, such as oxygenation and acidity of the blood. In addition, it receives inputs from the cortex and limbic system regarding behavioural and emotional factors. Based on these various inputs, the hypothalamus either increases or decreases activity within the autonomic nervous system and the various organs it controls.

Autonomic processes

The autonomic nervous system comprises two subsystems, known as the sympathetic and parasympathetic nervous systems. These arise in the medulla oblongata in the brain stem and travel down the spinal cord. At various points along the spinal cord, they link with other nerves connected to target organs such as the heart, arteries, skeletal muscles and colon. The *sympathetic system* is involved in arousal, and its activity within the brain and spinal cord is controlled by norepinephrine. High levels of norepinephrine result in increased arousal and activation of the target organs. The *parasympathetic system* is involved in calming or reducing arousal, and its activity is controlled by levels of a neurotransmitter called acetylcholine. The two systems tend to work antagonistically and the level of physical activation of the individual at any one time is a function of the relative dominance of each system.

Endocrine responses

Neurotransmitters act quickly, but are unable to maintain activation for long. To enable a sustained response to stress, a second system is activated by the sympathetic nervous system. High levels of sympathetic nervous system activity cause part of the adrenal glands, known as the adrenal medulla which are situated above the kidneys, to release hormonal counterparts of the neurotransmitters norepinephrine and epinephrine into the bloodstream. These travel to the target organs, are taken up by receptors, and sustain the action initiated by the neurotransmitters.

When the emotion of stress is experienced, the sympathetic nervous system gains dominance, activates the body and prepares it to deal with physical damage. At its most dramatic, this response is known as the *fight–flight response*. At such times, sympathetic activity is clearly dominant, the heart beats more quickly and more powerfully, blood is shunted to the muscles and away from the gut (hence the experience of 'butterflies'), skeletal muscles tense in preparation for action, and so on. The individual may shake, pace or want to engage in some form of physical activity. This ancient response is clearly advantageous at times when the causes of stress are acute and life-threatening: chronic activation in response to long-term stress or short-term activation at inappropriate times, such as while in a supermarket or bus queue, is more problematic.

Drug therapies

Activation of brain systems is dependent on the activity of individual neurons, which are, in turn, mediated by the amount of neurotransmitter available at the postsynaptic receptor site. Too much and the system is overactive; too little, and it is underactive. The goal of drug therapies is to ensure appropriate levels of key neurotransmitters. They do this by one of two actions:

- *Increasing the availability* of the neurotransmitter by preventing re-uptake at the synapse, preventing degradation within the synaptic cleft, or replacing low levels of a particular neurotransmitter with its pharmacological equivalent. Drugs that increase the action of a neurotransmitter are known as **agonists**.

- *Decreasing availability* of the neurotransmitter by depleting levels of the available transmitter or replacing the active transmitters with an inert chemical. Drugs that inhibit the action of a neurotransmitter are known as **antagonists**.

Drugs are usually administered by mouth or injection into muscles, and then enter the bloodstream. They enter the brain by permeation from the small blood vessels that pass through it. Designing drugs to influence brain activity has not proven easy. The brain is protected from infection and other blood-borne insults by the blood–brain barrier. In the rest of the body, drugs pass from the blood vessels to target sites through pores in the walls of the blood vessels. The blood vessels in the brain lack these pores, and drugs have to pass directly through the cells of the blood vessel wall. This mechanism means that only drugs using relatively small molecules can pass this barrier, and even then their perfusion will be less than in the rest of the body.

Treating depression

Drugs that increase norepinephrine: MAOIs

The first potent antidepressants to be developed were known as monoamine oxidase inhibitors (**MAOIs**). These prevent degradation of norepinephrine (and to a lesser extent, serotonin) by monoamine oxidase within the synaptic cleft and help sustain its action. As was the case of a number of early psychiatric treatments, the discovery of the antidepressant qualities of MAOIs was accidental. Their first use was in the treatment of tuberculosis, where they were found to improve mood in those treated. MAOIs have since become a standard treatment for depression, with a success rate of about 50 per cent.

Despite this, MAOIs have to be used with some caution. As well as working in the brain, they prevent the production of monoamine oxidase in the liver and intestines, where it breaks down tyramine, a chemical that can result in potentially fatal and sudden increases in blood pressure if allowed to accumulate within the body. In order to prevent this, people who take MAOIs have to avoid foods such as cheeses, red wines, Marmite, bananas and some fish that contain tyramine. Eating these foodstuffs may trigger a sudden and potentially fatal rise in blood pressure. Some newer MAOIs, known as reversible selective MAOIs, have been developed that avoid these problems. However, as more recent research has suggested that serotonin is more important in the aetiology of depression than norepinephrine, treatment has mostly changed to drugs that affect serotonin levels: the **tricyclics**, selective serotonin re-uptake inhibitors (**SSRIs**), and selective serotonin and norepinephrine re-uptake inhibitors (**SNRIs**).

Drugs that increase serotonin: tricyclics, SSRIs and SNRIs

Three drug groups increase serotonin levels by inhibiting its re-uptake into the presynaptic terminal: the tricyclics (for example, imipramine, amitriptyline), SSRIs (for instance, fluoxetine, sertraline), and SNRIs (venlafaxine, milnacipran and duloxetine). Tricyclics and SNRIs also increase levels of norepinephrine.

The first tricyclic, imipramine, was used initially as a treatment for schizophrenia. It was unsuccessful in this, but did reduce levels of depression in many people. Between 60 and 65 per cent of those who take tricyclics do experience some improvement of symptoms (Hirschfeld 1999). Their effects can take ten or more days to become evident, probably as a result of an initial reduction in the amount of serotonin produced at the presynaptic terminal in response to more being available within the synaptic cleft. Improvements in mood occur as the system adapts to the drug and begins to release normal amounts of serotonin again, with re-uptake prevention finally resulting in an increase in available serotonin. It is important to maintain a therapeutic regime for some months after changes in mood have been achieved: about 50 per cent of users will relapse within a year if tricyclic use is prematurely stopped (Montgomery et al. 1993).

SSRIs are a more recent pharmacological treatment. They increase serotonin levels without affecting norepinephrine levels, which may increase following treatment with tricyclics. Although they may not be more effective than tricyclics, they have fewer side-effects such as constipation and dry mouth and are less dangerous in overdose. Rocca et al. (1997), for example, found that 56 per cent of people who took tricyclics reported an uncomfortably dry mouth, compared with 8 per cent treated with SSRIs. Tricyclics and SSRIs are the most commonly used pharmacological treatments of depression; MAOIs may have therapeutic effects on some individuals who do not respond to these drugs, but the potential risks associated with their use generally make these a second-line treatment. Of concern is evidence of a characteristic SSRI discontinuation syndrome (Tamam and Ozpoyraz 2002). It is usually mild, commences within one week of stopping treatment, resolves spontaneously within three weeks, and consists of a number of physical and psychological symptoms, of which the most frequent are dizziness, nausea, lethargy and headache. Restarting use of an SSRI leads to resolution within 48 hours. To minimize this risk, SSRIs, like other antidepressants, need to be withdrawn gradually. Because SNRIs work on both serotonin and norepinephrine levels, they appear to be more effective in the treatment of depression than are SSRIs. However, like tricyclics, they may have more severe side-effects and discontinuation symptoms (Sir et al. 2005; Stahl et al. 2005).

Side-effects such as a dry mouth may appear somewhat trivial, but they can have a significant impact on those taking these drugs, as one user pointed out:

> The worst thing about the drug was the dry mouth I got with it. And when I say 'dry mouth', I really mean it. My mouth and lips were dry all the time. I wanted to drink all the time, so I could refresh my mouth. But that didn't help much – so I ended up chewing gum all the time – and I hate gum! It may not sound much, but when you are already feeling down, it just adds to the bad feeling.

Another woman, who benefited from taking SSRIs, commented on a, perhaps, less obvious side-effect.

> Taking these drugs was great – I felt so much better on them. But one problem did arise. When I was depressed, the last thing I wanted to do was to have sex with my husband. Now, I can't wait . . . but the most frustrating thing is I can't climax! We have great fun, but it is so frustrating!

Research box 3

Loerch, B., Graf-Morgenstern, M., Hautzinger, M. et al. (1999) Randomised placebo-controlled trial of moclobemide, cognitive-behavioural therapy and their combination in panic disorder with agoraphobia, *British Journal of Psychiatry*, 174: 205–12.

The authors noted that both pharmacotherapy and psychotherapy have proven effective treatments of panic disorder, but that it was still not clear which approach was more effective, either alone or in combination. The study intended to inform this debate, comparing the effectiveness of a new generation of MAOIs (moclobemide) with cognitive behavioural therapy and a combination of both approaches in the treatment of panic disorder plus agoraphobia.

Method

Participants were people between 18 and 65 years old who met DSM-III criteria for panic disorder plus agoraphobia. They had to have had at least one panic attack in the previous week and to have a 'moderate' degree of agoraphobia. Potential participants were excluded if they had other psychiatric problems. Participants were randomly allocated to one of:

- moclobemide plus CBT
- moclobemide plus clinical management (i.e. regular visits to prescribing psychiatrist)
- placebo plus CBT
- placebo plus clinical management (what the authors termed a 'double placebo').

Medical treatment and drug placebo were provided for a period of eight weeks, and then withdrawn over a further two weeks. The CBT involved nine, 50-minute, sessions plus two therapist-led exposure sessions averaging 6 hours in week 3.

Assessment

Primary outcome measure was self-report agoraphobic avoidance measured by the Fear Questionnaire (FQ) agoraphobia sub-scale, the Mobility Inventory (MI) and Disability Scale (DSS).

Secondary outcome measures were psychiatrist-rated assessments: Clinical Global Impression and Clinical Impression of Change, and the Hamilton depression and anxiety scales. Finally, participants kept a diary of the frequency, duration and severity of panic attacks. All measures were taken at baseline, and during weeks 4, 8 and 10 of therapy and one, three and six months following the end of therapy.

Results

Of 123 people in the University of Mainz anxiety treatment centre, 55 met the criteria for the study. Their mean age was 35 years, and the mean duration of the panic disorder, 73 months.

Thirteen participants dropped out of the study over the treatment period, resulting in a final sample of 42 people. Drop-out was highest in the moclobemide plus clinical management group (44 per cent) and lowest in the placebo plus CBT group (7 per cent). Table 3.2 shows some of the key outcomes at the end of therapy.

These, and other data including the frequency of panic attacks, show a consistent trend. Participants who received CBT either alone or in combination with moclobemide showed significant improvements. Those treated with moclobemide showed no evidence of gain, and the combination of drug plus CBT treatment was no better than CBT alone. Six-month follow-up data showed a continued superiority for CBT over moclobemide, although by this time the combined intervention proved the most effective. The percentage of participants in each group to be clinically improved (e.g. a score of less than 10 on the FQ-A scale) and not to have received further treatment over the 6-month follow-up period was 89, 18, 0 and 0 per cent of those receiving moclobemide plus CBT, placebo plus CBT, placebo plus clinical management and moclobemide plus clinical management, respectively.

Table 3.2 Mean scores on key outcomes before and after therapy

Measure	Moclobemide + CBT	Moclobemide + CM	Placebo + CBT	Placebo + CM
FQ–A				
Baseline	19.00	24.38	25.36	27.27
10 weeks	6.71	19.25	7.21	19.18
MI				
Baseline	3.05	3.34	3.61	3.45
10 weeks	1.84	2.94	1.86	2.96
HAX				
Baseline	23.57	24.44	22.14	23.91
10 weeks	11.43	19.88	11.86	20.82

CBT = cognitive behavioural therapy
CM = clinical management
FQ–A = Fear Questionnaire agoraphobia sub-scale
HAX = Hamilton Anxiety Scale
MI = Mobility Inventory

Discussion

The high drop-out and lack of effectiveness of moclobemide suggest this form of treatment alone is of minimal benefit to people with agoraphobia plus panic disorder. However, and in contrast to its initial impact, combining the drug with CBT resulted in the best long-term outcomes. Why this should be is not clear. The authors speculate that moclobemide may have induced a number of side-effects such as restlessness and agitation that could not be discriminated from anxiety symptoms. This may have resulted in a high drop-out and high reported symptoms, which abated after its withdrawal to reveal a longer-term benefit. What is clear, though, is that CBT is central to any treatment of panic disorder or agoraphobia.

Emerging problems

The introduction of SSRIs was not without problems. Perhaps the most widely known controversy has related to one of the first of this type of drug to be widely available – Prozac (otherwise known as fluoxetine). This was described by its makers as the first of a new generation of side-effect-free antidepressants. In addition, it rapidly gained a reputation as the only antidepressant that could not only help people who were depressed, but also improve the quality of life of people who were not. It seemed to increase confidence, sociability and to reduce shyness and social anxiety. As a result, it became widely prescribed in the USA, among both those who were depressed and those who needed the emotional lift that it provided.

This initial success was soon mitigated by a series of claims alleging that

Prozac had far more side-effects than were initially reported by its makers (see www.prozactruth.com), the most dramatic of which involved significant behavioural disinhibition that could result in either self-harm or violence towards others. Some of the links with violence were of a secondary nature. Lipinski et al. (1989), for example, reported significant levels of akathisia, a condition involving marked agitation and high levels of impulsiveness, in between 10 and 25 per cent of people who were prescribed Prozac. This may potentially be associated with suicide or aggression. Rothschild and Locke (1991), for example, reported the case histories of three people who felt suicidal and attempted suicide while being prescribed Prozac. Perhaps the most notorious association between Prozac and violence was the case of Joseph Wesbecker, who shot 20 people in his former workplace, 8 of them fatally, before killing himself while he was taking Prozac (Geoffrey 1991). It is important to note that small case studies and sensationalist stories cannot be considered convincing evidence of a link between Prozac and dangerous behaviour, but they have increased the publicity surrounding prescription of the drug.

More empirical studies have indicated a smaller potential risk associated with Prozac than these initial studies may have indicated, and even these are open to alternative explanations. Jick et al. (1995), for example, identified over 170,000 people who had been prescribed one of ten antidepressants over a five-year period. They then compared suicide rates across the various types of antidepressant, reporting them as the 'rate of suicide per 10,000 person years'. The lowest rate of suicide, 4.7, was found among people taking Lofepramine; the mean rate was 10.8 suicides per 10,000 years. The highest rate of suicide was found among those taking Prozac: 19.0 suicides per 10,000 years. The authors noted that many people taking Prozac were at particularly high risk of suicide as a result of factors other than their medication, including a history of feeling suicidal and poor outcome on other antidepressants. After accounting for these factors, the increased risk of suicide in those taking Prozac was less apparent, although suicide rates remained a little higher than the average

More recently, Gunnell, Saperia and Ashby (2005) reported the results of a meta-analysis of drug company data on suicide, suicidal thoughts, and self-harm following treatment with a variety of SSRIs or a placebo. Their findings were based on data from over 40,000 individuals in 477 trials of drug effectiveness. Despite this large number of people, their findings were surprisingly equivocal, with evidence of both a protective and risk-enhancing effect across a number of trials. The relative risk (compared with placebo) for suicide was 0.85, indicating a modestly reduced risk – but the 95 per cent confidence intervals ranged between 0.20 and 3.40, indicating a wide variety of outcomes across trials. A similar picture was found for self-harm and suicidal thoughts. They concluded on this evidence that 'more research is required', but that any very small increase in risk should be balanced against the effectivness of SSRIs in treating depression. Fergusson et al. (2005) found no evidence of any greater risk of suicide associated with SSRIs in comparison with tricyclics in a meta-analysis of the relevant trials. In addition, Yerevanian et al. (2004) found that suicide rates did not differ across SSRIs and tricyclics, and that suicide rates were higher following discontinuation of both SSRIs and tricylics than during active treatment.

Treating anxiety

Drugs that enhance the action of GABA: the benzodiazepines

Although their mode of action is not fully understood, a group of drugs known as benzodiazepines was found in the 1960s to be an effective treatment of anxiety. Benzodiazepines appear to enhance the action of GABA, but do not bind to the same postsynaptic receptor sites: the natural neurotransmitter that binds to these sites has not yet been identified. This class of drugs replaced the use of low doses of barbiturates, which made people drowsy, could prove fatal as they led to respiratory failure, and were highly addictive.

The first benzodiazepine was known as chlordiazepoxide (Librium). The best known, Valium, was marketed several years later. By the mid-1980s, benzodiazepines were the most widely prescribed **psychotropic medication**. However, their prescription has not been without cost. When their use is stopped, levels of anxiety frequently return to pre-morbid levels or above (Power et al. 1990). Sudden withdrawal of these drugs typically results in the rapid recurrence of previous symptoms combined with withdrawal symptoms, including sweating, shaking, nausea and vomiting. As a consequence of this, up to 80 per cent of people who stop taking benzodiazepines after a long period of use relapse and require further treatment. Many people have to be gradually withdrawn from the drugs over extended periods of time – often many months. In general, the shorter the **half-life** of a drug, the more sudden and severe any withdrawal symptoms (see Table 3.3).

Benzodiazepine use has also been associated with a number of undesirable side-effects, including drowsiness, memory loss, depression and aggressive behaviour including acute rage (Curran 1991). Long-term use may result in irreversible changes. Despite these concerns, benzodiazepines are still regularly prescribed, but now on a more short-term basis than previously. As well as impacting on sites within

Table 3.3 The half-life of various benzodiazepines

Benzodiazepine	Time to peak blood level (in hours)	Half-life (in hours)
Alprazolam	1–2	9–20
Chlordiazepoxide	1–4	24–100
Clonazepam	1–4	19–60
Diazepam	1–2	30–200
Flurazepam	0.5–1	40–250
Lorazepam	2–4	8–24
Nitrazepam	0.5–7	15–48
Oxazepam	2–3	3–25
Prazepam	2.5–6	30–100
Temazepam	2.5	3–25

Source: adapted from Bezchlibuyle-Butler and Jeffries (2003)

the brain such as the limbic system, they provide a relaxant effect as a result of their effect on GABA within the spinal cord.

Drugs that increase norepinephrine and serotonin
There is increasing evidence that some anxiety conditions, and in particular panic disorder, are mediated, at least in part, by norepinephrine. For these conditions, treatment with antidepressants has proven more effective than with traditional anxiolytics (Bakker et al. 1999). Treatment is usually with tricyclics rather than MAOIs, for safety reasons: although the primary effect of tricyclics is on serotonin, they also increase norepinephrine levels. Serotonin itself may also be involved in the aetiology of anxiety disorders such as panic and obsessive-compulsive disorder. As a result, these disorders are increasingly treated with both tricylics and SSRIs (Ballenger 2004).

Treating schizophrenia

Biological theorists have implicated dopamine in the aetiology of the positive symptoms of schizophrenia. Individuals with these symptoms do not show raised levels of dopamine but appear instead to have an excessive number of dopamine receptor sites on the postsynaptic terminal, making them overreactive to normal levels of dopamine. The goal of therapy is usually therefore to reduce the number of receptor sites accessible to the dopamine by filling them with inert drugs that mimic dopamine's chemical composition. A less frequent intervention involves reducing the amount of available dopamine.

Drugs that reduce dopamine levels
The phenothiazines The origin of the present pharmacological treatment of schizophrenia lies in the observations made in the 1940s by a French surgeon, Henri Laborit, that one of the drugs he used as an antihistamine had a profound calming effect on his patients prior to surgery. The drug was called chlorpromazine. By the early 1950s, this was used experimentally with patients with psychotic symptoms, and rapidly became established as the primary treatment of schizophrenia.

Chlorpromazine belongs to a class of drugs variously known as **phenothiazines**, neuroleptics or major tranquillizers. They work by blocking the dopamine receptors in the postsynaptic receptor sites. Unfortunately, while successful in the short term, their use results in a proliferation of dopamine receptor sites (Strange 1992), adding further to the sensitivity of the postsynaptic receptors and resulting in the need for long-term treatment. They also have a number of significant side-effects. For these reasons, clinicians maintain people with schizophrenia on the lowest effective dose or gradually reduce and stop medication after a period of time in which the individual is functioning normally (see Chapter 6).

The side-effects occur as a result of the drugs' impact on the extrapyramidal areas of the brain, including the substantia nigra. These areas are involved in the control of motor activity and coordination. The most common **extrapyramidal symptoms** are Parkinsonian symptoms. These include stiffness in the arms and legs, facial expressions that are fiat and dull, and tremors, particularly in the hands. These symptoms can usually be relieved by drugs that reverse the effects of phenothiazines or a reduction in the amount of drug prescribed. About 20 per cent of those who take phenothiazines for an extended time develop a second condition, known as tardive dyskinesia (APA 2000). Its primary symptoms include involuntary writhing or tic-like movements of the face or whole body. Facial movements include involuntary chewing, sucking and writhing of the tongue in and out of the mouth. Body movements include jerky, purposeless movements of the arms, legs and torso. Its severity varies between a single symptom and a severe whole body problem. These symptoms are difficult to treat and can be irreversible. If detected early, and treatment is stopped immediately, most symptoms will remit. However, many symptoms are similar to those found in schizophrenia and may not be observed – or even result in increased phenothiazine being prescribed. The longer an individual has taken phenothiazines, the less likely their symptoms are to remit, even after the cessation of therapy.

Reserpine   A second approach to the treatment of schizophrenia involves reducing the amount of dopamine available to be released into the synaptic cleft. The action of a drug known as reserpine is to inhibit the synthesis of dopamine. Once existing stores have been utilized it can take up to two weeks for them to return to normal levels during treatment with reserpine.

Drugs that reduce NMDA levels
One additional form of drug has proven effective in the treatment of schizophrenia. Atypical neuroleptics were initially thought to have their action through their impact on NMDA receptors, which are thought to be involved in the development of schizophrenia. Drugs such as phencyclidine (PCP 'angel-dust') and ketamine are thought to increase activity in these receptors and cause symptoms similar to those of schizophrenia. Their activity seems to be blocked by drugs such as clozapine and risperidone (Morimoto et al. 2002). There is evidence that these drugs may also reduce dopamine activity, possibly indirectly through the drugs' influence on serotonin levels, which may inhibit dopamine release at times of stress (Pehek et al. 2006).

These atypical neuroleptics are likely to prove a first-line treatment of schizophrenia in the future, as they may not only be more effective than phenothiazines but also cause significantly fewer extrapyramidal symptoms (Tandon and Fleischhacker 2005). Success rates with phenothiazines of about 65 per cent are typical: for the new drugs the success rate is about 85 per cent (Awad and Vorungati 1999). Unfortunately, the medication also carries some costs. Between 1 and 2 per cent of those who take the drug will develop agranulocytosis, a potentially fatal reduction in white blood cells, resulting in a need for all those prescribed these drugs to have regular blood tests so they can be withdrawn before this disorder becomes problematic.

Adherence to drug treatments

Any drug can achieve its potential only if it is taken regularly and at therapeutic levels. This is not always the case: up to 50 per cent of people prescribed psychotropic medication either do not take the recommended dose or do not take the drug at all (a figure, incidentally, that reflects a more general failure to adhere to recommended medication of all types within the general population). This may be a failure of memory. About 15 per cent of people forget at some time to take their medication when one tablet is prescribed, 25 per cent forget when two or three are prescribed, while 35 per cent of people forget if five or more tablets are prescribed (Ley 1997). One way of preventing this type of lack of adherence is to provide slow-release medication by **depot injection**, which requires those receiving it to have injections at regular intervals, rather than remember to take tablets several times a day. Phenothiazines are often given using this route.

More conscious decisions whether or not to take tablets are often based on a form of cost–benefit analysis, in which the benefits of taking medication, usually in terms of relief from symptoms, are weighed against the costs of taking it, usually the side-effects that accompany use of the drug. The more side-effects a drug has, the less likely those prescribed it are to adhere to its use, particularly where there are no immediate changes in symptoms when doses of a drug are taken or missed, as is the case for many psychiatric drugs. An example of this can be found in the findings of Demyttenaere et al. (1998), who found that 36 per cent of people prescribed the tricyclic amitriptyline failed to take their medication, compared with 6 per cent of those prescribed the SSRI fluoxetine. Level of depression was not predictive of drop-out. However, younger men who experienced severe side-effects were least likely to take the medication.

Not surprisingly, some side-effects are more problematic than others. Lingjaerde et al. (1987) listed a hierarchy of side-effects that people receiving phenothiazines considered most troublesome. In ascending order, these were sleepiness, increased fatiguability, weight gain, tension or 'inner unrest', and concentration difficulties. Extrapyramidal effects, which were the main concern of the prescribing psychiatrist, were rated as relatively unimportant. When asked whether they preferred depot or tablet medication, up to 80 per cent preferred depot (Desai 1999). Other factors may also be involved. Day et al. (2005) found that a poor relationship with the prescriber, experience of coercion during admission, and low insight predicted a negative attitude towards treatment. This finding is consistent with the findings of Myers and Branthwaite (1992), who found that adherence was greatest when clients and not the doctor chose the times when they took their drugs. Finally, Sirey et al. (2001) found high adherence to medication to be associated with lower perceived stigma of taking drugs, higher self-rated severity of illness, being aged over 60 years, and absence of 'personality pathology'.

Thinking about . . .

Taking medication has both benefits and costs. We may experience a relief from symptoms, but at the same time experience a number of side-effects. Most of these are relatively innocuous – although they may have a significant impact on the individual. The dry mouth associated with some antidepressant medication, for example, sounds relatively trivial, but in reality is a significant and uncomfortable consequence. The side-effects of some other medication types may have a longer-term and more significant impact on health. Of note in this context is that these side-effects are frequently experienced immediately an individual starts taking medication – the benefits may take some time, often weeks, before becoming evident.

So, what would influence your adherence to medication? Would you accept significant side-effects in the hope of future gain – and if so, for how long? Many people have an 'against medication' bias. If you do, how severe would any mental health problem have to be before you decided to take medication?

Electroconvulsive therapy (ECT)

Electroconvulsive therapy (ECT) is the brief discharge of an electric current through the brain with the aim of inducing a controlled epileptic convulsion to achieve an improvement in an abnormal mental state. Its origins lie in observations made in the 1930s that stunned pigs appeared particularly sedated and quiet in abattoirs, and justified by the suggestion that people who had epilepsy rarely evidenced any form of **psychosis** and that mood following epileptic seizures often improved.

Extrapolating from these observations, physicians attempted to induce epileptic fits in an attempt to treat mood disorders, initially using injections of camphor to provoke seizures – a process that proved fatal in a number of cases. An alternative approach was pioneered by two Italian psychiatrists, Ugo Cerletti and Lucio Bini, who found that they could induce seizures by applying electrical currents to patients' heads, and began their treatment of schizophrenia. Cerletti later abandoned ECT and sought alternative treatments as a result of his concerns over the physical damage, including jaw dislocation and broken bones, and neurological effects such as memory loss that resulted from the seizures provoked by his treatment.

Until the 1950s, ECT involved placing electrodes on each temple and passing an electric current of between 65 and 140 volts through these 'paddles' for half a second or less. This provoked an epileptic fit lasting from half to several minutes. Initially, this was given 'straight', that is, with the patient fully conscious. Vigorous convulsive muscle activity frequently led to bone fractures until the introduction of the muscle relaxants given prior to ECT. As awareness of this paralysis led to high levels of anxiety on the part of the recipient, this was soon accompanied by administration of an intravenous barbiturate to render them unconscious during the procedure, a process known as modified ECT. More recently, the electrodes have been placed over the non-dominant hemisphere only, a process known as unilateral ECT. This is thought to result in fewer side-effects. Although schedules of treatment vary, ECT is typically administered either two or three times a week in courses ranging from 4 to 12 treatments. Less commonly, it is given fortnightly or monthly for six months or longer to prevent relapse, as continuation or maintenance ECT.

Use of ECT

The use of ECT peaked and then began to decline substantially in the 1950s following the introduction of a range of psychotropic drug treatments. Nevertheless, its use is still recommended by psychiatric authorities for treatment of depression that is resistant to pharmacological intervention or where there is a strong likelihood of suicide (Freeman 1995). A recent systematic review of the use of ECT for people with schizophrenia (Tharyan and Adams 2005) also concluded that when combined with treatment with antipsychotic drugs, ECT may be a useful therapeutic option when rapid global improvement and reduction of symptoms are necessary or where individuals show limited response to medication alone. Even though this initial beneficial effect may not last beyond the short term, they suggested there is no clear evidence to refute its use for people with schizophrenia.

Just how ECT achieves any benefits remains unclear, although work by Ishihara and Sasa (1999) suggests that it may increase the sensitivity of postsynaptic neurons to serotonin in the hippocampus, increase levels of GABA and reduce levels of dopamine. These data explain the impact of this one procedure on both depression and schizophrenia.

The ECT controversy

The use of ECT has not been without controversy, and the literature seems to be divided largely into those who enthuse over its use and those who vehemently oppose it. Measured debate is less frequent. Those against its use oppose it on moral grounds as well as question its effectiveness. Thomas Szasz (1971), for example, argued that electricity as a form of treatment 'requires the sacrifice of the patient as a person, [and] of the psychiatrist as a clinical thinker and moral agent'. This negative view is endorsed by a number of psychological organizations, including the British Psychological Society, which considers that the use ECT should be prohibited in Britain. Even the psychiatric authorities that endorse its use have acknowledged the controversy. The NIH (1985) Consensus Statement observed that ECT had been used inappropriately to treat disorders where there was no evidence of effectiveness and that many of these efforts proved harmful. It also noted that the use of ECT as a means of managing unruly patients, exemplified in the film *One Flew over the Cuckoo's Nest*, contributed to its perception as an abusive instrument of behavioural control for patients in mental institutions. Issues of effectiveness are considered in the chapters on depression and schizophrenia, where ECT has been most widely used. The rest of this section considers some of the evidence of side-effects associated with ECT.

There are a number of short-term risks associated with ECT. First, those associated with being given an anaesthetic, and second, risk associated with fitting. Adverse events are rare, but do occur. The NIH Consensus Statement suggested a rate of up to 4.5 deaths per 100,000 treatments, a risk comparable to the use of short-acting barbiturate anaesthetics in other conditions. They also noted that the risk of physical injury was much less than in the past, with a complication rate of 1 per 1300 to 1400 treatments. Problems included tooth damage, vertebral compression fractures, uncontrollable fitting, peripheral nerve palsy and skin burns. Some people also perceive ECT as a terrifying experience, or regard it as an abusive invasion of personal autonomy. Some experience a sense of shame because of the social stigma they associate with it (NIH 1985).

Effect on memory

Perhaps the most problematic outcome of ECT is its effect on memory. People who have ECT typically experience an acute phase of confusion following treatment: it can take them five or ten minutes to remember who they are, where they are or what day it is (Friedberg 1977). It also impairs the ability to learn and retain new information for a period of time following administration and may impact adversely on memories of events that occurred months or even years before treatment. Squire and Slater (1983), for example, found that three years after receiving ECT, many people reported that their memory was not as good as it was six months before their treatment and thought that this decrement was related to having received ECT.

More objective studies of the impact of bilateral ECT have identified measurable long-term decrements in memory following its use. However, proponents of ECT note that the shift from bilateral to unilateral ECT has resulted in fewer memory problems. This defence was tested by Lisanby et al. (2000), who followed 55 people with major depression, randomly allocated to either unilateral or bilateral ECT. Prior to treatment, they obtained detailed autobiographical and impersonal memories and then tested recall of these memories immediately following the course of ECT and at two-month follow-up. A control group who did not have depression or ECT underwent the same testing procedures. All those who received ECT recalled fewer personal and impersonal memories, and in less detail, than controls on both testing occasions. By the second assessment, differences between the two groups who received ECT also emerged: those given bilateral ECT recalled less than those who had unilateral ECT.

Given the problems associated with ECT, a number of researchers and clinicians have attempted to find alternative methods to achieve the same clinical results – but without the unwanted side-effects. Transcranial magnetic stimulation (TMS) appears to be one such approach. The process involves passing a series of electrical pulses close to the brain. The coil is held on the scalp – no actual contact is necessary – and the magnetic field passes through the skull and into the brain. Small induced currents can then make brain areas below the coil more or less active, depending on the settings used. TMS can influence many brain functions, including movement, visual perception, memory, reaction time, speech and mood. The obvious effects of TMS last for very short times following stimulation. However, there is some evidence that the procedure may have longer-term effects on mood – and may prove an alternative approach to the use of ECT. In one relevant study, Schulze-Rauschenbach et al. (2005) compared TMS with unilateral ECT in the treatment of major depression. Treatment response was comparable: 46 per cent of people treated with ECT and 44 per cent of those treated with TMS group showed significant clinical improvements. More encouragingly, while patients treated with ECT showed evidence of memory deficits, those treated with TMS showed no decrement and even improvements in memory. Quite how TMS impacts on mood is not clear. However, animal studies suggest it may result in increases in serotonin and a number of other neurotransmitters including dopamine (Zangen and Hyodo 2002; Kanno et al. 2003).

Psychosurgery

The modern practice of psychosurgery began in the 1930s, when two Portuguese neurologists, Egas Moniz and Almeida Lima, began severing connections to and from the frontal lobes in people with 'psychoneuroses'. By 1936, the procedure had been developed into what was termed a prefrontal leucotomy (sometimes referred to as a lobotomy). This operation was initially fairly crude, as the surgeon had to estimate where to lesion the brain without any form of neuro-imaging and did so freehand. However, it has gradually become more precise in its anatomical location and procedures. Between 1936 and 1961, over 10,000 people received this type of treatment in the UK. Of these, an estimated 20 per cent of people with schizophrenia and about 50 per cent of those with depression gained some degree of benefit (Malizia 2000). However, 4 per cent died as a result of surgery, 4 per cent developed a severe loss of motivation and up to 60 per cent developed 'troublesome' personality changes, while 15 per cent developed epilepsy. Despite these problems, this approach had many advocates, probably because there were no viable alternatives to this treatment for much of this time.

Rates of psychosurgery have fallen dramatically since effective therapeutic alternatives have become available. Now, only about 20 operations are conducted in the UK each year, and only for conditions that have proven unresponsive to a variety of alternative treatments. New, more specific, surgical procedures have also been developed, including the stereotactic subcaudate tractotomy and stereotactic cingulotomy. Stereotactic interventions involve a device called a stereotactic frame which is placed over the brain during operations and, in combination with neuro-imaging, allows highly accurate lesions to be conducted. Neurosurgeons now use a 'conservative' approach, creating small initial lesions, which can be added to with later operations should this be required.

Most lesions are created with heated electrodes, with the exception of the subcaudate tractotomy which involves placing radioactive rods in the target area, which destroy parts of the subcaudate brain area through a brief burst of radioactivity before becoming inert. It is usually used for the treatment of severe, intractable depression. Stereotactic cingulotomy is the most commonly used procedure for the anxiety disorders, including obsessive-compulsive disorder (see Chapter 7). The operation is conducted under general anaesthetic and involves placing electrodes into the cingulate bundle in each hemisphere. The tips of the electrodes are then heated to 85 degrees centigrade for about 100 seconds.

Availability of psychosurgery

Psychosurgery is banned by law in some countries, for example Germany, and in some US states. To be given this form of treatment in the UK, an individual has to be resistant to all other attempts to treat the condition. In treating depression, for example, a candidate for surgery would typically have made more than two serious suicide attempts, have had an initial onset at least 18 years previously, and their present episode would have lasted seven years without a period of remission of at least six months. They would have received over 30 ECT treatments, unusually large doses of antidepressants, and be severely depressed on psychometric testing (Malizia and Bridges 1991). In England and Wales, a panel of three representatives appointed by the **Mental Health Act Commission** is required to assess that the person is providing full consent to the operation and that they are likely to benefit from it. In Scotland, this safeguard is evoked only if the person is detained for treatment against their wishes.

Post-operative effects

Since the advent of the newer operations, mortality has dropped to one in a thousand cases, and post-operative epilepsy to between 1 and 5 per cent (Jenike 1998). In addition, there is no evidence of reduced intellectual function following surgery. Indeed, many people perform better on psychometric testing following surgery than before, perhaps because their depression is lifted and/or they are no longer taking antidepressant medication. Similarly, there is no evidence of significant 'personality changes' following neurosurgery, despite the potential for damage to the frontal lobe, which is considered by many to control functions considered fundamental to an individual's personality. The tests typically given in these studies do not test for subtle frontal lobe deficits, however, and Jenike (1998) acknowledged that the possibility of such damage cannot be excluded.

A number of people commit suicide following surgery. Whether this is a result of the surgical procedure or would have happened without this intervention is difficult to judge. It is possible that some people who view the operation as the treatment of last resort may commit suicide after disappointing results. Certainly, there is no evidence of this being a direct consequence of surgery. Jenike et al. (1991) found that 4 of a series of 33 individuals who underwent cingulotomy for the treatment of obsessive-compulsive disorder (OCD) committed suicide in the 13 years following the operation. All four experienced severe depression with prominent suicidal ruminations prior to surgery. The percentage of individuals to make a significant recovery following some form of psychosurgery is reported in Table 3.4.

How psychosurgery achieves these therapeutic gains is not fully understood. In OCD, it may sever the brain systems driving the behaviours (see Chapter 7). However, preliminary evidence suggests that people with OCD do not improve immediately following surgery. It may take several weeks or months before any benefits are observed. Jenike (1998) speculated that secondary nerve regeneration or metabolic alterations in brain areas other than those actually lesioned may be involved in any changes. What these may be, however, is unclear. This lack of understanding of what surgeons are actually doing provides critics of this approach with strong concerns about the nature and use of psychosurgery (www.antipsychiatry.org).

Table 3.4 Summary of published outcome data for neurosurgery

	'Good' outcome (%)		
Procedure	Depression	OCD*	Anxiety
Stereotactic subcaudate tractotomy	53	44	43
Cingulotomy	34	56	50
Capsulotomy	60	93	
Stereotactic limbic leucotomy	55	67	27

* OCD obsessive-compulsive disorder
Source: adapted from Jenike (1998)

Chapter summary

1 The brain is divided into a number of anatomical areas, most of which are in some way related to functions that influence mood or behaviour.

2 Damage to most brain areas will result in deficits that may be evident as emotional or mental health problems.

3 Activity within the brain is mediated by neurotransmitters, which act at the neuronal synapse.

4 Neurotransmitters mediate the activity within brain systems that are responsible for mood and behaviour. The most important to mental health are serotonin, dopamine, GABA and norepinephrine.

5 Drug therapies affect the activity within brain systems by increasing or decreasing levels of neurotransmitters. Antidepressants increase the amount of serotonin (and to a lesser extent norepinephrine); anxiolytics increase levels of GABA; and neuroleptics decrease levels of dopamine.

6 ECT involves passing an electrical current through the temporal lobes of the brain to induce a seizure.

7 Treatment with ECT remains controversial; although it is now much safer than previously, it still evokes strong emotional arguments, among both those who support its use and those who oppose it.

8 ECT does appear to be linked to significant measurable memory problems, that last a significant period of time. A new alternative, transcranial magnetic stimulation, may prove equally effective and have fewer such side-effects.

9 Psychosurgery is now used only in extreme cases of OCD or depression.

10 Psychosurgery achieves a moderate degree of clinical benefit in a population where previous, more conservative, treatments have failed, but carries with it a small but significant risk of subtle cognitive deficits.

11 How psychosurgery acts to relieve symptoms is not clear. It may interfere with activity within brain systems that mediate OCD or depression. However, the time frame in which changes occur following surgery indicates the possibility of other, as yet unknown, mechanisms.

For discussion

1 Is ECT a degrading and dehumanizing form of treatment, or a useful alternative to drug and psychotherapy treatments?

2 Drug treatment for schizophrenia carries both risks and benefits. What considerations should a doctor have when prescribing phenothiazine medication?

3 Would you consider having ECT or psychosurgery if others thought you might benefit from either treatment?

4 If offered a choice, would you opt for a medical or psychological treatment for a mental health condition that could be treated with either approach?

Further reading

Healy, D. (2004) *Psychiatric Drugs Explained*. Edinburgh: Churchill Livingstone.

Jenike, M.A. (1998) Neurosurgical treatment of obsessive-compulsive disorder, *British Medical Journal*, 163 (Suppl. 35): 75–90.

Ratey, J. (2001) *A User's Guide to the Brain*. Boston, MA: Little, Brown.

Tharyan, P. and Adams, C.E. (2005) Electroconvulsive therapy for schizophrenia, *Cochrane Database of Systematic Reviews*, Issue 2.

4

Beyond the individual

Very few of us live isolated lives that do not involve interacting with other people or the wider society. These interactions impact on our mental well-being. Good relationships, for example, appear to be protective against mental health problems. Poor relationships or living in a stressful environment increase our risk for such problems. This chapter considers two important social factors that influence mental health: the family and the social environment in which we live. It then considers how some of these problems may be ameliorated through family therapy or the use of health promotion and other public health interventions. The chapter then goes on to consider how cultural factors may influence the presentation and treatment of a number of mental health problems. By the end of the chapter, you should have an understanding of:

- Theoretical models of the family and family problems
- Interventions that involve the whole family
- The impact of social and cultural factors such as socio-economic class, gender and ethnicity on mental health
- How mental health problems may present and be treated across differing cultures
- How health promotion and public health programmes may improve the mental well-being of individuals and populations.

Family models of mental health disorders

Family models of mental health disorders and their treatment are based on systems theory. This views the family or other social groups as an interrelated set of individuals. The behaviour of each person within the system does not occur in isolation. Instead, behaviour follows a principle of circularity in which no one behaviour is seen as starting or being the outcome of events. The behaviour of X affects Y, whose behaviour reciprocally affects X, whose response to this affects Y, and so on. Behaviours form a continuous causal loop, with no beginning or end-point. Change within this continuous set of behaviours can be achieved by intervening at any point in the system.

Systemic therapy

This chapter considers two systemic therapies that have emerged from very different theoretical perspectives: structural family therapy and strategic family therapy. Other forms of family therapy are described in the following chapters as appropriate.

Structural family therapy

The structural school of family therapy was initially developed by Salvador Minuchin (1974). The core premise of this school of family therapy is that families that operate well have a clear structure. When a family lacks such a structure, the family will fail to deal with problems that it is presented with either internally or from outside sources. This lack of structure may not be apparent to the family: they may not present complaining of family problems. More typically, one person from the family is seen as having mental health problems. According to Minuchin, this 'identified patient' is a symptom of a dysfunctional family, and the family as a whole would benefit from change.

According to Minuchin, families develop structures in order to carry out roles. One important structure is the family rules that govern the way in which people relate to each other within the family. The father, for example, will relate to different people in different ways at different times: partner, father, disciplinarian, friend, and so on. The rules that regulate these various relationships differ. However, each is governed by overt and covert rules.

Minuchin also identified a series of elements that combine to determine each family's organization and style of interaction. Subsystems are small units within the family that share a common element: generation, gender, interest, and so on. One individual may be a member of several subsystems. Boundaries exist between subsystems and between the family and the outside world. According to Minuchin, clear boundaries are required to allow subsystems to carry out their specific functions and to develop autonomy and a sense of belonging. Problems arise when these boundaries are incorrectly established within families. Diffuse boundaries are highly permeable and information flows readily between subsystems. In such cases, family members are extremely close. Indeed, they may become too close, leading to a state of enmeshment in which individual members do not experience a state of autonomy or independence. Conversely, boundaries that are too rigid and which prevent information flow between subsystems result in a process of disengagement and emotional detachment between family members.

Subsystems are organized hierarchically. The parental subsystem is generally considered to be superordinate to others, such as sibling subsystems, and to have an executive function. It makes key family decisions. There may also be disruptions or temporary subsystems established, in the form of alliances. Here, members of different subsystems cooperate, typically on a short-term basis. Father and son may combine forces to influence the mother, and so on. These alliances, particularly if they are long term, are thought to disturb the family hierarchy and to be an indication of dysfunction.

Minuchin identified the characteristics of functional families as having clear boundaries, appropriate hierarchies, and sufficiently flexible alignments to adjust, change and foster individuals within them. Dysfunctional families have the opposite constellation of characteristics. According to Minuchin, when an individual presents with problems seen as requiring therapy, these 'symptoms' actually represent systemic problems. Minuchin's group associated particular diagnoses with specific types of family dynamics. Minuchin et al. (1978), for example, identified the characteristic of 'anorexic families', as being enmeshed, overprotective, rigid and conflict-avoidant, with unexpressed parental conflict. According to Minuchin, the stresses associated with an adolescent's push for independence within such a family increase the risk of the parental conflict becoming overt. To avoid this, the adolescent develops anorexic behaviours to prevent total dissension within the family. These behaviours may hold the family together as it unites around the 'identified patient' and deflects attention away from parental conflict.

The goal of therapy is to identify where these dysfunctions lie and to change them: to establish a 'normal' family structure in which the parental subsystem has executive powers, the boundaries between and around generations are clear, and long-term alliances do not exist. Each family member should have age-appropriate independence while still feeling part of the family.

Structural family therapy is behavioural, directive and dynamic. The therapist is active within therapy sessions. They may move about, change the positions of family members to develop or disrupt alliances, interrupt particular allegiance patterns and align with different members of the family. Treatment of the family involves three elements:

- challenging the family's perception of reality
- providing alternative possibilities that make sense to them
- once they have tried out new patterns of transactions, developing new relationships and structures that are self-sustaining.

The therapeutic process involves a series of stages:

1 *Joining with the family:* in this, the therapist enters the system, joining or establishing rapport by accommodating to the family's culture, mood, style and language. The therapist may physically sit within the family and engage with them.

2 *Evaluating the family structure:* here, the therapist examines boundaries, hierarchies and alliances. This may be a very dynamic process. Individuals or subsystems are observed interacting using role play. The therapist may even set up conditions for these to be real interactions. Minuchin et al. (1978), for example, frequently held therapy sessions with the families of children with anorexia at lunchtime, when the family would be invited to have a meal together. These sessions could demonstrate, for example, the inability of parents to work together to encourage their child to eat, or a shifting pattern of coalitions between each parent and the child. This may then lead on to discussion among family members about the reasons for these various behaviours.

3 *Unbalancing the system:* during this phase, the therapist deliberately unbalances existing, dysfunctional, behavioural patterns in order to put the family into a state

of disequilibrium. This process is highly directive and may involve the therapist aligning him or herself with different subsystems or alliances. An example of this process can be found in the case of a depressed woman who was pessimistic and hopeless at the start of a therapy session, but whose mood improved as she vented her feelings of frustration with her husband and her husband's family, who were critical and demanding of her. Rather than remain neutral, as would be the case in most one-to-one therapies, the therapist began to take sides with her husband, sympathizing with the problems he was having trying to keep everyone in the family happy, but also suggested that the two of them sat down and attempted to establish limits on the intrusiveness of his family on their relationship.

4 *Restructuring operations:* once the system has been unbalanced, attempts follow to establish a normative family structure. This may involve a series of strategies, including:
   (a) *actualizing family transactional patterns:* this involves developing more appropriate transactional patterns through strategies including role play, guided practice, and physical manipulation of individuals into appropriate subsystems (by, for example, sitting mother and father together and combining to interact with members of other systems);
   (b) *escalating stress:* this involves blocking recurrent inappropriate transactional patterns, and developing conflict in order to encourage new alliances within more appropriate subsystems.

It is assumed that any changes are mutually reinforcing and that the family will continue to develop without the need for further intervention. Therapy may nevertheless continue at weekly intervals for several months. One advantage of this approach is that it presents a clear model of therapy. Targets and goals are clearly stated. The process of change and the strategies through which they can be achieved are well delineated. However, its simplicity may also be a disadvantage, and many new therapists attempt to restructure the family before they have sufficient grasp of family rules. The application of too rigid a blueprint of family functioning can have the effect of imposing the therapist's solution on the family, which may, of course, be incorrect.

Strategic family therapy

The strategic model of family therapy, led by (among others) Watzlawick et al. (1974), also focused on the interactions between family members. However, rather than the structure of the family, the approach considered the problem-solving strategies that families use, typically in response to poor or unsuccessful adjustment at critical points in the family life cycle, as key to understanding family problems.

They noted that when a family faces a problem, its members typically interact in repetitive ways and use previously used strategies to deal with the problem. If this is successful, the problem is resolved. Where these strategies are unsuccessful, some families will adopt novel approaches in their attempts to resolve the problem. Others may continue to apply the same unsuccessful strategy to try to achieve change. Where this occurs, the attempts at problem resolution may themselves become the problem: perhaps more so than the original problem. An example of this process can be found in the man who responds to his wife's lack of engagement with him with upset and anger. In his anger, he attempts to persuade his wife to be more forthcoming in their relationship. However, in response to his anger, she becomes more withdrawn and avoidant, which results in him becoming more angry, her becoming more avoidant, and so forth. Here, his anger used in an attempt to change the original problem has become part of the problem, not the solution – as has the woman's withdrawal. It is important to note that *both* repetitive responses actually exacerbate the problem – not just his anger, which is what individual therapy may focus on.

The goal of therapy is to identify and change these repetitive and, ultimately, destructive, attempts at problem resolution. The family's tendency to look for a cause of the problems and to attribute them to one individual is minimized, as this is seen as contributing to, rather than helping, the problem. The strategic school placed significant emphasis on both verbal and non-verbal communication between family members. All behaviour was thought to act as a form of communication. One cannot fail to communicate: inaction provides a message just as much as action.

The goal of strategic therapy is to disrupt behavioural cycles that maintain the problem, and to introduce the conditions for more appropriate transactional patterns. Therapy follows a number of discrete stages:

1   Detailed exploration and definition of the difficulties to be resolved.
2   Developing a strategic plan of action to break up the sequences of interactions that are maintaining the problem.
3   Delivery of the strategic interventions – often involving homework between therapy sessions, the goal of which is to disrupt the problematic sequences.
4   Feedback on the outcome of these interventions.
5   Reappraisal of the therapeutic plan, including revision of homework or other interventions employed.

The style of the therapist is one of emotional distance from the family. To avoid confrontation, they may adopt a one-down approach rather than expert position. They also do not insist that the whole family attends therapy sessions: they will work with whoever attends. Therapy focuses on two key strategies of change: positive reframing and paradoxical interventions.

• *Positive reframing* involves placing a positive interpretation on the behaviours that are contributing to the problem. That is not as difficult as it may sound because, according to the strategic therapists, these behaviours are erroneous but genuine attempts at resolving a problem. In this way, a couple who are constantly antagonistic towards each other may be told that the good thing about their arguing is that it shows they both have sufficient commitment to the relationship to continue fighting in an attempt to make it work. The goal of reframing is to challenge the family's perception of the presenting problem and to encourage them to redefine and give a new meaning to it. Having redefined the problem, the family can no longer apply the same solutions, and new solutions and patterns of interaction become possible.

• *Paradoxical interventions* involve those involved in the therapy being asked to engage in tasks that are paradoxical or contrary to common sense. The arguing couple, for example, may be asked to *continue* arguing – perhaps linked to the positive reframe of 'because this shows your continuing attachment to each other'. By the use of paradox, the therapist creates a therapeutic bind by suggesting that there are good reasons why it is advisable for change *not* to occur: while hoping to have the opposite effect. The paradox is intended to give the problem a new meaning so that those involved will be forced to decide on change or no change – itself a change within the system.

A number of paradoxical strategies have been identified. The above example is known as *symptom prescription*. A similar technique, known as *pretending*, involves a family member deliberately and consciously pretending to have a particular problem, with the family enacting their usual pattern around the presenting 'symptom'. Again, this is meant to disrupt the normal family interactions and facilitate behavioural change. The approach has a number of strengths, and the strategic group have reported some impressive therapeutic gains (Watzlawick et al. 1974). However, the ethics of the approach have been strongly questioned, as the power lies with the therapist and the method of treatment is not clear to its recipient. Box 4.1 illustrates two differing interpretations of one problem from both structural and strategic perspectives.

How effective is systemic therapy?

Systemic therapy involves the family, and sometimes extended family, with usually two or more therapists. The latter may not be obvious to the family, but they will know of their presence. Often a team of therapists sits behind a one-way mirror and tracks the progress of therapy. They may discuss issues raised within the session, identify the nature of the interactions among family members and develop intervention strategies. They provide support to the therapist in the room with the family, who may be too involved in managing the process of therapy to notice all the complex interrelationships that occur. These observers may take an active role. They may communicate with the therapist in the room, either by telephone or by the therapist stepping out of the room for consultations with them, and share developing formulations about the nature of the problem. They may even tell the therapist to take a particular action or ask a specific question. The experience of family therapy is therefore very different from that of individual therapy, as is reflected in these participants' negative and positive responses to an initial therapy session:

I found it unpleasant and uncomfortable. We didn't all want to be there, and when we did get there, it was not at all clear what was going on. I didn't feel it right that we were watched by people through a mirror. You can't see their reaction to what's going on . . . that is really uncomfortable. I didn't like it at all. I don't think we'll come back.

It was weird, and not what I expected. The therapist was moving about talking to us all. He even got some of us to move around! Not what you expect. I thought he or

Box 4.1 Jane's anorexia: an example of structural versus strategic therapy
Strategic and structural approaches view the problems that people have quite differently.
Here are two formulations of the problems associated with anorexia.

A structural approach

Jane is an adolescent girl diagnosed as having anorexia in a family: the 'identified
patient' indicative of structural problems. The therapist has heard how the mother
and father try to encourage her to eat, but have so far failed to do so. The therapist
diagnosed the issue as one in which the family has failed to accommodate her
transitional stage from adolescence. The parents are observed as powerless to
persuade her to eat, and seem to put their differences aside and unite in their
concern to get her to eat.

A structural view of this situation would be that the family is enmeshed: they are
overly concerned about their daughter's behaviour and so close to her that they
deprive her of her independence and decision-making autonomy. The power invested
in the girl to control the family has inverted the power hierarchy within the family, and
the parental system is weak: they cannot get her to eat.

The goal of therapy is to remedy these deficiencies, in particular, to strengthen
the parental subsystem and restore the appropriate power hierarchy. One way in
which this may be achieved is for the therapist to actively change the structure and to
support the parents in their attempts to control the behaviour of their daughter.

A strategic approach

A different formulation of the problem may be gained by a strategic approach.
One possible formulation is that as Jane entered adolescence she tried to gain
more autonomy and independence. However, her parents were overprotective and
controlling and did not accommodate to these changes. She therefore started to diet
as an expression of control and autonomy. However, her dieting and loss of weight
simply increased her parents' concern over her health and increased their desire to
control her and ensure she ate 'properly'. Accordingly, they increased their attempts
at controlling her eating. As a direct consequence, she rebelled and escalated her
diet, which, in turn, increased her parents' concern and protective behaviour, which
. . . The cycle continues. The pattern of interaction that is established is the main
concern of the strategic therapist – not the initiating problem.

she would be quiet and make us take it in turns to talk to them. . . . not move around
and interrupt and things . . . It was unnerving to know that people were watching
through the mirror. But you couldn't see them, and I began to forget about them,
especially when we were dealing with difficult things in the therapy session.

This chapter has described two very different approaches to working with families;
there are many other approaches, some of which will be described in subsequent
chapters. Evaluation of the effectiveness of systemic interventions is therefore not a

simple question. Different chapters in this book will show that systemic therapy has proven successful in the treatment of conditions as varied as schizophrenia, alcohol- and drug-related problems and anorexia: on occasion, it is more effective than individual therapy. A more statistical overview of the effectiveness of this approach can be found in the results of a meta-analysis reported by Shadish et al. (1993). They synthesized the results of 163 randomized trials, and found systemic (family or marital) therapy to be effective in the treatment of a wide range of problems including conduct disorder, phobias, schizophrenia, sexual problems and depression. The strategic model described above was one of the most effective interventions, with a success rate of about 65 per cent. The structural approach of Minuchin was generally less effective, although it has been used with some difficult-to-treat groups, including people with anorexia. Later reviews, such as that of Asen (2002), have confirmed this optimism, with consistent evidence of systemic therapy being effective in disorders as wide-ranging as anorexia, mood disorders and schizophrenia.

Psychosocial explanations of mental health problems

Risk for mental health problems has been linked to a number of social and economic factors. The results of the British Psychiatric Morbidity Survey (Jenkins et al. 1998) provided evidence typical of the wider findings. The authors conducted diagnostic interviews on 10,000 people who were either living in their own home or homeless and roofless. Among the former, they found relatively high rates of neurotic disorders (various types of depression or anxiety) among women, those living in urban settings, unemployed people, and separated, divorced or widowed individuals. Men were three times as likely as women to be dependent on alcohol, and twice as likely to be dependent on drugs. Unemployed people were twice as likely to abuse alcohol as employed people and five times more likely to be dependent on other types of drugs. Psychoses were more prevalent among urban than rural dwellers. The prevalence of neurotic disorders among hotel residents was 38 per cent; among night shelter residents, the prevalence was 60 per cent; among those sleeping rough, rates were 57 per cent. Rates of psychoses and alcohol and drug dependence were similarly high. Less dramatically, there is consistent evidence that mental health problems are more prevalent among the less well-off than among the better-off in most developed countries (Fryers et al. 2005).

Socio-economic status

Social causation versus social drift

Two hypotheses have been proposed to explain findings of higher rates of mental health disorders among people in the lower socio-economic groups than among the economically better-off. *Social causation models* suggest they result from higher levels of stress experienced by the less well-off: that is, low socio-economic status 'causes' mental health problems. The *social drift model* opposes this view. It suggests that mental health problems lead to a decline in socio-economic status. According to this model, when an individual develops a mental health disorder, they become less economically viable. They may be unable to maintain a job or the levels of over-time required to maintain their standard of living. They therefore drift down the socio-economic scale: that is, mental health problems 'cause' low socio-economic status.

The evidence generally favours the causation hypothesis. Indeed, where there is social drift, this has been found to precede rather than follow episodes of depression (Moos et al. 1998). These effects may even be intergenerational. Ritsher et al. (2001) followed a cohort of people whose parents had either experienced an episode of major depression or were depression-free. They hypothesized that if the social causation model held, the children of blue-collar parents were at increased risk of developing depression. If the social selection model held, having depressed parents placed participants at risk of a low socio-economic status. Their data supported the social causation hypotheses. The children of blue-collar workers were more than three times as likely to develop a major depressive disorder as those of white-collar workers. Parental depression did not predict the socio-economic status of their offspring. Nor was there any evidence of drift following the onset of depression.

These findings should not be surprising. The lower the individual is within the social structure, the greater the reported exposure to stressful life-events, hassles and problems, and the greater the emotional impact they have (House et al. 1991). Not having a job also appears to have negative effects on mental health. Ferrie et al. (2001), for example, found that insecure re-employment and unemployment following redundancy were associated with significant increases in minor psychiatric problems and high use of family doctors.

Differential vulnerability

Not only do people in the lower socio-economic groups experience more stresses than the better off, but they often have fewer resources to help them cope with them. Hobfoll's (1989) *conservation of resources model* proposed that mental and physical health are determined by the amount of resources available to the individual. These may be economic, social (for example, family support), structural (such as housing), or psychological (for instance, coping skills, perceived control). A high level of resources is health protective. Low levels of resources place an individual at risk for mental health problems.

As well as more economic resources, people in higher socio-economic groups also appear to have more social and psychological resources known to be protective against mental health problems than the less well-off. Turner et al. (1999), for example, found that people in higher socio-economic groups reported higher levels of self-esteem and personal control over events than those in lower socio-economic groups. Both are known to be protective against depression. Social support, which is highly protective against a number of mental health problems (Kawachi and Berkman 2001), is also generally less available to those in the lower socio-economic groups. Ruberman et al. (1984), for example, found that measures of life stress, depression and social isolation were greatest among those with relatively few years in education. Similarly, Marmot et al. (1991) found that fewer male blue-collar workers than white-collar workers reported having a confidant whom they could trust with their problems, or from whom they received practical social support.

Relativity issues

While social stress and lack of resources appear to be direct causes of many mental health problems, some theorists have argued that it is not an absolute lack of resources that results in stress or mental health problems. Rather, it is the knowledge that one is under-resourced in comparison to other groups within society. If everyone 'is in the same boat', a lack of resources is not problematic. This type of hypothesis has been derived from studies which have examined the physical health of whole populations. These have found that the highest levels of premature mortality among western countries are not found among the poorest countries. Rather, they are found among the countries where there are the greatest disparities between rich and poor. Japan and Cuba, which perhaps represent the extremes of wealth across the western countries, both have low levels of premature mortality (see Wilkinson 1992). Both have relatively flat income distributions. Countries where the distribution of income is greater, such as the USA and the UK, have less healthy populations. These and other similar data led Wilkinson (1992) to suggest that we engage in some form of comparison of our living conditions with others in society, and that knowledge of a relative deprivation in some way increases risk of disease. Such a relationship is likely to be mediated through adverse mood states and stress, although studies of these processes are in their infancy, and the hypothesis has yet to be fully tested. However, there is emerging evidence that negative social comparisons may impact particularly on the health of men, and those in the lower middle incomes – below this level of income, absolute poverty may be the primary determinant of health (Aberg Yngwe et al. 2003).

Gender differences

A number of theories have attempted to explain consistent findings of higher levels of mental health problems among women than men. One common argument suggested that these differences may be more apparent than real, and stem from women's willingness to report psychological distress and men's relative unwillingness to do so. This theory has not been substantiated, however, and a number of well-conducted prevalence studies have consistently found gender differences in rates of mental health problems when random populations have been closely interviewed about the presence of psychiatric symptoms (Weich et al. 1998). Other theories have suggested similar mechanisms to those used to explain socio-economic differences in health: differential exposure and vulnerability to stressors.

Differential exposure

The differential stress hypothesis suggests that women encounter more stress in their lives than men, and as a result are more prone to mental health problems. What evidence there is suggests that women experience more hardship in their work and family roles than men (Rieker and Bird 2000). In addition, women encounter more role strain and spillover between the demands of work and home. Even when working full-time, women tend to do more work in the home than their partners. The resultant stress may place them at increased risk for stress-related and mental health problems. These issues were clearly demonstrated in the findings of Lundberg et al. (1981), who found that female managers' stress hormone levels remain raised following work, while those of male managers typically fell. This effect was particularly marked where the female managers had children. It seems that men compensated for a hard working day by relaxing when they came home, while women continued to cope with the demands of family and home. These differences in exposure to stress may be exacerbated by women's lack of support or control within the family or at work.

Women are also more subject to physical assault within the family, rape, and other traumatizing events than men. Although these events may be relatively uncommon, they may profoundly affect those involved and contribute to higher overall rates of anxiety or depression among women. Cloutier et al. (2002), for example, found that 19 per cent of their representative sample of women in North Carolina had been the subject of sexual assault at some time in their life. These women were two and a half times more likely to report 'poor mental health' than women who had not experienced this. A final source of stress among women may be poverty. Strickland (1992) suggested that 75 per cent of those living in poverty were mothers and children. Vulnerability to mental health problems as a result of low socio-economic status may therefore particularly impact on women.

Differential vulnerability
An alternative approach to this issue suggests that women may be more vulnerable to some types of stress than men. Elliott (2000), for example, suggested that women have a higher dependence on the support provided by social networks than men, and may be differentially affected by events that disrupt them. Related to this may be problems associated with the loss of attachment to the extended family, as children are more mobile and increasingly move from the family home as they mature. Finally, Simon (1995) suggested that women may react more strongly to work and family strains than men because of the importance that these roles have to their sense of worth.

Minority status

Minority status can be conferred by a number of factors: ethnicity, sexual choices, appearance, and so on. However, it is usually taken to mean obvious differences as a result of ethnicity. Considering issues of ethnicity is not without its dangers. Nazroo (1998), for example, warned that ethnicity encompasses a variety of issues: language, religion, experience of races and migration, culture, ancestry and forms of identity. Each of these may individually or together contribute to differences between the mental and physical health of different ethnic groups. It is dangerous to reify 'ethnicity' as a single factor which alone impacts on mental health. Any brief review of the relevant literature can therefore only scratch the surface of a complex literature and suggest some issues that may explain some differences in some mental health problems across some minority groups.

Differential exposure
One explanation for higher levels of mental health problems among social minorities is that they are exposed to more stress than the majority groups as a consequence of their minority status. One general stress to which many people in ethnic minorities are

exposed is that associated with low socio-economic status. Indeed, some commentators have suggested that any distress resulting from being within an ethnic minority is the result of occupying lower socio-economic groups, not being part of an ethnic minority *per se*. Ulbrich et al. (1989), for example, used data from a survey of 2115 adults to explore the role of race and socio-economic status on mental health in the USA. The minority group of interest here was African-American people. Overall, they found that occupational status, but not race, was related to distress. Other studies have found a more direct link between race, ethnicity and stress, not mediated by economic status (Williams 1999).

There are a number of social stressors to which minority social groups are uniquely exposed. One obvious stressor is that of racial prejudice. In an interesting examination of the effects of this type of stress, Clarke (2000) found that among a sample of young African-American women, the more they reported experiencing racism, the greater their rises in blood pressure during a task in which they talked about their views and feelings about animal rights. They took this to suggest that they had developed a stronger emotional and physiological reaction to general stress as a result of their long-term responses to racism.

A third source of stress experienced by ethnic minorities may be that resulting from tensions as individuals adopt or consciously reject some of the norms or mores of other cultures, including those of the host culture. Both may result in feelings of alienation, rejection by other members of the larger or one's own culture, and consequent mental health problems. In one study of this phenomenon, Lai (2004) studied Chinese immigrants to Canada, and found that the highest levels of depression were among those who established more cultural barriers against the new culture, and who had a higher level of identification with traditional Chinese cultural values.

Minority status is not just conferred by visible differences. Sexual minorities also experience prejudice that may impact on their mental health. Cole et al. (1996), for example, found that healthy gay men who concealed their sexual identity were more likely to experience poor mental and physical health than those who were able to express their sexuality. The same research group found social rejection influenced mental health and even disease progression in HIV-infected men. Those who experienced social rejection evidenced greater immune system dysfunction and less time to a diagnosis of AIDS.

Wider cross-cultural issues

The previous section considered how being a member of minority population may impact on mental health. But there are also a variety of factors that vary across cultures that may influence when and how people may present with mental health problems, and what form of treatment they seek. Any differences between cultures have not always been benign. As late as the second half of the last century, many Europeans and Americans believed that so-called 'primitive' people, including people from Africa, Native Americans, and some eastern countries, differed from western people in their capacity to think, process emotions and to cope with the demands of western civilization. Ironically, perhaps, these populations also reported relatively low levels of mental disorders – a phenomenon which was attributed to their primitive brain and the simple society rather than the result of some protective factor (Oda et al. 2005). Thankfully, such overtly racist (and incorrect) views have now been discarded, although differences between cultures in their presentation, causal attributions and treatments of various mental health disorders can be found.

Presentation of problems

Not surprisingly, perhaps, many common conditions present in ways that reflect the culture in which they are situated. Members of the Inuit population, for example, may develop a condition known as *kayak angst* – a feeling of panic associated with being alone in a kayak in the Arctic wastes. This may be termed 'agoraphobia with panic disorder' in societies where there are lots of houses and busy streets, and no kayaks. Mental distress may also result from exaggeration of culturally specific normative behaviours or concerns. In Japan, where ritual and politeness are extremely important, a condition known as *taijin kyofusho* is an incapacitating fear of offending or harming others through one's own awkward social behaviour, glancing at their genital areas, or imagined physical defect (Kirmayer 1991).

Similar problems may also present quite differently in various parts of the world. One of the key differences across cultures is the greater or lesser emphasis placed on physical symptoms as either a metaphor for, or means of expressing, emotional distress. It is generally acknowledged that people from eastern cultures tend to 'somatize' their distress, talking about it in terms of physical symptoms, while people from western cultures talk more about psychological symptoms. An example of this type of expression can be found in the Korean word '*hwa-byung*' which means 'fire illness' and can equally be epigastric pain or anger due to interpersonal conflict.

In China, presentation of mental health problems through physical complaints is common. Kua, Chew and Ko (1993) for example, reported that 72 per cent of people, later found to have a mental health disorder, initially presented with physical symptoms. The most common were chest or abdominal discomfort and headache. Kleinman reported a similar phenomenon in a study of a group of Taiwanese people with 'depressive syndrome' (1977: 5). Eighty-eight per cent of them initially complained only of physical symptoms – and did not report any emotional or psychological problems when directly asked about them. Twenty-eight per cent rejected the idea that they were depressed even whey they had experienced symptom relief following antidepressant medication. In a similar group of American patients, only 4 per cent presented complaining of physical symptoms.

In a study of this phenomenon in different ethnic groups within one country, in this case, the UK, Bhatt, Tomenson and Benjamin (1989) found that people from an Indian culture were more likely to attribute mental health problems to physical causes than were an indigenous English comparison group. Similarly, Gada (1982) found that depressed patients from an Indian background were more likely to report somatic symptoms and show evidence of hypochondriasis than were depressed indigenous British patients. Conversely, guilt feelings, obsessional and paranoid symptoms were significantly less frequent than among the indigenous British patients. Later research by Commander et al. (2004) in a similar population found no differences between indigenous British people and South Asian people in their beliefs about the nature and cause of their anxiety or depression. Such an explanation may suggest that some of the findings reported here may be framed in time, and may change as cultural influences change.

Kleinman (1977) suggested that differing presentations between cultures do not result from a misinterpretation of symptoms. Rather, they reflect social beliefs, norms and attitudes towards mental health problems. He argued that people from cultures that stigmatize mental health problems or where treatments for such problems are usually somatic, are more likely to report physical problems rather than mental ones. An example of this process is provided by Kirmayer et al. (2004), who reported a study of Vietnamese people who had emigrated to Canada. Many of them expressed emotional distress in terms of a condition they termed *uat u'c*. This was described in terms of having bodily aches, being cold and depleted of energy. However, further discussion with these individuals revealed that their symptoms resulted from a predicament that involved indignation over a social injustice that could not be denounced because of their status within the social hierarchy and a need to maintain social harmony by not complaining about this injustice. Similarly, Karasz (2005) examined conceptual models of depressive symptoms in South Asian and European immigrants to the USA. Participants were presented with a vignette describing depressive symptoms and then asked about their understanding of the symptoms presented. The Asian people identified the problem in the vignette in social and moral terms, and suggested treatment should involve self-help and non-professional help. The Europeans typically held one of two models. The first was similar to that of the Asians; the other emphasized biological explanations including 'hormonal imbalance' and 'neurological problem'.

More radical differences in beliefs about the nature of mental health problems have been found in a variety of non-western countries, including those in Africa and Asia. In Malaysia, Razali (1995) found that 53 per cent of people with mental health problems attributed them to supernatural agents, such as witchcraft or possession by evil spirits. Interestingly, belief in supernatural causes of mental illness was not significantly associated with age, gender, level of education or occupation. A second example can be found in research from Zimbabwe, reported by Patel et al. (1995), who found that angered ancestral spirits, evil spirits and witchcraft were potent causes of mental health problems. Similar levels of belief in supernatural causes of mental health problems were found in Nigeria by Adebowale and Ogunlesi (1999), although they also found that 17 per cent of people attributed their mental health disorder to biological factors, and 23 per cent believed their condition was the result of psychosocial factors. The latter beliefs were more common among urban than among rural dwellers, suggesting that beliefs about the cause of mental health disorders may change as people become aware of alternative causal explanations. This change from traditional models of mental health problems to more western understandings has been tracked over time in Kerala, southern India, where Halliburton (2005) reported a transition from explanations of mental health problems in terms of spirit possession to more western understandings of 'depression' and 'tension' over time.

Research box 4

Nakane, Y., Jorm, A.F., Yoshioka, K. et al. (2005) Public beliefs about causes and risk factors for mental disorders: a comparison of Japan and Australia, *BMC Psychiatry*, 21(5): 33.

The authors note that surveys of the public in a number of western countries have shown a predominant belief in social stressors as the primary cause of mental disorders. However, they noted this issue has received little research attention in other parts of the world and few cross-cultural comparisons have been reported. This study attempted to add to this literature by conducting surveys of general populations' beliefs about the causes and risk factors for depression and schizophrenia in Australia and Japan.

Method

Questionnaire

Participants were shown one of four vignettes describing a person, either male or female, with major depression, major depression with suicidal thoughts, early schizophrenia or chronic schizophrenia. The vignettes provided sufficient symptoms to 'satisfy at a minimal level these diagnostic criteria'. They were asked to rate, using a 5-point scale, the likelihood of a number of psychological and biological factors, both in the present and past, being the cause of the problems. Factors included a virus or infection, genetics, day-to-day stress, the recent death of a person close to them, being badly treated as a child, weakness of character, and losing one or both parents while young. They were also asked to rate the importance of a number of 'risk factors' including gender, being under 25 years of age, poor, divorced or separated, and so on.

Survey methods

A household survey was conducted on Australian adults aged 18 years or over. Households were sampled from 250 census districts in urban and rural areas throughout Australia. Researchers attempted to interview the person in each household with the most recent birthday. A target of 4000 interviews was planned. To try to achieve this, the researchers visited 18,957 households, and conducted a total of 3998 interviews. A similar process was followed in Japan, with households approached until 2000 interviews were conducted. The number of households visited was not recorded.

Key findings

Both samples were similar to the two countries' populations' age, marital, educational, and gender distribution. Any deviations from these norms were identified and statistically corrected for, so the comparisons were meaningful between population norms. Table 4.1 shows the percentage of Japanese and Australian respondents to judge each cause as 'likely' or 'very likely' to lead to the four conditions. Although no statistical analyses were reported, it appears that the Japanese population was more likely to endorse the role of the trait characteristics of 'nervous person' and 'weakness of character', while Australians were more likely to endorse the role of biological factors such as a virus or genetics. Data on what the authors described as risk factors

Table 4.1 Percentage of Japanese and Australian populations to endorse each explanation as likely or very likely

Cause	Depression	Suicidal	Acute schizophrenia	Chronic schizophrenia
Virus or infection				
Japan	6.2	6.6	7.2	7.2
Australia	50.5	41.4	32.1	33.6
Stress				
Japan	93.6	91.8	92.0	91.2
Australia	96.8	95.7	89.6	86.6
Close death				
Japan	79.8	81.4	73.4	74.0
Australia	96.3	94.8	87.4	83.3
Traumatic event				
Japan	82.6	79.6	78.2	80.8
Australia	93.9	92.7	86.5	82.8
Childhood problems				
Japan	81.0	82.0	88.2	89.0
Australia	91.3	95.0	90.8	91.4
Inherited or genetic				
Japan	34.6	34.0	34.2	43.8
Australia	68.0	68.4	70.0	73.7
Nervous person				
Japan	81.4	77.4	74.0	81.8
Australia	67.9	65.6	58.1	56.9
Character weakness				
Japan	73.6	69.2	73.4	82.0
Australia	43.0	46.1	39.7	35.1

are not reported here in detail. However, more Australians than Japanese people considered poverty to be a risk factor for both depression and schizophrenia.

Discussion

There were clear differences between the cultures' causal beliefs, with the most stark differences being the higher frequency of the belief among Australians that biological factors and poverty contributed to risk for mental health problems, while more of the Japanese people endorsed personality traits. According to the authors, one culture focused on uncontrollable and external factors; the other was more likely to 'blame' the individual for their mental health problems. Nevertheless, there were more commonalities in beliefs about causal factors than dissimilarities. It would have been interesting to see whether there were any differences between people with different levels of education or of different ages, to see whether cultural or generational factors influenced beliefs. However, these analyses were not reported.

Help seeking

Not surprisingly, the beliefs individuals hold about the cause of any problem will influence the type of help they seek to cope with it. Razali and Najib (2000), for example, found that 69 per cent of Malay patients in their sample had sought help from traditional healers called a *Bomoh* before consulting a psychiatrist. Similar patterns of help seeking also occur in a number of African countries. Abiodun (1995) found that the first point of contact for about one-third of patients attending a mental health service in Nigeria had been a traditional or religious healer. By contrast, Appiah-Poku et al. (2004) found that only 6 per cent of Ghanaian people within a population of users of psychiatric services had seen a faith healer before coming to the service. Again, these data allow the possibility of shifting cultural understandings of the causes of mental health problems changing the type of help that is sought. To put these data in context, Elkins, Rajab and Marcus (2005) found that 44 per cent of their sample of US psychiatric in-patients had tried to treat their condition by the use of herbal therapies before seeking professional help; 30 per cent had used spiritual healing.

Thinking about . . .

Imagine waking up feeling miserable, sad, finding it difficult to face the day. But how serious do these feelings need to be before you seek help? Do they have to last a week, a month, before you seek help? And who do you tell about your problems? Your doctor? Your friends? And when you do tell people, how much do you confide and how do you describe your problems?

Admitting both to yourself and others that you have a physical or mental health problem is not always easy. Private people, in particular, may find it difficult to admit to other people that they are experiencing problems. But what factors influence when and how an individual decides to tell others about any emotional distress they are experiencing – and how much they tell? Culture is only one factor that determines when and how such problems are reported. What other factors will influence this process? Personality? The social context within which an individual lives? The strength of the support available to the individual?

Treatment

Non-western approaches to the treatment of mental health problems may differ significantly from that familiar to most westerners. Treatment by a *Bomoh*, for example, differs according to their diagnosis of the problem. If the condition appears to be caused by a spell, the *Bomoh* finds out the ingredients of the spells and removes or neutralizes them. If the problem is caused by ghosts or evil spirits, they try to drive out or defeat them. This involves going into a trance, carrying out exorcism, communicating with spirits and reciting special prayers or verses from the Koran. Traditional Chinese treatments may involve the use of herbs and diet therapy. Kleinman (1997) described the treatment one Chinese man had to treat his recurrent feelings of grief and loneliness following a number of bereavements, and depression following financial losses on the stock market. He attributed his symptoms to not having enough blood, and was treated with tonics to 'increase blood' and with symbolically 'hot' food to correct his underlying humoral imbalance. He was also considering treatment with acupuncture.

Psychological therapy across cultures

Obviously, the type of treatment provided has to be consistent with the beliefs and culture from which an individual comes. So far, the chapter has considered gross differences in treatment across cultures and beliefs systems. At a more micro-level, cultural issues need to be considered within any psychological therapy when these larger cultural differences do not prevent its practice. Care must be taken to work within the cultural framework and understandings an individual brings with them to therapy. Key issues that have to be considered include:

- *The language of therapy:* although some therapy may be undertaken through the use of interpreters, the ideal is that it is undertaken in the native language of the client. This allows the therapist to understand and respond to the full meaning, including metaphorical meanings, of what is said.

- *The type of communication appropriate for the culture:* cultures may differ in terms of norms related to self-disclosure, privacy and confidentiality. If boundaries are inadvertently or unknowingly crossed, this will significantly impact on the effectiveness of any intervention.

- *Cultural beliefs and behavioural norms:* these may differ across cultures and have to be taken into account when considering what constitutes abnormal behaviours or emotional responses to events. Hearing voices, for example, may be quite acceptable, even laudable, in some cultures but be regarded as an indication of mental health problems in others.

- *Beliefs about the causes of mental health problems:* if these differ, then therapy will prove difficult if not impossible. Some cultures, for example, may ascribe problems to the individual, who may become the focus of any intervention; others may consider mental health problems to result from social factors, where others may be more involved in treatment.

- *The limits of change imposed by cultural factors:* if the therapist places too much emphasis on individual change, 'growth' and expression of the self when treating an individual from a highly socio-centric culture, this may prove distressing both to the individual and to those around them.

- *When and how to discuss issues of race and culture:* this may not be an issue if client and therapist are from the same culture, but may have to be addressed if they differ.

Preventing mental health problems

Health promotion

According to the World Health Organization (1996), health promotion involves a variety of complex interventions at differing levels, aimed not just at preventing ill-health, but also at promoting positive health. This perspective involves:

- having a holistic approach to health
- respecting diverse cultures and beliefs
- promoting positive health as well as preventing ill-health
- working at a structural (societal) not just individual level
- using participatory methods.

Removing the jargon, this means that health promotion should work not just with individuals, but also at a societal level to bring about improvements in health. It works with communities to meet their particular health needs, and attempts to improve health and quality of life, not just prevent disease. It can work at a legislative level, with communities, and groups and individuals within them. It can be conducted by a variety of people, some of whom would label themselves as workers in health promotion, many of whom would not. Some examples of the range of health promotion activities that can be conducted, in this case to minimize levels of alcohol-related problems, are outlined in Table 4.2. Here, interventions are aimed at the whole population of drinkers as well as those who drink to excess.

Therapeutic interventions

The majority of health promotion initiatives in the context of mental health have involved attempts to improve access to psychiatric and psychological care, by reaching out to groups with poor access to health care and who have high levels of mental health problems: the economically deprived, people without housing, and so on. Other interventions have been aimed at preventing relapse in people already identified as having a mental health problem (Secker 1998). In the USA, such an approach has increasingly been advocated for social minorities such as Native Americans who experience high levels of mental health problems and drug use. The approach adopted by the US system suggests that such interventions always need to be individualized in the clinical setting according to each person's age, gender, race, ethnicity and culture (Department of Health and Human Services 1999).

Psychosocial interventions

More radical approaches to mental health promotion go beyond the individual and consider how societal conditions impact on mental health. The link between poor mental health and socio-economic inequalities has led some commentators to suggest that the most compelling intervention strategies to reduce mental health inequalities

Table 4.2 Examples of differing levels of health promotion aimed at minimizing alcohol-related harm

Level of approach	Examples of practice
Whole population	
Central government	Establishing drink–drive laws: reduces harmful effects of alcohol consumption
	Taxation: high taxation reduces consumption
	Government guidelines on consumption limits
Local government	Local police policies on public houses and drink–driving
	Licensing of new pubs and drinking time limits
Media	Drink–drive campaigns
	Television programmes on the harmful effects of alcohol and promoting sensible drinking
Supermarkets/shops	Giving priority to low-alcohol drinks on the shelves
Population of drinkers	
Individual pubs/brewers	Establishing local minibus services to prevent drink–driving
	Provision of low alcohol beers
	Discouraging the obviously intoxicated from drinking alcohol (in the USA, a bartender can be sued for an incident – e.g. car accident – involving a drunk individual if they served them alcohol while visibly drunk)
Supermarkets/shops	Policing of drinking-age requirements for purchase of alcohol
Problem drinkers	
Health care/social services	Provision of detoxification services
	Therapy to prevent excess alcohol consumption
	Therapy to prevent relapse in people who have successfully stopped or reduced their excess drinking

are likely to be social, economic and political. From an economic perspective, strategies should include measures to reduce unemployment to the lowest possible level. The Swedish economic model identified a series of strategies that have proven effective in maintaining high levels of employment, including proactive employment exchange, high quality training aimed at providing skills required by the employment market, recruitment incentives for employers, and the right to temporary public employment in the last resort. Davey Smith et al. (1999) called for a series of differing economic measures. They argued for the implementation of 'affordable' basic income schemes as a means of ending poverty. These could take the form of a payment received by every person or household to provide a minimal income, with the amount paid based on age and family status. In addition, they suggested that all benefits to families with children which receive income support should be increased to avoid the next generation being disadvantaged from birth. They noted that a quarter of all children are born to mothers under the age of 25 years, and that the government should ensure that those under this age receive no fewer benefits than older individuals – as they did at the time of their paper. It is beyond the scope of the present volume to comment on the strengths and weaknesses of various economic systems. However, they have significant implications for mental health and should, therefore, form a legitimate area of influence for those involved in health promotion and public health.

Using the media

One in four people is likely to experience mental health problems in their lifetime, of whom only a minority will access professional help (Jenkins et al. 1998). The mass media provides a means of accessing such individuals. One example of this approach was reported by Barker et al. (1993). They reported the outcome of a series of seven, 10-minute, programmes, covering a variety of mental health topics. An audience survey indicated that viewing the series led to attitudinal, but not behavioural, changes: probably as much as could be expected given the brevity with which each subject was dealt with. The effects of a more substantial television series, 'Pssst . . . the really useful guide to alcohol', which aimed to encourage sensible drinking, were reported by Bennett et al. (1991). The programmes were designed to attract younger drinkers, and involved both media personalities and experts in educating viewers about what was meant by sensible drinking and providing models of sensible drinking: Rowan Atkinson, for example, provided humorous reminders of weekly sensible drinking limits. One of the presenters gradually cut his consumption over the course of the programme. Surveys conducted before and after the programme suggested that the series improved knowledge of what was meant by sensible drinking among the general population, and resulted in a modest shift of attitudes among moderate–high drinkers towards drinking less. The impact of a more explicitly 'mental health' programme, this time in South Africa, was reported by Wessels et al. (1999). They recorded over 3000 telephone calls asking for information on mental health issues following a television series which described and explained the signs and symptoms of a variety of mental health problems. Most calls related to depression and anxiety.

Public education

Another health promotion approach involves providing relatively simple psychological interventions that are open to all: usually in the form of **stress management** classes. Brown et al. (2000) assessed one such programme. They ran eight free full- or half-day stress management workshops in a leisure centre following a publicity drive as part of the 'Healthy Birmingham 2000' programme. These taught attenders relaxation and other strategies for controlling their stress. Their comparison groups comprised people who took part in a day-long programme focusing on sessions on healthy eating, alcohol awareness and physical exercise and a group of people on a waiting list for future workshops. The event proved very popular and attracted both people who had seen a health professional, usually their GP, about stress-related problems and those who had not. The intervention also proved successful. Compared with baseline levels, participants in the full-day workshops showed significantly greater reductions in stress and anxiety three months following the workshop than those in the comparison groups: an impressive result given the relative brevity of the intervention and the wide range of people attending.

The working organization can also provide a setting in which people can learn stress management skills. One survey (Fielding and Piserchia 1989) found that about a quarter of large companies in the USA provide some form of stress management classes for their workers. In general, these have proven effective, although Oldenburg and Harris (1996) noted that they attracted only between 10 and 40 per cent of the workforce, and that many of those that attend had little to gain, while many anxious individuals did not attend them.

Setting up and running these types of workshops, while of benefit to those who attend, are relatively time-consuming and costly, so some groups have begun to explore alternative, more cost-effective approaches. One exciting approach is to provide stress management training or other psychological therapies online. A quick search on the Internet will show the hundreds, if not thousands, of private therapists who provide such a service. These tend to focus on treatment rather than prevention. However, larger-scale prevention projects are also being set up. One example of this is an interactive web-based stress management programme set up by Unilever, which can be accessed through health clinics or online to interested individuals throughout Europe. This provides a structured approach to reducing stress as well as targeting behaviours that increase risk for heart disease, including an exercise programme and dietary advice. A more targeted approach was reported by Matano et al. (2000), who set up a website to provide advice on how to cut down alcohol consumption for a single large worksite. As with the Unilever project, levels of usage and its effectiveness have yet to be evaluated, but the potential for such interventions is impressive.

Organizational interventions

So far, the preventive approaches discussed have focused on helping people cope more effectively with the stress in their lives. A higher level intervention may involve reducing the causes of those stresses. While large-scale societal changes to improve mental health have proven difficult to implement and are constrained by political and economic factors, one area that can be more easily manipulated is the workplace.

One of the few worksite stress management projects to adopt a systemic approach to reducing stress was reported by Maes et al. (1998). Their intervention focused on modifying key aspects of the working environment in order to enhance mental well-being throughout the workforce of a major industrial producer. Their intervention drew upon studies that identified working conditions that can enhance both the well-being of workers and work production levels, including individuals working within their capabilities, avoiding short and repetitive performance tasks, having some control over the organization of work, and adequate social contact in the work situation. With these factors in mind, they attempted, within the constraints of production, to change the nature of each worker's job to bring it closer to the ideal. In addition, they trained managers in communication and leadership skills and identified methods through which they could recognize, and then prevent or reduce, individual stress within the workforce. Although measures of 'stress' were not taken as part of the research programme, these changes resulted in an increase in the quality of work and lower absenteeism rates: both indicative of an increase in well-being at work.

A second, and very important, organization in which preventive services may be established is the school. A number of interventions have been aimed at school-children of all ages. Some involve working directly with children to teach them coping skills. The Promoting Alternative THinking Strategies programme (PATHS: Greenberg and Kusche, 1998), for example, taught children how to understand and regulate their emotions through the use of cognitive strategies similar to those discussed in Chapter 3. This proved effective in improving social problem-solving, emotional understanding, self-report of conduct problems, teacher ratings of adaptive behaviour, and cognitive abilities related to social planning and impulsivity for up to two years following the intervention. Other interventions may work at a higher level and involve changes to the wider school environment. The School Transitional Environment Project (STEP) (e.g. Felner et al. 1993), for example, changed the school environment to make it less threatening to students during transitions from lower to higher schools. It aimed to reduce the complexity of the new school environment, to make teachers more supportive and to create a stable support mechanism through a consistent set of peers and classmates. This broad environment change resulted in significantly lower levels of stress and anxiety, depression and delinquent behaviour than in schools where these changes were not instituted. It also proved more effective than a teaching programme focusing on generic coping and problem-solving skills on measures of adjustment to school change and academic performance.

Chapter summary

1   Both small and large social groups and other social factors impact on levels of mental health conditions.

2   Family models of mental health note the reciprocity between family members, and that mental health problems arise as a consequence of interactions between family members.

3   Structural family therapy adopts a model of a well-functioning family, based on the boundaries between units within the family. It uses behavioural strategies to shift dysfunctional families towards this model.

4   Strategic family therapy has no model of appropriate functioning. It uses two strategies of change: positive reframing and paradoxical manipulations.

5   Three major social variables impact on levels of mental health within the population: socio-economic position, gender and minority status.

6   Explanations for these differences include differences in levels of stress and coping resources and, perhaps, processes of social comparison.

7   Cultural factors may influence the causal explanations for mental health problems and the treatment individuals from differing cultures seek.

8   Proponents of radical health promotion suggest that health inequalities can best be addressed through economic and political changes.

9   Those involved in promoting mental health have typically done so using more
    circumscribed interventions including using the media and open access classes to
    teach stress coping skills. Some projects have also addressed working and school
    environments to make them less stressful.

For discussion

1 All conditions treated with family therapy can also be treated by one-to-one
  therapy. What are the advantages and disadvantages of each approach?
2 How effective is a white middle-class therapist likely to be when providing
  therapy for someone from a different social class and culture? How can they
  alter the approach they take with such an individual?
3 Consider how you could promote mental health within the wider population
  or specific groups, such as working mothers or students.
4 If mental health disorders result at least in part from social conditions, should
  psychologists be actively involved in attempts to influence public health
  policy and relevant government decisions?

Further reading

Dallos, R. and Draper, R. (2005) *An Introduction to Family Therapy: Systemic Theory and
    Practice*. 2nd edn. Buckingham: Open University Press.
Elliott, M. (2000) Gender differences in the causes of depression, *Women and Health*, 33:
    163–77.
Kirmayer, L.J. (2001) Cultural variations in the clinical presentation of depression and anxiety:
    implications for diagnosis and treatment, *Journal of Clinical Psychiatry*, 62 (Suppl. 13):
    22–8.
Secker, J. (1998) Current conceptualisations of mental health and mental health promotion,
    Health Education Research Theory and Practice, 13: 57–66.
Turner, R.J., Lloyd, D.A. and Roszell, P. (1999) Personal resources and the social distribution
    of depression, *American Journal of Community Psychology*, 27: 643–72.

PART II
Specific issues

5

Somatoform disorders

This chapter explores some of the psychological conditions in which the relationship between psychological processes and physical processes is most apparent. It explores four conditions which fall under the heading of somatoform disorders. At a quick glance, the first two conditions, somatization and hypochondriasis, appear very similar as they both involve the reporting of inappropriately high levels of physical symptoms, and some clinicians have argued that they overlap in a number of ways. However, there are key differences between them. Somatization disorder involves the experience and reporting of recurrent and frequently changing physical symptoms, which cannot be explained by any known medical condition and may raise some concern. Hypochondriasis is excessive *fear* of illness and the belief that one has an undiagnosed physical disease. It may involve checking or seeking medical reassurance as a means of reducing fear.

The other two conditions to be considered in the chapter are more easily distinguishable. The first of these, body dysmorphic disorder, involves an excessive dissatisfaction with one's body or particular body parts. Finally, the chapter examines one of the most intriguing psychosomatic conditions, in which an individual may develop extreme and disabling physical symptoms, such as paralysis or blindness, with no apparent physical cause. By the end of the chapter, you should have an understanding of:

- The nature and aetiology of each condition from a number of theoretical perspectives
- The types of interventions used to treat each disorder
- The relative effectiveness of each of these interventions.

Somatization disorder

Somatization may be described as the experience and reporting of physical symptoms that cause distress but lack corresponding physical pathology and cannot be explained by physical examination, laboratory tests or diagnostic techniques. DSM-IV-TR (APA 2000) identified the following diagnostic criteria that need to be met to result in its diagnosis:

- A history of many physical complaints beginning before the age of 30 years which occur over a period of several years and result in treatment being sought or significant impairment, including:
    - four *pain* symptoms: a history of pain related to at least four different sites or functions (e.g. head, abdomen, menstruation, sexual intercourse)
    - two *gastrointestinal* symptoms: a history of at least two gastrointestinal symptoms other than pain (e.g. nausea, bloating, or intolerance of several foods)
    - one *sexual* symptom: a history of at least one sexual or reproductive symptom other than pain (e.g. sexual indifference, irregular menses, excessive menstrual bleeding)
    - one *pseudoneurological* symptom: a history of at least one symptom suggesting a neurological condition (e.g. impaired coordination or balance, difficulty swallowing or lump in throat, double vision).
- Either:
    - the symptoms cannot be fully explained by a known general medical condition or the direct effects of a substance, or
    - when there is a related general medical condition, the physical complaints or resulting impairment are in excess of what would be expected.
- The symptoms are not intentionally feigned or produced.

Of note is the age at which symptoms typically start – well before the age of onset of most chronic diseases – and the wide variety of symptoms necessary for a diagnosis to be assigned.

Prevalence

Most of us report some sensations or symptoms that are not related to illness at some time or other. The American Epidemiologic Catchment Area study (Kroenke and Price 1993), for example, found that about a quarter of the general population had experienced some degree of somatic symptoms with no obvious cause, including joint pains, headache and fatigue at some time in their life, and that these were sufficient to trigger a change in lifestyle, use of medication or seeing a doctor. Similarly, Bridges and Goldberg (1985) found that about 20 per cent of new primary care consultations were for somatic symptoms for which no specific cause could be found. This background of symptom reporting makes if difficult to assess levels of hypochondriasis – where the level of symptoms has become pathological. However, Creed and Barsky (2004) estimated that, at any one time, between 0.1 and 0.7 per cent of the general population could be diagnosed with somatization disorder. Among people in general medical wards, Fink, Hansen and Oxhoj (2004) estimated the prevalence of somatization as 5.2 per cent, with a significant difference between the rates among men and women (3.8 and 7.5 per cent respectively). It is often accompanied by high levels of depression or anxiety (Henningsen et al. 2003).

Health complaints where no obvious medical cause can be found are often considered a modern phenomenon, the results of the stress of 'modern life'. However, this may not be true. Eriksen et al. (2004) investigated the frequency of such complaints in three groups of individuals: Norwegians, Aborigine Mangyans living under 'primitive conditions' on a small island in the Philippines, and urban people living on the same island. To their surprise, both island populations reported more musculoskeletal problems, fatigue, mood changes and gastrointestinal symptoms than did the Norwegian sample.

So far, the chapter has assumed that somatization is the result of individual psychological processes. But some cultures may 'somatize' more than others, or report psychological symptoms in terms of physical states (see Chapter 4). An example of this is afforded by the Korean word '*hwa-byung*' which is translated as 'fire illness' and may refer to symptoms of epigastric pain, but may equally refer to anger due to interpersonal conflict. In western countries, less dramatic, but still important differences in presentation of symptoms may also occur. In Britain, for example, people who originate from the Indian sub-continent are more likely to attribute mental health problems to physical causes, and report them in terms of physical illnesses, than indigenous British people (Bhatt et al. 1989). Care must be taken when considering these explanations for distress. If such expressions of distress are used within a culture of agreed meaning, this may prove an effective way of communication. However, if patients try to explain their distress to doctors from a different culture who are unaware of these cultural differences, this may result in erroneous efforts to diagnose and treat non-existent physical conditions – or inappropriately suggest a 'diagnosis' of somatization, which more accurately reflects cultural differences in reporting of emotional distress.

Mrs T was a 45-year-old secretary who repeatedly presented at her family doctor complaining of bizarre and medically unexplainable symptoms. She was referred to a clinical psychologist, to whom she recounted some of her symptoms. Of interest, is that she was seen by the psychologist on a number of occasions, during which the description of her symptoms changed, seemingly in response to discussions with the psychologist. One key example of this was that while she initially denied that her symptoms were related to stress, once presented with a stress-based explanation of her symptoms, this was seamlessly built into her description of her symptoms:

I don't know what's the matter with me. But I know that it is serious . . . and I worry that it cannot go on much longer. I have problems from my head to my toes. My tongue feels like it is tasting metal and it fizzes. That's all I can describe it as . . . it fizzes. I cannot eat because it feels so bad. And if I do, my stomach fizzes and is so painful and I feel sick. I have nearly stopped eating. (In fact, she had not lost weight since the onset of her symptoms some months previously.) The pain is here . . . and here. I can feel it now. It fills me, it bubbles up and moves along my stomach. I think it's stress affecting it from my brain. I can feel the nerves running down my body. They are hot and spiky feeling.

I sometimes feel dizzy and worry that I will fall over. I feel faint, my eyes go blurry, and I feel pale. Nothing really sets this off . . . it just happens. I worry about my symptoms all the time. When I am at work I sit and think about them. I ask my colleagues to look at me to show them my symptoms – to see how I am. I don't know how long I can still go to work. I am thinking about giving up. The people at work are really helpful. They listen to me. But my husband is fed up of me telling him about it. He says that it's all nonsense . . . and that I should listen to the doctor when he says there is nothing wrong with me. I keep trying to tell him how I feel, but he doesn't understand how I feel. I feel frightened that I will die. I know that I have had my problems a long time and that if something bad was going to happen it probably would have by now. But they scare me just the same. I have never had things like this. I've not had any illness, so why this should happen now I don't know. [According to her family doctor, this was far from the case – her medical notes were 'inches thick': i.e. she had been a frequent attender over many years.]

I would love to have a scan. The tests I have had have found nothing. But there are other tests that doctor can give me. They may show what the problem is . . .

Aetiology of somatization disorder

A psychobiological model

The simplest biological model of somatization suggests that people with the disorder have a biologically mediated sensitivity to physiological activity within the body, which they report as 'symptoms'. The biological pathways through which this may occur are not as yet clear – and not all evidence supports the notion of this hypersensitivity (e.g. Sherman et al. 2004). Nevertheless, Rief et al. (2004) speculated that dysregulation of amino acids and serotonin may contribute to somatization. The group compared levels of various amino acids including tryptophan (a precursor to serotonin; see Chapter 3) in patients with somatization disorder, with and without depression, and normal controls and found that low levels of tryptophan were associated with high levels of somatization independently of the presence of depression. They took these data to suggest that the serotonergic system may be involved in a process of sensitization of neurones that leads to a state of **hyperalgesia**, which forms the basis of chronic somatization.

Along with this potential biological sensitivity, individuals with somatization disorder may interpret bodily functions in a catastrophizing manner (Rief et al. 1998). That is, they may misperceive normal body sensations or emotional signals as evidence of dangerous somatic processes. In this way, biological processes may be augmented by psychological processes. These psychological processes may be influenced by a variety of factors, including childhood events and personality.

Childhood learning

Somatization may have its roots in early childhood experiences. There are several retrospective studies indicating that adults who report high levels of somatic symptoms with no obvious cause are more likely to have witnessed more illness in family members than is the norm, including:

- excessive somatic complaints by parents
- excessive illness or complaints of illness from other family members
- excessive family complaints of pain.

In addition, there is some evidence of relatively high levels of somatization among people with a history of family members with physical handicap or deformity. In one study of this phenomenon, Craig, Cox and Klein (2002) compared the (self-reported) history of three groups of women who were either chronic somatizers, had a long-term illness, or were healthy. Somatizing mothers were three times more likely than the other women to have witnessed a parent having a physical illness. The children of these somatizing mothers were, in turn, more likely to report health problems than were the children of the medically ill or healthy women, and had more consultations with family doctors. These consultations were associated with maternal somatization, maternal childhood adversity, and the child's tendency to worry about their health. In a second study with the same women, Craig et al. (2004) demonstrated the subtle way in which parents can focus on health-related issues. In their study, they observed the women playing with their 4–8-year-old children in a structured play setting. Somatizing mothers were emotionally flatter and gave their children less attention than the other mothers during both play tasks. However, they were more responsive to their child than the other mothers when they played with a medical box.

Craig et al. (1993) suggested the childhood experience of illness is more likely to result in somatization where it is associated with lack of parental care (Craig et al. 2002) and sexual abuse (Modestin et al. 2005). Specific childhood trauma may also increase risk for specific sets of symptoms. Sexual abuse, for example, may lead to complaints of abdominal and pelvic pain in adulthood (Barsky et al. 1994). This emphasis on acute and severe trauma has been questioned by, among others, Lackner, Gudleski and Blanchard (2004), who found that higher levels of rejection and/or hostility among fathers (not mothers) were more correlated with somatization than was abuse, suggesting that low-level, long-term, neglect may lead to similar problems to those arising from more dramatic factors. According to Craig et al. (1993), these predisposing factors contribute to risk of somatization through psychological processes:

• lack of care or neglect increases risk of an emotional disorder such as anxiety or depression
• high levels of illness behaviour among parents predisposes children to interpretations of their emotional symptoms as indicative of physical illness.

A third related factor suggested by Latimer (1981) is that expressions of physical health problems may be reinforced by parents who themselves view the cause of symptoms to be more physical than emotional. As a consequence, the child learns to express their emotional distress in terms of physical symptoms as this gains more attention and is responded to more than complaints of psychological distress. This may be evident in the findings of Craig and colleagues discussed above. All three predisposing factors suggest that the experience of stress by people with this history will result in the expression of their distress in physical terms.

Personality

Most research on the relationship between personality and somatization has focused on the role of **alexithymia**, whose key defining characteristic is difficulty in identifying and describing feelings and in distinguishing between feelings and bodily sensations. A number of studies have found a high prevalence of alexithymia among people with somatoform disorder. Lipsanen et al. (2004), for example, found a significant correlation between measures of somatization and alexithymia in a large non-clinical sample. Jones et al. (2004) also found some (but not all) patients with **functional dyspepsia** had slightly higher scores on measures of alexithymia than a comparison group with no health problems. Similarly, Duddu, Isaac and Chaturvedi (2003) found that mean alexithymia scores in individuals with somatoform disorder were significantly higher than for normal controls. However, both groups had mean scores within the non-alexithymic range. In addition, and apparently paradoxically, people with alexithymia in the somatoform disorder group were *more* likely to give a psychological explanation of innocuous bodily sensations than those with low levels of alexithymia. Summarizing the available evidence, while alexithymia may be related to the somatization, the strength of this association may be less than may have been previously thought.

There is some evidence that other personality factors – perhaps developed as a consequence of the type of upbringing discussed above – may be associated with somatization. Noyes et al. (2001), for example, found that more somatizers met the diagnostic criteria for obsessive-compulsive disorder, and scored more highly on psychometric measures of self-defeating, depressive and neurotic personality types than people in a general medical comparison group. Neitzert, Davis and Kennedy (1997) also found neuroticism and depression to be associated with levels of symptom reporting.

Psychoanalytic explanations

Classic Freudian explanations of physical symptoms focus on sudden inexplicable presentations of physical symptoms – conversion disorder – and are considered later in the chapter. Post-Freudian explanations of somatization reflect the evidence described earlier in this section. According to Guthrie (1996), deficiencies in the early mother–child relationship leave the individual with an inability to use their imagination and language to describe and control stress and distress. This results in a limited fantasy life, difficulties in processing emotional experiences, and a susceptibility to somatic complaints. This leads to difficulties in developing appropriate relationships in adulthood. Any relationships the individual does develop are either chaotic or symbiotic. In the latter, they form a relationship with someone who adopts the role of carer – and they adopt the role of invalid. The physical symptoms they report therefore act both as a way of coping with intolerable emotional feelings and as a means of eliciting the care of their partner.

Treatment of somatization disorder

Pharmacological treatment

In one of the very few studies to investigate the pharmacological treatment of somatization disorder, Noyes et al. (1998) reported an uncontrolled trial of treatment using an SSRI. Twenty-nine people with a variety of somatoform disorders were treated. However, only seven had a diagnosis of somatization disorder. Of these, four evidenced moderate improvements, at least in the short term. So, there is some preliminary evidence of a therapeutic benefit for SSRIs, but more trials are needed to confirm this.

Psychological interventions

Just as with pharmacological treatment of somatization disorder, there are relatively few studies of the effectiveness of psychological interventions. The condition is often reported as difficult to treat. However, a number of uncontrolled studies using cognitive behavioural programmes involving education, relaxation response and cognitive restructuring have been shown to be of some benefit (e.g. Nakao et al. 2001). In a more controlled study, Lidbeck (2003) reported on the effectiveness of a programme involving a thorough physical examination, education about psychological and physiological stress symptoms to enable cognitive restructuring, and relaxation training. In comparison with no treatment, this programme achieved reductions in cognitive worries and medication usage both immediately following treatment and at six-month follow-up. A year later, participants in the intervention group maintained their improvements on measures of health worry, and also reported gains on measures of generalized anxiety and depression.

Hypochondriasis

For a diagnosis of hypochondriasis to be made, DSM-IV-TR (APA 2000) states that the following symptoms should be present for at least six months:

- preoccupation with fears of having, or the idea that one has, a serious disease based upon misinterpretation of bodily symptoms
- the preoccupation persists despite appropriate medical evaluation and reassurance
- the preoccupation with fears is not of delusional intensity and is not restricted to a circumscribed concern about appearance.
- the preoccupation causes clinically significant distress or impairment.

This description of the disorder, however, is not accepted by everybody. Fink et al. (2004), for example, noted that the definition overlaps with a number of other diagnoses, and (perhaps as a consequence) is therefore rarely used in practice. They suggested an alternative set of symptoms that maintain the spirit of the original diagnosis but which have less overlap with others:

- preoccupation with the idea of harbouring an illness or with bodily function
- rumination about illness
- suggestibility
- unrealistic fear of infection
- fascination with medical information
- fear of prescribed medication.

People with hypochondriasis significantly exaggerate the dangerousness of bodily signs and symptoms and believe they are more likely either to have or to develop a particular illness than is justified on basis of any evidence. They are highly sensitive to information that suggests the possibility of them having a disease, and frequently seek what they consider to be confirmation of their worries from a variety of sources. By contrast, they are highly resistant to reassurance: appropriate information, education and explanation typically fail to reduce any fears of disease (Lucock et al. 1997). This fear seems limited to threats to health and is not evidence in other areas of life. Barsky et al. (2001), for example, found that hypochondriacal patients' perception that they were likely to develop various diseases was greater than those of a comparison group of patients from a primary care setting. However, they did not consider their risk of succumbing to accidents and criminal victimization as being any greater. Similarly, Haenen et al. (2000), reported that while their 'normal' comparison group felt equally threatened by both health- and non-health-related threats, individuals with hypo-chondriasis were more threatened by health-related threats than others.

Prevalence of hypochondriasis

Rates of the disorder in the general population are relatively low. In a meta-analysis of data available at the time, Creed and Barsky (2004) suggested prevalence levels of between 0.03 and 2.8 per cent among the general population. Fink, Hansen and Oxhoj (2004) estimated the prevalence of hypochondriasis among people admitted into general medical wards to be 3.5 per cent, with markedly different rates between men and women (1.5 and 6.0 per cent respectively).

Aetiology of hypochondriasis

Genetic factors

There seems to be a genetic predisposition to at least some elements of hypochondriasis. Gillespie et al. (2000), for example, examined the genetic risk for developing what they termed somatic distress. They gave measures of anxiety, depression, phobic anxiety, somatic distress and sleep difficulty to 3469 Australian twins aged 18 to 28 years, and found that 33 per cent of the genetic variance in somatic distress was due to specific gene action unrelated to depression or phobic anxiety. Thus, their data suggest a unique genetic contribution to the reporting of somatic distress, and that this is not simply a manifestation of a more general propensity to anxiety or depression.

Psychosocial factors

Many of the risk factors for hypochondriasis overlap with those thought to increase risk for somatization disorder. Rates of physical and sexual abuse among people with hypochondriasis are higher than among comparison groups (e.g. Barsky et al. 1994), as are reports of inadequate or inattentive parenting (Bass and Murphy 1995). Other studies have reported high levels of childhood sickness (Craig et al. 1993) and parental overprotection and encouragement of sick-role behaviour (Parker and Liscombe 1980). Noyes et al. (2003) found that hypochondriacal symptoms were positively correlated with all the insecure attachment styles they measured, especially the fearful style. These same symptoms were positively correlated with self-reported interpersonal problems and negatively correlated with patient ratings of satisfaction with, and reassurance from, medical care.

Personality factors

In a review of personality traits associated with adult somatization, Kirmayer, Robbins and Paris (1994) noted that various abnormal traits have been linked to hypochondriasis, but that few systematic studies have been conducted. Perhaps the strongest association is with neuroticism (Noyes et al. 2003).

Interpersonal theory

Reflecting the overlap between the various somatoform disorders, the model of hypochondriasis proposed by Stuart and Noyes (1999) is similar to the model of somatization of Craig and colleagues. That is, they consider it to involve seeking emotional care from professionals as well as family and friends, through the reporting of physical complaints or symptoms. According to Stuart and Noyes, this results from anxious and insecure attachments established early in life with the individual's parents. As in the case of somatization, lack of parental care or an adverse early environment may cause a child to view others as unreliable caregivers. The one way of gaining attention that these children may have is through complaints of physical symptoms, as their parents are unresponsive to complaints of psychological distress. Thus, a cycle of complaints about physical symptoms, reinforced by parental attention, is established, which becomes the primary way of gaining adult attention and feelings of attachment. This has two outcomes. First, the child learns to use complaints of physical symptoms to gain attention and perhaps love. Second, the child fails to learn other ways of eliciting care and attention from their environment. As an adult, therefore, the still insecurely attached person may communicate his or her need for care through complaints of illness. Unfortunately, these attempts at support seeking are frequently not responded to, and even viewed with some suspicion, which only serves to reinforce the original fear of lack of attachment and supportive relationships.

Hypochondriasis as threat

The model developed by Warwick and Salkovskis (1990) focused on the immediate cognitive processes involved in hypochondriasis. They suggested that current life stresses or simply noticing bodily signs can activate previously latent cognitive schemata about health and disease – probably developed in childhood as a result of circumstances described above – that are faulty, unduly alarming, or pessimistic. This leads to a number of sequelae:

- *Selective attention to information supporting this schema:* an increased focus on internal physiological factors such as heart rate, gastric motility, and so on. People with hypochondriasis may also focus on observable bodily signs such as lumps, bumps and moles, and bodily products such as sputum, faeces, and so on.

- *Cognitive errors:* disconfirmatory information, such as medical reassurance (even when sought) is ignored, rumination about the consequences may occur – usually in some catastrophic form.

- *Physiological changes:* autonomic activity may increase due to the anxiety, resulting in change in bowel habits, sleeping, and so on. Each will confirm the health problem.

- *Behavioural responses:* these may involve safety behaviours such as repeated checking, self-examination, taking unnecessary preventive medication, and so on. People with hypochondriasis may avoid activities that trigger health rumination or seek family or medical reassurance that 'all is well'. Safety behaviours, like those in obsessive-compulsive disorders, maintain the problem, as the individual feels emotionally more secure following their execution – leading to an operantly conditioned reinforcement of the checking behaviour (Mowrer 1947 – see discussion in Chapter 2) – and never learns that a failure to engage in them will not lead to disastrous outcomes.

Threat plus symptom sensitivity

A variant of the threat model is one of threat combined with symptom sensitivity. That is, people with hypochondriasis are both physiologically more aware of any physical sensations they may have than are most individuals, and are more likely to label these sensations as symptoms of some underlying medical condition. In this process, benign bodily sensations are mistakenly attributed to a suspected serious disease. This focuses their attention on their symptoms, which increases their awareness of them, reinforcing the individual's suspicion that they are seriously ill. Evidence for this extension of the model is not strong. Barsky et al. (1995) found that people with hypochondriasis did not differ significantly from a 'normal' comparison group in their accurate awareness of heart beat. Within each sample, the only statistically significant association found was a moderate *negative* correlation between heart beat awareness and the severity of hypochondriasis. So, the results actively countered the threat plus symptom sensitivity model. Despite this, the hypochondriasis group considered themselves more sensitive to benign bodily sensations and reported more somatic symptoms than the non-patient comparison group. This negative finding was echoed by Steptoe and Noll (1997) who found a negative correlation between hypochondriacal concerns and accuracy of perception of sweat gland activity. Further evidence against the model was reported by Haenen et al. (1997) who found that tactual sensitivity to non-painful stimuli in people with hypochondriasis and healthy subjects did not differ, although those with hypochondriasis, again, considered themselves more sensitive to bodily sensations than others.

Thinking about . . .

One of the jokes often said about medical students as they go through their training is that they experience every illness they encounter – or at least they think they do. Luckily, most of them recover from these non-existent illnesses before developing the next. But this reaction to health and health risk information may have implications for many more people. We are increasingly made aware of our health and the health risks associated with our behaviour, our genetic make-up, and the environment in which we live. We know that many people who go through health checks become worried about their long-term health even when they are told that they have no health problems – it seems that for some vulnerable people, just being made aware of their personal risk evokes high levels of health anxiety. So, while some may benefit from health advice, others simply become worried about their health. As well as creating a health-conscious society, are we also creating a health-anxious one?

Treatment of hypochondriasis

Pharmacological treatment of hypochondriasis

Until the late 1980s, the general consensus among clinicians was that pharmaco-therapy would not benefit people who experienced hypochondriasis. However, the similarities between hypochondriasis and obsessive-compulsive disorder have led to the use of SSRIs in an attempt to treat it. A number of case reports have found these drugs to be of benefit. There is, however, only one published report of a placebo-controlled trial of SSRIs in hypochondriasis at the time of writing – and this was only a small study. In it, Fallon et al. (1996) randomized 20 participants to a placebo medication or an SSRI (fluoxetine). Short-term findings indicated that of 10 patients given fluoxetine, 6 were virtually symptom-free, compared with only 1 of 6 patients treated with placebo. In a subsequent study with no placebo control, the same group reported that 57 per cent of patients given fluoxetine reported significant short-term benefits.

Cognitive treatment of hypochondriasis

Psychological treatment for hypochondriasis can be difficult, particularly where individuals hold a strong belief in their having a physical disease. One way this has been addressed is through the use of a variety of techniques generally used in cognitive behavioural interventions, including:

- *Behavioural hypothesis testing:* this can involve working with a client to investigate the reality of their symptoms. If someone has a fear of a muscle-wasting disease, for example, they may predict that they would become extremely weak if they engage in even light exercise. With some encouragement, this hypothesis can be tested – and hopefully be found to be inaccurate.

- *Reducing checking and medical consultation:* in order to reduce safety behaviours in general, and use of medical support in particular, the client may reduce checking behaviour and medical consultations – or delay them. This is similar to the approach taken in obsessive-compulsive disorder and phobias. That is, exposure plus response prevention (see Chapter 7). They may also develop a realistic strategy for when to seek medical help.

- *Cognitive challenge:* this involves techniques to counter some of the catastrophic thoughts that an individual may have about their symptoms. Thus, fear that one has a serious heart problem may be based on the experience of chest discomfort, heart missing a beat, and breathlessness. These experiences may be contextualized and made less threatening by reframing:
  - 'Most heart beats change rhythm from minute to minute.'
  - 'It's normal to become breathless following exertion – especially if you are unfit.'
  - 'I've had these symptoms before, and although they made me worried, they did not lead to any problems.'

In one of the first studies to evaluate the effectiveness of this approach, Clark et al. (1998) compared their cognitive treatment programme with a non-specific behavioural stress management programme which targeted stress-related cognitions and emotions but not those specifically related to health concerns. Comparisons with a waiting list control group showed both treatments were more effective than no therapy. Initially, the interventions had specific benefits: cognitive therapy was more effective than behavioural stress management on measures of hypochondriasis, but not on measures of general mood disturbance. However, one year after treatment, while people who had received both interventions remained significantly better than before treatment, there were few differences between them.

A second study to use this approach, reported by Barsky and Ahern (2004), randomly allocated people with hypochondriasis into either a usual care control group or six-session active cognitive behavioural intervention. At 6- and 12-month follow-up, participants in the active intervention reported significantly lower levels of hypochondriacal symptoms, beliefs, and attitudes and health-related anxiety than those in the control group. They also reported significantly less impairment of social role functioning and activities of daily living. A very different approach was adopted by Papageorgiou and Wells (1998), who examined the effectiveness of training patients with hypochondriasis to distract away from their worrying thoughts. In a series of three case reports, this resulted in improvements both in mood and in illness-related thoughts and behaviours lasting at least six months following treatment.

Body dysmorphic disorder

Many of us have some degree of dissatisfaction with our body. In a widely cited survey of over 4000 people, the magazine *Psychology Today*, for example, found that 56 per cent of women reported being dissatisfied with their appearance. Major sources of dissatisfaction were their abdomens (71 per cent), body weight (66 per cent), hips (60 per cent), and muscle tone (58 per cent). Sixty-three per cent of men were unhappy with their abdomens, 52 per cent unhappy with their weight, 45 per cent unhappy with their muscle tone and 38 per cent unhappy with their chest size (http://cms.psychologytoday.com/articles/pto-19970201-000023.html). Significantly fewer of us are so unhappy that this dissatisfaction reaches pathological proportions. Bohne et al. (2002), for example, found that while 74 per cent of American university students reported having body image concerns, only 29 per cent were preoccupied by them, and only 4 per cent met DSM-IV criteria for body dysmorphic disorder. Not surprisingly, perhaps, rates are higher among people seeking plastic surgery. Aouizerat et al. (2003) reported a 9 per cent prevalence rate for body dysmorphic disorder in their sample of patients having plastic surgery. Sadly for these people, surgery rarely improves their feelings about themselves.

Body dysmorphic disorder – sometimes referred to as dysmorphophobia – involves a preoccupation with an imagined defect in appearance. In addition, people with the disorder experience significant levels of negative thinking, self-criticism, anxiety and depression. DSM-IV-TR (APA 2000) stated the following criteria must be met for a diagnosis of body dysmorphic disorder to be given:

- Preoccupation with an imagined defect in appearance. If a slight physical anomaly is present, the person's concern is markedly excessive.

- The preoccupation causes clinically significant distress or impairment in social, occupational or other important areas of functioning.

- The preoccupation is not better accounted for by another mental disorder.

Levels of distress can be such that many people with this diagnosis experience major depression, social phobia, obsessive-compulsive disorder, and substance abuse (Sobanski and Schmidt 2000). In one study (Phillips et al. 1993), 30 per cent of people with the condition said they avoided social contact because of the disorder: 17 per cent reported having made at least one suicide attempt. The condition may prevent normal social, economic and sexual relationships. Veale et al. (1996), for example, found that 74 per cent of their sample of people with body dysmorphic disorder with an average age of 33 years were not married, while 50 per cent did not have a job. The typical age of onset appears to be in adolescence and early adulthood (e.g. Veale et al. 1996). About 10 per cent of people who develop body dysmorphic disorder will also be given a diagnosis of anorexia (Philips 1996).

Concerns can involve preoccupations with the face (such as scars, spots, discoloration, acne, or the shape or size of the nose, mouth, eyes, etc.), the hair (fears of receding hairlines), or the size and shape of any other body part, including hips, buttocks, legs and hands. Men tend to be concerned about their body build, genitals and hair. Women focus on their hips, breasts and legs (Perugi et al. 1997; Phillips and Diaz 1997). Typical behaviours include:

- frequent checking of appearance in mirrors or other reflecting surfaces
- camouflaging the perceived defect with clothing, make-up or posture
- seeking surgery, dermatological treatment or other medical treatment
- attempts to convince other people of the deformity
- skin picking

- measuring the disliked body part
- excessive dieting or exercise
- avoiding social situations in which the perceived defect may be exposed
- feeling very anxious and self-conscious around other people because of the perceived defect.

The belief in a defect can be so strong it may border upon being a delusion. DSM-IV-TR suggests that where this is the case, the disorder may best be considered a psychotic, delusional, disorder. By contrast, Phillips (2004) adopted a dimensional view (see Chapter 2), suggesting that those people whose strength of beliefs are so great that they may be considered delusional are no different except in strength of belief from other people with the non-delusional disorder – and should therefore not be considered under a separate diagnosis.

A second suggestion is that body dysmorphic disorder may be considered a variant of obsessive-compulsive disorder (see Chapter 7). The preoccupations held by people with body dysmorphic disorder resemble obsessions, in that they are anxiety-producing, recurrent and difficult to control. Repeated checking or other procedures to reduce anxiety are also similar to obsessive-compulsive disorder. More tangential, but still relevant, are findings that both psychological (exposure plus response prevention) and pharmacological (SSRIs) treatments used to treat obsessive-compulsive disorder have also proven effective in treating body dysmorphic disorder. There is also evidence that family members with body dysmorphic disorder are more likely than the norm to have a relative with obsessive-compulsive disorder. Despite these similarities, a number of important differences have been found between the two disorders that suggest that body dysmorphic disorder is associated with greater psychopathology (see Cororve and Gleaves 2001). People with body dysmorphic disorder experience:

- poorer insight than people with obsessive-compulsive disorder
- higher co-morbidity with major depression
- higher rates of social phobia and psychotic disorder diagnoses
- higher suicide attempt rates due to the disorder.

A third approach has considered whether body dysmorphic disorder may be a form of eating disorder – or that both body dysmorphic disorder and eating disorders lie on a continuum of disorders relating to body image distortion. Cororve and Gleaves (2001) made a case for this conceptualization, including:

- Both body dysmorphic disorder and eating disorders involve excessive concerns about physical appearance in addition to body image dissatisfaction and distortion. The location of concerns may differ – eating disorder patients are primarily concerned with lower body areas or overall weight and shape; people with body dysmorphic disorder are more preoccupied with localized features. Nevertheless, concerns over physical appearance are central to the condition.

- Body dysmorphic disorder includes intrusive thoughts about appearance and an overemphasis on the importance of appearance for relationships and self-worth, avoidance of places, and other activities (Rosen and Ramirez 1998).

Countering this classification is the key issue that body dysmorphic disorder involves a preoccupation with appearance whereas eating disorders involve preoccupations with eating and appearance – although eating may be considered a specific means of reducing distress unavailable to people with concerns about, say, hair loss. In addition, body dysmorphic disorder is equally prevalent in men and women – eating disorders are much more prevalent in women. This may reflect cultural issues that drive more women to have weight concerns than men (see Chapter 12). More problematic is that this model considers eating disorders to be primarily driven by weight concerns. As we see in Chapter 12, weight and appearance concerns may form only part of the clinical picture – at least in the case of anorexia.

Research Box 5

Phillips, K.A., Pagano, M.E., Menard, W. et al. (2005) Predictors of remission from body dysmorphic disorder: a prospective study, *Journal of Nervous and Mental Diseases*, 193. 564–7.

Although body dysmorphic disorder is relatively common, its course has received very little investigation. This study attempted to provide some relevant evidence. In it, the authors examined predictors of remission from body dysmorphic disorder in a one-year prospective study. Their key hypotheses were that more severe symptoms and the presence of major depression would predict a relatively poor prognosis. They also hypothesized that a more severe form of body dysmorphic disorder, in which individuals' strength of belief in their body's abnormality is so severe that it may be considered delusional, would have a worse prognosis than its 'non-delusional variant'.

Method

Some 176 participants took part in the study. Inclusion criteria were DSM-IV-diagnosed body dysmorphic disorder or its delusional variant and being aged 12 years or older. The only exclusion criterion was the presence of an organic mental disorder. The initial evaluation comprised the Structured Clinical Interview for DSM-IV (SCID-I) to assess Axis I disorders and the SCID-II to assess Axis II personality disorders (see Chapter 1). In addition, they gained information on clinical features (e.g. age of onset and duration), and past and current treatment. Severity was assessed with the Yale–Brown Obsessive-Compulsive Scale Modified for Body Dysmorphic Disorder and the Psychiatric Status Rating Scale for Body Dysmorphic Disorder. Finally, participants were assessed with the Brown Assessment of Beliefs Scale, to assess the delusionality of body dysmorphic disorder beliefs.

Follow-up interviews were conducted one year after the intake interview using the Longitudinal Interval Follow-Up Evaluation (LIFE) to collect detailed information on the course of their problems. This measure obtains information on symptom severity, diagnostic status and treatment received. This report presents data for the 161 subjects who met full DSM-IV body dysmorphic disorder criteria at intake and also had one year of follow-up data.

Results

Of the 161 participants, 70 per cent were female, and the mean age at intake was 33 years. The mean age at onset of body dysmorphic disorder was 16 years, and the mean duration of body dysmorphic disorder was 16 years.

Participants had a 0.09 probability of fully remitting from body dysmorphic disorder over the year of follow-up, and a 0.21 probability of partially remitting. Multiple regression revealed a number of independent predictors of outcome. More severe symptoms at intake strongly predicted a lower likelihood of partial or full remission from body dysmorphic disorder as did a longer duration of the disorder as did the presence of a co-morbid personality disorder. Many variables, however, did not influence the likelihood of remission: gender, race/ethnicity, socio-economic status, being an adult versus an adolescent, age of onset, delusionality of body dysmorphic disorder symptoms, the presence of major depression, a substance use disorder, social phobia, obsessive-compulsive disorder or an eating disorder at intake. Outcome was also not significantly predicted by receiving mental health treatment during the follow-up period or by receiving non-mental health treatment such as surgery or dermatologic treatment.

Discussion

This study, the first longitudinal study of body dysmorphic disorder's course, found that the condition was unusually chronic – more so than similar studies have found for mood disorders, panic disorder, generalized anxiety disorder, and even personality disorders. The more severe the problem at entry into the study, and the longer its duration prior to treatment, the lower the likelihood of remission. The five most commonly co-morbid Axis I disorders, including major depression, did not predict outcome. However, having a personality disorder did. The finding that participants who received mental health treatment during the follow-up period were no more likely to achieve significant improvements than those who did not was disappointing, indicating the difficulties of treating the disorder. In keeping with other literature, it was perhaps less surprising that people who received other forms of treatment, including surgery and dermatologic treatment, were also no more likely to improve than those who did not.

Aetiology of body dysmorphic disorder

Socio-cultural factors

There has been little systematic research into the social and cultural factors associated with the development of body dysmorphic disorder. However, given the importance placed on physical appearance in society, it is not unreasonable to suspect that societal beliefs and attitudes towards appearance influence risk for body dysmorphic disorder. There is certainly evidence that the media can influence our perceptions of what is healthy and what is attractive. These concerns may differ across cultures. An example of this can be found in western males' increasing preoccupation with muscularity, known as muscle dysmorphia or more colloquially as the 'Adonis complex'. Levels of this problem are rising significantly among European and American males, but it is very rare among Far Eastern countries (Yang et al. 2005). Of interest is that European and American magazines frequently portray undressed and muscular men: in Far Eastern countries, this occurs much less frequently. This led Yang and colleagues to suggest that increasing levels of muscle dysmorphia reflect western traditions emphasizing muscularity and fitness as a measure of masculinity, increasing exposure of western men to muscular male bodies in media images, and a greater decline in traditional male roles in the West, leading to a greater emphasis on the body as a measure of masculinity. Despite these societal influences and changes, most people do not become as obsessed or concerned about their appearance as people with body dysmorphic disorder. Other factors may give rise to a specific vulnerability to such influences. What contributes to this vulnerability is largely speculative at present.

Psychoanalytic models
A psychoanalytic view of the development of body dysmorphic disorder suggests that the disorder arises from an individual's unconscious displacement of sexual or emotional conflict or feelings of guilt and poor self-image to specific parts of the body (Sobanski and Schmidt 2000). The displacement is thought to occur because the underlying problem is so threatening to the ego that it is unconsciously displaced into the more psychologically manageable issue of appearance. The body part of concern, such as the nose, may represent another, more emotionally threatening, body part, such as the penis (Phillips 1996).

A psychological model
Rosen (1996) suggested a key factor in the development of body dysmorphic disorder involves critical events or traumatic incidents that involve an individual's appearance. The most common example is being teased about weight or size (Biby 1998), with many people with body dysmorphic disorder reporting repeated criticism about their appearance from members of their own family. More general vulnerability factors may involve being neglected as a child, leading to feelings of being unloved, insecure and rejected (Phillips 1991). Other trauma, such as sexual abuse or assault, may also be involved. As with some other somatoform disorders, many people with body dysmorphic disorder also report having experienced a physical injury or illness. According to Rosen, these critical events activate dysfunctional assumptions about the normality of physical appearance and the implications of appearance for personality, self-worth and acceptance. In one exploration of this phenomenon, Osman et al. (2004) conducted a semi-structured interview with people with body dysmorphic disorder and 'normal' controls. During the interview, the people with body dysmorphic disorder evidenced more spontaneously occurring negative appearance-related images than did control participants. These images were linked to early stressful memories.

Once established, the disorder may be maintained by selective attention to perceived physical problems or information that supports this belief. People with body dysmorphic disorder become hypervigilant for any minor changes that occur in their appearance. In addition, Rosen suggested that rehearsal of negative and distorted self-statements about physical appearance results in them becoming automatic and believable. Finally, the positive emotional responses associated with avoidance, checking and reassurance-seeking behaviours reinforce and maintain the condition (Mowrer 1947; see Chapter 2). Buhlmann, Etcoff and Wilhelm (2006) provided experimental evidence of some of the cognitive distortions held by many people with body dysmorphic disorder. In their study, people with body dysmorphic disorder and a 'normal' control group completed two questionnaires accompanying facial photographs of people in various everyday situations. One questionnaire included self-referent scenarios ('Imagine that the bank teller is looking at you. What is his facial expression like?'); the other included other-referent scenarios ('Imagine that the bank teller is looking at a friend of yours . . .'). They were asked to identify the emotion evident in each face. Overall, people with body dysmorphic disorder had more difficulty identifying emotional expressions in self-referent scenarios than did the comparison group. They also misinterpreted more expressions as contemptuous and angry in self-referent scenarios than did controls.

Biological explanations

There have been relatively few studies of the biological underpinning of body dysmorphic disorder. The role of serotonin has been implicated in its aetiology as a result of the effective treatment of the condition using SSRIs (see below). This conclusion has been supported by a small amount of experimental evidence. In one case report, Barr, Goodman and Price (1992) followed a woman who was placed on a diet low in tryptophan (a serotonin precursor). This resulted in a dramatic increase in symptoms. Similarly, Craven and Rodin (1987) reported a significant worsening of symptoms following the chronic abuse of a drug known as cyproheptadine, which reduces the uptake of serotonin at the postsynaptic receptors and can be used to treat serotonin toxicity.

A biopsychosocial model

Veale et al. (1996) focused on both biological and psychological factors that may predispose an individual towards low self-esteem and body dysmorphic disorder. Their model echoes the previously outlined model. However, it suggested that psychological factors may combine with biological factors to result in body dysmorphic disorder. In this model, fears of rejection, especially during adolescence, are believed to be biologically influenced, probably involving serotonin dysregulation. In addition, Veale et al. argued that rigidly held beliefs about appearance may be difficult to change, as there is evidence that most people favour both overt beauty and more subtle symmetries across left and right sides of the body thought to indicate health. Scheib, Gangestad and Thornhill (1999) found that such symmetry correlated significantly with age of first sexual experience and number of sexual partners. Veale and colleagues argued that these fundamental concerns may prove highly resistant to change.

Psychological treatment

The most common psychological treatment strategies for body dysmorphic disorder are cognitive behavioural. Exposure to avoided situations can include exposure to the sight of the individual's own body or showing their perceived defect in social situations. Often, exposure programmes follow hierarchies of increasingly difficult to cope with body parts or avoided situations (as discussed in the context of phobias in Chapter 2). Prevention of checking or self-reassuring behaviours is used to counteract checking rituals. Finally, cognitive restructuring, in which dysfunctional thoughts are identified and then challenged, is a key component of any intervention. The effects of these interventions are generally positive. Cororve and Gleaves (2001) concluded from their review of both controlled and uncontrolled studies of cognitive behavioural treatments that clinically significant benefits were found for both body dysmorphic disorder symptoms and associated problems such as depression, poor body image, self-esteem, and anxiety both after treatment and at longer-term follow-up. Many of the studies into the treatment of body dysmorphic disorder are uncontrolled clinical cases. However, in one controlled study Rosen, Reiter and Orosan (1995) followed 54 people with body dysmorphic disorder during a baseline no treatment phase and then group cognitive behavioural therapy comprising eight 2-hour sessions. Therapy involved modification of intrusive thoughts of body dissatisfaction and overvalued beliefs about physical appearance, exposure to avoided body image situations and elimination of body checking. Body dysmorphic disorder symptoms were 'eliminated' in 82 per cent of people in the intervention group immediately following the intervention and in 77 per cent at follow-up. This compared with a 7 per cent improvement reported in the baseline, no-treatment, phase.

Conversion disorder (hysteria)

Long known as hysteria or hysterical conversion, the American Psychiatric Association now calls this condition conversion disorder. DSM-IV-TR (APA 2000) provides the diagnostic criteria for this diagnosis to be assigned, including:

- One or more symptoms or deficits affecting voluntary motor or sensory function that suggest a neurological or other general medical condition.
- Psychological factors are judged to be associated with the symptom or deficit because the initiation or exacerbation of the symptom or deficit is preceded by conflicts or other stressors.
- The symptom or deficit is not intentionally produced or feigned.
- The symptom or deficit cannot, after appropriate investigation, be fully explained by a general medical condition, or by the direct effects of a substance, or as a culturally sanctioned behaviour or experience – note this excludes some of the somatoform presentations of other psychological disorders such as depression.

People with conversion disorder often present with striking neurological symptoms such as weakness, lack of coordination, tremor, paralysis, sensory disorders or memory loss, in the absence of any pathology that could be responsible. Less common symptoms include somatosensory disorders and skin changes. Many people appear unconcerned about their symptoms – a characteristic sometimes labelled *la belle indifférence*. Perkin (1989) estimated that up to 4 per cent of those attending neurology outpatient clinics in the United Kingdom have conversion disorders. Bendadis and Allen Hauser (2000) estimated that 10–20 per cent of patients referred for treatment of epilepsy in the USA have what they termed 'psychogenic non-epileptic seizures'. The prevalence of conversion disorders within the general population is even harder to estimate than those within specific medical populations. However, Favarelli et al. (1997) found a rate of 0.3 per cent among a relatively small population sample of 673 individuals. The condition may also present with others. Crimlisk and Ron (1997) estimated that up to 50 per cent of people with conversion disorder could be assigned a second diagnosis of depression: up to 16 per cent could be assigned a diagnosis of anxiety. The prognosis is not good. Crimlisk et al. (1998) followed 73 people with medically unexplained motor symptoms for six years. Only three people had subsequently been given a medical diagnosis in this time, indicating an initial misdiagnosis. Seventy-five per cent of their cohort had been diagnosed with a 'psychiatric disorder'; 45 per cent had been diagnosed with a personality disorder. The presenting symptom was unchanged in 14 per cent of people, and had worsened in 38 per cent of cases.

The term hysteria has a long history – and was originally derived from the Greek word for uterus. Initially, it was used to label a condition thought to occur as a result of the uterus literally wandering through the body, resulting in symptoms as varied as feelings of suffocation, coughing, dramatic fits, paralysis of the limbs, fainting spells, sudden inability to speak, persistent vomiting and inability to take in food. Treatment involved encouraging the womb back to its proper place often through physical manipulation.

More recently, the condition came to prominence in the First World War, when many soldiers in the trenches developed a condition known as 'shell shock', of which the most prominent features were blindness, paralyses, contractures, **aphonia**, anaesthesias and profound amnesias. The initial interpretation of these symptoms was that they resulted from micro-haemorrhaging in the brain, as a consequence of the shock wave created by exploding shells – hence the term 'shell shock'. Subsequently, doctors noted that the majority of soldiers with the condition had not been close to any explosions, that there was no evidence of any brain haemorrhages among those who had died and been subjected to autopsy, and that the condition could occur among recruits who had not yet been to the battlefield. As a result of this, the condition became thought of as a psychological, rather than physical, one. Interestingly, social and cultural factors appear to have influenced diagnosis and outcome following detection of the problems. Officers were less likely to develop these problems than enlisted men, but when they did they were more likely to be taken from the trenches and receive long-term treatment than the enlisted men, even when their symptoms were relatively minor.

Aetiology of conversion disorder

Social processes

Other social factors may be involved in the development of conversion disorder. The condition has been described as contagious, in that the sight or knowledge of one person with unexplained symptoms may trigger similar symptoms in others, particularly in situations where many people are grouped together and placed under some form of stress. One such incident among US Army recruits, was reported by Struewing and Gray (1990). They referred to the process as an epidemic, which occurred over a 12-hour period following evacuation of 1800 men from their barracks owing to a suspected toxic gas exposure – which turned out to be a false alarm. Despite the lack of toxin in the atmosphere, over two-thirds of the recruits developed at least one respiratory symptom, and 375 were evacuated by air ambulance for immediate medical investigation; 8 were kept in hospital. Two weeks after the incident, 55 per cent of a sample of this group reported developing at least one symptom, including cough, light-headedness, chest pain, shortness of breath, headache, sore throat or dizziness. Those who reported the most, or the most severe, problems reported high levels of physical stress, mental stress, and awareness of rumours of odours, gases and/or smoke. More recently, Cassady et al. (2005) reported on five girls from an Amish community who developed debilitating voluntary motor deficits, anorexia and weight loss. Four experienced neck weakness with inability to hold up their heads. The onset of symptoms followed a period of particular stress within the community, and showed some improvement in four of the cases following family therapy.

Psychoanalytic explanations

Early psychoanalytic explanations of conversion disorder (or hysteria as it was then known) considered the condition to reflect anxiety aroused by unconscious conflict being converted into physical symptoms. Freud (Freud and Breuer 1984) thought that one ego defence mechanism against high levels of distress was to convert this distress from psychic to physical symptoms. Perhaps the most famous case he reported was that of Anna O, who was initially treated by Joseph Breuer. Anna O was a 21-year-old woman who became ill while nursing her terminally ill father. Her own illness began with a severe cough, and subsequently included paralysis of the extremities of the right side of her body, contractures, disturbances of vision, hearing and language, lapses of consciousness and hallucinations. Breuer noticed that when Anna told him the content of her daytime hallucinations, while under hypnosis, she became calm and tranquil. He considered this to be way of expressing the 'products' of her 'bad self': a process of emotional catharsis. Breuer further developed his understanding of her symptoms following a period of time when Anna O stopped drinking, and quenched her thirst by eating fruit and melons. At this time, she recounted in one of her sessions how she had been disgusted by the sight of a dog drinking out of a glass. Soon after this revelation she asked for a drink. Breuer took this to indicate that insight into the factors associated with the beginning of symptoms was a key issue in relieving them. This became a focus of later hypnotic sessions.

The twist in the story came from Freud's analysis of the situation. He noted that Anna specifically required Breuer to provide the therapy, and that when she was in a hypnotic state, she needed to feel his hands to ensure he was there. In addition, one of the symptoms she developed was being pregnant with his child. Freud took this as an indication that she was in love with Breuer – and that her secret sexual desires were the cause of these hysterical symptoms. In fact, Freud considered conversion disorder to result from an unresolved Electra complex (see Chapter 2). In this, the young girl is sexually attracted to her father. If her parents' responses to this are harsh or disapproving, the girl's feelings are repressed. This leads to a preoccupation with sex, at the same time as an avoidance of it. If these sexual urges occur later in life, the defence mechanism evoked can involve conversion of the sexual impulses into physical symptoms.

Behavioural explanations

The behavioural explanation of conversion symptoms is that they are functional and under the control of the individual expressing them. They are functional in the sense that their enactment leads to some sort of benefit or reinforcement – the obvious one in the case of the Anna O being the attention given to her by Breuer, while the men in the trenches potentially avoided being killed as a result of being taken to hospital away from the front-line trenches. In arguing this case, Miller (1999) suggested that it is very difficult to determine from an external standpoint what is motivated, controllable, voluntary behaviour and what is not. However, he argued that some notable cases of conversion disorder seem to be faked and under voluntary control – albeit it in a rather clumsy way.

One apparent example of this process was reported by Zimmerman and Grosz (1966), who asked someone with hysterical blindness to identify which one of three visual stimuli was being presented to them. He performed this task at a level consistently below chance – a finding that may be considered unusual, because if he was unable to see, he should have performed at chance levels, not below chance. Zimmerman and Grosz then presented the stimuli in a non-random order (left–centre–right: left–centre–right, etc.), and the person was informed of which stimulus had been presented on each trial following their attempt to identify it. This is a task for which one would expect a blind person to learn the sequence and perform at above-chance levels. The participant in their study did not. Finally, when he was allowed to overhear a comment by a confederate of the experimenter that 'the doctors reckon that the patient can see because he makes fewer correct responses by chance than a blind man would make' (1966: 259), his performance improved to chance levels. Miller speculated that this indicated the individual was dissimilating.

This argument can also be made from an anatomical perspective. Merskey (1995) noted, for example, that patients with hysterical aphonia (inability to speak) may be able to cough – yet both processes require the vocal cords to function normally. If an individual can cough, there are no anatomical reasons for them not being able to talk. Similarly, some patients with an inability to move their limbs may show evidence of tensing both the apparently affected muscles and those which prevent movement of the limb. Again, this suggests that some sort of voluntary processes are at work. Despite these cases, Miller (1999) acknowledged these findings do not necessarily mean that all people with these phenomena are faking.

Hysteria as a form of hypnosis

An opposing interpretation of the findings that Miller (1999) considered to be evidence of dissimilation was proposed by Oakley (1999). He argued that some, at least, could be considered to be evidence of some form of hypnotic processes at work. He noted a number of similarities between hysterical conversion and hypnosis:

- *Similarities in 'symptoms':* many of the conditions that can be established in hypnosis are similar to frequently reported conversion symptoms, including motor paralysis (inability to rise from a chair, move an arm, etc.), loss of touch or pain sensation, blindness, and the generation of pain sensations.

- *Lack of concern over symptoms:* both hypnotized individuals and at least some people with conversion disorder express a lack of concern over their strange symptoms.

- *Involuntariness:* the deficits or physical states that are associated with both conversion disorder and hypnosis involve a degree of involuntariness. People report that they would like to, for example, move their hand, but cannot. This has long been reported and is perhaps best phrased by someone from the nineteenth century (Paget 1873), who commented: 'They say "I cannot"; it looks like "I will not"; but it is "I cannot will" ' (cited in Oakley 1999).

- *Apparent malingering and display of 'implicit knowledge':* both conditions can appear as if the individual is deliberately faking their symptoms. They may also have 'implicit knowledge'; that is, they may respond as if they do not have the deficit while still reporting it. Hysterically deaf individuals, for example, may raise their voice when their speech is masked by white noise, while the speech of hypnotically deaf people is disrupted by delayed auditory feedback, as is the case in non-hypnotized individuals. Both imply some sort of knowledge and response to stimuli that they apparently cannot sense. The performance of the hysterically blind individual reported by Zimmerman and Grosz (1966) proves further evidence of this implicit knowledge. Miller suggests this could be evidence of faking. However, Oakley had a different explanation. Oakley proposed that these types of data could suggest that any of the mechanisms responsible for both hysterical and hypnotic blindness occur at a late stage in processing of visual material. Becoming aware of visual stimuli involves a series of processes before we become consciously aware of any stimulus: reception of information in the visual cortex, transmission of this information to the temporal and parietal lobes where the location and type of stimulus are determined, and then to the prefrontal cortex where this information is integrated with memories. All this occurs before we are aware of having seen a stimulus. It is possible that processes/deficits associated with hypnosis or conversion disorder occur before we become consciously aware of the stimulus, but allow some form of apparently conscious response to stimuli.

Oakley suggested that if we accept from these data that there are some commonalities between the conversion hysteria and hypnosis, there may also be common neurological processes occurring in both. What evidence we have from neurological studies suggests that the experience of people with conversion disorder do at one level mirror the experience of people asked to produce similar states during hypnotic trances. In one study of this phenomenon, Marshall et al. (1997) investigated the neural processes that occurred in a lady with conversion disorder when asked to move her paralysed left leg, using functional MRI scanning:

- *Preparing* to move her leg resulted in activation of her left premotor cortex and both cerebellar hemispheres – the same processes that occurred when she was preparing to move her non-paralysed right leg. The authors interpreted this as an indication of her 'genuine' preparation to move her left leg.

- When *trying* to move her leg, there was activation of the normal movement-related brain areas including the left dorsolateral prefrontal cortex and both cerebellar hemispheres. There was no activation of the right premotor areas or the right primary sensorimotor cortex necessary for movement. However, areas of the brain not usually involved in movement *did* show activation – in the right cingulated cortex and right orbitofrontal cortex. The authors proposed that this activation somehow inhibited movement of her left leg.

Marshall et al. suggest that the desire to move was evidenced by the activation of the movement-related areas of the brain. However, this activation was somehow over-ridden by other neurological activity: not 'I cannot' or 'I will not' but 'I cannot will'. These findings reflect similar processes found in people placed under hypnosis and who are given hypnotic commands mimicking the paralysis of conversion disorder. That is, the parts of the brain that should be used to instigate movements are activated; however, other, normally inactive, parts of the brain also become active and seem to inhibit the movement that would otherwise result (Halligan et al. 2000).

These neurological processes can be partially explained by cognitive models developed by, among others, Shallice (e.g. 1988). Shallice suggested that our decision making involves a hierarchical cognitive system, controlled by a supervisory control system. The overarching control of responses to environmental events is provided by a central executive. At a lower level, mental functioning comprises a series of learned behavioural sequences. These are guided by action schema stored in long-term memory. They enable routine behaviours, and are relatively uncontrolled by the central executive. Action at this level is guided by processes which we are not aware of – they are unconscious. The executive becomes involved in active planning and decision making only when the learned behavioural sequences are insufficient to cope with our responses: when there are no pre-existing action schemata. A major function of the executive is to exert attentional control: to focus attention on demanding tasks, and away from distracting stimuli. According to Shallice, any mental processing involving the central executive becomes part of our conscious awareness, and any actions that follow its activation are thought of as voluntary. Processing below this level (the learned behavioural sequences) is unconscious. These processes explain, for example, the commonly reported phenomenon of having driven a car for many miles, and yet having no real recollection of the journey. The process of driving can be relatively automatic and, if the driver focuses their attention on other things, may happen at an unconscious level and be filtered out from conscious awareness.

Oakley (1999) moved further than this to suggest that not all those elements being processed by the central executive come into consciousness. Indeed, one of the functions of the executive is to select from a range of processing which ones come into awareness: those that are relevant to current actions or concerns are selected, those less relevant remain unconscious. He also suggested that so-called negative hypnotic phenomena, such as analgesia, blindness and paralysis, may occur under hypnosis as a result of the executive system withholding sensory information from our awareness following suggestions from an external source. Because we are unaware of this selection, any failure to move or lack of sensation is thought of as involuntary. By contrast, action sequences may also occur as a result of processing the executive does not allow into awareness; so an individual may make apparently 'involuntary' movements which they consider to have been out of their control. In this way, hypnotic phenomena are the result of selective awareness governed by the central executive. Oakley suggests that conversion symptoms may result from the same processes. In this case, the executive 'chooses' in some way to allow or disallow various information into awareness. This may be the result of a variety of unconscious 'internal dynamics and motivations in the interests of providing a solution to what may be an otherwise insoluble psychological problem' (1999: 260).

Stress as a precipitant to conversion disorders
Oakley's concept of conversion disorder as a consequence of individuals facing an otherwise insoluble problem hints at the role that stress may have as a precipitant to this disorder. Relatively few controlled studied have studies this in any detail. However, what studies have been conducted confirm this hypothesis. Harris and colleagues (e.g. 1996) have found people with *globus pharyngis* (a persistent sensation of a lump in the throat) to have higher levels of anxiety and to have experienced more adverse life-events in the year preceding onset than controls with medical problems thought to have no psychosomatic content. Singh and Lee (1997) found that 72 per cent of a sample of people with conversion disorder reported serious concurrent stress: 28 per cent reported a history of sexual abuse. However, while stress may form a precipitant to the development of conversion disorders, this cannot be the only cause of the condition. Many other mental health problems are triggered by stress, and the levels of stress reported by people with conversion disorder do not seem to differ from those reported by people with other conditions, such as depression (Roelofs et al. 2005). What the other factors are is not clear. Sar et al. (2004) found that many people with conversion disorder reported relatively high levels of childhood emotional and sexual abuse, and physical neglect. However, a majority of their sample had not experienced these problems (and many people with other disorders have), so a long-term route to increased risk of conversion disorder (as opposed to other stress-related disorders) has yet to be understood.

Treatment of conversion disorder

Studies of interventions in conversion disorder are largely uncontrolled studies of cohorts of patients with the disorder or case studies. At the time of writing, few randomized controlled trials – the gold standard of intervention research – had been conducted. This can makes it difficult to ascribe any successes found in the published research to the specific intervention as any changes may be due to placebo effects or non-specific therapy effects. Such caution may be increased following the findings of Letonoff, Williams and Sidhu (2002), who described three cases of psychogenic paraplegia, with symptoms including complete loss of motor control and sensation in the lower extremities and incontinence. Each individual 'ambulated out of the hospital without assistance', albeit up to several months following their diagnosis, with no other treatment than being told that their test results and medical examinations indicated no physical problems. Nevertheless, a number of case studies (e.g. Wald et al. 2004) have shown cognitive behavioural interventions, including imaginal exposure to trauma memories (see Chapter 9), to be of some benefit. A different approach was taken by Ataoglu et al. (2003). They used a therapeutic technique called paradoxical intention (see Chapter 4), in which individuals are encouraged to maintain or even exacerbate their symptoms. They compared this approach with use of an anxiolytic, diazepam, in 30 patients diagnosed with pseudoseizures. Of the 15 patients who completed paradoxical intention treatment, 14 showed some improvement; of the 15 treated with diazepam, 9 showed improvements, while 6 maintained their symptoms at the end of six weeks of treatment.

One of the very few randomized trials of treatments of conversion disorder was reported by Moene et al. (2003). They assigned patients with motor conversion disorders with symptoms including paralysis, gait disturbance, coordination problems, aphonia, and pseudo-epileptic seizures either to a waiting list control or active treatment. Treatment involved 10 sessions of hypnosis focusing on suggestions of symptom reduction and age regression to enable emotional insight. The waiting list control group design did not allow long-term follow-up measures to be taken. However, at the end of therapy, patients in the intervention condition showed significantly more improvement on video-based measures of their disorder than those in the control group.

Chapter summary

1   Somatization disorder is characterized by the experience and reporting of physical symptoms that cause distress but lack corresponding physical pathology.

2   At any one time, between 0.1 and 0.7 per cent of the general population could be diagnosed with somatization disorder.

3   Biological models of the disorder suggest it results from a sensitivity to physical sensations perhaps due to dysregulation in the serotonergic system. This sensitivity may be added to by catastrophic interpretation of these sensations.

4   Psychological models suggest somatization results from modelling of somatic complaints by parents and gaining attention of parents by reporting physical problems. In time, individuals may come to express emotional distress through reporting physical symptoms.

5   There are relatively few reported treatment studies, although there is preliminary evidence that treatment with SSRIs or cognitive behavioural therapy may be of benefit.

6   The key symptom of hypochondriasis is a preoccupation with fears of having, or the idea that one has, a serious illness – in the absence of contrary medical evidence.

7   As with somatization disorder, hypochondriasis may involve seeking emotional care through complaints of physical health problems.

8   Warwick and Salkovskis considered hypochondriasis to be a response to immediate threat that triggers health concerns established earlier in life. These become the focus of attention and cause considerable distress.

9   The main treatment for hypochondriasis is generally cognitive behavioural, although there is some evidence that SSRIs may be effective.

10 Body dysmorphic disorder involves a preoccupation with an imagined defect in appearance, often with high levels of negative thinking, self-criticism, anxiety and depression.

11 The disorder may be linked to increasing social and interpersonal expectations of high levels of physical attractiveness.

12 Developmental psychological theories suggest that the condition is triggered by critical or traumatic incidents that involve an individual's appearance, and is maintained by selective attention to perceived physical limitations.

13 Low levels of serotonin may also be implicated in the disorder.

14 Treatment studies are rare and usually involve cognitive behavioural therapy.

15 Conversion disorder presents as a neurological or sensory disorder that is disabling but has no physical cause.

16 Despite the phenomenon being observed for many years, its aetiology is poorly understood. Explanations vary from being a deliberate behaviour under the control of the affected individual to being a form of self-hypnosis. Both may be precipitated by stress, although why this should lead to conversion symptoms in particular is not understood.

17 Treatment studies are rare but suggest that cognitive behavioural and hypnotic treatments may be of some benefit.

For discussion

1   How may childhood factors translate into somatization disorders, and what factors may maintain them once established?

2   Why are somatization disorders hard to treat?

3   Are the somatization disorders distinct disorders or simply the end of a spectrum of health or appearance concern most of us experience at some time?

4   What factors may contribute specifically to the onset of a conversion disorder? Do these differ from those that trigger a variety of other mental health disorders? What other factors may contribute to the disorder?

Further reading

Ballas, C.A. and Staab, J.P. (2003) Medically unexplained physical symptoms: toward an alternative paradigm for diagnosis and treatment, *CNS Spectrum*, 8 (12 Suppl. 3): 20–6.

Brown, R.J. (2004) Psychological mechanisms of medically unexplained symptoms: an integrative conceptual model *Psychological Bulletin*, 130: 793–812.

Eriksen, H.R. and Ursin, H. (2004) Subjective health complaints, sensitization, and sustained cognitive activation (stress), *Journal of Psychosomatic Research*, 56: 445–8.

Wilhelmsen, I. (2005) Biological sensitisation and psychological amplification: gateways to subjective health complaints and somatoform disorders, *Psychoneuroendocrinology*, 30: 990–5.

6
Schizophrenia

Schizophrenia is one of the most controversial psychiatric diagnoses. Over time, debates have addressed whether a distinct state of schizophrenia actually exists, whether it results from genetic or environmental causes, and whether it should be treated using drug therapy, electroconvulsive therapy, or more social or psychological approaches. This chapter will address each of these issues. By the end of the chapter, you should have an understanding of:

- The nature of schizophrenia
- Alternative understandings of the 'symptoms' of schizophrenia
- The possible causal role of genetic factors, the family and psychosocial factors
- Neuronal and neurotransmitter models of the disorder
- Psychological models of the experiences of people diagnosed as having schizophrenia
- Differing approaches to the treatment of schizophrenia and their effectiveness.

The condition now labelled schizophrenia was first described by Kraepelin ([1883] 1981) using the term *dementia praecox*. This label was chosen to indicate that it was a progressive and deteriorating illness with no return to pre-morbid levels of functioning. Some years later, Bleuler (1908) identified four fundamental symptoms of what he termed the group of schizophrenias (literally, 'split mind'): ambivalence, disturbance of association, disturbance of mood and a preference for fantasy over reality. In retrospect, many of these people may actually have been suffering from a number of neurological disorders including a form of encephalitis known as *encephalitis lethargica* (Boyle 1990).

The nature of schizophrenia

The exact nature of schizophrenia remains hotly disputed. However, the consensus view is that it comprises a number of related disorders characterized by fundamental distortions of thinking and perception. Disturbances in thought processes are usually the most obvious symptom of schizophrenia. Conversations may lack coherence, jumping from topic to topic and idea to idea in an apparently incoherent manner. People with schizophrenia may use **neologisms** or make bizarre associations between words. They may feel that someone is putting thoughts into their mind and lose track of their conversation or thoughts, perhaps not completing sentences. They may have deluded and sometimes bizarre beliefs about themselves or others. These may include *delusions of control* (both being able to control others or being controlled by others), *delusions of grandeur* (believing they are rich, famous, talented) and *delusions of reference* (believing the behaviour of others is directly related to them: glances, looks, laughter, are all seen as being directed at the individual). People with schizophrenia may also experience hallucinations, the most frequent of which are auditory. Their content may vary from the benign to the persecutory. The emotions that such people experience are often described as *flattened*. That is, they experience a general lack of emotional responsiveness, although they may be prone to apparently inappropriate mood states such as anger or depression as a consequence of internal thoughts or hallucinations.

Personal experiences

The experiences of people with schizophrenia vary markedly, as does the degree to which any experiences interfere with their life. Many people experience delusions over long periods without any significant impact on their life; for others, the experience may be much more problematic. Two examples of this may be found in the experiences of Michael and David. Michael was a middle-aged man diagnosed with schizophrenia some years ago who was living a relatively normal life in a small flat in Cardiff. One of his delusional beliefs was that he is being attacked by lasers from an unknown, probably extraterrestrial, source:

> The lasers attack me. They aim for my head. I know when they are firing because I have pains when they hit me. They don't fire at me all the time. They come and go. I don't know what I have done to have them do this to me. But it's been going on for years. They usually hit me in the head, so I wear protection against it when they fire. I wrap metal foil over my head so it reflects the lasers away . . . that way they can't get to me . . . I think they are aliens that do this . . . The last time they fired at me was Sunday morning. They woke me up – the lasers – with my head really hurting. I couldn't get out of bed because of the pain. I had to wear protection and take my time to get going because of the pain . . . That was bad. Usually I can stop the lasers with the metal, but it can get through sometimes.
>
> [It is perhaps not coincidental that Michael had spent much of Saturday night drinking beer in a local pub.]

A more acute and devastating set of delusional beliefs resulted in David being admitted to hospital as he was running naked down the middle of a city road proclaiming that he was the son of God come to save us from our sins. At the time he was brought into casualty he was proclaiming:

I am the messiah! I am David, David, the saviour . . . I will save you from the sins you have committed that commit you to the heat of the hell not heaven of the Lord my God. You cannot hold me . . . God is angry with you, the world, the whole round . . . the devil will take you for your sins of holding me here . . . the nine that follow will kill you for holding the son of God in your hall . . . I have come to save the world . . . you cannot hold me . . . By the writings of Methuselah and the prophets and God and Jesus I am here. God speaks to me! Not you! And he is angry at the wickedness of the world and the work of the people and the things they have done . . . the sins, things . . . wings of angels will come for me to take me away from this hall.

About 1 per cent of adults are diagnosed as having some form of schizophrenia (APA 2000). Prevalence rates appear stable across countries, cultures and over time (but see the discussion of cultural relativity in Chapter 1), with the onset of problems typically beginning between the ages of 20 and 35 years. On average, women develop the condition three to four years later than men and show a second peak of onset around the menopause. It is an episodic disorder, with periods of acute problems frequently separated by periods of remission, and still has a relatively poor prognosis. Harrow et al. (2005) found that only 40 per cent of their cohort of people diagnosed with schizophrenia in Chicago had one or more periods of recovery over a 15-year period. In a similar Dutch study, Wiersma et al. (1998) reported that two-thirds of people with a diagnosis of schizophrenia followed up over the same period had at least one relapse, and after each relapse one in six did not recover: one in ten committed suicide over the course of the study. Factors associated with a good prognosis included an acute onset, the presence of an identifiable stress trigger, a predominance of positive symptoms (see p. 144), good social support and no family history of schizophrenia. Rosen and Garety (2005) found having a job to be a protective factor against relapse following a first episode of schizophrenia. They suggested that this may provide a direct protective benefit, as well as being an indicator that factors associated with holding down a job identified by Wiersma and colleagues, such as having an acute onset without a longer-term deterioration, may also influence longer-term outcome.

DSM diagnostic criteria for schizophrenia

For a diagnosis of schizophrenia to be made, DSM-IV-TR (APA 2000) states that two or more of the following symptoms should be present for a significant period of time during a one-month period:

- delusions
- hallucinations
- disorganized speech: frequent derailment or incoherence
- grossly disorganized or **catatonic behaviour**
- negative symptoms: **flattened mood**, **alogia** or **avolition**.

Only one of these symptoms is required if the delusions are bizarre or the hallucinations comprise a voice keeping up a running commentary on the person's behaviour or thoughts, or involve two or more voices conversing with each other. A second criterion is that the symptoms result in significant impairment. Four sub-types of schizophrenia, in which differing symptoms predominate, have been identified:

- *Disorganized:* in this, disorganized speech and behaviour, and flat or inappropriate mood are the dominant features.

- *Paranoid:* the commonest type of schizophrenia, characterized by stable, paranoid delusions. Auditory hallucinations may support these delusional beliefs. Disturbances of mood and speech, and catatonic symptoms, are not prominent.

- *Catatonic:* characterized by marked psychomotor disturbances. The condition varies among extreme excitement, stupor and waxy flexibility in which the individual may be placed in a position which they maintain for several hours. They may also evidence automatic obedience. These individuals may experience a dreamlike state accompanied by vivid hallucinations. It is now rarely seen in industrial countries, though it remains common elsewhere.

- *Residual:* characterized by an absence of prominent delusions, hallucinations, disorganized speech, or grossly disorganized or catatonic behaviour. There is, however, continuing evidence of a disturbance, indicated by the presence of negative symptoms or two or more of the key symptoms in an attenuated form (Table 6.1).

Alternative view of the symptoms

A different way of thinking about schizophrenia from the DSM diagnostic criteria is to examine which symptoms cluster together, and to examine any underlying mechanisms that contribute to these symptom clusters. Factor analysis of the signs and symptoms of the various sub-types of schizophrenia has identified three clusters of symptoms, known as disorganized, positive and negative symptoms (Liddle et al. 1994), each of which may have different psychological and biological causes:

- The disorganized cluster is characterized by disorganized speech, behaviour and flat or inappropriate mood (or 'thought disorder').

Table 6.1 Some of the most frequent symptoms of acute schizophrenia

Symptom	% of cases
Lack of insight	97
Auditory hallucinations	74
Ideas of reference	70
Flattened affect	66
Suspiciousness	66
Delusions of persecution	64
Thought alienation	52

- The positive cluster includes hallucinations and delusions.

- The negative symptoms denote an absence of activation, and include apathy, lack of motivation, or poverty of speech.

Deconstructing schizophrenia

The DSM-IV-TR criteria for a diagnosis of schizophrenia differ markedly from those of DSM-III, which differ from the alternative definitions of schizophrenia suggested by Liddle et al. (1994). This difficulty in establishing exactly what schizophrenia is presents clinicians and researchers with significant problems when developing aetiological models or treatment approaches. So great is this difficulty that many scientists and clinicians have begun to question whether schizophrenia exists in any form, let alone how it is defined by DSM.

A dimensional perspective

Associated with schizophrenia – in what are frequently referred to as the schizophrenic spectrum disorders – are a number of apparently more stable personality types, each of which contains some of the symptoms of schizophrenia, but at a less problematic or significant level. These include the *schizoid personality*, in which the individual neither desires nor enjoys close relationships, frequently chooses solitary activities, has little interest in having sexual experiences with another person, appears indifferent to the praise or criticism of others, and shows emotional coldness, detachment or flattened mood. People with *schizotypal personality* frequently experience **ideas of reference** (believe other people are talking about them), have odd beliefs that influence behaviour and are inconsistent with sub-cultural norms, and unusual perceptual experiences, including bodily illusions. They may engage in odd thinking and speech, show suspiciousness or paranoid ideation, show inappropriate mood, appear eccentric, lack close friends, and experience excessive social anxiety (APA 2000). These and other personality disorders are considered in more depth in Chapter 11. However, the existence of these personality types suggests that each of the symptoms of schizophrenia can vary across individuals and only achieve a significant level in some – opening the possibility of a dimensional view of schizophrenia (see Chapter 1) rather than it being an all or nothing dichotomous condition as exemplified by DSM.

A further issue of relevance here is that the experiences of people diagnosed with schizophrenia, or even disorders of the schizophrenic spectrum, are not exclusive to them. Many people who do not come to the attention of the psychiatric services also hear voices. What distinguishes between people who seek help for their 'problem' and those who do not appears to be differences in their responses to the voices and their ability to cope with them. Positive coping strategies include setting limits to the time spent listening to voices, talking back to them, and listening selectively to more positive voices (Romme and Escher 1989).

Schizophrenia as multiple disorders

An even more fundamental problem with the DSM concept of schizophrenia is that different people, given the diagnosis, can present with very different experiences and problems: only two, potentially quite different, symptoms need be present to achieve a diagnosis of schizophrenia. This contradicts the notion of a disorder that has one underlying mechanism: if this were the case, all people should present with the same cluster of symptoms. A related point is that different people with schizophrenia respond to different medications, including **neuroleptics**, lithium and benzodiazepines. Others fail to respond to any of these medications. Accordingly, the course and treatment of the condition vary considerably across individuals. As Bentall (1993: 227) noted, 'We are inevitably drawn to an important conclusion: "schizophrenia" appears to be a disease which has no particular symptoms, which has no particular course, and which responds to no particular treatment.' On these grounds, he suggested that the diagnosis has no validity and that the concept of schizophrenia should be abandoned. Rather than attempting to explain multiple syndromes, future efforts should focus on explanations of particular behaviours or experiences: each of the various symptoms of 'schizophrenia' should be considered as a disorder in its own right, with differing underlying causes and treatments.

Having argued that attempts to link widely differing experiences under the rubric of 'schizophrenia' present significant problems, a number of the following sections of the chapter reflect a more traditional perspective, and review research based on DSM or similar definitions of schizophrenia. Some may argue that this type of research is doomed to failure as it is seeking to identify causal factors for a condition that does not exist. More positively, it may still indicate some of the factors that increase risk or provide effective treatment for some or all of the experiences now considered under the rubric of schizophrenia. It also indicates some of the problems faced by theorists trying to explain common factors that contribute to the diverse experiences of people diagnosed as schizophrenic. As the research almost exclusively focuses on people with a diagnosis of schizophrenia, this term will be used throughout the sections, despite concerns about the validity of the concept.

Aetiology of schizophrenia

Genetic factors

Schizophrenia has been at the centre of a scientific debate concerning the role of nature and nurture in the development of mental health problems. Perhaps the dominant model of the aetiology of schizophrenia has considered it to have a biological cause, driven by genetic factors, although this has been hotly debated by those who favour environmental explanations. Evidence relating to genetic factors has therefore been closely scrutinized and has not been without controversy.

Early genetic studies indicated that the risk for schizophrenia among relatives of an identified 'case' correlated with the degree of shared genes. Table 6.2 summarizes the findings of some early family studies, although weak study designs may have resulted in an overestimation of the strength of the family linkages (Tsuang 2000). More recent and methodologically sound studies (e.g. Kringlen 1993) have reported concordance rates for schizophrenia in MZ twins of between 30 and 40 per cent and between DZ twins of 10–15 per cent, suggesting a part-genetically mediated risk for schizophrenia. While this evidence shows that schizophrenia runs in families, it does

Table 6.2 Risk for schizophrenia (definite and probable) of relatives of people diagnosed with schizophrenia

Relationship	Percentage shared genes	Risk (%)
General population	N.A.	1
Spouses of patients	N.A.	2
Third-degree relatives	12.5	
First-degree cousins		2
Second-degree relatives	25	
Uncles/aunts		2
Nieces/nephews		4
Grandchildren		5
Half-siblings		6
First-degree siblings	50	
Parents		6
Siblings		9
Children		13
Siblings with one schizophrenic parent		17
Dizygotic twin		17
Monozygotic twin	100	48
Children with two schizophrenic parents	100	46

Source: adapted from Tsuang (2000)

not necessarily mean that it has a genetic causation (see Chapter 1). Those closest to the affected individual may share a similar environment to them, or be affected by their behaviour. Attempts to disentangle environmental from biological issues have led to a number of studies comparing the risk for schizophrenia among relatives or twins of adopted-away children

Close examination of these studies reveals a far from clear set of evidence. The Danish Adoption Studies (Kety et al. 1975), for example, traced the biological relatives of 34 adopted children who later developed schizophrenia and those of 34 control cases with 'clean pedigrees', and compared the prevalence of schizophrenia among them. Interestingly, they found only one person diagnosed as having chronic schizophrenia among the relatives of either cases or controls. Only when they extended the diagnoses assigned to one of schizophrenic spectrum of disorders comprising numerous diagnoses including borderline state, inadequate personality and uncertain schizophrenia did differences between the groups arise. Using these diagnoses, they found nine affected relatives in the families of the cases and two among the controls. This, some critics (e.g. Roberts 2000) have argued, provided no evidence that schizophrenia *per se* is inherited. Roberts also noted that at least some of the diagnoses assigned were taken from hospital notes and not confirmed by the research team, and that at least one person's reported diagnosis changed from inadequate personality to borderline schizophrenia over the course of two reports by the same research team. Worse was to come: subsequent reading of this individual's notes showed an initial diagnosis of bipolar disorder (see Chapter 8: Rose et al. 1984).

A more recent study of genetics reported by Tienari et al. (2000) compared rates of schizophrenia in the adopted-away offspring of both mothers diagnosed with schizophrenia and those without the diagnosis. Risk for schizophrenia was four times greater among the children of the women diagnosed as having schizophrenia than among the children of the comparison mothers: a total **incidence** of 8.1 per cent versus 2.3 per cent. However, this was not entirely due to genetic factors. Using data from the same study, Wahlberg et al. (2000b) reported an interaction between genetic and environmental factors. Children of women diagnosed with schizophrenia who lived in households where there was good communication between the family members were not at increased risk of thought disorder. By contrast, the children of women diagnosed as having schizophrenia who were placed in families with evidence of communication deviance were at greater risk of developing schizophrenia than those with 'normal' mothers who were placed in such households. That is, the development of schizophrenia seemed to depend on both genetic risk *and* communication deviance within the adoptive family. Importantly, any communication deviance seemed to predate the adoption, and was not a consequence of the child's behaviour.

Together, these and other data have generally been seen by biological theorists as supporting a model in which genetic factors influence risk for schizophrenia but do not form the single causal agent. They form a vulnerability factor rather than a causal factor. The search for the location of genes that increase risk of schizophrenia has also failed to yield definitive results, although loci on a dozen chromosomes have been implicated as likely sites (Tsuang 2000). Even genetic advocates such as Corsico and McGuffin (2001) have admitted that identifying the genetic linkages of schizophrenia presents 'great difficulties'. When considering the role of genetics in schizophrenia, one final cautionary note should be borne in mind: 89 per cent of individuals diagnosed with schizophrenia have no known relative with the disorder. Other factors are clearly implicated in the development of the disorder.

Biological mechanisms

The dopamine hypothesis

Much of the neurological research attempting to identify the causes of schizophrenia has been conducted on people who already are known to have the condition. This makes sense in some ways. But it provides significant problems for interpretation of many of the data. Johnstone (2000), for example, contended that any findings of neurological differences between people with schizophrenia and those without it may not indicate that these differences cause the condition. Rather, they may be explained by the effects of medication and/or the stress of experiencing vivid hallucinations or holding strong delusional beliefs.

Despite these provisos, a number of biological models of schizophrenia have been proposed. The first plausible theory involved the dopamine systems of the brain. Neurons mediated by dopamine are found in the limbic system, in a brain area known as A10, with links to the thalamus, hippocampus and frontal cortex, and the substantia nigra. The key feature of the dopamine hypothesis is that the experiences of people diagnosed with schizophrenia result from either an excess of dopamine, or the receptors at neuronal synapses being supersensitive to normal amounts of dopamine. Evidence generally supports the latter, but either way this theory suggests that at least some of the experiences of schizophrenia may result from excess activity in those parts of the brain controlled by dopamine.

Evidence of increased dopamine activity comes from a number of converging types of study (Lieberman et al. 1990):

- Amphetamine use increases dopamine levels and can produce experiences that mimic the positive symptoms of schizophrenia. Small controlled doses of amphetamines can produce schizophrenic-like symptoms in at least some naïve subjects. These experiences may continue long after cessation of taking the drug. They do, however, mirror only one particular type of schizophrenia: paranoid schizophrenia.

- Some of the most effective drugs for treating both amphetamine psychosis and schizophrenia are the neuroleptic drugs known as phenothiazines (see Chapter 3), which block transmission of dopamine by preventing its uptake at the postsynaptic receptor site.

- Post-mortem evidence has shown a marked increase in dopamine receptor sites in people with schizophrenia in comparison with 'normal' controls, suggesting a supersensitivity to dopamine. How much of this is a consequence of medication and how much the disease process is in dispute.

Other evidence is less supportive of the dopamine hypothesis (Duncan et al. 1999):

- No direct evidence of pathologic dopamine neuronal activity has been consistently demonstrated, such as increased levels of dopamine, its metabolites or its receptors, that are not the potential results of antipsychotic drug treatment.

- One of the most effective antipsychotic drugs, clozapine, appears to work by its impact on the serotonin and not dopamine systems. This suggests that other neurotransmitters may be involved in schizophrenia.

- A substantial proportion of people with schizophrenia are resistant to treatment with neuroleptics, suggesting that dopamine systems may not always be involved in its aetiology.

- Schizophrenic-like experiences are rarely induced in 'normal' individuals when they are administered drugs that increase dopaminergic activity.

- Neuroleptics are only partially effective in alleviating the negative symptoms of people diagnosed with schizophrenia.

These conflicting findings may reflect problems in trying to collapse a number of differing biological processes under the rubric of one condition which may present quite differently in different people. However, instead of trying to identify specific biological substrates with specific psychological experiences, biological theorists continue to attempt to provide a model which explains all the experiences of schizophrenia. One way they have done this is to extend the number of neurotransmitters implicated in its aetiology. Duncan et al. (1999), for example, suggested that NMDA and serotonin dysregulation may also contribute to the disorder (see discussion of the mode of action of atypical neuroleptics in Chapter 3).

Neurological substrates

As well as errors in neurotransmitter levels, some studies suggest that negative, disorganized, and some positive symptoms may result from damage to the neural systems themselves (Basso et al. 1998). The most common findings of brain scans of people diagnosed with schizophrenia include enlarged cerebral **ventricles** and decreased cortical volume especially in the temporal and frontal lobes compared with normal scans. Post-mortem examinations have revealed reductions in neuron density and size in the limbic, temporal and frontal regions and that the connections between neurons are relatively disorganized. The various affected brain areas include systems that influence attention, memory and mood (limbic system), planning and coordination (frontal and prefrontal lobe), and acoustic and verbal memory (temporal lobes).

The length of time a person experiences any problems before receiving drug treatment is a significant predictor of long-term outcome. Lieberman et al. (1990) took this to indicate the neuronal degeneration is a progressive deterioration, resulting in a diminished ability of the individual to respond to antipsychotic medication. Provide treatment too late, and the degree of neuronal damage is too great to allow full recovery. Biological theorists have proposed a number of potential causes for any neural damage, as described next.

Excess dopamine   In an extension of the dopamine hypothesis, Lieberman et al. (1990) suggested that the initial trigger to a first episode of schizophrenia may involve increased dopaminergic activity, which results in positive symptoms. However, continued excessive dopamine activity leads to degeneration of the neurons in the dopamine systems, leading to exceptionally low levels of dopamine activity and, hence, negative symptoms. While this theory is still widely advocated, not all evidence is supportive. Ho et al. (2005), for example, noted that the hippocampus appears particularly sensitive to damage through a variety of chemical pathways. Accordingly, they argued, if high levels of dopamine were to damage neural systems within the brain, then the longer any episode of schizophrenia occurred without treatment, the more damage to the hippocampus should occur – and any damage that did occur could be attributed to dopaminergic or other neurotoxic processes associated with schizophrenia, rather than any treatment regimen. To explore this issue, they examined the relationship between the time following untreated initial diagnosis of schizophrenia and hippocampal volume in 105 individuals. The average duration of symptoms prior to treatment was over a year. They found no relationship between duration of symptoms and hippocampal volume, providing no support for the neurotoxic impact of dopamine.

One explanation for Ho's negative findings may be that any damage occurs rapidly at an early stage of the disorder. Evidence for this can be found in the work of Pantelis and colleagues (see Pantelis et al. 2005) who have found evidence of significant pathological changes at a very early stage in the development of schizophrenia – including during the transition from people being 'well' to a first episode of schizophrenia. In one study by this group, Wood et al. (2005) compared hippocampal volumes of 79 male subjects at, what they termed, ultra-high-risk of schizophrenia with those of 49 healthy male volunteers. The high-risk participants had significantly smaller hippocampal volumes than the comparison group. So, the dopamine causes neuronal damage theory has been supported.

Viral infection There is consistent evidence that children born in the winter months are more at risk of developing schizophrenia than those born in the summer (Torrey et al. 1997). Why this should be the case is not clear. However, the best guess is that neural damage as a result of viral diseases, which are more prevalent during the winter, may be a causal factor. Supportive evidence was reported by Jones and Cannon (1998), who found that young children who had viral infections were five times more likely to develop schizophrenia than those who did not. Similarly, Takei et al. (1995) found that female (but not male) foetuses exposed to an influenza virus five months before birth were at increased risk of developing schizophrenia in adulthood than those that were not exposed. Larger studies in whole populations have not always supported these findings, however. While some studies have found the incidence of schizophrenia to be higher among cohorts of adults born close to times of childhood viral epidemics, this is not always the case (Battle et al. 1999).

Pregnancy and delivery complications Pregnancy and delivery complications may also cause subtle brain damage that increases risk for schizophrenia. In a meta-analysis of 11 studies reporting relevant data, Geddes et al. (1999) compared data on 700 children who went on to develop schizophrenia and 835 controls. A number of delivery complications were implicated by their data, including low birth weight, prematurity, requiring resuscitation or being placed in an incubator, lack of oxygen, and premature rupture of the membranes.

Maternal stress A number of studies have also implicated maternal stress in the development of schizophrenia. Van Os and Selten (1998), for example, found that the children of Dutch women who experienced bombing during the Second World War during their pregnancy were at increased risk for schizophrenia in comparison to control populations who did not. Interpreting these data is somewhat complicated as not all women may have experienced stress as a consequence of these factors. In addition, the cause of any relationship between maternal stress and subsequent disorders is far from clear. It could be mediated through hormonal changes at times of stress, changes in health behaviour such as smoking or alcohol use, delivery complications or some other mechanism.

Substance abuse

So far, the chapter has identified a number of factors that either increase risk of developing schizophrenia or explain the chronic degenerative changes associated with the condition. They have not considered what may actually trigger particular episodes. Such triggers may be psychological (see below). However, one biochemical trigger may also be implicated. Amphetamines can cause transient psychotic experiences and precipitate relapse of an existing psychotic condition (Satel and Edell 1991).

Evidence that cannabis consumption can also increase risk of schizophrenia may be found in a longitudinal study of nearly 45,000 Swedish people reported by Andreasson et al. (1987). Those who used cannabis at the age of 18 were more likely to be admitted to hospital with schizophrenia over a 15-year follow-up period than those who did not. In addition, there was a dose–response relationship between the frequency of smoking cannabis and the risk of developing schizophrenia: the more cannabis smoked, the greater the risk of developing schizophrenia.

Reviewing this, and subsequent evidence, a meta-analysis by Henquet et al. (2005) found that young heavy cannabis users were at double the risk of non-users of developing schizophrenia. Evidence from work by Caspi et al. (2005), suggests the possibility that this risk may be largely specific to individuals with a particular genetic make-up (a functional polymorphism in the catechol-O-methyltransferase (COMT) gene). A potential biochemical route through which cannabis exerts this influence has also been determined. The active metabolite of cannabis (delta-9 tetrahydro-cannabinol) raises levels of cerebral dopamine and might precipitate psychosis. People with the early experiences of schizophrenia may also take cannabis as a form of self-treatment to alleviate either negative experiences or depression (Peralta and Cuesta 1992), reversing the causal link.

Psychosocial factors

The highest population rates of schizophrenia are among those in the lower socio-economic groups. Eaton et al. (1989), for example, calculated that individuals in the lowest socio-economic group were three times more likely to be assigned a diagnosis of schizophrenia than those in the highest. This type of finding could have (at least) two implications. Either socio-economic status is a risk factor for schizophrenia, or schizophrenia is a risk factor for low socio-economic status: social causation versus social drift (see Chapter 1). Fox (1990) analysed both his own long-term data and those of other published work and found no evidence to support the social drift hypothesis. It seems that low socio-economic status is generally a cause rather than a consequence of schizophrenia.

One explanation for this finding is that the relatively high levels of stress associated with low socio-economic status may trigger the onset of schizophrenia in vulnerable individuals. This speculation is supported by findings that up to 24 per cent of episodes of schizophrenia seem to be precipitated by some acute life stress (Tsuang et al. 1986).

Long-term stresses also increase risk of initial onset of the condition. One long-term stressor may be the family in which the individual lives. One of the first theories to consider this issue identified the relationship between the child and their mother as a critical factor in schizophrenia. This psychoanalytic theory, developed by Fromm-Reichman (1948), suggested that schizophrenia is the outcome of being raised by a mother who appears warm and self-sacrificing, but is in reality self-centred, cold and domineering – the so-called *schizophrenogenic mother*. Fromm-Reichman suggested that the mixed signals that such a mother gives out confuses the child and makes their world difficult to interpret, a process that eventually leads to chaotic behaviour and cognitions. A similar theory was subsequently proposed by Bateson et al. (1956).

Their 'double-bind' theory suggested that some parents frequently deal with their children in contradictory and confusing ways. They may, for example, tell their children they love them in a tone of voice that implies the opposite, or ask them to do incompatible things: 'I think you should go out more often with your friends: please stay with me . . .'. Frequent exposure to these contradictory demands may confuse the person, and eventually prove so stressful that it results in the experience of schizophrenia. Both models have some logic, but they have little evidence in their support.

One family theory has proven more robust. A critical element in the family process seems to be the degree of family criticism that the individual experiences. According to this model, the expression of high levels of negative emotional expression, hostility or criticism may trigger a relapse in someone who has already had at least one episode of schizophrenia. The classic study of this phenomenon, now known as high negative expressed emotion (NEE), was conducted by Vaughn and Leff (1976) in a study of readmission rates of people with schizophrenia discharged from the Maudsley Hospital during the 1970s. Their findings were dramatic: those who were discharged to low NEE households were much less likely to relapse than those whose home was rated high in NEE. The effect of this type of environment is related to the amount of time it is experienced. Individuals who spent fewer than 35 hours a week in the home environment, because they went to work or to a day centre, were significantly less likely to relapse than those who were exposed to these conditions for more than 35 hours a week. Since then, these findings have been replicated in a number of countries and cultures (Miklowitz 2004).

The majority of studies have considered high negative expressed emotion to be a trigger to relapse – not a trigger to a first episode. As such, the high expressed emotion environment is often thought of as a consequence of the family coping with an individual within it whose behaviour may be at odds with family values and processes. In this model, high negative expressed emotion is not a direct 'cause' of episodes of schizophrenia. Rather, it lies within a circle of causality, being both a response to 'difficult' or inexplicable behaviour and a contributor to its development. In keeping with this family process, levels of negative expressed emotion tend to be higher in families where odd behaviour is seen as wilful and under the control of the individual, and lower where any odd behaviour is attributable to an illness or an uncontrollable cause (e.g. Yang et al. 2004). Evidence that family processes may also trigger the initial onset of schizophrenia in vulnerable individuals can be found in the Wahlberg et al. (2000b) study described earlier in the chapter.

From a wider perspective, the International Pilot Study of Schizophrenia (e.g. Leff et al. 1992) suggested both social and cultural factors may influence both the presentation of schizophrenia and its outcome. Of particular note was that the clinical and social consequences of the disorders were far less negative in developing countries such as Nigeria and India than in the more industrialized countries – suggesting there is less stigmatization of schizophrenia in these countries and that the presence of extended family networks and fewer societal pressures may provide an effective moderator of symptoms.

A psychobiological model

So far, the evidence has implicated dopamine, subtle brain damage, and stress in the aetiology of the wider set of experiences of people diagnosed with schizophrenia. What it has not done is explain the episodic nature of the disorder or how psycho-social factors influence its course. The dopamine hypothesis can be extended to account for the stress–schizophrenia link, as there is evidence from animal studies that levels of dopamine increase at times of stress (Walker and Diforio 1997). In addition, rats sensitized by chronic amphetamine administration show increased behavioural responses and rises in dopamine levels in response to stress more than control animals (Duncan et al. 1999). Together, these data suggest a possible stress-vulnerability model of schizophrenia involving three broad stages:

- The first stage is one of disordered neuronal development resulting from genetic, natal or perinatal factors. These problems underlie subtle early cognitive, motor and social impairments. They provide a *vulnerability* for schizophrenia.

- These deficiencies may lead to the second stage, which occurs in adolescence and early adulthood. At this time, stressful but normal human experiences result in increases in dopamine activity. As a consequence of this neuronal disorganization, dopaminergic neuronal systems become sensitized to existing levels of dopamine and become more reactive to them, resulting in the positive symptoms of schizophrenia. The greater the stress experienced, the greater the risk of dysregulation and onset of schizophrenia.

- If prolonged or recurrent, high levels of dopamine can lead to the degeneration of neurons, leading to structural damage, and the onset of negative symptoms.

Accordingly, the dysregulation that underpins schizophrenia may be a consequence of both biological factors that increase vulnerability and may contribute to its chronicity, and stress factors that trigger or exacerbate the condition. Even this biopsychosocial model is too 'biological' for some critics (e.g. Johnstone 2000) who have argued that there are no compelling grounds to assume any biological underpinnings to either schizophrenia or its 'component' elements. They still do not feel the necessity to combine biological and psychological elements, arguing for a psychosocial rather than biopsychosocial model.

Psychological models

Rather than attempt to identify factors that trigger 'episodes' of 'schizophrenia', psychological models of schizophrenia typically attempt to explain the processes that underlie each of the different types of experience reported by people assigned the diagnosis.

Theory of mind
One of the most encompassing psychological models of schizophrenia was initially developed by Frith (e.g. Frith and Corcoran 1996). He proposed that our under-

standing of the social world around us depends on being able to interpret the causes of our own actions and the actions of other people. In social situations, we interpret others' verbal and non-verbal signals in order to try and understand what they are thinking, feeling, what they believe, what is conjecture, what is real, and so on. In order to do so, theory of mind suggests we first of all need to understand our own cognitive processes – the way *we* interpret our world – and then need to translate this knowledge onto the actions of others. A failure in this process makes it difficult to understand the social signals during any interaction and to understand the full meaning of any conversation – to understand the world we inhabit.

Frith suggested that a key element of schizophrenia is that individuals with this disorder do not have a fully intact theory of mind. They cannot fully understand their own cognitive processes: in particular, they can have difficulties in monitoring their own intentions – leading to feelings of passivity and being out of control of their own actions. Other phenomena associated with this problem include the belief that thoughts are being placed in an individual's mind by others, and auditory hallucinations. In addition, individuals with this problem cannot understand the minds of other people, and therefore find it difficult to interpret what other people are thinking or feeling. This may lead to delusions of paranoia and reference. Finally, because such individuals find it difficult to interpret their world, they may become withdrawn and isolated in order to avoid any distress or confusion such attempts may engender. The degree to which these problems exist may vary across individuals. According to Frith, some people with a diagnosis of schizophrenia may have a complete inability to represent other people's mental states. In this, they may be similar to autistic people. Others, including people with paranoid delusions, have some understanding that other people have minds and motivations, but make significant errors due to an inaccurate or poorly developed theory of mind.

This theory has significant implications for a variety of processes involved in the symptoms of schizophrenia. It also provides a number of experimentally testable hypotheses. Not surprisingly, therefore, a number of studies provide supportive evidence, while others are less supportive. Such studies typically attempt to identify how well people diagnosed with schizophrenia can understand other people's mental states – often through the use of analogue studies. These can involve quite complex cognitive tasks. One of the simpler methodologies has involved exploration of the understanding of jokes which involve deception – and therefore require an intact theory of mind to understand. In one such study, Marjoram et al. (2005) presented 20 people diagnosed with schizophrenia and 20 controls with 63 single-image cartoons. Thirty-one of these were considered to be 'theory of mind cartoons', in that understanding the joke required an attribution of ignorance, false belief or deception to one of its characters and, therefore, an analysis of their mental state. The other jokes were more slapstick in nature and subsequently did not require theory of mind capabilities for their correct interpretation. People with a diagnosis of schizophrenia showed less understanding of both types of jokes than the control group – as has been found elsewhere. In addition, they showed significantly less understanding of the theory of mind jokes than the slapstick cartoons, and less understanding of them than the comparison group, suggesting some impairment in their theory of mind. Craig et al. (2004) used two tasks to measure theory of mind in people with paranoid delusions and healthy controls. The first assessed their ability to infer an individual's intentions based on hints within a short written passage; the second measured their ability to detect 'cognitive emotions' such as being embarrassed or pensive (which require inferences about other people's beliefs or intentions to fully understand) from photographs of faces showing only the eye region. People with a diagnosis of schizophrenia performed least well in both tasks.

In a more clinical study of this phenomenon, McCabe, Leudar and Antaki (2004) analysed recordings of interactions between mental health professionals and people diagnosed with chronic schizophrenia during outpatient and cognitive behavioural therapy sessions. In these interactions, it was evident that some of the people recognized that they and the health professionals did not share their beliefs about particular issues. They were also able to attribute emotions and appropriate causes of emotions to other people. One participant stated that he did not tell people when he had 'funny' thoughts come into his head because he was aware that other people did not have such thoughts and he felt ashamed having them. The expression of shame – which is a socially determined emotion – showed an awareness both that other people were different and that they would consider his thoughts to be odd. Accordingly, this study found no evidence of a deficit in theory of mind in this particular sample of people.

Summarizing the available data, Brüne (2005) suggested that there is good empirical evidence that theory of mind is impaired in schizophrenia and that many psychotic symptoms, such as delusions of alien control and persecution, may best be understood as resulting from difficulties in monitoring one's own intentions and relating to other people's intentions. More cautiously, he also noted that we still do not understand how any impairment fluctuates between acute and stable periods within the disorder or how it affects individual's use of language or social behaviour.

Hallucinations as a failure of attention

A number of explanations for hallucinations have been based on an early theory of attention and memory developed by Broadbent (1971). Early work (e.g. McGhie and Chapman 1961) suggested that people with schizophrenia were experiencing a failure to filter out irrelevant and unwanted stimuli: they could not filter out, or decide, which were appropriate or inappropriate elements of their environment to attend to. As a consequence, they felt overwhelmed by sensory experiences and found it difficult to concentrate and respond to their environment appropriately. This approach was extended by Hemsley (e.g. 1996), who considered many of the symptoms of schizophrenia to result from two key failures of processing:

- an impairment of the rapid and automatic assessment of sensory input
- a breakdown in relationship between stored memories and current sensory input.

He suggested that we choose what to attend to within our sensory field as a consequence of our previous experience. We store in our memory what Hemsley referred to as 'regularities', that is, stored information that determines our expectations or interpretations of a situation. This regulates our reactions in similar but novel situations. These processes occur rapidly and automatically and allow us to focus our attention on what is important within our environment, and what is not. As a result of these stored memories, we know what to attend to when we go into a shop to buy a pair of shoes, when we play football, and so on. According to Hemsley, these automatic processes do not occur in people with schizophrenia, and the individual is unable to focus their attention appropriately. They attend to everything within their environment, and become overwhelmed by sensory information. Three key problems arise from this sensory barrage:

• Hallucinations result from a failure to filter out redundant information and from giving all stimuli equal weight.

• One's own thoughts cannot be distinguished from external stimuli – and can be perceived as an external voice.

• Delusions occur when trying to impose meaning on a barrage of confusing internal and external stimuli.

This model explains the positive symptoms of schizophrenia. But Hemsley was also able to explain some of the negative symptoms. He suggested that symptoms such as social withdrawal, impoverished speech, and flat affect may arise either as a consequence of, or as a coping strategy with, the sensory overload. Evidence for some of the key elements of the theory can be derived from a number of sources. One source of support stems from studies of people with speech hallucinations. There is consistent evidence that people with hallucinations have difficulty in identifying the spacial location of sounds, and are less accurate than controls in determining the meaning of words when said against a background of white noise – despite being highly confident of the meaning they attach to such sounds (e.g. Bentall and Slade 1985). In one investigation of this phenomenon, Hoffman et al. (1999) examined the performance of three groups of people during a variety of tasks. Those involved had either a history of hallucinations, a diagnosis of schizophrenia with no history of hallucinations, or were 'normal' controls. They took part in a masked speech tracking task with three levels of superimposed phonetic noise. Participants were asked to repeat the sentences they heard, as they heard them – to assess grammar-dependent verbal working memory. They also took part in a non-verbal tracking task to assess any differences in attention between the three groups. People with a history of hallucinations performed less well on the speech tracking task, but were not impaired on the non-verbal tracking task. The authors took this to indicate that hallucinated voices in schizophrenia arise from disrupted speech perception and verbal working memory systems rather than from non-language cognitive or attentional deficits. Rossell and Boundy (2005) subsequently found that people who hallucinated were particularly poor at distinguishing words with an affective meaning – leaving them susceptible to misinterpreting emotionally laden words in ordinary life.

In a study of the neurological processes that may contribute to this phenomenon, McGuire et al. (1996) used positron emission tomography to measure brain activity of people with a history of hallucinations, people with a diagnosis of schizophrenia with no such history, and 'normal' controls while they took part in a number of tasks. In the first condition, in which participants were asked to simply talk to themselves in their head, there were no differences in brain activity between the groups. However, when they were asked to imagine someone else talking in their head, people who had experienced hallucinations showed different brain activity from both other groups. This group showed reduced activation in the left middle temporal gyrus and the rostral supplementary motor area regions – which were strongly activated in both other groups. As this area is implicated in the monitoring of inner speech, they took this deficit to be a neurological substrate of the failure to identify the source of verbal information and for the hallucinations this group experienced.

A cognitive model of delusions

An alternative, and symptom-specific, example of a psychological approach to explaining the experiences of people diagnosed with schizophrenia can be found in the cognitive model of delusions developed by Bentall and colleagues. Perhaps the most common understanding of these beliefs is that they are qualitatively different from the those held by 'ordinary people'. Berrios (1991), for example, argued that delusions are 'empty speech acts' that refer neither to the world nor to the self: they are not symbolic of anything. By contrast, clinicians such as Bentall (e.g. Bentall et al. 2001) have argued that delusions are at the extreme end of a continuum of types of thought that runs from 'ordinary thoughts' to those that are bizarre and impossible, but all of which are the end-product of similar cognitive processes. Cognitions, including delusions, are seen as an interpretation of events, maybe even rational attempts to make sense of anomalous circumstances. While the thought content may be out of the ordinary, the psychological processes underpinning it are not.

Bentall and colleagues have focused particularly on explanations of one form of delusion involving persecutory beliefs. Their research has indicated that people with these types of belief have cognitive distortions which differ in their specific content, but are similar in type to those associated with many other disorders. Bentall et al. (2001), for example, found that people who experienced persecutory beliefs were more likely than depressed people or participants with no mental health problems to recall threatening themes in stories they were given to read as part of a memory test. They took this to indicate a bias in their interpretation of events generally, not just those events that referred or happened to them directly.

The model of persecutory beliefs developed by this group (Bentall et al. 2001) drew on the humanistic concepts of the actual and ideal self. They suggested that many people with schizophrenia have a poor self-image and experience significant discrepancies between their actual- and ideal-self, that is, how they see themselves and how they would like to be. These discrepancies may be maintained by attentional and attributional biases, in particular, by considering negative events or outcomes of their behaviour to be the result of personal deficiencies. An awareness of the discrepancy between ideal- and actual-self may result in depression. Persecutory beliefs may occur as the result of a struggle to minimize the discrepancy. According to Bentall and colleagues, when discrepancies between actual- and ideal-self are activated by negative life-events or other triggers, the individual tries to minimize this discrepancy by shifting this attribution onto others, as a form of psychological defence: 'I think I am OK, even though others don't'. It may be less distressing for the individual to think that others think poorly of him or her than to accept their own feelings of inadequacy.

Bentall and colleagues further suggest that the natural history of schizophrenia within the family can be explained by this model, as attributional styles may be learned from other family members, and parental criticism may precipitate relapse by triggering actual–ideal self-discrepancies. Evidence for this model is outlined in the Research box 6.

Research box 6

Kinderman, P., Prince, S., Waller, G. et al. (2003) Self-discrepancies, attentional bias and persecutory delusions, *British Journal of Clinical Psychology*, 42: 1–12.

The authors tested Bentall's ideal-self versus actual-self model of persecutory beliefs described in the main text. They explored whether increasing the salience of threat through completion of a Stroop task with many threatening words would result in the attentional biases and changes in self-perception hypothesized by the model.

Method

The study group comprised three groups of participants: 13 people experiencing persecutory delusions (based on case notes and consultation with staff), 11 people with a diagnosis of depression, and 13 attendees of a general practice clinic with no history of mental health problems.

Assessments

Participants first used the Self-concept Checklist which comprised 30 positive and 30 negative self-descriptive words. This assessed participants' beliefs about how 'you actually are' (self-actual), 'how you would ideally like to be' (self-ideal), and 'how other people think you actually are' (other-actual). By subtracting one score from another, they computed participants' self-actual:self-ideal discrepancy and self-actual:other-actual discrepancy scores. Participants then completed an adapted emotional Stroop task. Each task involved colour naming two lists of 48 words, one of which comprised words representing one of five types of threat and the other of which comprised neutral words. The threats were: sociotropy threat (e.g. isolated, abandoned), autonomy threat (e.g. powerless, dependent), physical threat (e.g. pain, hurt), ego-threat (e.g. ridiculed, insulted), self-directed ego threat (e.g. failure, stupid). After completing the Stroop task, participants once more completed the Self-concept Checklist.

Results

Table 6.3 shows discrepancy scores at the first and second administration of the Self-concept Checklist for each group. Before administration of the emotional Stroop task, there were no significant differences between the groups in terms of their self-actual: self-ideal and self-actual:other-actual discrepancies. However, after the Stroop task, significant differences between the groups emerged. These showed evidence of the attributional changes hypothesized by Bentall. That is, among participants with persecutory beliefs, the discrepancy between self-actual and self-ideal was reduced. Conversely, showing a shift to an external negative evaluation, this group showed significant increases in self-actual:other-actual discrepancies. These changes did

Table 6.3 Discrepancy scores for the Self-concept Checklist

Discrepancy	Control	Depression	Paranoid
Time 1			
Self-actual:self-ideal	−11.62	−26.09	−20.69
Self-actual:other-actual	0.46	8.27	8.54
Time 2			
Self-actual:self-ideal	−8.08	−34.91	−8.31
Self-actual:other-actual	2.77	−10.09	18.92

not occur in either of the comparison groups. The group with persecutory delusions also experienced significantly more interference with the colour-naming task when reading the threat words than either other group, indicating a greater focus on the meaning of the words than experienced by the depressed or normal controls.

Discussion

The study had two key findings. First, the experience of threat resulted in a reduction in discrepancies between what people with paranoid delusions wanted to be like and what they considered themselves to actually be like, at the same time as increasing the difference (in a negative direction) between what they considered themselves to be like and their beliefs about what others thought of them. This was unique to this group and not found in either the clinical comparison or the normal group. Second, this was a dynamic, responsive, process. The discrepancy between self-actual and other-actual held by people with persecutory delusions did not differ from that experienced by people with depression before the priming task. Only after it did they differ. This suggests that people with such delusions may only experience significant cognitive distortions when placed under situations of personal threat.

A trauma model of hallucinations

Romme and Escher's (1989) model of hallucinations considered hallucinations to be a normal response to traumatic events, particularly bereavement and sexual or physical assault. They considered that their function is to draw attention to emotional traumas that need resolving and to provide a defence against the emotional upset associated with the memories by placing them into the third person. This may be considered a form of dissociation similar to that involved in the processing of traumatic memories discussed in Chapter 9. The goal of therapy should therefore be to help people develop strategies to understand the meaning of the voices they are hearing, not to rid the person of their voices. This approach has received little empirical attention. However, one key element of their model is that many people experience hearing voices. What distinguishes people who become 'patients' and those that do not is that non-patients perceive their voices as predominantly positive, are not alarmed by them, and feel in control of the experience (Honig et al. 1998).

Despite the lack of scientific data in support of their model, Romme and Escher have had a significant impact on the normalization of the experiences of people with schizophrenia and supporting people who hear voices. The 'hearing voices network' (http://www.voicesforum.org.uk/index.htm), inspired by their work and supported by them, provides support to people with this type of experience. It started in Holland in 1987, with the second network established in the UK. Since then, networks have been established in several European and Asian countries, Australia, and the USA. The aims of the network are:

- to raise awareness of voice hearing, visions, tactile sensations and other sensory experiences
- to give men, women and children who have these experiences an opportunity to talk freely about this together
- to support anyone with these experiences seeking to understand, learn and grow from them in their own way.

Support is provided through self-help groups, training sessions for health workers and the general public, an Internet discussion site and a telephone helpline.

A coping model

A final approach to considering the experiences of people diagnosed with schizophrenia is that they are the end-point of a sequence of poor coping strategies in the face of life stresses. Analysis of the 'early signs' that indicate the future onset of what DSM would term an episode of schizophrenia often presents a pattern of behaviours involving withdrawal from friends and family, spending increasing amounts of time socially isolated perhaps in one room, poor sleep leading to tiredness to the point of exhaustion, losing the structure of the day and perhaps starting to take drugs to relieve distress and low mood (see Box 6.1). These conditions are not so far removed from conditions of sensory deprivation which are known to result in delusional thinking and hallucinations in most people. This model suggests that the experiences of people diagnosed with schizophrenia are perhaps not so far removed from those of other people. It may be that their eventual 'relapse' is more the inevitable end of a sequence of poor coping behaviours that places them at risk of unusual experiences rather than the onset of a 'disorder' that is removed from the experience of the rest of the population.

Treatment of schizophrenia

Antipsychotic medication

Most people diagnosed with schizophrenia receive some form of medication, although dosages may be reduced or even discontinued during periods of remission. Chlorpromazine, haloperidol and clozapine are three of the most commonly used drugs (see Chapter 3 for a review of their mode of action and effectiveness). Their most striking effect is one of sedation. They also have a direct effect on hallucinations and delusions, although their effectiveness varies markedly between individuals. Chlorpromazine and haloperidol seem to affect only the positive symptoms of schizophrenia: clozapine, an atypical neuroleptic, is more successful in treating both positive and negative symptoms, and is often effective when other treatments fail (see, e.g., Sharafi 2005).

Antipsychotic medication has been so successful in treating people with schizophrenia that their typical hospital stay during an acute episode has declined to less than 13 days, when formerly it was months, years, even a lifetime. Nevertheless, while antipsychotic drugs may be an important protective factor against relapse, relapse rates of 40 per cent in the first year following treatment initiation and 15 per cent in successive years are typical (Sarti and Cournos 1990). Overall, they appear to delay relapse rather than prevent it.

The use of antipsychotic drugs is not without problems. They have a variety of side-effects that frequently lead those receiving them to minimize or stop their use. Side-effects of chlorpromazine, for example, include a dryness of mouth and throat, drowsiness, visual disturbances, weight gain or loss, skin sensitivity to sunlight, constipation and depression. More problematic, however, are what are known as extrapyramidal symptoms. These include the symptoms of Parkinsonism and tardive dyskinesia (see Chapter 3), which have been estimated to affect over a quarter of individuals who receive medium- to long-term neuroleptic treatment. Treatment by clozapine or other atypical neuroleptics does not carry this risk, but those who receive it may be at risk of a condition known as **agranulocytosis**, which results in significant impairment of the immune system.

Adherence to antipsychotic drug regimes can be as low as 25 per cent among people living in the community (Donohue et al. 2001). This does not seem to be associated with socio-demographic variables, severity of the disorder, or even the extent to which people experience extrapyramidal symptoms. Instead, low adherence seems to be related to attitudes towards medication, expectations of drug effectiveness, available social support, and the quality of the therapeutic alliance. Poor memory may contribute to accidental adherence.

Strategies to maximize adherence include education, developing a high quality therapeutic alliance, and the use of memory aids for those with a poor memory. **Depot injections** may also be of benefit, as these have a relatively long active therapeutic life, and involve the client in less day-to-day decisions about taking oral medication. One relatively new strategy to educate and motivate people to take medication is known as motivational interviewing (Miller and Rollnick 2002). This neutral approach does not involve attempts at persuasion to take medication. Instead, it encourages the client to choose whether or not to take their medication as a result of a careful exploration of the costs and benefits of their medication use. This process provides some degree of control to the client, maintains or improves the therapeutic alliance as the therapist is not seen as coercive, allows any misunderstandings about medication to be identified and corrected, and seems to be more effective in encouraging drug use than direct attempts at persuasion (Coffey 1999). In one exploration of this approach, Kemp et al. (1998) compared motivational interviewing designed to increase adherence to medication with routine care following relapse. The group which received the motivational approach showed higher levels of adherence to the drug regimen and lower readmission rates over an 18-month period. This positive finding compares well against even quite sophisticated education programmes involving several sessions, which have not proven so effective (e.g. Byerly et al. 2005).

Minimizing drug usage: early signs

The psychological and physical consequences of long-term drug treatment of schizophrenia have led clinicians to seek innovative methods by which medication usage can be minimized. One approach, involving 'early signs', is based on findings that many people with schizophrenia and their families can detect subtle changes in behaviour and mood that precede a relapse (see Box 6.1). Herz and Melville (1980), for example, found that 70 per cent of people with schizophrenia and 93 per cent of their families were aware of such changes. These experiences frequently followed a regular and predictable order, the progression of which typically occurred in a period of less than one month, but in some cases may appear up to one year before the onset of significant problems. The 'early signs' approach assumes that while a person is well, they may be placed on a reduced level of drug treatment or even withdrawn from medication completely. When they experience changes that indicate risk of relapse, these should trigger the individual to seek help (often following a prearranged care plan) and to receive intensive drug and/or psychological therapy to prevent relapse and maintain their recovery (Birchwood et al. 2000).

This approach can be effective. Gaebel et al. (2002), for example, compared outcomes in 363 people with schizophrenia who received either intermittent (early signs intervention) or continuous medication following either a first episode or multiple episodes of schizophrenia. Those people treated using the early signs approach used less medication over a two-year period than those in the continuous medication condition. Despite this, there were no differences in effectiveness between the treatments on measures of psychopathology, social adjustment and subjective well-being.

Box 6.1 Early signs of relapse

Birchwood and colleagues (2000) ask clients to tick off a checklist of 'early signs' which they experience at different times within a process of relapse. Others ask them to identify them through discussion. Here are some of the early signs identified by a number of people using this approach, roughly in the order in which they occur at times up to several months before any obvious 'relapse':

Sean

- sleeping later in the morning
- reduced contact with people – staying in
- loss of interest in music
- anxiety
- smoking and drinking more
- paranoia – think I'm being poisoned
- depression
- erratic eating
- stop shaving
- litter around the house – don't clean up, live in a mess
- fear
- mental exhaustion – peripheral hallucinations, flashes of light and dark.

Tony

- abusing drugs and alcohol
- distrusting people
- hostile towards people
- sleep deprivation
- erratic mood swings
- comfort eating
- tired and lethargic
- alienation from friends and family
- crying
- racing thoughts
- anger and violent behaviour towards parents
- smoking cannabis during work hours
- find it difficult to separate thoughts from reality
- washed-out on jobs – verbally abusive
- lack of concentration

Electroconvulsive therapy

Electroconvulsive therapy (ECT: see Chapter 3) has been a front-line treatment of schizophrenia in the past, and has achieved some success. A meta-analysis by Tharyan (2002) concluded that about half those treated with ECT showed short-term improvements in general functioning when compared with those given placebo. This effect, however, did not last. Moreover, ECT is less effective than antipsychotic drug treatment. Combining antipsychotic drugs and ECT is of benefit only in the short term, and only one out of every five to six people appears to benefit. For these reasons, ECT in the treatment of schizophrenia has largely been curtailed, with an increased emphasis on medication and psychosocial treatments. However, some have still advocated its use when other treatments have proven unsuccessful (Tharyan and Adams 2005).

Psychological approaches

Psychoanalytic approaches
One of the first psychosocial treatments of schizophrenia was developed by Harry Stack Sullivan in the early part of the twentieth century. Sullivan (1953) considered schizophrenia to involve difficulties in living arising from problems in personal and social relationships, and that 'personality warps' were the lasting residue of earlier unsatisfactory personal experiences. His treatment approach involved examination of the individual's life history and the historical roots and current ramifications of their maladaptive interpersonal patterns, evident in their relationship with their doctor and in daily life. Characteristic difficulties were thought to include a basic mistrust of others, and a marked ambivalence in relationships, with swings between a long-

ing for, and a terror of, close relationships. Resolution of this conflict through the psychotherapeutic process was thought to result in improvements in psychosis, and maturation of the patient and their non-psychotic personality. While Sullivan's interventions were important, as they encouraged the psychological treatment of people with schizophrenia, the approach has been found to be less effective than supportive therapy, and is no longer carried out.

Family interventions

The recognition that high NEE was contributing to relapse in schizophrenia resulted in a number of studies of family interventions targeted at its reduction. In one of the earliest of these, Leff and Vaughn (1985) randomly assigned people with schizophrenia who had at least 35 hours per week face-to-face contact with family members in a high NEE household to a family intervention or usual care condition. The intervention included a **psycho-educational programme** that focused on methods of reducing NEE within the household, family support and the opportunity for family therapy. The programme was highly successful. Nine months after the end of therapy, 8 per cent of the people in the treatment group had relapsed, in contrast to 50 per cent of those in the comparison group. By two-year follow-up, 40 per cent of the treatment group and 78 per cent of the control group had relapsed.

A similar therapeutic approach was adopted by Falloon et al. (1982). Their intervention included education about the role of family stress in triggering episodes of schizophrenia and working with the family to develop family problem-solving skills. Their results were equally impressive. At nine-month follow-up, 5 per cent of the people in families receiving treatment had relapsed, in contrast to 44 per cent of those receiving standard medical treatment. By two-year follow-up, relapse rates were 16 per cent and 83 per cent respectively. On the basis of this and other related evidence, Pharoah et al. (2000) concluded that family interventions reduce risk of relapse by about half in comparison with standard medical care. They also noted that family interventions decreased the frequency of admissions to hospital, time spent in hospital, and improved compliance with medication regimens.

Cognitive behavioural therapy

Two forms of cognitive behavioural therapy are increasingly being used with people with a diagnosis of schizophrenia. The first, stress management, involves working with individuals to help them cope with the stress leading to or associated with psychotic experiences. The second, known as belief modification, involves attempts to change the nature of delusional beliefs the individual may hold.

Stress management Stress management approaches involve a detailed evaluation of the problems and experiences an individual is having, their triggers and consequences, and any strategies they may use to cope with them. Problems are identified and the therapist and client work together to develop specific coping strategies to help the client cope more effectively with them. Potential strategies include cognitive techniques such as distraction from intrusive thoughts or challenging their meaning, increasing or decreasing social activity as a means of distraction from intrusive thoughts or low mood, and using breathing or other relaxation techniques to help the client to relax (see Chapter 2).

One key group that these techniques have been used with are people who are at particularly high risk of a first episode of schizophrenia. In an attempt to prevent this, McGorry et al. (2002) randomized such individuals into what they termed a needs-based intervention, involving supportive psychotherapy focusing on social, work, or family issues or low-dose risperidone therapy combined with CBT (termed a specific preventive intervention). Each intervention lasted for six months. By the end of treatment, 36 per cent of the people who received needs-based intervention progressed to first-episode psychosis compared with 10 per cent in the specific preventive intervention group.

Other studies have evaluated interventions intended to promote recovery *following* an acute episode of schizophrenia. In one such study, Tarrier et al. (2000) randomly assigned individuals to either drug therapy alone, or in combination with stress management or supportive counselling. The stress management intervention involved 20 sessions in ten weeks, followed by four booster sessions over the following year. By the end of the first phase of treatment, those who received this intervention evidenced a greater improvement than those in the supportive counselling group, while people who received only drug therapy showed a slight deterioration. One-third of the people who received stress management achieved a 50 per cent reduction in psychotic experiences; only 15 per cent of the supportive counselling group achieved this level of benefit:15 per cent of the stress management group and 7 per cent of the supportive counselling condition were free of all positive symptoms. None of those in the drug therapy group achieved this criterion. One year later, there remained significant differences between the three groups, favouring those in the stress management condition. Evidence of a one-year gain was also reported by Startup et al. (2005) following a similar intervention. However, by two-year follow-up, although people in the Tarrier study who received only drug therapy had significantly more problems than those in the active treatment groups, there were no significant differences between the stress management and supportive counselling groups.

Belief modification   Belief modification involves the use of two cognitive interventions, verbal challenge and behavioural hypothesis testing, to counter delusional beliefs and/or hallucinations. Verbal challenge encourages the individual to view a delusional belief as just one of several possibilities. The person is not told that the belief is wrong, but is asked to consider an alternative view provided by the therapist. New possibilities may then be tested in the 'real world' as appropriate. A similar process is used to challenge hallucinations, focusing on the patient's beliefs about their power, identity and purpose. Behavioural hypothesis testing involves challenging any thoughts in a more direct, behavioural, way (see also discussion of these issues in Chapter 2).

Reflecting the novelty of this approach, the number of studies to evaluate this type of intervention is relatively small. Nevertheless, Jones et al. (2000) conducted a meta-analysis on the results of four randomized controlled trials of belief modification, and found that it reduced both the frequency and the impact of hallucinations. In addition, while it had only a minimal impact on measures of conviction in delusional beliefs, it did reduce the amount of distress associated with them. Overall, people who were taught ways of challenging their delusional beliefs or hallucinations were half as likely to relapse as those who were not.

Three of the studies analysed by Jones et al. (2000) involved specific interventions. One of them, reported by Haddock et al. (1998), compared a cognitive approach involving challenging the content of auditory hallucinations with one based on distracting from them. Both treatments were equally effective in the short term, reducing the frequency of hallucinations and minimizing their impact on daily life. However, those who were taught to challenge the content and nature of the hallucinations reported stronger beliefs that the voices were their own thoughts than those in the distraction condition. Jakes, Rhodes and Turner (1999) evaluated the impact of CBT on 18 people with long-term delusions. Of these, six reported reduced conviction in their delusions during cognitive therapy and not during the control period. Seven participants showed no evidence of change. Five patients showed a variable response. More recently, Warman et al. (2005) followed the outcomes of a group cognitive behavioural intervention. The study followed only six individuals, but it evidenced gains on measures of delusions as well as depression, anxiety and hopelessness over an 11-month period.

A more multifaceted intervention was reported by Drury et al. (2000). Their intervention involved both individual and group cognitive therapy in which participants learned to cope with delusions and hallucinations. In addition, they took part in a six-month long family psycho-education programme and an activity programme including life-skills groups. The effects of this intervention were compared with those of an activity programme involving participants in sports, leisure and social groups. The short- and mid-term impacts of the intervention were impressive. Those in the active therapeutic programme recovered more quickly following the relapse that brought them into therapy. By nine-month follow-up, 56 per cent of the control group still had moderate or severe problems, in comparison to 5 per cent of the intervention group. By five-year follow-up, however, there was no evidence of any long-term differences between the two groups on measures of relapse rates or levels of positive symptoms. To achieve longer-term benefits, it may be necessary to introduce a second, perhaps less extensive, 'booster' intervention.

Chapter summary

1 Schizophrenia is one of the most disabling mental health disorders.

2 DSM identifies four types of schizophrenia: disorganized, paranoid, catatonic and residual.

3 An alternative classification system identifies two clusters of symptoms. Positive symptoms include hallucinations, delusions and thought disorder, and negative symptoms are those related to a general lack of motivation.

4 Concerns over the nature of schizophrenia have led some to argue that the concept can no longer be considered valid. Instead, they have argued that the various experiences of people diagnosed as having schizophrenia would be better considered as separate and unrelated factors.

5   There is no exclusive 'cause' of schizophrenia, although a number of factors have been implicated, including genetics and social and family stress.

6   The biological bases for schizophrenia include disruption of the dopamine system and neuronal degeneration, partly as a consequence of perinatal factors, partly due to excess dopamine.

7   Psychological models adopt a dimensional view of the disorder and attempt to understand the psychological processes that contribute to the experiences of people diagnosed with schizophrenia rather than to identify triggers to a 'condition' in which the individual differs categorically from the norm.

8   Theory of mind explanations of schizophrenia attempt to explain a wide range of symptoms of people diagnosed with schizophrenia, and attribute the condition to an inability to monitor and understand one's own thought processes and those of others.

9   More cognitive explanations of delusions suggest they may form an attributional process, to help people cope with negative self-evaluations.

10 Treatment is largely with phenothiazines such as chlorpromazine and newer drugs including clozapine. These seem to delay rather than prevent the onset of further problems.

11 The high level of side-effects associated with these drugs has led to a number of innovative strategies to minimize their use, including the relapse prevention strategy known as 'early signs'.

12 Drug therapy may be significantly augmented by family therapy, particularly for those who live in a high NEE environment, which has been shown to profoundly alter the course of schizophrenia.

13 Newer cognitive techniques may also be of benefit, although their long-term benefits are yet to be evaluated.

For discussion

1   Is the diagnosis of schizophrenia a valid one?

2   Should people with schizophrenia receive genetic or family counselling when planning a family?

3   Should family or cognitive therapy form the first-line treatment for schizophrenia, with drug therapy used only if this is unsuccessful?

Further reading

Bentall, R.P., Corcoran, R., Howard, R. et al. (2001) Persecutory delusions: a review and theoretical integration, *Clinical Psychology Review*, 21: 1143–92.

Birchwood, M., Fowler, D. and Jackson, C. (eds) (2000) *Early Intervention in Psychosis*. London: Wiley.

Boyle, M. (2002) *Schizophrenia*. London: Routledge.

British Psychological Society (BPS) (2000) *Recent Advances in Understanding Mental Illness and Psychotic Experiences*. Leicester: BPS.

Haddock, G. and Lewis, S. (2005) Psychological interventions in early psychosis, *Schizophrenia Bulletin*, 31: 697–704.

National Institute for Clinical Excellence (2002) *Schizophrenia: Core Interventions in the Treatment and Management of Schizophrenia in Primary and Secondary Care – Clinical Guideline 1*. London: NICE. (http://www.nice.org.uk/pdf/CG1NICEguideline.pdf)

7

Anxiety disorders

Anxiety is a useful emotion. Without it, we are likely to be reckless and engage in dangerous activities that could lead to harm or even death. It therefore has strong survival benefits for both the individual and the species. However, when levels of anxiety become inappropriately high, they stop being a proportionate response to the threats within the environment and become problematic to the individual experiencing them. The anxiety disorders lie at the extreme end of the distribution of anxiety within the population. They fall under the DSM category of neurotic and stress-related disorders. This chapter will focus on four diagnoses within this group: generalized anxiety disorder, simple phobias, panic disorder and obsessive-compulsive disorder. Each represents a differing response to either diffuse or specific causes of anxiety. By the end of the chapter, you should have an understanding of:

- The nature and aetiology of each condition from a number of theoretical perspectives
- The types of interventions used to treat each disorder
- The relative effectiveness of each of these interventions.

Generalized anxiety disorder

The chapter starts by considering the most pervasive anxiety disorder. DSM-IV-TR (APA 2000) defines generalized anxiety disorder (GAD) as excessive or ongoing anxiety and worry, occurring on more days than not, over a period of at least six months. In addition:

- The person finds it difficult to control the worry.
- The anxiety and worry are regularly associated with three or more of the following:
  - restlessness or feeling keyed up or on edge
  - being easily fatigued
  - difficulty concentrating or mind going blank
  - irritability
  - muscle tension

  –   sleep disturbance.
- The anxiety, worry or physical symptoms cause significant distress or impairment.

The worries reported by people with GAD usually relate to minor or everyday matters, which they may acknowledge as such, but nevertheless find difficult to control. In the USA, the prevalence of GAD within the general population is 2.1 per cent, while 4.1 per cent of the population will develop the disorder in their lifetime. Rates are highest among women, middle-aged people, people living alone, and of low income (Grant et al. 2005). GAD usually begins in childhood or adolescence. Once established, it tends to be a chronic disorder: up to 80 per cent of people diagnosed with GAD report having been worried or anxious all their lives (Butler et al. 1991).

Aetiology of generalized anxiety disorder

Genetic factors

The influence of genetic factors on the risk of developing GAD appears to be modest. Hettema et al. (2001b), for example, obtained a lifetime history of GAD through interviews with 3100 twin pairs. Concordance rates between the pairs were relatively low, leading them to estimate the heritability of GAD to be about 15–20 per cent across both sexes. Other studies have found no differences in concordance rates between MZ and DZ twins. Nevertheless, a meta-analysis by Hettema et al. (2001a) indicated a heritability coefficient of 0.32, suggesting that genetic factors influence the risk of whether an individual will develop GAD.

Biological mechanisms

Chronic anxiety appears to be associated with overactivation of a brain system involving the septohippocampal system and the Papez circuit (see Chapter 3). Gray (1983) called this the behavioural inhibition system (BIS), because activation of these brain circuits is thought to interrupt ongoing behaviour, and redirect attention to signs of threat or danger. According to Gray, the BIS receives information about the environment from the sensory cortex. It then checks this against predictions it makes about future changes. When a mismatch occurs, the system is activated and the individual experiences the emotion of anxiety.

In GAD, the criteria for such discrepancies may be 'set' too low, resulting in the individual constantly responding to perceived mismatches and the system being chronically activated. This system appears to be mediated by norepinephrine and serotonin, and is linked to the sympathetic nervous system via the amygdala and hypothalamus (see Chapter 3). Accordingly, it can initiate and maintain high levels of arousal when activated. A final brain and neurotransmitter system involved in anxiety is associated with the GABA receptors which control activity within the hypothalamus and sympathetic nervous system. Low levels of GABA result in high levels of activation of these neuronal pathways, resulting in the fight–flight response at times of high stress (see Chapter 3).

In contrast to panic disorder (see below), measures of sympathetic nervous system reactivity suggest this system is actually less reactive to acute stress in people with GAD than in 'normal' people, perhaps as a consequence of chronic activation. This lack of reactivity appears to be related to norepinephrine levels. People with GAD show a subnormal response to drugs that influence norepinephrine levels, which may indicate that the receptivity of norepinephrine at the postsynaptic site has become less sensitive to the norepinephrine, perhaps as a result of high levels at some previous time (Spiegel and Barlow 2000).

Psychoanalytic explanations

Freud distinguished two routes to general anxiety in adulthood, both of which have their roots in childhood: too rigorous punishment and overprotection. He suggested that both 'neurotic' and 'moral' anxiety begin when the child is repeatedly punished for, or prevented from, expressing their id impulses. This leads them to believe that such impulses are dangerous and have to be controlled. In adulthood, when parental control is no longer available, the individual feels high levels of fear that their id impulses will not be controllable and they may take actions they do not want to. By contrast, if a child is protected from threats and frustrations, it will not develop defence mechanisms adequate to dealing with the demands of adult life. As a consequence, relatively small threats result in feelings of high levels of anxiety.

Evidence relating to these explanations is mixed. Chorpita and Barlow (1998), for example, found overprotectiveness, excessive punishment and critical comments as a child to be associated with high levels of anxiety in adulthood. By contrast, Raskin et al. (1982) found no relationship between excessive discipline or parental protection and the development of GAD. However, even if these factors do contribute to GAD, they do not require a psychoanalytic explanation. A more cognitive explanation may be that they result in the child believing they have little control over their environment or come to consider it as particularly punishing or threatening, both of which may predispose them to GAD.

Humanistic explanations

A further explanation of any link between parental control and the development of GAD is provided by the humanists. Humanists consider GAD to occur when individuals fail to accept themselves for who they are. As a consequence, they experience extreme anxiety and are unable to fulfil their potential as a human being. According to Rogers (1961), this negation of self arises from the childhood experience of excessive discipline. If the individual is subject to criticism and harsh standards as a child, they adopt the standards of those around them, and receive conditional positive regard for doing so (see Chapter 3). They subjugate their own beliefs and desires and try to meet these externally imposed standards by repeatedly denying or distorting their true thoughts and experiences. Despite such efforts, threatening self-judgements can break through and cause intense anxiety. While theoretically elegant, this theory has not been subject to empirical testing, and the importance of these processes is largely unknown.

Socio-cultural factors

Social stress influences the prevalence of GAD. It is more prevalent among people in lower socio-economic groups than the more economically advantaged (Blazer et al.

1991). Ethnic minority groups, who tend to occupy the lower socio-economic groups and who may experience additional pressure because of their ethnicity, also experience relatively high levels of GAD. Levels of GAD are higher in urban than rural countries and rise and fall in parallel with major societal changes, including war and political oppression (Compton et al. 1991). As coping with the demands of everyday living becomes more complex, so too does the proportion of the population experiencing GAD. Prevalence levels in the USA, for example, rose from 2.5 per cent in 1975 to 4 per cent by the early 1990s (Regier et al. 1998). Finally, GAD can be triggered by adverse or traumatic life-events. Blazer et al. (1987) found that men who reported four or more stressful events in the preceding year were eight times more likely to develop GAD than those who reported three or fewer.

Surprisingly few studies have considered longer-term antecedents to GAD – and these have found little evidence of a particular role of childhood trauma. Bulik, Prestcott and Kendler (2001), for example, investigated retrospective reports of child sexual abuse in women who had experienced either major depression, generalized anxiety disorder, bulimia nervosa, panic disorder, or alcohol or drug dependence. Although many of the women reported experiencing childhood sexual abuse, this was not uniquely predictive of any diagnosis. Wilhelm et al. (2004) found an association between separation anxiety and GAD in adulthood, raising the possibility that childhood fears of separation and poor attachment may contribute to longer-term problems of GAD. However, supportive evidence is lacking. Finally, poor marital relationships in adulthood may influence the outcome of GAD, with poor relationships predicting a poor response to therapy (Yonkers et al. 2000).

Cognitive behavioural explanations
The fundamental behavioural model of the acquisition and maintenance of anxiety is that of Mowrer (1947). His two-factor model stated that fear of specific stimuli is acquired through classical conditioning, and maintained by operant conditioning That is, a classically conditioned fear response is maintained by avoidance of the distress associated with a conditioned aversive stimulus. The feelings of relief when this occurs form an operant conditioning process that reinforces avoidance of the feared object. Avoidance also inhibits the extinction process by preventing the individual experiencing the feared situation in the absence of negative consequences (see Chapter 2 and below for more discussion of this issue).

While an effective model of the acquisition and maintenance of specific fears, the model cannot easily explain the diffuse anxiety associated with GAD, and more cognitive models have been developed to account for this phenomenon. According to Beck (1997), people who experience high levels of generalized anxiety initially interpret a relatively small number of situations as dangerous and threatening. Over time, they apply these assumptions to more and more situations and develop an increasingly generalized anxiety. Beck identified a number of cognitive schemata that underpin this anxiety, including 'a situation or a person is unsafe until proven safe', and 'it is always best to assume the worst'. As a consequence of such thoughts, the individual becomes alert to the possibilities of danger and threat throughout their everyday life, and responds with the emotion of anxiety. The process may also work in reverse. Beck noted a form of reasoning he called emotional reasoning, which suggests that if we feel an emotion such as anxiety in certain situations, this leads us to have cognitions that support this anxiety: 'If I am feeing anxious, there must be something to be anxious about here.' Thus, the individual may find themself in a cycle of negative emotions driving negative cognitions, which in turn drive negative emotions, and so on. According to Beck, the origin of these cognitive biases arises in childhood, with their activation in adulthood being triggered by issues that mirror those in which the child had felt threatened, and then expanded to a wider set of stimuli or situations.

An alternative cognitive model of GAD was developed by Wells (1995), who proposed that the core feature of GAD was excess worry. He identified two types of worry experienced by people with GAD:

- *Type 1 worries* are the typical worries that most of us experience, albeit at an amplified level: worries related to work, social, health and other issues.
- *Type 2 worry*, or 'meta-worry', involves the negative appraisal of one's own worries: 'Worrying will drive me mad . . .', 'I worry about my worries taking me over . . .'.

Type 1 worries are relatively common in population samples. Type 2 worries are common in samples of people with GAD. Wells (1995) therefore suggested that individuals with GAD are defined by high levels of Type 2 worries.

The clinical picture is more complex than this, however, as despite these negative beliefs about their worries, people with GAD also hold some positive ones: 'Worrying helps me cope with my problems . . .'. As a result, they may be motivated to continue worrying, despite the discomfort experienced while doing so. In this way, worrying acts both as the cause of their stress and as a means of coping with it. In the light of this, people with GAD frequently try to avoid the need for worry in the first instance, although this can be difficult because of the wide range of stimuli that may trigger them. Other coping strategies commonly used to reduce worries, once initiated, include reassurance seeking, distraction, and attempts at controlling thoughts. The latter may, ironically, actually increase the accessibility of worries. This combination of processes led Dugas, Marchand and Ladouceur (2005) to suggest that the central elements of GAD are an intolerance of uncertainty, positive beliefs about worry, poor problem orientation, and cognitive avoidance.

Claire provides an example of the worries and meta-worries that people with GAD experience:

> It's a family joke, but it's true . . . one day we set off from home to shop in Nottingham – a journey of about an hour and a half . . . and from the minute we got in the car I was worried about where we were going to park, what the traffic would be like when we got there, and so on. I just worried the whole trip and drove my family mad. It sounds funny, but it's true!
>
> I worry about everything and nothing. I worry if the kids are late back at night. They know I worry, so they really try to be back on time. I've given them a mobile phone so they can ring me if there are any problems or if they are going to

be late . . . and they do because they know I'll be in a right state when they get home if they don't. I worry about the food – I won't eat it if it's over the recommended date even though my husband assures me that that's OK and we're not going to get any disease. You name it,

I'm sure I've worried about it. It does get me down . . . I can see me worrying myself into an early grave . . . But I can't stop worrying. My husband says 'Just get on with things, try not to worry.' But I can't. I sit and knit or watch the television in the evening trying not to worry about things, but once something's on my mind it's really difficult to stop – however hard I tell myself to. I worry about my health – the slightest thing, and I'm off to the doctor. I know I'm going to worry about things when we have stopped talking. Sometimes it really feels as if I'm going mad. It does get me down, because every day I cannot relax and just get on with things like most people. Mind you, I think many people worry too little . . . just cruise through life without a care in the world . . . that can't be right either . . .

What sounds even more mad is that I worry about NOT worrying. What if the worrying I do does stop bad things happening? I know it doesn't really, but I could never forgive myself if something happened to the children and I had just been getting on with things and didn't have their safety in mind. I could never forgive myself. What sort of a person would that make me – not caring for them when they were in danger?

Treatment of generalized anxiety disorder

Cognitive behavioural treatment

Behavioural treatments of GAD initially involved exposure to feared situations combined with a procedure known as response prevention – much as in the treatment of phobias (see below and Chapter 2). In this, the individual was exposed to their feared situations, frequently in a graded manner starting with the least feared. On each occasion, they remained in the presence of the feared object until they were no longer anxious: that is, they were prevented from using their escape response. This was thought to extinguish the fear response as the individual learned the lack of association between the stimulus and its expected negative consequences.

Unfortunately, while effective in the treatment of some other anxiety disorders, these methods proved of little value in the treatment of GAD as the situations that threatened people with GAD were so diffuse. Cognitive behavioural interventions did not prove effective in the treatment of GAD until they incorporated three key strategies:

- cognitive restructuring of anxiety-provoking thoughts
- relaxation training
- worry exposure assignments.

Cognitive restructuring involves identifying the cognitions leading to anxiety and challenging any inappropriate assumptions. Strategies may be rehearsed in the therapy session before being used in the situation in which the client feels anxious. Relaxation training involves a structured programme of learning to physically relax and to slow and control breathing at times of anxiety. Worry exposure follows an exposure and response prevention approach. Many people with GAD attempt to mentally block or distract from negative or catastrophic thoughts. As a result, they fail to extinguish the associated anxiety, and continue to be worried by the thoughts in the long term. Worry exposure involves the individual focusing on their frightening or catastrophic thoughts or images for increasing periods of time, eventually up to between 25 and 50 minutes. Anxiety typically rises then falls, as the images are held and the individual habituates to them.

This approach has proven relatively effective. Butler et al. (1991), for example, reported that 42 per cent of participants in a cognitive behavioural programme achieved clinically significant changes in behaviour, cognitions and anxiety, compared with only 5 per cent of those who received only behaviour therapy involving exposure and response prevention methods. Similarly, Borkovec and Costello (1993) found this approach to be more effective than relaxation alone or non-directive counselling. At 12-month follow-up, they found 58 per cent of people who received the combined intervention were relatively symptom-free compared with 33 per cent of those in the relaxation only group, and 22 per cent of those receiving non-directive counselling.

Psychoanalytic therapy

One study has examined the effectiveness of psychoanalytical therapy in the treatment of GAD, comparing it with a cognitive intervention (Durham et al. 1994). Psychoanalytical therapy involved the exploration and understanding of the individual's problems within the context of their current relationship, their developmental context and in terms of the transference and resistance within the therapeutic relationship (see Chapter 2). The cognitive behavioural approach followed that described above. Levels of contact were similar across both interventions. Cognitive behavioural therapy proved significantly more effective than psychotherapy, both immediately following therapy and at six-month follow-up. By this time, 76 per cent of those receiving cognitive therapy were 'better' or 'very considerably' improved; 42 per cent of those in psychoanalytic therapy achieved the same levels of success. Using a more conservative criterion of 'return to normal functioning', the results were less supportive of analytic therapy: 20 per cent of those receiving psychoanalytic therapy achieved this criterion in comparison with 66 per cent of those in the cognitive therapy condition. Drop-out from therapy was much lower in the cognitive therapy group than in the analytic therapy condition: 10 versus 24 per cent respectively.

Pharmacological therapy

Benzodiazepines have frequently been used in the treatment of GAD, achieving an overall success rate of about 35 per cent (Davidson 2001). A further 40 per cent of people show moderate improvement but still have some symptoms of GAD. However, benzodiazepines bring with them a number of drawbacks, particularly when used in the long term, including impaired cognitive performance, lethargy, drug tolerance and dependence, depression and relapse upon withdrawal, and are no longer considered the drug treatment of choice (Davidson 2001). Not only are tricyclics and

SSRIs safer, but also they are more effective than benzodiazepines. Both types of antidepressant appear equally effective, although the lower number of side-effects associated with SSRIs is generally considered to make them the pharmacological treatment of choice. Rocca et al. (1997), for example, compared the effectiveness of the tricyclic imipramine, the SSRI paroxetine, and a benzodiazepine in the treatment of GAD. From the fourth week of treatment, both antidepressants proved more effective than the anxiolytic. However, the levels of side-effects were greater among those prescribed the tricyclic, as were the drop-out rates (31 versus 17 per cent) making paroxetine the most effective treatment.

Pharmacological versus psychological therapy

Studies comparing the efficacy of benzodiazepines (diazepam and lorazepam) and cognitive approaches have shown similar or greater initial gains in the pharmacologically treated groups, but that the cognitive approach is more effective in the medium and long term. Power et al. (1990), for example, evaluated a number of treatments including cognitive therapy alone, diazepam alone and drug placebo alone. Significant treatment gains were found in 85 per cent of those treated with cognitive therapy, 68 per cent of those treated with diazepam and 37 per cent in the placebo condition. Six months after the end of treatment, most of those in the cognitive therapy group had maintained their therapeutic gains, while many of those receiving medication had relapsed, presumably because they had not learned to control the symptoms of anxiety masked by the use of benzodiazepines until their withdrawal. The percentage of people to achieve complete recovery at this point were 70, 40 and 21 per cent respectively.

Simple phobias

A simple (or perhaps more accurately, specific) phobia is an unrealistic fear of a specific stimulus. DSM-IV-TR (APA 2000) states the following criteria must be met for a diagnosis of a phobia to be met:

- Marked and persistent fear that is excessive or unreasonable, cued by the presence or anticipation of a specific object or situation.
- Exposure to the phobic stimulus almost invariably provokes an immediate anxiety response, which may take the form of a panic attack.
- The person recognizes that the fear is excessive or unreasonable.
- The phobic situation(s) is avoided or endured with intense anxiety or distress.
- The avoidance, anxious anticipation, or distress in the feared situation(s) interferes significantly with the person's normal routine or they experience distress about having the phobia.
- In individuals under age 18 years, the duration is at least 6 months.

The DSM further notes that phobic responses can occur in response to a variety of types of stimuli, including animals, natural environmental factors (heights, water), blood-injection-injury, specific situations (aeroplanes, lifts), and 'other' situations including fear of vomiting, contracting an illness, and so on. More complex disorders, such as a phobic fear of social situations and agoraphobia receive separate diagnoses. Agoraphobia is linked to panic disorder, and will be discussed later in the chapter.

Phobias are often considered relatively trivial mental health disorders. However, this is not necessarily the case. While most of us are aware of someone with a mild spider phobia which does not significantly influence their life, the author has clinical experience of working with one woman with a spider phobia who, during the summer months, was unable to leave any of the rooms in her house (or any other building she was in) without first having reassurance that there were no spiders outside the door. When her family were not at home, she was effectively a prisoner in one room in her house – at least during the summer months. Similarly, people with a phobia of cars or other means of travel can have severely constrained lives.

About 7 per cent of men and 16 per cent of women are likely to experience a phobia of some kind at some time in their life (Kessler et al. 1994). The most prevalent fear is that of snakes: about 25 per cent of the population have some degree of fear of them. Fear of dentists is also widely prevalent: between 3 and 5 per cent of the population report such a fear (Kent 1997). The gender-ratio for risk of developing a phobia differs according to the type of phobia. Between 90 and 95 per cent of people with an animal phobia are women – other phobias such as blood-injury phobia are less gender-specific. The age of onset for phobias tends to follow a particular pattern, with phobias relating to animals, blood-injury, dentists and natural environments beginning in childhood, while others such as claustrophobia and agoraphobia typically start in adolescence and early adulthood (Öst 1987).

Some common and not so common phobias are:

Mysophobia	Fear of germs or contamination
Claustrophobia	Fear of enclosed spaces
Trypanophobia	Fear of injections
Monophobia	Fear of being alone
Helminthophobia	Fear of (parasitic) worms
Taphephobia	Fear of being buried alive
Triskaidekaphobia	Fear of the number 13
Ailurophobia	Fear of cats
Aviophobia	Fear of flying
Arachnophobia	Fear of spiders

Phobias such as a fear of snakes or spiders seem universal. Why this should be so is considered later in the chapter. The nature and prevalence of other phobias, however, appear to be influenced by cultural factors. Agoraphobia, for example, is much more common in the USA and Europe than in other areas of the world (Kleinman 1988). A very specific social phobia common in Japan but almost non-existent in the West is known as *taijin kyofusho*, an incapacitating fear of offending or harming others through one's own awkward social behaviour, glancing at their genital areas or imagined physical defect (Kirmayer 1991). The focus of this phobia is on the harm to others, not on embarrassment to the self as in social phobias in the West. As such, *taijin kyofusho* appears to be a pathological exaggeration of the modesty and sensitive regard for others that, at lower levels, is considered proper in Japan.

Aetiology of phobias

Psychoanalytic models

According to Freud (1906), phobias act as a defence against the anxiety experienced when impulses formed by the id are repressed – resulting in a displacement of the repressed feelings onto an object or situation with which it is symbolically associated. These become the phobic stimuli and the individual is able to avoid dealing with their repressed conflicts by avoiding them. These conflicts often involve childhood trauma or conflict. The most famous case of a phobia discussed by Freud is that of Little Hans. Hans was a 5-year-old boy who was afraid of horses, and avoided leaving the house for fear of being bitten by one. He also developed a specific fear of the blinkers and muzzles on horses' faces. Freud considered his fears to relate to his Oedipus complex (see Chapter 2), in which a boy develops an intense sexual love for his mother and fear of his father – from whom he fears castration. Freud's interpretation of Hans's problems was that he was having sexual fantasies about his mother, and he feared his father's retaliation. He therefore displaced the fear of his father onto horses who reminded him of his father. A more prosaic explanation for these fears may have been his witnessing an incident in which a horse fell down in the street in front of him resulting in a conditioned fear response – as suggested by the behavioural model of phobias (see below). A more general psychodynamic approach in which the feared object or behaviour is seen as symbolic of other fears or issues – such as agoraphobia as a response to feeling trapped within a marriage – may be less sexually charged than Freud's interpretation of phobias but of relevance to more modern psychodynamic therapists (Barber and Luborsky 1991).

Behavioural models

Early behavioural models of phobias considered them to be the result of conditioning experiences. As discussed in Chapter 2, they were based on the premise that conditioning experiences may influence emotional as well as behavioural responses to stimuli. According to this model, phobias result from a conditioning experience in which the inappropriately feared object or situation is associated with the experience of fear or anxiety at some time in the past. The conditioned stimulus subsequently evokes a conditioned fear response. The conditioning process can be so powerful when acute fear is experienced, that it may require only one conditioning experience to result in a long-term fear response that is difficult to extinguish. Being in a car crash, for example, may result in a phobic reaction to being in a car, and subsequent avoidance of being in a car or driving. This response has three components:

- a *behavioural* element involving avoidance or escape from the feared object
- high levels of *physiological arousal* evident through a variety of symptoms including physical tension, increased startle response, tremor or sweating and driven by the sympathetic nervous system
- the *emotion* of anxiety and fear.

The most famous early example of the conditioning of a phobic response was Watson and Raynor's (1920) conditioning of 'Little Albert', discussed in Chapter 2.

The **classical conditioning** model of phobias is adequate in its description of the process of acquisition of anxiety and phobias. However, it is less able to explain why they are maintained over long periods, as repeated exposure to the feared object or situation in the absence of any negative consequences should lead to a reduction of anxiety through the process of extinction. Mowrer's (1947) two-factor theory combined both classical and operant processes to provide an explanation of this phenomenon. He noted that once a phobic response is established through classical conditioning processes, the affected individual tends to avoid the feared stimulus. This has two consequences. First, it prevents the classical conditioning process of extinction, as the individual does not experience the conditioned stimulus under conditions of safety. Second, because avoidance itself produces feelings of relief (i.e. it is reinforcing), the avoidance response is strengthened by operant conditioning processes. In this way, anxiety is potentially maintained over long periods.

By the 1970s, conditioning theories of the acquisition of fear and other emotional responses were finding it increasingly difficult to account for emerging experimental and clinical findings (e.g. Davey 1997):

- Many people with a phobia were unable to identify any traumatic conditioning incident. This seems particularly true of some animal phobias and fear of heights and water. Murray and Foote (1979), for example, found that less than 10 per cent of snake phobics had been attacked or bitten by a snake. By contrast, over 90 per cent of people reporting a dental phobia had at least one painful episode at a dentist (Davey 1989).

- Many people who are exposed to a trauma do not go on to develop a phobia. Only about 16 per cent of people who attend hospital following a serious road traffic accident, for example, go on to develop a phobia or fear of travelling by car (Mayou et al. 2001).

- Many common phobias are to relatively benign stimuli (e.g. spiders).

- Many common phobias are to stimuli rarely if ever directly encountered by most individuals (e.g. snakes).

- By contrast, rates of phobias to many frequently encountered and potentially frightening stimuli (e.g. traffic, knives, guns) are relatively low (e.g. Seligman 1971).

- Phobias tend to 'run' in families. This may imply some level of genetic transmission (see below). However, there is evidence that the major mechanism through which this occurs is that of **vicarious learning**, in which young children learn fear from observation of a parent expressing fear in the presence of certain stimuli. Many other people presenting with phobias also report this phenomenon (e.g. Menzies and Clarke 1995).

More recent models of the aetiology of phobias retain the conditioning element of the early models but have added a number of other processes. The most important of which is the inclusion of cognitive variables as mediators of the acquisition of a phobias, the strength of fear elicited by the feared stimulus, and the potential time course of the problem.

A cognitive behavioural model

The cognitive behavioural model of phobias developed by Davey (1997) still suggests that one route through which we can acquire and maintain phobias involves direct conditioning experiences as suggested by the behavioural model. However, he added to the behavioural model by identifying a number of factors that may influence the *acquisition* of phobias:

- The degree of familiarity with the feared stimulus. The more trauma-free associations the individual has had with a particular stimulus, the less likely they are to develop a phobia if that stimulus does become associated with high levels of arousal and fear: a process known as latent inhibition (e.g. De Jong et al. 1995). Conversely, the more any negative emotions are associated with a particular stimulus prior to a traumatic event, the more likely an individual is to develop a phobia.

- An association between a stimulus and a traumatic outcome can be learned as a result of information from other people or from observing someone else experience the contingency between a particular stimulus and the experience of fear. Such fear may be more easily extinguished than fear acquired through direct experience of fear in the presence of a particular stimulus – but if observed over many occasions, may still result in a severe phobia.

- The previous beliefs and expectancies an individual holds about a stimulus may influence their reaction to a traumatic situation and their likelihood of developing a conditioned fear response/phobia.

A number of factors that influence the *maintenance* of phobias, include:

- Subsequent experience with the feared object/situation. As predicted by Mowrer (1947), the more experience with a feared object or situation in which nothing disastrous occurs, the more quickly will the phobia extinguish.

- Socially/verbally transmitted information about the feared stimulus can influence fear. Unfortunately, it seems easier to increase fear by telling people that the stimulus is more fearful than they expected – or appeared at the time – than to reduce fear through reassurance that it is less frightening than expected (Davey et al. 1993).

- Cognitive rehearsal of the fear. Many people with phobias focus on, rehearse and generally overestimate the possible adverse outcomes that may occur should they encounter the feared stimulus. The more they do so, the stronger the fear reaction tends to be when they encounter the stimulus in real life (Davey 1995).

- By contrast, the use of appropriate coping strategies can reduce the impact of a frightening event is known as threat devaluation. Davey (1999) identified a number of cognitive processes through which this can be achieved, including:

- *downward comparison:* 'Other people are worse off than me'
- *denial:* 'This really did not happen to me'
- *cognitive disengagement:* 'This problem isn't important enough to worry myself about'
- *faith in social support:* 'I have family or friends who can help me deal with this'.

Biological/evolutionary model

A second influential theory that has been used to account for the non-random distribution of phobias is known as preparedness theory (Seligman 1971). Seligman proposed that some phobias or fears are more easily acquired as a result of their evolutionary usefulness than others. He contended that at some time in our evolutionary history it was beneficial to have a fear of potentially dangerous stimuli such as snakes, small animals, and so on – stimuli he termed 'phylogenetically relevant cues'. As a result, we may be hardwired, or biologically prepared, to react fearfully to stimuli that were once threatening to prehistoric man. Note that Seligman did not suggest we have an inborn fear of snakes, spiders, and so on. Rather he suggested that we acquire fear more easily to such stimuli following some form of conditioning experience than we do to others. The theory has four key predictions (Merckelbach and de Jong 1999):

- The most prevalent phobias should be to stimuli present and potentially dangerous in a pre-technological age: this does seem to be the case (Merckelbach and de Jong 1999).
- Fear of these stimuli is easily acquired (and more easily than other phobias): again, this may the case. Marks (1977), for example, provided an example of a woman who was looking at a picture of a snake at the time she was involved in a car accident. She become phobic to snakes, but not to cars.
- Because of their biological significance, they are non-cognitive.
- They resist extinction: experimental work by Öhman and colleagues (e.g. Öhman 1986) found that once a conditioned response to phylogenetically relevant stimuli was established in the laboratory, it took longer to extinguish than other conditioned phobias.

Thus, although not all the evidence is strongly supportive of the model (see Merckelbach and de Jong 1999), the general consensus seems to be that some evolutionary/ genetic processes may be involved in the acquisition of phobias.

Genetic factors

The core of the preparedness model is that there is some genetic predisposition to a phobic response to certain stimuli. What evidence there is does suggest some degree of heritability of phobias. Skre et al. (2000) investigated levels of common phobic fear in the twins of people who were treated for some sort of phobia. Their final sample comprised 23 monozygotic and 38 same-sex DZ twin pairs. They scored each twin for severity of various phobias and found the phobia scores were more strongly correlated between MZ twins on measures of agoraphobia, social phobia and animal phobias than among DZ twins. Using statistical modelling to partial out the effects of environment, they calculated a genetic heritability of 0.47 for common phobic fear of small animals and a heritability of 0.30 of agoraphobic fear. However, there was no evidence of heritability for the fear of 'nature phenomena' and situational fear. These findings support both a model of modest genetic contribution to at least some phobias and a predisposition to a fear of small animals in particular. Hettema et al. (2005) also found evidence of two genes that contributed independently to two broad groups of disorders: panic-generalized-agoraphobic anxiety and specific phobias. They also found a significant environmental contribution to the development of each disorder.

Biological mechanisms

The expression of any genetic risk of developing phobias may be expressed through high levels of autonomic reactivity. A central element of the phobic response is a high level of physiological arousal, triggered by hypothalamic activity and mediated by the sympathetic nervous system (see Chapter 3). This response is driven by the neurotransmitter and hormone norepinephrine, and to a lesser extent, epinephrine. When the emotion of anxiety is experienced, these both activate the body and prepare it to deal with physical damage (see Chapter 3). At its most dramatic, this response is known as the fight–flight response. At such times, the heart beats quickly and power fully, blood is shunted to the muscles and away from the gut (hence the experience of 'butterflies'), skeletal muscles tense and blood pressure rises. These and other processes prepare the body for rapid and dramatic action. In the case of panic disorder, this may be apparent through running away from a feared situation, or shaking, breathlessness and dizziness as the person **hyperventilates**. The feeling of palpitations can be so extreme that it can lead to fear of having a heart attack.

People at high risk of developing phobias may have a genetically mediated excessive sympathetic response to environmental events, which makes them more likely than others to become physiologically aroused when faced with potentially frightening situations. The one exception to this occurs in people who have a phobia concerning blood-injury or injection. When they encounter these stimuli they typically experience an initial acceleration in heart rate, followed by a rapid reduction in heart rate and blood pressure. As a consequence they experience nausea, dizziness and may faint in such situations – up to 70 per cent of such individuals report having fainted at some time (Öst and Hellström 1997).

The predominant model of phobias relates to autonomic arousal. Little has been considered in terms of neurotransmitter processing such as GABA and serotonergic mechanisms – perhaps because their short-term, and specific, activity during a phobic response is difficult to measure. However, as these appear to be involved in other anxiety conditions they may also be involved in simple phobias, but strong evidence is lacking.

Treatment of phobias

Behavioural treatments

The premise underlying the behavioural treatments of phobias, involving systematic desensitization and flooding, was outlined in Chapter 2. Both involve exposure to the feared stimulus either directly (flooding) or in a series of hierarchical stages (systematic desensitization). The aim of these approaches is either to condition a feeling of relaxation and lack of fear with the previously feared stimulus – a process known as counter-conditioning – or to extinguish the fear response by repeated presentation of the feared object in the absence of any harm. These approaches may be augmented by teaching people skills such as relaxation or cognitive strategies to counter negative expectations and fear of catastrophic outcomes. The effects of these additions have been mixed – with both treatment gains and losses – suggesting that exposure and direct experience of the lack of harmful consequences are the key to cognitive behavioural treatment of phobias.

Systematic desensitization and flooding have long been considered the primary interventions to treat phobias, and following early work in the 1970s, much of the relevant research has involved attempts at fine-tuning this approach and making it cost-effective. One strand of research has focused on the effects of single-session exposure to the feared stimulus. These sessions may be fairly lengthy – sometimes over three hours. However, they can be effective with a variety of phobic problems including fear of spiders, snakes, heights, blood and injuries, and even flying (Hellstrom et al. 1996). In one study of its effectiveness, Hellstrom et al. reported the outcomes of a group treatment of 42 people with a spider phobia. These people were randomly assigned into two conditions: small groups of 3–4 people and larger groups of 7–8 people. They each received one three-hour session in which the principles of the treatment – based on flooding – were explained to participants. They watched as the therapist was exposed to the spiders and coped with their fear. They were then encouraged to handle four spiders and shown how to cope with this experience. The percentage of people to make clinically significant improvements was greater in the small than in the large group. Immediately after treatment, 82 per cent of the small group had made clinically significant improvements; 70 per cent of the large group had made the equivalent changes. By one-year follow-up, the equivalent percentages were 95 and 75 per cent respectively.

A second strand of research has focused on minimizing contact between client and therapist in programmes of systematic desensitization. The effects of this 'self-directed exposure' have varied from being as effective as therapist-led exposure to significantly worse. Öst, Salkovskis and Hellström (1991), for example, compared the effectiveness of a single three-hour therapist-led session with that of a self-exposure programme involving use of a therapy manual given to participants. The single session group did far better than the client-determined therapy, with success rates of 71 per cent in the therapist-led therapy and 6 per cent in the self-directed exposure group – this despite all but one of the participants in the self-directed exposure group reporting using the manual and exposing themselves to their feared stimulus (in this case, spiders).

A third strand of therapy has involved the use of virtual reality. In one study of this approach, Walshe et al. (2003) first tested how involved people with a fear of travelling by car following an accident became in a computer simulation or virtual reality world of driving. Those who became involved (i.e. reported anxiety) were then treated using a virtual reality exposure programme involving up to 12 one-hour sessions. The group improved significantly on measures of travel distress, avoidance and maladaptive driving strategies. This approach is clearly more expensive and complex than the treatment for spider phobia described above. However, in phobias such as car or aeroplane phobias where exposure to controlled or safe 'live' exposure may be difficult to establish, it may be of some benefit.

Pharmacological treatments
According to Hayward and Wardle (1997), opinion on the benefits of pharmaco-logical treatment of phobias is mixed, with many people feeling that they are of little benefit. Indeed, the general belief appears to be that behavioural methods are the treatment of choice for specific phobias. As a consequence, many major reviews of the pharmacological treatment of anxiety (e.g. Ballanger 1999) do not even address the pharmacological treatment of specific phobias.

Panic disorder

A panic attack is a period of intense fear or discomfort that reaches a peak within ten minutes, and is associated with at least four symptoms that include breathlessness, palpitations, dizziness or trembling, feelings of choking, nausea and tingling sensa-tions in the arms and fingers. As noted earlier, this may be a severe element of a phobic response. It may also be given a separate diagnosis in DSM of panic disorder (APA 2000). To be given this diagnosis, the individual will report recurrent unexpected panic attacks, at least one of which has been followed by one month (or more) of one (or more) of the following:

- persistent concern about having additional attacks
- worry about the implications of the attack or its consequences (e.g. losing control, having a heart attack, 'going crazy')
- a significant change in behaviour related to the attacks.

A common feature of a panic attack is known as hyperventilation, which involves rapid short inhalations and exhalations. As a result, carbon dioxide is rapidly exhaled and not absorbed through the lungs into the bloodstream, and oxygen is over-absorbed, leading to the symptoms described above. As the breathing response is triggered by high levels of carbon dioxide within the circulation, the physiological trigger to breathe does not occur, resulting in feelings of shortness of breath, which encourage further over-breathing. It is at times such as this that the eponymous 'brown bag' can come in useful. Placing one over the mouth and nose ensures that the person re-breathes the carbon dioxide they are exhaling, increases its absorption from the lungs into the blood, stabilizes the breathing pattern and stops the symptoms.

Charles Darwin provided one of the first descriptions of a panic attack, when he described one of his own. He was not unusual: about one-quarter of the general population will experience an occasional and unexpected panic attack at some time. However, the number of people achieving the diagnostic criteria for panic disorder is much less. Wittchen and Essau (1993), for example, estimated that about 2 per cent of the general population will develop repeated panic attacks, diagnosable as panic disorder. The condition is universal and consistent across geographical and cultural boundaries, although triggers to panic may vary across cultures. In the Arctic, a fear of being alone, known as *kayak angst*, and a Chinese anxiety syndrome involving the fear of penile retraction into the body resulting in death known as *koro*, show striking similarities to panic disorder.

Aetiology of panic disorder

Genetic factors
Evidence that risk for panic disorder has a genetic component can be found in studies such as that of Torgersen (1983), who found concordance rates of 31 per cent between MZ twins, and zero concordance between DZ twins. Similarly, Kendler et al. (1993) found concordance rates among female MZ twins of 24 per cent and 11 per cent between DZ twins. These and other data placed within a meta-analysis by Hettema et al. (2001a) indicated that panic disorder has a heritability coefficient of 0.40, suggesting that genetic factors will have some influence on whether an individual develops panic attacks. Specific genes related to panic disorder are being investigated (e.g. Shimizu et al. 2005), but remain somewhat elusive.

Biological mechanisms
As with simple phobias, the central element of the panic response is a high level of physiological arousal, triggered by hypothalamic activity and mediated by the sympathetic nervous system. This response is driven by the neurotransmitter and hormone norepinephrine, and to a lesser extent epinephrine. Two further biochemical systems also seem implicated in the development of panic disorder. The effectiveness of tricyclics and SSRIs in treatment studies has implicated the role of serotonin in the disorder, although the exact nature of the relationship between panic and serotonin levels is far from clear. The success of modern benzodiazepines in treating the condition has also implicated a role of GABA. The amygdala is involved in the generation of fear (see Chapter 3), and its activity is controlled by GABA: low levels of GABA lead to high levels of fear (Goddard et al. 2001). GABA receptors also control activity within the hypothalamus, and hence the sympathetic nervous system.

Social factors
As with GAD, high levels of social stress increase risk for panic disorder. The highest rates of panic disorder are among widowed, divorced or separated individuals who live in cities. Limited education, early parental loss, or physical or sexual abuse also increase risk for the disorder (Ballenger 2000), as do many of the factors that increase risk for GAD (see above). Not surprisingly, childhood anxiety, which may be related to poor attachment with parents, also predicts panic disorder in adulthood (Biederman et al. 2005).

Psychological explanations
Psychoanalytic and humanistic theories do not discriminate between panic disorder and GAD, and the models outlined above hold for both disorders. Both explanations also receive limited empirical support, as people with panic disorder frequently recall

their parents being overly concerned for and protective of them as a child (Parker 1981). Mowrer's (1947) model of fear acquisition and maintenance can provide only a partial explanation of panic disorder, as it assumes high levels of conditioned anxiety to be triggered by the presence of a feared stimulus. It has difficulties in explaining high levels of anxiety in the absence of an obvious stimulus: a defining characteristic of panic disorder.

More recent aetiological models have considered how cognitions can lead to episodes of panic in the absence of any obvious trigger. The most influential of these cognitive models is that of Clark (1986), which identified three triggers to panic attacks:

- fear-related cognitions related to a particular stimulus or situation
- high levels of physiological arousal associated with different emotional states
- other events that may result in a physical disturbances.

According to Clark, each of these factors triggers the central cognitive element of panic disorder, which is the interpretation of bodily sensations in a catastrophic fashion. The sensations that are misinterpreted are mainly those involved in the normal anxiety response. Other triggers include tension and arousal associated with other strong emotions such as anger, raised heart rate as a result of caffeine ingestion, and so on.

Catastrophic misinterpretation involves perceiving these sensations as more dangerous than they really are, in particular believing they are signs of serious physical or mental health problems. These thoughts lead to activation of the fight–flight response involving an increase in levels of physiological arousal, which is again interpreted in a catastrophic fashion ('Yes, my heart really is pounding: I really am heading for a heart attack'). These anxiety-laden cognitions lead in turn to a further increase in arousal and its associated bodily sensations (including high heart rate, sweating, shaking), which lead to further levels of anxiety: a vicious circle which culminates in a panic attack (see Figure 7.1). People who make such catastrophic interpretations of relatively benign symptoms are considered to have high levels of anxiety sensitivity: they literally fear the symptoms and experience of fear more than do people who acknowledge the presence of such sensations but do not respond so catastrophically.

Once an individual has developed a tendency to interpret bodily sensations catastrophically, two further processes contribute to the maintenance of panic disorder. First, because they are frightened of certain sensations, they become hypervigilant and repeatedly scan their body checking for them. This internal focus of attention results in them noticing sensations that most people would not be aware of. Once noticed, these are taken as further evidence of the presence of a serious physical or mental disorder. Second, safety behaviours, usually involving not entering a feared situation, or leaving it at the onset of symptoms, tend to maintain the individual's negative interpretations. Such avoidance, the second stage of Mowrer's model, prevents the individual from learning that the symptoms they have experienced are not as dangerous as they consider, and prevents the extinction process. The case of Sue provides an example of these processes:

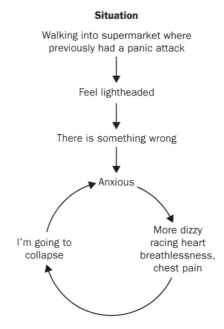

Figure 7.1 The panic cycle

When did it begin? I remember my first panic – who wouldn't? It was in the car park in Tesco's. I remember feeling a bit faint. I thought I was going to pass out. I thought I would look such a fool if I did. Stupid to pass out in a car park. And everyone would look at me . . . Now I know it was a panic attack. But when it happened I didn't have a clue what was going on. I felt bad for no reason . . . I didn't think I was going to die or anything like that, but I was frightened I would collapse and end up in hospital. I think I could have got over it OK, but the next time I went shopping, I began to think about things again. I wondered whether there was anything about Tesco's or shopping that might bring it on again. Perhaps I had pushed myself too hard . . . I was in a bit of a rush when it happened – I don't know. They weren't very sensible thoughts, really. But I suppose they began to wind me up. Anyway, the next time I went shopping . . . yes, I had another attack. That was it really, I just thought, 'I'm not going there again.' So I started to shop in other places, but I began to worry that the same thing would happen, and then I had another panic while I was out, and that just confirmed my worries.

In the end, it got easier to stay at home out of the way than to go out. I quite like it at home. I feel safe, and I watch TV without any hassle. My friends come and see me, so it's not as if I don't have a life. I was never one for going out much. If I go out, then I worry before I set off, and while I am out. I often have a panic, so it's just not worth going out. I can get to the local shop if I go with my husband. And I can go in the car with him – as long as I don't have to get out. But I don't like to go far . . .

The example of Sue fits Clark's (1986) model of the development of panic disorder. She also hinted at a further factor that can contribute to the development of the disorder or its associated problems: a process known as secondary gain. Being restricted to the house was quite pleasant for Sue. She gained sympathy from her husband and quite enjoyed being at home. These secondary rewards contributed to the maintenance of her avoidant behaviour once it had been initiated.

Clark's model has been experimentally tested in a number of ways. These have examined key elements of the theory:

- Cognitions can trigger panic in vulnerable individuals.

- People with panic disorder are more likely to panic if they experience unusual physical symptoms within an experimental setting than are people without the disorder.

- If people with panic disorder experience unusual symptoms and are given appropriate explanations, they will experience less panic than those without such an explanation.

Perhaps the most dramatic evidence of the first of these elements comes from what is now a rather old study reported by Clark et al. (1988). They asked a group of individuals with panic disorder and 'normal' controls to read out loud a series of pairs of words. Some of these pairings included combinations of body sensations and catastrophic feelings or thoughts typically made by individuals while panicking: 'breathless – suffocate', and so on. Each group was asked to rate their anxiety before and after reading the cards and to rate any changes in any panic symptoms. The manipulation proved unexpectedly powerful. Ten out of the twelve people with panic disorder, but no controls, had a panic attack while reading the cards.

Investigation of the second and third elements of the theory has frequently involved use of an experimental paradigm known as respiratory challenge. In it, participants breathe in air with higher than usual levels of carbon dioxide (various studies use between 5 and 50 per cent carbon dioxide mixture). This induces feelings similar to those that occur during hyperventilation: shortness of breath, lightheadedness, tingling in arms and legs, and so on. There is consistent evidence that following this procedure, people with panic disorder are significantly more likely to panic than are people with obsessive-compulsive disorder, generalized anxiety disorder, or depression (Telch et al. 2003).

This panic may be moderated if individuals are given a non-catastrophic explanation for any symptoms they experience. In one study of this effect, Rapee et al. (1986) gave different information about the sensations likely to be experienced as a result of a single inhalation of 50 per cent carbon dioxide and 50 per cent oxygen to people with panic disorder. Half their participants were given a detailed explanation of all the possible sensations they could experience, and told they resulted from inhalation of the gas. The others were given no explanation of what to expect. As expected, participants in the detailed explanation group reported less catastrophic cognitions and less anxiety than those in the naïve condition.

Stop and think . . .

We often talk about risk factors for various disorders, but rarely if ever think about *protective* factors. We know some: men benefit from being married (the advantage is less for women), women benefit from having a wider support system. But what factors may be protective, in both the long and the short term, against the anxiety disorders so far discussed in this chapter?

Treatment of panic disorder

Cognitive behavioural interventions

Some of the most successful treatment programmes for panic disorder have been based on Clark's aetiological model. Clark et al. (1994), for example, developed a two-phase treatment approach. The first phase involved teaching clients the cognitive model of panic. The second phase involved three elements:

- relaxation to reduce physiological arousal at the time of stress
- cognitive procedures to change panicogenic cognitions
- behavioural procedures in order to control panic symptoms.

Relaxation involves learning to physically relax and to slow and control breathing. These techniques can be applied before potential panic attacks, for example when approaching a situation where a panic attack has occurred previously, and during them. Cognitive procedures include self-instruction and cognitive challenge. Self-instruction training involves developing a series of 'calm-down' statements the client can use at times when they are feeling panicky. These pre-rehearsed statements may include reminders that their symptoms will not actually result in their feared outcome and to use coping strategies such as relaxation. Cognitive challenge involves identifying the cognitions contributing to panic, and trying to challenge any inappropriate assumptions. The goal of the behavioural procedures is to teach the individual, through direct experience, that the outcome they fear at times of panic will not actually happen. Increasingly, therapists instigate the symptoms of panic within the therapy session and practise its control through the use of cognitive and relaxation techniques. Symptoms may be generated by a variety of procedures, including reading lists of words linking bodily sensations and catastrophic outcomes, and hyperventilating. These behavioural experiments can be used to show how thoughts and behaviours influence symptoms previously considered the result of unknown factors and allow rehearsal of cognitive and relaxation panic control strategies. Once control over symptoms has been achieved within the therapy sessions, these skills can be used in real-life situations. This may be done in a graduated process, starting with relatively easy circumstances and moving on to more difficult ones.

Over 80 per cent of individuals are typically panic-free at the end of therapy using this approach, in contrast to about 12 per cent of those in no-treatment control groups. Clark et al. (1994), for example, reported outcomes following cognitive behavioural therapy, applied relaxation, the tricyclic imipramine and a **waiting list control** period. Participants in the cognitive therapy group took part in 12 sessions over a period of three months, followed by up to three booster sessions over the following three months. Imipramine was withdrawn after six months. At one-year follow-up, all three treatments proved more effective than no treatment. However, cognitive therapy was the most successful at this time, with 85 per cent of individuals being panic-free, in contrast to 60 per cent of those who received imipramine or who were taught relaxation. Of note is that 40 per cent of those receiving imipramine and 26 per cent of those receiving relaxation sought an alternative therapy in the year following the intervention. Only 5 per cent of the cognitive therapy group did so.

Of interest is that this form of intervention may be effectively provided over the Internet. In one exploration of this process, Schneider et al. (2005) gave people with panic disorder or phobias access to one of two self-help programmes, combined with brief back-up telephone contact with a clinician, via the Internet. One programme involved a cognitive therapy programme similar to that of Clark and colleagues, with specific planned exposure to feared situations. The second group experienced a briefer CBT intervention and did not have a planned exposure programme. By the end of therapy, both groups evidenced significant benefits on a variety of measures, and did not differ in the level of improvement achieved. However, by one-month follow-up, those in the first treatment group, involving a planned exposure programme, showed more consistent gains.

Research box 7

Rollman, B.L., Belnap, B.H., Mazumdar, S. et al. (2005). A randomized trial to improve the quality of treatment for panic and generalized anxiety disorders in primary care, *Archives of General Psychiatry*, 62: 1332–41.

One key issue facing the provision of mental health services is how best to treat people as early in the time course of their problems as possible, and how to provide any treatment in a cost-effective manner. The authors of this report set out to examine these issues, investigating the outcomes following a series of telephone contacts between people with anxiety problems and a 'non-physician health professional'.

Method

The research was conducted at four primary care practices in Pittsburgh. Consecutive patients aged 18–64 years were screened for potential anxiety problems, and exclusion factors of dementia, psychosis, alcohol dependence and communication problems. Those that met these criteria, and who provided informed consent, completed the PRIME-MD Anxiety Module. This assessed the presence or absence of symptoms of panic or generalized anxiety disorder. If these were present and the person was neither receiving treatment from a mental health professional nor had a history of bipolar disorder, then they completed the Hamilton Anxiety Rating Scale (SIGH-A) and the 7-item Panic Disorder Severity Scale (PDSS). Those that achieved the clinical cut-offs for these measures then took part in the treatment trial.

Participants were randomized into either usual care or active intervention. In the intervention arm, a care manager telephoned each participant to conduct a detailed mental health assessment, provide basic psycho-education about panic disorder or generalized anxiety disorder as appropriate. They were offered one of three treatment approaches: a workbook designed to teach self-management skills for managing panic or generalized anxiety disorder with telephone follow-up to review lesson plans; a guideline-based trial of anxiolytic pharmacotherapy, usually an SSRI; or referral to a community mental health specialist. Participants' family doctors were advised of the treatment plan and could add their support if the patient attended their surgery.

Assessments
Telephone assessments were made at baseline, 2, 4, 8 and 12 months following recruitment. At baseline, the researchers assessed socio-demographic status, mental and physical health-related quality of life, the presence of major depression, and the severity of depressive symptoms. They also assessed use of medication and mental health speciality visits, emergency department usage, hospitalization for any cause, and employment status. These measures were repeated at each assessment time.

Results

Some 191 participants were randomized to either the intervention or usual care control condition. Of these, between 65 and 75 per cent completed each subsequent assessment. During the first six months following study enrolment, intervention patients had a median of seven telephone contacts with the care manager. Eighty per cent accepted the anxiety self-management workbook, although the data suggest some were receiving pharmacological treatment at the same time. Levels of drug therapy and attendance with a mental health specialist did not differ by treatment assignment. Key findings were that at 12-month follow-up, intervention patients reported reduced anxiety ($p < 0.05$) and depressive symptoms ($p < 0.05$), and improved mental health-related quality of life ($p < 0.01$) relative to people in the usual care group. They also reported greater improvements in hours worked per week ($p < 0.05$) and fewer work days absent in the past month ($p < 0.05$). Of the 91 patients who were employed at baseline, more intervention patients than usual care patients remained working at 12-month follow-up (94 per cent versus 79 per cent: $p < 0.05$).

Discussion

Compared with the outcomes achieved by usual care for panic disorder and generalized anxiety disorder, the telephone-based collaborative care intervention significantly reduced anxiety and depressive symptoms, improved mental-health-related quality of life, and improved employment patterns over the 12-month course of follow-up. These favourable outcomes were achieved without increasing the number of physician contacts by patients compared with the usual care control condition.

Pharmacological interventions

Both benzodiazepines and SSRIs have proven effective in the treatment of panic disorder, at least in the short term, although attempts to combine the drugs to achieve additional benefits have proven disappointing (e.g. Seedat and Stein 2004). SSRIs, for example, have reduced the frequency of panic attacks to zero in 36–86 per cent of people treated using them (Kasper and Resinger 2001).

At least one study has shown drug therapy to be more effective than cognitive therapy within this time frame. Bakker et al. (1999) reported a study comparing the relative efficacy of an SSRI (paroxetine), a tricyclic (clomipramine) and cognitive therapy in the treatment of panic disorder. Paroxetine proved more effective than cognitive therapy over the 12-week intervention period. While this outcome is notable, it is important to note that the therapeutic gains reported were achieved while on the drug. The problem with drug treatments is often one of relapse once they are stopped. Relapse rates as high as 50 and 60 per cent have been reported following withdrawal of benzodiazepines and of between 20 and 50 per cent following withdrawal of tricyclics and SSRIs (Spiegel et al. 1994). In addition, long-term use of benzodiazepines may result in problematic withdrawal symptoms and exacerbation of anxiety to beyond pre-medication levels (see Chapter 3). Antidepressants also have a number of side-effects that result in drop-out rates of between 25 and 50 per cent (Gould et al. 1995): reported drop-out rates from cognitive therapy vary between 15 and 25 per cent. The hypervigilance associated with panic and anxiety disorders may mean that those treated are highly sensitized to any side-effects, and that *any* medication is likely to result in high levels of reported side-effects.

Combining interventions

Given the potential short-term gains of benzodiazepines and the long-term benefits of cognitive behavioural therapy, a number of clinicians have considered the effectiveness of combining the two approaches. The results of such studies have generally been disappointing, and combined interventions have not achieved the benefits that may be expected. Barlow et al. (2000), for example, found significant gains six months following the end of all therapy in 32 per cent of participants who received cognitive therapy, 20 per cent of those prescribed imipramine and 26 per cent who received a combination of drug and psychological therapy.

The reason for these disappointing results may lie at the heart of the mechanisms of change in cognitive therapy and pharmacotherapy. Central to change in the cognitive model is a reduction in catastrophic beliefs and increased control over symptoms at times when anxiety or panic were previously experienced. These are achieved by learning to cope with the symptoms of panic through challenging catastrophic beliefs and the use of relaxation at times of potential panic. The use of anxiolytics may prevent either of these from occurring, as use of the drug inhibits the arousal and catastrophic cognitions central to panic. Once off the medication, recipients may once more experience the arousal in response to environmental or physical cues, which triggers catastrophic thoughts they have not learned to cope with, and the problem may reappear. Worse, when their symptoms reappear, they may feel more out of control and less confident in their ability to cope with them than previously (Westra and Stewart 1998).

Obsessive-compulsive disorder (OCD)

Obsessive-compulsive disorder is a chronic and disabling condition. It typically involves intrusive thoughts that some form of harm will occur if the individual does not perform certain acts or rituals, the performance of which results in a reduction of the anxiety. Fear of contamination, that one's thoughts can harm others, and eternal damnation are relatively common. Behaviours or thoughts to counter these fears, often referred to as safety behaviours, can include ritual and repeated washing, to the point of developing skin problems, checking up to 20 or more times that an action has actually been done, and engaging in ritual behaviour or thoughts. DSM-IV-TR defines obsessions and compulsions in the following ways:

Obsessions

- Obsessions are recurrent and persistent thoughts, impulses or images that are experienced as intrusive and inappropriate and that cause marked anxiety or distress.
- In addition:
  - these are not simply excessive worries about real-life problems
  - the person attempts to ignore or suppress them with some other thought or action
  - the person recognizes that they are a product of his or her own mind.

Compulsions:

- Compulsions are repetitive behaviours (for example, hand washing, checking) or mental acts (such as praying, repeating words silently) that the person feels driven to perform in response to an obsession or according to rules that must be applied rigidly.
- The behaviours or mental acts are intended to prevent or reduce distress, or to prevent some dreaded event or situation; they are not connected in a realistic way with what they are designed to neutralize or prevent or are clearly excessive.

Rachman (2003) identified some of the more common obsessions as concerning:

- *aggressive actions:* thoughts of harming or harm coming to family or children
- *sexual acts:* fear of inappropriate acts or gestures ('I will molest a young child'), images of sex with inappropriate partners
- *blasphemous acts:* a fear of making sacrilegious gestures in a holy place, pollution of prayers with impure thoughts.

He also identified some of the safety behaviours in which people with obsessive-compulsive disorder often engage to counter particular concerns, some of which are summarized in Table 7.1.

To be assigned a diagnosis of obsessive-compulsive disorder, compulsions must cause marked distress, last at least one hour a day, or significantly interfere with the person's normal routine functioning. An example of the nature of obsessive-compulsive disorder and the problems associated with it is afforded by Stephen, who

Table 7.1 Frequent concerns and safety behaviours reported by people with obsessive-compulsive disorder

Concern	Safety behaviour
Concern with cleanliness (dirt, germs, contamination)	Excessive and ritualized bathing, washing, cleaning
Concern about body secretions (saliva, urine, stool)	Rituals to remove contact with body secretions, avoid touching, etc.
Sexual obsessions (forbidden urges or aggressive sexual actions)	Ritualized and rigid sexual relationships
Obsessive fears (harming self or others)	Repeated checking of doors, stoves, fire alarms, locks and emergency brakes; when driving, retracing route for fear of having run over someone
Concern with exactness (symmetry, order)	Ritualized arranging and rearranging
Obsessions with health (something terrible will happen and lead to death)	Repeating rituals (checking and rechecking vital signs, rigid dietary intake, constantly checking for new information about health, death and dying)

was a factory worker frightened of catching venereal disease from 'contaminated' parts of his work area that he believed someone with this problem had touched – some months ago. To avoid this, he engaged in a number of protective behaviours, including turning on taps using his elbows, waiting by doors so that someone else would open them and using disposable towels to avoid the possibility of contamination. Because the man had been in his work area on one occasion, he washed his hands frequently through the day to make sure no stray contamination affected him. On each occasion he washed his hands until his skin was raw and bleeding. If he touched an area he 'knew' to be contaminated, he became extremely anxious and had to wash his hands repeatedly until he could reassure himself that he was not contaminated and reduce his anxiety. He described his situation as follows:

> I am frightened to touch anything M has been in contact with – well I won't touch it. I know he had venereal disease and he could have AIDS, and you know how it can spread . . . and you cannot, like, avoid it. It's invisible – and I can't take the risk of coming into contact with it. I was really angry when he came into where I work. It's one thing avoiding things when I could kick doors open, but when I knew he had touched my workbench, I was horrified . . . because I didn't want me and my family to get the disease, and I didn't know how to avoid it. I washed and scrubbed it down with disinfectant and rubbed my hands raw – but you can never guarantee that things are entirely clean. So, I start each day by cleaning my work area, hands, and arms for security . . . to protect me and my family from the dirt that this man has spread . . . Once that's done, I can relax . . . I've got eczema on my hands because of the washing and they get really sore but it's worth it. It stops me worrying about things – and that's a lot worse. If I worry I think about getting

AIDS and dying and my family dying. I just can't stop until I've got things sorted.

From the minute I come into work, I get really anxious. I get anxious on the way to work, because I have to face the risk of catching venereal disease . . . it feels such a relief when I have finished washing, even though my hands are sore. I wash before I go home, and I take my clothes off before going into the house when I get back from work. I put them in the washer and wash them straight away – my wife can't touch them . . . I have a shower before I do anything else and wash myself thoroughly. I would never forgive myself if I brought the disease into the house . . . I leave my shoes outside.

I don't care if other people use my work bench – unless they work with M. I don't worry for them – that's for them to look out for. But if they don't get a disease it doesn't reassure me, because I know that these things are hidden . . . just because they don't seem to have the disease doesn't mean they don't have it. If they know M, then I have to redo the washing, because I worry that they may be contaminated.

Aetiology of obsessive-compulsive disorder

Genetic factors

Evidence of a genetic risk for obsessive-compulsive disorder is mixed. Carey and Gottesman (1981), for example, reported an 87 per cent concordance between MZ twins and a 47 per cent concordance for DZ twins, supporting a part genetic explanation for risk of the disorder. By contrast, Andrews et al. (1990) found no evidence of higher concordance in MZ versus DZ twins. Family studies have also produced mixed results. While a number of these have reported higher than population levels of obsessive-compulsive disorder among the relatives of people identified as having the disorder, Black et al. (1992) found that 2.5 per cent of their large sample of relatives of people with obsessive-compulsive disorder had the disorder: a figure similar to the 2.3 per cent prevalence among their control group and population norms.

Biological mechanisms

Biological theorists have identified two interconnected brain systems that are implicated in obsessive-compulsive disorder. The first is a loop connecting the orbito-frontal area, where sexual, violent and other primitive impulses normally arise, to the thalamic region, where the individual engages in more cognitive and perhaps behavioural responses as a result of this activation. A second loop connects the orbito-frontal region to the thalamic region, but via the corpus striatus. The striatal region is thought to control the degree of activity within the systems. It tends to filter out high levels of activity within the orbito-frontal area so that the thalamus does not over-respond to these initial impulses. In obsessive-compulsive disorder, it may fail to correct overactivity in the orbito-frontal–thalamic loop, and as a result the individual over-responds to environmental stimuli, and is unable to prevent their cognitive and behavioural responses to them. The first system appears to be mediated by the excitatory neurotransmitter glutamic acid. The second system appears to be mediated by a number of neurotransmitters including serotonin, dopamine and GABA.

Psychoanalytic explanations

Freud (1922) considered obsessive-compulsive disorder to be the result of the individual's fear of their id impulses and their reactive use of ego defence mechanisms to reduce the subsequent anxiety. This 'battle' between the two opposing forces is not played out in the unconscious. Instead, it involves explicit and dramatic thoughts and actions. The id impulses are typically evident through obsessive thoughts, while the compulsions are the result of ego defences. Two ego defence mechanisms are particularly common in obsessive-compulsive disorder: undoing and reaction formation. *Undoing* involves overt behaviours designed to counter the feared outcome: washing to avoid contamination, and so on. *Reaction formation* involves the adoption of behaviours diametrically opposed to the unacceptable impulses. The compulsively clean individual, for example, may harbour strong 'inappropriate' sexual compulsions that are countered by their cleanliness and orderliness.

Freud considered obsessive-compulsive disorder to originate in difficulties associated with the anal phase of development. He suggested that children in this stage gain gratification through their bowel movements. If their parents prohibit or curb this pleasure through, for example, over-zealous potty training, this may result in a state of anger and aggressive id impulses expressed through soiling or other destructive behaviour. If the parents respond to this with further pressure, and if they embarrass the child in attempts to encourage toilet training, the child may feel shame and guilt as a consequence of their behaviour. So, the pleasure of the id begins to compete with the control of the ego. If this continues, the child may become fixated in this stage and develop a obsessive personality. Traumas experienced in adulthood may result in a regression to this stage if the passage through it is incomplete.

Not all psychodynamic theories are in agreement with Freud, although all agree that the disorder represents competition between aggressive impulses and attempts at controlling them. Kleinian analysts suggest that as a consequence of stress some individuals may lose the ability to see both good and bad in the same object. Rather, they consider it to be either good *or* bad: there is a *splitting* of good and bad with no shades of feelings in between. Obsessive-compulsive disorders arise where the individual protects themself against these 'bad' thoughts that would make them a 'bad' person through the use of obsessional behaviours.

Behavioural explanations

The behavioural model of obsessive-compulsive disorder is based on the two-process model of Mowrer (1947): fear of specific stimuli is acquired through classical conditioning and maintained by operant processes. What differentiates obsessive-compulsive disorder from a phobic or panic disorder is that anxiety arises in conditions from which the individual cannot easily escape. As a result, reductions of distress are achieved by engaging in covert or overt ritual or obsessive behaviours, including repeated checking or hand washing, or repetition of cognitive or behavioural sequences designed to reduce the anxiety associated with the particular stimulus. These form escape or avoidant behaviours, and reduce anxiety in the short term. However, they maintain longer-term anxiety and avoidant behaviour, as the affected individual fails to learn that no harm will occur in their absence. The individual also attempts to prevent initial contact with a feared stimulus.

Cognitive explanations

Two distinct types of cognitive theories have tried to explain the phenomena associated with obsessive-compulsive disorder. Cognitive deficit theories (Reed 1985) suggest that obsessional behaviour results from a general failure in cognitive control, and inadequate memory and decision-making abilities. Critiquing this approach, Salkovskis and Kirk (1997) argued that these theories fail to adequately address a number of features of obsessive-compulsive disorder. In particular they noted:

- People with obsessive-compulsive disorder do not appear to have general memory and decision-making problems: their problems are situation-specific. Although they may, for example, check many times that the door of their house is locked, they may have no problems locking a kitchen cupboard door.

- Similarly, people with obsessive-compulsive disorder may be frightened of a specific type of contamination or contamination from a particular source. They do not have a general problem in deciding what is clean and what is dirty.

- Obsessional individuals show no evidence of memory problems outside areas directly linked to their obsessional problems. They may check because of *concerns* about their memory, not because of any actual inabilities.

Salkovskis's own model (Salkovskis and Kirk 1997) is a development of the behavioural models of obsessive-compulsive disorder. He suggested that obsessions are intrusive cognitions which the individual interprets as indicating they may be responsible for harm to themselves or others unless they take some form of action to prevent this. This belief leads to a state of fear or distress which the individual tries to reduce by (1) trying to suppress these thoughts: and (2) taking actions intended to reduce their responsibility for any negative outcomes: safety behaviours. This may also be accompanied by a high level of expectation that an unwanted event will occur – and is more likely than if other people were responsible: 'I know that if I don't wash my hands I will spread contamination – if you don't wash your hands, this is less likely.'

Wells (2000) suggested that people with obsessive-compulsive disorder often blur the boundaries between thoughts and events or thoughts and actions. They may believe, for example, that having a thought about an event will make that event happen ('If I think of the devil, the devil will appear') or that thinking about an event in the past must mean that it has actually happened ('If I think I have abused her, I probably have'). He termed these inappropriate linkages thought-event fusion.

Unfortunately, attempts at suppression of intrusive thoughts paradoxically make them more frequent and salient (stop reading, sit quietly, and try not to think of a pink elephant in the next minute, and see for yourself). In a rather more empirical test of this phenomenon, Salkovskis and Kirk (1997) reported a series of single-case studies in which people with obsessive-compulsive disorder used a diary to record the frequency of intrusive thoughts during alternate days in which they either attempted to suppress their thoughts or not. They found a clear difference in the number of intrusive thoughts during each phase of the study: during 'suppression' days, levels of intrusive thoughts were about double the rate reported on non-suppression days. This inability to choose not to think about particular thoughts leads to engaging in other forms of safety behaviours, designed to reduce the threat associated with particular thoughts. Salkovskis identified a number of safety behaviours, including:

- *Compulsive behaviour:* includes excessive washing to remove the threat of contamination, ritual or repeated checking, and so on.
- *Neutralization:* often a cognitive equivalent of the compulsive behaviour. This can involve counting to a certain number or thinking a specific thought to counter the original thought. Thoughts related to evil or harm may be countered by repeating phrases such as 'Jesus cares for me' several times, and so on. Neutralization may also involve covert behaviours – such as looking at white (pure) walls to counter sexual thoughts, facing north to the head of Jesus to counter irreligious thoughts, and so on.
- *Avoiding situations* related to the obsessional thoughts.
- *Seeking reassurance:* includes asking others for reassurance that the expected feared outcome will not happen.
- *Diluting or sharing responsibility:* a form of reassurance involving asking others to take some responsibility for action or reassurance that, for example, the individual is not fully responsible for potential harm to others or preventing this harm.

Engaging in each of these strategies may reduce anxiety in the short term, as the individual feels relief once they have occurred. Unfortunately, they maintain long-term anxiety, because the individual never experiences the expected harm not occurring in their absence. They therefore cannot learn or gain confidence that not using them will not result in harm (as discussed earlier in the behavioural model: Mowrer 1947).

Treatment of obsessive-compulsive disorder

Behavioural and cognitive behavioural approaches

Behavioural treatment of obsessive-compulsive disorder typically involves exposure and response prevention. In this, the individual is exposed to their feared stimulus, frequently in a graded manner, and then helped to prevent avoidance through their use of escape rituals, for example, 'contaminating' hands and then not washing them. This is thought to extinguish the fear response as the individual learns the lack of association between the occurrence of harm-related thoughts and any expected negative consequences. Relaxation may also be taught to help people cope with the high levels of physiological arousal associated with the fear response.

Many clinical studies using this approach achieved moderate success, although complete remission was achieved by less than half of those who engaged in such programmes (Salkovskis and Kirk 1997). Behavioural treatments were also difficult to apply to people who ruminated or who had no ritualistic behaviour, and treatment refusals and drop-outs were relatively common. Accordingly, as models of the disorder have evolved, so have the treatment programmes, which now focus increasingly on the cognitive factors that maintain the disorder.

The cognitive approach still involves exposure to a feared stimulus and response prevention. However, these procedures are augmented by a number of cognitive strategies, including:

- challenging inappropriate thoughts
- mind experiments
- behavioural hypothesis testing
- thought stopping.

Mind experiments allow the individual to test the validity of their expectations, particularly focusing on the threat associated with their thoughts. Someone who is frightened that their thoughts may kill someone, for example, may be encouraged to test the reality of this assumption by a mind experiment in which the therapist and then client test out this assumption by thinking the feared thoughts – hopefully with no negative effects!

Thought stopping is the converse of cognitive challenge. In it, the client is taught to distract from their thoughts rather than challenge their content. Learning thought stopping involves a progressive series of steps. Initially, the client relaxes in a comfortable chair and is asked to think about the thoughts they wish to distract from. Once this is established, the therapist interrupts this train of thoughts by, quite literally, startling the client from them (by saying 'Stop!' loudly and making a loud noise). At this juncture, the client is asked to concentrate on a pre-prepared image or thought totally different from their initial ones. This process is repeated, gradually reducing the strength of external stimulus and then making this an internal cue in which thinking the word 'Stop' is associated with a transition from threat-based thoughts to some other image or thought. The goal is to make distraction a classically conditioned response that the individual can trigger when they feel overwhelmed by their anxiety-provoking thoughts.

Comparisons between behavioural and cognitive approaches have failed to consistently identify which is the superior – indeed, one study found a cognitive intervention to be less effective than a behavioural one. McLean et al. (2001) compared the effectiveness of a purely behavioural intervention (exposure and response prevention) and a cognitive intervention involving challenging cognitions thought to underpin the disorder, with a particular focus on inflated responsibility, overestimation of threat, and intolerance of uncertainty. The researchers defined a measure of clinical recovery as evidence of a 'reliable' reduction in symptoms and being 'in the dysfunctional range'. Using these criteria, 16 and 38 per cent of participants in the cognitive and behavioural groups respectively had made significant recoveries by the end of treatment. At three-month follow-up, the figures were 13 and 45 per cent respectively. Unfortunately, the method of cognitive therapy used in the study may not have been optimal. In the behavioural programme, participants were exposed to their feared stimuli on several occasions in the presence of the therapist, and remained with them without responding with safety behaviours until their anxiety had significantly diminished, facilitating the extinction of their anxiety response (and possibly resulting in cognitive change: see Chapter 2). In the cognitive intervention, participants were similarly exposed to the feared stimuli, but only to practise their cognitive skills. They did not remain with the feared stimulus until their fear had diminished. Participants may have left the presence of the feared stimulus while still highly anxious. This procedure may therefore have maintained or even exacerbated their initial levels of anxiety and obsessional behaviour. The relative failure of the cognitive approach may therefore be of no surprise. No difference in effectiveness between cognitive and behavioural therapy was reported by Cottraux et al. (2001) when cognitive therapy involved challenging assumptions underlying the obsessional behaviour, but did not use exposure and response prevention methods. Finally, Van Oppen et al. (1995) found cognitive therapy combined with exposure and response prevention to be superior to behaviour therapy. It seems that 'pure' cognitive interventions without exposure/response prevention are less effective than exposure/response prevention alone. However, a combination of both approaches may be most effective. This outcome is in keeping with Teasdale's (1993) assertion that cognitive changes made in therapy sessions are relatively transient: only when they are behaviourally validated will any changes become fully integrated into the individual's cognitive schema.

Pharmacological interventions

Until the advent of SSRIs, the pharmacological treatment of choice for obsessive-compulsive disorder was clomipramine, a tricyclic. This has been shown to be effective in the treatment of obsessive-compulsive disorder independent of any affect on mood. The Clomipramine Collaborative Study Group (1991), for example, found an average 40 per cent reduction in obsessive-compulsive disorder symptoms following treatment with clomipramine, in comparison with improvements of up to 5 per cent achieved by placebo. Where the effectiveness of clomipramine and SSRIs has been directly assessed, both treatments seem to be equally effective, and to have similar levels of side-effects (Freeman et al. 1994). Most people relapse after prematurely discontinuing treatment, and it may take many months before a maximum response is achieved. Pato et al. (1988), for example, reported that 16 out of 18 people treated with clomipramine relapsed within seven weeks of stopping taking the drug, despite some of them having been on the drug for over a year.

In the strongest comparative study of the efficacy of both drugs and exposure plus response prevention, Foa et al. (2005) compared the effects of clomipramine an intensive four-week long programme of exposure and response prevention followed by a further eight weekly sessions, a combination of both, and a pill placebo. By the end of therapy, all the active treatments proved superior to the placebo intervention. The least effective intervention was the clomipramine. The most effective intervention was exposure plus response prevention – which had no additional benefit of being combined with clomipramine.

Surgical approaches

Treatment of obsessive-compulsive disorder by surgery is generally performed only in people with severe problems that have not responded to other treatment approaches. The most common surgical procedure for people is stereotactic subcaudate cingulotomy (see Chapter 3). This has proven of some value in this limited group of individuals. Jenike et al. (1991), for example, reported that 25–30 per cent of a series of cases improved significantly following surgery. However, 9 per cent developed epilepsy, while 10 per cent committed suicide. Whether this was as a result of changes in mood as a result of surgery, disappointment at the failure of the treatment of last resort, or pre-existing suicidal ideation was not clear. In one of the relatively few studies to use a control group in an evaluation of the surgical treatment of obsessive-compulsive disorder, Tan et al. (1971) investigated the effects of a bimedial leucotomy, a procedure no longer used owing to its high level of adverse effects. At five-year follow-up, 50 per cent of the patients who had surgery were rated as 'much improved' on measures of obsessive symptoms, compared with 23 per cent of those in their medical treatment group. For measures of anxiety, the corresponding figures were 89 and 63 per cent. This remains one of the few studies of the long-term outcomes of psychosurgery in obsessive-compulsive disorder. How psychosurgery achieves its effects is unclear, although the best hypothesis is that it severs connections between the orbito-frontal and thalamic areas, damping down the activity within this circuit and hence the obsessive-compulsive disorder symptoms.

Chapter summary

1 Generalized anxiety disorder (GAD) is an excessive, long-term, diffuse and inappropriate anxiety.

2 Levels of GAD vary according to the social and economic stress across the population and time.

3 It is partly genetically mediated via the septohippocampal system and Papez circuit, in the behavioural inhibition system. Activity of this system is dependent on levels of norepinephrine, serotonin and GABA.

4 Psychoanalytic explanations consider GAD to arise from excess punishment or protection during childhood. These lead to distorted id impulses or inadequate defence mechanisms.

5 Humanists consider GAD to be the result of deviation from the pathway to self-actualization as a result of conditions of worth imposed by others distorting the idealized self, and then the actual self.

6 Cognitive models of GAD emphasize the role of worry and meta-worry in maintaining anxiety.

7 Pharmacological treatment may be equally or more effective than psychological therapies in the short-term. Cognitive therapies are most effective in the long term.

8 Simple phobias are an unrealistic fear of a specific stimulus: DSM identifies four

types: animals, natural environmental factors, blood-injection-injury, and other situations.

9   Psychoanalytic models suggest that phobias result from anxiety impulses when id impulses are repressed.

10 Behavioural models consider the condition to stem from negative conditioning experiences.

11 Cognitive behavioural models consider the condition to arise from a variety of potential causes, including conditioning and vicarious learning, and to be moderated by factors including previous experience of the feared stimulus and the use of naturally occurring coping strategies.

12 Seligman has argued that the potential to develop some phobias may be hardwired into our brains – preparedness theory.

13 Phobias involve high levels of autonomic system arousal. As yet, there is little evidence of more general neurotransmitter dysregulation in the condition.

14 Behavioural or cognitive behavioural treatments appear to be the most effective treatment for the condition.

15 Panic disorder occurs when an individual experiences repeated unexpected panic attacks.

16 It has a modest genetic heritability, and is mediated by high levels of norepinephrine and low levels of GABA.

17 Cognitive models provide an explanation of the triggering of panic in the absence of obvious triggers: people with the condition experience catastrophic cognitions in response to internal, usually physiological, stimuli.

18 Cognitive behavioural interventions appear to be the most effective treatment for the disorder.

19 Obsessive-compulsive behaviour is the result of anxiety triggers the individual is unable to avoid.

20 Psychoanalytic theories and cognitive theories agree that compulsions form part of a repertoire of safety behaviours the individual uses to reduce the threat associated with the anxiety. They disagree about their nature and causes.

21 The symptoms of obsessive-compulsive disorder appear to result from lowered serotonin levels and raised dopamine levels, affecting the functioning of areas of the frontal cortex and basal ganglia.

22 Cognitive behavioural therapy combining exposure/response prevention and cognitive restructuring may prove the most effective treatment for obsessive-compulsive disorder, although evidence is mixed, and many people do not benefit from this or pharmacological therapy.

23 Relapse following the cessation of pharmacological therapy is common.

24 Psychosurgery may be the treatment of last resort for obsessive-compulsive disorder.

For discussion

1 What strategies may increase or decrease levels of worry in GAD?

2 What factors would indicate either psychological or pharmacological approaches being the treatment choice in people with an anxiety condition?

3 How important are cognitive processes in the development of anxiety disorders?

4 Each of the anxiety disorders described appears to be mediated by different biological substrates. With this in mind, consider whether the various conditions should be seen as differing presentations of similar, related disorders, or whether they are, in fact, unrelated disorders.

Further reading

Baer, L. (2002) *The Imp of the Mind: Exploring the Silent Epidemic of Obsessive Bad Thoughts.* New York: Plume Books.

Wells, A. (2000) *Emotional Disorders and Metacognition: Innovative Cognitive Therapy.* Chichester: Wiley.

Western, D. and Morrison, K. (2001) A multi-dimensional meta-analysis of treatments for depression, panic, and generalized anxiety disorder: an empirical examination of the status of empirically supported therapies, *Journal of Consulting and Clinical Psychology*, 69: 875–99.

8
Mood disorders

Mood disorders are those in which depression is a significant symptom. What determines the differing diagnostic categories are the causes of depression and conditions with which it coexists. Major depression is a condition in which the individual experiences a significant degree of impairment as a result of depression. Seasonal affective disorder is a condition also involving periods of depression. It differs from major depression in that, as its name implies, it is a seasonal condition, occurring only in winter. Finally, bipolar disorder is a condition in which the individual fluctuates between periods of profound depression and manic behaviour. The chapter also considers the causes of suicide (not all of which are associated with depression) and treatment of people who have unsuccessfully attempted suicide. By the end of the chapter, you should have an understanding of:

- The nature and aetiology of depression, seasonal affective disorder and bipolar disorder from a number of theoretical perspectives
- The causes of suicidal behaviour
- The types of interventions used to treat each disorder
- The relative effectiveness of each of these interventions.

Major depression

DSM-IV-TR (APA 2000) defines a major depressive episode as the presence of at least five of the following for at least two weeks:

- depressed mood
- markedly diminished interest or pleasure in almost all activities
- significant weight loss or gain, or increase in or loss of appetite
- physical agitation
- fatigue or loss of energy
- feelings of worthlessness or excessive guilt

- reduced ability to think, concentrate or indecisiveness
- significant distress or impairment.

Depressed people are characterized by emotional, motivational, physiological and cognitive problems. They feel low in themselves and gain no pleasure from their usual activities. They are frequently unmotivated to take voluntary action, often spending considerable time in bed or withdrawing quietly from the company of others. They may be markedly slow in their activities or speech. They generally hold negative views about themselves and marked pessimism about the present and future. They may feel out of control and unable to change their situation. Some, but by no means all, will experience suicidal thoughts or actions. Depressed people often report confused or slow thoughts, and difficulties in retaining information or solving problems.

About 5 per cent of the European population will be clinically depressed at any one time (Paykel et al. 2005); 17 per cent will experience significant depression at some time in their life (Angst 1999). About a quarter of depressive episodes last less than one month; a further 50 per cent resolve in less than three months. Between 25 and 30 per cent of people remain depressed one year after onset, while nearly a quarter remain depressed for up to two years. The typical age of onset of a first episode of depression is between the ages of 24 and 29. Women are at least twice as likely as men to report depression, with lifetime prevalence rates among women being 26 per cent compared with 12 per cent for men (Keller et al. 1984).

Aetiology of major depression

Genetic factors

Although there have been some negative findings, there is an increasing consensus that genetic factors influence risk for major depression. McGuffin et al. (1996), for example, found that MZ twins had a 46 per cent chance of being concordant for depression, while DZ twins had a concordance rate of 20 per cent. Similarly, Wender et al. (1986) compared rates of depression in the relatives of adult adoptees who developed depression and a group of adoptees matched on measures of age, socio-economic status and time spent with biological mother, who did not. The relatives of adoptees who had experienced depression were 8 times more likely to have had a period of major depression and 15 times more likely to have attempted suicide than the biological relatives of index cases. Levels of mild depression did not differ across the groups. Genes thought to be associated with depression include those involved in the synthesis of serotonin from tryptophan (Gizatullin et al. 2006) and the transmission of serotonin at the synapse (Surtees et al. 2006).

Biological mechanisms

Both norepinephrine and serotonin have been implicated in the aetiology of depression (see Chapter 3). It was initially thought that low levels of either neurotransmitter impacted on mood. This simple model is now being challenged by recent data. It seems that mood is the result of an interaction between both serotonin and norepinephrine systems. It may even be the result of interactions between these and other brain systems. Rampello et al. (2000), for example, argued that mood is a consequence of an imbalance between several neurotransmitters, including serotonin, norepinephrine, dopamine and acetylcholine. It is possible that serotonin provides overall control of a variety of brain systems, and that low serotonin levels disrupt activity within these systems which results in depression. The major brain area involved in depression is the limbic system. According to the psychobiological model, these processes are triggered by both social and psychological factors, with genetic factors influencing the degree of stress required from each domain before an episode of depression is triggered.

Socio-cultural factors

A number of social stresses have been shown to increase risk for depression. Prevalence rates of depression are relatively high among the poor, ethnic minorities and those with poor social or marital support (Jenkins et al. 1998). Many people experience a combination of factors that make them particularly prone to depression. Brown and Harris (1978), for example, found that working-class women who had three or more young children, lacked a close confidante, had no outside employment, and whose father had died while they were young, were more prone to depression than those with the opposite constellation of circumstances. Economically deprived individuals tend to experience more negative life-events than those who are better-off, and may have fewer social and financial resources with which to deal with them (House et al. 1991). Many people in minority ethnic groups may have to cope with adverse economic circumstances. In addition, they may have to contend with issues of prejudice and integration with the majority population that can cause significant stress (Clarke 2000). More acute life stresses, such as divorce or separation, may also trigger episodes of depression. Conversely, a good social support network can be protective (Paykel 1994).

Explanations of why more women report depression than men vary. Initially dismissed as a reporting bias, there is now mounting evidence that there are real gender differences in the prevalence of depression (Weich et al. 1998). Social explanations of these phenomena suggest that women now experience more responsibilities and lower quality of life than men. Women tend to have lower-status jobs and have more spillover between work and home (Bird and Rieker 1999). That is, when they finish work they are more likely than men to take on the domestic role and continue working. Women may also be more subject to cultural pressures, including those to conform to western ideals of attractiveness, than men, adding further to their stress. A more psychological explanation suggests that women are more likely to attribute failure to personal characteristics than are men, making them more prone to self-blame and low self-esteem. In addition, Holen-Hoeksema (1990) argued that when men experience circumstances that may lead to depression, they are more able to distract from any negative thoughts than women, who are more likely to focus on issues and their possible causes, increasing the salience of potentially depressing cognitions. Among the elderly, illness may also contribute the onset of depression. Tsai et al. (2005), for example, found that having a respiratory disease, poor cognitive function, poor social support network, dissatisfaction with their living situation, perception of poor health status, and perceived income inadequacy were significant predictors of depressive symptoms in their sample of Taiwanese older adults.

Psychodynamic explanations

Freud ([1917] 1957) considered depression to be a similar process to grieving. During grieving, the individual regresses to the oral stage of development as a defence mechanism against overwhelming distress. This involves complete dependence on the loved one, as a consequence of which they merge their identity with them and symbolically regain the lost relationship. In addition, through a process known as introjection, they direct their feelings for the loved one into themselves. These feelings may include anger as a result of unresolved conflicts. This reaction is generally short-lived, but can become pathological if the individual continues to introject their feelings in the long term, leading to self-hatred and depression.

Freud suggested that 'normal' depression results from an imagined or symbolic loss. Events are seen as somehow removing the love or esteem of important individuals, and the depressed person introjects their negative feelings towards the individual who is seen as rejecting them. Those most prone to depression are people who fail to effectively progress though the oral stage of development (see Chapter 2), because they are either gratified too much or too little at the time. Such people remain dependent on others for love and approval through their lives, and are susceptible to events that trigger anxieties or experiences of loss.

Behavioural explanations

Behavioural theories of depression typically focus on operant conditioning processes. Lewinsohn et al. (1979), for example, suggested that depression is the result of a low rate of positive social reinforcement. This leads to low mood and reductions in behaviour intended to gain social rewards. The individual withdraws from social contacts, an action that may actually result in short-term increases in social contact as they gain sympathy or attention as a result of their behaviour. This may establish a further reinforcement schedule, known as *secondary gain*, in which the individual is rewarded for their depressive behaviours. This phase, however, is usually followed by a reduction in attention (further reducing the frequency of rewards available from the environment) and mood.

Learned helplessness

As noted in Chapter 2, there has been a shift from behavioural to cognitive behavioural explanations of the emotional disorders. This may be exemplified by the changes made to Seligman's (1975) **learned helplessness** theory over time. Seligman's initial theory suggested that depression results from learning that one's physical or social environment is beyond one's personal control. The term learned helplessness stemmed from animal experiments in which animals were typically placed in an area from which they could escape, for example by jumping over a low barrier. Following a mild electric shock, the animals quickly learned to jump over the barrier to avoid it. However, when they were prevented from doing so by being placed in a harness, they eventually stopped trying to avoid the shock even when the possibility of escape was open to them. They had learned that they could not avoid the shock, and expressed their helplessness by inertia and not trying to change the situation. A number of studies used differing procedures to induce learned helplessness both in animals and humans. Those that went through these procedures evidenced 'symptoms' similar to clinically depressed individuals, including lack of motivation, passivity and disrupted learning.

Cognitive explanations

Learned helplessness/hopelessness   Seligman's behavioural model of depression was revised in the late 1970s by Abramson et al. (1978), partly in response to the developing paradigm of cognitive psychology. The revised learned helplessness theory suggested that depression – or more accurately, hopelessness – was the result of three key attributional processes in response to both positive and negative events:

- *Internal/external:* is the outcome the result of some aspect of the individual, or some outside cause?
- *Stable/unstable:* will the result happen every time, or is it changeable or random?
- *Global/specific:* does the outcome occur in all situations, or only in specific instances?

According to the revised model, individuals prone to depression tend to view negative events or outcomes as internal, stable, and having global causes ('It's my fault, it will always go wrong . . . and this is just typical of my life'). By contrast, positive outcomes are attributed to external, unstable, specific causes: 'Things went well, but no thanks to me. It was luck and won't happen anywhere else in my life.' That is, they have a negative attributional style. Abela and Seligman (2000) stated that these attributions will result in depression only if they produce a sense of hopelessness, that is, a belief that the individual has no response available to them that will alter their situation coupled with an expectation that desirable outcomes will not occur.

There is significant evidence to show that depression is concurrently associated with the negative attributions identified by Abramson and colleagues. However, associations between attributions and mood do not show that a particular attributional style leads to, or causes, particular mood states. For that, longitudinal evidence is required. A number of studies have now begun to report such data. Abramson et al. (2002) followed a group of several hundred students, after measuring their attributional style. Those students found to have a negative attributional style were seven times more likely to become clinically depressed over a two-year follow-up period than those with a more optimistic style. This risk was further magnified among those students who tended to ruminate about their negative thoughts. Similar findings, but over a much shorter time period, were reported by Kwon and Laurenceau (2002) who followed a cohort of students after completing a measure of attributional style, who then reported daily hassles and depressive symptoms over a period of ten weeks. Their findings revealed that attributional style was not predictive of the number of daily hassles reported. However, a negative attributional style predicted greater depressive symptom reactivity in response to those hassles.

A schema model of depression   Matching these changes in the learned helplessness model, behavioural explanations of depression have largely been superseded by cognitive ones, the best known of which is that of Beck (1997) (but see also discussion of the work of Bower and Ellis in Chapter 2). Beck argued that depression results from inaccurate cognitive responses to events that affect us. In depression, the immediate responses to such events are what Beck termed automatic negative thoughts. These seem immediate and valid, and are often accepted as true. However, they systematically misinterpret events in ways that lead to depression. Errors that typify such thinking include overgeneralization, selective abstraction and dichotomous thinking (see Table 8.1). They influence what Beck referred to as the *cognitive triad*: beliefs about our self, events or other people that affect us and our future.

According to Beck, our conscious thoughts are distorted by underlying depressogenic schemata (schema in the singular). These are unconscious underlying beliefs about ourselves and the world that influence conscious thought and are established during childhood. Negative events in childhood, such as parental rejection, for example, establish negative cognitive schemata about the self and the world. For most of the time, these beliefs are not particularly salient, or else the individual would be chronically depressed. However, when we encounter stressful circumstances in adulthood, and particularly those that echo previous childhood experiences (divorce or separation, for example, reflecting earlier experiences of parental rejection), underlying negative schemata are activated, influence our surface cognitions, and lead to depression (see Figure 8.1).

There is good evidence that some negative schemata are more accessible at times of low mood than at other times. Others may remain salient throughout the life course (see discussion of schemata models of personality disorder in Chapter 11). Whether either type of schemata is irrevocably established in a critical period during childhood has been questioned by Meichenbaum (1985) who suggested that schemata are more malleable than this, and change as a consequence of events over the life course. Determining which explanation is right has proven extremely difficult. Clinical

Table 8.1 Some examples of Beck's depressogenic thinking errors

Absolutistic thinking	Thinking in 'all-or-nothing' terms: 'If I don't succeed in this task, I am an absolute failure. I am either the best teacher, or I am nothing . . .'
Overgeneralization	Drawing a general (negative) conclusion on the basis of a single incident: 'That's it – I always fail at this sort of thing . . . I can't do it!'
Personalization	Interpreting events as personal affronts or obstacles: 'Why do they always pick on ME . . .? That's how it always feels, even when I'm not to blame.'
Arbitrary inference	Drawing a conclusion without sufficient evidence to support it: 'They don't like me . . . I could tell from the moment we met . . .'
Selective abstraction	Focusing on an insignificant detail taken out of context: 'I thought my lecture went well. But that student who left early may have been unhappy with it. Perhaps the others were as well but didn't show it . . .'.

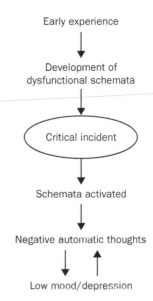

Figure 8.1 Beck's developmental model of cognitive and behavioural precursors to depression

practice has shown that some negative schemata beginning in childhood endure over long periods, and can be difficult to change. However, this does not necessarily reflect a childhood critical period when such schemata are laid down. An alternative explanation may be that childhood beliefs are maintained by continuously distorted interpretations of events, perhaps because nothing happens to make the individual question their initial assumption. Indeed, an individual's own behaviour may result in these beliefs being reinforced. A girl who does not believe that her parents love her, for example, may react against them and cause them to treat her more severely or rigidly than would otherwise have been the case, providing some support for the initial belief. Over time, this belief and its associated behaviours may spill over to other relationships, resulting in relationship problems that continue for many years. Here, the schemata laid down in childhood are maintained in adulthood not because of a critical period, but because the woman's behaviour as an adult continued to elicit responses that reinforced her childhood beliefs.

There is a strong reciprocity between mood and cognition: negative cognitions lower mood, and low mood increases the salience of negative cognitions. Depressive thoughts, for example, can be triggered in non-depressed subjects following mood induction techniques in which people read aloud a series of adjectives describing negative mood states. In a clinical population, Boury et al. (2001) found a significant correlation among the number of negative automatic thoughts, number of core beliefs, and the severity of depression. In addition, the frequency of negative cognitions influenced the duration of depression. However, there has been some debate as to whether cognitive distortions contribute to the *initiation* of clinically significant episodes of depression or simply follow its onset.

The answer now seems that both are true. Lewinsohn (1988) found that negative thinking, self-dissatisfaction and high life stress preceded an episode of depression; poor social relationships and reductions in positive rewards accompanied it. Similarly, Rush et al. (1986) found that women who continued to hold negative cognitions at the end of a period of treatment for depression were more at risk of relapsing than those who were more positive by the end of therapy. More recently, Abela and D'Alessandro (2002) asked applicants to a Canadian university to complete measures of depressed mood and dysfunctional attitudes between one and eight weeks before receiving their admissions decision. This measure was preceded by a priming task (completion of a questionnaire focusing on negative life events) designed to activate latent depressogenic schemata. Two months later, following the decision to accept or reject them from entry into the university, participants completed measures of depressed mood, negative views of the self and negative views of the future. Consistent with Beck's theory, dysfunctional attitudes at baseline predicted increases in depressed mood immediately following a negative admissions outcome.

Depressive realism

One final commentary on cognitive models of depression suggests that depressed individuals may actually be 'right', and the rest of us 'wrong'. The depressive realism hypothesis (Haaga and Beck 1995) suggests that depressed people may actually be more accurate in their world evaluations than those who are not depressed. A number of experimental tests have supported this theory. Depressed individuals, for example, are more accurate than non-depressed people in their evaluations of how favourably or unfavourably others judge them and in their judgements of how much control they have in an experimental situation (Alloy and Abramson 1979). Those going through therapy for depression may actually benefit as a result of their cognitions becoming *less* realistic, albeit more positive.

Treatment of major depression

Biological interventions

Antidepressants   There are now two types of antidepressant in general use in the treatment of depression (see also the related section of Chapter 3 for discussion of SNRIs). A third group of antidepressants, known as **monoamine oxidase inhibitors (MAOIs)** proved reasonably effective, achieving clinically significant changes in about 50 per cent of the people prescribed them. However, the dangers associated with their use (see Chapter 3) have meant they are used less as other drugs have become available. Now, the two key drug therapies are tricyclics and **SSRIs**. The two drugs seem equally clincally effective, with between 60 and 65 per cent of individuals who take them reporting significant improvements in mood (Hirschfeld 1999). Anderson (2000) agreed with this overall conclusion, although noting that tricyclics may even be superior in the context of in-patient treatments. Where SSRIs gain their advantage is in their side-effect profile. Rocca et al. (1997), for example, reported 56 per cent of users complaining of a dry mouth following treatment with tricyclics compared with 8 per cent treated with SSRIs. The percentages to report constipation were 39 and 8 per cent respectively. Anderson (1998) reported that 14 per cent of people on tricyclics discontinued their use due to adverse side-effects in comparison with only 9 per cent of those receiving SSRIs. Whichever type of drug is given, it is important to maintain a therapeutic regimen for some months after therapeutic gains have been achieved, as about 50 per cent of users will relapse within a year if their use is prematurely stopped (e.g. Hollon et al. 2005). The association between SSRIs and suicide is discussed in Chapter 3. Another caution over the use of SSRIs has focused on their potential impact on rates of breast cancer, following a report in the early 1990s that one SSRI, fluoxetine, increased the growth rate of breast tumours in rodents. Reassuringly, there has been no evidence of this in large human population studies (Coogan et al. 2005).

St John's wort   A radical shift from traditional pharmacology is found in treatments using extracts of the plant *Hypericum perforatum*, more popularly known as St John's wort. Its mode of action is little understood, but it does seem to benefit those receiving it. A meta-analysis conducted by Linde and Mulrow (2002), for example, identified 14 trials that compared preparations of hypericum against placebo or antidepressant medication. The percentage of people to clinically improve following treatment with hypericum preparations and placebo were 56 per cent and 25 per cent respectively. Comparisons with antidepressants revealed few differences in benefit, with clinical gains in 50 per cent of those treated with hypericum compared with 52 per cent with standard antidepressant treatment. Of those treated with a combination of hypericum and antidepressant, 68 per cent evidenced clinically significant improvements. St John's wort seemed to be more acceptable to those prescribed it than standard pharmacological medication, with drop-out rates due to side-effects averaging 2 per cent among those prescribed hypericum in contrast to 7 per cent of those receiving standard antidepressants.

St John's wort does have some side-effects, including gastrointestinal discomfort, fatigue, dry mouth, dizziness, skin rash and hypersensitivity to sunlight. Of more concern is that it may also interfere with the effectiveness of indinavir, a protease inhibitor used in the treatment of AIDS; cyclosporin, an immunosuppressive drug used to protect patients from organ rejection after heart transplantation; and warfarin, an anticoagulant. As a result, its use has to be limited in some cases.

Electroconvulsive therapy

Evaluations of the effectiveness of ECT have, in the past, compared its effectiveness with that of pharmacotherapy in a general population of depressed people. More recently, the success of antidepressants in treating depression, and a concern over the acceptability of ECT as a first-line treatment (see Chapter 3), have resulted in it being used increasingly as a second-line treatment for those individuals who do not respond to pharmacological, and perhaps psychological, treatments: so-called treatment-resistant cases. At this point, ECT does appear to have some benefit, and given the lack of response to other treatments, any gains at this point may be considered a success (McCall 2001).

Perhaps more controversial has been the question whether ECT should be continued over an extended period of time to maintain initial improvements in mood, or whether drug therapy is sufficient. Gagné et al. (2000) explored this issue by comparing outcomes over a period averaging about three years in a group of people initially treated with ECT and then maintained on either antidepressants or anti-depressants plus ECT. ECT was initially delivered once-weekly, and then gradually increased to once-monthly. Their findings appeared to support the use of mainten-ance ECT: 7 per cent of those receiving continuation ECT plus antidepressant com-pared with 48 per cent of those receiving only antidepressants relapsed over this time. However, they also noted that participants in the ECT condition received more time with their doctor than those who received medication as a result of their clinic visits. In addition, those who did not attend their ECT clinic were vigorously followed up and encouraged to attend, potentially resulting in more immediate remedial action should the individual have started to become depressed than among those treated only with antidepressants. Both may have contributed to the better outcome in this group.

Psychological interventions

Cognitive therapy The seminal cognitive treatment of depression was developed by Beck (1977). Despite its name, cognitive therapy has its historical roots in the behavioural treatment of depression, and still maintains a strong behavioural element. It typically involves a number of strategies, including:

- *an education phase* in which the individual learns the relationships between cognitions, emotions and behaviour
- *behavioural activation* and *pleasant event scheduling* to increase physiological activity, and engagement in social or other rewarding activities
- *cognitive rehearsal* in which the individual develops and practises cognitive or behavioural strategies to help them cope with behavioural hypothesis testing or other situations that have previously been problematic
- *behavioural hypothesis testing* in which the individual deliberately tests the validity of their negative assumptions, in the hope of disproving them.

Despite the emphasis on cognitive causes of depression, treatment may first involve a behavioural technique, involving increased engagement in physical activities. For those who are profoundly depressed, this may simply involve planning times to get out of bed, go to the shops, and so on. For those who are less depressed, it may involve engaging in social or 'pleasant' activities. Cognitive factors are usually addressed only after the client has experienced some improvement in energy or mood. At this time, they are taught to identify 'faulty thinking' that leads to low mood and to use cognitive challenges to counter it. In addition, the client is typically given homework to do between sessions, usually involving some form of behavioural hypothesis testing or practice in the use of new coping skills. Hypothesis testing involves direct, behavioural challenges of negative cognitions. Someone who is not sure they will be able to cope with a particular situation, for example, may be encouraged to enter the situation and try to cope with it. Such tasks should be selected with care. The therapist, at least, should be confident the client will be able to cope with the situation, as failure will reinforce negative expectations: the very thing the task was set up to disprove. Because there can be a significant risk of relapse in the year following cessation of therapy, one or two 'booster' sessions during this period can be a useful means of preventing relapse.

By the mid-1980s, there was a general consensus that cognitive therapy was at least as effective as antidepressant therapy in the treatment of both moderate and severe depression. This consensus was broken following publication of the results of the most influential treatment trial so far conducted. The National Institute of Mental Health (NIMH) Treatment of Depression Collaborative Research Program (Elkin et al. 1989) was a particularly important trial as it was the first to compare two psychological treatments, cognitive therapy and **interpersonal psychotherapy** (based on humanistic principles), with both pharmacotherapy (imipramine) and a placebo drug intervention. By the end of the 16-week treatment phase, all the interventions appeared to be equally effective. The only between-group differences to reach statistical significance indicated that the pharmacological intervention was significantly more effective than the placebo intervention. Of those in the interpersonal psychotherapy condition, 55 per cent were clinically 'improved', in comparison with 57 per cent in the active drug intervention, 51 per cent in the cognitive therapy group and 29 per cent in the placebo group. For those who were severely depressed, cognitive therapy proved significantly less effective than pharmacotherapy.

This secondary finding caused a significant amount of debate and discussion, not least because its results led both the American Psychiatric Association and the US Agency of Health Care Policy and Research to recommend against the use of cognitive therapy for more severe cases of depression. However, the results have been questioned from a number of perspectives. Psychiatrists were puzzled by findings that the effectiveness of the placebo was much greater than is typically found. Psychologists were surprised that the cognitive intervention proved less effective than in earlier studies. So much so, that Jacobson and Hollon (1996) suggested that it had been implemented by insufficiently skilled therapists at some sites. Subsequent data have also challenged this short-term finding. DeRubeis et al. (1999), for example, compared the short-term outcomes of antidepressant medication and cognitive behaviour therapy in people with severe depression in sub-groups of four major randomized trials. In contrast to the NIMH study, both cognitive therapy and pharmacotherapy fared equally well in the short-term treatment of people with severe depression.

The long-term results of the NIMH study were also more favourable to the psychological interventions (Shea et al. 1992) – and here may lie their advantage over pharmacological therapy. Relapse rates following discontinuation of drug therapy are often much higher than those following cognitive therapy, even when the initial treatment is successful. In one study of this phenomenon, Hollon et al. (2005) compared outcomes in three groups of patients over a period of one-year. The first group comprised people who had been successfully treated with cognitive therapy, which was then discontinued. The second group comprised individuals successfully treated with medication, which was also discontinued. The final group comprised a group of people successfully treated with medication, which was then withdrawn and replaced with a placebo. Relapse rates in the following year were 31 per cent following cessation of cognitive therapy, 47 per cent among those who continued on placebo intervention, and 76 per cent on those who received neither medication nor placebo. Two hypotheses for the relative successes of cognitive therapy have been that it results in enduring changes in dysfunctional attitudes or assumptions. This hypothesis has received little support, and more evidence seems to suggest that rather than these general long-term, global, cognitive changes, the changes are in the types of thoughts that are activated when the individual is experiencing mildly depressed mood. That is, when mood is lowered, the individual no longer accesses the types of depressive thoughts that led to their episode of depression. Instead, people implement the behavioural and cognitive strategies they used to reduce their previous episode of depressed mood.

Thinking about . . .

The discussion about the effectiveness of cognitive behavioural therapy raises a number of issues. One key issue seems to be the effectiveness of cognitive therapy when conducted by people away from centres of excellence. Jacobson and Hollon (1996) contended that the reason cognitive therapy did not fare well in the Shea et al. (1992) study was because the therapists involved were not based in a centre of excellence, and may not have been sufficiently skilled. This argument raised a number of concerns for the author. First, because he too was not working in a centre of excellence, did this mean that any therapy he provided was likely to be ineffective? Second, as most people work away from such centres, does this mean that we should just abandon any hope of intervening and simply prescribe medication – a much simpler process?

At a wider level, most of the psychological treatment research reported is based in research environments, where people with co-morbidity are excluded from any intervention as, frequently, are those who fail to engage effectively in therapy. Many of the people clinicians see in the 'real world' do not present with such 'pure' problems. People with depression may also be anxious, live in depressing environments, have failed to engage in therapy previously offered, and so on. They are frequently more difficult to treat than many of the people who engage in the treatment trials. So, how much do the results of these trials transfer to real people working in real health care environments? What hope do we have of helping these people? Are you an optimist or a pessimist?

Suicide

Suicide is not an affective disorder. Nor is it uniquely associated with depression. Nevertheless, it is an important topic and is more strongly associated with depression than any other mental health disorder considered in this text, which is why it is discussed in this chapter.

Suicide rates vary across countries. For example, Russia has an annual rate as high as 40 per 100,000 people, while Greece has as few as 4 per 100,000 (World Health Organization: www.who.int). They also vary over time and across genders. Among British women, for example, suicide rates have fallen since the early 1970s; among men, a decline in suicide rates between 1960 and 1975 has been followed by a steady increase over the subsequent ten years (McClure 2000). In 2000, the UK rates were 11.7 suicides per 100,000 men and 3.3. per 100,000 women – a substantial difference. Attempted suicide is particularly common in young people: two-thirds of all cases are below the age of 35 years of age (Hawton 1997). Suicide is the third leading cause of death among American young people aged between 15 and 24 years (Anderson and Smith 2003), with particularly high rates among American Indian and Alaskan natives (Centers for Disease Control: www.cdc.gov/ncipc/wisqars).

Only about half of those who commit suicide have an identified mental health problem, the most common being depression, substance-related disorders and schizophrenia. About 15 per cent of those with each disorder kill themselves (Meltzer 1998). Suicide is less strongly associated with severe than with moderate levels of depression, as those who are severely depressed may lack the volition to act on their feelings. Indeed, people who are depressed may kill themselves as their depression begins to lift because they are still hopeless but have some increased impulsivity and motivation.

Bronisch and Wittchen (1994) reported that 56 per cent of their sample of people with a diagnosis of depression reported thinking about death, 37 per cent reported a wish to die and 69 per cent had suicidal ideas. However, these thoughts were not exclusive to depressed individuals: 8 per cent of a comparison group who had never been assigned a psychiatric diagnosis reported having suicidal ideas, and 2 per cent had made a suicide attempt. Suicide in people with schizophrenia is more often a result of demoralization than the result of hallucinations or delusions. Other risk factors include being male, single, living alone, poor sleep, impaired memory and self-neglect (Bronisch 1996).

The psychological characteristics of individuals who attempted suicide often involve feelings of hopelessness (Stewart et al. 2005), worthlessness, guilt, despair, depressive delusional symptoms, inner restlessness and agitation (Wolfersdorf 1995). Individuals at risk are also more likely to have pre-morbid characteristics that include high levels of impulsivity, irritability, hostility and a tendency to aggression, as well as a history of alcohol or drug abuse which may exacerbate these characteristics (Dumais et al. 2005). Gunnell et al. (2005) also found that men with low intelligence were at more risk of suicide than those of higher intelligence, perhaps reflecting a limited ability to solve problems while going through an acute life crisis or suffering from mental health problems.

Research box 8

Liu, X., Tein, J.Y., Zhao, Z. et al. (2005) Suicidality and correlates among rural adolescents of China, *Journal of Adolescent Health*, 37: 443–51.

The rate of suicide in China is about 23 suicides per 100,000 head of population – about double the global average. Among young adults, suicide accounts for 19 per cent of all deaths. In contrast with western countries, the highest rates are among women, especially in rural areas. This study investigates some of the reasons for this high rate in a survey of rural adolescents in the Shandong province of China.

Method

The survey sampled 1400 students aged 12 to 18 years (200 students from school grades 6–11) from five schools considered 'average high schools' for the area. Participants completed questionnaires in their classroom during regular school hours. Three trained interviewers distributed them to the classes, and all students attending school that day in the target class were asked to complete the questionnaires. From a total of 1400 students, invited to participate, 1362 returned completed questionnaires; 822 boys, and 540 girls, with a mean age of 14.6 years. Most of their parents were farmers with only primary or junior school education.

Measures

Measures used were as follows:

* suicidality was measured using two adapted questions from the Self-report Child Behavior Checklist (YSR)
* depressive symptoms were measured by the depression sub-scale of the YSR
* aggression was measured using the aggression sub-scale of the YSR
* life stress was measured using the Adolescent Self-rating Life Events Checklist (ASLEC). This lists 27 negative life-events from home, school, peer relationships and health domains.
* external locus of control
* child characteristics and family variables included age, gender, perceived health status, number of friends, boarding, quality of relationships with parents, and so on.

Results

Participants were divided into three groups according to their score on the suicidality scale: suicide ideation only ($n = 167$), suicide attempts ($n = 96$), non-suicidal ($n = 1052$). Females were more likely to report suicidal ideation than males (22 versus 17.5 per cent), as were older students (10.3 per cent of 12–13-year-olds versus 32.7 per cent among 18-year-olds). Rates of suicide attempts also increased with age: 2.3 per cent of 12–13-year-olds reported having attempted suicide in the last six months, 11.5 per cent of 18-year-olds had done so; 17 per cent of females aged 18 years old reported having tried to kill themselves.

Logistic regression found a number of risk factors to be associated with both suicidal ideation and suicide attempts, including: being older, boarding in school during weekdays, less physical exercise, elevated depression and aggression scores, higher levels of life stress over the past year, an external locus of control, poor family relationships, and poor relationships with parents. Perceived poor health, chronic disease and poor academic performance were also associated with increased risk for suicide attempts. Being female was associated with risk for suicidal ideation.

Discussion

These data seem disturbing and dramatic. However, they compare with US data, which indicates that about 20 per cent of adolescents report having suicidal ideation, and 8 per cent make a suicide attempt during any one year. They also are consistent with increased risk for suicidal ideation and suicide attempts in older adolescents found in western countries. The data linking adverse life stresses with suicidal ideation are also consistent with data from other countries. However, the authors suggest that academic pressures may be particularly high for Chinese adolescents, especially those living in rural areas, as this is seen as the only way for them to leave the relative poverty of rural living. The challenge may be to develop preventive interventions to minimize the risk for these negative outcomes.

Aetiology of suicide

Socio-cultural factors

Suicide rates are lowest among those who are married or co-habiting, and highest among divorcees. Three times as many women attempt suicide as men: conversely, three times as many men actually succeed in their attempt. About 60 per cent of attempted suicides occur after the individual has been drinking alcohol (Royal College of Psychiatrists 1986).

The types of problems that trigger attempted suicide vary according to age. Hawton's (1997) summary of the data suggested that 72 per cent of adults who committed or attempted suicide had difficulties in interpersonal relationships, 26 per cent had employment problems, 26 per cent had difficulties with children, while 19 per cent had financial problems. By contrast, high levels of emotional lability and sexual problems may make some adolescents particularly prone to suicide. Remafedi et al. (1998), for example, found that 28 per cent of homosexual or bisexual males but only 4 per cent of heterosexual male adolescents had ever considered or attempted suicide. For females, the corresponding figures were 21 and 15 per cent. Among older people, suicide may occur as a consequence of increasing disability: 44 per cent of one sample of elderly people apparently committed suicide to prevent being placed in a nursing home (Loebel et al. 1991). Suicide among those who have recently been bereaved is also frequent.

A recent phenomenon has been the development of suicide pacts made through the Internet, often between people who did not previously know each other, and often using information about suicide from suicide websites. However, this is not a new phenomenon. Although suicide pacts account for less than 1 per cent of the total number of suicides in the UK (Brown and Barraclough 1997), one pact occurs, on average, every month (Rajagopal 2004). In contrast to the Internet pacts, the relationship between individuals in most is typically exclusive, isolated from others, and the immediate trigger is frequently a threat to the continuation of the relationship, such as the impending death of one member. Both people involved typically employ the same method.

A more theoretical social model of suicide was developed by Durkheim ([1897] 1951) who identified three types of suicide: anomic, altruistic and egoistic. According to Durkheim, *anomic suicide* occurs when the social structure in which an individual lives fails to provide sufficient support for them, and they lose a sense of belonging – a state known as anomie. High levels of anomie occur at times of both societal and personal change, including economic stress, immigration and social unrest. *Altruistic suicide* occurs when an individual deliberately sacrifices themself for the well-being of others or the community. Finally, *egoistic suicide* occurs among those not governed by the norms of society, who are outsiders or loners in a more permanent state of alienation than those who commit anomic suicide.

Psychoanalytic explanations

According to Freud ([1920] 1990), suicide represents a repressed wish to kill a lost love object, and is an act of revenge. Hendin (1992) identified a number of other psychoanalytic processes that may lead to suicide, including ideas of effecting a rebirth or reunion with a lost object as well as self-punishment and atonement.

Cognitive explanations

Many people who attempt suicide have deficits in memory and problem-solving skills, even in comparison with non-suicidal depressed individuals (Schotte and Clum 1987). These deficits may make it difficult for such individuals to cope with stressful circumstances effectively and more likely that they will use ineffective coping strategies, including suicide.

A more elaborate cognitive model of suicide was developed by Rudd (2000), based on Beck's model of emotional disorders and his own clinical experience. According to Rudd, the components of the underlying cognitive triad are the self as worthless, unloved, incompetent and helpless, others as rejecting, abusing, judgemental, and the future as hopeless. In contrast to depression, where sadness predominates, the suicidal individual may experience a range of emotions including sadness, guilt and anger. Thoughts may focus on revenge, but this will not lead directly to suicidal behaviour. Thoughts and emotions associated with suicide occur at the same time as high levels of physiological arousal and agitation: the profoundly depressed non-aroused individual will not have the motivation to attempt suicide. Risk of suicide varies over time, with periods of acute risk interspersed with lower levels of risk. High levels of risk occur when multiple risk factors converge. These may include situational stress, activation of negative schemata, emotional confusion and deficient coping skills.

Here are the desperate words of a married woman close to suicide, for whom the events of many years previously held a continuing and damaging influence:

> I just can't go on . . . I'm bad . . . dirty . . . The things I did before were bad. I did things with men that I shouldn't, even at the age of 6 . . . that makes me a whore . . . That's why I was raped at 11. I'm dirty, bad . . . a tart . . . and I can't keep trying to change, to be good. Whoever I love I make feel bad because I am me . . . because I am dirty. I can't do anything to change things because I am bad, dirty. I can't think of a way out of things. I've tried for 30 years not to be bad. But I can't stop it. There's so many things I have done that make me bad . . . I just can't make myself good. There's nothing to live for. My husband and my daughters . . . They'll get along without me. They don't need me. I make them unhappy and when I am gone they will be happy again. They don't deserve to have me pulling them down, making them unhappy. That's why the best thing to do is to kill myself . . . end my misery and theirs.

Treatment of attempted suicide

Problem-solving therapy

People who attempt suicide and have a mental health problem may benefit from treatment of this disorder regardless of its influence on their mood or behaviour. They may also benefit more directly from addressing the factors that contributed to their suicide attempt. One way through which this can be achieved is the development of strategies to cope more effectively with the problems they face. The key elements of this approach include:

- both client and therapist gaining a good understanding of the nature of the problems
- identifying in what ways the situation could be improved: the desired goals (such as better relationship with partner)
- identifying strategies by which these goals can be attained (for example, talking more, going out together, and so on).

This approach can be used with individuals as well as couples and even families. Therapy sessions may be frequent in the early stages of therapy, and then more widely spaced as the individual begins to cope better with their problems. Therapy may also involve relatively few sessions: partly because this may be the only form of therapy acceptable to those who attempt suicide, partly to facilitate early client independence (Hawton 1997).

Evaluations of the effectiveness of this approach have generally supported its use. Indeed, in a meta-analysis of psychosocial interventions following suicide attempts, Van der Sande et al. (1997) found problem-focused and cognitive behavioural interventions to be the only interventions to prove effective in this group. In one study of these approaches, Salkovskis et al. (1990) compared a brief, five-session cognitive behavioural and problem-solving approach with routine outpatient care. In the six months following the intervention, 25 per cent of those in the active intervention group engaged in at least one further suicide attempt, in comparison with 50 per cent of those who did not receive the intervention. More recently, Brown et al. (2005) found that people who participated in a ten-session cognitive therapy intervention were 50 per cent less likely to re-attempt suicide than participants in a usual care group over an 18-month follow-up period: 24 per cent of the cognitive therapy group and 42 per cent of the usual care group made at least one subsequent suicide attempt over this period.

Seasonal affective disorder (SAD)

Seasonal affective disorder (SAD) was recognized as a distinct disorder by Rosenthal and colleagues only in the mid-1980s (Rosenthal et al. 1984). DSM-IV-TR (APA 2000) described it as having the following characteristics:

- a regular temporal relationship between the onset of an episode of depression and a particular time of year
- full remissions occur at regular times of the year
- two major depressive episodes that fit these criteria have occurred in the previous two years
- any seasonal depressive episodes outnumber the number of nonseasonal episodes of depression.

The characteristics of SAD appear to be quite different from major depression, and include increased appetite and carbohydrate craving, an associated increase in weight, and increased duration of sleep, as well as other depressive symptoms. Winter episodes typically begin in November and last about five months. The depression is seldom severe enough to require absence from work. Symptoms frequently include sadness, decreased activity, anxiety, work problems and day-time tiredness. Along with these may be increased sleep, poor quality of sleep, increased weight, carbohydrate craving, decreased libido and increased appetite (Magnusson and Partonen 2005). Age of onset is typically between the ages of 20 and 30 years. It may prove a chronically recurring problem: up to 42 per cent of patients have recurring episodes for up to 11 years following initial onset, some of which may occur in winter and some of which may become non-seasonal (Thompson et al. 1995). The prevalence of SAD within the population has been found to vary between less than 1 per cent and more than 10 per cent depending on the country in which rates are measured. In the northern hemisphere, prevalence rates are higher in northern countries, and lower in southern countries (Magnusson and Partonen 2005). Symptoms get worse if people move from south to north and improve if they move in the opposite direction (Rosenthal et al. 1984). The opposite pattern of findings occurs in the southern hemisphere.

Those whose symptoms are so severe that they receive a diagnosis of SAD may be a subset of a larger group of people who experience a variety of negative symptoms over the winter. Less dramatic seasonal changes in activity and weight levels occur within the general population. Terman (1988), for example, reported that 50 per cent of the general population reported lowered energy levels, 47 per cent reported increased weight, while 31 per cent reported decreased social activity in the winter months; 25 per cent reported that these changes were sufficiently marked to signify a personal problem.

Aetiology of seasonal affective disorder

Explanations of SAD are almost uniquely biological.

Genetic factors

Reflecting the relatively recent interest in SAD, there are few studies examining the role of genetic factors in its aetiology. However, Madden et al. (1996) examined concordance for SAD in a large sample of MZ and DZ twins. They also measured a number of environmental variables and were able to determine the relative importance of genetic and environmental variables. They concluded that about 29 per cent of the variance in the risk for developing SAD was attributable to genetic factors. Interestingly, given the apparent different aetiology between non-seasonal depression and SAD (see below), there is some evidence that genetic factors may be related to serotonergic transmission (Sher 2001).

The melatonin hypothesis

Melatonin has been implicated in SAD. It is a hormone whose release is triggered from the pineal gland in the base of the brain by darkness, and is found mainly in the midbrain and hypothalamus. It controls sleep and eating. In mammals that are living wild, the release of melatonin as the nights get longer reduces their activity, slows them down, and prepares them for winter rest or hibernation. According to the melatonin theory of depression, it has the same effect in humans, although most of us are able to override its effects and carry on without problems. However, some individuals appear particularly vulnerable to increased levels of melatonin in the winter months and experience a significant slowdown, evident in the symptoms of SAD (Blehar and Rosenthal 1989). In the reverse of SAD, some individuals seem to be affected by low levels of melatonin in the summer and experience periods of high mood and elation. Evidence of the role of melatonin is somewhat conflicting. While some studies have found an association between levels of melatonin and the onset and severity of SAD, this is not always the case, and its role in the aetiology of SAD is not yet fully understood.

Circadian hypothesis

In a twist to the melatonin hypothesis, Lewy et al. (1998) suggested that rather than the level of melatonin being the determinant of mood, it is the times at which it is secreted that are important in the onset and maintenance of SAD. In their circadian hypothesis, they suggested that 'normal' depression can result from poor sleep resulting from disruption of the circadian wake–sleep cycle. In the case of SAD, they suggested that changes in the times of dawn and dusk in the transition from summer to winter affect the time that melatonin is released, shifting the circadian rhythm of sleep, and taking it out of alignment with other biological rhythms. The goal of therapy is to rephase the wake–sleep cycle to that of the summer. According to Lewy and colleagues, this may be achieved through exposure to light early in the morning, which helps maintain the summer wake–sleep cycle and delays the secretion of melatonin until later in the day. This, combined with earlier times of sleep in the evening, should prove an effective treatment for SAD. Their own work supported this hypothesis, with findings that light therapy in the morning was more effective than if it was provided in the evening: an effect that seems to hold as long as the individual maintains their summertime waking and sleeping times (Lewy et al. 1998).

Serotonin hypothesis

The final hypothesis suggests that at least some of the mechanisms underlying SAD may not be peculiar to this particular syndrome, and may be those that underpin other forms of depression. A number of factors tie serotonin to the aetiology of SAD. Serotonin is involved in the control of appetite and sleep, and is a precursor to melatonin. Serotonin levels vary seasonally, and reducing serotonin levels by removal of a precursor to serotonin known as tryptophan from the diet results in depressive symptoms during the summer in people who typically develop winter SAD (Neumeister et al. 1997). Further evidence of a role for serotonin has come from treatment trials involving SSRIs. Both sertraline and fluoxetine have proven moderately effective in the treatment of SAD. However, these are generally not as effective as light therapy (Partonen and Lonnqvist 1998) or may work best with people who have not responded to light therapy (Pjerk et al. 2004), suggesting that while serotonin levels may be implicated in SAD, they do not provide the entire picture.

Treatment of seasonal affective disorder

The recognized treatment of SAD is known as 'bright light' treatment which serves to lower levels of melatonin. In this, the individual is typically exposed to high levels of artificial light, varying from 2500 lux for a period of 2 hours to 10,000 lux for half an hour each day over a period of between one and three weeks. For comparison, light in the house typically measures 100 lux or less. Outside lux levels may vary between 2000 lux or less on a rainy winter day and 10,000 lux in direct sunshine. Exposure is increasingly done in the morning to help shift individuals into an appropriate melatonin day–night rhythm.

These interventions can be effective. In a meta-analysis of the relevant studies Terman et al. (1989) reported significant improvements in 67 per cent of people with mild SAD, and 40 per cent of those with moderate to severe levels, treated with light therapy: results that were significantly better than those of placebo treatments. Sumaya et al. (2001) reported a trial in which participants were subject to three conditions in a random order: (1) a therapeutic dose of 10,000 lux for 30 minutes daily for one week: (2) a non-therapeutic dose of 300 lux over the same time period (placebo): (3) and a no-treatment period. After light treatment, 50 per cent of those receiving the active treatment no longer met the criteria for depression. Levels of depression did not change following either the placebo or no-treatment phases. More recently, studies have tried to find the optimal wavelength of the light people should be exposed to in order to improve their mood. In one such study, Glickman et al. (2006) compared the effects of short wavelength light (blue light) against dim red LED lights. The blue light proved the more effective of the two. Despite these successes, not all studies have proven light therapy to be effective. Wileman et al. (2001) randomly allocated people with SAD to either an active (four weeks of 10,000 lux exposure) or what they considered to be a placebo (four weeks of 300 lux) condition. Immediately following treatment, 30 per cent of those in the active treatment and 33 per cent of those in the placebo treatment were no longer depressed; 63 per cent of those in the active group and 57 per cent of the placebo group showed 'significant' improvements. The authors took this to indicate either a high level of placebo response among people with SAD, or that the threshold for light therapy was lower than initially thought.

Although light therapy remains the pre-eminent treatment for SAD, some people prefer to take medication – perhaps because they find it difficult to get up in the morning and use the light therapy. SSRI medication results in greater improvements than those achieved by placebo (Pjerk et al. 2005) and achieves significant gains among people who have benefited little from light therapy (Pjerk et al. 2004).

Bipolar disorder

People with bipolar disorders experience both depression and periods of mania. According to DSM-IV-TR, mania involves at least three of the following:

- inflated self-esteem or grandiosity
- decreased need for sleep

- more talkativeness than usual or pressure to keep talking
- flight of ideas or the experience that thoughts are racing
- distractibility
- increased activity or psychomotor agitation
- excessive engagement in high-risk activities.

Manic individuals move rapidly, talk rapidly and loudly, and their conversation is often filled with jokes and attempts at cleverness. Flamboyance is common. Judgement is often poor, and individuals may engage in risky and other behaviours that they regret when less manic. They may also become extremely frustrated by the actions of others, whom they see as preventing them achieving their great plans. Of interest is that while many people appear extremely happy while in a manic episode, this may not always be the case.

DSM-IV-TR described two types of bipolar disorder:

- *Bipolar disorder I:* individuals typically experience alternating episodes of depression and mania, each lasting weeks or months. Some individuals may experience several episodes of either mania or depression, separated by periods of 'normality', in sequence. Some people may swing between depression and mania in one day.
- *Bipolar disorder II:* depressive episodes predominate. The individual may swing between episodes of hypomania (an increase in activity over the normal, but not as excessive as mania) and severe depression. In addition, they will not have experienced an episode of mania.

Between 1 and 2 per cent of the adult population will experience bipolar disorder at any one time, with disorder I being the more prevalent (Bebbington and Ramana 1995). While the overall prevalence among men and women does not differ, women seem to have more depressive and fewer manic episodes than men and to cycle between these episodes more frequently (APA 2000). As with major depression, the prevalence of the condition differs according to social and cultural circumstances. Grant et al. (2005) found an overall prevalence within the US population of 2 per cent. However, the prevalence was higher among Native Americans, young adults, people who were living alone following separation or bereavement, and those in lower socio-economic groups. Prevalence rates were lowest among Asian and Hispanic people. The first episode of bipolar disorder usually occurs between the ages of 20 and 30 years. Over half of those who have an initial episode of major depression and at least 80 per cent of those who have an initial episode of mania will have one or more recurrences (APA 1994). Each episode may last days, weeks or, in some cases, years. The seriousness of the disorder tends to increase over time, although after about ten years there may be a marked diminution in severity.

Aetiology of bipolar disorder

Genetic factors

An early review of the genetics of bipolar disorder by Allen (1976) reported overall concordance rates for MZ twins of 72 per cent, while concordance rates for DZ twins averaged 14 per cent. More recently, these estimates have been reduced to 40 per cent and between 5 and 10 per cent respectively (Craddock and Jones 1999). Attempts to identify the locus of the genes that contribute to risk for the disorder have suggested that it may lie on chromosomes 4, 6, 12, 13, 15, 18 and 22 (Berretini 2000), suggesting a multi-gene contribution to risk. A number of other studies have found small positive associations between genes influencing serotonin metabolism and bipolar disorder (see Levenson 2005).

Biological mechanisms

Given the role of serotonin and norepinephrine in depression (and the genetic evidence referred to above), it would seem logical to assume that they also play a role in mania. However, the biological model that has emerged is not as simple as may have been expected. Data on norepinephrine are consistent with a simple model of mood disorders. High levels of norepinephrine are associated with elevated mood and mania; low levels result in depressed mood. No such relationship has been found for serotonin levels. Indeed, mania has been associated with low levels of serotonin (Mahmood and Silverstone 2001) – just as in depression. This finding is perhaps relevant to psychological studies that suggest manic behaviour may be somehow 'masking' depressed mood. Data such as these have led some researchers to suggest a *permissive theory of bipolar disorder*, in which low serotonin levels somehow permit the activity of norepinephrine to determine mood. Low serotonin combined with low norepinephrine results in depression; combined with high norepinephrine, it results in mania.

A second model of bipolar disorders moves from consideration of neurotransmitters to the electrical conduction of whole neurons. Two processes involved in nerve transmission may be implicated: disturbances in activity of second messengers known as *phosphoinositides*, that instigate the firing of nerves including those involved in moderating mood, and altered sodium and potassium activity in the same neurons (see Chapter 3). In mania, second messenger activity or sodium and potassium transport across the cell membrane may be excessive and result in overactivity of the neuron system; in depression, there may be low activity in the neurons (Lenox et al. 1998).

A third factor that may contribute to bipolar disorder involves actual damage to the neurons. Sassi et al. (2005) found evidence of neuronal abnormalities in the prefrontal cortex of young people with bipolar disorder – similar to those found in adults with the disorder. Because this was found in both groups, they concluded that this damage was unlikely to represent long-term degenerative processes, and was more likely to reflect an underdevelopment of dendritic connections and synaptic connections. By contrast, Nugent et al. (2006) found evidence of neuronal damage in adults in parts of the brain, including the amygdala and hippocampus. These structures within the limbic system contribute to control over emotions and emotional behaviour. They suggested that repeated stress and elevated **glucocorticoid** secretion may have contributed to neuronal damage, and dysfunctional processing of these brain areas. The damage to these and other neurons appears to lead to marked cognitive decrements in individuals with bipolar disorder including deficits in executive functioning and verbal memory (Sobczak et al. 2002).

Psychoanalytic explanations

Psychoanalysts view mania as an extreme defence mechanism to counter unpleasant emotional states or unacceptable impulses. Katan (1953), for example, suggested that as periods of mania frequently follow states of depression, the conflict in mania may be of a similar nature to that in depression. People who pass from depression into mania maintain their preoccupation with a real or fantasized loss. In the manic state, this anxiety is externalized. Aggressive drive is directed outwards, and the individual reacts to external objects in the same manner as introjection directs anger inwards in depression.

Cognitive models

The cognitive model of unipolar depression has been adapted to explain bipolar problems by two research groups. Newman et al. (2002) suggested that schemata can act in a 'bidirectional' manner in people with bipolar disorder. A schema related to being loved, for example, may have two poles – 'I am totally unlovable' versus 'Everybody loves me.' Depending on mood and any relevant life-events, both positive and negative, either one of these poles may be activated. A second cognitive model (Lam et al. 2003) suggested two key beliefs underpin the condition:

- The ability to achieve goals – 'If I try hard enough, I should be able to excel at anything I attempt.'
- A lack of dependence on others – 'I do not need the approval of other people to be happy.'

According to Lam, success in achieving goals leads to euphoria, and a positive feedback loop in which vulnerable individuals continue to try to achieve different goals in an attempt to maintain or enhance the positive emotional state they have achieved through their success. In order to do so, their behaviour becomes increasingly goal-driven and the views of others are disregarded. Failure to achieve their goals results in the onset of low mood and a downward cycle of behaviour. Countering this model were the findings of Scott et al. (2000) who found people with bipolar disorder (while neither depressed nor manic) reported higher levels of interpersonal dependence and stronger needs for social approval than controls. Of course, it is possible that these needs differed at times of depression or mania.

As in psychoanalytic models, the third cognitive model of Winters and Neale (1985) suggested mania is a defence reaction against depression, arguing that a combination of low self-esteem and unrealistic standards of success may drive both depressive and manic episodes. According to Winters and Neale, when individuals with this constellation of cognitive schemata experience an adverse event, they experience either the emotions of depression and cognitions related to low self-esteem, or a defensive reaction against them, in which they adopt the *manic disguise* through which they report normal self-esteem levels. Why such individuals adopt differing strategies at different times is unclear. However, it may be a result of the acceptability of each response to those around the affected individual. Where the expression of negative emotions is unacceptable, they may adopt a manic coping style, which may be rewarded by continued or even increased social contact with important others. Despite this social reinforcement, however, the individual may eventually be unable to continue with these behaviours, and their depression may 'break through'. They then swing into a depressive episode.

In one of the few experimental tests of the manic defence hypothesis, Lyon et al. (1999) compared the attributions made by people with bipolar disorder who were either manic or depressed and 'normal' controls, in response to hypothetical positive and negative events. Both groups of people with bipolar disorder attributed personal responsibility for more negative events and for fewer positive events than those in the control group. By contrast, when asked to endorse a number of positive and negative attributes as descriptors or 'self', both controls and people with mania endorsed largely positive items. Those in the depressed group endorsed mostly negative items. On a subsequent memory test of these words, however, people who were both manic and depressed recalled more negative words than the normal controls. Lyon and colleagues took this pattern of results to indicate that while people with mania explicitly made positive attributions about themselves, underlying this was a set of negative beliefs about self: the manic defence.

These experimental data are in accord with the experience of Christina, who had experienced significant mood swings for many years. When she was in a manic phase, she typically wore livid coloured clothes, used bright and excessive make-up, and was generally hyperactive, gregarious and had difficulty in concentrating on one thing at a time. She looked like she was having fun. Talking to her about her experiences gave a different impression:

> I know it looks like I'm having fun, being happy and all that. But it's not how I feel. I feel driven by things, it's like there's something in me driving me, making me do things wild. Like the make-up, it's all over my face, and I don't like it but I do it. I feel really down sometimes while I'm acting all manic. It's not like I choose to though, it's like it's happening despite how I feel – it's not happy. I really don't like it. And I don't like people around thinking I'm happy too . . . it's really weird.

Treatment of bipolar disorder

Lithium therapy

Standard antidepressants are typically not used in the treatment of bipolar disorder, as they may provoke rapid mood swings rather than stabilize mood – although when combined with atypical antipsychotic medication (see Chapter 3), this risk may be reduced (Thase 2005).

Instead, lithium bicarbonate tablets are typically used to moderate mood swings. Lithium typically achieves this within 5 to 14 days in about 60 per cent of cases, and has to be taken continually to minimize risk of the onset of depression or mania. Suppes et al. (1991) reported relapse rates 28 times higher among individuals who stopped taking lithium when not experiencing symptoms than those who continued its use. How it achieves these therapeutic gains is unclear. It may act on all three processes that appear to influence mood: increasing serotonin activity, regulating the activity of second messengers, and/or correcting sodium and potassium activity within the neuron.

Despite its therapeutic potential, the effectiveness of lithium in clinical practice has been less than was hoped for, possibly because of poor adherence to recommended treatment regimes. Between 18 and 53 per cent of those receiving treatment do not adhere to the recommended regime (Guscott and Taylor 1994). Reasons for this include side-effects of weight gain, problems with coordination and tremor, excessive thirst, and memory disturbances. Psychological factors include a dislike of medication controlling mood, feeling well and seeing no need for medication, and missing the highs of hypomania. In addition, many users complain of a 'damping down' of all emotions all the time, which they find problematic. A further caution is that the window between ineffective and toxic doses of lithium is narrow. Too high a dose will result in lithium intoxication, the consequences of which include nausea, vomiting, tremors, kidney dysfunction and, potentially, death. Accordingly, levels of lithium have to be regularly monitored by blood testing, a further disincentive to adherence.

A final aspect of research into the effectiveness of lithium has revealed how a surprisingly large number of psychosocial factors moderate its effectiveness. Kleindienst, Engel and Greil (2005) found that high social status, good social support, and adherence to taking the medication each contributed independently and positively to the effectiveness of lithium therapy. By contrast, living in a high expressed emotion environment (see Chapter 6), neurotic personality traits, and stressors including unemployment and other adverse life-events, contributed to a poor response to lithium.

Cognitive behavioural approaches

The biological model of bipolar disorder has been dominant for some years, and it is only recently that attempts to change the course of the disorder using cognitive behavioural methods have been attempted. One approach has evaluated the effectiveness of psycho-educational programmes. In one such study, Colom et al. (2003) randomly allocated people with bipolar disorder either to group psycho-education or unstructured group meetings. The educational programme proved more effective than the unstructured programme over a two-year follow-up period: 35 per cent of those in the educational group versus 25 per cent in treatment group respectively were hospitalized over this period.

A second approach has been to evaluate cognitive behavioural therapy to avoid relapse. Scott et al. (2001), for example, randomly allocated people with bipolar disorder into treatment with lithium either alone or in combination with cognitive therapy. The cognitive therapy involved three elements:

- an educational phase to prepare people for the cognitive approach
- a focus on cognitive behavioural methods of symptom management including establishing regular activity patterns and time management, as well as challenging dysfunctional thoughts
- anti-relapse techniques involving developing strategies for managing medication, individual coping strategies to deal with stress, or seeking help at times of the onset of signs of relapse.

Each intervention lasted six months. By this time, those in the combined intervention showed more improvements on measures of general functioning and depression than those in the drug treatment group. The data on relapse were equally impressive. Those who received the combined intervention were 60 per cent less likely to relapse than those in the drug-only condition. Lam et al. (2003) also found that cognitive therapy plus drug therapy proved more effective than drug therapy alone. Over a one-year follow-up, those who received the additional intervention experienced fewer relapses and hospitalizations, with relapse rates of 44 per cent in the cognitive therapy group and 75 per cent in the drug-only group.

An third approach has been to work with families – justified by reports such as Kleindienst, Engel and Greil (2005), who showed the role of family dynamics in predicting relapse. Miklowitz et al. (2003) reported an intervention designed to improve communication, problem-solving and coping strategies training within the family, comparing this with standard care and a brief two session family intervention. At two-year follow-up, those receiving the family therapy experienced fewer relapses than the standard care group (71 per cent versus 47 per cent). The benefits were greater in individuals living in a high expressed emotion environment. Rea et al. (2003) compared family and individual interventions and found that the family intervention proved superior in the long term. Relapse rates were 60 per cent among those who received the individual intervention and 28 per cent of those who received the family intervention.

Chapter summary

1 Major depression involves significant psychological impairment lasting at least two weeks. About one-third of the people who become depressed will remain depressed one year later.

2 Psychodynamic explanations consider depression to result from the symbolic loss of love or esteem. Negative feelings towards the responsible person are internalized and result in depression.

3 Socio-cultural explanations focus on differentials in stress and coping in different social groups.

4 Genetic factors contribute to the risk of depression.

5 Low levels of serotonin may result in depression as a result of a loss of control over a number of brain systems, including those mediated by norepinephrine and dopamine.

6 Behavioural theories suggest that depression is the result of a lack of social reinforcement.

7 Cognitive theories consider negative automatic thoughts and dysfunctional schemata to be causal.

8 Both pharmacological and cognitive interventions appear to be equally effective in the short-term treatment of depression. Cognitive interventions may be more effective in the long term.

9 St John's wort may prove an effective natural therapy.

10 ECT may be effective for some 'treatment-resistant cases', but continued use of ECT to maintain any gains remains controversial.

11 While individuals with serious mental health problems may be at increased risk of suicide, so are individuals without such disorders.

12 In adults, the primary trigger to a suicide attempt is interpersonal problems.

13 Freud considered suicide to be an attempt at revenge on a hated individual.

14 Cognitive explanations suggest that poor problem-solving skills and feelings of being worthless and rejected combined with situational stress, emotional confusion and high levels of physiological arousal place an individual at risk of committing suicide.

15 Interventions that increase problem-solving skills appear to reduce the risk of suicide.

16 SAD appears to result from disordered melatonin and circadian rhythms.

17 Bright light therapy appears to be the most effective treatment for SAD.

18 Bipolar disorder is the result of neural mechanisms involved in the transmission of information along the neuronal axis.

19 The primary treatment of the disorder involves lithium medication, although cognitive behavioural and family interventions also appear to be of significant benefit.

For discussion

1 Jacobson and Hollon (1996) argued that the short-term findings of the NIMH depression study were flawed as a result of the inexpert implementation of cognitive therapy. Given the spread, and possible dilution, of therapist skills away from centres of excellence, is this an argument for the use of pharmacological therapies in preference to the psychotherapies?

2 Consider why the relapse rate among people with depression treated with antidepressants is significantly higher than that among people treated with cognitive therapy.

3 Is SADness in winter a common phenomenon? If so, why?

Further reading

Clark, D., Beck, A. and Alford, B. (1999) *Scientific Foundations of Cognitive Theory and Therapy of Depression*. New York: Wiley.

DeRubeis, R.J., Gelfand, L.A., Tang, T.Z. et al. (1999) Medications versus cognitive behavior therapy for severely depressed outpatients: mega-analysis of four randomized comparisons, *American Journal of Psychiatry*, 156: 1007–13.

Lyon, H.M., Startup, M. and Bentall, R.P. (1999) Social cognition and the manic defense: attributions, selective attention, and self-schema in bipolar affective disorder, *Journal of Abnormal Psychology*, 108: 273–82.

Power, M.J. (2005) Psychological approaches to bipolar disorders: a theoretical critique, *Clinical Psychology Review*, 25: 1101–22.

Sohn, C.H. and Lam, R.W. (2005) Update on the biology of seasonal affective disorder, *CNS Spectrum*, 10: 635–46.

9

Trauma-related conditions

This chapter focuses on three types of problems that may occur as a result of significant trauma experienced by the individual either as an adult or child. The first, post-traumatic stress disorder (PTSD), is widely acknowledged as a natural response to being involved in or seeing highly traumatic events. The other two conditions explored in the chapter are rather more controversial. Indeed, their very existence has been called into question. The chapter explores evidence relating to two apparent responses to childhood trauma: hidden and recovered memories, and dissociative identity disorder (DID), previously known as multiple personality. By the end of the chapter, you should have an understanding of:

- The nature and treatment of post-traumatic stress disorder
- The controversy surrounding 'recovered memories'
- The controversy surrounding dissociative identity disorder
- Treatment approaches used in DID.

Post-traumatic stress disorder (PTSD)

The DSM-IV-TR criteria for a diagnosis of PTSD are that the individual has experienced or witnessed an event that involved actual or threatened death or serious injury, or a threat to the physical integrity of self or others, and that their immediate response involved intense fear, helplessness or horror. In the longer term, the individual must have experienced three clusters of symptoms lasting one month or more:

- *Intrusive memories:* the trauma is re-experienced through intrusive thoughts, flashbacks or nightmares. Such review may be deliberate as the individual ruminates about the traumatic event. Images may also spring unbidden to mind, in the form of flashbacks. These images often feel as real as the event, but may be fragmentary or partial. Emotions and sensations associated with the trauma may be relived with similar intensity to those felt at the time. Images are often described as if being in a film of the incident. Initially, the person may feel they are actually 'in' the film: as they recover, they feel they are watching the film as an outside observer. That is, they begin to, almost literally, feel more detached from the trauma.

- *Avoidance:* the adoption of activities or behaviours to avoid reminders of the traumatic event. This may involve mental defence mechanisms including being unable to recall aspects of the trauma, emotional numbness, or detachment from others, as well as physically avoiding reminders of the trauma.

- *Arousal:* persistent feelings of over-arousal that may be evidenced by irritability, being easily startled or hypervigilant, suffering insomnia, or having difficulty concentrating.

The triggers of PTSD vary widely, and include war experiences, childhood sexual and physical abuse, adult rape, and natural and technological disasters. Perhaps the most frequent cause of PTSD is road traffic accidents: about 20 per cent of those involved develop some degree of PTSD (Ehlers et al. 1998). About 1 per cent of men and 2 per cent of women in the general population will have PTSD at any one time (e.g. Perkonigg et al. 2000). Prevalence rates among groups that regularly encounter traumatic events are much higher. Bennett et al. (2005), for example, found a prevalence rate of 22 per cent among emergency ambulance personnel, while rates among combat veterans from Vietnam are as high as 30 per cent for men and 27 per cent for women (Kulka et al. 1990). PTSD often begins within a few weeks of the precipitating event, but can recur after symptoms have faded as a result of further trauma or life-events as diverse as trauma anniversaries, interpersonal losses, and changes in health status. Of the three key symptoms, re-experiencing appears to decrease most rapidly: people in whom hyperarousal is the dominant symptom appear to have the worst prognosis (Schell et al. 2004). According to Freedy, Resnick and Kilpatrick (1992), an adult's risk for distress will increase as the number of the following 'risk' factors increases:

- female gender
- aged 40 to 60 years old
- little previous experience or training relevant to coping with disaster
- low socio-economic status
- for women, the presence of a spouse at the time of the trauma, especially if he is significantly distressed
- psychiatric history
- severe exposure to the disaster, especially injury, life threat and extreme loss
- living in a highly disrupted or traumatized community
- secondary stress

Here is the story of Ron, which shows how both the situation and the reaction of the people around him can contribute to the development of PTSD.

At the time this happened, I was working in a small hut on an industrial estate.

They had been building some more units and had a crane on a lorry to lift things around the site. This was right next to our office. You couldn't see it, because there were no windows on that side of the hut, but you knew it was there . . . I don't know why, but on the day of the accident they were using the crane without stabilizing it by putting the legs onto the ground. The upshot of this was that the crane toppled over and fell onto the building I was in. The first we were aware of things was a lot of shouting and mechanical noises we now know were it toppling. Then there was a great crash and the arm of the crane smashed through the building. I was in there with my mate. Amazingly, neither of us were actually hit by the thing. But we were both trapped by debris from the building. I think I was knocked out for a while because I cannot remember in detail what happened, but it could only have been for a minute or two. I wasn't hurt too badly, but I was trapped. The worst part of it all, was just having to wait to get out. I was frightened that the gas pipes were fractured and the image of dying in a fire went through my mind. I hate being unable to move and all sorts of things went through my head about what would happen to me while I couldn't move. I felt really frightened until I could hear people coming to dig us out, and they lifted the heavy stuff off me and I could move . . .

Once I was out, I went to the sick bay and was sent home. I told them I was OK, just 'cos I wanted to get home and get out of it. I was driven home and spent the rest of the day like a zombie. I just phased out. I didn't want to talk about it. Kept myself to myself. I slept OK. I hate missing work so I went in the next day. My mates took me to look at the hut, and they were saying how lucky we were to get out alive. Everyone I met said the same thing! I know they were being friendly, but that made things worse, and I began to think about things more and more. I felt shaky and sick . . . In the end, I had to go home.

The nightmares began a couple of days later. I dreamt that I was in the building – this time I was watching the crane fall even though I didn't in real life and felt trapped as it hit. Each dream was terrifying and I woke up sweating and breathing hard. I could dream two or three times a night. I had to get up and watch TV, have a cup of tea and fag to help me calm down after them . . . I couldn't go back to sleep. I took about eight or nine weeks off work because of all this. I was just too knackered to work.

I was also pretty uptight during this time. I'm usually very easy going. But I ran into problems with the wife because I was so difficult to live with . . . The dreams gradually got better and I forced myself to go back to work. I had a few panic attacks when I went back to start with because I was working in a temporary building which had no windows, so I panicked at the thought of things that were happening outside. The new office has large windows, and that's OK for me now.

9/11 and PTSD

The destruction the World Trade Center buildings by Al Qaeda on 9 September 2001 led to a number of scientific papers on its psychological impact on the general population – focusing particularly on the outcome of being involved in or witnessing a highly traumatic event. Galia et al. (2003) conducted psychiatric telephone surveys one month, four and six months after the event throughout the population of New York. The prevalence of what they termed 'probable PTSD' directly related to the attacks declined from 7.5 per cent one month after the event to 0.6 per cent five months later. The prevalence of PTSD symptoms was highest among people who were directly affected by the attacks – but a significant number of people who were not directly affected by the attacks also met criteria for probable PTSD. Predictors of PTSD symptoms included worries about future terrorist attacks and reduced self-confidence, reduced feelings of personal control, guilt/shame and helplessness/anger, and low levels of social support (Piotrkowski and Brannen 2002; Simeon et al. 2005). Ahern et al. (2002) examined the impact of the television coverage of the events, and found that more frequent viewing of television images was associated with a higher risk for PTSD and depression. People who both watched the events on television and knew someone involved in them were at particularly high risk of both PTSD and depression. One key image that seemed to influence rates of PTSD was the image of people 'falling or jumping' from the building. The prevalence of PTSD among individuals who repeatedly saw this image was 17.4 per cent: 6.2 per cent of those who did not see this image developed PTSD.

Among children in New York, the attack increased the risk for a number of mental health problems. Hoven et al. (2005) measured levels of psychopathology in a large-scale survey of schoolchildren in New York six months following the events, and found higher than normal levels of agoraphobia, separation anxiety and PTSD. Girls experienced higher levels of distress than boys. Direct exposure to events, exposure of a child's family member, and a prior history of trauma increased the risk of some form of mental health problem. As with adults, exposure to events through the television contributed to risk for PTSD. Lengua et al. (2005) found that 8 per cent of the children in their sample of children in Seattle, who had only seen the events on the television, met criteria 'consistent with PTSD'. As in the Hoven study, girls experienced more emotional problems than boys.

Aetiology of post-traumatic stress disorder

Biological factors

The brain systems involved in PTSD are thought to be those involved in processing emotions and memory, in particular, the amygdala and hippocampus. The hippocampus is responsible for storing and retrieving the memories. It is linked to the amygdala, the area of the brain particularly associated with the formation of conditioned fear responses. Both the hippocampus and the amygdala are activated either in establishing memories of the event and its associated emotions, or in recalling them.

Two stress hormones appear particularly implicated in establishing traumatic memories: norepinephrine and cortisol. Increases in these hormones generally enhance memory, although the levels that may occur at times of traumatic stress may actually be toxic to brain tissue and result in neuronal death, damaging the memory systems. The hippocampus, for example, may experience damage following severe trauma, leading to reductions in its size, which do not recover following treatment or resolution of the trauma (Lindauer et al. 2005). Norepinephrine release has been found to produce high states of arousal and fear, and intense visual flashbacks in some, but by no means all, cases (Leskin et al. 1998). Brewin (2001) speculated that flashbacks may occur when information is transferred from the amygdala to the hippocampus. The sympathetic nervous system (see Chapter 3), controlled by the hypothalamus and levels of norepinephrine, is responsible for the high levels of physiological arousal associated with the condition.

Conditioning models

The conditioning model of PTSD (Foa and Kozak 1986) is based on Mowrer's (1947) two-factor theory, that is, it considers PTSD to be a classically conditioned emotional response. According to Foa and Kozak, associations are stored in neural networks (see Chapter 2), linking emotions, cognitions and perceptual memories. As such, re-exposure to similar contexts or stimuli evokes memories of the event and the conditioned fear response. Avoidance of reminders of the trauma not only prevents distress, but also prevents habituation of the fear response to stimuli associated with the event (Mowrer 1947). As a result, occasional and accidental encounters with relevant stimuli result in flashbacks and other cued memories. Chemtob et al (1988) proposed a similar model to that of Foa, but suggested that memories of the incident are maintained within a neural network which is permanently activated (as opposed to being activated by environmental and emotional cues) and causes the individual to function in 'survival mode', resulting in the symptoms of hyperarousal which form a key element of PTSD as well as re-experiencing.

A schema model of PTSD

The first schema model of PTSD, developed by Horowitz (1986), was strongly influenced by psychoanalytic theory. He proposed that PTSD occurs when the individual is involved in events that are so horrific they cannot be reconciled with the individual's view (schema) of the world. The belief that one may die in an incident, for example, may shatter previous beliefs of invulnerability. The individual feels unsafe and vulnerable. To avoid this ego-damaging discrepancy, defence mechanisms of numbing or denial are evoked. However, these compete with a second innate drive, known as the completion tendency. This requires the individual to integrate memories of trauma into existing world models or schemata: either to make sense of the memories according to currently held beliefs about the world or to change those beliefs.

The completion tendency maintains trauma-related information in active memory in an attempt to process it. Defence mechanisms try to stop these memories entering consciousness. The symptoms the individual experiences are the result of fluctuating strengths of these competing processes. When the completion tendency breaks through the defence mechanisms, memories intrude into consciousness in the form of flashbacks, nightmares and unwanted thoughts or emotional memories. When the defence mechanisms are effective, the individual experiences periods of numbness or denial. Once the trauma-related information is integrated into general belief systems, the symptoms cease.

Research box 9

Bricre, J., Scott, C. and Weathers, F. (2005) Peritraumatic and persistent dissociation in the presumed etiology of PTSD, *American Journal of Psychiatry*, 162: 2295–301.

The authors noted that a number of studies have shown traumatized individuals to frequently experience dissociative symptoms, such as depersonalization, amnesia or fugue states, immediately following the trauma. This is thought to be a defensive process through which an individual develops the capacity to separate him or herself from the distress associated with memories of traumatic events. However, there is some evidence that it may increase risk for PTSD in the long term. What is not clear, however, is whether dissociation immediately around the time of the trauma, or more extended dissociation following the trauma, contributes to such risk. The present study explored this issue.

Study 1

A group of 52 trauma-exposed residents were recruited through newspaper advertisements and flyers. Participants were individually interviewed with the Clinician-Administered PTSD Scale and completed questionnaires including the Peritraumatic Dissociative Experiences Questionnaire, the Dissociative Experiences Scale and the Detailed Assessment of Posttraumatic Stress. The average age of this sample was 35.9 years: 86.5 per cent were women. Fourteen (26.9 per cent) were found to have PTSD on the Clinician-Administered PTSD Scale.

   Univariate ANOVA results revealed that when they were considered individually, scores on the Peritraumatic Dissociative Experiences Questionnaire, the Dissociative Experiences Scale and the sub-scales for peritraumatic distress and trauma-specific dissociation were all associated with the presence of PTSD. When the unique contribution of each variable was evaluated by discriminant analysis, i.e. with control for all other variables in the equation, all but one of these variables emerged as meaningful discriminators. The discriminant function coefficients indicated that although scores on the Dissociative Experiences Scale and the peritraumatic distress and trauma-specific dissociation sub-scales continued to be meaningful discriminators of PTSD, scores on the Peritraumatic Dissociative Experiences Questionnaire were no longer related. That is, dissociation close to the trauma was not predictive of the development of PTSD after controlling for the presence of longer-term dissociation.

Study 2

This involved 386 participants from a general population who had experienced significant trauma and had been involved in the development of the Detailed Assessment of Posttraumatic Stress – a questionnaire previously developed by the research team. This study was a random mailed survey of individuals with cars or telephones in the USA and had a response rate of 11 per cent. The average age of this traumatized sub-sample 45.2 years: 52.3 per cent were men.

   In the second study, a stepwise logistic regression analysis revealed that PTSD was unrelated to demographic variables at step 1 but was associated with exposure to sexual and physical violence at step 2; peritraumatic distress, peritraumatic dissociation and persistent dissociation at steps 3, 4 and 5; and disengagement and emotional constriction at step 6. That is, each variable made a significant contribution to the prediction of PTSD, even when all variables entered at prior steps were taken into account. Significantly, peritraumatic dissociation remained a significant predictor at step 4 even after trauma exposure and post-traumatic distress were already entered into the regression equation. However, when all variables were considered simultaneously (i.e., after step 6), peritraumatic distress and peritraumatic dissociation were no longer related to PTSD, whereas persistent dissociation, disengagement, and emotional constriction were. Trauma-exposed individuals with non-clinical levels of persistent dissociation had a 2.9 per cent likelihood of having PTSD, whereas those with clinical levels had a 56.5 per cent likelihood of having PTSD.

Discussion

As reported in other investigations, univariate analyses indicated that peritraumatic dissociation was a significant predictor of PTSD status. However, this relationship ceased to be significant in both studies once persistent dissociation was taken into account by multivariate analyses. Overall, the findings of both studies suggest that the primary risk for PTSD is not so much whether an individual dissociates during (or soon after) a traumatic event, but whether such dissociation persists over time. The time frame of this response appears to be critical.

A process model of PTSD

Brewin (2001) added a second level of information processing to the model proposed by Horowitz. According to Brewin, the individual can both deliberately choose to address their traumatic memories, and memories may also come to consciousness without deliberate recall. These processes involve two differing memory systems:

- *Verbally accessible memories (VAMs):* this system involves memories of the incident that can be deliberately accessed. They tend to be fragmented, based on normal recall processes, and therefore can be changed as the person processes information about the traumatic incident. They may, for example, become less traumatic as the individual reframes the incident as being less threatening than they initially thought; they may become more traumatic if they later consider the event to have been more personally threatening.
- *Situationally accessible memories (SAMs):* these memories cannot be deliberately accessed, but come to consciousness in response to cues that remind the individual of the incident – including activation of the VAM system. They may also occur when the brain is not actively processing information – most commonly at night in the form of nightmares. They feel as if they are 'in the event' and cannot be deliberately changed.

According to Brewin, resolution of PTSD requires both sets of memories to enter the normal memory system. By this time, they are still accessible but do not carry the high levels of emotional content associated with both VAMs and SAMs. Resolution of VAMs involves deliberate recall and reframing of information. This leads to an integration of the VAMs with their pre-existing beliefs and models of the world, and restores a sense of safety and control over both self and the world. Activation of the SAMs is also required, and the SAMs gradually change over time and become less emotion-laden and frightening. Changes in SAM representations may occur through the integration of new, non-threatening information or, more frequently, through the creation of new SAMs. As SAMs may be triggered through conscious processing of VAMs, this process may occur naturally. Both these processes are similar to the completion tendency described by Horowitz. Thus, the model includes elements of the schema theory of Horowitz, as PTSD resolves when memories of the event are integrated within pre-existing memory structures and elements of Foa's fear network in terms of the representation of memories.

Empirical investigation of these processes can be difficult. However, Brewin and colleagues have been able to find differences in the types of memories people provide from VAMs and SAMs. In two studies, Hellawell and Brewin (2002, 2004) asked people to recall and write a narrative of the trauma that led to their PTSD and then to identify which parts to the narrative were based on flashback memories (SAMs) and which were based on 'ordinary' memory (VAMs). In the first study, they found that narrative involving flashback memory was associated with higher levels of autonomic and behavioural arousal (as observed by a researcher) than writing based on ordinary memories. In the second study, they found that writing based on flashback memories was more detailed, made more mentions of death, fear, helplessness and horror. It was also more likely to be written in the present tense than memory sections written from ordinary memory. By contrast, sections written from ordinary memory tended to mention more 'secondary' emotions such as guilt and anger, which may have been experienced following the incident rather than at the time of its occurrence.

Brewin suggested that the hippocampus is the neural centre involved in process-ing VAMs. The amygdala may be involved in processing the more emotionally laden SAMs. Brewin, like Horowitz, suggested that emotional processing results from a drive towards resolution of conflict between previously held schemata and new information. The activation of SAMs provides the detailed information needed to allow cognitive readjustment to the trauma. Once integration has been achieved, the symptoms of PTSD will resolve.

A psychosocial model

Rather than focus on just the immediate cognitive processes involved in PTSD, Joseph et al. (1995) explored a wider set of factors that influence the development and course of the disorder. These included:

- *Event stimuli:* iconic representations of the event held in immediate memory.
- *Event cognitions:* memories that provide the basis for re-experiencing phenomena or intrusive memories – Brewin's SAMs.
- *Appraisals and reappraisals:* the individual's thoughts about the incident – Brewin's VAMs. These involve interpretation of information relevant to the incident, drawing on past representations and experiences. They may take the form of automatic schemata linked to strong emotional states triggered by stimuli associ-ated with the trauma or more considered attempts to think through and perhaps

reappraise the meaning of the event. Key appraisals that influence the outcome are appraisals related to guilt, control and self-blame.

- *Coping attempts:* flashbacks and emotional memories of the event may result in coping attempts intended to minimize emotional distress. These usually take the form of avoidance of reminders, memories or similar emotions and activities to those associated with the event. Coping strategies may also involve attempts at inhibiting unwanted memories.

- *Personality:* this will influence the type of cognitions and emotions experienced at the time of a traumatic incident, the appraisals made in response to it, and subsequent coping strategies. Accordingly, personality has a significant impact on whether or not the individual develops PTSD and its course.

- *Social support:* an important mediator of the response to trauma, perhaps because talking to other people helps the individual assign new meanings to the event and provides support for the expression of negative emotions.

According to Joseph et al. (1995), traumatic events result in immediate cognitions that give rise to extreme emotional arousal. This arousal interferes with immediate processing of these cognitions. As a consequence, they are held in specific memory networks, as a result of their personal salience and the difficulty of storing in general memory outlined by Horowitz. These cognitions correspond to those of Brewin, and involve memories that are not available to conscious awareness and memories that can be deliberately accessed. These form the basis of the re-experiencing phenomena, and are influenced by the nature of the trauma, the core assumptions and beliefs an individual has about the world, elements of the situation which presented the most threat, and the personality of the individual. In other words, the nature of the post-traumatic symptoms will reflect both the nature of the trauma to which an individual was exposed, and the nature of the individual.

The appraisal an individual makes at the time of the event will influence its impact on them. Some stimuli may be judged by all individuals as threatening and dangerous; others less so. Reappraisal of the situation, envisaging more or less threatening outcomes may also influence outcome. If an individual reflects on events, and thinks that, in the cold light of day, they were less threatening than they appeared at the time, they may experience fewer symptoms and their PTSD will have a shorter duration than if they do not lessen the threat, or even exaggerate the level of threat they experienced. Two key attributions about the event, whether made at the time or subsequently, will also impact on the development of PTSD: attributions of having potential control over an event but failing to take it ('I could have done something to stop it – and I didn't') which is linked to the emotion of shame and guilt. In one study of these processes, in victims of violent crime, Andrews et al. (2000) found shame and anger to be key predictors of levels of trauma one month following a key incident, and shame to be predictive of symptoms six months following the incident. Similar findings have been reported following a variety of traumatic incidents, including sexual abuse (Feiring et al. 2002) and being stalked (Kamphuis et al. 2003). Together with feelings of loss of core beliefs and values, distrust, alienation from others and a sense of being permanently damaged, these responses have been termed the 'experience of mental death', and Ebert and Dyck (2004) labelled them the core feature of PTSD.

The appraisals an individual makes may also influence their coping strategies. Strong feelings of guilt may be associated with intrusive thoughts and images. Shame may evoke attempts at avoidance and denial – which may result in a paradoxical increase in symptoms. Beliefs that an individual is unable to cope with strong emotions may also lead to avoidance of potentially stressful situations and prevent the individual from learning that they can, indeed, cope with such emotions. Good social support will generally lessen the symptoms of PTSD, partly, perhaps, because this supports rehearsal and positive reappraisal of event-related cognitions (Joseph et al. 1996). In one study of this phenomenon, Andrews et al. (2003) measured levels of available positive support and negative responses from other people in both male and female victims of violent crime. Women reported significantly more negative responses from family and friends, which contributed to higher levels of PTSD symptoms six months after the event.

Finally, the type of appraisals and coping efforts may be guided by trait, personality, variables. Two personality constructs appear to be particularly associated with the development of PTSD. Negative affect, or neuroticism, has been found to be predictive of the development of PTSD symptoms in some studies (e.g. Bennett et al. 2001). It may be predictive of PTSD as it is indicative of a propensity to appraise events as negative and threatening, and to dwell on such events. Studies have also found an association between the avoidance and numbing symptoms of PTSD and **alexithymia** (e.g. Fukunishi et al. 1996), characterized as a paucity of emotional experience and awareness, with an associated poverty of imagination and a tendency to focus upon the tangible and mundane (especially perhaps the physical symptoms of emotional responses). This may inhibit the processing of emotional experiences into general schemata and place the individual at risk for recurrent memories of the frightening event.

Thinking about . . .

The outcomes of traumatic events, or even the experience of PTSD, are not all negative. Calhoun and Tedeschi (1999) identified a more positive outcome, they termed post-traumatic growth. These changes include improved relationships, new possibilities for one's life, a greater appreciation for life, a greater sense of personal strength, and spiritual development. People who experience post-traumatic growth frequently report an increased sense of their own capacities to survive and cope with whatever life throws at them. They also may find themselves becoming more comfortable with intimacy and having a greater sense of compassion for others who experience life difficulties. A commonly reported change is that people begin to value the smaller things in life more and also to consider important changes in the religious, spiritual and existential beliefs they may hold. They may also change their life goals in the light of their traumatic experience.

Most psychological research and interventions in relation to traumatic issues focus on pathology. Perhaps both should focus more on understanding and facilitating positive growth . . .

Treatment of post-traumatic stress disorder

Preventing PTSD by psychological debriefing

Psychological debriefing is a single-session interview conducted immediately follow-ing a traumatic event intended to help those involved cope with their emotional responses to the trauma and prevent the development of PTSD. It involves encour-aging the individual to talk through the event and their emotional reactions to it in a detailed and systematic manner. It is thought to aid integration of incident memor-ies into the general memory system. Debriefing is now regularly offered following traumatic incidents, despite increasing questions about its effectiveness. Rose et al. (2002), for example, concluded from their meta-analysis of four well-conducted ran-domized controlled trials of debriefing that it not only may be ineffective in prevent-ing PTSD, but also may actually increase risk for the disorder. None of the studies using this method found a reduced risk for PTSD in the three to four months follow-ing the incident. The two studies that reported longer-term findings found that those who received debriefing had nearly twice the risk of developing PTSD than those who did not receive the intervention. That is, debriefing seems to inhibit long-term recovery from psychological trauma. A number of explanations have been proposed for these findings, although each remains speculative:

- 'Secondary' traumatization' may occur as a result of further imaginal exposure to a traumatic incident within a short time of the event.

- Debriefing may 'medicalize' normal distress, and increase the expectancy of developing psychological symptoms in those who would otherwise not have done so.

- Debriefing may prevent the potentially protective responses of denial and dis-tancing that may occur in the immediate aftermath of a traumatic incident.

Although psychodynamic approaches have been used to some benefit with people with PTSD (Marmar 1991), the most frequently used interventions in the treatment of PTSD are based on cognitive behavioural principles.

Exposure techniques

The principles underpinning exposure methods in the treatment of PTSD are that the individual will ultimately benefit from re-exposure to memories of the event and their associated emotions. The conditioning model suggests that distress lessens as the individual's emotional response to these memories habituates over time. A more cog-nitive explanation is that exposure leads to reconciliation between memories and the meaning of the traumatic event and pre-existing world schemata. Only by accessing and processing these memories will resolution occur.

Exposure therapy may lead to an initial exacerbation of distress as upsetting images, previously avoided where possible, are deliberately recollected. To minimize this distress and to prevent drop-out from therapy, Leskin et al. (1998) recommended a graded exposure process in which the individual initially talks about particular elements of the traumatic event at a level of detail they choose over several occasions until they no longer respond with a stress response. Any new, and potentially more distressing, memories are avoided at this time, and become the focus of the next levels of intervention. Reactivation of memories by this procedure involves describing the experience in detail, focusing on what happened, the thoughts and emotions experienced at the time, and any memories that the incident triggered. This core approach may be augmented by a variety of cognitive behavioural techniques, including relaxation training and cognitive restructuring. Relaxation may help the individual control their arousal at the time of recalling the event or at other times in the day when they are feeling tense or on edge. Cognitive restructuring may help the individual address any distorted cognitions they had in response to the event and make those thoughts less threatening ('I'm going to die! . . . It felt like I was going to die, but actually that was more my panic than reality . . .'). Wells and Sembi (2004) focused on teaching people to minimize the rumination that can be a particularly distressing element of PTSD, and which may serve to maintain PTSD symptoms, using active distraction techniques.

A number of studies have shown exposure-based therapy to be superior to no treatment and alternative active interventions including supportive counselling and relaxation therapy without exposure (Keane et al. 1989). Foa et al. (1991), for example, randomly allocated female rape victims to either a waiting list control condition, self-instruction training, supportive counselling or an exposure programme. Participants in each of the active interventions evidenced greater gains than those in the waiting list condition. Immediately following the intervention period, participants in the self-instruction training condition fared best. By three-month follow-up, however, those in the exposure programme reported significantly fewer intrusive memories and less arousal than participants in the other conditions. Similar results were reported by Marks et al. (1996) in a comparison of relaxation, exposure alone, cognitive restructuring alone, and exposure plus cognitive restructuring. By the end of the intervention phase, all the other treatments proved superior to relaxation, with no differences in effectiveness between them. By three- and six-month follow-up, the exposure programme proved superior. It seems that self-instruction and other cognitive techniques may help participants cope with the anxiety and other emotions evoked in the early stages of exposure programmes, while exposure to traumatic memories is critical to long-term benefit. The optimal treatment seems to involve a combination of self-instruction training or other cognitive strategies in the early stages of therapy combined with gradual exposure to traumatic memories.

Treating people with PTSD may not require large amounts of specialist training. Gillespie et al. (2002) taught health care staff with minimal background in cognitive behavioural therapy how to provide an exposure-based intervention for PTSD in response to a large bomb which exploded in the small Northern Irish town of Omagh in 1998. Staff received a two-day workshop plus telephone contact with an expert in the treatment of PTSD and therapy supervision. The effectiveness of their intervention was similar to those reported in previous studies involving expert therapists.

Eye movement desensitization and reprocessing (EMDR)
The most recent, and controversial, treatment of PTSD, known as EMDR, was discovered by chance by Shapiro (1995). She noticed that while walking in the woods

her disturbing thoughts began to disappear, and when recalled were less upsetting than previously. This change was associated with her eyes spontaneously moving rapidly backwards and forwards in an upward diagonal. Since then, the procedure has been developed into a standardized intervention and subject to a number of clinical trials in the treatment of PTSD.

Treatment typically involves recall of target memories by the client as visual images along with a negative cognition that goes with the image, framed in the present tense ('I am terrified'). The client next rates the strength of emotion evoked by this process. They are then asked to track the therapist's finger as it is moved increasingly quickly back and forth across their line of vision. After 24 such movements, the client is instructed to 'Blank it out' or 'Let it go', and asked to rate their level of emotion. This procedure is repeated until the client experiences minimal distress to the presence of the image and negative cognition. If no changes occur, the direction of eye movements is changed.

EMDR incorporates exposure to elements of the trauma stimulus. An important question is therefore whether the addition of the eye movements enhances the effect of exposure. This does not seem to be the case. While EMDR is certainly more effective than no treatment, it appears no more effective than standard exposure programmes. Davidson and Parker (2001) used meta analysis to examine the effectiveness of EMDR in the treatment of PTSD in comparison with no treatment, non-specific treatment and the exposure methods described above. While their analyses indicated a modest benefit for EMDR when compared with no treatment or non-specific treatments, its benefits were similar or less than those resulting from exposure approaches. In one such study, Devilly and Spence (1999) randomly allocated people with PTSD into either an exposure-based programme combined with cognitive challenge of irrational trauma-related cognitions or EMDR. Combining data from a number of measures of PTSD revealed a clear advantage for the exposure group in comparison to EMDR immediately after the intervention was finished, and at two-week and three-month follow-up. The differences between the two groups became greater over time. Subsequently, Taylor et al. (2003) found that, compared with EMDR and relaxation training, exposure therapy produced significantly larger reductions in avoidance and re-experiencing symptoms, and was quicker in achieving these successes.

Pharmacological interventions

A variety of drug types have been used in the treatment of PTSD to some effect, including antidepressant MAOIs, SSRIs and tricyclics (see Chapter 3). Stein et al. (2002), for example, conducted a meta-analysis on nine short-term studies of antidepressants in the treatment of PTSD. The overall effects of the interventions showed SSRIs to achieve significantly greater improvements than placebo on measures of functioning and the core PTSD symptoms of intrusion and avoidance.

Recovered memory

The prevalence of reported child sexual abuse is frighteningly high. Wilsnack et al. (2002), for example, reported data from a representative US sample of women.

Twenty-two per cent reported having sexually coercive experiences while growing up; of these, 69 per cent indicated that they felt they had been sexually abused. Only 2 per cent reported remembering the abuse with the help of a therapist or other professional person. Arreola et al. (2005) found that between 11 and 22 per cent of gay men reported experiencing sexual abuse before the age of 13 years.

Since the late 1980s, a number of clinicians have argued that many adults who were traumatized as children had repressed all memories of these events, and that these memories could be recovered only in the course of psychological therapy. In a seminal text, Bass and Davis (1988) argued that such repression is not unusual, and advised therapists to accept their 'recovered memories' of sexual abuse, and to suspend disbelief even if they found some parts of their history doubtful. Memories have been recovered in considerable detail up to 40 years after the alleged trauma. Individuals may describe partial or complete memory loss for periods of months or years while they are growing up. Between 20 and 60 per cent of women either in therapy or who have completed therapy report periods of forgetting some or all of the abuse they have experienced (e.g. Loftus and Ketcham 1994). Individuals identified as abusers, usually parents or other family members, frequently deny the episodes and claim that they have been wrongfully accused: that is, that the recovered memories of abuse are false memories. Recovered or false, the negative impact these accusations can have on families is often profound.

Explanations of recovered memory

The recovered memory phenomenon has engendered considerable controversy and debate. Three differing explanations for this phenomenon have been proposed.

Accurate accounts
Recovered memories are accurate accounts of previously forgotten events, and should be accepted as such even in the absence of corroborative evidence. Explanations of why these memories are apparently forgotten focus on both unconscious mechanisms that prevent the laying down of easily retrievable memories at the time of any traumatic incident and problems of recall. The first involves a process known as dissociation. This is an altered state of consciousness in which ordinary perceptual and cognitive functioning is impaired: events feel unreal and distant from the individual. Dissociation may occur during the traumatic experience and act as a defence that prevents the individual from experiencing the full emotional impact of what is happening. Retrieval of associated memories is poor, as little if any ordinary conscious processing took place at encoding. What memories there are may be fragmented, but vivid and intense. Hunter (1997) described three forms of dissociation that have been reported by child abuse victims: (1) out-of-body experiences in which events were seen as happening to someone else who looked like the victim; (2) conscious attempts to 'blank out' memories of the assaults during or after they had happened; and (3) the creation of an imaginary world to which the respondent could escape and feel safe during or after the abuse. Failure to recall events is thought to be the result of denial and long-term dissociation that prevent the retrieval of information once in memory stores.

Illusions

Recovered memories are illusions: false memories resulting from the therapy process itself (Zola 1998). Such memories are 'implanted' by therapists who have decided that the patient is an abuse victim and who use therapeutic techniques to persuade the client to remember these forgotten episodes of abuse in order to 'recover'. The likelihood of suggestive influences leading to memory errors is increased by the perceived authority and trustworthiness of the therapist, and their repetition and plausibility.

Normal forgetting

Recovered memories are not 'special', but are the result of normal forgetting (e.g. Loftus and Ketcham 1994). This explanation may be particularly relevant to single traumatic episodes, but has more difficulty in accounting for the forgetting of repeated traumatic episodes.

Evidence of recovered memory

Protagonists on each side of the debate have interpreted research findings both to support their case and question those who disagree with them. The debate has drawn on research related to normal memory processes as well as more clinical issues.

Age at time of incident

Recovered memories are sometimes described from before the age of 2, and often in significant detail (Loftus and Ketcham 1994). Morton et al. (1995), for example, reported that 26 per cent of allegations involved abuse that began when the claimant was aged between 0 and 2 years old. This, argue opponents of recovered memory, makes such memories unlikely to be accurate. Most people are unable to recollect experiences from the first two to three years of their lives, as the cortical areas that eventually become the sites for permanent memory storage are undergoing a process of maturation at this time that makes them unable to process and store information needed for long-term recall.

Evidence of emotionally intense memory distortion

Some clinicians (e.g. Terr 1991) have argued that trauma-related memories are not subject to the normal processes of memory decay and distortion over time, and are therefore more accurate than 'normal' long-term memories. This claim can be challenged, partly by the mechanisms of avoidance and dissociation described above that are thought to interfere with the accurate perception of events. Empirical evidence also suggests this is not the case. Neisser and Harsch (1992), for example, asked students one day after the *Challenger* disaster, in which a space shuttle burst into flames on lift-off, to describe their personal memories of the event: where they were at the time of the incident, and so on. Two years later, when asked to redescribe their memories, the accounts of one-third of the students differed substantially from their initial memories. Of note was that there was little relationship between the accuracy of recalled 'facts' and students' confidence in their ability to recall them. The *Challenger* disaster may not have been sufficiently traumatic for those not directly involved to result in unchangeable memory traces. Whether more salient emotional events can evoke differing memory processes is unclear, although a number of case studies in which long-term emotional memories show discrepancies with actual events suggest not (Zola 1998). Of course, this argument may challenge the accuracy of recall of events, but not statements as to whether or not particular incidents actually happened.

Corroboration

Gaining corroborative evidence of child sexual abuse is clearly problematic. Nevertheless, Feldman-Summers and Pope (1994) found some degree of corroborative evidence in 47 per cent of the cases they examined, including the abuser acknowledging some or all of the remembered abuse or someone else reporting abuse by the same perpetrator. Similar levels of corroboration, 41 per cent, were reported in an unrelated survey of British clinical psychologists (see Brewin and Andrews 1998).

Conditions of recall

Clearly, if recovered memory is a therapy-generated phenomenon, the majority of memories should reappear during therapy. This does not always appear to be the case. Feldman-Summers and Pope (1994) found that although over half such memories were recovered in the context of therapy, 44 per cent of their respondents stated that recovery had been triggered exclusively in other contexts. By contrast, Goodyear-Smith et al. (1997) reported summary data from several papers indicating that in over 80 per cent of cases of sexual abuse, memories had emerged while complainants were undergoing psychotherapy.

Attempts to forget

A key factor in the repressed memory debate is the assumption that those who remember childhood trauma as an adult have used unconscious coping mechanisms that result in them 'forgetting' the trauma they have undergone. If this is the case, then one would assume that a significant percentage of people who undergo other traumas as a child would engage in similar coping strategies and have similar problems of recall. Evidence to suggest this may not be the case can be found in studies of children who have gone through traumatic events which are a matter of historical record, including kidnap, the Holocaust and witnessing parental murder, and can accurately recall them (see Zola 1998). In each case, there was no evidence of repressed memory; indeed, many people had very vivid and detailed recall of events they would like to have been able to forget.

Proponents of the repressed memory hypothesis counter these data by suggesting that sexual abuse is different from other trauma and that it has specific and unique consequences for coping. They argue that because abuse is usually carried out by parents or significant others rather than strangers and occurs in isolation rather than with companions, the effects are unique. One proponent of this argument, Freyd (1996), argued that sexual abuse of children is more than a trauma, it is a betrayal, and that 'betrayal trauma' is more prone to repression than other types of trauma. According to her model, sexual abuse by a trusted caretaker will be more likely to be repressed than sexual abuse by a stranger. Evidence in support of this hypothesis was reported by Pope and Feldman-Summers (1992) who surveyed a representative population of US psychologists. Seventy-nine people reported having been abused at some time: 32 reported forgetting this abuse for a period of time. Of this group, 56 per cent reported that it involved sexual abuse by a relative, 37 per cent reported that it involved sexual abuse by a non-relative, providing some evidence in support of the model. While other surveys (e.g. Schultz et al. 2003) have reported similar findings, this result has not always been replicated, including in a sample of adults with documented abuse as children (Goodman et al. 2003).

Evidence of the creation of false traumatic memories

Those who argue against the concept of recovered memory suggest that such memories result from therapists planting suggestions of childhood abuse in people to whom this has not happened. There is a large body of evidence suggesting this is a possible explanation for at least some cases of recovered memory. In a naturalistic example of this, Piaget (1954) as an adult was able to recall in some detail memories of his being kidnapped as a child of 2 years of age. This despite the event never having occurred, and being a story told to him by a family nurse. More experimental evidence has been provided by Loftus and Coan (1998). In one study, adults were asked about childhood events, one of which had never occurred, in the presence of other family members, who 'reminded' them of the event during the interview. Subsequently, 6 of the 24 participants in the study 'remembered' the false episode as real and provided additional details about it. Using a similar method, Hyman et al. (1995) asked college students about various childhood events that had never happened, including an overnight hospitalization for an ear infection. At the end of the first interview, in which no participants 'recalled' the false events, they were encouraged to try to remember more information about them before the next interview. During a second interview, a quarter of the participants remembered detailed information about the false event.

Retraction

Although the percentage of people to do so is unknown, many people who recall traumatic memories eventually retract these memories and claim that the events never actually occurred: that they are a consequence of within-therapy processes. Here, for example, is the testimony of Clare, who retracted her claims of sexual abuse by a family member. Her story here focuses on the power that her therapist had over her, how he shaped her 'memories', and how she came to recognize his negative influence over her:

> Looking back, it's difficult to see how things could have got this far, and been so destructive. How could a relationship with a therapist become the only – the total – focus of my life for three years? How could I have sold my soul, my very self, to another human being? How could I have fallen under the spell of a man who, it turns out, had problems in his own life; a man so inadequate himself that he needed me and others to be 'sick' in order for him to be powerful and strong. I trusted this man with my life – my soul. I shared everything with him – my dreams, the desires of my life. I confessed my sins to him. He was my partner, mother, father, sister, best friend, and teacher. My role model. He was everything

to me. Whatever he said, I agreed with. How could he be wrong? My life became so linked with his life, my ability to think for myself disappeared. I thought what he wanted me to think. I believed what he wanted me to believe. I became what he wanted me to become.

Overview of the evidence

Brewin and Andrews (1998) considered the evidence relevant to each of these explanations. They suggested the present state of the evidence is as follows:

- The age at which the majority of events are said to have occurred extends beyond the period of the infant amnesia.
- Corroboration occurs with reasonable frequency given the nature of the alleged incidents.
- The content of most recovered memories concerns a variety of events known to occur with reasonable frequency, and is not limited to child sexual abuse.
- Well-trained therapists not using inappropriate techniques have reported clients recovering memories.
- The context of recall is not limited to the therapist's office.

On this basis, Brewin and Andrews suggested that the evidence is not sufficient to rule out the possibility that recovered memory may genuinely occur, at least in some cases, and that each case should be taken on its own merit. Nevertheless, because there is serious doubt over the accuracy of at least some recovered memories, a number of professional bodies have developed guidelines about how clinicians should respond to reports of 'recovered memory'. Those of the Australian Psychological Society (www.psychosociety.com.au) are typical:

- 'Memories' that are reported either spontaneously or following the use of special procedures in therapy may be accurate, inaccurate, fabricated or a mixture of these.
- The level of belief in memories, all the emotion associated with the memory, does not necessarily relate to the accuracy of the memory.
- The available scientific and clinical evidence does not allow accurate, inaccurate or fabricated memories to be distinguished in the absence of independent corroboration.

Psychologists/therapists should:

- be alert to the ways they can shape the memories reported by clients through the expectations they convey, the comments they make, the questions they ask, and the responses they give to clients
- be aware that clients are susceptible to subtle suggestions and reinforcements, whether intended or unintended

- be empathic and supportive of the reports of clients, while ensuring they do not jump to conclusions about the truth or falsity of their recollections
- inform any client who recovers a memory of abuse that it may be an accurate memory of an actual event, may be an altered or distorted memory of an actual event, or may be a false memory of an event that did not happen.

Dissociative identity disorder (DID)

A defining characteristic of individuals with a diagnosis of dissociative identity disorder (DID) is that they behave as if they possess two or more distinct identities or person-alities, known as *alters*. In contrast to the past, where people with DID (or multiple personality as it was previously known) reported relatively few alter personalities, the average number of alters now reported is about 15, and some individuals exhibit more than 100. According to DSM-IV-TR, the diagnostic criteria for DID are:

- the presence of two or more distinct identities or personality states, each with its own relatively enduring pattern of perceiving, relating to and thinking about the environment and self
- at least two of these identities or personality states recurrently take control of the person's behaviour
- inability to recall important personal information that is too extensive to be explained by ordinary forgetfulness
- the disturbance is not due to the direct physiological effects, substance abuse or a general medical condition.

The number of alters depends on a number of factors, such as the severity and time period of the abuse. Each alter has a job within the system. Most alters protect the host personality from memories of the trauma. It is common for each alter to guard a particular memory. Some alters are aware of other alters; others do not know of their existence. Most alters do not see themselves in the physical body they are in: children see themselves as 4 feet tall, girls see themselves as women, and so on. They may be of different nationalities and races. Some may speak different languages. Alters may have different facial expressions and different mannerisms. There are many different kinds of alters and all systems are different, but there are some of the more common types of alter, here described by someone living with a partner who experienced DID (www.mpdfriends.homestead.com):

- *Host:* this person can either be the original birth child, or can be an alter that is the main personality presented to the outside world.
- *Original birth child:* this person may be awake and functioning, or said to be asleep. This person is sometimes referred to as the core personality.
- *Child alters:* child alters (or 'littles' as they are affectionately known) can range from the age of an infant upwards. These are the alters that took much of the abuse, and often carry a large number of memories. They display behaviour that

is appropriate for their age. Often they carry much pain, both physical and emotional.

- *Teens:* most systems have teen alters. These alters were often the ones who went to school, and were out for those years.

- *Gatekeepers:* some systems have a gatekeeper, who directs and has control of the body. They may also control the length of time an alter is in body. They do not often come out themselves, but just seem happy to observe and direct the others.

- *Internal self helpers:* these internal self helpers keep the alters safe. They usually know all the alters and the details of the abuse the alters endured. They are very helpful in therapy, and help the therapist understand why a particular alter feels the way they do, or decide the action of a particular alter. They also decide what information is passed to other alters and to the host.

- *Protectors:* protectors protect (!) the system from outside threats. They can usually talk hard, or fight, or do whatever is necessary to keep the system safe. They often use anger as a defence. They are especially protective of the child alters.

Switches between alters often result from some sort of stress or upset, which causes another alter, usually a protector alter, to emerge. Stresses can include comments by others, seeing the abuser, an unexpected touch, arguments and aggression – even having sex. Sel (1997) suggested that the individual has an ecosystem of alters who compete with each other to gain control over the output channels. The alter that most successfully maintains an emotional equilibrium is most likely to be best adapted. When the individual moves to a different context, different cognitive schemata may be more adaptive and the dominant alter will switch.

Aetiology of dissociative identity disorder

The nature and, indeed, existence of 'true' DID have been as hotly debated as the existence of recovered memories, and the arguments are very similar (see, for example, Piper and Merskey 2004). Such is the level of debate that even some experimental studies of this disorder remain neutral about its nature and aetiology. Elzinga et al. stated, for example, that they adopted a 'pragmatic stance . . . without making a priori claims about the nature of so-called "identities"' (2003: 237). Some contend that its existence is self-evident, and that there are too many people experiencing these symptoms to deny the reality of the problem. Others reject the concept, arguing that the symptoms are invented by the individuals reporting them, or even implanted in their consciousness by over-zealous therapists. The two dominant theories of DID are that it is either the result of childhood trauma (e.g. Gleaves 1996) or a socially constructed system created by the affected individual and shaped by the therapist (e.g. Spanos 1994).

Childhood trauma
There are relatively few studies of DID – perhaps because of the low prevalence of the condition. However, what evidence there is suggests that it is associated with child-

hood trauma. Boon and Draijer (1993), for example, reported that 94 per cent of the series of people diagnosed with DID in their sample reported a history of childhood physical and/or sexual abuse. Proponents of the childhood trauma model (e.g. Gleaves 1996) suggest that the experience of severe trauma during childhood produces a mental 'splitting' or dissociation as part of a defensive reaction. The abused child learns to dissociate, or enter a self-induced hypnotic state, placing the memory of the abuse in the subconscious as a means of coping with the trauma. These dissociated parts of the individual 'split' into alter personalities that, in adulthood, manifest themselves to help the individual cope with stressful situations and express resentments or other feelings that are unacceptable to the primary personality. This model fits well with the models of hypnosis outlined in Chapter 5.

Taking a similar approach, Putnam (1997) proposed a developmental model of these phenomena. He suggested that traumatic environments prevent children from completing the developmental task of consolidating an integrated sense of self from what he termed the 'discrete behavioural states' – involving cognitive and emotional functioning – which predominate in infancy. He suggested that normal caregiving environments facilitate integration of these differing states into a single integrated whole. Trauma actively inhibits this integration. Instead, the child develops a series of separate states that are adaptive to their parental behaviours.

Socio-cognitive model

By contrast, socio-cognitive theorists (e.g. Lilienfield et al. 1999; Spanos 1994) have argued that DID is a set of beliefs and behaviours constructed by the individual themself in response to personal stress, therapist pressure and societal legitimization of the construct of 'multiple personality'. They suggest that DID has become a legitimate way for many people to understand and express their failures and frustrations, as well as a tactic for the manipulation of others. According to this account, individuals diagnosed as having DID learn to portray themselves as possessing multiple selves and to reorganize and elaborate on their personal biography to make it consistent with their understanding of what it means to be a 'multiple'. That is, they actively construct their various selves. They have further argued that psychotherapists have contributed to the development of this disorder by encouraging clients to construe themselves in this way and by providing official legitimation for the different identities their patients enact.

The two poles of this argument are perhaps best considered in a large review by Spanos (1994) in which he gave the socio-cognitive critique of the disorder, and the defence of the psychiatric model provided by Gleaves (1996). The next four sub-sections consider their arguments in some detail, with data from other reviews added as appropriate.

Problems of prevalence The prevalence of DID has changed over time, increasing substantially since the 1980s. Spanos (1994) argued that if DID were a naturally occurring state, this degree of change would not occur, and that it represents an increase in the social construction of the condition by therapists and clients. Spanos further noted that among 'investigators who are sympathetic to DID', diagnostic rates are extremely high. Modestin's (1992) survey of Swiss psychiatrists, for example, suggested that about 1 per cent of cases seen within their psychiatric system were diagnosed as having DID. He also found that while 90 per cent of the psychiatrists he surveyed had not seen a case of DID, three reported seeing more than 20 people with the disorder: 66 per cent of the cases were reported by less than 0.1 per cent of the psychiatrists surveyed. He suggested that these clinicians may have either misidentified symptoms as evidence of DID or encouraged their clients to construct various manifestations of the disorder.

Gleaves responded to this argument by suggesting that it is not surprising there were differences in observation rates among differing clinicians. According to Gleaves, this may have been a result of different referral rates, an unwillingness among some clinicians to give a diagnosis of DID, and a reluctance among the same clinicians to ask the questions that would lead to this diagnosis being assigned. He also suggested that the increase in reported prevalence may be a function of previous misdiagnoses as a result of it being a relatively new diagnostic category, increased awareness of the prevalence and problems of child abuse, and increased interest in dissociative states. Finally, he suggested that a critical factor may simply be the trend towards a lessening of scepticism about the condition among therapists. He cited a number of studies involving large numbers of patients and clinicians (e.g. Ross et al. 1989) in which the diagnosis of DID was more evenly spread across psychiatrists than the study of Modestin (1992). He also noted that there are now several methods of assessment of DID, all of which have been found to have high reliability and inter-rater agreement (Steinberg et al. 1993). This consistency of diagnosis using standardized measures should indicate a reliable diagnosis, unbiased by therapist beliefs.

Teaching multiplicity   Spanos's most critical attack on clinicians who diagnose DID is that they lead their patients either covertly or overtly to report the presence of alters. He noted that proponents of DID have described a large body of symptoms that indicate the possible presence of the disorder and justify probing to confirm a diagnosis, including depression, periods of missing time, headaches and impaired concentration. One clinician even argued that a smooth complexion may be indicative because the regular switching between personalities prevents the formation of wrinkles. Merskey (1992) suggested that highly leading and suggestive procedures are frequently used, to the point that some therapists insisted to doubting patients that they were multiples and supplied them with the names of their alters. Allison and Schwarz (1980) contended that clients are frequently reluctant to accept they are multiples and, under these circumstances, should be actively persuaded by their therapist.

The generation of alters often occurs in the privacy of the consultation following use of hypnotic techniques. Spanos (1994) argued that the use of persuasive techniques or suggestion while under hypnosis may itself result in some individuals reporting alters and subsequently behaving as if they were 'multiples'. The role of hypnosis in generating alters was challenged by Gleaves (1996), who noted that the percentage of patients diagnosed with DID following hypnosis varied between 4 and 27 per cent across studies. Ross and Norton (1989), for example, found no differences between the clinical presentation, symptomatology, or number of alters, of people who were, or were not, treated using hypnosis.

Finding evidence of suggestion in clinical sessions is difficult, as their content is rarely made public. However, Spanos was able to review the transcripts of the interview of a suspected murderer, Ken Bianchi, who was found to have DID by Schwarz (1981) and who confessed to a murder perpetrated by an alter named Steve. Spanos argued that the instructions given to Bianchi led him to report having an alter, as they repeatedly informed him that there was another individual within, who could be addressed. When Spanos et al. (1985) used this procedure with naïve participants under hypnosis in an experimental study, most participants enacted the symptoms of DID by adopting a different name, referred to their primary personality in the third person, and displayed amnesia for their alter personalities after termination of the hypnotic interview. The participants maintained their role successfully in a second session by exhibiting marked and consistent differences between their primary and secondary personalities on a variety of psychological tests.

Gleaves (1996) responded to findings such as this by arguing that while they raise interesting questions about the capacities and workings of the human mind, they do not indicate that DID is necessarily created within the therapy session. According to Gleaves, these analogue studies produced phenomena that were only superficially similar to DID. Participants did not experience any of the established features of DID, such as episodes of time loss, depersonalization or derealization, or hearing voices, in any of these studies. According to Gleaves, just because some people can replicate some of the symptoms of DID does not invalidate the concept: a person may replicate depression, anxiety and so on, without challenging the reality of the condition.

Further evidence countering the role of the therapist in developing a diagnosis of DID can be found from studies showing significant evidence of DID pathology prior to any therapist contact. Coons et al. (1988), for example, reported that amnesia (a core symptom of DID) was present in all 50 of their sample of people with DID at the time of their first presentation to the mental health system. Gleaves (1996) also reported evidence of symptoms including journals in differing handwriting or memories of dissociative experiences going back to childhood. Some of this evidence could be verified by family members and friends. By contrast, Piper and Merskey (2004) noted that relatives of people with DID have usually not seen evidence of multiple identities before treatment.

Motivation, legitimation and DID Spanos (1994) argued that people may seek or collude with a diagnosis of DID as a means of gaining the support of their therapist and others. He suggested that the idea of being a multiple may provide some people with a viable and face-saving way to account for personal problems as well as a dramatic means of gaining concern and attention from significant others. Spanos suggested that people who seek help and are diagnosed with DID are often unhappy and insecure people with a strong investment in gaining the interest and approval of their therapist. By contrast, therapists are highly valued by their clients and their suggestions are treated seriously. This combination of therapists 'on the look-out' for signs of DID and clients wanting to create a good impression with their, valued, therapist may result in a gradual shaping of responses to fit those of DID. Spanos (1994) did not claim that people with DID are necessarily faking their multiplicity.

Rather, they have come to adopt a view of themselves that is congruent with the view conveyed to them by their therapist, to adopt and believe in their presentation as someone with multiple alters.

The wider social environment may also be supportive of their diagnosis. Spanos argued that support for DID has almost taken on the characteristics of a social movement. People with DID and therapists participate regularly in workshops and conferences, and both those affected and their therapists frequently have access to national newsletters that provide ongoing legitimization for the multiple-self enactments. All this may reinforce the presentation of self as someone with multiple alters. Gleaves (1996) contended that this is not always the case, and that therapy is not always easy for patients with DID. Many people with the symptoms of DID experience hostile reactions from professionals and public alike. Many are told they are lying or faking, or even that their therapist is crazy.

Gleaves noted that some protagonists have suggested that some people with DID are seeking attention. By contrast, he contended that many are actually secretive about their condition and conceal their disorder for fear of being labelled crazy and typically have an avoidant style that inhibits disclosure of their abuse histories (Kluft 1994). This speculation was supported by Fink and Golinkoff (1990), who found that people with DID evidenced relatively low levels of histrionic behaviours and emotional lability, and were more intellectualized, obsessive and introvert than a comparison group of people without the disorder. However, while this may indicate a general unwillingness to portray themselves to the general public as DID sufferers, it does not counter the argument that expression of multiple personalities develops over time as a result of therapist–client interactions.

DID and child abuse   Findings that people with DID report extremely high rates of childhood sexual or physical abuse (e.g. Ross et al. 1991) has led some theorists to suggest that dissociation as a result of repeated sexual abuse is almost a defining characteristic of DID. In response to this, Spanos (1994) argued that the apparently high level of association between child sexual abuse and the phenomenon of DID may both be spurious and the result of therapist and client beliefs about the nature of the phenomenon. He suggested that:

- Child sexual abuse is relatively common in the USA, and rates are particularly high among those who seek psychiatric help. High rates among people who develop DID may therefore be indicative of these high background rates rather than indicative of risk for DID.

- Because some clinicians consider a history of sexual abuse to be a possible sign of DID, they may be more likely to expose abused than non-abused patients to hypnotic interviews and other procedures that result in 'multiplicity'.

- Some patients with DID do not remember being abused until their multiplicity is discovered in the course of therapy. Any recovered memories should be treated with some caution (see above).

- Therapists may disbelieve DID patients who claim not to have been abused and may be probed repeatedly in an attempt to unearth such memories. When patients believe they may be fantasizing, their uncertainty may be presented to them as evidence that they are unwilling to face the fact of their abuse (Bliss 1986).

- Many patients with DID report not just sexual abuse but also that this was ritualistic and long-term. These histories are usually identified following a series of leading questions under hypnotic suggestion, and none have been found to be substantiated.

- Some of the data related to abuse are not in accordance with data on memory recall and typical patterns of abuse. Ross et al. (1991) reported on the age of earliest sexual abuse reported by their patient group. Over a quarter reported being abused before the age of 3 years, and 10 per cent reported being abused before the age of 1 year. These ages are much younger than is typical in cases of sexual abuse (see Chapter 10) and prior to the establishment of neural substrates that permit long-term recall (see p. 247).

Experimental evidence

Although not addressed in the debate between Gleaves and Spanos, a key issue in the medical explanation of DID is that memories remain 'locked' within certain alters and do not leak out into other states. Thus some alters, at least, are protected against memories of traumatic events – and in adulthood, memories of events that occur are thought to remain within the memory system of the alter that experiences them, and not spread into other memory systems. This phenomenon could provide a test of the DID diagnosis, as it allows experimental testing with clear hypotheses. In one study of this issue, Elzinga et al. (2003) assessed both implicit and explicit memory performance in 12 people with DID. In their study, they presented participants with 96 words, half of which had a threatening or sexual connotation; half of which were neutral. Participants were instructed after each presentation to either remember or forget the presented word, as forgetting them would aid their recall of the other words in a subsequent memory test. They then completed an interference task, following which they were instructed to change state. All participants reported they achieved this change, and the new state (alter) reported that they had no conscious recall of the words they had previously been exposed to. They then took part in an implicit memory test in which 48 words were flashed 'briefly' on a computer screen followed by a mask of letters for one second. They were then asked to guess what word had been presented. Following a second interference task, participants were then presented with the stems of the previously presented words and asked to complete them. Finally, participants were asked to switch back to their original state and this sequence of testing was repeated. Their findings indicated a significant reduction of explicit memory between states. Participants were more likely to recall words they had been asked to recall when in the same state than when in a different state from the state in which they were presented with the words. However, the second alter still remembered significant numbers of words. Levels of recall of emotional to-be-remembered words, for example, were 36 per cent in the same state and 21 per cent in the second state. In addition, there was no evidence of any differences across states on their measure of implicit memory. These data, although not involving childhood trauma, show some transfer of information between states, and potentially counter the argument of a compartmentalized memory, with each memory system specific to different personalities.

To add to the difficulties of interpreting these type of data, Huntjens et al. (2005) examined memory between people with DID, 25 controls, and 25 people asked to simulate DID. As expected, the people with DID showed evidence of inter-identity amnesia, and more so than the 'normal' controls. However, controls asked to simulate amnesia performed as badly as people with a diagnosis of DID. On this basis, they argued that such studies cannot provide evidence for, or against, inter-state amnesia. With these and similar results in mind, Merckelbach, Devilly and Rassin came to similar conclusions, arguing that studies of alters are open to multiple interpretations, and 'in no way refute an interpretation of alters in terms of metaphors for different emotional states' (2002: 481).

Treatment of dissociative identity disorder

Not surprisingly, both Spanos (1994) and Gleaves (1996) disagreed over the treatment of DID. Spanos contended that the goal of treatment is to help clients accept that their alter identities are real personalities rather than self-generated fantasies. Gleaves contended that the opposite is true. He argued that the central goal of treatment should be to help the individual understand that the alters are in fact self-generated, not to convince them that they are real people. He argued that therapists working with people with DID should emphasize the fundamental nature of the disorder as a difficulty in integrating various aspects of the personality rather than a profusion of personalities (Fraser 1992).

Even among therapists who accept the reality of the multiple selves, the goals of therapy differ. Some (e.g. Spiegel 1993) suggest the goal of therapy is to move the individual towards a sense of integrated functioning. This can be achieved by:

- recalling repressed memories
- detraumatizing these memories so that recall does not result in reversion to other alters
- integrating the alters and primary personality.

Techniques such as psychodynamic therapy and hypnosis have been used to help individuals recover memories from the past (e.g. Kluft 1999). These approaches have to be used with care because the individual may revert to another alter when exposed to traumatic memories. In addition, some alters may take on a 'protective' role and attempt to protect the primary personality from suffering the pain of recalling traumatic experiences by, for example, becoming self-destructive or aggressive (see Kelly 1993).

Once memories have been recovered or recalled, they can be detraumatized using exposure techniques similar to those used in the treatment of PTSD. Because the reaction of someone with DID is to avoid recall of memories, this type of exposure work is difficult, and the traumatic nature of the memories may usefully be minimized at any one time. Advocates of EMDR suggest that this may form a useful intervention when used in combination with relaxation techniques, as this technique is thought to assist the person recall memories without the full-blown emotional effects (but see the cautionary results in relation to PTSD).

For most therapists, the ultimate goal of therapy is to integrate the various alters into one cohesive personality, a process known as fusion. In this state, the person is aware of all their behaviours and thoughts and accepts them as their own. Oke and Kanigsberg (1991) used a combination of play, guided imagery, life skills teaching, projective techniques and group therapy to help bring awareness and understanding of other selves, and through this eventually achieve cohesion between all alters. Unfortunately, the effectiveness of this and similar types of intervention is limited to descriptions of interventions with no outcome data or case reports, which by their very nature tend to be positive (few therapists like to broadcast their failures widely, and most journals are biased against publishing 'negative results'). Their efficacy or otherwise has yet to be fully investigated. Fifteen years on from this early study, interventions to treat DID are usually reported as case studies. Kellett (2005), for example, found the use of cognitive analytic therapy (see Chapter 3) to be effective in the treatment of one case.

A fundamental cautionary note about such efforts has come from people with DID themselves. Many sub-personalities reject integration as a therapeutic goal, as they see integration as a form of death (Spiegel 1999). In support of this stance, Rossel (1998) argued that in a disintegrating postmodern world, it is of little benefit to attempt to achieve integration. Instead, the individual should be open to the experience of shifting between alters, which should be construed as a positive and comfortable experience, not a negative, destructive one.

Chapter summary

1 PTSD has three central symptoms: (1) intrusive memories; (2) attempts at avoidance of these memories; and (3) high levels of arousal.

2 The neurological substrates of PTSD are the amygdala and hippocampus that together mediate fear and memory, and link the two together. High arousal is mediated by the sympathetic nervous system.

3 The conditioning model of PTSD provides a partial explanation of the phenomenon, but cognitive models such as that of Brewin provide a more in-depth understanding.

4 Clinical incident debriefing is often provided at traumatic incidents. Evidence is mounting that this may actually inhibit long-term recovery from psychological trauma.

5 Exposure methods may prove the best intervention for PTSD, particularly when combined with strategies to help clients cope with any emotional distress triggered by the therapeutic process.

6 EMDR appears to be of no more benefit than exposure methods.

7   Since the 1980s, an increasing number of people have begun to report recovered memories of trauma, usually sexual trauma, experienced in childhood.

8   Three explanations have been proposed to account for this phenomenon: (1) the memories are real and have been hidden as a result of a number of unconscious self-protective mechanisms; (2) they are the result of therapists shaping clients' apparent recall of past events that did not in reality occur; and (3) they are incidents forgotten as a result of normal forgetting processes.

9   Arguments about which of these explanations are correct have focused on a number of issues: the age at the time of the incident, distortions in memory over time, mixed levels of corroboration of events, and experimental evocation of false memories.

10   Brewin and others have suggested that while some memories may be false, others may be truly repressed and recovered. Each case should be considered on its own merits.

11   The clinical model suggests that DID is a response to repeated childhood sexual trauma involving severe dissociation at the time of the trauma, resulting in the development of 'alters' or alternative personalities.

12   The socio-cognitive model suggests this is a response to therapist and social pressure to behave in a way that suggests multiple personalities.

13   Debate about which of these models is the better has focused on differing explanations of the prevalence of the disorder, whether therapists can 'teach multiplicity', social and therapist pressures to present with DID, and the relationship between childhood abuse and DID.

14   While some cases of DID may be created by the process of therapy, others may represent a 'real' clinical condition. Each case should be considered on its own merits.

For discussion

1   How should we treat people following a major trauma?
2   What factors may contribute to the development of PTSD?
3   Is there such a thing as 'recovered memory'?
4   What are the causes of DID?

Further reading

Brewin, C.R. and Holmes, E.A. (2003) Psychological theories of posttraumatic stress disorder, *Clinical Psychology Review*, 23: 339–76.

Gleaves, D.H. (1996) The sociocognitive model of dissociative identity disorder: a reexamination of the evidence, *Psychological Bulletin*, 120: 42–59.

Gleaves, D.H., May, M.C. and Cardena, E. (2001) An examination of the diagnostic validity of dissociative identity disorder, *Clinical Psychology Review*, 21: 577–608.

Piper, A. and Merskey, H. (2004) The persistence of folly: a critical examination of dissociative identity disorder. Part I. The excesses of an improbable concept, *Canadian Journal of Psychiatry*, 49: 592–600.

Spanos, N.P. (1994) Multiple identity enactments and multiple personality disorder: a socio-cognitive perspective, *Psychological Bulletin*, 116: 143–65.

10

Sexual disorders

There are two categories of sexual disorders: *sexual dysfunctions*, which involve a problem in sexual response, and *paraphilias*, which involve repeated and intense sexual urges, behaviour or fantasies in response to objects or situations that society deems inappropriate. This chapter examines both types of problems. It considers problems that some people experience during the sexual act, focusing on the male problem of failing to achieve an erection and its female 'equivalent', known as vaginismus, and considers how these may be treated. It then describes the aetiology and treatment of paedophilia and transvestism. Finally, the chapter considers the problems faced when an individual questions their very sexual identity and wishes to change it: gender identity disorder. By the end of the chapter, you should have an understanding of:

*   The nature and aetiology of erectile dysfunction, vaginismus, paedophilia, transvestism and gender identity disorder
*   The types of interventions used to treat each disorder, and their relative effectiveness.

Sexual dysfunctions

The sexual dysfunctions are those that involve a problem with the sexual response. They include disorders of desire, such as an aversion to sexual activity and low sexual drive, problems of orgasm including premature ejaculation in men and a failure to achieve orgasm in both men and women. Here, two conditions are considered: erectile dysfunction in men, and a condition known as vaginismus in women. Both problems markedly interfere with, or may prevent, the sexual act. Both are treatable using relatively simple behavioural and pharmacological interventions.

Erectile dysfunction

A DSM-IV-TR diagnosis of erectile failure requires persistent or recurrent inability to gain or maintain an adequate erection until completion of sexual activity, which results in marked distress or interpersonal difficulties. It is a fairly common disorder, particularly among older men, although younger men are not immune. Laumann et al. (1999) reported a 7 per cent prevalence among men aged 18–29. The prevalence rate was 9 per cent for men aged 30–39, 11 per cent for those aged 40– 49 and 18 per cent for those aged 50–59. Some of the causes of erectile dysfunction are physical, including high blood pressure, and the long-term effects of drugs such as alcohol, heroin, marijuana and cigarettes. However, Masters and Johnson (1970) found a relevant physical condition in only 7 out of 213 men they assessed; the most common causes of the problem are psychological. These may be immediate or remote:

- *immediate:* performance anxiety, lack of adequate stimulation, relationship conflicts, lack of partner intimacy, poor partner communication
- *remote:* childhood sexual trauma, unresolved partner or parental attachments, sexual identity or orientation issues.

Aetiology of erectile dysfunction

Psychodynamic explanations
According to Janssen (1985), erectile failure results from an oedipal conflict constellation involving fear of castration or incest, uncertainties in sexual identity, incestuous object choices, latent homosexual tendencies and fear of aggressive-phallic impulses. These may develop as a result of factors that inhibit appropriate passage through the oedipal stage of psychosexual development (see Chapter 2). In a case example, Janssen described one man who reported that as a child his mother had turned to him to discuss matters relating to her relationship with his father. When his father became aware of this, he became angry and abused his mother. The client feared that he too would become the focus of his father's wrath and experienced a conflict in wanting to defend his mother, but to avoid confrontation with his father. This prevented his successful resolution of the oedipal conflict. In adulthood, the fear of his aggressive father prevented him developing appropriate emotional and sexual relationships with women. Treatment involved dealing with his relationship with his father, not any explicit sexual function.

Cognitive explanations
In a more cognitive explanation, Bancroft (1999) argued that anxiety adversely affects sexual performance as a result of cognitive and perceptual factors. He suggested that men's sexual excitement depends on a delicate balance between excitatory and inhibitory mechanisms. Two key inhibitory processes are performance anxiety and fear of negative outcomes. Both may lead to a process coined by Masters and Johnson as *spectating* in which the individual becomes so concerned by the adequacy of their performance or the consequences of potential failure that they distract from sexually arousing cues, and lose their erection. Evidence in support of Bancroft's model can be found in a number of laboratory studies which have shown performance demand to increase sexual arousal in most men, but to have the opposite effect on those with erectile dysfunction. In addition, the presence of non-sexual stimuli is more disruptive to men with the disorder than those without (Cranston-Cuebas and Barlow 1990).

Many men set themselves inappropriately high levels of performance to which they aspire. Zilbergeld (1992), for example, noted that men frequently buy into the fantasy that their performance is the 'cornerstone' of every sexual experience and that a firm erection is the key element of every sexual encounter: views not necessarily subscribed to by their female partners. According to Zilbergeld, a failure to achieve this ideal results in fears of dysfunction, loss of masculinity, and declining interest in their partner.

Treatment of erectile dysfunction

Anxiety reduction and desensitization

The classic treatment programme for erectile failure, known as *sensate focusing*, was developed by Masters and Johnson (1970). It involves a structured approach, designed to take the stress out of the sexual act. It begins with the couple learning to touch each other in pleasurable ways, but with a mandate not to touch each other's genitals. Their goal is to enjoy the intimacy of touch, not to give or receive sexual pleasure. Once couples are comfortable with non-genital sensate focusing, they are directed to gradually make genital contact and to give and receive pleasure doing so. At this time, they are still mandated not to attempt intercourse, nor for the male to try to achieve or maintain an erection (although this typically occurs). Finally, when the couple are comfortable with this level of intimacy, they may progress to full inter-course. This is a frequently applied intervention; although there are relatively few studies of its effectiveness, it is generally considered to be highly effective (Hawton et al. 1986).

Cognitive techniques

There are relatively few formal assessments of cognitive interventions in the treatment of erectile failure, although Goldman and Carroll (1990) reported the outcomes of a number of workshops in which participants were given appropriate sexual information and inappropriate cognitive concerns were challenged. Participants showed signifi-cant changes in knowledge and attitudes towards sex, and reported increased sexual frequency and satisfaction in the short term; no long-term data were reported.

Interpersonal interventions

Hawton et al. (1992) reported that the most important predictor of outcome follow-ing a programme of sensate focusing and graduated stimulation techniques was the couples' ratings of marital communication before treatment. Three domains are the main foci of interpersonal interventions (Rosen 2001):

- status and dominance issues
- intimacy and trust
- loss of sexual attraction.

Each of these may be more or less salient in the lifetime of a sexual relationship. Status and dominance issues may be salient when one partner loses a job or achieves promotion; intimacy or trust issues may be salient following an affair, while loss of sexual attraction may follow weight gain or some other physical or psychological changes. Following an intervention addressing these factors, Hawton and colleagues reported that 70 per cent of couples reported a positive outcome.

Medical approaches

Perhaps the best-known pharmacological treatment for erectile failure is sildenafil, more popularly known as Viagra. This works on the smooth muscle of the penis. It is an inhibitor of the enzyme phosphodiesterase type 5 (PDE5) which normally breaks down cyclic guanosine monophosphate (cGMP), a chemical that brings about smooth muscle relaxation, and maintains the erectile response. It is generally effective in treating erectile dysfunction, whatever the cause. Goldstein et al. (1998), for example, reported that 70 per cent of men treated with Viagra reported improvements in the quality and frequency of erections; 70 per cent of attempts at intercourse were successful, in comparison with 22 per cent of attempts by those treated with placebo. PDE5 is predominantly found in the penis. However, it is also found in other areas of the body. As a consequence, about 16 per cent of users experience headaches, 10 per cent experience facial flushing, with other effects such as gastrointestinal upset and alterations in colour vision being somewhat rarer. One of the more dramatic side-effects was thought to be the onset of a heart attack, but this is now thought to be a result of exercise, not the drug (Holmes 2000). One of the benefits of Viagra is that it enhances the sexual response rather than initiates it. Erection therefore follows sexual stimulation, and does not immediately follow taking the drug, as is the case in some alternatives. Erection may also be achieved by vacuum pumps, direct injection of drugs into the penis and the use of prostheses. Each method has achieved some success, and many continue to be used, but less so in the light of the development of Viagra and similar drugs (Ralph and McNicholas 2000).

Vaginismus

Vaginismus is the recurrent or persistent involuntary spasm of the musculature of the outer third of the vagina that prevents sexual intercourse. It can cause considerable distress or interpersonal difficulties. It is thought to be one of the most common of the female psychosexual dysfunctions, although its exact prevalence rate among the general population is unknown. About 20 per cent of women experience occasional pain during intercourse, but less than 1 per cent are thought to have vaginismus (Heiman and LoPiccolo 1988).

Aetiology of vaginismus

Psychoanalytic explanations

Classic psychoanalytic theory considers vaginismus to result from unresolved psychosexual conflicts in early childhood. Women with the condition have been characterized as fixated or regressed to the pre-oedipal or oedipal stages. According to Abraham (1956), in less severe cases, women are not able to transfer their libidinal energy from their father to their husband/partner. In more severe cases, women remain fixated on their mothers, and have a poor prognosis.

Behavioural explanations

According to behavioural theory, vaginismus is a phobic reaction to actual or imagined negative experiences related to penetration. Fear or anxiety concerning penetration results in high levels of sympathetic nervous system activity, one of the results of which is involuntary vaginal muscle spasm. These fears may, in part, arise from ignorance of sexual issues. Three other factors may increase the fear reaction (Ward and Ogden 1994). First, a mother who is frightened of intercourse may pass a fear of pain to her daughter. Second, the experience of sex may be painful for the affected woman, and memories of pain trigger the symptoms: nearly three-quarters of women with vaginismus in Ward and Ogden's sample reported this type of fear. The third issue involves a fear of punishment related to sexual guilt. Ward and Ogden found that many women with vaginismus experienced sexual guilt, stemming from a belief that 'sex is wrong', which led to a fear of punishment for engaging sexual acts. Childhood sexual trauma and a background of religious orthodoxy may also contribute to the conditioning of fear or guilt in relation to intercourse.

Treatment of vaginismus

Psychological approaches

One way of reducing anxiety associated with the sexual act is through the use of sensate focus techniques, with a gradual progression to genital touching. However, the most common treatment of vaginismus involves systematic desensitization together with the use of graded dilators. This may be conducted in combination with education, homework assignments and cognitive or relaxation therapy. In this procedure, the woman, and in some cases a physician, inserts dilators of gradually increasing size into the vagina until the woman is relaxed and the involuntary spasm is not triggered by the entry of an object into the vagina. When she is able to accommodate a fairly large dilator, the woman may be encouraged to keep it in place for several hours every night. This type of approach has proven very effective. Masters and Johnson (1970), who pioneered this approach, reported complete success with no relapse in the treatment of 29 women with this condition.

The paraphilias

Defining which of the various forms of sexual activity is 'normal' and 'abnormal' is not unproblematic. However, a number of sexual behaviours are generally considered to be 'abnormal'. These are referred to as the paraphilias, which include behaviours that are legal, such as fetishism and transvestism, and some that are illegal, in particular, paedophilia (see Table 10.1).

Many people who engage in paraphilic behaviour do not experience distress as a result, nor do they seek help to change the nature of their sexual interest. As a consequence, people who engage in unusual sexual behaviour may be considered as at the

Table 10.1 Some of the more prevalent paraphilias

Fetishism	Recurrent intense sexual urges, sexually arousing fantasies or behaviours that involve the use of non-living objects, often to the exclusion of all other stimuli; common fetishes are to women's underwear, boots and shoes
Exhibitionism	Recurrent urges to expose the genitals to another person of the opposite sex – often while having sexually arousing fantasies
Voyeurism	Recurrent and intense urges to secretly observe unsuspecting people as they undress or have intercourse
Sadomasochism	Sexual stimulation through the act of being humiliated, beaten, bound or otherwise made to suffer, or being the one to inflict such acts
Frotteurism	Repeated and intense sexual urges to touch and rub against non-consenting others

edge of the distribution of sexual interests rather than disordered. With this in mind, DSM-III stated that any paraphilic behaviour had to result in distress on the part of the individual before a diagnosis of a 'disorder' be assigned. However, following strong criticism of this *laissez-faire* approach, DSM-IV stated that paedophilia was to be considered a disorder regardless of the perpetrator's emotional reaction to their behaviour. In its latest version, DSM-IV-TR states that exhibitionism, frotteurism, sexual sadism and voyeurism are also now to be considered 'disorders' if the person acts on their desires, even though their behaviour may not cause them any distress or 'impaired functioning'. The medicalization of sexual behaviours is increasing. Relatively few people receive a diagnosis of paraphilia, but the number of specialist websites and other services suggests that these behaviours are more prevalent than this would suggest.

Aetiological explanations have tried to identify common pathways to all the paraphilias. Accordingly, while the next sections consider the aetiology and treatment of paedophilia and transvestism in some detail, the general process by which these conditions develop could be applied to all the paraphilias.

Paedophilia

DSM-IV-TR defined paedophilia as 'recurrent intense sexual urges and sexually arousing fantasies involving sexual activity with a prepubescent child or children' and that the person has acted on these urges, or the sexual urges or fantasies cause marked distress or interpersonal difficulty. In addition, the person has to be at least 16 years old and at least 5 years older than the other child or children involved. Note the emphasis on the victim's sexual maturity, not age. Legal definitions lay clear boundaries as to the age at which consenting couples may have intercourse. Violation of these limits will result in an individual being termed a sex offender, but not a paedophile unless the other child is pre-pubescent.

Paedophilic behaviours vary. Some paedophilic individuals may look at and not touch a child. Others may want to touch or undress them. When sexual activity occurs, it often involves oral sex or touching the genitals of the child. In most cases, except incest, there is no penetration. Where sex is penetrative, it is usually with older children and may involve threats or force. More typically, however, paedophilic individuals depend on persuasion, guile and 'friendship' (Murray 2000). Paedophilic individuals who are attracted to females usually prefer 8–10-year-olds, while those attracted to boys prefer slightly older children (APA 1994). Most are relatives, friends or neighbours of the child. Greenberg et al. (1993) reported that 33 per cent of people who engaged in paedophile behaviour abused only boys, 44 per cent only girls, and 23 per cent abused both boys and girls.

Prevalence levels of paedophilia are extremely difficult to determine. Most surveys report the prevalence of people who have been sexually abused rather than the prevalence of perpetrators. Barbaree and Seto (1997), for example, calculated that at least 7 per cent of US females and 3 per cent of males have experienced some form of childhood sexual abuse, although some surveys suggest even higher prevalence rates.

Research box 10

Frei, A., Erenay, N., Dittmann, V. et al. (2005) Paedophilia on the internet – a study of 33 convicted offenders in the Canton of Lucerne, *Swiss Medical Weekly*, 135: 488–94.

The authors note that the Internet is now a means of quickly and easily obtaining child pornography, but that little is known about its users. The study took advantage of a Swiss police action involving 1300 inhabitants of Switzerland who were customers of an illegal American provider of child pornography on the Internet, 'Landslide Production Inc'. Users accessed child pornography by paying a monthly fee of $29.95. To do so, they had to provide their name, address and credit card number. In August 2001, the Swiss Federal Police started a nationwide inquiry, named 'Genesis', and were able to identify the Swiss users of this website. The aim of their study was to examine the characteristics of these users.

Method

The Genesis investigation revealed that 38 people from Lucerne had used Landslide Production Inc. Thirty-five files were accessed by the researchers, who examined:

- *sociodemographic variables:* age, origin, home, profession, marital status and number of children
- *criminological variables:* motive, prior convictions, insight concerning illegality and legal consequences
- *psychosexual variables:* the kind of sexual activity depicted
- *time spent on illegal activities.*

Findings

All offenders were male. Their mean age was 39.8 years (range 25–69 years). A summary of other characteristics is reported in Table 10.2.

Table 10.2 Summary of characteristics of Swiss Internet paedophiles

Profession	%	Children	%	Marital status	%	Motive	%
Academic/ supervisor	33	Adult children	9	Divorced, separated or widowed without intimate partner	12	Boredom	9
Blue-collar worker	12	Infant	3	Girlfriend	3	Coincidence	9
Employee	39	No children	60	Married	27	Curiosity	51
Self-employed	12	One child	6	Unmarried without known intimate partner ever	33	Fascination	3
Unemployed	3	2–3 children	21	Unmarried or divorced, living in common-law marriage	24	Indulging in violence	3
						Investigation	15
						Sexual	6
						Unclear	3

There was little evidence of any prior psychiatric treatment in the files. One offender committed suicide. The house search of one offender revealed that, as a pool attendant, he had installed a video recorder in the women's changing rooms of the public swimming bath where he worked and had taken pictures of the women while they were changing. Another offender had used a video camera to peep under the skirts of women in public places. The estimated range of time spent downloading and looking at pornography varied between 1 and 1320 hours. In 19 cases, the time spent was less than 100 hours. Only seven of the offenders admitted they had masturbated while watching the pictures, but they did not say which ones. The percentage use of differing levels of pornography was: erotica (surreptitiously taken photographs of children in play areas or other safe environments showing underwear or some level of nudity), 9 per cent; erotic posing, 3 per cent; explicit sexual activity, 3 per cent; gross assault (sex with an adult), 45 per cent; and sadistic/bestiality, 27 per cent.

Discussion

These data are shocking in that many of those involved are 'people like us'. They have families, hold down responsible jobs, and so on. Despite having paid to access the websites, and apparently for long periods of time, it is noteworthy that the reasons for accessing it frequently implied an accidental or relatively disinterested reason for doing so. Fifty-one per cent of those involved claimed to have accessed the site as a result of 'curiosity'. Nine per cent implied that they did not really mean to access the site at all. This fits with the use of cognitive distortion and self-justification of such behaviour discussed in the chapter.

Aetiology of paedophilia

Theories of the aetiology of paedophilia are limited and focus more on social and psychological factors than on biological ones. These split into long-term background factors and proximal factors that form more immediate triggers to such behaviour.

Long-term risk factors

Many child sex offenders report that their early parent–child relationships were disruptive and/or that they have experienced childhood sexual abuse: up to 67 per cent of respondents in one survey (Hanson and Slater 1988). Similarly, in a matched comparison between male paedophile and 'healthy' individuals, Cohen et al. (2002) found that 60 per cent of paedophiles reported experiencing adult sexual advances as a child. This compared with 4 per cent of the comparison group. These data are extremely difficult to validate. Many people who engage in paedophilic behaviour have a vested interest in reporting such events as a way of minimizing their own responsibility for their actions or gaining the sympathy of others. Attempts at validation by asking the alleged perpetrators are equally likely to result in misreporting. In an attempt to minimize these problems, Dhawan and Marshall (1996) used detailed interviews and questionnaire methods to try to corroborate or challenge any misreporting. They concluded that 50 per cent of imprisoned people who engaged in paedophile activities had been sexually abused as children. What this, of course, does not explain is why such episodes predict later sexual offences. If these incidents were particularly traumatic, one might expect a rejection of sexual relationships with children in order not to repeat the trauma.

Behavioural theories (e.g. Barbaree 1990) suggest that child offenders develop a strong sexual attraction to children following pairings of sexual arousal and images of children. These associations typically occur in early adolescence, and may initially be accidental. However, they may be strengthened by masturbation to images of children and the use of pornography. In a partial test of this model, Barbaree and Marshall (1989) measured the sexual response to pictures of female children and mature women among men who had either sexually abused children not in their family, committed incest, or claimed to have no sexual interest in children. Their findings were somewhat surprising. Less than half of the non-familial offenders and only 28 per cent of those who had committed incest were more sexually stimulated by pictures of young women than those of mature women. In addition, 15 per cent of men who reported no sexual interest in children were more sexually aroused by pictures of children than of mature women. While the conditioning model may hold for some individuals, it does not hold for all.

These data indicate that sexual interest is not the only factor that influences the sexual choices of paedophilic men. Another important factor may be a failure to develop satisfying psychological and sexual relationships with adults. Many people who engage in paedophile behaviour report high levels of loneliness, perhaps arising from inadequate attachment styles developed as children (Ward et al. 1996). As a result, some seek out intimacy with children, with whom they find it easier to instigate both a physical and non-physical relationship, and who are easier to control. However, this is certainly not the case for all those who engage in paedophile behaviour, emphasizing that the route to paraphilias differs widely between individuals. Nevertheless, Finkelhor's (1984) 'preconditions theory' of paedophilia identified these factors as key to the condition. He suggested that paedophilia is the result of four factors:

- Sex with children is emotionally satisfying.
- Sex with children is sexually satisfying.
- An inability to meet sexual needs in a more socially appropriate manner.
- Disinhibited behaviour at times of stress (see below).

Proximal factors
Pithers (1990) added to these background factors by examining the more immediate antecedents to any sexual offence. He suggested that the desire to engage in paedophile behaviour is frequently triggered by low mood as a result of stress or conflict. As a result, individuals seek some way of decreasing these negative feelings, and allow themselves to enter a high-risk situation. This may appear the result of seemingly irrelevant decisions that place them in increasing proximity to potential victims. Once in this situation, they are overwhelmed by the potentially powerfully rewarding feelings associated with paedophile acts. They focus on these rather than the long-term negative outcomes to the situation, and as a result engage in some form of paedophile behaviour. Once the immediate 'rush' has receded, they may once more experience remorse, but feel out of control of their behaviour, a negative mood state that may trigger the cycle again.

Up to two-thirds of those imprisoned for sexual offences either deny or minimize their own role in the offence. Barbaree (1991) identified three types of denial:

- complete denial that anything took place
- admission of sexual relations, but denial that it was an offence
- admission of physical contact but denial of any sexual elements.

He also noted three types of minimization, involving denial of harm to the victim, the extent of previous offences, and responsibility for offences. Common cognitive distortions are that children are as interested in sex as adults, that they seek out sex with adults, and that they enjoy and benefit from the experience. Some of these may be truly believed by the individual. Others may be deliberate falsification, to minimize negative reactions from others (see Box 10.1). Implicit tests of attitudes are, perhaps, more revealing. In one study of this, using the implicit association test, Mihailides et al. (2004) found that child sex offenders were more likely to implicitly endorse 'children as sexual beings', 'uncontrollability of sexuality' and 'sexual entitlement-bias' beliefs than other types of offender and non-offenders.

Box 10.1 Differing paedophile behaviours

Not all people who engage in paedophile acts have the same motivation and act in the same way. Here are two contrasting cases, with very different outcomes.

John

John was a 30-year-old man, admitted to hospital as a result of a period of severe depression. Prior to his depression he had been a teacher in a school in the north of England. Although there was no evidence that he had engaged in paedophile acts with any children, his name was found on a distribution list for child pornography kept by a paedophile ring. His house was raided and paedophile materials were found in it. He was therefore charged by the police, and found guilty of using child pornography. The school at which he worked was notified of this outcome and he was immediately dismissed from his job.

He was married at the time that this occurred, but was immediately asked to leave the marital home and his wife began divorce proceedings. He moved to London, where he could be 'lost among the crowd' and had some family contacts. There he became profoundly depressed, and was admitted to hospital where he entered into therapy for his depression. After he began to trust his therapist, he started to tell his story.

He admitted to the use of child pornography for sexual pleasure, and that he was particularly turned on by pictures of young boys. His marriage had been functional and pleasant, but not sexually satisfying. He had had a number of age-appropriate homosexual relationships prior to his marriage, but these had generally ended disastrously. He was aware that his sexual interest was inappropriate and felt ashamed by it. He did not try to condone his behaviour, but thought that while he had no physical contact with young boys, even using photographs in this way was exploitative and morally unacceptable. His depression was a consequence of the loss of his job and his marriage, the probability that he would never find work again, and the shame he felt as his behaviour had been made public. He lived alone and avoided company other than his immediate family. He left his flat only rarely, and deliberately avoided places where children might congregate.

Because he found his sexual interests inappropriate and shaming, he was motivated to engage in therapy. He began a programme of masturbatory reorientation. In this, he began to masturbate to images of young children to achieve sexual excitement, before shifting the focus of his images to those of more mature boys or young-looking men. He found the image of one young-looking male Hollywood star (who will remain nameless!) particularly exciting. This programme worked very well, and he found that he could become sexually excited by the images of age-appropriate men.

Despite these gains and the claims he made about only using child pornography, his behaviour followed the pattern suggested by Pithers (1990) on at least one occasion. At this time he was feeling depressed, and decided to go for a walk, which drew him 'accidentally' to a shopping area frequented by local schoolchildren, and 'he happened to pass by a [public] toilet' when a young boy walked into it. At this point, he was excited by the thought of seeing the young child expose himself, and followed him into the toilet. There, he watched him use the urinal. The child was unaware of his presence, and there was no social or physical contact with him. Nevertheless, the incident highlighted the need to set up a relapse prevention programme, in which he drew up a list of alternative behaviours to do when he felt depressed or the need for sexual excitement. The alternative behaviours he engaged in were fairly limited, and included calling his family on the telephone or visiting them, and focusing on chores or tasks about the house. The one thing that he determined not to do was to leave the house, to walk randomly about, as this inevitably would lead to his 'accidentally' walking into high-risk areas. Both interventions progressed well after this point, and he was eventually discharged.

Stephen

By contrast, Stephen was more manipulative in his behaviour. He was a man in his late fifties, already living in London at the time of his offences. His history was one of befriending single mothers with adolescent daughters. After a (short) period of time, he had typically moved in with these women, and encouraged their daughter to join them in bed in the morning, so 'they could be a proper family'. When this was an established habit and the woman was not present, he had succeeded in having sexual intercourse with at least two of these girls. He came into therapy a few months before he was due in court. It quickly became clear that he considered his behaviour to be acceptable and justified. He told his therapist that he considered he was helping these girls in their sexual journey, 'because it was better that a sexually experienced man bring them into the sexual world rather than some spotty adolescent who would fumble around and not know what he was doing'. He stayed in therapy for a few sessions, all the time claiming that his behaviour was justified, and then stopped attending immediately before his attendance in court. He did not attend court, and could no longer be found at his flat.

Treatment of paedophilia

Social constraints

One way in which society has dealt with issues of paedophilia has been to try to control – not treat – the actions of paedophiles. A number of laws have been instituted to facilitate this process in the UK, including:

- *The Sex Offenders Act 1997:* lists all people convicted of acts 'of a sexual nature involving an abuse of power, where the victim is unable to give informed or true consent'. It covers a range of offences, including rape, incest, child abuse and indecent assault. Offenders have to register with the police and notify them of any changes in their name and address. People who do not register can be imprisoned or receive a £5000 fine. People stay on the register for differing times, depending on the nature of their conviction. People who receive a non-custodial sentence or caution stay on the list for five years: those given sentences of 30 months or over stay on indefinitely.

- *Crime Sentence Act 1997:* allows for sex offenders who are convicted of a second serious sex offence to be automatically given a life sentence.
- *Crime and Disorder Act 1998:* gives police extra powers against sex offenders, allowing them to apply for a 'Sex Offenders Order' for any offender who can reasonably be considered a public risk. Courts can impose conditions on offenders, such as banning them from places where children are likely to come together, such as parks and schools.

Thinking about . . .

In some states in the USA, a law unofficially called Megan's Law provides information about the presence of a child sex offender in the neighbourhood. This may involve the individual involved telling his neighbours that he is a paedophile and leaving a notice in their window with this information on. This does not happen in the UK at present, although schools or youth clubs can be made aware of the presence of a convicted offender by the police. Where names have been publicized, for example, through a series of photographs in the *News of the World* newspaper, the high publicity given to these issues apparently led to a number of attacks on people suspected of being paedophiles. In one instance, in South Wales, the house of a doctor who worked with children – a paediatrician – was mistakenly attacked. Clearly, there are a number of issues raised by these facts:

- How do we ensure that the risk of paedophiles accessing and assaulting children is minimized?
- How to we counter the need to ensure the safety of children with the physical safety and rights of people who may or may not have committed paedophile acts?

Where do *you* stand on these issues?

Treatment programmes

As sexual activity with young persons is against the law, treatment is usually initiated in a prison or a secure forensic facility. Even here, engagement in treatment programmes is not compulsory, and only about 25 per cent of those offered treatment choose to engage in treatment programmes.

Physical treatments

Physical treatments suppress sexual urges and behaviour, but do not change the object of sexual desire. Two surgical procedures, castration and neurosurgery, are no longer considered ethically acceptable. However, chemical approaches involving administration of drugs that block the production or action of androgens, hormones that influence the male sexual response, remain in use. These have achieved modest results. Berlin and Meinecke (1981), for example, followed 20 men treated with androgen-blocking drugs; 3 repeated their offences while taking medication, and relapse rates were high following cessation of therapy. A major problem for anti-androgen treatments is that between 30 and 100 per cent of the people prescribed these drugs do not take them

(Barbaree and Seto 1997). Many of those who stop taking them presumably do so because they want to re-offend, as they do not change any of the beliefs or attitudes that drive deviant sexual behaviours. In addition, the drugs have a number of side-effects, including weight gain and reducing the size of testes, which may discourage their use. Finally, these treatments are effective only in individuals with abnormally high testosterone levels. Most people who engage in paedophile acts do not have these levels of testosterone, so would not benefit from the treatment even if they were fully compliant with the therapy.

Behaviour therapy

Both aversion therapy and masturbatory reconditioning methods have been used in the treatment of paedophilia. In aversion therapy, an inappropriate sexual stimulus is paired with an aversive event such as mild electric shock or strong aversive odour. This process is thought to condition a negative emotional state to the presence of the sexual stimulus. Most studies show some reduction of arousal to stimuli of young children. However, this may not result in reductions in offences. Rice et al. (1991), for example, followed 136 non-familial child molesters, 50 of whom received aversion therapy, following their discharge from a maximum security prison. Over a period of about six years, 31 per cent were convicted of a new offence. Recidivism rates were no lower among those who received aversion therapy than those who did not.

Masturbatory reconditioning involves the individual initiating a sexual response through the use of their favoured sexual images. Once they have achieved an erection, they switch to more appropriate images, such as a naked woman or man. They continue to masturbate to orgasm, when they concentrate deeply on this image. This approach may be combined with a graded series of 'normal' images, from less to more typical of the desired sexual focus. This approach has a number of advantages over aversion therapy. First, it is less ethically challenging and more acceptable to potential recipients. Second, it does not involve laboratory equipment and can be practised between therapy sessions. Although there is little empirical evidence of its effects, it is considered to be moderately effective (Laws and Marshall 1991).

Relapse prevention

Relapse prevention involves teaching the individual to do the following:

- identify situations in which they are at high risk of offending behaviour
- get out of the risky situation
- consider lapses as something to be learned from
- identify factors that led to relapse and plan how these could be avoided in the future.

The relapse prevention programme described by Marques et al. (2000) is typical of its type. It involved an intensive in-patient programme conducted in a secure forensic hospital and a one-year support programme following discharge. Participants were given sexual education and taught general coping skills such as relaxation, stress and anger management, as well as social skills. More specific interventions included identifying the behaviours that preceded offending behaviour and addressing how these may be interrupted. It also dealt with issues of responsibility and minimization. Over a five-year follow-up, this intervention had a known re-offence rate of 10.8 per cent in contrast to the 13 per cent rate among those who did not receive the intervention – a modest, but significant difference. The programme was most successful with offenders who had male victims, and less successful with those who had female victims, although why is not clear.

The effectiveness of therapy

Measuring the outcome of offender programmes is difficult. Self-report change must be treated with caution, and data on relapse are usually obtained from official records, which can measure only re-offending of which society is aware. Convincing research on the outcome of treatment programmes is therefore lacking. Despite this, Hall (1995) reported a meta-analysis on the effectiveness of a variety of interventions. Of note is that many people were excluded from both types of interventions for a number of reasons, including an extensive offence history, denial of offences, and behavioural disturbances while in prison. Overall, the most effective interventions were relapse prevention programme and hormonal therapy, with neither proving more effective than the other. Average known re-offence rates following taking part in relapse prevention programmes were 15 per cent over a period of three years, in comparison with an average rate of 35.5 per cent among those not involved in such programmes. With hormonal therapy, known re-offence rates were 22 per cent over an average of ten years: rates of those who received no intervention averaged 36 per cent. Hall (1995) noted that up to two-thirds of participants refused hormonal therapy, and 50 per cent of those who started then discontinued treatment. By contrast, only one-third of those offered relapse programmes either refused or dropped out of them. He took this to indicate that relapse prevention programmes may prove the treatment of choice. Summarizing these, and more recent data, in a meta-analysis, Kenworthy et al. (2004) concluded that there was good evidence that group cognitive behavioural therapy aimed at relapse prevention reduces one-year re-offence rates compared with standard care; psychoanalytic psychotherapy appeared to increase risk of recidivism.

Many offenders find discussion and disclosure of sexual abuse within therapy sessions are not easy. As a consequence, many people in therapy still avoid discussion of their behaviour – or attempt to downplay its significance (Frost 2004). In an attempt to engage more people in therapy, Marshall (1994) used a group approach to try to shift people from a state of denial or minimization to one where they accepted responsibility for their actions. The intervention comprised a series of group meetings, which participants entered as necessary and left when they had significantly improved. In it, they recounted their version of events that led to them being there, focusing on issues of blame and responsibility. Where there was evidence of denial or minimization, other group members were invited to challenge these interpretations, following which they retold their story taking account of these challenges and with less distortion. Marshall reported that those who went through this procedure showed significantly less denial and minimization than at baseline. While this appears a promising procedure, it is not clear how much the participants reported change simply to escape the group, and how many had made real and substantial changes.

Can we predict who will re-offend?

Identifying those who are at risk of re-offending is not an exact science. However, a number of clinicians have identified factors that may be predictive. Quinsey et al. (1995), for example, were able to correctly classify 72 per cent of re-offenders, as they had a previous criminal history, violent convictions, were unmarried, scored highly on a psychopathy checklist (see Chapter 11) and had a previous record of sexual offences. They suggested that these factors, combined with evidence of an individual's response to therapy, may inform decisions about length of sentence and release from prison. Once discharged from prison, sex offenders are now monitored by police and in some cases the public. A second screening scale has been reported by Seto et al. (2004) which was associated with an index of sexual arousal to stimuli depicting pre-pubescent children and re-offending. Despite this evidence, there is significant concern that the answers to any screening scale can be fabricated – particularly in cases where release from prison or hospital will be informed by any scores on such measures. For this reason, a more implicit (and therefore less prone to manipulation) measure developed by Gray et al. (2005) may prove more useful in clinical settings.

Transvestic fetishism

Transvestism involves wearing the clothing of the opposite sex. DSM-IV-TR defined transvestic fetishism as:

- recurrent, intense, sexually arousing fantasies, sexual urges or behaviours involving cross-dressing over a period of at least six months in a heterosexual male
- these fantasies, sexual urges or behaviours cause clinically significant distress or impairment in social, occupational or other important areas of functioning.

There is little evidence of an analogous form of the disorder in women. Boys who grow up to engage in transvestite behaviour do not engage in 'feminine' behaviours before puberty, nor do they cross-dress. Similarly, men who are transvestites are unremarkably masculine in their adult hobbies and career choices.

Transvestite boys usually begin cross-dressing at puberty, and rarely later than mid-adolescence. This typically results in sexual excitement, although many people report that they dress in this way because they like the feel of the clothes and that there is no sexual motivation to their behaviour. Some adolescents wear female clothes occasionally; others compulsively wear them under their masculine clothes. Attempts at passing off as a woman are rare in adolescence. However, cross-dressing is frequently accompanied by fantasies of being female, and these fantasies may form the nucleus of sexual fantasies. The prevalence of transvestism within the general population is rarely measured. However, Langstrom and Zucker (2005) found a prevalence rate of 3 per cent among men in a Swedish population sample.

In a survey of over 1000 adult transvestite men, Docter and Prince (1997) reported that 40 per cent of their sample experienced sexual excitement and orgasm 'always' or 'often' when they cross-dressed. Only 9 per cent of the sample said they never experienced this. Cross-dressing frequently elicits less and less sexual excitement as the individual grows older and may eventually have no discernible sexual association. However, the desire to cross-dress may remain the same or even grow stronger, and may be accompanied by feelings of comfort and well-being. Lack of opportunity to cross-dress can result in a lowering of mood and marked irritability. As a result, many transvestites continue to wear women's undergarments beneath the normal male clothes.

Among Docter and Prince's (1997) respondents, 87 per cent reported being exclusively heterosexual; 83 per cent were either married at the time of the survey or had been married; 32 per cent of their wives knew they cross-dressed before marriage; 28 per cent were completely accepting of the behaviour once they became aware of it, while 19 per cent were 'completely antagonistic'. It is common for transvestite men to stop cross-dressing in the early months or years of relationships with a new partner, although many revert to cross-dressing in time. Many enjoy 'normal' heterosexual intercourse. Others need props such as wearing feminine attire to achieve sexual pleasure.

As social reaction can be very negative to transvestic behaviour, cross-dressing usually takes place in arenas where such behaviour is acceptable, including the home and transvestite clubs or organizations. Nevertheless, Docter and Prince (1997) reported that 71 per cent of their sample had cross-dressed in public: 10 per cent had ridden on a bus or train while cross-dressed, 28 per cent had eaten in restaurants, 26 per cent used the ladies' toilet and 22 per cent had tried on feminine clothing in stores. When asked their preferred gender identity, 11 per cent preferred their masculine self, 28 per cent preferred their feminine self and 60 per cent preferred each equally.

Some people experience guilt and shame as a result of their feelings and behaviour. Such individuals may make repeated, frequently unsuccessful, efforts to overcome their perceived anomaly. They may destroy their wardrobe of feminine clothes, before acquiring new ones in the following weeks and months. This cycle may occur repeatedly in younger people who later become more accepting of their feelings. In Docter and Prince's sample, 70 per cent reported having purged their wardrobe on at least one occasion, and 45 per cent reported seeking counselling as a result of their feelings.

Aetiology of transvestic fetishism

Biological factors
There are surprisingly few studies of a biological cause of transvestism – and most are case studies rather than formal scientific studies. One such case, reported by Riley (2002), involved a 72-year-old man who was treated with a drug known as selegiline, an MAOI (see Chapter 3) which, among other actions, increases serotonin and dopamine activity. Following this treatment, the man developed a frequent impulse to wear women's clothing – despite never having had this desire previously. The drug was withdrawn, and his urge to wear women's clothing stopped. However, this is one of the very few studies of biological mechanisms – more social and psychological risk factors for transvestism have been identified, although the body of evidence from which these risk factors have been drawn is limited.

Parental relationships

Various, often contradictory, family theories of transvestism have been proposed. Newcomb (1985) found that transvestite men were more likely than other hetero-sexual men to characterize their parents as less sex-typed and more sex-reversed in terms of dependence and affiliation. This suggested some form of modelling process may be involved. However, men who become transvestites tend to adopt typical masculine roles as a young child, countering this type of theory. A second theory suggested that the principal maternal influence in transvestism is one of hostility and anger towards males. Zucker and Bradley (1995) noted evidence that boys who develop transvestism have higher separation rates from their mothers than is the norm, suggesting this reflected their mothers' aggressive attitudes towards men.

Behavioural models   One school of thought suggests that transvestism results from being cross-dressed during childhood, particularly by mothers or other female figures, as a form of punishment – a process known as 'petticoat punishment'. A number of case examples have been published (Stoller 1968), although it is not clear why an adult should choose to adopt a behaviour used to punish them as a child as a sexual fetish. Stoller argued that this may represent a form of mastery over the punishment. However, a number of clinicians have claimed that incidences of forced cross-dressing are rare, and that it is usually the child who initiates such behaviour. More conventional reinforcement models (Crawford et al. 1993) suggest that if a child is exposed to women's clothing and enjoys the feel of them or masturbates while wearing them, this may establish a reinforcement process that results in the continuation of this behaviour.

Psychoanalytic models   Ovesey and Person (1973) suggested that the psychoanalytic processes that lead to transvestism occur after an individual has consolidated their sense of maleness. Their mother is typically warm and supportive, their father distant and threatening, even verbally or physically abusive. As a result, the mother turns towards her son for gratification not forthcoming from her marriage. She is seductive in her closeness to the boy, but at the same time encourages his cross-dressing either overtly or covertly. In doing so, she is thought to be gratifying herself sexually, but repressing her real (sexual) interest by denying his masculinity. The child is gratified by her intimacy, but also feels guilty. He assumes that his mother wishes to dress him as a girl in order to placate his father. The intimacy of his mother and the perceived rivalry of his father prevent a successful resolution of the oedipal complex (see Chapter 2).

After childhood, the individual seeks to preserve the mother as a dependence object, and is attracted to women like his mother who will accept or even encourage cross-dressing. Adult transvestites resort to cross-dressing under periods of stress and wear female underclothing as a protective device. Female clothes provide protection in three ways:

- they symbolize the mother and perpetuate dependence and continued need for her protection

- they symbolize auto-castration, a token submission to male competitors, which wards off their retaliation

- they disguise masculinity to disarm rivals.

The clothes conceal the penis, the symbol of masculine power, and deny hostile intent. They allow the individual to avoid detection by their rivals, which not only allays anxiety, but even confers on the individual an inflated sense of masculinity. Ovesey and Person (1973: 69) went so far to suggest that 'the transvestite is Superman in drag!'

Treatment of transvestic fetishism

Transvestism is not a condition that requires treatment. Nevertheless, people whose behaviour is affecting their relationships or who find their behaviour unacceptable may seek treatment. Marital problems often lead to attempts at behavioural change and the initiation of therapy. Wives often have negative feelings towards their husband's behaviour even when they know about it early in their relationship (Bullough and Weinberg 1988).

Treatment usually focuses on the sexual elements of transvestite behaviour, and includes aversion therapy and modification of sexual fantasy. Some aversion programmes have proven moderately successful. Marks et al. (1970) reported that two-thirds of participants in electrical aversion therapy improved with treatment, up to a follow-up period of two years. This compared with one-quarter of a control group who did not receive the intervention. A second approach to the treatment of transvestism involves masturbatory retraining. Here, the individual masturbates using his preferred sexual object, including female props worn either by the individual or his partner, before reverting to images of more 'normal' sex objects immediately before and at orgasm. Again, a number of case descriptions and uncontrolled studies have shown this method to have been used with good effect (Laws and Marshall 1991). More recently, Chiang et al. reported significant changes following a cognitive behavioural programme instituted following the individual developing 'severe moral anxiety' (1999: 299). The individual involved did not respond to psychodynamic therapy, but a combination of supportive and cognitive therapy proved of some value, at least in the short term.

Gender identity disorder

In contrast to transvestism, where men dress as women, but accept their male identity, individuals with gender identity disorder believe themselves to have been born the wrong sex. DSM-IV-TR defines the disorder as:

- a strong and persistent cross-gender identification

- persistent discomfort with one's sex, or a sense of inappropriateness in the gender role of that sex

- clinically significant distress or impairment in social, occupational or other important areas of functioning.

In adolescents and adults, gender identity disorder is manifested by a preoccupation with the belief that they are born 'the wrong sex' and a desire for the removal of primary and secondary sex characteristics. Many people with this disorder opt for surgery to change their body to what they consider to be their appropriate sex. They become transsexuals. Others do not take such a radical step, but dress and try to pass themselves off as a member of their desired sex. People with gender identity disorder are often sexually attracted to people of the same sex, which they interpret as conventional heterosexual preference. There are no prevalence data of the condition within the general population. However, what little evidence there is suggests that people with gender identity disorder are highly likely to experience clinically significant distress at some period in their life (Hepp et al. 2005).

Most adults with gender identity disorder report a history of consistent cross-gender behaviour in childhood. Boys may reject the rough-and-tumble play and prefer the company of girls. They frequently dress in women's clothing and insist they will grow up to be a girl. Some claim their penis and testes are disgusting and hope they will somehow change into female genitalia as they grow older. Girls may reject urinating in the sitting position, and assert that they do not want to grow breasts or menstruate. They may reject typical girls' clothing. Green and Blanchard (1995) reported that these behaviours and attitudes are usually detected before the age of 3 years. These characteristics are not static, however, and many children adopt more gender-appropriate behaviours and identities over time. Some adults may also spontaneously change their gender identity (Marks et al. 2000), although such occurrences are rare.

Aetiology of gender identity disorder

Genetic factors
One of the very few studies of the genetic processes in gender identity disorder, reported by Coolidge, Thede and Young (2002), found 2 per cent of their sample of over 300 MZ and DZ twins showed some evidence of gender identity disorder symptomatology based on self-report measures. Applying statistical modelling to their data, they found that 62 per cent of the variance in reported symptoms could be attributed to biological factors; 38 per cent was attributable to environmental factors. These data led the investigators to suggest that the causes of gender identity disorder were primarily biological – not psychological.

Biological factors
The biological processes through which these genetic effects may be mediated remains unclear. Studies of sex hormonal disturbance in adulthood are surprisingly difficult to conduct, because many people with gender identity disorder take hormones of the opposite sex either as part of a treatment programme or by purchasing them on the black market. Despite these interpretive difficulties, what evidence there is does not support a hormonal explanation. Summarizing the evidence, Gladue (1985) reported few, if any, hormonal differences between men with gender identity disorder, male heterosexuals and male homosexuals. Similarly negative results have

been found in women. Meyer-Bahlung (1979) found some women with gender identity disorder had elevated levels of male hormones, but most did not.

A variant of the hormonal explanation is that abnormal levels of prenatal hormones may influence behaviour, and possibly gender identity. This may affect both sexes. The female children of women who have taken precursors to male hormones during pregnancy to prevent uterine bleeding tend to express high levels of tomboyish behaviour in preschool years (Ehrhardt and Money 1967). Boys whose mothers have taken female hormones while pregnant tend to be less boyish than their peers and to engage less in rough-and-tumble play (Yalom et al. 1973). However, there is no evidence that either group of children dislike their gender.

Although a number of studies have failed to find any differences between the brains of people with and without gender identity disorder, one study did show evidence to suggest a neurological substrate to this disorder. Zhou et al. (1995) conducted autopsies on the brains of six people who had changed their sex from male to female. They found an area of the brain, known as the bed nucleus of stria terminalis (BST), to be much smaller than is typically found in men. Indeed, the size of the BST matched that typically found in women, which is usually about half the size of that found in men. In a further investigation of this phenomenon, Kruijver et al. (2000) examined the number of somatostatin-expressing neurons in the BST. They found the same pattern of neurological findings. The number of these neurons in the BSTs of male-to-female transsexuals was similar to those in the females' BST, while the number of these neurons of a female-to-male transsexual was in the male range. What this difference actually means is not clearly understood, although the BST is known to regulate sexual activity in male rats. It is possible, therefore, that this may contribute in some way to gender identity disorder.

A number of research groups have attempted to measure whether any neuronal differences between people with and without gender identity disorder are reflected in cognitive processes. In one such study, Haraldsen et al. (2003) found that people with gender identity disorder who had not received any hormonal treatment performed on cognitive tests in which there are typically sex differences in performance (including rotation, visualization and verbalization tasks) in ways that were predicted by their biological sex, not their gender identity – suggesting few neurological differences between people with gender identity disorder and those without such issues. This contrasts with other studies that have shown a closer relationship to the gender identity than the biological sex. However, these have generally tested individuals who have had some form of hormonal treatment. The one exception to this was reported by Cohen-Kettenis et al. (1998) who found that males with gender identity disorder had less functional brain lateralization than a male comparison group, and had a more 'feminized' brain structure. Interestingly, studies in which performance on cognitive and other tasks has been assessed during hormone therapy for gender identity show how susceptible to hormonal treatment the brain is. Van Goozen et al. (1995), for example, found that among women transforming to men, administration of androgens was associated with significant increases in aggressiveness, sexual arousability and spatial ability, and reduced scores on verbal fluency tasks. For the male-to-female group, the opposite constellation of outcomes was observed: anger and aggression proneness, sexual arousability and visuo-spatial ability decreased, while verbal fluency improved.

Psychoanalytic explanations

Psychoanalytic explanations suggest that male transsexuals have an ambiguous core gender identity. According to Ovesey and Person (1973), male transsexualism originates from extreme separation anxiety early in life before the individual has fully established his own sexual identity. To alleviate this anxiety, the individual resorts to fantasy of symbiotic fusion with the mother. In this way, mother and child become one and the danger of separation is nullified. In the transsexual's mind, he literally becomes the mother, and to sustain this fantasy attempts to revert his core identity from male to female.

To explain the desire for the removal of the penis, Ovesey and Person (1973) noted that the transsexual does not experience castration anxiety, as do most boys. Instead, they experience anxiety that continues until they *are* castrated. The penis is clear evidence that they have failed to psychically fuse with the mother. For the same reason, they reject the act of homosexuality, as this would also acknowledge them as male. They prefer to reject any sexual experience, and generally have little or no experience of sex, even masturbation. In sum, the motivation for security takes priority over motivation for sexuality, as a result of fear of early maternal abandonment.

Early life conditioning

Perhaps the most widely accepted theory of gender identity disorder is that of early life conditioning. Parents of people with gender identity disorder frequently report that they encouraged and gave attention to their child when he or she cross-dressed. This appears to be particularly relevant in boys, where they may be taught how to wear make-up and other feminine behaviours (Green 1987). More subtle factors may also be at play. Girls who exhibit high levels of tomboy behaviour tend to have parents who do the same, and to choose their father as their favourite parent. This allows the possibility of learning such behaviours from their parents and being rewarded for expressing them (Zucker et al. 1994).

Conditioning experiences may also explain why more children than adults are identified as having gender identity disorder. Early life experiences are dominated by family. However, as an individual grows up, they are subject to influences of a wider range of people: peers, school teachers, and so on. It is possible that such exposure results in differing reinforcement processes in which the individual is punished for behaving in 'inappropriate' ways. The competing strengths of each reinforcement system may determine whether or not the individual does or does not behave in gender-discrepant ways. While this approach can explain the development of non-gender-typical behaviours, it has more difficulty in explaining the extremely strongly held beliefs about their gender that such people hold, and their resistance to any form of psychological therapy.

Treatment of gender identity disorder

Psychological therapies

Most people with gender identity disorder are resistant to psychotherapy. As a result, there are no clinical trials reporting attempts to change gender identity. However, a number of case reports indicate that behaviour and attitudes can be changed should the individual wish, or even when they do not seek help. Barlow et al. (1973) reported an intervention with a 17-year-old boy who chose not to proceed with sex reassignment surgery. The intervention included teaching 'male' behaviours, mannerisms and social skills. It proved successful: by the end of therapy, the individual felt no discrepancy between his biological and psychological sexual identity. A second intervention involved a 5-year-old boy who had been cross-dressing for a period of two years before the beginning of therapy (Rekers and Lovaas 1974). The parents were required to initiate a behavioural programme in which they encouraged masculine behaviour, including playing with masculine toys and rough-and-tumble. They also actively discouraged female behaviours such as playing with dolls. The programme was successful in changing the boy's behaviour up to a two-year follow-up. This suggests that there is some malleability in the development of behaviours associated with gender identity disorder.

Surgery
Many people with gender identity disorder request sex reassignment surgery. This involves a complex, staged process. For male-to-female transitions, treatment starts at least a year before surgery (see Box 10.2). First, the individual starts taking the female hormone oestrogen that results in a number of physical changes, including the development of breasts and a softening of the skin. Fat may shift from the shoulders to the hips in feminine fashion.

Box 10.2 Problems of gender identity disorder

Access to sex change surgery in Britain is limited. At times of inadequate resources for health care, this type of surgery is given a low priority, and many people with gender identity disorder can find it extremely difficult, if not impossible, to obtain this treatment from the National Health Service. Many people who choose to have surgery do so by paying privately for it, through specialist private companies such as TRANSFORM, who provide an assessment of the individual's suitability for gender reassignment, hormone therapy, support for a year while they await surgery and try to live as someone of the opposite sex, and then surgery and post-surgery support.

Simon was a 30-year-old man just beginning this process. He had been to the initial assessment and accepted as a possible 'case', and had begun hormone therapy at the time of the interview in which he described what led him to seek gender reassignment and the frustrations he had experienced on the way:

> I am so angry. I know I have the wrong body, and no one can convince me that I am wrong. As long as I can remember, I have felt this way. I wanted breasts, to be a girl, to have a period – to get rid of my penis. I envy them so much . . . I have tried to go along with things, not to be as I am. It's really pretty frightening admitting it and having to go the whole way like I want to. But it's what I want . . .
>
> I married someone just to try and conform. I love her as well. Not in a physical way, though. We don't have sex . . . she isn't really a sexual person so that's all

right. That's why I began to see her. She isn't very attractive, but she's a good person, so it feels good that she's with someone like me, where sex isn't a big deal. It doesn't feel right, but we are good friends and we get on well. I tried to keep things a secret. I have – had – a place in my wardrobe where I keep women's clothing. I put it on when she is at work. It feels so natural and fantastic. It's the only time I felt I was really me, and how I wanted to be. I had a wig, make-up and stuff so I could really feel like a woman. It was secret, but she came home when I was wearing it one day, and so I had to explain some of how I feel and what I want. She knows I want to change my sex. We're going to live together until I do, even though my body is going to change with the hormones. But she wants to live with me despite it. I don't know what will happen and how we'll feel in time, though . . . I wear the clothing and the wig at home all the time now, now she knows. She's OK about it . . . I'm not a 'trannie' [transvestite] though, because I want more – just dressing up isn't enough. They are just men playing at being women. I want and have always wanted to be a proper woman.

It has been so frustrating getting so far. I went for an interview at Charing Cross Hospital and they agreed to put me on their programme, but the local health people wouldn't pay for it, even though I had letters from my GP and a psychiatrist saying I needed it. So I had to go to TRANSFORM. I went to see them and they agreed to give me an assessment by a psychologist, and he agreed to put me on the programme. And that was great . . . but I had no money, so I couldn't do it straight away. I felt so low at the time . . . very depressed. I really needed it, but no one would let me get on with things. I was pretty close to suicidal . . . I thought things would never change . . . and I couldn't tell my wife why I was so low . . . I'm still on antidepressants now . . . I think they're the only thing keeping me going . . . I still don't know how I'm going to pay for surgery . . . I would sell the house but that's not fair on my wife, so I'm happy I'm on the hormones and beginning to see changes, but I can't see how I will go the whole way . . . but I won't be happy unless I do, because emotionally it all feels so right.

Once initiated, hormones are taken indefinitely. At the same time, the person will undergo electrolysis to rid them of masculine hair patterns. They are also trained to raise the timbre of their voice. At this early stage, some people may also have cosmetic surgery to alter facial features such as their chin or larynx to make them appear more feminine. Most of these changes are reversible. More enduring changes are usually held back for at least a year during which the individual is required to live as a woman. Only if this 'trial period' is completed successfully will the final surgery be conducted. This involves amputation of the penis and construction of an artificial vagina. This will permit normal sexual intercourse.

For female–male reassignment a similar process is followed. Hormone therapy changes body shape, redistributing fat, as well as deepening the voice. However, surgery is more arduous and the end results are less successful. The penis that can be constructed is generally small and not capable of a normal erection. Accordingly, sexual intercourse is not possible without the use of artificial supports. Surgery may also include bilateral mastectomy and hysterectomy.

The social and psychological outcomes of surgery are generally good. Summarizing the data to date, the Wessex Institute for Health Research and Development (1998) reported that two years after surgery, people who received sex reassignment surgery engaged in more visits to family and friends, eating out, sport and sexual activity than those who did not receive surgery. They also made modest gains on outcomes including social drinking, work record and cinema/theatre attendance. Y.L.S. Smith et al. (2001) followed a cohort of adolescents, who either did or did not receive sex reassignment surgery, for a period of four years. By this time, none of those who received surgery regretted their choice and they were considered to be functioning psychologically and socially 'quite well'. Those who did not receive surgery generally did less well, although they showed modest improvements on measures as diverse as gender dysphoria and body dissatisfaction. These gains, however, were of a different order of magnitude to those made in the group treated with surgery. Positive outcomes in uncontrolled studies have been reported in domains such as cosmetic appearance, sexual functioning, self-esteem, body image, family life, social relationships, psychological status and satisfaction. The small number of serious postoperative incidents includes requests for reversal, hospitalization and suicide. New problems may also emerge following reassignment surgery. Some individuals may need to come to terms with painful loss, including jobs, families, partners, children and friends, as a result of their gender change. Many people are forced to move away from a familiar environment and, despite being confident in their gender role, may have difficulties with social adaptation and acceptance by others.

Of interest is that the changes following hormonal treatment are not only physical, but also include cognitive changes. Van Goozen et al. (1995), for example, reported on the effects of sex-hormone therapy on behaviour and cognitive processes. Among women transforming to men, administration of androgens was associated with significant increases in aggressiveness, sexual arousability and visuo-spatial ability, and reduced scores on verbal fluency tasks. For the male-to-female group, the opposite constellation of outcomes was observed: anger and aggression proneness, sexual arousability and visuo-spatial ability decreased, while verbal fluency improved. Men transforming to women undergoing oestrogen therapy have also shown improved paired associate learning scores compared with a similar group not receiving oestrogens (Miles et al. 1998).

Chapter summary

1   There are two broad categories of sexual disorder: disorders of response (including erectile dysfunction and vaginismus) and disorders of desire, the paraphilias.

2   Erectile dysfunction can be the result of physical factors, but is frequently the result of psychological ones. Common factors include anxiety, often as a result of distorted beliefs about sexual performance, and 'spectating'.

3   Vaginismus is also triggered by anxiety.

4 Treatment using sensate focus and graded exposure methods is effective in both disorders.

5 Paraphilias are generally considered to be the result of conditioning processes in childhood, although specific paraphilias may have multiple casual factors.

6 Paedophilia may result from conditioning processes, poor adult attachment and sexual relationships, an emotional congruence with children, and processes such as justifying cognitions that support the behaviour.

7 Many people imprisoned as a result of paedophile behaviour do not enter treatment programmes. For those that do, cognitive behavioural programmes that address the cognitions supporting the behaviour and develop strategies for dealing with high-risk situations appear the most effective treatment. Masturbatory reconditioning may also alter the object of sexual pleasure. Hormonal therapies may be effective as long as the drug is taken, but compliance is low and relapse, once the drug is stopped, is high.

8 Transvestic fetishism is not a 'disorder' that requires treatment, but some people chose to seek treatment due to social and marital pressures.

9 Transvestism is usually considered to be the consequence of conditioning processes, and treatment involves reconditioning using masturbatory retraining techniques. Aversive approaches are rarely used for ethical reasons.

10 Gender identity disorder occurs when an individual feels that they are the incorrect gender and wishes to change it.

11 Gender identity disorder is poorly understood. No evidence of biological determinants has been found, and psychological models struggle to provide adequate explanations of the condition.

12 People with gender identity disorder are generally resistant to psychological therapy and most eventually seek surgery and hormonal treatments, following which most enjoy a better quality of life.

For discussion

1 Is transvestism a true sexual 'disorder'?

2 Given the difficulties of treating people who engage in paedophilic behaviour, should those people remain in hospital or some other institution to protect society from them? If they are released into society, should the public be made aware of where they live?

3 Consider the argument that applying behaviour modification principles to make a young person's behaviour more gender-appropriate is simply reinforcing cultural stereotypes, is unethical and is against the best wishes of the child, who should be free to express his or her own sexuality and behave in a way that they choose.

4 Could enforced celibacy as an adult increase risk for paedophilia? If so, how?

Further reading

Kenworthy, T., Adams, C.E., Bilby, C. et al. (2004) Psychological interventions for those who have sexually offended or are at risk of offending, *Cochrane Database of Systematic Reviews*, Part 3.

Murray, J.B. (2000) Psychological profile of pedophiles and child molesters, *Journal of Psychology*, 134: 211–24.

Tierney, D.W. and McCabe, M. (2002) Motivation for behavior change among sex offenders: a review of the literature, *Clinical Psychology Review*, 22: 113–29.

11

Personality disorders

Personality disorders affect an individual for much of their life. A number of these disorders have been identified, some of which, such as the schizoid or schizotypal disorders, have some of the features of other, more disabling, conditions – but not to such a degree that a formal diagnosis can be assigned. Others, including borderline personality or psychopathy, differ markedly from any other DSM diagnoses. The chapter begins with a discussion of the validity of the concept of personality disorders as distinct 'disorders', before considering a general theory explaining their development. The chapter then considers each of three clusters of personality disorders, with a particular focus on two conditions that have received the most attention from psychologists: borderline personality disorder and the associated diagnoses of antisocial behaviour and psychopathy. By the end of the chapter, you should have an understanding of:

- Issues related to all personality disorders
- Challenges to the diagnostic category of personality disorder
- A general theory of personality disorders
- The type A, B and C personality disorder clusters, with particular focus on:
  - borderline personality and its treatment
  - the aetiology and treatment of antisocial behaviour and psychopathy.

Introduction

Personality disorders are also known as axis 2 disorders within DSM (see Chapter 1), in that they are thought to be stable long-term conditions. DSM-IV-TR (APA 2000) defines such disorders as an enduring pattern of inner experience and behaviour that deviates markedly from the expectations of the individual's culture in at least two of the following: cognition, mood, interpersonal functioning or impulse control. The pattern is inflexible and pervasive across a range of personal or social situations and is long lasting. Its onset can be traced back to adolescence or early childhood. It is usually, but not always, associated with significant distress or impairment. DSM-IV-TR identified ten personality disorders in three clusters, although the overlap between the disorders is so great that it can be difficult to distinguish one from another, raising concerns about the reliability and validity of such diagnoses:

- Cluster A: '*Odd or eccentric*' – paranoid, schizoid and schizotypal
- Cluster B: '*Flamboyant or dramatic*' – antisocial, histrionic, narcissistic, borderline
- Cluster C: '*Fearful or anxious*' – avoidant, dependent, obsessive-compulsive.

Personality disorders are often accompanied by other disorders of mood. Depending on the study, between 24 and 74 per cent of people diagnosed with a personality disorder also have major depression, and between 4 and 20 per cent have bipolar depression. Co-morbidity with anxiety disorders is also very common (Grant et al. 2005). Antisocial and narcissistic disorders are generally thought to be more prevalent in men, and histrionic and borderline disorders more prevalent among women (APA 2000).

By definition, personality disorders are traits that are relatively stable over time. However, Loranger et al. (1994) found that many of these disorders appear to be less stable than first thought. Dependent and schizotypal 'personalities', for example, appear to be quite unstable even over relatively short time periods, while prevalence levels of antisocial personality and dependent personality fall as age increases, suggesting some moderation of these traits over time. Similar findings have been reported for people diagnosed within the cluster C, fearful or anxious, personalities. In one of the longest follow-ups yet reported, Paris and Zweig-Frank (2001) reported the 27-year outcomes of a cohort of individuals diagnosed with borderline personality disorder. By this time, only 5 out of 64 individuals in the cohort met the criteria for the diagnosis: 10 per cent had committed suicide over the follow-up period.

Diagnosis of personality disorders has, until recently, been somewhat arbitrary. Widiger et al. (1987), for example, reported that 55 per cent of people diagnosed as having borderline personality using DSM-III criteria could also have been diagnosed as having schizotypal disorder. Similarly, Morey (1988) found that 33 per cent of people diagnosed with schizotypal disorder also met the diagnostic criteria for having narcissistic personality disorder, while 59 per cent met the criteria for avoidant personality disorder and paranoid personality disorder. The change to DSM-IV and DSM-IV-TR and the development of structured clinical interviews have improved levels of diagnostic agreement, which now match those of the major diagnostic categories of depression, anxiety, schizophrenia, and so on. Maffei et al. (1997) reported inter-rater reliability statistics based on diagnoses using a standardized diagnostic interview with lower limit of 0.83 for obsessive-compulsive disorder and 0.98 for a diagnosis of narcissistic disorder. Nevertheless, Zimmerman (1994) found only modest test–retest reliability statistics of between 0.11 for schizotypal disorder and 0.84 for antisocial disorder over a period of one year. This indicates either poor diagnostic reliability or significant changes in symptoms – contrary to the notion of an invariant personality type.

A dimensional approach

Personality disorders may be considered as distinct 'disorders' – this is certainly the model taken by DSM. However, there have been challenges to this approach. Some (e.g. Trull 2005) have argued that people with these traits should not be assigned a categorical diagnosis identifying them as 'disordered' or mentally ill (see Chapter 1). The characteristics and experiences of people with these 'disorders' are not distinct from those of 'normal' individuals. They may therefore better be considered as at the extreme of the distribution of personality characteristics rather than categorically different from the norm. Here is a hypothetical profile, suggested by the five-factor model of personality (Costa and McRae 1995), for antisocial personality disorder which received empirical support in a cohort of adolescents by Lynam et al. (2005):

- *Low neuroticism:* lack of appropriate concern for potential problems in health or social adjustment; emotional blandness.
- *Low extraversion:* social isolation, interpersonal detachment and lack of support networks; flattened affect; lack of joy and zest for life; reluctance to assert self or assume leadership roles, even when qualified; social inhibition and shyness.
- *Low openness:* difficulty adapting to social or personal change; low tolerance or understanding of different points of view or lifestyles; emotional blandness and inability to understand and verbalize own feelings; alexithymia; constricted range of interests; insensitivity to art and beauty; excessive conformity to authority.
- *Low agreeableness:* cynicism and paranoid thinking; inability to trust even friends or family; quarrelsomeness; too ready to pick fights; exploitive and manipulative; lying; rude and inconsiderate manner alienates friends, limits social support; lack of respect for social conventions can lead to trouble with the law; inflated and grandiose sense of self; arrogance.
- *Low conscientiousness:* underachievement: not fulfilling intellectual or artistic potential; poor academic performance relative to ability; disregard of rules and responsibilities can lead to trouble with the law; unable to discipline self (such as stick to diet or exercise plan) even when required for medical reasons; personal and occupational aimlessness.

Not only can the dimensional view be argued on theoretical and philosophical grounds, it also may be better at predicting outcome than the DSM categorical approach. Ullrich et al. (2001), for example, found that scores on personality tests were better able to predict subsequent offending behaviour than categorical diagnoses of antisocial personality disorder. Heumann and Morey (1990) also found dimensional scores to be more reliable across clinicians than categorical diagnoses following DSM criteria.

A cognitive model of personality disorders

Although there are ten personality disorders (or personality types), Beck et al. (1990) attempted to develop a single, unitary, explanatory model for the development of them all. In doing so, they adopted an evolutionary perspective. They suggested that key neuro-cognitive responses, including those affecting perception, mood and behaviour, are genetically pre-programmed and that these responses may be adaptive in some evolutionary stages, but less adaptive in others. Competitive behaviour, for example, may be of benefit at times of scarcity but not at times of social cohesion and mutual cooperation.

According to Beck and colleagues, what we term personality disorders are the inappropriate expression of these pre-programmed responses. They suggested that it is not the behaviour *per se* that is problematic, but the individual's lack of adaptability and responsiveness to the environment. Most of us learn to adapt our behaviour as a result of life experiences, particularly those in childhood. For some people, however, childhood experiences may maintain or reinforce inappropriate pre-programmed responses. The naturally shy child, for example, whose parents' response is to be over-protective, may not experience any other way of dealing with the world. As a result, they may fail to develop alternative coping skills and come to believe that the only way to survive in the adult world is to be dependent and subservient. Adult personality is the combined result of these pre-programmed responses and childhood experiences. Rigid cognitive schemata develop over time, each of which governs behaviour. Beliefs of 'being bad', for example, will lead to self-punishment; beliefs of 'not being worthy of love' will result in the avoidance of closeness, and so on.

As in his model of depression, Beck considered the core schemata that drive personality disorders to be the cognitive triad concerning the self, others and the future. Instead of being episodically activated, as in the case of depression, those underlying schemata are more chronically activated in people with personality disorders. By placing these schemata as the central driving factor in all personality disorders, the cognitive model of personality disorders provides an explanation for an apparently diverse set of attributes and behaviours. The content of the schemata may vary, as a result of different child and adult experiences (and perhaps the pre-programmed neuro-cognitive responses), but the underlying structures are the same. Some of the key beliefs for the different personality 'types' include:

- Avoidant personality
    - *self:* socially inept and incompetent
    - *others:* potentially critical, uninterested and demeaning
    - *beliefs:* the self as worthless and unlovable: 'If people get close to me, they will discover the real me and reject me – that would be intolerable.'
- Dependent personality
    - *self:* needy, weak, helpless and incompetent
    - *others:* need a strong 'caretaker' in an idealized way; can function well in their presence, but not without them
    - *beliefs:* 'I need other people – specifically a strong person – in order to survive.'
- Schizoid personality disorder
    - *self:* self-sufficient and a loner
    - *others:* intrusive; closeness provides an opportunity for others to fence the individual in

–   *beliefs:* 'I am basically alone'; 'I can do things better when I am unencumbered by other people.'

According to Young and Lindemann (1992), the schemata most involved in personality disorders are those that relate to the need for security, autonomy, desirability, self-expression, gratification and self-control. Once formed, they become self-fulfilling, and are maintained through three different processes: schema maintenance, schema avoidance and schema compensation. Schema maintenance involves resistance to information or evidence that would disconfirm the schema through cognitive distortions and self-defeating behavioural patterns (see also Ryle's model of psychopathology discussed in Chapter 2). Avoidance involves avoiding situations that may test or provide information counter to the schema. Finally, schema compensation involves overcompensating for a negative schema by acting in the direction opposite to the schema's content. This may reinforce the initial schema, as the outcome of such actions may not be positive. A shy woman, who believes herself unattractive to men, yet acts flirtatiously, for example, may find herself in situations in which she feels unsafe, or hurt by men drawn to her flirtatiousness who reject her when they find her withdrawn and quiet, thus supporting her schema of being unattractive. Although much successful clinical work has been based on the schema model, until recently there have been few experimental studies of the phenomenon. However, what studies have been conducted support the schema models developed by both Beck and Young (e.g. Jovev and Jackson 2004; Arntz et al. 2005).

Cluster A diagnoses

According to DSM-IV-TR, paranoid disorder involves a pervasive distrust and suspiciousness of others such that their motives are interpreted as malevolent. It begins in early adulthood. To be assigned a diagnosis, four of the following need to be present. The individual:

- suspects, without sufficient basis, that others are exploiting, harming or deceiving them
- is preoccupied with unjustified doubts about the loyalty or trustworthiness of friends or associates
- is reluctant to confide in others because of unwarranted fear that the information will be used maliciously against them
- reads hidden demeaning or threatening meanings into benign remarks or events
- persistently bears grudges and slights
- sees attacks on their character or reputation that are not apparent to others and is quick to react angrily or to counterattack
- has recurrent suspicions, without justification, regarding fidelity of spouse or sexual partner.

Schizoid disorder presents as a pervasive pattern of detachment from social relationships and a restricted range of expression of emotions in interpersonal settings, beginning in early adulthood. Four of the following have to be present for a diagnosis to be assigned. The individual:

- neither desires nor enjoys close relationships, including being part of a family
- almost always chooses solitary activities
- has little, if any, interest in having sexual experiences with another person
- takes pleasure in few, if any, activities
- lacks close friends or confidants other than first-degree relatives
- appears indifferent to the praise or criticism of others
- shows emotional coldness, detachment or flattened affectivity.

Finally, schizotypal personality disorder is defined as a pervasive pattern of social and interpersonal deficits marked by acute discomfort with, and reduced capacity for, close relationships. In addition, individuals may experience cognitive or perceptual distortions and show eccentricities of behaviour. A diagnosis requires the presence of five or more of the following:

- ideas of reference (excluding delusions of reference)
- odd beliefs or magical thinking that influence behaviour and are inconsistent with sub-cultural norms
- unusual perceptual experiences, including bodily illusions
- odd thinking and speech (e.g. vague, circumstantial, metaphorical, overelaborate, or stereotyped)
- suspiciousness or paranoid ideation
- inappropriate or restricted affect
- behaviour or appearance that is odd, eccentric or peculiar
- lack of close friends or confidants other than first-degree relatives
- excessive social anxiety that does not diminish with familiarity and tends to be associated with paranoid fears rather than negative judgements about self.

The prevalence of these various disorders within the general community varies, according to different studies, between 0 and 4.5 per cent for paranoid personality disorder, 0 and 4.1 per cent for schizoid personality disorder, and 0 and 5.1 per cent for schizotypal personality disorder (Torgersen et al. 2001).

Each of these disorders involves some of the manifestations of schizophrenia. As such, they fit into a range of conditions known as the schizophrenia spectrum disorders – a linkage that stemmed from early observations of the relatives of people identified with schizophrenia, among whom there were relatively high rates of cluster A personality disorder (Nigg and Goldsmith 1994). Interestingly, though, few people diagnosed with these personality disorders go on to be diagnosed as having schizophrenia. These characteristics have also been found to be higher than average among the relatives of people with depression, allowing the possibility that they are associated with other disorders than schizophrenia (Squires-Wheeler et al. 1993).

Perhaps not surprisingly, given the linkage with schizophrenia, factors associated with the development of schizophrenia, including prenatal exposure to famine, influenza and even cold temperatures, have also been considered in the development of these disorders (see Parnas et al. 2005). Genetic studies have identified high concordance rates for each of the disorders between MZ twins (see Parnas et al. 2005). In one of several longitudinal studies, the Copenhagen High-Risk genetic risk study (Parnas et al. 1995), followed the offspring of women with a diagnosis of schizophrenia and those of a 'normal' comparison group of children from the age of 15 to 42 years. Twenty-one per cent of the children of schizophrenic mothers were assigned a cluster A personality diagnosis, compared with 5 per cent of the children in the comparison group. Of particular note is that among the children of the women diagnosed with schizophrenia, those exposed to a particularly stressful environment in childhood were most likely to be subsequently diagnosed with schizophrenia. Those who were exposed to a moderately stressful environment were more likely to be assigned a diagnosis of personality disorder, suggesting a gradient of risk based on both genetic factors and the degree of exposure to stress – a finding in keeping with the diathesis-stress model. Data such as these have led genetic theorists such as Meehl (e.g. 1990) to suggest that the core personality disorder is genetically mediated, while risk for schizophrenia involves further genetic influences and high environmental stress factors.

Treatment studies of cluster A disorders are relatively rare – perhaps because people who could be assigned these diagnoses rarely seek treatment, and when they do, this may be related to associated problems such as depression. With this in mind, Parnas et al. (2005) noted that antipsychotic medication may be of some benefit, but that adequate controlled trials of any psychotherapy or alternative medical treatments were lacking.

Cluster B diagnoses

Borderline personality disorder

DSM-IV-TR defines borderline personality disorder as a pervasive pattern of instability of interpersonal relationships, self-image and affect, and marked impulsivity. It begins in early childhood and its key characteristics include five of the following:

- frantic efforts to avoid real or imagined abandonment
- a pattern of unstable and intense personal relationships characterized by alternating between idealization and devaluation
- identity disturbance: markedly and persistently unstable self-image
- impulsivity in at least two areas that are potentially self-damaging (such as substance abuse, reckless driving)

- recurrent suicidal behaviour or self-mutilating behaviour; may involve repeated threats or gestures
- chronic feelings of emptiness
- inappropriate intense anger or difficulty in controlling anger
- transient stress-related paranoid ideation or severe dissociative symptoms.

About 2 per cent of the US population are thought to have this disorder, and about 75 per cent of these are thought to be women (APA 2000). It typically begins in adolescence and continues through adulthood. Thoughts of suicide and suicide attempts are common: up to 10 per cent of people with this disorder eventually commit suicide (e.g. Zanarini et al. 2005). Self-harm, in particular cutting of arms, legs or torso, burning or other mutilatory acts, is also common. This is usually in response to experiencing negative emotions such as anger or anxiety, attempts to block painful memories, or as a cry for help. These behaviours may also be used in a manipulative manner, to control relationships or the behaviour of others around them. People with the disorder often have intense, over-involved relationships, and have a deep fear of being rejected. This may result in them becoming panicky at the thought of being isolated, and they may engage in self-destructive behaviour to try to maintain relationships that are disintegrating ('If you leave, I will hurt myself . . .'). As with other personality disorders, it is not as immutable as was once thought. Zanarini et al. (2005), for example, found that over a six-year period, nearly three-quarters of people initially given this diagnosis could no longer be assigned the diagnosis. Only 6 per cent of these people experienced a 'relapse'.

Aetiology of borderline personality disorder

Biological factors

Genetic studies suggest that risk for borderline personality disorder may be, in part, a consequence of genetic factors, although the evidence is not strong. It is also methodologically flawed. Dahl (1994), for example, noted that the relevant evidence was based on studies that failed to carry out reliability assessments of diagnoses assigned to relatives of index cases, did not exclude other potential diagnoses, and/or used inappropriately low cut-off scores on a diagnostic scale. Despite the lack of genetic evidence, a number of studies have investigated neural and neurochemical mediators the condition. In one such study, Tebartz van Elst et al. (2003) found that the hippocampi of people with borderline personality disorder were 20 per cent smaller than those of a 'normal' comparison group, while their amygdalas were 24 per cent smaller. There is also evidence of damaged or a poorly functioning frontal cortex (De la Fuente et al. 1997), which may be related to dysregulation of serotonin within this system (New et al. 2004). This may contribute to a lack of inhibition in the regulation of aggression. Reports of the effectiveness of antipsychotic medication in the treatment of at least some cases of borderline personality disorder (e.g. Rocca et al. 2002) suggest that dopamine may also be involved in its presentation.

Socio-cultural factors

Risk for personality disorder is increased by a number of social factors. People with borderline personality are more likely than the general population to have been neglected by their parents, to have had multiple caregivers and to have experienced parental divorce, death or significant childhood trauma such as sexual abuse or incest. In one study of this phenomenon, Bandelow et al. (2005) found that people with borderline personality disorder reported much higher levels of traumatic childhood experiences such as sexual abuse, violence, separation from parents, childhood illness, and other factors than a matched, 'normal' comparison group.

Psychological processes

Psychological processes translate the social factors considered above into individual experiences. One significant outcome of these, or less dramatic, events may be poor attachment and bonding with parents – both of which may contribute to the development of borderline personality disorder (Nickell et al. 2002). Of interest in relation to these findings were those of Zweig-Frank and Paris (2002) who followed a cohort of people diagnosed with borderline personality disorder for 27 years and found that while reports of parenting quality and childhood abuse or trauma did not predict the long-term outcome of the condition, a measure of parental bonding did. From a psychoanalytic viewpoint, object relations theorists (e.g. Kernberg 1985) suggest that as a result of negative childhood experiences, the individual develops a weak ego and needs constant reassuring. They frequently engage in a defence mechanism known as *splitting*, dichotomizing objects into 'all good' or 'all bad' objects, and fail to integrate the positive and negative aspects of self or other people into a whole (Klein 1927; see also Chapter 2 in this volume). This inability to make sense of contradictory elements of self or others causes extreme difficulty in regulating emotions as the world is constantly viewed as either 'perfect' or 'disastrous'.

Cognitive theorists (e.g. Young and Lindemann 1992) argue that negative childhood experiences translate into maladaptive schemata about self-identity and relationships with others. These include beliefs that 'I am bad', leading to self-punishment; 'No one will ever love me', leading to avoidance of closeness; and 'I cannot cope on my own', leading to overdependence. Self-harm may be maintained by operant processes: successful control of other people's behaviour by threats of self-harm reinforces its use as a means of coping. Strong negative emotions experienced as a consequence of catastrophic or other negative beliefs may also lead to episodes of self-harm. Many people with borderline personality feel numbness or dissociation immediately before or while they harm themselves. Self-harm may therefore provide a means of escape from unbearable emotions, and may not be accompanied with feelings of physical pain. Other people, who feel confused and out of control, may find any pain they experience a form of self-validation of their own status and self-identity (see Table 11.1). According to the cognitive model, the use of self-harm to avoid emotional pain or to manipulate others is indicative of high levels of interpersonal anxiety, low self-esteem and a lack of alternative coping strategies to deal with personal stress.

Table 11.1 Example of an episode of self-harm and the development of alternative coping strategies

What happened before self-harm?	Two hours before meal with parents. They were stuck, not talking to each other. I felt stuck in the middle: couldn't eat
Feelings leading up to the self-destructive act	Numbness
Associated thoughts	I feel nothing. I am nothing
Self-destructive behaviour	Cut thighs with a razor blade
Feelings	No one feeling; pain on cutting
Associated thoughts	At least I feel pain: I can feel something
Consequences	More marks on thighs
	Blood on clothes
	Feel ashamed
	Hate self
Alternative to cutting	Go to bed and sleep or listen to loud music
	Tense my muscles really hard
	Melt ice cubes in my hand

Source: Davidson (2000)

Treatment of borderline personality disorder

Psychological approaches

Treatment of people with borderline personality is not easy, and there are relatively few controlled trials examining the effects of therapy. Roth et al. (1998) tried to establish some overall goals of therapy and some guidelines for who may benefit most from it. They suggested the following:

- Psychotherapy is more likely to be effective for less severe personality disorders.

- In individuals under the age of 30 years, the greatest risk comes from suicide. Prevention of this, rather than 'cure', may form a legitimate therapeutic target.

- Individuals with good social support, chronic depression, who are psychologically minded, and with low impulsivity, are most likely to benefit from 'talking therapies'.

- People who have high levels of impulsivity are most likely to benefit from a 'limit-setting' group or a therapist who is supportive of their attempts to struggle with uncontrollable impulses.

- Commitment and enthusiasm of the therapist may be of special significance, and finding the 'right' therapist for the 'right' patient is particularly important.

Because of the complex facets of the disorder, including the threat of self-harm, therapy with people with personality disorder is necessarily complex and the approaches used should be governed by the individual's ability to cope with particular therapeutic issues. Sometimes the severity of their problems brings people with borderline personality disorders into hospital. It may be useful for such people to spend some time in hospital during the early stages of therapy, as they may find these sessions so stressful they either drop out or harm themselves in some way. The hospital can provide a safe environment, where their behaviour can be observed and controlled, and both therapist and client have the security of knowing that any impulsive self-harming behaviour will be seen and dealt with should it occur.

Cognitive therapy The core of cognitive therapy is the identification and modification of cognitions and underlying schemata that drive inappropriate behaviours, using an approach known as schema therapy (Young 1999) or the cognitive analytic approach of Ryle described in Chapter 3. These approaches may combine with a number of other strategies, including developing problem-focused plans to cope with urges to self-harm, mood disturbances, suicidal feelings, improving relationship problems, and so on. The issues addressed in therapy and the strategies used are dependent on the most pressing and problematic behaviour at the time (Davidson 2000).

One of the most important therapeutic aims is to minimize risk of self-harm. This involves identifying the antecedents to episodes of self-harm, the thoughts and feelings that accompany them, and their consequences (see Table 11.1). Each of these forms a potential point of intervention, including preventing the need to self-harm or engaging in alternative behaviours at times of high risk for self-harm. Alternatives to self-harm often involve a high intensity action, such as listening to loud music, or painful, but not personally damaging, behaviours such as squeezing a ball until the muscles ache. Where there is risk that an episode of self-harm will escalate into a serious attempt at suicide, specific strategies may be used to minimize this risk, including problem solving and identifying reasons for living (see Chapter 8).

Evidence of the effectiveness of these approaches is still gradually accumulating. However, they do seem to be effective. In a series of case reports of schema therapy, Nordahl and Nysaeter (2005) reported significant gains following therapy in six patients, three of whom no longer showed evidence of borderline personality disorder at one-year follow-up. Brown et al. (2004) achieved similar gains in a larger group of patients who received weekly cognitive therapy over a period of one year, and who still showed clinical gains some six months later. In the one of the few controlled trials that has been reported, Van den Bosch et al. (2005) found improvements on measures of parasuicidal and impulsive behaviours, and in alcohol use six months after completion of a one-year programme of cognitive therapy relative to treatment as usual.

Emotional awareness training According to Farrell and Shaw (1994), people with borderline personality lack the ability to understand and describe their emotional state. Emotional awareness training is a structured programme to try to teach such awareness. Once this is achieved, according to Farrell and Shaw, the individual will have greater emotional stability and be more able to regulate arousal, resulting in more effective problem solving and interpersonal functioning. The programme works through a hierarchy of emotional awareness, starting with awareness of bodily sensations, through awareness of the body in motion and arousal, awareness of extremes of emotion and differentiation and integration of conflicting emotions, to an understanding of more pervasive and less extreme emotions. A basic exercise would involve the individual standing at the far end of a room, and then taking slow steps towards the therapist. As they walk, they are asked to describe any physical sensations they experience. Over repetitions of the exercise, they are asked to draw links between their feelings during the exercise and feelings outside the session. More advanced sessions involve monitoring thoughts, behaviours and emotions, and use of distress reduction skills. There are, as yet, no controlled trials of the effectiveness of this intervention (see Box 11.1).

Box 11.1 Sarah's borderline personality disorder

Here is a therapist's view of working with someone identified as having borderline personality disorder, using an interesting 'no-treatment' approach.

Sarah was 31 years old and had just moved back to live with her parents 'for a while'. The referring psychiatrist had judiciously refused to apply the label of borderline personality disorder on the grounds of its future potential for harm – nevertheless the referral letter bore the hallmarks: 'emotionally unstable', 'manipulative', 'potentially aggressive and violent' – an occasional 'self-harmer' with a history of involuntary treatments and involvement from a variety of professions including psychiatry, clinical psychology, social work, housing and the police.

What would you be expecting? Well, the Sarah I met in that initial meeting was so anxious she could hardly speak. She didn't look me in the eye once. At the end of the session, during which we mostly talked about everyday things, I asked her if she'd like to meet again next week.

'What do you think?' she said.

'Well, it's up to you.'

'Do you think it'll help?'

'I've really no idea – it might do and it might not.'

Thus started our first negotiation of competence – a central feature of our 'no-therapy' therapy. Sometimes we met in a consulting room, sometimes we went shopping, sometimes we went to an Internet café – it was her choice. We drank coffee, talked about whatever Sarah wanted to talk about, and throughout that time I tried to refrain from assuming responsibility for her well-being or conduct in any way. One of the things that she decided she wanted to do with our time was to get the hang of email and the Internet. But she was a perfectionist, and when things went wrong, she seemed engulfed by feelings of failure, anxiety and blame ('This f**king computer's shit'). What seemed to work best at these times was to contain, minimize and normalize . . .

'Hey, maybe it's just a glitch – I remember when I first started to use the net . . . [tale of woeful incompetence]' . . . and slowly but surely those major setbacks became minor setbacks as her confidence began to grow.

I learned that, for Sarah, the world seemed a black and white place – good or bad, triumph or disaster. Nowhere was this more apparent than in her chaotic personal relationships – a world of angels and devils. Sarah would model herself entirely on new-found friend(s), who were invariably seen as the embodiment of wisdom and goodness . . . that is, until the friend would begin to withdraw from this lopsided, burdensome and exhausting 'godlike' position. Then Sarah, faced with her biggest fear of all – rejection – would wreak a vengeance that had left several ex-friends in hospital. This was the point of 'no therapy' – of avoiding that mantle of competence and expertise that invited Sarah, with her negligible self-esteem, to define herself as 'the other' – i.e. incompetent and unknowing. Even an invitation to 'collaboratively work on issues' would have been an example of me defining the overall framework, thus taking an 'expert' role. The point of this intervention was simply to attempt a stable relationship, undistorted by oppositional roles – in other words the focus was on process, not content. When this had been achieved then maybe – just maybe – we could entertain the idea of 'therapy'. Yet this stability in itself would be an achievement. Thus I found myself continually, at least in the early stages of our 'no therapy', having to be aware of, and step aside from, assigned roles (e.g. 'expert', 'the competent one', 'rescuer') – because to accept them would be to allow Sarah to play out the opposite (not knowing, incompetent, needing to be rescued).

One of my most valuable resources was variations on 'I don't know'. This didn't mean avoiding things, it meant staying neutral and modelling comfort with uncertainty and shades of grey:

'So what do you think of the death penalty?'

'It's a complex issue – I really don't know.'

'But what about for people who kill children?'

'Well, some would say they deserve it, others might say that two wrongs don't make a right – it's a tricky subject. What do you reckon?'

An issue I initially found problematic was giving useful information without falling into the role of 'teacher'. My solution was to offer a range of options:

'So if I wanted to be a landscape gardener what should I do?'

'Blimey . . . well I suppose some people might look in the Job Centre, others might check out courses somewhere like Green College, others might buy a lawnmower and stick a note in the local Post Office. Some folks might do something completely different . . .

'I've no idea what would be the best option.'

'Hmmm, I might check out Green College. What do you think?'

'Who knows, they might have something useful.'

So it went on, with Sarah making steadily more competent decisions about her life. And how did I celebrate this new-found competence? Outwardly, I didn't. Why? Because Sarah was liable to lose herself in aiming to please others – when the only person she'd really benefit from putting first was herself:

'I went to Green College to look at courses the other day – what do you think about that?'

'Crumbs, I've no idea – never been there. Any good?'

'Yeah – I might try and sign up for one . . .'

Look again at the conversation above – what was I being invited to say? 'That's great'? 'Nice one, Sarah'? 'Go for it'? But then who would she potentially have been pleasing if she signed up? Herself – or me? At first, working in this way felt awkward and counterintuitive because it appears to partly deny the values that bring people into the 'caring' professions: that is, caring, concern, empathy and helping. However, it's the unsophisticated utilization of these qualities that seems most harmful to those who tend to attract the borderline label.

Sarah's life experiences had taught her that she was bad, sick, irresponsible and unlovable – that things she attempted of her own accord would be judged wrong, that she was to blame, she would be punished, and that taking control and responsibility was too dangerous to risk. For me there was initially the sense of a vacuum where her self-belief and confidence should have been and, at first, avoiding being 'sucked in' and used to fill that gap required a constant state of vigilance. Sarah was supremely skilled at subtly handing over the initiative – after all she'd spent her childhood learning, for the sake of her own safety and survival, to do exactly that.

After about nine months of 'no therapy' Sarah informed me that she wouldn't be requiring my services any more, as she was starting a job at the Botanical Gardens and it would be difficult to make the sessions. Additionally, she had started to feel that our work was 'going nowhere'. She was right – she had already got there. She was making competent, responsible decisions about her life of her own accord. And, crucially, I hadn't asked or demanded them (or indeed anything) of her – I had simply refrained from making them for her.

Additionally, she was able to end our relationship without guilt or recrimination, and, as far as I knew, that was a first. She had come wanting 'to be wrapped up in cotton wool and kept safe', but left appreciating 'you giving *me* the control' in a supportive (rather than hostile – like her childhood) environment. We never got as far as therapy, and that was fine.

Pharmacological treatment

Since the 1980s, there have been relatively few controlled trials of the effectiveness of drug therapy in borderline personality. These have had mixed and contradictory results. Soloff et al. (1993) found that a major tranquillizer, haloperidol, reduced a broad spectrum of symptoms, including anxiety, hostility and paranoid ideation. These benefits were not replicated in a subsequent study by the same group. Tricylics have proven ineffective, even in treating depressive symptoms. Indeed, some people have experienced an increase in suicidal threats, suicidal ideation and aggressive behaviour after taking them (Soloff et al. 1986). Accordingly, while some individuals may be helped by major tranquillizers, including the newer drugs such as reserpine (see Chapter 3), pharmacotherapy has so far not provided a consistently effective treatment for borderline personality disorder. Some aspects of the disorder may be treated with specific medication, however. Rinne et al. (2002), for example, found that treatment with the SSRI, fluvoxamine, proved successful in reducing rapid mood shifts, but not impulsivity and aggression in women with a diagnosis of borderline personality.

Research box 11

Van den Bosch, L.M., Koeter, M.W., Stijnen, T. et al. (2005) Sustained efficacy of dialectical behaviour therapy for borderline personality disorder, *Behaviour Research and Therapy*, 43: 1231–41.

There are very few studies of the effectiveness of any psychological interventions in the treatment of borderline personality disorder. This Dutch study provides some relevant evidence. It reports six-month follow-up data following a successful cognitive behavioural intervention previously reported by this group.

Method

This study was a randomized controlled trial involving 58 women with borderline personality disorder with and without substance abuse problems. Participants were initially randomized to either 12 months Dialectical Behaviour Therapy (DBT) or treatment as usual. The inclusion criteria were: female, aged 18–65 years, a diagnosis of borderline personality disorder according to the Structured Clinical Interview for DSM-IV. The exclusion criteria were: a DSM diagnosis of bipolar disorder or (chronic) psychotic disorder, insufficient command of the Dutch language, and severe cognitive impairments.

Treatments

Patients assigned to the DBT condition received 12 months of treatment according following a treatment manual. This involved weekly individual cognitive behavioural psychotherapy sessions and weekly skills training groups. Individual therapy focused primarily on motivational issues, including the motivation to stay alive and to stay in treatment. Group therapy taught self-regulation and change skills, and self and other acceptance skills (the latter being core to DBT).

Assessments

In the previously reported study, treatment conditions were compared after a 12-months treatment period on measures of treatment retention, the course of suicidal, self-mutilating and self-damaging impulsive behaviours. In the current study, both treatment groups were compared six months after discontinuation of DBT on measures of self-mutilating behaviour, impulsive behaviour, alcohol abuse, use of soft drugs (cannabis) and hard drugs (cocaine, heroin, amphetamines). Impulsive acts, suicidal behaviours and substance abuse were measured using the impulsivity and parasuicide sections of the BPD Severity Index (BPDSI). Parasuicidal/self-mutilating behaviours were measured using the Lifetime Parasuicide Count.

Results

After 12 months of DBT, significant differences were found in DBT and usual care groups on measures of impulsive behaviour, self-mutilating behaviour and alcohol consumption. All these behaviours decreased more in the DBT group compared with the control group ($p < 0.05$). These treatment effects were sustained in the first six months following treatment discontinuation. By contrast, no initial and sustained effects were found for measures of parasuicidal behaviour, and the use of soft and hard drugs. Finally, in the 12-month follow-up, it was shown that, although fewer participants in the DBT group (7 per cent) than participants who received usual care (26 per cent) attempted suicide during the year, this difference was not statistically significant (χ^2, $p = 0.064$). During the 6-month follow-up period, only one patient of the DBT group (4 per cent) attempted suicide, compared with six participants of the control condition (19 per cent). This difference again showed no statistical significance (χ^2, $p = 0.08$).

Discussion

Dialectical Behaviour Therapy was developed specifically to keep people with borderline personality disorder alive and to reduce life-threatening behaviour. When the study was started it was expected that DBT would prove to be superior to usual care on measures of severe, life-threatening impulsive behaviours. Because they limited the treatment programme to one year, the authors did not expect a reduction of depression, hopelessness or other core features of the pathology in patients with borderline personality disorder. They argued that the serious and persistent character of the disorder would make such an effect unlikely. Based on earlier DBT research and research on other cognitive behavioural therapies, they nevertheless expected the effect on life-threatening behaviours to sustain at follow-up. Their findings corroborated this expectation. However, they also demonstrated that the participants who received DBT condition showed no improvement during the 6-month follow-up period following the end of therapy. The data suggest that a longer follow-up period might even have shown an extinction of the effect of DBT – suggesting that any therapy may need short booster sessions following its cessation.

Antisocial personality and psychopathy

The terms antisocial personality and psychopathy are often used interchangeably. Indeed, the DSM-IV-TR category of antisocial personality disorder was intended to combine diagnoses of antisocial personality and psychopathy, which DSM-III did not. Critics of DSM-IV-TR have argued that it has not succeeded in this attempt, and that the two conditions are not synonymous: they have different characteristics and long-term outcomes. According to Hare et al. (2000), DSM-IV-TR still describes an individual who is criminally antisocial. By contrast, psychopathy refers to an individual who not only has these characteristics, but also experiences a poverty of both positive and negative emotions, and is motivated by thrill-seeking as much as by any other gain. Antisocial behaviour tends to reduce with age; psychopathic behaviour does not.

DSM-IV-TR defines antisocial personality as a pervasive pattern of disregard for, and violation of, the rights of others occurring from the age of 15 years. Its core characteristics include:

- repeatedly performing acts that could lead to arrest
- repeated lying, use of aliases, or conning others for personal profit or pleasure
- impulsivity or failure to plan ahead

- reckless disregard for the safety of self or others
- consistent irresponsibility: repeated failure to sustain work or honour financial obligations
- lack of remorse for others.

People with antisocial disorder have been described as having a developmental delay in moral maturity and cognitive functioning (Davidson 2000), and tend to operate at a concrete rather than abstract level of intellectual functioning. As a consequence, they lack problem-solving skills, and tend to act impulsively with little consideration of long-term consequences. They often believe they can do exactly what they want and that other people are there to be exploited for their benefit. Prevalence rates of anti-social personality are as high as 3.7 per cent (Widiger and Corbitt 1995). Antisocial personality appears to remit with age: few if any people over the age of 45 years are diagnosed with the disorder (Swanson et al. 1994).

Without specific DSM diagnostic criteria, those who distinguish between anti-social behaviour and psychopathy generally use Hare's (1991) diagnostic criteria to define psychopathy. These identified two major clusters of behaviours characteristic of people with psychopathy: emotional detachment and an antisocial lifestyle. Emotional detachment involves a lack of capacity to process emotional information, and a con-sequent lack of understanding and disregard for the emotions of others. It is Hare's defining characteristic of psychopathy. Using this definition of psychopathology, Hare found that up to 80 per cent of criminals could be categorized as having anti-social personality disorder: only between 15 and 25 per cent met the criteria for psychopathy (Hare et al. 2000), a finding that supported his argument of clinical differences between the two conditions.

Aetiology of antisocial personality and psychopathy

The apparent confusion between antisocial personality and psychopathy has meant that the relevant literature often confuses the two concepts. Some studies of antisocial personality include within them what Hare and others would consider to be psycho-pathy. Other studies specifically focus on psychopathy as defined by Hare. As psychopathy is linked to an 'antisocial lifestyle', it is perhaps not surprising that many of the factors that predispose to antisocial behaviour are also associated with psycho-pathy. What distinguishes psychopathy from the antisocial personality are distinct neurological factors that are uniquely associated with the emotional detachment and limited range or depth of emotions central to the condition. Accordingly, this section first considers factors that increase risk for antisocial behaviour or personality, before considering the neurological factors that contribute uniquely to the development of psychopathy.

Genetic factors
Genetic studies of families have found it difficult to discriminate between genes for problem drinking, criminality and antisocial behaviour, all of which seem to be closely related. Nevertheless, at least two adoptee studies have implicated genetic factors in

moderating risk of antisocial behaviour. Crowe (1974) reported that adopted-away children of women prisoners with antisocial personality disorder had higher rates of antisocial personality than control adoptees without this family history. Similarly, Cadoret (1982) found that rates of antisocial behaviour were higher among adopted adolescent females with a biological relative who engaged in antisocial behaviour than a matched group of adolescents without this family history. Risk for engaging in antisocial behaviour was further increased if the environment of the adoptive family was 'adverse', indicating an interaction between social and genetic factors in the development of antisocial behaviour. Evidence of both a genetic and environmental contributor to antisocial behaviour has also been found for children living with their parents (Button et al. 2005). Further support for a role of genetic factors for specific aspects of psychopathy was reported by Blonigen et al. (2005), who used statistical modelling techiniques to identify the contribution of genetic influences on the behaviour of 626 pairs of 17-year-old twins. They found genetic risk for what they termed fearless dominance and impulsive antisociality.

Biological mechanisms
High levels of impulsivity, irritability, aggression and sensation seeking are associated with low levels of serotonin. Low levels of sympathetic activity at times of stress may also be implicated in antisocial behaviour (Raine et al. 1998), perhaps because they predispose the individual to fearlessness and thrill seeking as a means of increasing arousal levels. High levels of testosterone may also be implicated in criminality (see Dolan 1994).

Socio-cultural factors
Social factors clearly influence the probability of an individual engaging in antisocial behaviour and being diagnosed with antisocial personality. Henry et al. (2001), for example, found that lack of emotional closeness within the family and poor parenting at the age of 12 years was predictive of both violence and delinquency at the age of 17 years. Perhaps the longest longitudinal study is the Cambridge Study in Delinquent Development (Farrington 2000). This was able to identify childhood factors that were predictive of antisocial personality and adult convictions up to the age of 40 years. The most important childhood predictors were similar to those of Henry et al. (2001): a convicted parent, large family size, low intelligence or school attainment, a young mother and disrupted family. Family factors may also contribute to the lack of emotion associated with psychopathy. It has been suggested that the sustained experi-ence of negative emotional events during childhood results in the individual learning to 'switch off' their emotions in response both to negative events that occur to them and to their behaviours that affect others. While family influences are clearly import-ant, external influences may also impact on the individual. Henry et al. (2001) found that having violent peers at this time was also predictive of later violent and non-violent delinquency. Similarly, Eamon and Mulder (2005) found that impoverished neighbourhood and school environments, exposure to deviant peer pressure, and parenting practices involving physical punishment and excessive monitoring of behaviour by their mothers (perhaps as a consequence rather than cause of their antisocial behaviour) were related to antisocial behaviour among Latino adolescents

in the USA. In an attempt to quantify the degree to which family and peer factors contribute to antisocial behaviour, Eddy and Chamberlain (2000) followed a group of offenders over a two-year period. Family management skills and deviant peer association accounted for 32 per cent of the variance in antisocial behaviour over this period. Borduin (1999) summarized the non-family antecedents of antisocial behaviour as:

- *peer relations:* high involvement with deviant peers, poor social skills, low involvement with pro-social peers
- *school factors:* poor academic performance, drop-out, low commitment to education, poor academic quality and weak structure of school
- *neighbourhood and community:* criminal sub-culture, low organizational participation among residents, low social support and high mobility.

The prevalence of antisocial behaviour is increasing over time in many countries, virtually doubling over a period of 15 years in the USA to about 3.6 per cent of the general population. There are also marked differences in its prevalence across countries, ranging from about 0.14 per cent in Taiwan to over 3 per cent in countries such as New Zealand. These various findings led Paris (1996) to speculate that Asian cultures are protective against antisocial personality as a result of their family structure, which is typically highly cohesive with clear limits on acceptable behaviour – the opposite constellation of characteristics to those implicated in the development of antisocial behaviour.

Cognitive models
Children within family systems that increase risk of antisocial behaviour do not have clear limits set to their behaviour. As a result, they frequently fail to internalize the controls on their behaviour that other children adopt. These types of environment may also foster beliefs about the individual and the world that support antisocial behaviour. Dodge and Frame (1982) suggested that all children develop routine responses that guide their behaviour: antisocial children develop aggressive and antisocial scripts and few pro-social ones. Lopez and Emmer (2002), for example, found that adolescents who engaged in crime believed aggression to be an effective and appropriate response to threat. Liau et al. (1998) and Sukhodolsky and Ruchkin (2004) found that specific beliefs led to specific behaviours. Liau and colleagues found that beliefs concerning overt antisocial behaviour ('People need to be roughed up once in a while') were associated with overt but not covert antisocial behaviour. Conversely, beliefs related to covert behaviour ('If someone is careless enough to lose a wallet, they deserve to have it stolen') led to covert but not overt antisocial behaviour. Sukhodolsky and Ruchkin found a higher frequency of aggressive acts was significantly associated with higher levels of anger and stronger beliefs that physical aggression is an appropriate course of action in conflicts in a sample of Russian adolescents. Non-aggressive antisocial behavior was associated with approval of deviancy, but not with anger or beliefs legitimizing aggression. Similar scripts may underpin adult behaviour of psychopaths. Beck et al. (1990), for example, identified

their core beliefs as 'people are there to be taken', and the strategy derived from this to be one of attack. Other core beliefs included:

- Force or cunning is the best way to get things done.

- We live in a jungle and the strong person is the one who survives.

- People will get at me if I don't get them first.

- I have been unfairly treated and am entitled to get my fair share by whatever means I can.

- If people can't take care of themselves, that's their problem.

Neurological mechanisms in psychopathy

Converging evidence suggests that the deficits in emotional processing associated with psychopathy are linked to damage to the limbic system, which inhibits the processing of emotional information. Laakso et al. (2001), for example, used brain imaging techniques to gain accurate data on the brain anatomy of 18 habitually violent psychopathic offenders. They found a strong negative association between the size of hippocampus and scores on the Hare Psychopathy Checklist, suggesting that damage in this area, which is involved in the acquisition of conditioned fear, may explain the lack of fear associated with psychopathic behaviour.

These data are added to by the findings of Kiehl et al. (2001) who used brain imaging to study activity within the limbic system in response to an 'affective memory task'. In it, three groups of participants (criminal psychopaths, criminal non-psychopaths and 'normal' controls) were asked to rehearse and remember lists of either neutral words or words describing negative emotions, and to identify these words in a subsequent recognition task. Psychopaths had significantly less activity within their limbic systems and greater activation of the frontal lobes while processing negative emotional words than the other groups, suggesting that the psychopaths and non-psychopaths used quite different brain systems to process emotional information. Birbaumer et al. (2005) extended this work to examine neurological processes while participants received painful pressure following presentation of various stimuli. The presentation of these stimuli before the pain meant that 'normal' participants learned to expect pain, reported some anxiety about these expectations, and developed a conditioned 'pain' response to these stimuli – evident through increased sweat gland activity when presented with the stimuli. During the acquisition phase of the study, they showed enhanced differential activation in the limbic–prefrontal circuit (amygdala, orbitofrontal cortex, insula and anterior cingulate). By contrast, psychopaths displayed no significant activity in this circuit, failed to show any conditioned 'pain' response and reported no anxiety.

Treatment of antisocial personality

Psychological interventions

Although there are a number of potential intervention types and focuses for people labelled as having antisocial personality disorder, treatment trials have almost exclusively focused on criminal behaviour and violence in adolescents. As such, they may be considered better as programmes designed to change criminal behaviour than antisocial personality *per se*. The consensus of these studies is that the classic 'boot camp' or incarceration does not work. More effective interventions appear to be those targeting the family. Borduin (1999), for example, described a multi-systemic, family-based approach, the goal of which was to provide participants with the skills to help them cope with family and extra-family problems. Family interventions aimed to improve parenting skills, encourage parents to support their child, and reduce levels of parental stress within the household. Parents were encouraged to develop strategies to monitor and reward progress at school, and to establish home-work routines. Peer-oriented interventions were designed to increase affiliation with pro-social peers through participation in youth group meetings, organized athletics and after-school activities. Sanctions were applied following associations with deviant peers. Cognitive behavioural interventions focused on teaching social and problem-solving skills. Interventions generally lasted up to five months, with initial sessions occurring as frequently as once a day, before tailing off to weekly as therapy progressed.

This approach has achieved significant success rates. Henggeler et al. (1992), for example, compared it with monitoring and general counselling in a group of 'serious juvenile offenders', most of whom had committed some form of violent crime. Immediately following the intervention, participants in the multisystemic intervention had improved their family and peer relationships more than those in the comparison condition. By one-year follow-up, they had also been arrested less frequently and had spent less time in prison: an effect that held up to the two-year follow-up. In a four-year follow-up of a similar trial by the same group, Borduin et al. (1995) reported a halving of the known recidivism rate among those who received the intervention compared with a control group (21 versus 47 per cent) four years after the intervention.

One problem faced by this type of intervention is that the parents frequently do not initiate or disengage from therapy. With this in mind, Nock and Kazdin (2005) examined how a brief intervention could enhance parent participation in this type of intervention. They used a technique they developed and called participation enhancement intervention. This used some of the principles of a technique known as motivational interviewing (Miller and Rollnick 2002) combined with providing parents with information about the importance of attendance and adherence, eliciting motivational statements about attending and adhering to treatment, and helping parents to identify and develop plans for overcoming barriers to treatment that may arise over the course of treatment. The total time of the intervention was between 4 and 45 minutes and formed part of the first three therapy sessions. It also proved effective. Parents who received the intervention reported higher levels of treatment motivation, attended more treatment sessions, and engaged more in the treatment than those in a control group.

Pharmacological interventions
A number of pharmacological interventions have been used to treat individuals who present with delinquent or antisocial behaviour. Some have proven effective, particularly in the treatment of aggression. Lithium, for example, has been shown

to reduce the number of impulsive aggressive episodes among offenders in an American correction centre, although only a quarter of the young offenders treated evidenced more than modest behavioural changes. By contrast, chronic aggressive behaviour among the older inmates was completely suppressed by lithium treatment, returning to baseline levels on placebo (Sheard 1971). SSRIs have also been suggested as a means of controlling impulsive aggression, but there are as yet no controlled trials of their efficacy. How these interventions would compare with psychological programmes in which individuals are taught to control their anger is not known.

Treatment of psychopathy

Psychopathic individuals do not seek treatment, and most interventions have occurred within prison or other custodial settings. As a result of their lack of motivation to change, psychopathy has often been considered an untreatable condition, although there have been some voices of dissent from this somewhat negative viewpoint. Of interest are three review papers of the treatment of psychopathy published within two years of each other and reviewing essentially the same literature. Salekin (2002) conducted a meta-analysis on data from 42 treatment studies, and concluded that while ECT and therapeutic communities were relatively ineffective interventions, good results could be achieved following psychoanalytic and cognitive therapy. Evaluating much the same literature, Reid and Gacono (2000) were more pessimistic in their conclusions and could find no evidence of consistent therapeutic gain following any form of treatment. Similarly, Wong and Hare (2002) concluded that, of the 74 empirical studies they could identify, only two were adequately conducted, and that the evidence was so weak that it remained unclear whether any intervention can be effective.

Measuring the effectiveness of programmes to treat psychopathy is problematic. A defining characteristic of psychopathic individuals is that they tell lies and are manipulative. Self-report measures should therefore be treated with considerable caution. Even behavioural measures cannot be relied on. The results of a study by Seto and Barbaree (1999) illustrate the problem. Their study examined the impact of a relapse prevention programme for sexual offenders similar to those described in Chapter 10. Participants included a range of people, not just psychopathic individuals. Their report focused on the relationship between apparent progress made within therapy as a function of in-session behaviour, homework quality, and therapist ratings of motivation and 'progress', and the frequency of reoffending following treatment. Among non-psychopathic individuals, greater within-therapy improvements were predictive of lower levels of offences following discharge from prison. By contrast, there was a *positive* association between apparent progress in therapy and the frequency of offences committed by the psychopathic individuals who took part in the programme: greater apparent progress was associated with higher offence rates. It seems that these people were able to learn the responses that the therapists considered indicative of progress and were able to simulate them. Those that were best at this simulation were also the most likely to re-offend. Therapy did nothing to change the underlying motivation of their behaviour.

Thinking about . . .

At present, few psychiatrists treat psychopaths. Most consider psychopathy an untreatable condition – as the evidence reviewed here suggests. But new UK legislation being prepared by the government will not only require psychiatrists and other health professionals to treat psychopaths . . . it will also give them the right and responsibility to treat them within some sort of secure setting if they believe that the individual will (at some unspecified time in the future) behave in a way that puts others at risk – whether or not they have ever done so in the past. Of course, this then makes the psychiatrist legally responsible should they choose not to place that person in a place of care and some 'inappropriate' behaviour were to occur.

So, psychiatrists and others may be placed in a situation where they are having to treat a condition that cannot be treated . . . and/or place people in some secure place also unspecified – in case they commit some form of offence.

Does this seem unreasonable? Or should society, acting through health professionals, be able to control the actions of potentially 'dangerous' individuals?

Psychoanalysis

A number of early studies of the treatment of psychopathic individuals involved psychoanalytic methods (Salekin 2002). These were virtually all case studies, and none compared the intervention with any other form of treatment or changes within a control group. Case histories are generally considered with some caution, as clinicians typically report their treatment successes, not their failures, so they represent a biased sample of cases. The successes reported in these studies may therefore not indicate the likely success rates among an unselected group of individuals, and do not provide strong evidence for the effectiveness of psychoanalysis in this population.

Therapeutic communities

Therapeutic communities were first developed under the leadership of Maxwell Jones in the UK in the late 1940s. They provide an intensive 24-hour-a-day intervention to change psychopathic behaviour. Those within them are made responsible for the physical and emotional care of others within the community. The group itself establishes acceptable and unacceptable behaviours. Members are required to accept the authority of the group, and to submit to its sanctions if they disobey the rules. Communities are loosely based on Rogerian principles (see Chapter 2), and try to inculcate high levels of honesty, sincerity and empathy.

One of the best evaluations of the effectiveness of this approach was reported by Rice et al. (1992). They focused on a therapeutic community situated within a maximum security prison. The programme was led by those within it, and comprised 80 hours of intensive group therapy each week, intended to help participants develop empathy and responsibility for their peers. Those who responded well led therapeutic groups and became involved in administering the programme. All participants were involved in decisions about who was released or transferred from the programme.

Participants had little contact with professional staff. Nor did they have much opportunity for diversion: access to television or even informal social encounters were severely limited. Participation in the programme was compulsory: disruptive behaviour, for example, resulted in entry into a sub-programme in which the individual discussed their reasons for not wanting to be in the programme, but they were ultimately expected to resume participation. The authors noted that some of these programme characteristics would now not be ethically acceptable, but that the programme was well regarded at the time it took place in the 1960s and 1970s.

The programme accepted both psychopaths and non-psychopaths, who were followed up for an average of ten years after discharge. Analyses compared the outcomes on psychopathic individuals, non-psychopathic participants and a matched control group who did not enter the community. Their results were similar to those reported by Seto and Barbaree (1999). Non-psychopathic individuals were less likely to offend following discharge than those in the control group. By contrast, psychopathic individuals who participated in the programme were more likely to engage in violent crime following discharge than those in the control group, with known recidivism rates of 78 versus 55 per cent respectively. The therapeutic community approach may actually have taught psychopathic individuals how to manipulate others more effectively – an unexpected and unwanted result.

Cognitive interventions

Cognitive behavioural interventions may not be immune from this paradoxical outcome. Hare et al. (2000) examined the outcome of a number of short-term, prison-based, cognitive behavioural programmes including anger management and social skills training. Their data revealed that the interventions had little effect on re-offence rates of most psychopathic individuals. However, among offenders with particularly high levels of psychopathy, re-offence rates rose following treatment. Again, it seems that these courses taught these people how to be 'better psychopaths'.

Despite these negative results, a number of research groups have considered how the goals and strategies of cognitive behavioural therapy could be adapted to treat psychopathic individuals. Beck et al. (1990) attempted to define the realistic goals of such interventions. They noted that the individual will continue to act primarily out of self-interest, and that the goal of therapy should therefore be to help them act in ways that are functional and adaptive within these limits. Cognitive challenge, which lies at the heart of the intervention, may therefore not only address core schemata such as 'I am always right', or 'Other people should see things my way', but also question whether antisocial behaviour is in the individual's own interest. Participants in therapy may, for example, be encouraged to question whether behaving in a way that assumes 'other people should see things my way' causes interpersonal friction which interferes with their own goals, and to change their behaviour if this is the case. This approach allows client and therapist to work together towards agreed goals.

Wong and Hare (2002) developed a substantial cognitive behavioural approach to the treatment of psychopathy, involving interventions at both an institutional (prison) and individual level. Their intervention was problem-focused and addressed issues specific to psychopathic individuals. Key elements of the programme included the following:

- *Support of pro-social attitudes and behaviour:* many psychopathic individuals within an institution seek out others with similar views who will reinforce their own beliefs. To minimize the risk of this happening, Wong and Hare (2002) suggest that a 'pro-social milieu' is established within the institution. This may be achieved by high-status individuals within the programme modelling positive attitudes and encouraging them in others, and encouraging group reinforcement of pro-social behaviours. Note that the results of Rice et al. (1992) suggest that this may not be easy to establish.

- *Changing dysfunctional behaviours – aggression, manipulation, intimidation:* strategies to achieve change include self-instruction training (Meichenbaum 1985: see Chapter 2 in this volume) to prevent overreacting to situations in which the individual feels inappropriately threatened or angry, and interpersonal skills training where these are lacking and contributing to the use of intimidation or other dysfunctional behaviours. These may be taught through role play and reinforcement of appropriate behaviour.

- *Learning to take responsibility for one's actions:* the intervention here involves a detailed analysis of the factors that lead up to offences, and identifying where the individual made choices that ultimately lead to offending. This also forms the core of relapse prevention training (see Chapters 9 and 12), as information here both encourages the individual to take responsibility for the actions that led to offending behaviour and to identify strategies to avoid them in the future.

The programme also examined strategies for minimizing substance misuse and helping the individual gain work skills or develop leisure activities to help avoid boredom once discharged, as this may trigger antisocial behaviour. Finally, the programme addressed the social network into which the individual is discharged following their stay in prison. Attempts to maintain or re-establish links with supportive family or other means of social support were recommended, although family contacts may be conducted with some caution, as relationships with family members are frequently poor. Evidence of the effectiveness of these therapeutic approaches has yet to be reported.

Cluster C diagnoses

Cluster C diagnoses subsume what may be termed neurotic disorders. According to DSM-IV-TR, avoidant personality is characterized by social inhibition, feelings of inadequacy, and hypersensitivity to negative evaluation. It begins in early adulthood and the individual has at least four of the following features. They:

- avoid occupational activities that involve significant interpersonal contact, because of fears of criticism, disapproval, or rejection
- are unwilling to get involved with people unless certain of being liked
- show restraint within intimate relationships because of the fear of being shamed or ridiculed
- are preoccupied with being criticized or rejected in social situations
- are inhibited in new interpersonal situations because of feelings of inadequacy

- view themselves as socially inept, personally unappealing, or inferior to others
- are unusually reluctant to take personal risks or to engage in any new activities because they may prove embarrassing.

A person with a dependent personality has the following characteristics. They:

- have difficulty making everyday decisions without an excessive amount of advice and reassurance from others
- need others to assume responsibility for most major areas of his or her life
- have difficulty expressing disagreement with others because of fear of loss of support or approval
- have difficulty initiating projects or doing things on his or her own (because of a lack of self-confidence in judgement or abilities rather than a lack of motivation or energy)
- go to excessive lengths to obtain nurturance and support from others, to the point of volunteering to do things that are unpleasant
- feel uncomfortable or helpless when alone
- urgently seek another relationship as a source of care and support when a close relationship ends
- are unrealistically preoccupied with fears of being left to take care of himself or herself.

Finally, the characteristics of the obsessive-compulsive personality are that the individual:

- is preoccupied with details, rules, lists, order, organization or schedules to the extent that the major point of the activity is lost
- shows perfectionism that interferes with task completion (e.g. is unable to complete a project because his or her own overly strict standards are not met)
- is excessively devoted to work and productivity to the exclusion of leisure activities and friendships
- is over-conscientious, and inflexible about matters of morality, ethics or values
- is unable to discard worn-out or worthless objects even when they have no sentimental value
- is reluctant to delegate tasks or to work with others unless they submit to exactly his or her way of doing things
- adopts a miserly spending style towards both self and others; money is viewed as something to be hoarded for future catastrophes
- shows rigidity and stubbornness.

The prevalence of cluster C disorders in the general population varies from between 1 and 8 per cent depending on the disorder and study (Tyrer 2002). The linkage between the conditions is not as strong as that within the cluster A group, and a number of factor analyses have found little or no overlap between the characteristics of obsessive-compulsive personality disorder and the others (e.g. Costa and McCrea 1992). There is also considerable overlap between the diagnostic criteria for the anxious personality types and axis 1 diagnoses such as social phobia, depression and generalized anxiety disorder, making differential diagnoses difficult to achieve at times. So close are these diagnoses that Ralevski et al. (2005) suggested that avoidant personality disorder and social phobia are 'alternative conceptualizations of the same disorder'. Certainly, these personality types place individuals at significant risk of developing axis 1 (see Chapter 1) diagnoses of anxiety or depression. When people with these personality types go on to develop axis 1 disorders, they typically experience more severe problems than those individuals without such a background (e.g. Boone et al. 1999).

There are relatively few studies exploring the origins of cluster C personality disorders. However, work by Torgersen et al. (2000) indicated both genetic and biological pathways to the disorders based on their genetic study. They modelled the role of genetic and environmental factors in the development of a variety of personality disorders and found a significant genetic contribution to the development of dependent, avoidant and obsessive-compulsive disorders. Their analyses excluded a role for a familial environment in cases of avoidant and obsessive-compulsive disorders, but a mixture of both genetic and environmental factors contributed to the development of dependent personality. By contrast, Parker et al. (1999) found associations between retrospective ratings of parents as uncaring, over-controlling or abusive to be associated with anxious, cluster C, personality types. How much this reflected reality, and how much cognitive distortions cannot be determined. Similarly, Nordahl and Stiles (1997) found that patients diagnosed with obsessive-compulsive personality disorder reported lower levels of paternal care and higher levels of paternal overprotection than a 'normal' control group. By contrast, avoidant, dependent, and cluster A personality disorders were not associated with abnormal parental bonding.

There are also very few studies of treatment research related to the cluster C disorders. There is some evidence of a short-term benefit of treatment by MAOIs (Deltito and Stam 1989) and SSRIs (Fahlen 1995), although placebo-controlled, definitive studies are still lacking. Studies of the effectiveness of psychological therapies have involved sub-analyses of people with both personality disorders and axis 1 disorders in larger treatment trials or uncontrolled trials of cognitive behavioural therapy. Using the former approach, Tyrer et al. (1993) compared the impact of tricyclic antidepressants and cognitive behavioural therapy in patients with anxiety and depressive disorders, including some with cluster C personality type. Tricyclics fared best over a two-year follow-up period in this group. Gude et al. (2001) found some benefit over a one-year follow-up following brief treatment using schema-focused therapy, which attempted to change the core beliefs underpinning the personality, but there was no control group against which to measure progress. Subsequently, Svartberg et al. (2004) compared the effectiveness of two active therapies (short-term dynamic psychotherapy and cognitive therapy) in the treatment of a variety of cluster C disorders. Two years after treatment, 54 per cent of the people who received short-term dynamic psychotherapy and 42 per cent of those who received cognitive therapy showed clinically significant improvements.

Chapter summary

1 DSM identifies ten types of personality disorder in three clusters: A – odd or eccentric; B – flamboyant or dramatic; and C – fearful or anxious.

2 These may be better considered as extremes on a continuum of personality factors rather than distinct 'diagnoses'.

3 Beck's evolutionary model of personality disorders suggests they are the inappropriate maladaptive pre-programmed responses to environmental events, that result from an interaction between genetic and childhood factors.

4 Cluster A diagnoses are also known as the schizophrenia spectrum disorders, and include paranoid, schizoid and schizotypal disorders.

5 Meehl suggested that the core personality disorder is genetically mediated, while risk for schizophrenia involves further genetic influences and high environmental stress factors.

6 Borderline personality disorder belongs to the cluster B group. Its core elements are an intense fear of abandonment, difficulties in coping with strong emotions, and the use of self-harm as means of coping with strong emotions.

7 The origins of the disorder seem largely linked to experiences of childhood rejections and trauma that translate into strong negative self-schemata and dissociation as a means of coping with distress.

8 Borderline personality disorder is difficult to treat, although significant therapeutic gains have been made using cognitive behavioural techniques. The effectiveness of a method known as emotional awareness training has yet to be fully evaluated. The disorder seems resistant to pharmacological therapy.

9 Although DSM tried to combine psychopathy and antisocial behaviour under one diagnostic umbrella, critics such as Hare have argued that they are different conditions. The DSM diagnostic criteria describe someone who is criminally antisocial. Psychopathic individuals experience a poverty of emotions as well as engage in antisocial behaviour.

10 Antisocial behaviour seems primarily to be the result of adverse social circumstances.

11 Psychopathic individuals also have neurological deficits within the limbic system that inhibit emotional processing.

12 Family or systemic interventions appear to be effective in the treatment of antisocial behaviour.

13 Finding effective treatments of psychopathic behaviour has proven more difficult. Standard interventions may actually increase psychopathic behaviour. Beck and Wong have been developing cognitive therapeutic interventions that may prove more effective – although there is no data yet concerning their effectiveness.

14 Cluster C diagnoses include those of avoidant, dependent and obsessive-compulsive personalities.

15 These personalities appear to be the product of both genetic and family factors – although the role of family may be less than that of genetics according to Torgersen and colleagues.

16 Although there are few studies of the effectiveness of interventions for cluster C personalities, cognitive therapy and psychodynamic therapy both appear to be of benefit.

For discussion

1 Are the 'personality disorders' categorically different from the personalities of 'normal' people?

2 Should families whose dynamics increase the risk of their children developing personality (or other) disorders be routinely offered some form of therapeutic support?

3 Should psychopaths be treated or punished for their behaviour?

Further reading

Davidson, K. (2000) *Cognitive Therapy for Personality Disorders*. Oxford: Butterworth-Heinemann.

Livesley W.J. (2005) Principles and strategies for treating personality disorder, *Canadian Journal of Psychiatry*, 50: 442–50.

Salekin, R.T. (2002) Psychopathy and therapeutic pessimism: clinical lore or clinical reality?, *Clinical Psychology Review*, 22: 79–112.

Trull, T.J. (2005) Dimensional models of personality disorder: coverage and cutoffs, *Journal of Personality Disorders*, 19: 262–82.

12

Eating disorders

Most of us have 'gone on a diet' at some time in our lives or wished to change our shape. Many of us succeed, at least in the short term, although we often experience a gradual increase in weight as we get older. For some, the imperative to diet or change shape may be more extreme than the norm – and be diagnosed as an eating disorder. Two eating disorders are considered in this chapter: anorexia nervosa and bulimia nervosa. By the end of the chapter, you should have an understanding of:

- The nature of anorexia and bulimia
- The various aetiological explanations of both disorders, including genetic, social, familial and cognitive factors
- The nature and effectiveness of interventions conducted with people who have eating disorders.

Although both disorders present in quite different ways, they have a number of elements in common, and many people with anorexia may shift into bulimic eating patterns at some time. Both involve prioritizing weight control. There are also significant differences between the conditions. People with bulimia, for example, are rarely underweight and they value being sexually attractive, unlike most people with anorexia. The chapter first describes the two conditions. Then, it discusses the aetiological factors that the conditions have in common and those on which they differ. It finally considers the treatment of the two conditions.

Anorexia nervosa

First identified in the late nineteenth century, anorexia nervosa involves behaviours intended to keep the individual as thin as possible. Indeed, the defining characteristic of anorexia is being significantly underweight. DSM-IV-TR suggested a weight-based cut-off point for a diagnosis of anorexia as being 15 per cent below the normal weight for age and height. Weight loss and control are generally achieved using one of two methods: the classic, type 1, pattern of self-imposed starvation, and the type 2 pattern of binging and purging through vomiting or the use of laxatives. Where anorexia is discussed in this chapter it usually refers to the first of these two types.

The DSM-IV-TR criteria for a diagnosis of anorexia are:

- a refusal to maintain body weight above a minimally normal weight for age and height
- intense fear of gaining weight, even though underweight
- disturbed body perception, undue influence of weight or shape on self-evaluation, or the denial of the seriousness of current low weight
- cessation of menstruation if this has already begun.

Between 80 and 90 per cent of those who develop anorexia nervosa are female, with the typical age of onset being between 14 and 18 years old (Pike 1998). Rooney et al. (1995) estimated the prevalence of anorexia nervosa to be 0.02 per cent of the total population and 0.1 per cent of young females. For most people with anorexia, weight control is a long-term issue. Loewe et al. (2001), for example, found that 21 years after their initial admission, just over half of a cohort of women identified as anorexic were 'fully recovered', 21 per cent were 'partially recovered' and 10 per cent still met the full diagnostic criteria for anorexia. Few had sought help or any form of treatment, and 16 per cent were dead of causes related to anorexia.

Many people with anorexia go on to develop eating habits typical of bulimia nervosa: that is, maintenance of normal weight while still having abnormal eating and vomiting patterns. In contrast to many mental health disorders, the prevalence of anorexia is highest among women in the higher socio-economic groups, and among those who achieve high academic achievement. People with anorexia tend to score low on measures of assertiveness and self-esteem, and high in self-directed hostility (Williams et al. 1993).

Despite their avoidance of eating, most people with anorexia are preoccupied with thoughts of food. They may spend much of their time thinking about food, preparing it for themselves or others, or watching others eat. They may report dreaming about food, experience hunger pains and retain an appetite for food. High levels of exercise or other behaviours that consume calories are common weight-loss strategies. Most, but not all, people with anorexia have a distorted body image, considerably overestimating their body proportions, and have a low opinion of their body shape (Gupta and Johnson 2000). Psychological problems, including mild depression, obsessive-compulsive disorder and anxiety, are common among people with anorexia.

The control and reduction in weight associated with anorexia can result in a number of health consequences. The most immediate is the absence of menstruation (or amenorrhoea). Less obvious problems include anaemia, increased tooth cavities and gum infections, high blood pressure, reduced bone mineral density, low blood pressure, rough and cracked skin, and dry and brittle hair. Health problems may move to crisis in the form of metabolic and electrolyte imbalances that can be life-threatening. Across studies, between zero and 21 per cent of people with anorexia die as a consequence of their problems (e.g. Birmingham et al. 2005), with the most common causes of death being starvation and suicide. The brain may also show evidence of changes at times of severe starvation, with reductions in brain volume and increases in the amount of cerebrospinal fluid. Thankfully, Wagner et al. (2006) found these changes to be reversible in people recovered for over one year.

Bulimia nervosa

The DSM-IV-TR (2000) criteria for bulimia are:

- recurrent episodes of binge eating
- recurrent inappropriate compensatory behaviour, such as vomiting after eating, in order to prevent weight gain
- compensatory behaviours occur, on average, at least twice a week for three months
- undue influence of weight or shape on self-evaluation.

Many people with bulimia feel unattractive, have a fear of becoming fat, and consider themselves to be heavier than they actually are (McKenzie et al. 1993). Their attempts to avoid being overweight are more chaotic than in anorexia, and periods of controlled eating are frequently interrupted by repeated, relatively short episodes of uncontrollable eating. These are followed by behaviours designed to counteract the consequences of bingeing. The amount of food consumed in binges can be vast: up to and beyond 5000 calories at any one time. Food is not eaten for pleasure; indeed, it is usually eaten secretly, rapidly and barely tasted. Episodes are usually preceded by periods of considerable physical and psychological tension, and eating serves to reduce this tension. While bingeing, the individual may feel out of control, and episodes are typically followed by feelings of guilt, self-blame and depression. The weight of people with bulimia usually remains within the normal range, although it may fluctuate considerably over time.

Between 80 and 90 per cent of people with bulimia vomit after eating in an attempt to control their weight, one-third abuse laxatives, while others may exercise excessively (Anderson and Maloney 2001). Compensatory behaviours reduce discomfort and feelings of anxiety, self-disgust or lack of control associated with bingeing. Ironically, however, they frequently fail to prevent the calorific intake from much of the ingested food. Bulimia involves some risk to health. Repeated vomiting and laxative abuse can lead to problems including abdominal pain, digestive problems, dehydration, damage to the stomach lining and to the back of the teeth, where regurgitated acid can do permanent damage to the tooth enamel. The most serious outcome can be an electrolyte imbalance leading to renal damage and potentially fatal cardiac arrhythmias.

The prevalence of bulimia varies between 0.5 and 1 per cent of the population across community samples (Fairburn and Beglin 1994). However, among young women, rates are much higher. Up to 50 per cent of female students surveyed by Schwitzer et al. (2001) reported periodic binges; 6 per cent had tried vomiting; 8 per cent had used laxatives on at least one occasion. Few, however, engaged in these behaviours sufficiently frequently for them to be considered a disorder. In a population of slightly older women attending a family planning clinic, Cooper and Fairburn

(1983) found that 20 per cent reported at least one bulimic episode; 3 per cent had used it as a means of weight control (see Table 12.1).

Aetiology of anorexia and bulimia

Genetic factors

Genetic factors may contribute to risk for both anorexia and bulimia. Klump et al. (2001), for example, estimated 74 per cent of the variance in anorexic behaviours to be attributable to genetic factors, following a twin study in which they found 50 per cent of MZ twins and no DZ twins to be concordant for anorexia. Similarly, Kendler et al. (1991) found the rate of concordance for bulimia between MZ twins to be higher than that between DZ twins, although the concordance rates for both groups were relatively low: 23 and 9 per cent respectively. In addition to genetic risk for eating disorders, Keel et al. (2005) found evidence of shared genetic risk for both eating and anxiety disorders in a large-scale twin study involving nearly 700 twins. Genetic studies have now moved from family studies, indicating potential genetic processes, to examination of actual genes. Key genes identified as being involved in eating disorders appear to control serotonin metabolism, with particular attention given to the gene linked to various alleles of the serotonin 2A receptor gene (e.g. Ricca et al. 2002) – although other variants have also been studied. Evidence for the involvement of

Table 12.1 Differences between 'classic' anorexia nervosa and bulimia nervosa

Restrictive anorexia	Bulimia nervosa
Body weight significantly below age/height norms	Weight varies: underweight, overweight, close to age/height norms
Less likely to experience intense hunger	More likely to experience intense hunger
Less likely to have been overweight in the past	More likely to have been overweight in the past
More likely to be sexually immature and inexperienced	More likely to be sexually active
Considers behaviour as reasonable and 'normal'	Considers behaviour as abnormal
Less likely to abuse drugs or alcohol	More likely to abuse drugs or alcohol
Less likely to engage in deliberate self-harm	More likely to engage in deliberate self-harm
Tendency to deny family conflict	Acknowledges family conflict
Age of onset between 14 and 18 years	Age of onset between 15 and 21 years
Relatively independent	Seeks the approval of others; wants to be attractive to others
Weight loss is not driven by a wish to look 'feminine'	Accepts social concepts of 'femininity' and wishes to adhere to them
High self-control	Impulsive and emotional instability

genes involved in the regulation of other neurotransmitters, including dopamine and norepinephrine, is less strong (Hinney et al. 2004).

Biochemical mechanisms

The main brain area involved in the regulation of appetite is the hypothalamus, although other areas and factors in the gut also influence hunger and satiety. The lateral hypothalamus produces hunger when stimulated; surgical damage results in dramatic reductions in food intake and weight loss. Activation of the ventromedial hypothalamus triggers feelings of satiation and reduces hunger: for this reason it has been called the satiety centre.

The *set-point theory* (Keesey 1986) suggests that food intake and weight control are the result of a balance between these two parts of the hypothalamus and other metabolic processes, which try to maintain the body at a weight set-point. Eating excessively results in a variety of metabolic processes that burn calories and reduce hunger. Eating too little results in reductions in metabolic rate and increases in feelings of hunger. According to set-point theory, as an individual tries to diet and their weight begins to fall, hypothalamic activity reduces metabolic rate and increases the urge to eat. This combination of processes makes it difficult to lose weight. Successful dieting involves countering these processes, which remit in time and allow weight loss to occur. Perhaps here lies one of the differences between people with anorexia and those with bulimia. Individuals with anorexia learn to control their feelings of hunger and continue to control their diet whatever their symptoms. In doing so, they counter the effects of the hypothalamic control and continue to lose weight. People with bulimia, on the other hand, enter a constant battle against these processes: sometimes winning and sometimes losing. Activity within the hypothalamus is largely mediated by two neurotransmitters: dopamine and serotonin, which initiate, maintain, and then inhibit eating.

Dopamine   At the onset of or when anticipating eating, dopamine activity increases in both the lateral hypothalamus and the mesolimbic dopamine system – the primary reward system (see Chapter 3). Thus, the early stages of eating are both triggered and maintained by a direct effect on hunger and a feeling of pleasure. As eating continues, the dopaminergic activity is replaced by serotinergic activity, which reduces appetite and inhibits eating. Jimerson et al. (1992) suggested that people prone to binge eating may experience reductions in the levels of dopamine release (or be insensitive to the dopamine that is released) when they start eating. This may lead to binge eating as they attempt to achieve previous levels of satisfaction/reward from eating. Such speculation is supported by findings of low levels of HVA (a metabolite of dopamine) in the cerebrospinal fluid of people with bulimia (Kaye and Weltzin 1991). Surprisingly, perhaps, low levels of HVA have also been found in people with anorexia – both while showing eating restrictions and following recovery (Kaye et al. 1999). One explanation for the similarity of findings between people with anorexia and bulimia is that many of the studies of people with anorexia include people who binge and purge (type 2 anorexia) who may have some common biological features with bulimia. However, at present we can only conclude that dopamine appears to have a role in the eating disorders – although its exact role remains to be determined.

Serotonin   Animal studies have shown that when serotonin is released into either the ventromedial or lateral hypothalamus, animals stop eating and may starve despite the presence of food. Thus, high levels of serotonin lead to feelings of satiation and lower levels of eating – as well as improve mood. Low levels of serotonin result in excess eating and obesity – and low mood. This is not simply the result of serotonin's influence on the hypothalamus – areas such as the limbic system are also involved.

One explanation for the eating binges associated with bulimia has been that dieting reduces levels of tryptophan, a precursor to serotonin, leading to low mood and cravings for food high in tryptophan – carbohydrates such as chocolate, cakes and chips (Kaye et al. 1988). Eating these restores serotonin and mood levels to normal (Wurtman and Wurtman 1986). In support of this hypothesis, Kaye et al. (1988) found that women with bulimia typically stopped bingeing if their levels of tryptophan increased significantly following an eating binge: those whose tryptophan remained relatively low continued bingeing. In a related study, Goldbloom et al. (1990) found that following release into the synaptic cleft, bulimics' serotonin was more quickly reabsorbed by the initiating axon than that of normal controls, resulting in a reduced *availability* of serotonin at the receptor cells. In response to these findings, Jimerson et al. (1992) suggested that periodic binge eating may cause sudden increases in serotonin levels within the brain. This causes the receptors to become less sensitive to serotonin when released. This low sensitivity to serotonin means that the individual may become less responsive to normal levels of serotonin, requiring them to take in larger amounts of tryptophan to convert to serotonin in order to maintain emotional equilibrium.

Despite some supportive data, both theories have not always been supported by empirical evidence. Weltzin et al. (1995), for example, found no evidence of reduced levels of tryptophan prior to binge eating episodes in women with bulimia, and Jansen et al. (1989) found that levels of tryptophan in the foods typically eaten in a binge were actually quite low in tryptophan and were not a particularly effective means of increasing tryptophan levels. Behavioural studies also provide limited support for the hypothesis. Steiger et al. (2005) used hand-held computers to obtain repeated 'online' measurements of eating behaviours and mood in 21 women with bulimia. As expected, their mood was typically depressed before binge episodes. However, following bingeing, their mood deteriorated further.

People with anorexia typically have lower levels of serotonin metabolites in their cerebrospinal fluid than controls. However, this may be a consequence of their lack of dietary tryptophan (Kaye et al. 1988) Indeed, Kaye et al. (1991) found that when they were not starving themselves, people with anorexia had *higher* levels of serotonin levels than normal. This finding led Kaye (1997) to argue that reduced food intake may act as a means of reducing uncomfortably high levels of serotonin that may be associated with experiences such as feeling nervous or jittery. Unfortunately, more recent work in which serotonin use within the brain has been directly measured using brain imagery techniques (Kaye et al. 2005), found lower levels of serotonergic activity during periods of both starving and recovery among people with anorexia than among 'normal' controls. Brain areas involved include the frontal, cingulated, temporal and parietal cortical regions – which are involved in anxiety, behavioural control and body image. Together, these data suggest that while serotonin dysregulation may be involved in both bulimia and anorexia, as with dopamine, its exact role in either disorder is yet to be fully understood.

Socio-cultural factors

'Thin is attractive.' People with both anorexia and bulimia place a prime importance on shape and weight, probably because of a more general cultural emphasis placed on physical appearance within western society. Images of femininity and female attractiveness have shifted since the 1960s to a slimmer, less 'hour-glass' shape. The classic 'figure' portrayed in *Playboy* magazine, for example, has slimmed during the 1990s, with smaller hips, waist and bust measurements (Rubinstein and Caballero 2000). Not surprisingly, the prevalence of low body weight and eating disorders is particularly high among those groups where physical attractiveness or performance is placed at a premium, such as models, dancers and athletes. As social groups develop positive attitudes towards thinness, levels of eating disorders rise within them. In the USA, for example, as a high value on thinness has shifted from white upper-class women to those in the lower socio-economic groups and other ethnic groups, so has the prevalence of dieting and eating disorders (Striegal-Moore and Smolak 2000).

Judgements based on weight are not only aesthetic; attributions of a variety of personal attributes can be based on the appearance of the individual. Food, eating and weight are seen by many as moral issues, and body shape can be a major criterion of self- and other-evaluation (Wardle and Marsland 1990); many people hold prejudicial views against overweight individuals.

Over half the families in which an individual develops an eating disorder are likely to place a strong emphasis on weight and shape (Haworth-Hoeppner 2000). The mothers in such families are also more likely to diet and to be perfectionist than those in families where these disorders do not develop (Pike and Rodin 1991). Successful dieting may be one way of gaining acceptance from parents with high aspirations, particularly where the child has not 'succeeded' in other life domains. Not eating may make an individual important within the family, and give them some degree of control over other family members ('I'll eat if you . . .'). It may also provide a means of punishing them ('I'm not eating because you . . .'). A second consequence of anorexia is that it can lead the individual to be treated as a child, and allow them to avoid the responsibilities they would otherwise have to face; again, this may be most influential in families where there is a high emphasis on achievement.

A completely different model of anorexia is afforded by some family therapists, in which the person with anorexia is viewed as a symptom of a dysfunctional family. Minuchin et al. (1978) defined the characteristic of 'anorexic families' as being enmeshed, overprotective, rigid and conflict-avoidant. That is, there is conflict between parents which is controlled and hidden. According to Minuchin et al., adolescence is a stressful time for such families, as the adolescent's push for their independence within the family increases the risk of the parental conflict being exposed. The development of anorexia prevents total dissension within the family, and may even hold it together as the family unites around the 'identified patient'. The presentation of the young person as weak and in need of family support ensures that they become the focus of family attention and deflects it away from parental conflict.

Evidence for this theory is mainly based on the clinical experience of the Minuchin group of family therapists.

A final socio-cultural model suggests that both anorexia and bulimia may occur as a result of sexual abuse (Oppenheimer et al. 1985). According to this model, abuse results in the adolescent girl having strong negative attitudes towards her femininity, resulting in a rejection of the typical feminine shape and attempts to avoid it. This is most likely to occur around puberty. The evidence for this is not strong. Even though rates of sexual abuse are relatively high among people with eating disorders, it is not a defining characteristic, as they are no higher than those among people with mood, anxiety and other psychological disorders.

Psychological explanations

Weight-related schemata   Social factors translate into behaviour through cognitive processes. Despite the many differences in presenting problems, Fairburn's (1997) cognitive model proposed a similar cognitive disturbance in both anorexia and bulimia: a set of distorted beliefs and attitudes towards body shape and weight. Thinness and weight loss are prioritized, perhaps because of the high status given to looking thin and attractive, and the individual works to avoid weight gain and becoming fat. The underlying schemata involve judging one's self-worth on the basis of achieving a low body weight and being thin – so-called weight-related self-schemata.

Once weight-related schemata are established, they distort the way the individual perceives and interprets their experiences. Other people are evaluated not on the basis of personal qualities, but in terms of being thinner or fatter than the individual. All activities are assessed in terms of weight control, and any situation that leads to self-evaluation also results in an intensified focus on weight and shape. Any weight fluctuation has a profound effect on thoughts and feelings. For some people, their concerns and prioritizing control over their weight reflect a wider lack of self-esteem, a vulnerability to cultural messages about body weight (Stein and Corte 2003), and the desire to gain control over one aspect of their life. They hope to feel better about themselves if they are thinner – a process that leads them to be perpetually dissatisfied with their appearance and to be continually working to lose weight. Depression that may result from anorexic behaviour may intensify feelings of low self-esteem and increase dependence on controlling weight as a means of maintaining self-worth.

Both anorexia and bulimia may reflect different ways of coping with the same underlying cognitions. According to Fairburn (1997), people with anorexia are more able to sustain long-term control over their eating than those with bulimia, who are more chaotic and less consistent. He suggested that because of their restrictive dietary habits, individuals with both bulimia and anorexia are under significant psychological and physiological pressure to binge eat. To cope with these demands, both groups set a series of rules to govern their eating: when they should eat, what they can and cannot eat, and so on. These rules are typically perfectionist and difficult to achieve. Despite this, people with anorexia have sufficient self-control to be able to follow the rules they have set. By contrast, individuals with bulimia may on occasion fail to do so. This type of analysis is supported by personality studies (e.g. Cassin and von Ranson 2005) that have found both anorexia and bulimia to be consistently characterized by perfectionism, obsessive-compulsiveness, neuroticism, negative emotionality, and harm avoidance. However, anorexia is typically associated with traits of high constraint and persistence, while people with bulimia are more impulsive and sensation-seeking.

Once an individual with bulimia starts to eat, Fairburn suggests that they typically engage in dichotomous thinking ('I've eaten, so that's the end of my diet. What's the point of even trying to diet . . . ?') and a binge occurs. Binge eating also tends to improve low mood, and is thus in itself reinforcing (but see Steiger et al. 2005, discussed above). This is due to several effects, including drowsiness that follows eating large quantities of food and, in those who vomit, the feeling of relief and release of tension. These initial positive feelings are typically followed by feelings of disgust and shame at overeating, which results in a determined effort to follow the dietary rules set, which places the individual at risk of bingeing, and so the cycle continues (see Figure 12.1).

Initial attempts at weight loss may be triggered by a variety of factors, including critical comments about weight or appearance, teasing, or role confusion at the time of transition from child to woman. As well as cognitive processes, dietary changes may also be maintained by a number of reinforcement processes. Positive reinforcement may initially be experienced in the form of compliments on looking slim. As these comments turn to concern, they may still provide positive reinforcement as the individual gains attention from their family. One specific form of feedback may be particularly important: the daily or weekly reinforcement of the bathroom scales. These provide unequivocal feedback on performance. For people with low self-esteem, weight loss may provide one element of control and success in their life. Weight loss becomes equated with self-esteem and self-worth, perhaps more so

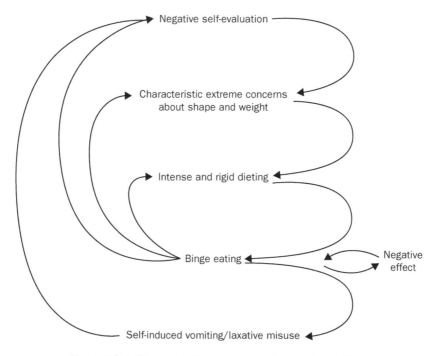

Figure 12.1 The cycle of bulimic behaviour and cognitions

than any other factor in life. Anorexic behaviours may also be driven by negative reinforcement processes. People with anorexia experience an intense fear of gaining weight. Avoidance of this fear, by restrictive eating, provides relief from such fears.

Distorted body image   A second cognitive model, involving a distorted body image, applies only to people with anorexia. This suggests that such people feel 'fat' even when their weight is actually clinically subnormal (Bruch 1982). Summarizing a plethora of research studies, Gupta and Johnson (2000) suggested that many people with anorexia considerably overestimate their body proportions, have a low opinion of their body shape, and consider themselves to be unattractive. By contrast, Slade and Brodie (1994) suggested that many of these reports represent an *emotional* reaction to their body shape rather than a perceptual experience. They suggested that those who experience an eating disorder are uncertain about their body size and shape, and only when they are compelled to make a judgement about these issues do they err on the side of reporting an overestimated body size. Skrzypek, Wehmeier and Remschmidt (2001) reached a similar conclusion, concluding from their summary of the relevant research that body image disturbance is not due to any perceptual deficit, but is based on 'cognitive-evaluative dissatisfaction'.

The restricted food intake achieved by people with anorexia may have biological effects unrelated to body size or shape that serves to perpetuate any cognitive distortions. Starvation affects a number of cognitive processes, resulting in poor concentration, concrete thinking, rigidity, withdrawal, obsessive-compulsive behaviour and depression. As a result, starvation may lead to a positive feedback loop in which people with anorexia become increasingly rigid in their beliefs and are unable to consider other ways of looking at their problem (Whittal and Zaretsky 1996).

Psychoanalytic explanations

Classic psychoanalytic theory provides a number of explanations for anorexia (Zerbe 2001). One explanation is that it stems from an unconscious confusion between eating and the sexual instinct. Some women may avoid eating as a means of, symbolically, avoiding sex. Another interpretation suggests that women with anorexia have fantasies of oral impregnation, and confuse fatness with pregnancy. Starvation reduces the risk of pregnancy. Yet another explanation is that anorexia reflects a regression to an earlier stage of development. The individual literally 'shrinks' in size. This, and the cessation of menstruation, are an unconscious rejection of adulthood and a wish to revert to a childhood state. Finally, anorexia is considered the result of an arrested psychosexual development. If the child is fixated in the oral stage, sexual anxieties and obsessions are likely to be expressed as disturbances of eating.

Integrating psychoanalytical and cognitive processes, Bruch (1982) argued that anorexia is the result of disturbed mother–child interactions that lead to ego deficiencies including a poor sense of autonomy and control, manifest through disordered eating patterns. According to Bruch (1982), some mothers fail to attend appropriately to their young child's needs, perhaps as a result of prioritizing their own needs over those of the child or misunderstanding their behaviour. They may, for example, provide food and intimacy at times that suit them rather than the child, or misinterpret the child's emotions or needs. As a result, the child may grow up confused and unaware of their own internal needs, not knowing for themselves when they are hungry or full, and unable to identify their own emotions. As a consequence of their confusion, they turn to external guides such as their parents, and appear to be 'model children'. However, they fail to develop genuine self-reliance and the experience of being in control of their behaviour, needs and impulses. They feel as if they do not own their own bodies. Adolescence increases their innate need to establish autonomy, but they feel unable to achieve this. To overcome their sense of helplessness, they seek excessive control over their body size and shape and eating habits. A number of studies have provided some support for Bruch's assertions. Steiner et al. (1991), for example, reported that many parents of young girls with anorexia tended to have fed them as a baby on their schedule rather than that of child. Fukunishi (1997) reported that many people with bulimia mistake emotions such as anxiety or upset as signs of hunger and respond to them by eating. Finally, Walters and Kendler (1995) reported that people with eating disorders tend to rely excessively on the opinions of others, and worry about how other people view them (see Box 12.1).

Box 12.1 Bulimia and anorexia

Here are two accounts of people with bulimia and anorexia. Despite both being concerned with eating-related disorders, the two discourses are completely different. The account of the person with bulimia centres on the drive to eat and the guilt and discomfort associated with it. That of the person with anorexia focuses on wider issues, in particular issues of revenge and control. The pathways to each disorder differ across people, so although these may be considered 'typical' accounts in some ways, the accounts of other people with the same disorder may differ markedly.

Bulimia

I think it's easier not to drink or take drugs than to eat normally. You can either take them or not. If you don't want to – you just avoid them. But eating is so different. You have to eat . . . and once you – well, I – start, it's so difficult to stop. I want to be slim and look good. And I like my food. So I say to myself OK. Today you will not eat till 6 o'clock and you will eat a healthy meal. So I start the day with good intentions.

But then I live for food. I can avoid eating at lunchtime – it's almost easy with people around me. But as the day goes on, I want food!! I don't feel hungry. But what happens when I get home, I just want to eat. It's on my mind, and I know there's food in the fridge – lovely ice cream . . . chocolate. God, I love chocolate! Why can't I like something healthy and low calorie?! I sit and watch the TV, but I'm thinking of food. I am now! Anyway, some nights I can get by, cook myself something reasonable – nights when I'm busy or interested in what's on TV or something. But other nights, I just go straight to the fridge and have a snack. Unfortunately, it's never a small one – what does that do to you? A couple of biscuits just doesn't work for me. So, I tend to snack on something big and calorific. Even that would be OK if I could stop there. But I tend to think, 'I've blown it now . . . I've begun to eat, so what's the point of stopping now?' Once I've blown away my good intentions, then I just give in to eating I suppose. So I eat and eat. I don't stop when I am full. I eat till I am bursting. I feel uncomfortable, and I know I'm bound to put on weight. I feel really guilty – another day when I haven't kept my good intentions. So, I make myself sick. I'm good at it. It's not difficult now. Then I feel better. At least I can relax and know that I won't put on weight. It feels such a relief. But I also know that I shouldn't have had to do it, so I feel guilty and vow that tomorrow I will control my eating and not need to do it. But, of course, tomorrow never comes . . .

Anorexia

My anorexia kicked in at age 13. I battled food issues for years before that. Mum was always on a diet – and I was often hooked into being her dieting partner, and sometimes competitor. Both our food struggles – I see now – only diverted our and the family's attention from the emotional turmoil permeating our household. I became the convenient whipping post of my parents' outbursts of anger, insecurities . . . I was hit a lot and verbally abused. At age 13, my parents cracked down and tried to totally control my life – friends, boyfriends – everything. That control pushed me over the edge . . . Dieting became an obsession for me. I dropped two stone in a month! The hunger was still there. Some days, all I thought about was food. But I was determined to conquer it. I strove for complete control – perhaps the only control I had. I felt repulsed if I ate – I had let myself down, lost control. I wanted to look good, to fit the ideal of womanhood. But a large part of the drive was revenge! I loved to see my parents' reactions to me starving. Dieting was no longer good, something to do with my mother . . . it was a weapon. Turning her own behaviour on her. They were partly angry because they could not control this part of me, and partly fear and worry. But I had control. They ranted, they shouted, and tried to get me to eat. But I wouldn't – not for them. I began to lose contact with my feelings. I wanted to starve to be in control, to prove I could do it, but also because I deserved to . . . because I hated myself.

Attachment theory suggests that some of these behaviours may be interpreted in terms of insecure attachment with a mother figure, leading to insecurity and anxiety at times of independence (Troisi et al. 2005). Ward et al. (2001) went further, and suggested that the mothers of adolescent girls with anorexia may transmit their anxious attachment patterns with their own mother to their daughters.

Interventions in anorexia

Given the multiple routes to anorexia, the optimal emphasis of treatment may vary considerably across individuals. Potential interventions include cognitive behavioural therapy, family therapy, insight-oriented psychotherapy, with each being complementary rather than competitive interventions. Interventions can be considered in two stages: first, initial treatment, usually in hospital, focusing on weight gain; and second, longer-term outpatient treatment focusing on sustained cognitive and behavioural change.

Promoting weight gain

In-patient care may be necessary where an individual's weight is seriously compromised: that is, less than 75 per cent of 'normal' for an individual's height and age. Interventions in hospital usually focus on providing extrinsic rewards for weight gain. This operant-based process involves gaining pre-specified rewards for pre-specified gains in weight, the most valued of which may be discharge from hospital on achieving a target weight. This avoids the danger of rewarding food intake, which may be subsequently vomited up and is therefore ineffective.

Some years ago, the nature of these rewards included access to a telephone or television. These are now considered to be basic rights, and removal of them would infringe such rights. Accordingly, the 'rewards' for eating are now typically defined by the individual and are more than the basic elements available to all in-patients. They may include increased social privileges, access to visitors, and exercise privileges. Calorific intake is gradually increased over time: too high an initial calorie intake may result in refusal to consume the calories. Nurses may also educate the individual about anorexia and provide more informal support and encouragement. Critical here is the reassurance that weight gains made at this time will not be translated into becoming overweight in the long run. Schwartz and Thompson (1981) reviewed the outcome of in-patient programmes such as this and found that at follow-up, there was a 6 per cent mortality rate from self-starvation, 49 per cent of people had recovered, 31 per cent had improved but still had an eating disorder, and 18 per cent showed no change from their original state.

Thinking about . . .

Before reading the next section, consider the implications of a failure to achieve any weight gain – or continued weight loss – during the first phase of treatment.

Most people with anorexia are intelligent and capable individuals. They choose to stop or minimize their eating. Do we, as health professionals or others, have the right to force them to eat, to prevent them engaging in what is their choice of behaviour? If someone is actively wishing not to have nutrition, should we force them to have food or put intravenous drips into their arm to improve their nutritional status? Or should we hope that they will eventually eat if their health becomes seriously compromised? It can be frightening to watch someone literally starving themself to death. But do we have the right to force them to eat or receive nutrition through drips in the knowledge that this will be distressing to the individual . . . and once it stops, the person is likely to continue to starve themself?

While a majority of people gain weight in this first phase of treatment, some continue to lose weight, possibly to the stage that this becomes life-threatening. This presents a significant clinical and ethical challenge to those involved in the care of such people. A key issue at this time is whether nutrition should be given against the affected individual's wishes. This debate has focused, in particular, on the competence or otherwise of people with anorexia to make what are truly life and death decisions. Some clinicians (e.g. Russon and Alison 1998) have argued that the majority of people with anorexia are mentally competent to make decisions about whether or not to eat. As a result, they suggest that it is inappropriate to treat them against their wishes, even if this leads to their death. Others (e.g. Treasure 2001), while accepting that force-feeding is inhumane and unacceptable, have pointed out that both it and other active treatments can be legally used with people with anorexia *in extremis*, as they are not mentally competent to make decisions that may result in their death.

Treasure (2001) identified four general principles that define whether an individual is competent under the law to make therapeutic choices or to refuse treatment. They must be able to do the following:

- take in and retain information relevant to their decision and understand the likely consequences of having or not having the treatment
- believe the information
- weigh the information in the balance as part of the process of arriving at a decision
- recognize they have a health problem and take action to remedy their condition.

According to Treasure, individuals with anorexia do not conform to these criteria and are therefore deemed, under law, incompetent to make medical decisions that may endanger their life. Accordingly, doctors have the right to treat the individual without their consent. This argument is in accord with legal precedents (Dyer 1997) that have stated that compulsory treatment of people with anorexia, including force-feeding, is both legal and may be necessary on occasion.

Cognitive behavioural approaches

The second phase of treatment involves interventions aimed at achieving and maintaining long-term behavioural change. Perhaps the most widely used cognitive behavioural approach was developed by Garner and Bemis (1985). This was divided into a number of phases, the first of which was intended to establish a working alliance with the individual. Garner and Bemis stated that at this time, it is critical that the individual's core beliefs are not directly challenged, as this is likely to result in a withdrawal from therapy. Instead, the therapist needs to align with the individual, recognize how their weight-control strategies are intended to fulfil important functions for them, and appreciate that these strategies have been partly successful. This may be linked to questioning whether they have achieved everything the individual intended, and evaluating the emotional and physical costs of extreme dieting. The first few sessions may be spent developing a list of the advantages and costs of their anorexic behaviour. There may also be exploration of the deeper schemata underlying this behaviour. Homework assignments may be used to gather data on how events influence thoughts and feelings, and to provide opportunities to practise different ways of interpreting weight- and eating-related events. Only once a working alliance has been achieved and the individual is motivated to at least consider change, can cognitive therapy begin.

Cognitive interventions may have multiple targets, including modifying inappropriate cognitions and developing autonomy. Emphasis may be placed on challenging perceptual/attitudinal distortions. While these may never change to perceptions of being thin, an awareness of distortions and an acceptance that they have some degree of exaggeration may help change the individual's willingness to eat. Autonomy may be encouraged by challenging negative cognitions and encouraging the individual to trust their own intuitions and feelings. Cognitive challenges encourage the individual to consider the high emotional cost of their behaviour, and help them to explore some of the more entrenched schemata that underpin this behaviour, such as the belief that body weight or shape can serve as the sole criterion for self-worth and that complete control of one's body is necessary. Participants in therapy may also be taught problem-solving techniques to help them deal with any crises that might occur more effectively.

Despite the life-threatening nature and chronicity of the problem, there are remarkably few controlled trials of the effectiveness of cognitive behavioural interventions in anorexia (Pike 1998). This may be because the chronic nature of the condition means that many people could take part in several treatment programmes over the course of their condition, making it difficult to ascribe changes in their behaviour to any one intervention. The long-term risk of serious harm if individuals are assigned to a no-treatment condition and high drop-out of most interventions also make it difficult to conduct standard trials.

What data there are, nevertheless, suggest that cognitive behavioural therapy may be an effective intervention. In an early trial, Channon et al. (1989) compared behavioural and cognitive behavioural approaches. Behavioural therapy involved a gradual exposure to avoided foods: cognitive behavioural therapy identified challenging dysfunctional beliefs about eating. There were few differences between the two interventions at both 6- and 12-month follow-up, although the authors suggested that the greater acceptability of cognitive procedures and the lower attrition rate associated with them made this the better of the two interventions. The study did not have a 'no-treatment' control as this was considered unethical, so the benefits of intervention over no intervention could not be determined. In a similar comparison, Treasure et al. (1995) compared the effectiveness of a cognitive and combined cognitive/psychoanalytic therapy. By the end of the one-year intervention, both therapies proved equally effective, with 63 per cent of participants having achieved a 'good' or 'intermediate' recovery. Pike et al. (2003) found cognitive behavioural therapy to be more effective than nutritional counselling in reducing relapse rates in people recovering from anorexia. The combined percentage of people to drop out of therapy and/or relapse over a one-year period was 22 per cent of those in the cognitive therapy condition and 73 per cent in the nutritional counselling condition. However, the findings of McIntosh et al. (2005) suggested that cognitive behavioural therapy may not always prove more effective than some alternatives. They compared the effectiveness of cognitive behavioural therapy, interpersonal therapy, and non-specific supportive clinical management. The latter was thought to be the baseline against which these active therapies were measured. However, it proved the most effective approach, with 56 per cent of the people in this condition showing significant improvement, compared with 32 per cent in the cognitive behavioural intervention, and 10 per cent of those in the interpersonal therapy. The authors were surprised by these findings, and speculated that the cognitive behavioural therapy may have failed as the cognitive rigidity of the people with anorexia may have made it difficult to achieve cognitive, and hence behavioural, change.

Family therapy approaches

A number of different family therapies have been used to treat anorexia, although all seek to change the power structure within the family by empowering parents, preventing alliances that cross generations, and reducing tensions and problems between parents. Note that this approach contrasts markedly with the cognitive behavioural interventions described above which encourage autonomy and personal control over eating.

Structural family therapy   One of the first family approaches to treating anorexia was reported by Minuchin et al. (1978; see Chapter 4 of this volume). They reported an 85 per cent success rate, although this has been viewed with some caution as it was based on a series of case reports with relatively young and 'intact' families rather than data from controlled trials. More recently, Russell et al. (1987) followed a similar therapeutic approach which focused on the underlying stresses within the family. The approach had three tasks. The first involved engaging the family in the therapy process. They termed the second part the refeeding phase. In this, the family was observed eating together to identify relationships, communication of support, and rules about food and eating. At this time, the 'identified patient' and their siblings were encouraged to align, in order to reinforce appropriate boundaries within the family. The final stage involved changes in the family system, including return of control over eating to parents, working to support cooperation between parents, and stopping alignments or collusion between one or other parent and the person with the eating disorder.

Russell et al. (1987) compared the effectiveness of this approach with that of individual supportive therapy in the treatment of people with both anorexia and bulimia. Their findings were somewhat disappointing. Although many of the people with anorexia achieved significant weight gain, most participants achieved only modest gains on more general measures of outcome. At one-year follow-up, 23 per cent of the participants were rated as having a 'good' outcome, 16 per cent had a 'moderate' outcome and 61 per cent had a 'poor' outcome. Family therapy proved more effective than individual therapy on measures of weight, menstrual functioning and psychosocial adjustment for participants whose problems began before the age of 19 years and where the duration of problems was less than three years. Individual therapy proved marginally more effective than family therapy for older participants.

Behavioural family therapy   Behavioural family therapy (Robin et al. 1995) combines systemic and behavioural therapy approaches. The goals of therapy begin with restoration of weight. Strategies to achieve this include changing eating habits and cognitive therapy to minimize body image distortions, fear of fatness, and feelings of ineffectiveness. Family interaction patterns such as conflict avoidance, enmeshment and overprotectiveness are also targeted. Therapy follows three phases. First, control over eating is taken away from the individual and given to the parents, to restore the family hierarchy. Parents are taught and encouraged to implement a behavioural weight-gain programme for their child, including making meals, regulating exercise and establishing consequences for following or not following the plan. Once weight gain has been achieved, therapy moves to the second stage. This combines three elements:

- cognitive restructuring of distorted body image and unrealistic food beliefs
- working with the family to alter enmeshment, coalitions and inappropriate family hierarchies (see Chapter 4)
- gradually giving control over eating to the person with the eating disorder.

Finally, the family may be taught problem-solving and communication skills. Robin et al. (1995) evaluated the effectiveness of their approach, comparing it with supportive individual therapy, in a group of female adolescents aged between 12 and 19 years. At one-year follow-up, both forms of treatment had positive effects, although there were no between-group differences. Subsequently, Eisler et al. (2000) compared 'conjoint family therapy' with 'separated family therapy'. Both used the behavioural principles outlined above. However, in the conjoint therapy, the therapists worked with the whole family together, while in the separated family intervention they worked with adolescent girls and their parents separately. Both interventions proved effective over the one-year-long period of treatment, achieving significant gains on measures of symptomatology such as bulimic symptoms, as well as on nutritional status and mood. Among participants from families where there was significant maternal criticism towards the adolescent, the separated family intervention proved most effective. These data are in accord with the findings of Perkins et al. (2005) who found that adolescent girls who did want not involve their parents in their treatment for bulimia considered their mothers to be more blaming and to hold a more negative attitude towards them than those who wanted them to be involved.

Psychoanalytic therapy

A number of case studies and uncontrolled studies have shown psychoanalytic approaches to the treatment of anorexia to be effective with adolescents with relatively minor problems. However, studies of the effectiveness of this approach compared with others are limited. Dare et al. (2001) provided one such comparison. Their psychoanalytic intervention was relatively time-limited, averaging 24 sessions over a one-year period. In it, the therapist took a non-directive stance, gave no advice about eating or other problems of symptom management. Instead, he or she addressed the conscious and unconscious meanings of the symptom (that is, not eating) in terms of the individual's history, the effects of the symptom and its influence on their current relationships, and the manifestations of these influences in their relationship with the therapist. Dare et al. compared the effectiveness of this approach with family therapy similar to that provided by Russell et al. (1987), an individually based intervention with elements of both analytic and cognitive approaches, and a low-contact support condition in which participants received no systematic therapeutic approach. Participants in the study had a relatively poor prognosis. They had a late age of onset, a long duration of problems, and had not improved with other therapies. Nevertheless, by the end of the year-long interventions, about one-third of the women in the active interventions no longer met the criteria for a diagnosis of anorexia. Only 5 per cent of those in the control group had shown such improvements. No one intervention proved more effective than the others.

Pharmacological interventions

Kaye et al. (2001b) reported an intervention in which women with anorexia were treated with either fluoxetine or placebo control. Of those on fluoxetine, 63 per cent achieved a 'good' response as a result of gains in 'appropriate weight maintenance', obsessionality, 'core eating disorder symptoms' and mood. Only 16 per cent of those in the placebo group achieved comparable gains. However, this positive finding may be rather optimistic, as Attia and Schroeder (2005) reviewed the evidence from all the controlled studies of the treatment of anorexia using antidepressants and neuroleptics then available, and found little evidence of benefit. More specifically, Ferguson et al. (1999) concluded that although treatment with SSRIs may prove effective in the treatment of depression that may coexist with anorexia, there is no evidence of consistent changes in 'core' anorexic symptoms. This finding of benefit in some of the peripheral symptoms was also found in a small study reported by Mondraty et al. (2005), that found that anorexic individuals treated with an atypical antipsychotic (see Chapter 3) reported fewer ruminations than those treated with a phenothiazine. In a meta-analysis comparing psychological and pharmacological therapies, Bacaltchuk et al. (2002) found overall remission rates of 20 per cent following treatment with antidepressants compared with 39 per cent following psychotherapy.

Research box 12

Keel, P.K., Dorer, D.J., Franko, D.L. et al. (2005) Postremission predictors of relapse in women with eating disorders, *American Journal of Psychiatry*, 162: 2263–8.

Between 22 and 51 per cent of people who recover from anorexia and bulimia are likely to relapse. The authors note that the identification of predictors of post-remission relapse could reveal key targets for the prevention of future episodes of these problems. Previous studies of women with bulimia have identified a number of post-treatment predictors of relapse, including higher frequencies of vomiting, higher dietary restraint, greater dissatisfaction with body image, and the over-importance of weight and shape. Studies of women with anorexia have reported few post-treatment predictors of relapse. The aim of this study was to examine the rates and predictors of relapse in women with eating disorders following full remission of their symptoms.

Participants

Participants were women seeking treatment for an eating disorder in Boston between 1987 and 1991. Inclusion criteria included: a DSM-III-R diagnosis of anorexia or bulimia, a minimum age of 12 years, and no evidence of organic brain syndrome or terminal illness. Of the 294 women who met these criteria, 250 (85 per cent) agreed to participate in the longitudinal study. Four participants dropped out between the intake and follow-up interview, leaving a study cohort of 246 women, of whom 136 (55 per cent) were diagnosed with anorexia nervosa and 110 (45 per cent) with bulimia nervosa. Ninety-six per cent of the participants received some form of treatment during follow-up. At the last follow-up, 229 (93 per cent) participants had been retained in the study group.

Method

Women who met the study inclusion criteria were interviewed to confirm the presence of each eating disorder and to assess their psychiatric history using the Schedule for Affective Disorders and Schizophrenia – Lifetime Version. Objective measures of height and weight were obtained during this intake interview. Follow-up interviews were conducted every six months during the first five years of the study and then annually during the remaining years. At follow-up assessments, the Longitudinal Interval Follow-Up Evaluation (LIFE) adapted for eating disorders was used to assess eating pathology, co-morbid axis I disorders, psychosocial function, and whether or not the individual had been receiving treatment. In addition, the following DSM-III-R cognitive symptoms were probed: fear of becoming fat, misperception of body weight or shape, and over-concern with weight or shape.

Results

Remission rates were 13 per cent among the women diagnosed with anorexia, and 75 per cent of those with bulimia: 36 per cent of these women with anorexia and 35 per cent with bulimia subsequently relapsed. These women were the focus of the analyses. Of note was the finding that many of the women who recovered from anorexia nervosa relapsed into a bulimic syndrome. None of the women who recovered from bulimia nervosa relapsed into an anorexic syndrome.

Multivariate modelling of predictors of relapse among the women with anorexia found the following predictors: psychosocial function, over-concern with weight or shape, misperception of body weight or shape, age, and receiving more individual psychotherapy. Univariate predictors of relapse among women with bulimia included worse psychosocial function, over-concern with weight or shape, and worse scores on the Global Assessment of Functioning Scale (a measure of more general psycho-pathology). Multivariate modelling found the following predictors: worse psychosocial function and over-concern with weight or shape.

Discussion

Overall, one-third of the women who recovered from either eating disorder relapsed. As in previous studies, predictors of relapse included an over-concern with weight or shape, suggesting that focused work on body image may help patients achieve lasting recovery from both behavioural and cognitive symptoms of eating disorders. The finding that higher levels of individual therapy were predictive of relapse in the women diagnosed with anorexia may imply that such therapy is of little value. However, as this therapy followed remission, it is likely that it was related to other psychological problems – suggesting that those who received it had more general psychological problems than those that did not receive it. In other words, it may be a marker for more severe psychological problems.

Interventions in bulimia

Cognitive behavioural therapy

In contrast to interventions in anorexia, those in bulimia are more structured, and have a better prognosis (Anderson and Maloney 2001). One of the pioneers of cognitive behavioural interventions in bulimia developed a three-stage approach (Fairburn 1997). The initial stage has two aims: first, to provide a rationale for the treatment, and second, to replace binge eating with a pattern of more regular eating. Eating is restricted to three planned meals a day, plus two or three planned snacks, none of which is followed by vomiting or other compensatory behaviours. This is not usually accompanied by weight gain. Indeed, reductions in the frequency of binge eating often result in weight loss. Distracting activities, such as having a bath or contacting friends, can be used to minimize the risk of bingeing. Once regular meals are established, the desire to vomit may reduce naturally. However, where this remains problematic, continued use of these inhibitory behaviours for an hour or so after eating may be necessary. Laxative and diuretic use should also be stopped at this time, with a phased withdrawal programme established for those who are unable to do so immediately. Knowledge that these strategies do not prevent food absorption aids this process. Towards the end of this phase, therapy sessions may involve both the client and key friends or relatives, with the intention of establishing an environment that will support behavioural change.

The second stage involves the using of both behavioural and cognitive procedures to counter concerns about shape and weight, and other cognitive distortions. Behavioural interventions may involve eating previously avoided types of food and, where necessary, increasing energy intake. This may be achieved by working up a hierarchy from relatively acceptable foods to those that initially invoke high levels of anxiety or desires to binge or purge. At the same time, clients are encouraged to identify negative assumptions about their shape and weight, and to find evidence in support or against them using cognitive challenge techniques.

Fairburn (1997) noted that many clients have a limited repertoire of such thoughts, triggered by a range of different circumstances. By repeatedly examining these thoughts and the circumstances that trigger them, their potency and automacity gradually decline. Further behavioural hypothesis testing may involve a gradual introduction of previously avoided and feared behaviours, including exposing body shape through wearing tight clothing, undressing at swimming baths, or even no longer undressing in the dark. The third stage involves maintenance of progress achieved in the first two stages and consideration of strategies to prevent relapse once therapy is terminated.

Cognitive behavioural therapy is considered the psychological treatment of choice for bulimia (Anderson and Maloney 2001), achieving good results in both the short and the long term. Wilson (1996), for example, reported that an average of 55 per cent of participants in cognitive behavioural therapy programmes no longer purged at the end of therapy, and those who continued to purge did so much less: an average of an 86 per cent reduction in purging. Long-term follow-up data are also encouraging. Fairburn et al. (1995) reported that 63 per cent of their sample had not relapsed at an average of nearly six-year follow-up. Comparisons of behavioural therapy and cognitive behavioural therapy suggest that both are equally effective in reducing binge–purging immediately following treatment. However, cognitive behavioural therapy is superior in reducing the 'core psychopathology' of distorted weight and shape and in maintaining long-term changes (Fairburn 1997). Disappointingly, this form of intervention did not prove effective when translated into a guided self-help programme conducted in primary care using family doctors as 'therapists' (Walsh et al. 2004).

Interpersonal psychotherapy

One other psychological approach appears to be particularly effective in the treatment of bulimia. Interpersonal psychotherapy (IPT) focuses exclusively on strategies for improving interpersonal relationships to the exclusion of any other therapeutic issues. Fairburn et al. (1993) found it to be less effective than cognitive therapy in the short term. However, by one-year follow-up, the differences between the two conditions were not significant, as a result of continuing improvements among those who received IPT. Remission rates at this time were 46 per cent for IPT and 39 per cent for cognitive behavioural therapy. The authors speculated that these gains in the IPT condition resulted from an improvement in self-worth and relationships, which made weight and shape much less important to the individual. As the effects of IPT are more indirect than cognitive methods, they took longer to become apparent. A second comparison of the two approaches was reported by Agras et al. (2000). They found a similar outcome. Cogntive therapy proved more effective than IPT at the end of a 20-week intervention, with 29 per cent versus 6 per cent fully recovered. However, by one-year follow-up, although the cognitive therapy still appeared more successful, the differences between the groups were no longer significant (40 versus 27 per cent).

Pharmacological interventions

Overall, antidepressant medications for bulimia decrease binge frequency by an average of 56 per cent, compared with an average decrease of 11 per cent following treatment with placebo (Jimerson et al. 1993). However, many people treated with antidepressants drop out of treatment due to drug side-effects. In addition, a significant relapse rate of between 30 and 45 per cent is typical in patients between four and six months following cessation of medication. Jimerson et al. (1993) summarized the data, suggesting that most people show at least a 50 per cent improvement following prescription of antidepressants, although only one-third will experience a sustained remission.

Three of five studies that have compared cognitive behavioural and pharmacological interventions found no differences in their effectiveness (Bacaltchuk et al. 1999). Two found cognitive behavioural interventions to be superior. Overall, long-term remission rates were 20 per cent for antidepressants and 39 per cent for cognitive approaches. In addition, drop-out rates were higher among those receiving antidepressants than among those receiving cognitive therapy: 40 versus 18 per cent. In one of the studies reported in this analysis, Agras et al. (1994) randomly allocated women with bulimia into a number of conditions, including a short-term course of antidepressants, cognitive behavioural therapy or a combined treatment. At four-month follow-up, both cognitive behavioural therapy and the combined treatment were superior to medication alone on measures of binge eating and purging. These advantages were maintained up to one-year follow-up. At this time, 18 per cent of those receiving antidepressant treatment were free of binge eating and purging, in comparison with 78 per cent of those receiving the combined treatment. The one exception to these findings of the superiority of psychological therapy was reported by Walsh et al. (2004) in their study of the treatment of bulimia using guided self-help in primary care. In this context, treatment with an SSRI (fluoxetine) proved more effective than psychological therapy. Fluoxetine may also prove a useful intervention among people who do not respond to cognitive behavioural interventions (Walsh et al. 2000).

Chapter summary

1 Anorexia is defined by the desire to achieve a body weight significantly below normal. This can be achieved in two ways: self-imposed starvation, or bingeing and purging.

2 Anorexia has a relatively poor prognosis, with long-term mortality rates of up to 16 per cent, and complete 'recovery' in just over half the cases.

3 Bulimia has a better prognosis, with most people achieving something like normal eating patterns.

4 Cognitive models suggest that both conditions are driven by cognitions which prioritize control over eating and weight control. The behaviour of people with each condition varies as a result of their abilities to control their responses to hunger. People who engage in type 1 anorexic behaviour are able to control their hunger; those who are bulimic occasionally give in to urges to eat, and compensate by purging.

5 Psychoanalytic models of anorexia suggest that it forms a rejection of sexual instincts and risk of pregnancy.

6 Bruch contested that anorexia arose out of chaotic parent–child interactions that leave the child confused about their own emotional and physical needs. They turn to their parents to provide feedback on their own feelings. At the time of adolescence, they seek but fail to achieve autonomy from their parents. As a response, they seek excessive control over their size and shape.

7 Socio-cultural models emphasize the role of social pressures in shaping young women's striving for thinness and the perfect body.

8 Family models suggest anorexia results from aberrant family dynamics. Minuchin, for example, suggested that the person with anorexia serves to maintain family cohesion as the family focuses on them and their needs, and ignores the dysfunctional relationship between their parents.

9 There appears to be a genetic risk for anorexia, possibly mediated through disorders of serotonin metabolism.

10 Interventions in anorexia usually involve two stages: first, weight gain to safe levels, and second, longer-term interventions involving cognitive behavioural

therapy, family therapy, psychotherapy or drug therapy. The best intervention for each individual may depend on the specific factors that led to their problems, with each of the psychological approaches being of benefit to some. The long-term prognosis, however, is not good.

11 Cognitive behavioural interventions are acknowledged as the treatment of choice in bulimia, with most people making significant long-term gains. However, in some contexts, pharmacological therapy using SSRIs may be advantageous.

For discussion

1 Should we actively treat people with anorexia who are close to dying as a result of their restrained eating, or should we respect their desire not to eat whatever the consequences?

2 Anorexia is perhaps one of the most difficult psychological conditions to treat. Given the success of cognitive behavioural techniques in other conditions, why should this not be the case in anorexia?

3 Bulimic behaviour could be considered a highly functional way of controlling weight. If this is the case, should it be treated only where the affected individual is distressed by their way of controlling their weight?

Further reading

Fairburn, C. and Brownell, K.D. (eds) (2005) *Eating Disorders and Obesity: A Comprehensive Handbook*. London: Europa Publications Ltd.

Grange, D. and Lock, J. (2005) The dearth of psychological treatment studies for anorexia nervosa, *International Journal of Eating Disorders*, 37: 79–91.

Russell, G.F. (2001) Involuntary treatment in anorexia nervosa, *Psychiatric Clinics of North America*, 24: 337–49.

Slade, P. and Brodie, D. (1994) Body-image distortion and eating disorder: a reconceptualization based on the recent literature, *European Eating Disorders Review*, 2: 32–46.

13

Developmental disorders

This chapter looks at three disorders within the diagnostic category of pervasive developmental difficulties. It describes three conditions in which difficulties in childhood are predictive of subsequent adult problems. It considers the problems associated with a variety of
disorders grouped under the broad category of learning difficulties. It then discusses the
aetiology and treatment of more specific conditions: autism and attention-deficit/
hyperactivity disorder (ADHD). By the end of the chapter, you should have an understanding of:

- Definitions and some of the causes of learning difficulties
- Aspects of the social and psychological care of people with learning difficulties
- The biological and psychological bases of autism
- The MMR vaccination and autism controversy
- Treatment of autism and autistic behaviours
- Factors that contribute to ADHD
- Biological and psychological treatments of ADHD.

Learning difficulties

Learning difficulties is a broad term that encompasses a variety of conditions whose
defining characteristic is a significant impairment of intellectual functioning. The
terms used to describe people with this condition differ across the world and in time.
In the UK, they have in the past been referred to as 'handicapped', 'subnormal' or
'retarded'. Now, all people with intellectual deficits, however profound, are referred to
as having learning difficulties. The reasons for these changing terms are not trivial:
they reflect attempts to minimize the prejudice often expressed in relation to this
group of people. In the USA, people with mild learning difficulties are referred to as
having learning difficulties, those with more profound deficits are still referred to as
having mental retardation.

  The first criterion for a diagnosis of having a learning disability is that its onset is
before the age of 18 years, to exclude the affects of trauma or other neurological

illness later in life. In addition, the individual needs to score significantly below the norm on intelligence tests. The usual cut-off score for this diagnosis is between 70 and 75 on the standard IQ test: two standard deviations below the population mean of 100. About 3 per cent of the population fall into this category. Within this category are a number of subcategories.

- IQ 50/55–70 *Mild learning difficulties:* includes about 85 per cent of people with learning difficulties. As children, they may be superficially indistinguishable from children with normal IQs, although their school performance shows they have clear learning difficulties. As adults, they are likely to be able to hold down unskilled jobs, although they may need help with social and financial issues.
- IQ 35/40–50/55 *Moderate learning difficulties:* includes about 10 per cent of people with learning difficulties. Within this group of people, learning difficulties are often combined with other neurological deficits, including problems with motor skills such as walking, holding implements, and so on. People in this group usually live independently within families or in group homes. Many have obvious brain damage and other pathologies.
- IQ 20/25–35/40 *Severe learning difficulties:* usually associated with genetically mediated physical abnormalities and limited sensorimotor control. Most people with severe learning difficulties live in institutions and require constant aid and supervision. As adults, they are typically lethargic and lack motivation. They may, nevertheless, communicate at a simple and concrete level.
- IQ < 20/25 *Profound learning difficulties:* profound mental and physical problems mean that people with this degree of difficulty require total supervision and nursing care all their lives. They cannot communicate using language and cannot get around on their own.

Although performance on IQ tests is frequently used to define the degree of learning difficulties, a critical issue is to what extent this affects the individual's ability to adapt to their environment. The second criterion for being identified as having learning difficulties is, therefore, evidence of a failure to develop the skills necessary to cope with the increasing demands placed on an individual as they grow older. Problems here may be the first sign of more pervasive problems.

Severe learning difficulties are more common among males than females. Mild learning difficulties are most common among males and those from economically deprived or adverse family backgrounds (Roeleveld et al. 1997). As the medical care of people with learning difficulties improves, the prevalence of older people with learning difficulties within society is increasing, at the same time as there are reductions in childhood prevalence resulting from increased prenatal screening and better child health care.

Aetiology of learning difficulties

Only about 25 per cent of cases of learning difficulty have an identified cause. These include:

- *genetic conditions:* including Down syndrome and Fragile X syndrome
- *infectious diseases:* including rubella, parental syphilis and encephalitis
- *environmental hazards:* including lead paint and exhaust fumes in leaded petrol
- *antenatal events:* including parental infections (including rubella), endocrine disorders such as hypothyroidism
- *perinatal trauma:* including asphyxia during birth.

For many people, there is no known biological cause. This is unsurprising, as IQ, like all other natural phenomena, follows a normal distribution within the population, with the exception of the so-called 'hump' within the lower end of the distribution that occurs as a consequence of biological causes (see Figure 13.1).

This does not mean that poor performance on IQ tests is totally biologically determined. Environmental factors, including quality of parental care, education and the social environment, can markedly influence IQ scores, academic performance and the development of adaptive skills, particularly for people with mild–moderate learning difficulties. Birch et al. (1970), for example, identified all children born with learning difficulties in Aberdeen between the years 1951 and 1955. Some 20 years later, they collected information from health and social services, and conducted interviews with the parents and the individuals themselves. Mild learning difficulties were significantly more prevalent in families from the lower socio-economic groups and families classed as unstable, defined by high levels of multiple carers, abuse and child neglect. No such relationship was found for more severe learning difficulties, which may be more biologically determined.

Down syndrome
People affected by Down syndrome are short and stocky in stature, and have typical facial characteristics, including upward-slanting eyes, sparse, fine straight hair, and a large furrowed tongue which protrudes as the result of a small mouth. They may also have a number of other less obvious characteristics, including serious heart malformations. All people with this condition have some degree of learning difficulty. Autopsy reveals brain tissue very similar to that found in Alzheimer's disease.

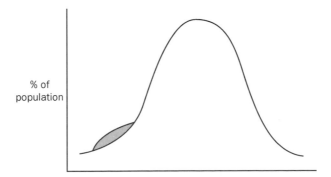

Figure 13.1 The genetic 'hump' within the distribution of IQ scores

Down syndrome is found in about 1 of 500–600 live births and has been detected in about 3 per cent of foetuses that spontaneously abort before 20 weeks' gestation. It occurs sporadically. People with the disorder are generally the children of parents without it, precluding an obvious genetic linkage. Because the risk of having a child with Down syndrome increases with the age of the mother, rising significantly in women giving birth over the age of 32 years, it was originally thought to be the result of an 'unfavourable' interaction between mother and foetus during pregnancy. However, it is now known to result from a chromosomal abnormality. People with Down syndrome have three, instead of two, chromosomes-21, leading to the more technical name of the disorder, trisomy-21.

This is the result of a process that occurs during the first few cell divisions that occur prior to fertilization. In trisomy-21, as the female egg cells duplicate, they fail to do so properly and some sex cells receive two chromosomes-21; some receive none. If these eggs are fertilized by a normal sperm, the resultant cells contain either three or one chromosome-21. The latter is not a viable combination and the developing cells are aborted. However, in the case of trisomy-21, the embryo and then the foetus remain viable and survive. The age-related risk is thought to be the result of some kind of metabolic or physical damage accumulated by the egg cells while lying in the ovaries for decades before ovulating. Although Down syndrome is considered to be untreatable, some aspects of the syndrome may respond to medical treatment. Van Trotsenburg et al. (2005), for example, found that treatment with thyroxine from immediately following birth may reduce the level of both motor and mental developmental delay during early childhood.

Fragile X syndrome

Fragile X syndrome affects approximately 1 in 1000 male and 1 in 2500 female births. This syndrome is caused by a defect within the FMR-1 (Fragile X mental retardation) gene located on the X chromosome. In Fragile X syndrome, a small region of the gene undergoes repeated, unnecessary duplications of a number of amino acids that result in a longer gene. When the number of repeats is small (fewer than 200) the individual often has no signs of the disorder. Where there are a larger number of repeats, the learning difficulties associated with Fragile X syndrome are observed. In families that show evidence of Fragile X syndrome, both the number of repeats and the length of the chromosome increase with succeeding generations, with a proportional increase in the severity of symptoms.

Because of the X-linkage, the frequency of the syndrome is greater in males than in females. This is because females typically have two X chromosomes, and males have one X and one Y chromosome. A female who inherits a chromosome carrying the Fragile X gene from either parent is likely to inherit a normal X chromosome from the other parent. This masks the presence of the Fragile X gene in a female. However, she may carry the gene and be capable of passing it on to her children. By contrast, because a male has only one X chromosome, if he inherits an affected X chromosome he will inevitably inherit the condition. This simple genetic model does not always hold, however: about 20 per cent of males who carry mutated forms of FMR-1 are either unaffected or only mildly affected. In addition, a single copy of the Fragile

X gene can be sufficient to cause the syndrome in some females. Why this happens is not understood.

Social interventions in learning difficulties

The lives of people with learning difficulties have been affected by socio-political factors as well as psychological and social interventions. One ideological movement, known as *normalization* (Wolfensberger 1972), has been particularly influential. This began in the 1960s in response to the poor institutional conditions in which many people with learning difficulties then lived. The movement called for people with learning difficulties to live a life as close to normal living conditions as possible, to have normal rhythms to their lives, and the means to establish and maintain behaviour as close to their cultural norms as possible. Under the rubric of *social role valorization* (Wolfensberger 1983), the movement subsequently called for the creation, support and defence of valued social roles for people with learning difficulties. These have led to five key aims of any service provided for people with learning difficulties:

- *Community presence:* people with learning difficulties live in the community, in normal houses, not institutions. To avoid 'pockets' of disability, housing is distributed through the community.
- *Choice:* people have the choices of accommodation, care and day-to-day routine, available to the 'normal' population.
- *Competence:* the competences of people with learning difficulties are acknowledged and maximized.
- *Respect:* people with learning difficulties are afforded the respect due to all other people within the population.
- *Participation:* people with learning difficulties have equal rights of participation in society, including access to work, leisure facilities, political activities and sexual relationships, as the rest of the population.

In the spirit of this integrated approach, children with learning difficulties are increasingly being taught in mainstream classes, and most adults with learning difficulties live in the community following the closure of large institutions. However, these changes fall short of the goals of normalization, and there is still work to do. Nearly two-thirds of British adults with learning difficulties, for example, continue to live with their family of birth – a significantly higher proportion than among the 'normal' population.

Schooling
Government policy within most western countries is that all children should be educated in ordinary schools, although in the UK at least, education authorities are left with substantial discretion, and many 'special schools' still operate. However, the number of children taught in them is gradually reducing: only 1 per cent of all British 5–15-year-olds were enrolled in special schools in 1998 (Emerson et al. 2001). This political and social policy is supported by the empirical evidence: educating children

with learning difficulties in mainstream schools with additional support seems to be at least as effective as placing them in segregated 'special' schools (Emerson et al. 2001).

Preparing for adulthood

The transition from school to adult life requires planning, as many people require some sort of social support in adulthood. Children leaving school are assessed and a care plan is drawn up, setting out how services will meet their continuing needs. Individual circumstances differ, but this process includes consideration of the following:

- future daytime activities: including possible further education, supported employment and attendance at day services
- living arrangements: choices may include remaining in the family home or moving to more independent living
- leisure opportunities
- physical health care needs.

Occupation and employment

Support in adulthood is usually provided through some form of day care or employment. In the UK, this has involved attendance at adult training centres. In them, the individual takes part in a number of 'productive' activities, including simple contract work for which they receive a token 'wage', simple skills training, sports, and arts and craft activities. These centres also provide day care for people with severe or complex disabilities.

More recently, significant effort has been given to placing people with learning difficulties into real working environments. One of the best models of this approach, known as the *supported employment model*, originated in the USA. It assumes that almost anyone can be employed if given sufficient support. It is colloquially known as a 'place, train and maintain' model, because the process involves identifying a job suitable to the individual, training them to do the job effectively, and then supporting them in the job, with decreasing levels of support as appropriate. This can be effective in increasing integration into the workplace, particularly where co-workers are prepared and receive appropriate training (Farris and Stancliffe 2001).

Living away from institutions

Most adults with learning disabilities continue to live in their family of origin. Others may live independently in rented accommodation. A number of other options are available, each providing differing levels of support, including the following:

- *Registered care homes:* have up to 20 residents, though between 3 and 6 is more typical; 24-hours-a-day support is provided. All personal care and meals are provided.
- *Shared housing:* usually for groups of three or four people; levels of support vary from staff visiting once or twice a week to 24-hours-a-day support. Residents

may do their own shopping, cooking, budgeting and housework, with some support from staff.

- *Cluster of flats or bedsitters:* self-contained units, usually on a single site but occasionally dispersed across a neighbourhood. Support staff are available, but residents are more independent than in other settings.

Psychological interventions in learning difficulties

Psychological interventions for people with learning difficulties usually have one of two goals: either to teach people the skills necessary to maximize their abilities or to reduce inappropriate behaviours. Both approaches are frequently based on the principles of operant conditioning, in which behaviour is shaped by a series of rewards and, less frequently, punishments. The remaining part of this section focuses on three interventions relevant to people with learning difficulties, starting with a programme aimed at preschool children. More programmes, developed for people with a combination of autism and learning difficulties, are described in the next section of the chapter.

Preschool behavioural programmes

Most children with learning disabilities live in their family home. Preschool programmes provide opportunities for teaching age-dependent skills necessary for when the child starts to attend school. One of the most widely used systems through which this is provided is known as *Portage*.

First established in the town of Portage, USA, this home-visiting service is now used in countries as far apart as India, Britain, Japan, as well as the USA. The teaching process first involves assessment of the child's abilities. Therapists and parents then work together to develop a training programme addressing six domains: infant stimulation, social development, communication speech and language, self-help, cognitive development and motor development. Once the programme is designed, the parent works with the child on a planned programme of skills training, with weekly visits by health professionals providing support and assessment of progress. Parental interventions are facilitated by the provision of cards describing in detail how to teach 580 behaviours. Each card has a behavioural description of a skill (such as 'Mary will place 6 pieces in puzzle with verbal prompt'), suggested teaching materials and the type of reinforcement to be used in its development. Despite its widespread use, there are relatively few formal evaluations of the approach. However, what evidence there is suggests it works. Revill and Blunden (1977), for example, reported significant acceleration in achieving skills and scores on a measure of mental development in a group of 19 children aged from 8 months to 4 years following implementation of the Portage programme.

Cognitive behavioural interventions

Older children and adults may also benefit from interventions designed to teach age-appropriate skills or to help them cope with the learning demands being placed upon them. People with learning difficulties may benefit from learning social skills involving complex social behaviours and how to respond appropriately to social cues. Corrigan

(1991), for example, reported outcomes of studies of the effects of this type of training in people with learning difficulties, psychosis and offenders. People with learning difficulties gained significantly from the intervention. They performed best on measures of skill during role play and maintenance of skills over time. They were, however, less successful in transferring these skills to situations beyond the training setting.

Self-instruction training (Meichenbaum 1985) can be used to help children cope more effectively with the learning process. Used in this way, it typically involves a five-stage procedure, in which the child learns to talk themself through the procedures necessary to learn a new skill or solve a problem: first, the teacher performs the task, speaking instructions aloud as they do so; second, the child performs the task, following instructions from the teacher; third and fourth, the child performs the task twice more, once while talking through the instructions and then whispering them; fifth, the child performs the task while thinking the instructions only. This approach can also be used to help reduce anxiety by including self-instructions that focus on anxiety-reducing statements as well as task-oriented ones. Kamann and Wong (1993), for example, used self-instruction to reduce maths-anxiety in children, 20 of whom had learning difficulties and 20 of whom were normally achieving children. Before the intervention, the latter group produced substantially more self-instructions aimed at reducing anxiety than did children with learning difficulties. Following training in the use of self-instructions, the children with learning difficulties produced levels comparable to the group of more able children. They also gained in their ability to work through mathematical problems.

Coping with challenging behaviour

Between 10 and 15 per cent of people with learning difficulties engage in challenging behaviours, that is, behaviours that transgress social rules, and usually involve aggression either towards themselves or others, destructive behaviours, or place the individual or others at risk of harm. These are now considered to be operantly conditioned behaviours, through which people with restricted abilities try to achieve some degree of control over their environment and the people around them: for example, by attracting attention or getting someone to stop an unwanted action. Because each of the challenging behaviours differs in its causes, nature and the type of intervention required, the effects of any intervention are not easily measured using the randomized controlled trials used to study interventions in many other conditions. Nevertheless, a number of broad principles for reducing the frequency and severity of challenging behaviour have been developed. Emerson (1998), for example, identified the following three key intervention approaches, none of which involves punishing the individual.

Enrich the environment   Reinforcement theory suggests that the rate of behaviours maintained by positive reinforcement should reduce as the background level of reinforcement increases. Enriching environments by increasing social interaction or providing more things to engage and interest the individual should therefore reduce challenging behaviours. In one study of this approach, Golding, Emerson and Thornton (2005) found an improvement in the challenging behaviours shown by a group of six men with mild to moderate learning difficulties when moved from an institution to a more enriched environment in a specialized community-based home. Following relocation, they found a significant increase in participants' domestic activity skills, a decrease in the occurrence of problem behaviours and an increase in engagement and staff contact.

Reduce exposure to the triggers to challenging behaviour   One simple way in which challenging behaviour can be prevented is to minimize or obviate its triggers. Touchette et al. (1985), for example, identified that one woman's outbursts were associated with her attendance at pre-vocational and community living classes. Rescheduling them resulted in an almost total cessation in the frequency of aggressive behaviour.

Teach or support alternative behaviours   Most challenging behaviour is considered to be functional, that is, it is engaged in in order to gain some end-point. A key intervention, therefore, involves teaching people how to gain their desired outcome without engaging in challenging behaviour. To be effective, the new behaviour has to achieve exactly the same outcome as the original behaviour and be a more 'efficient' way of achieving this goal. An example of this approach was reported by Steege et al. (1990), who taught two young children with severe multiple disabilities to press a micro-switch to activate a tape-recording of a request for a break from self-care activities, a process that led to marked reductions in self-injurious behaviour previously used to stop such activities.

Note that this list does not include the use of punishments, which would essentially punish the individual for attempting to gain some control over an aspect of their life.

Autism

Autism was first identified in 1943, and was differentiated from schizophrenia only in 1971. For a DSM diagnosis of autism to be made, a total of at least six symptoms must be present, with at least two from the first section and at least one from each of the second and third sections, with onset prior to age 3 years.

1   Impairment in social interaction:
   - impairment in the use of non-verbal behaviours, such as eye-to-eye gaze, facial expression and gestures, to regulate social interaction
   - failure to develop peer relationships
   - lack of spontaneous seeking to share enjoyment, interests or achievements with other people
   - lack of social or emotional reciprocity.
2   Abnormalities in communication:
   - delay in, or total lack of, the development of spoken language
   - in individuals with adequate speech, marked impairment in the ability to initiate or sustain a conversation
   - stereotyped and repetitive use of language or idiosyncratic language
   - lack of spontaneous make-believe play or social imitative play.

3   Restricted, repetitive and stereotyped patterns of behaviour, interests and
    activities:
    • inflexible adherence to specific, non-functional routines or rituals
    • stereotyped and repetitive motor mannerisms
    • persistent preoccupation with parts of objects.

In its severest form, autism occurs in about 4–15 individuals per 10,000 population.
There may, in addition, be a wider spectrum of milder problems that are more widespread through the population (Bailey et al. 1995). The abilities and difficulties of
people with autism vary considerably. Some people are able to take an active part
in society, with no deficits apparent to the casual observer, although the individual
may have significant problems in establishing and maintaining relationships. About
80 per cent of children with autism score less than 70 on intelligence tests, placing
them in the learning disabilities range. These deficits are quite specific, and relate to
abstract thought, symbolism and sequential logic. Some people may have isolated
skills that reflect great talent, including prodigious mathematical or memory skills, in a
condition known as '*idiot savant*'.

Core limitations of autism

The core limitations associated with autism are social isolation, communication
deficits and obsessive-compulsive or ritual behaviours.

Social isolation
Many children with autism act as if people have no special characteristics that distinguish them from inanimate objects. As babies, they do not respond to their mothers
when being touched or fed, and may reject attempts at cuddling by arching their back.
By the age of 2 or 3, they may form a weak emotional bond with their parents. Few will
initiate play with other children, and they are usually unresponsive to attempts by
other children to engage them in play. Attempts at achieving eye contact are usually
met with avoidance or movement away, and carry no social message (Mottronb et al.
2005). By contrast, children with autism may develop strong bonds with inanimate
objects, and carry them around with them if possible.

Communication deficits
About 50 per cent of children with autism never learn to speak. Those that do, have a
number of common abnormalities. One frequent speech characteristic is known as
echolalia: the repetition of words or phrases spoken to the child immediately, hours or
even days earlier. This is now thought to be an attempt at communication, and may be
associated with an event or stimulus. Repetition of the phrase, 'Do you want a sweet?',
for example, may indicate a learned association between the phrase and being given a
sweet. A second common characteristic is known as *pronoun reversal*. In this, children
refer to themselves in the third person. This may be associated with echolalia and
reflect how they have heard others speak about them (e.g. 'How are you, Mary?' –
'She's here . . .'). This is highly resistant to change, even after substantial training
programmes.

Obsessive-compulsive and ritualistic acts

Children with autism rarely engage in symbolic play. More frequently, they engage in repetitive, **stereotypic** and seemingly meaningless behaviour. These include ritualistic hand movements, such as flicking fingers across their face, or repetitive body movements, including rocking or walking on tip-toe. They may become upset if prevented from doing these behaviours or when minor elements of their daily routine are changed. Their play often has an obsessive flavour to it, lining up toys or constructing complex patterns with household objects.

Growing up

The prognosis of children with autism is mixed. Those with learning difficulties often make a poor adjustment to adulthood, and most need some level of supervised care. By contrast, those without learning difficulties frequently go on to achieve an independent life, gain employment and live independently. Some go on to make significant contributions in their lives. However, most continue to have significantly impaired social relationships and little understanding of social and emotional aspects of life. For a powerful description of the feelings and development of a 'high functioning autistic' (her phrase), it may be useful to go to a chapter by Temple Grandin, a professor at Colorado State University (available at www.autism.org/temple/inside.html). Here are some of her fascinating insights into her own condition, starting with her childhood frustration at not being able to speak:

> Not being able to speak was utter frustration. If adults spoke directly to me I could understand everything they said, but I could not get my words out. It was like a big stutter . . . My speech therapist knew how to intrude into my world. She would hold me by my chin and made me look in her eyes and say 'ball.' At age 3, 'ball' came out 'bah,' said with great stress. If the therapist pushed too hard I threw a tantrum, and if she did not intrude far enough no progress was made. My mother and teachers wondered why I screamed. Screaming was the only way I could communicate . . .
>
> I wanted to feel the good feeling of being hugged, but when people hugged me the stimuli washed over me like a tidal wave . . . I pulled away to avoid the all-engulfing tidal wave of stimulation. The stiffening up and flinching were like a wild animal pulling away. At age 18 I built a squeezing machine. This device is completely lined with foam rubber, and the user has complete control over the duration and amount of pressure applied. The machine provides comforting pressure to large areas of the body. It took me a long time to learn to accept the feeling of being held and not try to pull away from it . . . I almost never feel aggressive after using it. In order to learn to relate to people better, I first had to learn how to receive comfort from the soothing pressure of the squeeze machine . . .
>
> Shortly after my first menstrual period, the anxiety attacks started. The feeling was like a constant feeling of stage fright all the time. The 'nerves' were almost like hypersensitivity rather than anxiety. It was like my brain was running at 200 miles an hour . . . The 'nerves' were worse in the late afternoon and early evening.

They subsided late at night and early in the morning. There are two . . . ways to fight the nerves: fixate on an intense activity, or withdraw and try to minimize outside stimulation. Fixating on one thing had a calming effect. I used to write three articles in one night. While I was typing furiously I felt calmer. I was the most nervous when I had nothing to do.

Aetiology of autism

Genetic factors

Genetic studies of autism are difficult to conduct as the condition is so rare. Nevertheless, what evidence there is suggests a significant genetic component to the risk for autism. McBride et al. (1996), for example, reported that the siblings of people with the disorder are about 75 times more likely to develop the disorder than those without an affected sibling. Further data have been reported in twin studies, where concordance rates of between 60 and 91 per cent for MZ and 20 per cent for DZ twins have been reported (e.g. Bailey et al. 1995). The recurrence rate in siblings of affected children is approximately 2 per cent to 8 per cent, much higher than the prevalence rate in the general population but much lower than in single-gene diseases (Muhle et al. 2004). Any genetic model is, therefore, likely to be polygenic. According to Muhle et al. (2004), candidate genes include those that influence serotonin and GABA processes and are involved in speech and language processing.

Biological mechanisms

The opioid theory

It has proven difficult to find a biochemical model of autism. Until recently the most advocated theory, the opioid theory, suggests that the condition is the result of an early overload of the central nervous system by opioids. This is based on findings that certain behaviours found in autism, including stereotyped behaviour, can be artificially induced in animals following injection with opioid agonists. The excess opioids are thought to be the result of incompletely digested dietary gluten and/or casein found in barley, rye, oats and milk products (Reichelt et al. 1991). These result from a lack of chemicals within the gut known as peptidases which break down natural opioids found in these foodstuffs into innocuous metabolites. Unfortunately, what biological studies have been conducted have not always supported this theory. Hunter et al. (2003), for example, found no evidence of these opioid peptides in the urine of a sample of children with autism aged between 2 and 10 years. A number of studies have used drugs or dietary restrictions to inhibit uptake of opioids from the gut as a treatment of autism. These have met with limited success (see p. 355). However, treatment studies may provide only a tangential test of the opioid theory, as it is not clear whether any neurological changes resulting from this excess of opioids are reversible.

An emerging, and possibly stronger, candidate for some of the problems associated with autism is the dysregulation of serotonin both before and after birth. Reviewing the evidence, Whitaker-Azmitia (2005) suggested that in the early stages of development, when the **blood–brain barrier** is not yet fully formed, high levels of serotonin in the blood can enter the brain of genetically vulnerable foetuses and damage serotonin terminals during development. The loss of serotonergic nerve fibres persists throughout subsequent development and contributes to the symptoms of autism. Exactly where in the brain any damage may occur is still not fully investigated, but animal studies suggest that the amygdala, a brain region involved in fear-responding, and the hypothalamus, a brain region involved in social memory and bonding, may be particularly vulnerable to damage. The anterior cingulated area of the brain, which is involved in face recognition, social, cognitive and affective functions relevant to autism, may also be particularly damaged. Dysregulation of serotonin may continue into adulthood among people with autism (Chugani 2004).

MMR and autism   In the later 1990s, Wakefield et al. (1998) examined 12 children referred to hospital with a normal developmental history followed by an apparently sudden loss of cognitive skills accompanied by a number of abdominal symptoms. Symptom onset was reported to have followed the Measles, Mumps and Rubella (MMR) vaccination in eight of the children; nine were diagnosed as having autism. Each of these nine children was found to suffer from an inflammation of the bowel wall, known as lymphoid hyperplasia. Wakefield et al. suggested that this may have resulted in a failure to break down dietary gluten and/or casein and, hence, triggered the onset of autism. This finding, and the subsequent public fears of MMR, sparked a widespread controversy and significant reductions in the uptake of the MMR vaccination.

A number of subsequent reports have both supported and challenged Wakefield's conclusions. The same research group (Uhlmann et al. 2001) compared 91 patients with lymphoid hyperplasia and 70 controls without the condition. Of those with lymphoid hyperplasia, 75 were found to have the measles virus in their gut; only 5 of the control group had the virus. They concluded that this was evidence of a plausible link between measles, MMR and lymphoid hyperplasia – with its potential link to the onset of autism. Since then a number of findings which question the MMR–autism link have been reported. Taylor et al. (1999), for example, examined trends in births and any subsequent registration of children with special needs and disabilities since 1979 in the UK. They noted a gradual increase in the numbers of children with autism since this time, but no sudden increase coinciding with the introduction of the MMR vaccine, nor any evidence of a cluster of children with developmental regression occurring within two to four months of MMR vaccination. In an even more clear-cut study, Honda et al. (2005) reviewed the rates of autism diagnosed in the Kohuku area of Yokohama between 1988 and 2002. During this time, rates of MMR fell dramatically (for reasons not related to the autism scare) and no MMR vaccines were administered from 1993 onwards. By contrast, rates of autism rose throughout this period with the greatest increase beginning in the cohort of children born in 1993 – after the MMR vaccination was no longer given. These, and other data, led Demicheli et al. (2005) in their review of the evidence to suggest that exposure to MMR was unlikely to be associated with Crohn's disease, ulcerative colitis, autism or mumps.

So, why have some people been so convinced that MMR has caused their child to develop autism? Perhaps the answer lies in the coincidence of timing between the

MMR and the developmental history of autism. About 600,000 children receive the MMR vaccine in any year, mostly at the time that autism first becomes evident. It is possible that among these children, the identification of a small number of cases of autism will coincide with vaccination. This apparent association could have been exaggerated by the highly selective way in which children were identified and assessed in the Wakefield et al. (1998) study. In addition, it is possible that the link between receiving the MMR vaccine and the onset of symptoms made by parents may be inaccurate. It is usually difficult to identify the time of onset of symptoms of autism, and most people search for a 'cause' of such problems. If parents were to attribute their child's problems to the vaccination, this may result in unconscious memory biases and inappropriate linkages of behaviour with the timing of the MMR vaccination.

Psychodynamic explanations
Early psychological theories of autism focused on psychodynamic processes. Autism was seen as a form of escape from environments that lacked warmth and care. Bettelheim (1967), for example, suggested that children who develop autism have rejecting parents and are able to perceive their negative feelings. The infants learn that their actions have little or no impact on their parents' emotions or behaviour. They come to believe they have no power to influence the world, and so choose not to enter it. Instead, they build an 'empty fortress' of autism against this pain and disappoint-ment. Unfortunately, from Bettelheim's perspective, there is no evidence that the parents of children who develop autism differ from those of children who develop normally. Cox et al. (1975), for example, found that the parents of children with autism and those of children with problems in understanding speech did not differ in terms of emotional demonstrativeness, responsiveness to their children, or sociability.

A biopsychosocial model
A similar explanation is found in the psychobiological theory of Koegel et al. (2001). They suggested that children who develop autism lack motivation to engage with other people and, as a result, withdraw from social interactions. This may begin early in life as a result of neurological dysfunction. However, it can be exacerbated by carers' efforts to 'help' affected children by doing things for them regardless of their behaviour. Whatever the child does, they receive the same response from their environment. As a result of this, and because social interactions and communication are inherently difficult, they revert to early forms of communication such as crying or tantrums to get their needs met and avoid social interactions.

Treatment of autism

Pharmacological approaches
A number of psychoactive drugs have been used to treat the symptoms of autism. Perhaps the most commonly used drugs are neuroleptics, which block the effects of dopamine (see Chapter 3). Campbell et al. (1988), for example, found haloperidol to be more effective than placebo in decreasing levels of stereotyped behaviour and

withdrawal. In addition, it enhanced the effects of behavioural techniques used in developing the use of language, perhaps because it allowed the children to focus more on the learning process than previously. Similarly, the Research Units on Pediatric Psychopharmacology Autism Network (2005) reported significant benefits from the use of risperidone in the treatment of severe tantrums, aggression and/or self-injurious behaviour in a small group of adolescents with autism. To avoid the long-term adverse effects of neuroleptics, including tardive dyskinesia and Parkinsonism (see Chapter 3), the drugs may be used at relatively low dosage and episodically (five days on, two days off) and still be effective.

Tricyclics and SSRIs have also proven effective in reducing repetitive behaviours and aggression. McDougle et al. (1994), for example, found that half those treated with fluvoxamine (an SSRI) were rated as 'clinical responders' and showed significant reductions in repetitive behaviours. The National Institute of Mental Health study (Gordon et al. 1993) compared the effectiveness of two SSRIs, clomipramine and desipramine, with placebo in a group of children and adolescents with autism. Treatment with clomipramine resulted in more improvements on measures of repetitive behaviours, self-injury and aggression than placebo.

Opiate antagonists, such as naltrexone (see also Chapter 15), have been used with only modest effect. Perhaps the most consistent effect of naltrexone is a reduction in activity levels. It did not aid a behavioural programme conducted by Campbell et al. (1993), nor did it reduce self-injurious behaviour in a study reported by Willemsen-Swinkels et al. (1995). Indeed, in this study, treatment with naltrexone actually increased levels of stereotypic behaviour.

An alternative biological approach has been to reduce levels of dietary casein and gluten in order to reduce the extent to which opiates continue to be absorbed from the gut. Evidence of the effectiveness of this approach is not yet convincing. Knivsberg et al. (1998), for example, reported on the outcomes in a group of 20 children who either received or did not receive this restricted diet for a period of one year. They reported significant success, with improvements in the treated group relative to those who did not receive the diet on a combined measure of behaviour and communication. However, the relatively small number of children in the trial, together with a lack of statistical analyses and measures of the diet given to the children, makes these results somewhat preliminary, and there is little data to make any judgement about the effectiveness of this type of intervention (Millward et al. 2004).

Behavioural approaches

Many programmes to change behaviours associated with autism have involved direct reinforcement of behaviours such as speech or pro-social behaviours. In these, the therapist/trainer typically provides a cue, usually a question or command, to evoke a specific response. This may be physically prompted if necessary, and performance of the behaviour is reinforced by a tangible reward such as a sweet: 'Look at me' – move head to face therapist if necessary – reward with sweet. In some programmes, inappropriate behaviours such as self-injury may be followed by an aversive response, including mild electric shocks or exposure to the smell of ammonia (Koegel et al. 2001). Other, more ethically acceptable, programmes have implemented non-aversive procedures even in response to challenging behaviour. Gena et al. (2005) used both live and video models of appropriate behaviour and rewards for appropriate changes to both instigate and reward appropriate behavioural change. This type of approach has resulted in reductions in self-injury, aggressive behaviour and echolalia, and gains on measures of eye contact, vocalizations and toileting.

One of the key researchers in this area is Ivar Lovaas, who developed a highly intensive operant programme for children. In his initial study (Lovaas 1987), therapy continued for much of the children's waking hours both at home and in school, for a period of two years. Children were rewarded for being less aggressive and more socially appropriate: talking, playing with other children, and so on. They were also punished, on occasion, for engaging in challenging behaviour. They were taught with their peers, not in special groups. This intensive intervention was compared with a similar treatment maintained for only ten hours a week. The differences between the two groups were dramatic. By the end of the two-year programme, the average IQ of the intervention group was 83 points, compared with 55 in the less intense intervention; 12 of the 19 children in the intensive intervention group had IQs at or above the norm, compared with 2 out of 40 in the less intensive intervention. These findings translated to school performance, with 9 children in the intensive therapy group being accepted in the same age class as their peers: only 1 child in the less intensive therapy group achieved this. Four years later, the relative gains made by the children in the intensive therapy had been maintained.

These findings created considerable controversy and have been criticized on methodological grounds (e.g. Gresham and MacMillan 1998). One criticism was that assignment of subjects to treatment and control groups was not random, allowing the possibility that the groups differed on potentially important variables that may have been left uncontrolled. A second criticism was that the pre- and post-treatment measures were not the same for all children. A third criticism was that the study results have not been reliably replicated, nor has a more recently developed non-aversive version of Lovaas's treatment been shown to be effective (Gresham and MacMillan 1998). These criticisms have been strongly refuted by Lovaas (www.feat.org/lovaas). In addition, some studies (e.g. T. Smith et al. 2000) have achieved similar gains to those made in the original Lovaas study. Accordingly, while this approach may not always achieve the therapeutic gains achieved by Lovaas, it does form a potentially effective approach to the treatment of children with autism.

Koegel et al. (2001) further refined the operant approach by targeting a number of what they termed primary factors, which they considered to precede a number of consequent or secondary factors: poor communication skills, for example, typically precede severe behaviour problems. Interventions to improve language and communication skills could, therefore, prevent the need for interventions to deal with disruptive behaviour. Koegel and colleagues argued for targeting a variety of pro-social behaviours that facilitate communication, including improving eye contact, head positioning, reducing stereotypical movements and unusual facial expressions, as well as encouraging children to initiate social interactions.

A second innovation was based on the idea that the goal of any behavioural programme should not just be to modify one particular behaviour, but to increase the individual's motivation to engage in a number of similar behaviours. A key element of their behavioural programmes, therefore, was to provide rewards for behaviours similar to the target one. An example of the difference between this and previous conditioning approaches was reported by Koegel et al. (1988). In this, the traditional operant approach reinforced specified phonetic sounds, as they became increasingly word-like over time. To obtain reinforcement, the child had to produce responses that were at least as good as their previous responses. The newer approach reinforced any attempts to verbalize, however accurate or inaccurate the noise made. In a direct comparison between the two approaches, Koegel et al. (1988) found the newer method to result in more rapid gains in the use of appropriate speech and greater levels of pro-social behaviours than the traditional method.

A final innovation of their approach was to allow the child control over the reward they were given for engaging in the targeted behaviours. Perhaps the most extreme, and ultimately most rewarding, examples of this allowed the child to engage in stereotypical or ritualistic behaviours, which are intrinsically highly rewarding, as a reward for completion of other tasks. This strategy has been shown to reduce the incidence of aggressive tantrums and other 'off-task' behaviours (Charlop-Christy and Haymes 1998).

Attention-deficit/hyperactivity disorder (ADHD)

DSM-IV-TR identified three categories of attention-deficit/hyperactivity disorder (ADHD): problems of poor attention, hyperactive-impulsive behaviour and a combination of both. Most children with the disorder have both sets of problems. Criteria for each diagnosis are engaging in at least six of the behaviours in Table 13.1 over a period of at least six months.

For a diagnosis to be given, problem behaviours need to have begun before the age of 7 years, be present in school and home, and significantly impair functioning. Many children with ADHD have difficulty in getting on with their peers and establishing friendships. They fail to recognize when their behaviour is annoying others, and may make significant social mistakes. They can usually understand such issues in hypothetical scenarios, but have trouble translating this understanding into the 'real world' (Whalen et al. 1985). About 25 per cent of children with ADHD have some form of learning difficulty, and many are placed in special education units as a consequence of their disruptive behaviour. Children with ADHD are more likely to drop out of school than those without the disorder.

An estimated 3–5 per cent of children in the USA could be diagnosed as having ADHD (APA 1994). However, it is not a uniquely American or western problem. Kashala et al. (2005), for example, reported a prevalence level of 6 per cent among schoolchildren in the Democratic Republic of Congo. Some but not all problems abate as the individual grows older. Of children identified with ADHD, 40 per cent continue to have these problems in late adolescence, and about 10 per cent have some level of symptoms in adulthood (Mannuzza and Klein 2000). Between 1 and 6 per cent of adults meet the criteria for ADHD (Murphy and Barkley 1996). By this time, most people have learned to adapt to their symptoms and can hold down jobs.

Table 13.1 Key features of the ADHD diagnostic categories

Inattention	Hyperactivity-impulsivity
• Fails to pay close attention to details or makes careless errors in schoolwork, work or other activities	• Squirms in seat or fidgets
• Has trouble keeping attention on tasks or play	• Inappropriately leaves seat
• Doesn't appear to listen when being told something	• Has trouble playing quietly or engaging in leisure activity
• Neither follows through on instructions nor completes tasks, schoolwork or jobs (not due to oppositional behaviour or failure to understand)	• Runs or climbs inappropriately; in adolescents or adults, there may be only a subjective feeling of restlessness
• Has trouble organizing activities and tasks	• Appears driven or 'on the go'
• Dislikes or avoids tasks that involve sustained mental effort (e.g. homework, schoolwork)	• Talks excessively
• Loses materials needed for activities: books, pencils, tools, toys, and so on	• Answers questions before they have been completely asked
• Easily distracted by extraneous stimuli	• Has trouble waiting turn
• Forgetful	• Interrupts or intrudes on others

Diagnostic versus categorical understandings of ADHD

Many children exhibit some of the characteristics of those diagnosed as having ADHD. This indistinct line between what is 'ordinary' and what is 'pathological' behaviour, and the potential abuse of the diagnosis of ADHD as a justification for medicating disruptive children (see pp. 361–3), has led to strong arguments as to whether ADHD exists as a separate 'condition' or whether the behaviours that comprise ADHD are better thought of as being at the extreme end of the normal distribution of behaviour. That is, the condition may best be considered in dimensional rather than categorical terms (see Chapter 1).

Arguments favouring the dimensional approach are both clinical and empirical. Clinicians note that a child may have significant problems in one particular area, but may not receive help because they do not fulfil the 'diagnostic requirements' for ADHD and therefore may not be considered to have a 'problem'. Similarly, a diagnosis of ADHD may justify drug treatments where other approaches may be more beneficial to the child. Empirical evidence suggests that dimensional scores of behaviours subsumed within ADHD appear to be more predictive of outcome than categorical diagnostic judgements. Fergusson and Horwood (1995), for example, compared the predictive validity of dimensional and categorical ratings/diagnoses of ADHD to predict levels of substance abuse, juvenile offending and school drop-out in a cohort of New Zealand schoolchildren. They found a dose–response relationship between the number and severity of behaviours associated with ADHD and risk of each of these outcomes. Dimensional scores were more predictive of outcome than diagnostic category. These various findings suggest that the behaviours that comprise ADHD are better thought of as the end of a distribution of behaviours rather than categorically different from the norm.

Aetiology of attention-deficit/hyperactivity disorder

Genetic factors

Genetic factors appear to contribute to risk of developing ADHD. One early genetic study (Goodman and Stevenson 1989) found a 51 per cent concordance for ADHD between MZ twins and a 31 per cent concordance between DZ twins. More recent studies have found concordance between MZ twins to vary between 58 and 83 per cent compared with between 31 and 47 per cent for DZ twins, with heritability estimates for attention problems varying between 60 and 80 per cent (Wender et al. 2001). Meta-analyses or pooled data analyses have supported association between ADHD and polymorphisms in a number of genes that influence dopamine receptors and transporter processes (Thapar et al. 2005) as well as norepinephrine and serotonin transporter genes (Russell et al. 2005).

Biological mechanisms

The main characteristics of ADHD are thought to reflect problems with behavioural control and management. Impulsivity is not thought to result from an inability to attend, but is the result of problems in executive function: a failure to decide when actions should be taken and how they should be executed. This implicates dysfunction of the frontal lobe as central to the disorder, a hypothesis supported by findings of smaller frontal lobes among children with ADHD than among a 'normal' comparison group reported by Castellanos et al. (1996), which may also be associated with reductions in size of temporal grey matter, caudate and cerebellar areas of the brain (Castellanos et al. 2002).

The main neurotransmitter involved in ADHD seems to be dopamine. Data to support this hypothesis mainly stem from animal models and studies that have found drugs that increase dopamine levels to be most effective in reducing or even eliminating the symptoms of ADHD. These include various types of amphetamines, and indirect dopamine agonists. In addition, administration of l-dopa and tyrosine, which are precursors to dopamine, results in moderate to marked reductions in ADHD symptoms in about half the people with ADHD given them (Reimherr et al. 1987). It seems paradoxical that an amphetamine actually reduces levels of physical activity, but it appears to do so by increasing frontal activity and control over executive dysfunctions that underpin the behaviour. In fact, Sagvolden et al. (2005) suggested that dopamine dysregulation in three brain areas may lead to the key symptoms of ADHD:

- *mesocortical system:* deficient attention, poor behavioural organization
- *mesolimbic system:* shorter 'delay of reinforcement gradient', and deficient extinction. That is, low levels of dopamine lead to people with ADHD being more

influenced by short-term rewards and less able to behave in ways to gain delayed reinforcement. Thus, the short-term rewards of responding to immediate stimuli within the environment overwhelm any control over behaviour to gain delayed, longer-term rewards – leading to impulsiveness

- *nigrostriatal system:* clumsiness, and poor non-declarative, routine, habit learning.

A second, and still important, neurotransmitter involved in ADHD is norepinephrine. Evidence suggests that there is lower than normal norepinephrine activity within the prefrontal cortex of children with ADHD, which may amplify their responses to attended stimuli, and reduce responses to irrelevant stimuli. A final explanation has focused on the role of environmental toxins. Feingold (1979) suggested that salicylates, artificial colours and artificial flavours contribute to ADHD, although treatment using the Feingold diet, which is free from such additives, has proved effective only for a few children, and less so than medication (Hill 1998).

Psychological explanations
As noted above, ADHD can be characterized not by hyperactivity, but by high levels of impulsivity. According to Barkley (1997), children with ADHD do things other children think of doing, but don't actually do. The urge to act is not inhibited. The first response to a situation is the response that is taken. He suggested that the core of ADHD is a failure to inhibit inappropriate responses to environmental events. In addition to this, children with ADHD are more emotionally responsive to events than most children. They are poor at controlling feelings, and less able to tolerate negative emotions. Their emotions are driven by the moment and the object of their attention at that time. As a consequence, they have difficulties in maintaining goal-oriented behaviour, particularly when this is associated with some type of negative emotion. They have difficulty in sticking to a task in the expectation of future rewards or satisfaction on its completion. Schoolwork or other demanding and sometimes boring or frustrating tasks do not hold their attention and they move rapidly to other more immediately rewarding activities.

Barkley (1997) noted that as children grow older they use an internal dialogue as a means of self-control. This internalized language develops at around the age of 3–4 years, the time that ADHD is often first identified. This is not coincidental: Barkley suggests that children with ADHD have disorganized internal speech, which contributes to their disorganized responses to external events. Barkley noted that children with ADHD often appear 'chatty', but their conversation usually deals with the present rather than the future: thoughts do not lead to planning and future expectations. This disorganization also means that children with ADHD have difficulties in dealing with abstract issues. They find it hard to explain things: they do not get to the point, they talk around it. Of interest is that while Barkley (1997) provides a psychological perspective on ADHD, he considers it to have a biological basis, and to be largely the result of biochemical and neurological factors. He describes people with ADHD as *biochemical outliers*, acknowledging a dimensional view of their behaviour rather than a categorical one.

While Barkley's model is probably the most widely acknowledged psychological theory of ADHD, it is not without its critiques. Sagvolden et al. (2005), for example, suggested the biochemical processes that underpin ADHD are more complicated than implied by the relatively simple model of Barkley. They also disagreed on the fundamental processes underpinning the condition. Barkley suggested ADHD involves a failure to inhibit urges to respond to the environment. Sagvolden and colleagues suggested a more complex process involving poor attention and behavioural organization, a failure to learn appropriate behavioural sequences, and a sensitivity to short-term reinforcers and lack of response to longer-term outcomes that rewards rapid, poorly thought through, responses to environmental stimuli. In a more specific examination of the cognitive processes underpinning ADHD, Cornoldi et al. (2001) found that children with ADHD symptoms had working memory problems which led to them having difficulties in suppressing information that initially had to be processed, and subsequently excluded from memory, in order to perform a memory task effectively.

A biopsychosocial model

Bettelheim (1973) integrated biochemical models with social and psychological factors in a biopsychosocial model of ADHD. He suggested that ADHD develops when children with a biological predisposition to hyperactivity are raised in an environment with a strong authoritarian ethos or one where there is evident resentfulness at inappropriate behaviour. According to Bettelheim, if a child with a predisposition to hyperactivity is responded to with obvious frustration or impatience by their parents, they may feel unable to respond effectively to their parents' need for controlled behaviour and obedience. As both react to each other in negative ways, this may spiral into a continuous battle between child and parents, that spills over to other settings and eventually results in what may be termed ADHD.

Evidence of a role of family dynamics as a causal factor for ADHD is mixed. A.J. Smith et al. (2002), for example, found significant associations between conflictual child–mother relationships and the presence of ADHD. By contrast, although Rey et al. (2000) found an adverse family environment was associated with conduct disorder and oppositional defiant disorder, it was not associated with ADHD. In addition, although family relationships may be strained in families with a child who has ADHD, there is some evidence that parent–child relationships improve once treatment is initiated, suggesting that adverse or conflictual family environments are, at least in part, a response to the child's behaviour, not simply the originating cause (Tallmadge and Barkley 1983). These types of data contributed to the psychosocial model of Sandberg (2005), who suggested that ADHD is an adaptation to defective neurotransmission. The resulting behavioural style is usually maladaptive and not only increases vulnerability to adverse experiences, but also creates a context in which encountering adversity is more likely.

Treatment of attention-deficit/hyperactivity disorder

Pharmacological interventions

Perhaps the best-known pharmacological treatment of ADHD involves methylphenidate, better known as Ritalin. The combined results of studies investigating its efficacy suggest it achieves significant improvements in about 60 per cent of those prescribed it, compared with about 10 per cent of those prescribed placebo (Wender et al. 2001). The key benefit of Ritalin is that it moderates the symptoms of both inattention and hyperactivity, allowing the individual to focus more on educational, social and family issues. Pelham et al. (1993), for example, compared an eight-week school-based behaviour modification programme combined with Ritalin and the same programme combined with placebo in the treatment of a group of 8-year-old boys with ADHD. The behavioural programme involved a points system with both rewards for appropriate behaviour and 'costs' for inappropriate classroom behaviours. Acquisition of a fixed number of points could be exchanged for a variety of items chosen by the child. The effect of the behavioural intervention combined with Ritalin was significantly greater than when it was combined with placebo on measures of both class behaviour and academic performance.

The benefits of Ritalin can be dramatic. Here, a teacher describes the impact of Ritalin on one child and his classmates:

> He just came to us in Year 7, with a real history of paperwork behind him . . . poor behaviour, learning difficulties. He came to the school in September. We thought he had ADHD because he was beyond control, reason. He couldn't stay seated – or wouldn't – he wandered round the classroom, started wandering about the school. He was a powerful lad, and just pushed people out of the way that tried to stop him. By the end of November he had been seen by the doctor. He was given a diagnosis of ADHD and prescribed Ritalin. He stayed at home a couple of days, because he was pretty zonked out on it. Then he came back to school. The change was instantaneous. He was a difficult child, and he still had behavioural problems . . . but you could reason with him.
>
> You could sit him down and talk to him. He decided he liked learning, as for the first time he could understand what he was being taught. He started reading . . . which boosted his self-esteem . . . lots of these kids with ADHD have low self-esteem as they fail in school . . . Ritalin does allow them to access the curriculum. For the first time, they can concentrate on something and make progress. But when the medicine wears off you know about it. We start to give the mid-day dose at about a quarter to twelve. By this time, they [children with ADHD] have got more 'edgy', more loud. Lots of walking, winding people up: 'loud' is the predominant word . . . Sometimes you think the poor kids don't have a chance. It's difficult at home – and they may trash their room. But you think sometimes it's a response to real problems they have with their parents. Some of them are like their child: they go from 'down here' to sky high in seconds. It's got to be bad for the kids.

Ritalin is now widely used: so much so that some have argued that it is overprescribed, and used to control unruly or unwanted behaviour – not just ADHD. Indeed, some schools in the USA have refused to accept 'difficult' children unless they are treated with Ritalin. Such demands have led pressure groups such as Parents Against Ritalin to lobby the US Congress into considering a bill that prevents school officials from requiring a student take the 'behavioral drugs' in order to attend school (http://www.ritalinaddiction.com/). Ritalin's side-effects include loss of appetite, abdominal pain, weight loss, insomnia and increased heart rate. Retardation of growth may also occur during prolonged therapy in children. Of more concern may be the triggering of psychotic symptoms. Cherland and Fitzpatrick (1999) reported a 9 per cent prevalence of psychotic symptoms, including hallucinations and paranoia, among their sample of 192 children treated with Ritalin for ADHD, which ceased immediately on withdrawal of the drug. No psychotic symptoms were reported among children with ADHD who did not receive the drug. A final risk associated with Ritalin is its use as a drug of abuse, which is becoming increasingly common in the USA. As an amphetamine, it suppresses appetite, increases wakefulness and produces an emotional high. When abused, tablets are either taken orally or crushed and snorted. Some abusers dissolve the tablets in water and inject the mixture, which can cause complications as insoluble fillers in the tablets can block small blood vessels.

Thinking about . . .

Treatment with Ritalin has not been without controversy. Searching the web quickly identifies a number of sites of parents and others concerned about its use – one of which is cited in the main text. People worry about its over-prescription, that very young children are being placed on powerful medication, that schooling problems are becoming the remit of medical practitioners. Many people are 'against Ritalin' and similar drugs. But they can work . . . So, what are your views, and how would you feel if one of your children was put on this drug?

Other drug treatments are now emerging. The role of norepinephrine in ADHD has resulted in the development and use of a drug designed to increase levels of norepinephrine within the frontal lobe. Atomoxetine is a norepinephrine re-uptake inhibitor which may provide an alternative treatment to Ritalin – although comparative trials are still lacking. However, it does appear to be more effective than placebo in both children (Spencer et al. 2002) and adults (Faraone et al. 2005). Another form of treatment is provided by a drug known as Modafinil. This psychostimulant has been used for treating excessive daytime sleepiness associated with **narcolepsy**, and is now being used in ADHD. The mechanism of action of Modafinil is unknown, but, unlike other stimulants, the drug is highly selective for the central nervous system and has little effect on dopaminergic activity. It also seems effective in reducing the core symptoms of ADHD (Biederman et al. 2005).

Operant approaches

The behavioural intervention used by Pelham et al. (1993) and described above is typical of operant-conditioning-based interventions. These usually take the form of a token economy, in which the child is rewarded for engaging in specific pre-specified behaviours by receiving a token. Tokens can be collected and, when enough have been accrued, exchanged for a desired item. This approach has a number of variants, including charts on which stars are placed as a reward for appropriate behaviours and, again, exchanged for tangible rewards when enough are displayed. Although this type of intervention can be effective on its own, the results of studies such as that of Pelham and colleagues suggest that operant procedures may be most effective when used in conjunction with treatment by Ritalin.

Training attention

The attention training tasks used to treat head injuries described in Chapter 14 can also be used to help children with ADHD. Semrud-Clikeman et al. (1999), for example, examined the effectiveness of the Attention Process Training Programme (Park et al. 1999: described in more detail in Chapter 14) combined with training in problem-solving in a school setting with children identified as having problems in attention and not completing work. As a result of the training programme, the children improved on the training tasks, completed more tasks in class, and their teachers reported that they seemed more attentive. Using materials specifically developed for young children, Kerns et al. (1999) reported improvements in a group of 7–11-year-old children following a similar attention training programme. By the end of the training period, participants achieved better scores on untrained cognitive tasks, academic performance and on teacher reports of impulsiveness.

Environmental manipulation

As many of the behaviours associated with ADHD are seen as immediate responses to the environment, one way in which they may be influenced is by environmental manipulation. The ERIC (Educational Resources Information Center) Clearing-house on Disabilities and Gifted Education (www.ericec.org) set out some clear guidelines, including the nature of the learning environment, to help teachers work with children with ADHD. These included:

- seat students with ADHD at the front of the class with their backs to the rest of the class to keep other students out of view
- surround students with ADHD with good role models
- avoid distracting stimuli
- produce a stimuli-reduced study area for teaching (which other children can access) to avoid isolation.

In addition to these environmental factors, they considered a number of other factors, including guidelines for maintaining and enhancing self-esteem, responding to inappropriate behaviour, and the process of teaching, all of which contribute to best practice when teaching children with ADHD.

Working with families

As noted above, the families of children with ADHD experience significant levels of stress and upset. A number of studies have attempted to reduce family problems by working with the whole family. Barkley et al. (2001), for example, compared the effectiveness of problem-solving communication training alone or following training behavioural management skills in an attempt to minimize conflict within families. Problem-solving communication training involved teaching a five-stage process through which the family combined to deal with problems: defining the problem, brainstorming potential solutions, negotiating and deciding within the family which solutions to implement, and then implementing the solution. The behavioural skills management involved learning to change triggers or responses to disruptive behaviour using operant procedures. Both interventions proved equally effective in those that completed them. However, three times as many people dropped out of training where the problem-solving approach was used alone than when the combined intervention was used, suggesting that some form of combined intervention may be treatment of choice. More recently, Bjornstad and Montgomery (2005) reviewed the evidence concerning family therapy. They identified two large-scale well-conducted studies involving behavioural family therapy, one of which (Jensen et al. 1999) found no evidence of benefit of family therapy over usual care (an issue not addressed by Barkley et al.), and one (Horn et al. 1991) which found some benefit when compared with drug placebo. Thus, so far, family therapy appears to have limited benefits in the treatment of ADHD.

Research box 13

The MTA Cooperative Group (1999) A 14-month randomized clinical trial of treatment strategies for attention-deficit/hyperactivity disorder: multimodal treatment study of children with ADHD, *Archives of General Psychiatry*, 56: 1073–86.

The authors note that while a number of studies have examined the effectiveness of both pharmacological and psychological therapies in the treatment of ADHD, there have been no long-term comparisons of their effectiveness. This study filled this research gap.

Method

Some 574 children, aged between 7 and 9.9 years, with a diagnosis of ADHD were randomly assigned to one of four conditions, each lasting 14 months: medication management, behavioural treatment, combined medication and behavioural treatment, and community care. Each participant met the DSM-IV criteria for ADHD, and had lived with the same caregiver for at least six months. Referral into the study was through 'mental health settings', paediatricians, advertisements and school notices. Exclusion factors were that the family would be unable to fully participate in the study, but did not include other diagnoses such as conduct or oppositional disorder.

Assessments

Six outcome measures were used, with measures before and after the 14-month intervention:

- ADHD symptoms were measured by the parent- and teacher-completed inattention and hyperactivity scale of the SNAP
- Oppositional and aggressive behaviour was measured by parent- and teacher-completed oppositional/defiant scale of the SNAP
- Social skills were measured with the Social Skills Rating System (SSRS)

- Anxiety and depression were measured by the 'internalizing' scale of the SSRS and the anxiety scale of the Multidimensional Anxiety Scale for Children (MASC).

Interventions
- The behavioural intervention involved parent training following the method of Barkley described in the chapter, child-focused treatment comprising a behavioural programme modelling and rewarding appropriate behaviour and not rewarding inappropriate behaviour (as used by Pelham), and a school-based intervention in which teachers were taught classroom management techniques to control impulsive and haphazard behaviour. All the interventions were highly intensive at the beginning of the intervention period, but faded in intensity over time.
- Medication initially involved a double-blind variation of dosages of methylphenidate hydrochloride (Ritalin), given at breakfast, lunch and afternoon. Its impact on behaviour was observed by clinicians, and when they agreed the dosage appeared to be optimal, the blind was broken and this became the standard dose.
- The combined treatment involved both behavioural and medication treatment approaches.
- Community care involved feedback on baseline measures and information on local mental health facilities.

Results

Medication proved superior to psychological therapy on parents' and teachers' ratings of inattention, and teachers' ratings of hyperactivity and impulsivity. There were no differences between these groups on measures of classroom observer ratings of behaviour, parent and teacher ratings of aggression, child mood, social skills, and parent–child relationships. Combining the treatments had no additional impact: there were no differences between any of the scores of children in the medication-only group and the combined intervention. Finally, the combined and medical interventions were consistently superior to the community intervention on the measures of inattention and hyperactivity/impulsivity, and at least one measure of mood, oppositional behaviour and reading achievement. However, the psychological treatment was not.

Discussion

These data suggest a significant superiority of medication over psychological interventions. However, some caveats may be necessary. The medication was maintained over the entire period of the study. The psychological intervention was intensive at the beginning of the programme, but by 3–6 months prior to the end of the assessment period had reduced to one monthly contact. It is not clear how well the two active interventions fared when both were being conducted, or how quickly the benefits of the medication would dissipate once stopped. Pragmatically, though, these data suggest that unless one is concerned about the ethics of medication or its side-effects, this may prove the treatment of choice.

Working with adults who have ADHD

Self-management strategies

Adults with ADHD can be taught a number of self-management strategies to help them manage their attentional problems (Sohlberg and Mateer 2001). These include *orienting procedures* in which they regularly monitor their activities to ensure they focus on planned activities. An example of this approach may be the use of a watch that beeps every hour, reminding the individual to ask themselves, 'What am I currently doing? What was I doing before doing this? What am I supposed to do next?' An example of another orienting task, used for people who set off to drive somewhere and then forget their destination, is to routinely write down their destination, expected time of arrival, and the time at which it may be useful to ask for help if lost, at the beginning of every trip.

A second approach involves *pacing*. People with attention problems often experience fatigue or problems in maintaining concentration over extended periods of time. To combat this, they may benefit from pacing the demands they place upon themselves, by not setting too high standards of productivity and taking breaks at regular intervals. They can also be taught to monitor fatigue levels and take breaks at appropriate times rather than fighting through the fatigue and being unproductive. People with attention problems also find that they have difficulty in switching from one task to another. The *key ideas log* minimizes the problems associated with this by encouraging people with attention problems to quickly write down or tape-record ideas that spring to mind so they do not disrupt their ongoing task.

Environmental strategies

A final intervention involves thinking through the impact that environmental factors have on attention, and considering ways in which it can be modified to maximize cognitive performance (Sohlberg and Mateer 2001). Central to this approach is avoiding 'busy' or distracting environments and making use of 'quiet' environments when attention is required. This may involve, for example, shopping in quiet local shops rather than attempting to shop in bustling supermarkets. Further strategies may include minimizing the demand on attentional or organizational abilities, by setting up standing orders to pay bills or labelling cupboards to ensure maximum organization. The use of 'Do not disturb' signs both at home and at work may also help minimize distraction from ongoing tasks. While these types of approaches would seem logical and likely to be effective, their highly individual nature has meant that their effectiveness has largely been explored through individual case reports rather than controlled trials (Sohlberg and Mateer 2001).

Chapter summary

1 About 3 per cent of the UK population have learning difficulties.

2 Only about 25 per cent of cases of learning difficulty have an identified cause. These causes include genetic conditions, infectious diseases, environmental hazards and several perinatal factors.

3   Social factors contribute strongly to mild learning difficulties, less so to more severe problems.

4   Down syndrome and Fragile X syndrome are two common conditions resulting from differing genetic factors.

5   The principles of normalization and social role valorization ensure that people with learning difficulties achieve the same respect and rights as the rest of the population.

6   Care of people with learning difficulties includes both social and psychological interventions.

7   Psychological interventions are frequently based on operant conditioning approaches to skills learning or behavioural change, although cognitive behavioural interventions may also prove effective.

8   People with autism have difficulties in three areas: social interaction, communication, and obsessive-compulsive or ritualistic acts.

9   When combined with learning difficulties, these may profoundly affect the outcome of affected individuals.

10 The opioid theory of autism suggests that the disorder results from an overdose of opioids as a result of a failure to metabolize gluten and casein from the gut. The MMR vaccine was thought to contribute to this problem – but is no longer seen as a cause of autism.

11 A newly emerging neurological factor appears to be damage to the brain due to high levels of serotonin before birth affecting key brain regions regulating behaviours affected by autism.

12 Bettelheim's psychodynamic model suggests that autism is an escape from an adverse family environment.

13 The biopsychosocial model of autism proposes that the disorder results from a combination of lack of motivation to engage in social interactions combined with a lack of appropriate responses from the environment.

14 Lovaas's controversial behavioural treatment has proven moderately effective in the treatment of autism. Koegel and colleagues have developed a more strategic approach to such interventions.

15 Pharmacological interventions have also been shown to reduce a number of negative behaviours.

16 An estimated 3–5 per cent of children in the USA have ADHD.

17 ADHD seems to be driven by low levels of dopamine and serotonin and can be treated with drugs that increase these levels.

18 ADHD is driven by high levels of impulsivity, or lack of 'executive control'.

19 Barkley (1997) considered ADHD to reflect failures to control immediate impulses. By contrast, Sagvolden and colleagues considered the problem to reflect behavioural organization, an over-response to immediate reinforcers and a failure to learn routine behavioural sequences.

20 Family factors may also increase risk for ADHD, although relevant data are surprisingly sparse.

21 Treatment by Ritalin and atomoxetine have been shown to facilitate behavioural interventions and education in children and adults.

22 A variety of self-management programmes may be effective in treating adult ADHD.

For discussion

1 Do changes in technology and society help or hinder people with learning difficulties to cope with everyday living?

2 What are the implications for a family that has a child with a significant learning disorder?

3 What limits should there be to health professionals' responses to 'challenging behaviour'?

4 What are the implications for a family that has a child with ADHD?

5 Should all families of children with ADHD be encouraged to take part in family therapy to minimize the negative impact of an adverse family environment?

Further reading

Emerson, E., Hatton, C., Bromley, J. et al. (eds) (1998) *Clinical Psychology and People with Intellectual Disabilities*. Chichester: Wiley.

Emerson, E.C., Hatton, J., Felce, D. et al. (2001) *Learning Disabilities: The Fundamental Facts*. London: Mental Health Foundation.

Francis, K. (2005) Autism interventions: a critical update, *Developmental and Medical Child Neurology*, 47: 493–9.

Grandin, T. and Scariano, M.M. (1996) *Emergence: Labeled Autistic*. New York: Warner.

Murphy, K. (2005) Psychosocial treatments for ADHD in teens and adults: a practice-friendly review, *Journal of Clinical Psychology*, 61: 607–19.

Teeter, P.A. (2000) *Interventions for ADHD*. New York: Guilford.

14

Neurological disorders

Neurological disorders are the result of damage or degeneration of the brain following the onset of disease or trauma. This chapter focuses on the consequences of three types of disorder arising from two disease processes, Alzheimer's disease and multiple sclerosis (MS), and from head injury. In the case of Alzheimer's disease and MS, therapy is aimed at maintaining cognitive function and well-being in the face of a progressive deterioration of cognitive processes. Cognitive processes may be markedly impaired following head injury, but recover to some extent over time. Interventions here focus on maximizing the process of recovery and helping the individual cope with any residual cognitive deficits. By the end of the chapter, you should have an understanding of:

- The neurological processes that result in Alzheimer's disease and MS
- The psychological consequences of these diseases
- Interventions aimed at improving or maintaining both cognitive functioning and well-being as the diseases progress
- The immediate and long-term cognitive consequences of head injury
- Interventions used to maximize recovery following head injury.

Alzheimer's disease

Alzheimer's disease is the most common type of dementia, affecting between 5 and 10 per cent of those aged over 65 years, and at least 20 per cent of those aged over 80 years (Roca et al. 1998). Although generally a condition found in elderly people, this is not always the case. Indeed, Alois Alzheimer's first description of the condition in the early years of the twentieth century was of a middle-aged woman. DSM-IV-TR defined Alzheimer's disease as a progressive disease having the following characteristics (often summarized as the 4As):

- *amnesia:* loss of memory
- *aphasia:* language disturbance

- *apraxia:* impaired ability to carry out motor activities despite intact motor function
- *agnosia:* failure to recognize or identify objects despite intact sensory function
- *disturbance in executive functioning* (that is, planning, organizing, sequencing, abstracting).

To achieve a diagnosis of Alzheimer's disease, these deficits should cause significant impairment in social or occupational functioning and represent a significant decline from previous levels of functioning. Memory loss is progressive, with recent memories typically lost before remote ones, which are thought to be preserved as a consequence of rehearsal over life. However, as the disease progresses, even remote and emotionally charged memories are lost. Early forgetfulness becomes a pathologically poor memory for present events, daily routine, and even family members. Word-finding difficulties are common. In its final stages, Alzheimer's disease destroys the ability to communicate in any way.

In the early stages of Alzheimer's disease, levels of insight are high and most people are aware of their deficits. However, as the disease progresses, insight is lost, all sense of self seems to vanish, and the individual becomes completely dependent on others for care. Suspiciousness, paranoia and delusions are common. The individual may experience spontaneous changes in mood, including anger and irritability, as well as restlessness and agitation. Confusion is common, and may be worse at night when cues that may orient the individual in time and place are less obvious, and oxygen supply to the brain is at its least. Although most health care services aim to maximize the independence of the individual and maintain them in their own home, there may come a time when they are hospitalized. By this time, they may be confused for much of the time, incontinent, and respond only vaguely to their environment.

The duration of Alzheimer's disease from time of diagnosis to death can be 20 years or more: the typical duration is between 4 and 8 years. Over this time the individual will progress through the following stages:

- *Questionable dementia:* the individual begins to behave 'oddly' and relatives suspect there is a problem.
- *Mild dementia:* there is no question that there is a problem, but the affected individual is able to maintain independence.
- *Moderate dementia:* help is required for routine tasks; 'problem' behaviours such as wandering or aggression may be evident.
- *Severe dementia:* the individual becomes increasingly frail and eventually chair- or bed-bound.

Alzheimer's disease impacts not just on the individual with the disorder. Many elderly people, the preponderance of them women (Parker and Lawton 1990), care for people with dementia in their own home, often until the disease is far progressed. These people typically experience significant stress (see Box 14.1).

Box 14.1 Focus groups for mild–moderate dementia

Recently, one of my colleagues, Lucie Byrne, ran some focus groups exploring the factors that contributed to the quality of life of people with mild–moderate dementia. Below are some quotes taken from the focus groups, with people telling us what added to or took away from their quality of life. The quotes are actually quite unremarkable, and could be made by virtually anyone of any age. Importantly, what the participants did not say was that their failing memory made their quality of life any worse. Some said that it might in the future. In fact, this became the theme related to this issue: however bad people's cognitive abilities were, they were always said not to be affecting their quality of life at the time, but might in the future. This is not to say that loss of memory is not an issue and concern for people with dementia – and some people may become profoundly depressed as a result of their failing abilities. But many other things contributed to their quality of life – this did not hinge only on their cognitive abilities.

Husband/wife/partner

- Like I said, my husband is still there and so I'm all right.
- All I want is to be with my husband that I've been with practically since I left school.
- I think the majority would say if anything happens to the partner, there's nothing worse could happen, nothing worse could happen.

Children/grandchildren

- You got the love of a family and the grandchildren, like me.
- If I lost one of my children, I would be devastated.

Family

- Lack of friends or relations [would make the quality of life worse].
- I've got a good father and I had a good mother, but I'm afraid I've just lost my mum and dad, you know.

Your friends

- Lack of friends or relations, loneliness, all these things take away the quality of life.
- Friendship, that's very important, isn't it?

Feeling happy

- If you are happy, you are fair enough. Sometimes people are not happy and that must be awful.

Feeling that you are useful

- If you could do a good turn for anybody, do it, that makes the quality of life, don't it?
- If you see a dirty cup there, what's stopping you picking it up and just giving it a swirl, helping that poor lady there? . . . but people walk past . . . and I like [gestures angrily], that's my way.

Feeling content/satisfied

- Well, I could say nothing [could make the quality of life worse], I'm quite contented as I am.
- Whatever I do, I am contented with.

Feeling that you have had a good life

- I'm an extremely lucky person, I think.
- I suppose you don't know me, but over the years I've really enjoyed my life.

Aetiology of Alzheimer's disease

Genetic factors

Up to 50 per cent of first-degree relatives of a person with Alzheimer's disease will develop the disorder (Korten et al. 1993). Genes on chromosomes 14, 21 and in particular the apoE4 gene on chromosome 19 have been implicated in Alzheimer's disease. ApoE4 is one of several forms, or alleles, of the apoE gene, the others being apoE2 and apoE3. People who carry two apoE4 genes are about eight times more likely to develop Alzheimer's disease than those who have two of the E3 allele. The apoE4 gene may bring forward the onset of Alzheimer's disease by as much as 17 years (Warwick Daw et al. 2000). However, it is found in only 40 per cent of people who develop Alzheimer's disease and many people who carry the gene do not develop the condition. Three other genes have been identified as responsible for the rare early-onset familial form of the disease: the amyloid precursor protein (APP) gene, the presenilin 1 (PSEN1) gene, and the presenilin 2 (PSEN2) gene. Mutations in these genes, however, account for less than 5 per cent of the total number of cases of Alzheimer's disease (Rocchi et al. 2003).

Neurological processes

Alzheimer's disease is the result of premature degeneration of brain systems. Degeneration is progressive, and the course of Alzheimer's disease can be mapped against the geography of the brain affected. Problems typically initiate in the entorhinal cortex before proceeding to the hippocampus, and then gradually spread to other regions, particularly the cerebral cortex (Hedden and Gabrieli 2005). As the hippocampal neurons degenerate, short-term memory falters, as does the ability to perform routine tasks. As the disease spreads through the cerebral cortex, it begins to take away language.

The nature of the changes that occur appears to be both structural, including the development of beta amyloid plaques and neurofibrillary tangles, and to involve a number of neurotransmitters. Beta amyloid results from damage to amyloid precursor protein (APT), which lies within the neuron cell membranes. It is a member of a larger family of proteins which enclose cells and act as a barrier to control which substances go in and out of them. Damage to APT results in the formation of beta amyloid fragments, which may clump together to form amyloid plaques and cause neuronal death, perhaps because they form tiny channels in neuron membranes through which uncontrolled amounts of calcium can flow (Sinha et al. 2000). Neuro-fibrillary tangles comprise abnormal collections of twisted threads inside nerve cells. The chief component of these tangles is a protein called tau. In healthy individuals, this binds and stabilizes the microtubules that carry nutrients and molecules from the bodies of the cells to the ends of the axon. In Alzheimer's disease, tau is changed chemically, and this altered tau twists the microfilaments around each other to form tangles. The resultant collapse of the transport system causes errors in communication between nerve cells and neuronal death.

The most important neurotransmitter implicated in Alzheimer's disease is acetyl-choline: levels decline moderately in normal ageing but drop by about 90 per cent in people with Alzheimer's disease (Whitehouse et al. 1982). Acetylcholine is involved in memory formation and influences neuronal activity in the hippocampus and cerebral cortex. Other neurotransmitters may also be involved. Serotonin and norepinephrine levels are lower than normal in some people with Alzheimer's disease, which may contribute to sensory disturbances and aggressive behaviour (Zarros et al. 2005). They may also be linked to other psychological conditions associated with the early stages of Alzheimer's disease, including depression and anxiety.

Risk factors

Risk for Alzheimer's disease is determined in part by environmental factors, although their exact roles in its aetiology are little understood. One consistent risk factor appears to be a history of head injury (McDowell 2001). A previous hypothesis that exposure to high levels of aluminium may result in Alzheimer's disease has generally not been supported, although exposure to water massively polluted by aluminium in the UK may have resulted in a measurable decline in cognitive performance in a small number of people (Altmann et al. 1999). Smoking seems to be protective, even among those with a family history of dementia. Other protective factors include high levels of physical activity, moderate levels of red wine, and a diet high in vitamins B6, B12 and folic acid. High levels of consumption of fatty fish may also be of benefit. Huang et al. (2005) found that people who ate fatty fish at least twice a week were 41 per cent less likely to develop Alzheimer's disease than those that ate them less than once a month. A number of medications may also be protective, including non-steroidal anti-inflammatory drugs and oestrogen replacement therapy in post-menopausal women. One particularly important group of drugs which may prevent onset of Alzheimer's disease is known as statins. These drugs are typically used in the treatment of heart disease and reduce levels of cholesterol. Austen, Christodoulou and Terry (2002) estimated that they may reduce the risk of developing Alzheimer's disease by up to 70 per cent – although the mechanism of this protection is not understood.

Treatment of Alzheimer's disease

Pharmacological interventions

If reductions in acetylcholine cause Alzheimer's disease, increasing available acetyl-choline levels may reverse its symptoms. Drugs that do so prevent its breakdown in the synaptic cleft by acetylcholinesterase and increase uptake in the postsynaptic receptor (see Chapter 3). An important group of drugs, known as acetylcholinesterase inhibitors, such as donepezil, generally achieve short-term cognitive improvements, although they delay rather than prevent cognitive decline (e.g. Petersen et al. 2005). Unfortunately, many people taking them experience significant side-effects, most notably gastrointestinal tract disturbances, and up to 35 per cent of participants have been withdrawn from medication in clinical trials for this reason (Rogers et al. 1998). In addition, not all people respond to the treatment, although why this happens is unclear (Forette and Rockwood 1999). A second method of increasing acetylcholine levels is through ingestion of nicotine, which triggers the release of acetylcholine, and has been shown to improve memory in aged monkeys (Buccafusco and Jackson 1991). People with Alzheimer's disease have also shown short-term gains on a number of cognitive tasks and mood following injections of nicotine. However, there are, as yet, insufficient data to decide whether or not nicotine can prove effective in the treatment of Alzheimer's disease.

A different pharmacological approach involves attempts to block the production of beta amyloid within the brain. Evidence of the impact of this still relatively new treatment is now emerging. Sparks et al. (2005) compared the effectiveness of this type of drug with that of a placebo intervention in people with mild to moderate Alzheimer's disease. At one-year follow-up, the active intervention proved superior to placebo, with people in this condition showing less disease progression. Whether these initial improvements will be maintained for longer periods is yet to be assessed.

Psychological approaches

Psychological interventions aim to maximize quality of life and functional ability as the disease progresses. Support groups, involving other people with similar problems, may provide support or coping strategies in the early stages of Alzheimer's disease (Yale 1995). Three more formal therapeutic approaches are frequently used in its later stages.

Reality orientation Reality orientation (RO: Holden and Woods 1995) involves providing confused elderly people with relevant information to help them maintain an accurate understanding of the world. There are two types of RO:

- *24-hour RO* involves establishing an environment with multiple cues to orient the individual in time, place and person: large clocks and calendars, reminders of the name of an institution or ward, name badges, and so on. Social interactions with the person are also designed to provide relevant information ('Hello, Mr Jones. It's Tom here . . . It's really cold outside, like it usually is in January . . .'). Sentences are simple and specific, repeating information throughout the day and even within conversations.

- *Classroom RO* involves small groups of people meeting for between 30 and 60 minutes. Despite its name, these are held in comfortable rooms, with easy chairs and a relaxed atmosphere. Attenders are matched according to ability, and sessions involve discussion and information provision, with memory triggered by multiple cues and modes of information: newspapers, pictures, talking, and so on.

In their review of 21 controlled trials of RO, Holden and Woods (1995) concluded that RO achieved small but significant gains on measures of verbal orientation in comparison with no treatment or unstructured therapy. There appears to be limited generalization to other cognitive or behavioural skills, although Reeve and Ivison (1985) did report some improvements on measures of incontinence following a combination of classroom and 24-hour RO. Reality orientation may also combine with other treatments to maximize gains. Onder et al. (2005), for example, found both RO and donepezil contributed independently to cognitive gains made in a group of people with Alzheimer's disease.

Reality orientation may be replaced by a slightly different procedure, known as cognitive stimulation. A typical programme involves elements of RO combined with less structured approaches to facilitating cognitive processing, including reminiscence (see below). A key difference between the two approaches is that RO encourages rehearsal of knowledge. While this may occur in cognitive stimulation, more emphasis is placed on information *processing*. Thus, an activity known as 'faces' may ask group members 'Who looks the youngest?', 'What do these people have in common?', rather than 'Do you recognize these people?'. In one study of this approach, Spector et al. (2003) found evidence of increases in both quality of life and cognitive performance following one such programme relative to a control group who received no intervention.

Thinking about . . .

Whatever its outcome, RO can present difficulties for those trying to implement it, particularly when it may be necessary to remind people of distressing information. Many people with Alzheimer's disease, for example, forget about the death of a loved one, and in their confusion may start looking for them or demanding they come and see them. Proper adherence to RO involves a carer telling them that their loved one is dead. This can be devastating news and cause significant distress. Unfortunately, they may forget this information after a period of time and once more start looking for their loved one, requiring the carer to once more break the news of their loved one's death: a cycle that can be distressing for both the individual and carer. Is this fair and a reasonable way to treat people, or, in this case, is ignorance really bliss?

Validation therapy   As a consequence of this negative aspect of RO, Feil (1990) introduced a very different form of therapy. Validation therapy involves listening to the fears and concerns of the affected individual, taking time to fully understand their problems and to 'validate' them by valuing what they have to say. These conversations can provide opportunities to identify and modify any false beliefs, but this is not a core element of this approach. The focus is on listening and responding to the emotional rather than the factual content of what is said.

In group therapy, small groups of individuals may engage in discussions designed to elicit 'universal' feelings of anger, separation or loss (Bleathman and Morton 1992). Feil (1990) suggested that by verbalizing memories and thoughts and having them validated by the group, the person gains a feeling of being accepted. This emphasis on the need to deal with unresolved conflicts has elements of psychodynamic therapy, while the therapeutic use of empathy and acceptance of the individual's personal view of the world provide a strong humanistic element. Evaluation of the effectiveness of this approach is largely anecdotal or based on uncontrolled case histories. What evidence there is suggests it may be of benefit on measures of mood (see Neal and Briggs 2003), but whether it is better than other active interventions is not clear.

Reminiscence therapy There are three forms of reminiscence therapy (McMahon and Rhudick 1964). *Story-type reminiscence* involves remembering factual memories for pleasure. *Life-review* involves remembering and discussing memories, both good and bad, which come naturally to consciousness. Finally, *halo reminiscence* involves the repeated recollection of a particular situation involving guilt or despair. Life-review and halo reminiscence are thought to help resolve past conflicts.

Reminiscence therapy is based on Erikson's (1980) developmental model in which life-review is considered to occur naturally towards the end of life. This review may be generally positive or negative, with a resultant outcome of ego integrity or despair. In individual therapy, the therapist aids the individual through this already occurring self-analysis in order to make it more conscious and efficient. In group therapy, small groups review participants' lives through the use of prompts, including old photographs, television and radio broadcasts, and so on. As with validation therapy, there are few studies of the effectiveness of reminiscence therapy. Participants typically enjoy their involvement in reminiscence groups, and there are reports of small improvements in mood (Bohlmeijer et al. 2005) and increased self-esteem and life satisfaction (Lai et al. 2004) following group attendance. However, there is little evidence that it is more effective than other group activities.

Behaviour modification

Despite considerable interest in operant approaches to modifying the behaviour of confused elderly people, there are relatively few reports of its use and effectiveness. However, studies that have reported these procedures have generally proved effective. Burgio et al. (1988), for example, initiated a programme to increase appropriate toilet use and reduce incontinence which involved asking residents on a regular schedule whether they wished to go to the toilet and then reinforcing its use. This proved successful, although levels of self-initiated toileting actually fell over time, presumably as participants in the programme grew used to the system of prompts. Other programmes have reduced wandering, stereotyped behaviours, and increased social interaction and mobility (see Woods and Roth 1996). According to Woods and Roth, the critical element in the success of operant procedures in elderly people may not be the 'reward' for engaging in a particular behaviour. The use of prompts or cues to initiate behaviour may be more important.

One superordinate factor in providing care for confused elderly people is that the cognitive demands made of them are as minimal as possible (Woods and Bird 1999). Conversations should include short sentences, with repetition. Other relevant cues, such as pictures, may add to verbal information, but distraction with irrelevant information should be avoided. Cues should be simple and direct: an obvious line leading to the toilets and a picture of a toilet on the door, for example, may be more effective than the typical cue of a silhouette of a man or woman. Even people with mild–moderate dementia may find such socially based cues too subtle to interpret. Any cues may require training and repetition to enhance acquisition of relevant information. When taking an individual to the toilet, for example, the carer can talk the person through the process, and show the cues each time. In the home, safety can be maximized by a number of strategies that minimize the need for active planning, including installing storage heaters rather than gas fires, and so on.

Helping the carers

Caring for people with Alzheimer's disease at home places enormous strain on the carers, who are usually elderly themselves, and often in poor health. Many benefit from some form of support and help. This can be provided by voluntary bodies such as the Alzheimer's Disease Society in the UK, and short periods in which the affected person stays in hospital to provide a break for the carer. They may also benefit from other, more formal interventions.

In a meta-analysis of nine studies designed to help carers cope more effectively with their stress, Knight et al. (1992) concluded that both group and individual interventions reduced both perceptions of burden and feelings of depression. Gallagher-Thompson and Steffen (1994) subsequently contrasted cognitive behavioural and psychodynamic interventions in the treatment of depressed carers of elderly relatives. By the end of the intervention phase, both interventions proved equally effective: 71 per cent of participants no longer met the criteria for depression. However, those who had been in the caring role for a relatively short time benefited most from dynamic therapy. Those who had cared for their relative for a longer period gained most from the cognitive behavioural intervention. It may be that people relatively new to the caring role benefit from exploration of their new role and its implications, while those who have been involved for longer benefit from learning more practical techniques for coping with their day-to-day stress.

A second way of helping carers cope is to provide them with strategies to help them manage the behaviour of their relative more effectively. Pinkston et al. (1988), for example, showed carers how to manage a number of behaviours, including self-care, aggression and wandering. Over 75 per cent of the relatives showed some improvement in their behaviour following their carer's training, reducing the strain experienced by their carers.

Research box 14

Gitlin, L.N., Hauck, W.W., Dennis, M.P. et al. (2005) Maintenance of effects of the home environmental skill-building program for family caregivers and individuals with Alzheimer's disease and related disorders, *Journals of Gerontology. Series A, Biological Sciences and Medical Sciences*, 60: 368–74.

The authors of this study reported the long-term effects of an intervention designed to support people caring for someone with dementia. The Home Environment Skill-building Program (ESP) involved occupational therapists providing people caring for a relative with Alzheimer's disease with education, problem-solving and technical skills (including task simplification and communication) and simple home modifications. The intervention involved five, 90-minute home visits and one telephone session over a period of six months. This was followed by one home visit and three brief telephone sessions over the next six months.

Method

Caregivers enrolled into the study had to live with a person with dementia (the patient), be at least 21 years old, be a carer for over six months, and provide care for at least four hours a day. They were randomly assigned into either the active intervention or 'usual care'.

Participants

Some 190 caregivers started the study. By the one-year follow-up reported in this paper, 63 (33 per cent) of this group were no longer involved in the study. Many of those who dropped out from the study did so because of changes in their caring: 23 patients had gone to live in a nursing home, 20 had died. Only 20 dropped out from the study because they no longer wanted to be involved.

Measures

Five outcomes were assessed: the frequency of seven memory-related behaviours assessed using the revised memory-related problem behaviour checklist (rating the patient), caregiver upset in relation to the seven behaviours, days receiving support from family or friends, the Task Management Strategy Index to assess skill enhancement, and a five-item measure of mood, including: calm, upset, overwhelmed, and angry.

Results

The data reported add to published data from the six-month follow-up. By this time, significant six-month treatment gains on the measure of days receiving help and 'upset with memory-related behaviours', were no longer significant. Continued gains were found on measures of affect, and while the differences between the intervention and usual care groups were less than at six-month follow-up, there was some evidence of continued benefits on measures of effective strategy use and the frequency of memory-related behavioural occurrences.

Discussion

These data suggest that gains made at six-month assessment, following the intervention, were somewhat attenuated six months later. However, there was evidence of gains on measures of mood, and some maintenance of the use of skills taught on the course. More positively, the use of these skills appears to have had a modest impact on the frequency of the patients' problem behaviours – but not on the carers' need for support from family or friends. It is not clear why the intervention did not have a more clear-cut long-term benefit. Potential reasons may be that the intervention helped people cope with problems that were occurring at the time of the intervention but did not generalize to other problems, or that any skills were retained for only a relatively short period. More studies may be necessary to determine how intense any intervention or support has to be to have a longer-term benefit.

Head injury

Closed head injury occurs when an individual is struck on the head with no resultant damage to the skull or specific brain injury. This type of trauma usually results in the whole brain shifting within the skull at the time of the incident, resulting in diffuse damage. About half the cases of closed head injury result from road traffic accidents. The second highest cause is falls, particularly among frail elderly people and young children. Violence accounts for a further 20 per cent of cases, while sports injuries account for about 3 per cent. Alcohol consumption also adds to risk. People aged between 15 and 25 years old are most at risk. In the UK, there are up to 150 cases of closed head injury requiring hospitalization for every 100,000 people each year (Jennett 1996).

One simple index of the severity of injury is that of 'time to follow commands': that is, the time after trauma it takes the head-injured person to be able to respond to simple commands. Mild head injury is indicated by a time to follow commands of less than one hour; for moderate head injury this time is between one hour and 13 days; for severe head injury it is 14 days or more. Between 30 and 50 per cent of people will die as a result of severe head injury. About 10 per cent will still be in a 'vegetative' (non-responsive) state three months after the trauma, decreasing to about 4 per cent at six-month follow-up, and 2–3 per cent one year following injury.

For those who survive their injury and recover consciousness, recovery follows a typical pattern. The first phase involves a period of acute confusion and disorientation during which they are unable to form and retain new memories: *post-traumatic amnesia*. The longer the period of amnesia, the poorer the outcome. However, even a fairly long period of post-traumatic amnesia may not necessarily predict poor recovery. Jennett et al. (1981), for example, reported 'good' outcomes in 71 per cent of people who had post-traumatic amnesia lasting between one and two weeks.

Following resolution of post-traumatic amnesia, the majority of people with moderate or severe head injuries experience significant physical, cognitive and behavioural impairment. Most physical problems eventually resolve, although a minority of people continue to experience a wide range of symptoms including persistent muscle spasticity, impaired swallowing, and balance disturbances. About 5 per cent of those with moderate to severe closed head injury develop epileptic seizures: this compares with 35–50 per cent of people with penetrating head injuries. Risk for developing epilepsy continues to be higher than the population norm for as long as five years after the original trauma.

Cognitive and neuro-behavioural deficits are the most common residual symptoms of closed head injury. Diffuse brain injury results in a typical pattern of cognitive deficits, including slowed cognitive speed, decreased attention plus impaired memory, complex language skills and 'executive function' (Levin 1993). The latter includes problems in working memory, problem-solving, monitoring performance and organizing behaviour. Most recovery occurs in the first six months following injury, although recovery may continue more slowly for a further year. One month following injury, almost all people with moderate to severe injury have detectable cognitive impairments. Six months following injury about 8 per cent of those with moderate injury and 16 per cent of those with severe injury will require hospital care as a result of cognitive disabilities. The corresponding rates one year following injury are zero and 10 per cent. Only about a quarter of people with a severe head injury will ever return to work (Sherer et al. 2000).

Neuro-behavioural symptoms experienced by people with head injuries include increased irritability, headaches, anxiety, difficulty in concentrating, fatigue, restlessness and depression (Satz et al. 1998). These are more common than either physical or cognitive deficits and may have a greater impact on long-term outcome. One important feature of long-term recovery from head injury is a lack of self-awareness. Perhaps for this reason, relatives of people who have sustained a head injury frequently report more psychological changes than the affected individual. Relative reports include problems of slowness, irritability, fatigue, depression, rapid mood shifts and anxiety (Brooks et al. 1986). The long-term deficits of head injury can be profound and result in increased risk of divorce, chronic unemployment, economic strain and substance abuse. Perhaps not surprisingly, depression and suicide rates are higher among people with significant head trauma than population levels (Teasdale and Engberg 2001).

Cognitive rehabilitation following head injury

Rehabilitation following moderate to severe head injury involves a number of treatment approaches provided by a variety of health professionals. Medical treatments include pain control for headaches, drug treatment of epilepsy and surgical treatment for **hydrocephalus**. Physiotherapy may maintain muscle flexibility and strength, occupational therapy can teach skills necessary for self-care or return to some form of work. Speech therapists may work with the individual to improve their understanding and articulation of speech. From a psychological perspective, the main intervention is aimed at the cognitive and behavioural consequences of the trauma. The rest of this section will focus on some of the techniques used to improve cognitive function or help the individual cope with enduring cognitive deficits.

Coping with memory problems

A number of general techniques can improve memory, including memory drills, combining imagery with words to improve subsequent recall, and so on. Specific techniques have also been developed for use with people with head trauma. These have frequently involved very specific learning tasks. Wilson (1989), for example, used a preview, question, read, state and test (PQRST) model to improve encoding and recall of lists of words. This involved the participant examining the task, thinking about its requirements, and then reading a list of words over a number of trials both aloud and silently, before testing. The additional cognitive processing required in this approach was thought to enhance learning in comparison with simple repetition of lists of words. Unfortunately, memory gains made in such sessions frequently do not generalize beyond the specific memory task. In addition, as many people with head injuries underestimate their memory loss, attempts to implement such programmes are not always acceptable. Dobkin (1996) concluded that memory aids rather than memory 'treatments' may be the best approach to use (just as with people with MS and Alzheimer's disease). His list of possible memory aids included use of a tape-recorder or hand-written notes, palmtop computers, time reminders such as alarm clocks, phone calls or radio pagers, and the use of a personal organizer or orientation boards within the home.

People with significant impairment may need training in the use of memory aids. Sohlberg and Mateer (1989), for example, used a three-stage process of training to use a memory notebook. The first stage involved systematic training in the contents and purpose of the notebook. This was reinforced by a question-and-answer approach ('What are the five sections of your notebook?'). During the application phase, individuals practised using the book through role play. Finally, they used the book 'in real life'. Using this approach, it took one participant in their programme as long as 17 days to acquire the skills necessary to use the notebook.

Memory aids can be particularly helpful in reminding the individual to do various tasks they otherwise may have forgotten to do. Wilson et al. (2001), for example, evaluated the use of a paging system that reminded people with head injuries to do various tasks through the day. Most of those given the pager benefited both when they had it and during the seven weeks after returning it. Its use seems to have established behavioural patterns that were self-sustaining.

Improving 'executive functions'
A second problem that people face following head injury is a decrement in problem-solving skills. Interventions designed to compensate for this have focused on breaking down problem-solving into specific stages. One such model, which utilized a simple acronym, *IDEAL*, to trigger each phase, was developed by Bransford and Stein (1984):

I involved identification of the problem.
D involved defining the problem (its specific nature and causes).
E involved exploring alternative approaches to dealing with the problem.
A involved acting on the plan developed in stage E.
L involved checking on the effectiveness of any chosen plan.

People with head injuries may also be taught not to try to deal with multiple problems simultaneously, but to try to identify and deal with specific problems one at a time. Where people lose the attention required for problem-solving and other tasks, attention compensation training may be used. This involves the individual first identifying when they are losing concentration, and then using strategies such as self-instruction (Meichenbaum 1985: 'Come on now, pay attention here . . .') to help remain focused. External cues can also be useful in initiating behaviour (Wilson et al. 2001).

A number of standardized programmes have also been developed to remediate attention problems. The *Attention Process Training programme* (APT) of Park et al. (1999) did so by using a number of differing strategies. Sustained attention was trained by exercises including attention tapes that required listening for target words or word/number sequences and pressing a buzzer when identified, listening to a paragraph and testing comprehension, and mental arithmetic exercises. Shifting attention was trained by exercises including tapes that required identification of one type of target word followed by identification of another. Tasks were presented in order of difficulty and repeated until the individual was able to cope effectively with the task demands. If necessary, they were practised at home with the help of relatives as well as in the clinic. This type of approach has proven moderately effective. Most studies have shown gains on psychometric measures of memory or attention following such interventions. Less have looked at 'real-world' improvements, although there is some evidence that improvements can be made on measures as diverse as driving skills, independent living and return to work (Sohlberg and Mateer 2001). Some other strategies to increase attention or prevent distraction are discussed in the context of attention deficit disorder in Chapter 13.

Coping with negative emotions

Given the high levels of depression and suicide among people who have sustained a significant head injury, there is little doubt that many would benefit from some form of psychological or pharmacological intervention to help moderate their mood. The American National Institutes of Health (NIH Consensus Development Panel 1991), for example, noted that psychotherapy could be an important aid to emotional recovery, reducing depression and improving the low self-esteem associated with cognitive dysfunction. They suggested that such interventions should provide emotional support, explanations of the injury and its likely outcome, help achieve increased self esteem by maximizing gains towards achievable goals, reduce denial, and increase the individual's ability to relate to family and society. Despite this optimism, they noted that the use of psychotherapy has not been studied systematically in people with head injury, and its benefits therefore remain unproven. They also noted that while antidepressants may be of value in this population, people who have sustained head injuries are likely to experience more adverse side-effects from these drugs than the norm. This necessitates careful observation of those receiving such medication, and indicates that other therapeutic approaches should be selected where appropriate.

Helping the carers

People living with, and caring for, a person who has sustained a head injury may themselves experience significant stress and distress (Harris et al. 2001). While there is some evidence that strain on the family reduces as a consequence of improvements in cognitive deficits and health service input, there is a strong argument for the provision of services to help the family cope with the stress of caring for a person with a head injury more directly. Despite this, just as with studies to help people cope emotionally with the trauma and consequences of head injury, there are few studies of the effectiveness of such programmes, and most of these are uncontrolled and naturalistic studies. As a result, the impact of family or partner support programmes is difficult to judge (Sinnakaruppan and Williams 2001).

Multiple sclerosis (MS)

Multiple sclerosis is a neurological condition resulting from the destruction of the myelin sheath that surrounds all nerve cells within the brain and central nervous system. Where this destruction occurs, sclerotic plaques develop, which block or distort the normal transmission of nerve impulses. As this may occur in any part of the brain or spinal cord, the symptoms they cause differ markedly across individuals, and include loss of limb function, loss of bowel and/or bladder control, blindness due to inflammation of the optic nerve, and cognitive impairment. Muscular spasticity is a common feature, particularly in the upper limbs; 95 per cent of people with MS experience debilitating fatigue, which prevents any sustained physical activity in about 40 per cent of people. Nearly half the people with MS consider this to be their most serious symptom (Lechtenberg 1988). Between 30 and 50 per cent of people with the condition require walking aids or a wheelchair for mobility.

The course of MS differs across individuals. Onset before the age of 15 years is rare; 20 per cent of those who have MS have a benign form of the disease in which symptoms show little or no progression after the initial attack. A few people experience malignant MS, resulting in a swift and relentless decline and significant disability or even death shortly after disease onset. Onset of this type of MS is usually after the age of 40 years. The majority of people have an episodic condition, with acute flare-ups followed by periods of remission. Each flare-up is usually followed by a failure to recover to previous levels of function, resulting in a slowly deteriorating condition. Death is usually due to complications of MS, including choking, pneumonia and renal failure. Suicide rates are significantly higher among people with MS than in the general population (Sadnovick et al. 1991).

Susan provides a glimpse of what it feels like to have MS. At the time of our talk she was taking antidepressants for her depression and, as you will read, was having problems coming to terms with her disorder:

> I developed MS about four years ago. It was odd to start with. I didn't think I had anything serious, although you do worry about symptoms you don't understand. It started when I had some problems with my sight. I couldn't see as well as I used to be able to – it came on suddenly so I didn't think it was age or anything normal. I think at the time I was also a bit more clumsy than I had been – nothing obvious, but I dropped things a bit more than before. Nothing really that you'd notice unless other things were happening as well. I went to my GP about my eyes and he sent me to see a neurologist. He tried to reassure me that there was nothing too badly wrong and that he wanted to check out a few symptoms. But I began to worry then . . . you don't get sent on to see the hospital doctors unless there is anything really wrong with you. He suggested that he thought it might be MS, which was why he was not sending me to an eye specialist.
>
> I got to see the neurologist pretty quickly and she ran a few tests over a few weeks – testing my muscle strength, coordination, scans and so on . . . sticking needles into me at various times. The upshot of this was that I was diagnosed as having MS. My consultant told me and my husband together, and allowed us to ask questions about things. We also got to speak to a specialist nurse who has helped us over the years. She was able to take the time to tell us more than the doctor about what to expect and what support we could have. Although I think it was nice to hear the diagnosis from the doctor.

I must admit that I found it really hard to deal with things at the beginning – you don't know what to expect and perhaps you expect the worst. You hear all sorts of horror stories about people dying with MS and that. And no one can really reassure you that you won't have problems . . . Over the last few years, I've got to know my body and seen things getting worse. But it happens gradually and a lot of the time there are no changes. So that is reassuring that things aren't going to collapse too quickly and I won't be left incontinent and unable to feed myself for a long time – hopefully not ever!

The worse thing is the tiredness and clumsiness. My eyes have actually got better, thank goodness. I use sticks to get around the house. Sometimes I can walk a little out of the house. Often I have to take the wheelchair. I just get exhausted too quickly, there isn't a lot of point trying to walk, because I cannot go far . . .

I hate having MS. I used to take part in sports, go out, be lively. Now I can't do any of that. I'm tired . . . down a lot of the time. I think the two often go together. My memory was never that good, but now it seems to be worse than ever. I can hold conversations, but keeping my concentration up for a long time is difficult. So, people find you difficult to deal with. I know my husband feels that way. He married a lively, sporty, slim woman . . . now I'm lethargic, down, putting on weight because I eat and don't exercise – even though they tell me not to, so I can keep mobile and not develop skin problems. I don't go out very much because it's such a hassle in my wheelchair . . . cities were not designed for people in wheelchairs . . . and people don't like people in wheelchairs. You are ignored . . . and just want to say, 'Hey, I'm here. I have a brain you know . . .' I know this sounds sorry for myself. And sometimes I feel more positive. But I find living with uncertainty difficult. Will I have a bad day today? Will I have a flare-up – have to go to hospital, take mega-steroids, come out worse than when I went in? I guess you have to live for the day . . . but it can be difficult.

Aetiology of multiple sclerosis

Genetic factors

The lifetime risk of developing MS for the general population is 1 in 800. This increases to 1 in 50 for the children of affected individuals and 1 in 20 for their siblings. However, increased concordance among family members may not exclusively indicate a genetic aetiology. Siblings who both develop MS usually do so in the same calendar year rather than the same age, indicating the possibility of common environmental factors impacting on risk for MS (Haines and Pericak-Vance 1999). Other evidence of genetic factors are the markedly differing rates of the illness in different parts of the world (Rosati 2001). Multiple sclerosis is rare among a variety of groups including Uzbeks, Kazakhs, native Siberians, Chinese, Japanese, Africans and New Zealand Maoris. Rates of MS in Sardinia, and among Parsis and Palestinians are particularly high. Although these differences suggest a genetic contribution to risk for MS, the genes responsible for any transmission have so far proven difficult to find (e.g. Sotgiu et al. 2004; Fenoglio et al. 2005).

Biological mechanisms

The aetiology of MS is still not fully understood, although the favoured hypotheses are that it is the result of errors in the immune system or viral infection.

One chemical within the immune system, called *gamma-interferon*, is particularly implicated in MS: high levels of gamma-interferon co-occur with high levels of MS activity. How gamma-interferon affects the disease process is not yet fully understood, but it is likely that it stimulates production of cytotoxic T cells by the immune system that are responsible for attacking and destroying diseased or damaged body cells. These cells can attack cells directly and are usually able to discriminate between 'self' cells (those of the body) and 'non-self' cells (damaged or cancerous cells, or pathogens). In MS, it seems to be that the activated cytotoxic T cells wrongly identify the myelin sheath of nerve cells within the brain and spinal column as 'non-self', and attempt to destroy it. Viral infections may act as a trigger to the production of gamma-interferon: hence, the link between viral infections and MS.

Stress and MS

There is good evidence that stress can influence activity within the immune system. Given the possible role of the immune system in the aetiology of MS, it is possible therefore that stress may influence the onset and course of the condition. Evidence for the former was provided by Palumbo et al. (1998). They interviewed a group of people with MS and a healthy control group about the frequency and types of stress they had experienced in the year preceding the onset of disease or an equivalent time period. People with MS reported more stressful life-events than those in the control group, suggesting that these may have triggered its onset. Unfortunately, while these data are indicative of a stress–MS link, they cannot be considered definitive. Many people with serious physical illnesses try to find reasons why they have developed the disease at any particular time, a process known as 'the search for meaning'. As many people consider stress to be an important trigger to disease, this may make them more aware of stresses they have experienced or more likely to label events as stressful than people without the disease. Accordingly, any between-group differences in pre-disease stress may have been more apparent than real.

Longitudinal studies of the impact of stress on the progression of MS are easier to interpret and also indicate that stress may have a role in MS. In one such study, Mohr et al. (2000a) took various measures of stress and disease progression every four weeks over periods of up to 100 weeks in a group of people with MS. They found that increases in personal conflict or disruption to routine typically preceded increases in disease activity. Similarly, Ackerman et al. (2002) found that 85 per cent of the exacerbations in symptoms experienced by their cohort of women with MS were preceded by a period of stress. These typically occurred in the two weeks preceding the increase in symptoms. They estimated that participants were 13 times more likely to experience an exacerbation of their condition following an episode of stress than during periods of no stress. Of course, the exacerbation of symptoms may itself prove stressful. Schwartz et al. (1999) who found a bidirectional relationship between stress and MS: risk of disease progression increased as a consequence of stress, and increases in disease progression contributed to reported levels of stress – a vicious cycle between stress and disease progression.

Psychological sequelae of multiple sclerosis

Cognitive problems

As well as physical problems, people with MS frequently experience a number of cognitive deficits in memory, attention, conceptual reasoning, verbal fluency and abstracting abilities. Nearly half the people with MS complain of some degree of cognitive impairment and memory problems. The latter do not follow a distinct progression, but usually involve problems in retrieval from long-term memory storage: short-term and recognition memory is seldom impaired. Speed of information processing is also slowed in comparison to people without the condition, partly due to slowed psychomotor performance as a result of slowed neuronal activity (Brassington and Marsh 1999). Visual and auditory attention may also be impaired. Perhaps because of the cognitive deterioration they experience, subjective reports of cognitive deficits may differ markedly from more objective measures (Christodoulou et al. 2005).

Increasing cognitive deficits can be charted against progressive brain damage. Feinstein et al. (1993) conducted two-weekly cognitive assessments and magnetic resonance imaging (MRI) scans of brain lesions over a six-month period in a group of people with MS. Performance on the cognitive tasks varied as a function of disease progression as measured by the MRI. The test performance of participants whose MRI scans showed increasing lesions deteriorated over time, despite the practice effects of repeated administration. By contrast, those people whose MS did not progress either maintained or improved their scores. Damage to the corpus callosum, the bundle of fibres connecting both hemispheres of the cortex, appears implicated in a variety of cognitive impairments including visuo-spatial ability, and speed of problem-solving. Left parietal lesions are associated with impaired memory and learning (Huber et al. 1992).

Depression

The reported prevalence of depression among people with MS varies between 14 and 57 per cent, higher than among people with other neurological conditions (Schubert and Foliart 1993). About half the people who develop MS will be clinically depressed at some time during the course of the illness (Siegert and Abernethy 2005). Whether this is a direct result of neuronal damage or a psychological reaction to the experience of the disease is not clear. It may, of course, be both.

Perhaps the strongest indicator that depression can be the result of neurological changes is that depression can be the first sign of MS, preceding obvious neuro-cognitive symptoms by months or years (Berrios and Quemada 1990). Proponents of the neurological model have suggested that this is the result of sclerotic plaques in brain areas that mediate mood such as the limbic system, prior to any obvious disorder to which the individual will react. An alternative explanation could be that depression provides a trigger to the onset of MS (as may stress) rather than being an early indicator of its presence.

The findings of Dalos et al. (1983) also suggested a psychological causation. They reported a prospective study of the relationship between mood and disease progression, following 64 patients for a one-year period. Over this time, 90 per cent of people with progressive or relapsing MS developed depression, compared with 39 per cent of those with stable MS, and 12 per cent of a matched group of people with spinal cord injury. This pattern of results is consistent with a model of depression as a reaction to increasing and uncontrollable disability. Aronson (1997) provided further evidence of depression as a reaction to the physical and social consequences of disease: in their sample of people with MS, low mood was associated with unemployment, mobility limitations, fatigue, episodic exacerbations and interference with social activities.

Depression is not just a problem in itself. It may bring with it a number of negative health consequences. Johnston et al. (1999) reported a six-month longitudinal study of 38 people newly diagnosed with MS; 10 people died over the course of the study. Depressed mood at baseline was predictive of death, more rapid disease progression, and more severe disability at six-month follow-up. There was no association between severity of symptoms and depression at baseline, suggesting that depression predicted these outcomes independently of illness severity.

That depression predicts the degree of disability resulting from MS is not surprising. Depressed individuals are less likely to 'push' themselves to maintain independence or follow exercise regimes. Its impact on mortality is more difficult to explain. However, Johnston and colleagues provided three potential explanations for their findings. First, depressed people may behave differently from non-depressed people in ways that increase risk for disease progression: smoking more, eating less adequately or taking less care of themselves. They are also less likely to adhere to recommended treatments as closely as non-depressed people (Mohr et al. 2000b). Second, depressed individuals may differentially influence the behaviour of those around them, resulting in carers or health professionals giving less attention to their needs or restricting entry to aggressive treatments that may prolong life, as they may be considered too emotionally weak to cope with them. Finally, depression is associated with impaired immune functioning, which may directly affect disease progression. Which of these (or other) explanations is most appropriate is not yet understood.

In sharp contrast to the previous discussion, some people with MS experience periods of euphoria. This is found in people with advanced disease and is thought to be a consequence of scarring in the limbic system isolating it from frontal control, although this has not been confirmed by MRI studies (Minden and Schiffer 1990). Steroids used to treat MS during acute flare-ups may also trigger such episodes.

Treatment of multiple sclerosis

Psychological interventions in MS have two primary foci: first, to help people manage the cognitive and other symptoms of MS, and, second, to help people cope emotionally with the impact of the disease.

Coping with cognitive deterioration

Many of the memory aids used in dementia and head injury can also be used to help people with MS who have memory problems or problems of executive function. One additional strategy has been developed specifically for people with MS. Goldstein et al. (1992) suggested that *gist recall* can be a powerful aid to memory for people with MS. They noted that while people with MS may have trouble remembering specific details of events, they are able to remember the gist or basic elements of what occurred. According to this model, rehabilitation should focus on teaching people to encode and retrieve information according to its overall meaning rather than trying to remember the details of what may have occurred. How effective this is has yet to be fully evaluated.

Coping with emotional problems

A number of interventions can be used to help people cope with the symptoms of MS. One relatively simple method involves providing information about the likely course of the disease, as uncertainty is associated with lower mood. There is consistent evidence that more sophisticated interventions can also alleviate depressive symptoms experienced by people with MS. In a meta-analysis of the evidence, Mohr and Goodkin (1999) found both psychological and pharmacological treatments to be effective in treating depression, with no difference in benefits following either approach. Only five studies had been reported at this time, so any conclusions should be viewed with some caution. However, brief cognitive behavioural interventions appeared superior to both waiting list control and standard outpatient appointments. Larcombe and Wilson (1984), for example, randomly allocated 20 depressed people with MS into a cognitive behavioural or waiting list condition. The cognitive behavioural programme was based on Beck's depression treatment programme, and involved increased social interaction, pleasant event scheduling, and challenging cognitive distortions. People who took part in the intervention evidenced greater improvements in mood than those in a waiting list control group, both at the end of therapy and at one-month follow-up. The magnitude of reductions in depression reported was similar to those found in general psychiatric populations, suggesting there is nothing about depression in MS that makes it harder to treat than in people without MS. Similar gains were found by Visschedijk et al. (2004) following a similar group intervention.

Fatigue and poor mobility may make it difficult for many people with MS to attend outpatient therapy appointments. With this in mind, Mohr et al. (2000b) examined the effectiveness of a cognitive behavioural programme for the treatment of depression delivered by telephone. The intervention lasted eight weeks and involved a workbook with standardized assignments combined with telephone contacts. Assignments focused on identifying and modifying dysfunctional thoughts, increasing pleasant events, and developing strategies to manage fatigue. The latter included scheduling achievable amounts of exercise, scheduling breaks, and learning to identify physical cues to determine when to take breaks. The usual care control involved routine outpatient appointments. By the end of the intervention, participants in the cognitive behavioural programme reported lower levels of depression and were more likely to adhere to their interferon therapy than those in the normal care condition.

Pharmacological interventions

Medical interventions have been used to combat deteriorations in memory and depression in people with MS. Treatment of memory problems has mirrored treatment of Alzheimer's disease, by using donepezil. Krupp et al. (2004) found that twice as many participants reported improvements in memory following treatment with donepezil than when treated with placebo. Unfortunately, these improvements were not accompanied by improvements on objective tests of memory.

In terms of depression, Minden and Schiffer (1990) found desipramine (a tricyclic) to be superior to placebo. However, nearly half those in the trial experienced significant side-effects, even at less than optimum treatment levels of the drug. This sensitivity to medication has also been found in the treatment of depression following head injury, and may make psychological interventions the therapy of choice in such cases. Whatever the scientific evidence, pharmaceutical treatments are frequently prescribed for MS. Tremlett, Luscombe and Wiles (2001) found that, relative to a non-MS comparison group, people with MS were more likely to be prescribed a variety of medications including hypnotics, anxiolytics and antidepressants.

Chapter summary

1 Alzheimer's disease affects a significant proportion of elderly people.

2 It is characterized by a progressive process of cognitive and behavioural degeneration following a regular pattern as differing brain systems become involved.

3 The neurological processes underpinning the disorder appear to be neurofibrillary tangles and beta amyloid plaques. Reductions in levels of the neurotransmitter acetylcholine also appear to be implicated.

4 There is, as yet, no cure for Alzheimer's disease. In its early stages, interventions are aimed at maximizing cognitive abilities. As the illness progresses, interventions focus on minimizing cognitive load and maintaining independence.

5 Closed head injuries can result in profound and long-lasting cognitive deficits.

6 Psychological interventions in this population focus on cognitive retraining, although any gains often fail to generalize beyond the training context. Accordingly, many interventions incorporate the use of external aids to trigger routine behaviours as well as cognitive strategies for maintaining concentration.

7 Multiple sclerosis is a degenerative disease of varying course.

8 It impacts on both the cognitive and emotional life of people with the disease.

9 Interventions are therefore aimed at developing strategies for coping with both cognitive impairments and depression. Both appear to be effective.

For discussion

1 Many frail and elderly people act as carers for people with Alzheimer's disease. How can their stress be minimized?

2 Does cognitive retraining really provide meaningful benefit to people who have had a head injury, or are its effects too limited?

3 How may people with MS be helped to cope effectively with their disease?

Further reading

Brown, R.F., Tennant, C.C., Dunn, S.M. et al. (2005) A review of stress-relapse interactions in multiple sclerosis: important features and stress-mediating and -moderating variables, *Multiple Sclerosis*, 11: 477–84.

Cicerone, K.D., Dahlberg, C., Malec, J.F. et al. (2005) Evidence-based cognitive rehabilitation: updated review of the literature from 1998 through 2002, *Archives of Physical Medical Rehabilitation*, 86: 1681–92.

NIH Consensus Development Panel on Rehabilitation of Persons with Traumatic Brain Injury (1999) Rehabilitation of persons with traumatic brain injury, *Journal of the American Medical Association*, 282: 974–83.

Wilcock, G.K., Bucks, R.S. and Rockwood, K. (eds) (1999) *Diagnosis and Management of Dementia: A Manual for Memory Disorders Teams*. Oxford: Oxford University Press.

15
Addictions

Ask someone to describe an addict, and they will usually give a stereotypical description of someone addicted to 'hard' drugs such as heroin or cocaine. However, most chemical addictions are to legal drugs such as coffee, cigarettes and alcohol. People may also be addicted to a variety of behaviours, including exercise or gambling. For these people, the neurochemical reaction to their behaviour is similar to that induced by drugs. After a brief introduction to drugs and drug dependence, this chapter considers the aetiology, implications and treatment of three types of addiction: to alcohol, heroin and gambling. By the end of the chapter, you should have an understanding of:

- Why people take drugs, and the nature of dependence
- Factors leading to alcohol and opiate abuse, and gambling disorders
- The types of interventions used to treat each disorder, and their relative effectiveness.

Drugs and drug dependence

Many people take drugs, and start taking them at a relatively young age. In the UK, 41 per cent of 16-year-olds report having used cannabis, in comparison with 34 per cent of US, 10 per cent of Italian and 2 per cent of Greek teenagers (Hibell et al. 1997). Similar cross-cultural differences emerge when considering the use of cocaine in various European countries. Haasen et al. (2004), for example, found the percentage of individuals within a general population sample of people aged between 15 and 64 years having used cocaine on at least one occasion varied across countries: UK 5.2 per cent; Spain 4.9 per cent; Germany 2.3 per cent; Italy 1.1 per cent. Use of cocaine was highest among young people, socially marginalized groups such as the homeless and prostitutes, and opiate-dependent people in treatment programmes. Specific subcultures may also be associated with specific drug use. Participants in the rave culture typically report having used over ten drugs, including alcohol, cannabis, ecstasy, tobacco, LSD, amphetamine and cocaine (Forsythe 1996). Use of drugs among the wider population is considerably less, although about 25 per cent of the population report having used an illegal drug, most frequently cannabis, at some time in their life. Only 3 per cent of the drug-using population injects.

Drugs impact through changes in neurotransmitters within brain systems (see Table 15.1). With few exceptions, the quicker a drug's action, the more addictive it is. Cocaine, for example, was originally ingested by chewing coca leaves. This produced an increase in vigour and resistance to fatigue but little pleasure. More recently, it has been made into cocaine hydrochloride powder which, when taken nasally, impacts on the brain within 4–10 minutes of ingestion. Crack cocaine is a further refinement that allows it to be smoked and to impact on the brain in seconds. Each form of cocaine is thought to be increasingly addictive.

Problems arising from drug use defy simple categorization. They may be social, physical, legal, interpersonal or psychological. DSM-IV-TR (APA 2000) acknowledged these factors in its definition of 'abuse or harmful use of substances' as a maladaptive pattern of substance use leading to clinically significant impairment or distress and one or more of the following:

• failure to fulfil major role obligations at work, school or home
• use in situations in which it is physically hazardous
• legal problems
• social or interpersonal problems.

DSM-IV-TR also identified a more problematic level of dependence, in which the

Table 15.1 The neurotransmitters involved and 'addictiveness' of various drugs

Drug class	Neurotransmitter involved	Physical withdrawal problems	Psychological withdrawal problems
Mimic natural transmitters			
Opiates	Endorphins	+++	+++
Cannabis	Anandamide	+	+
Alcohol	GABA	+++	++
Nicotine	Acetylcholine	+	+++
Release transmitters			
Cocaine	Dopamine	++	+++
Amphetamines	Dopamine	+	++
Nicotine	Dopamine	+	+++
Ecstasy	Dopamine; serotonin	+	0
Block transmitters			
Barbiturates	Glutamate	+++	++
Psychedelics (incl. LSD)	Serotonin	+	0

Source: adapted from Nutt and Law (2000)

individual becomes psychologically or physically dependent on a particular drug. The key factor here is the development of a tolerance to the drug, involving a need for more of it to achieve the desired experience, and withdrawal symptoms if use of the drug is ceased. Other criteria include social impairment, devoting substantial time and effort to obtaining the drug, and a history of repeated, unsuccessful attempts to stop using.

Excess alcohol consumption

Alcohol is a socially sanctioned drug. Drunk at moderate levels, certain types of alcohol, such as red wine, may benefit health. Excess consumption may be harmful. Defining what is meant by excess alcohol consumption has proven far from simple. This confusion is illustrated by changes to health advice made by the UK government in 1995. Between 1986 and 1995 the recommended limits for weekly consumption were 21 units of alcohol or less for men, and 14 units or less for women. In 1995, a government committee established to review these guidelines recommended they be increased to 28 and 21 units per week respectively. These changes caused a furore and much criticism among alcohol experts, particularly as they were not based on any new evidence (see, for example, *British Medical Journal*, volume 293). Consequently, a number of health promotion and alcohol agencies have been reluctant to adopt these guidelines and there is a lack of clear advice concerning the recommended limits to consumption.

Acute intoxication can result in risk-taking or other behaviours that may damage both the individual or others. About 20 per cent of psychiatric admissions, 60 per cent of suicide attempts, 40 per cent of incidences of domestic violence and 15 per cent of all traffic deaths in the UK are associated with alcohol consumption (Royal College of Psychiatrists 1986; Edwards et al. 1994). Alcohol consumption has also been associated with an increased risk for violent crime, accidents at work, fatal and non-fatal driving accidents, drownings, burns and suicide (Allan et al. 2001).

Long-term dangers include physical health problems such as liver cirrhosis, hypertension and various cancers. Long-term excess consumption may also result in significant neurological problems. Wernicke's encephalopathy is caused by thiamine deficiencies common in heavy drinkers as a consequence of poor diet, and results from degenerative changes and small bleeds in the brain. Its symptoms include memory deficits, **ataxia** and confusion. If not treated, it may progress to a more problematic disorder known as Korsakoff's syndrome. This irreversible condition affects about 5 per cent of heavy drinkers and involves significant **retrograde amnesia** and **anterograde amnesia**. Anterograde memory deficits are usually the most marked problems, and individuals with the condition live a very 'minute-by-minute' existence, frequently **confabulating** in an effort to replace the memories they fail to sustain.

Problem drinking is usually the end-point of a progression from social drinking to drinking at times of stress or difficulty, through to an increasing 'need' to drink to cope with social or psychological problems or prevent the onset of withdrawal symptoms. In the early stages of dependence, individuals may need a drink at lunchtime to alleviate discomfort. As they become more dependent, they may need an early morning drink or one during the night to avoid withdrawal. Periods of abstinence of three to four hours may be difficult. Withdrawal results in a variety of symptoms, including tremor, nausea, sweating and mood disturbance. Delirium tremens ('the DTs') is the most extreme element of withdrawal. It usually begins within three to four days of abstinence and lasts between two and three days. It involves reductions in consciousness, impairment of memory, insomnia and frightening auditory and/or visual hallucinations.

The story of Anne is typical of many women who drink to excess:

First started drinking when I was 18. I was at college at the time – a part of the norm – drinking cider or lager at weekends. I met my first partner out drinking when I was about 22. We got into a crowd who were wine drinkers and so we started drinking more wine. He'd always been a heavy drinker – more than I ever did. And often as a result of his drinking he'd become quite violent towards me and arguments would follow after drinking. As a result of this, I began to drink more – to join him, to keep up. My violent marriage made me think about my childhood – which had been very unstable and unhappy for various reasons – and the more I brooded on that, the more I drank. I was drinking about two bottles of wine a night at this time. Drinking helped me cope with my marriage and memories of my childhood. It also made things in the relationship worse, of course.

By the time I was 28–29, the relationship had broken down, and my drinking fell a little – but not that much. Then one night, I was followed home by a man from a nightclub and sexually assaulted by him. My drinking escalated again. I felt I couldn't go out of the house. I was scared and felt trapped. I lost my job as a care worker with children and then I had nothing to keep me going, so I just drank through the day. I was drinking a couple of bottles of wine and perhaps a flagon of cider a day at this time. I did this for about six months or so, when I met my next partner, and I began to drink less. I managed to get another job. But the drinking was always there. I managed to get another job – as a health care assistant in an old people's home. I had a child – but things were never good in the relationship I suppose. For the last 20 years, things have pretty much been the same. I drink all the time – sometimes more, sometimes less. Drinking helps me forget my problems and go into oblivion – it blocks things out. And there's a lot to block out. I thought I had been an OK mother – perhaps not the best, but OK. But my son doesn't want to know me any more. My partner has long gone. I've had jobs on and off over this time – that last one, about eight years ago.

I feel guilty about my drinking. I've never really been there for my family – I've always been the drunk that doesn't fit in. I suppose if you are always drunk – quietly not loudly – you still can't do your best. Now, I stay in – I don't go out much. I'm ashamed when I go to the shops – people looking at me, talking about me. I feel they are looking at me – judging me. I don't feel good when I'm drunk, but I do feel in oblivion. I just sit there – or lie in bed all day. I'm drinking from the moment I get up – I have to control the tremors.

I want to stop drinking. I feel despair at the circle I'm caught up in – there's no way out. I try – I do all the right things from pouring the drink down the sink, going to the GP for help and so on. But when I stop drinking I get violent stomach cramps. I shake. I get headaches. I feel paranoid, that people are talking about me. I can't cope with these withdrawals, so I end up drinking again.

Since telling her story, Anne has been going through in-patient detoxification and a six-month programme in a residential setting involving both exploratory psychotherapy and a cognitive behavioural relapse prevention programme. At the time of writing all is going well.

Aetiology of excess alcohol consumption

Many people drink excessively for years without becoming dependent on alcohol. Most reduce their consumption as they grow older. Young men who drink excessively while single, for example, may moderate their consumption as they marry, have children and so on. Any explanation of alcohol-related problems needs therefore to explain factors that contribute to the early stages of alcohol use as well as why some people continue to use and then abuse alcohol. The biopsychosocial model appears to be the most appropriate model, as it may explain why some people are more prone to alcohol dependence than others, as well as the social and psychological factors that may independently and together lead to this state.

Genetic factors

There is some evidence of a genetic predisposition to alcohol problems. Prescott and Kendler (1999), for example, reported concordance for 'high lifetime alcohol consumption' of 47 per cent in MZ and 32 per cent in DZ twins. Adoption studies have also shown the adopted children of parents with alcohol problems to have higher rates of alcohol problems than those of parents without this history (e.g. Cadoret et al. 1995).

This evidence does not necessarily point to a gene for alcoholism: alcohol problems may be secondary to other genetically mediated traits, including poor impulse control or emotional problems. However, there is indirect evidence implicating a specific gene or genes related to alcohol dependence. Schuckit et al. (1996) found that individuals from families in which there were high levels of problem drinking had a lower physiological response to alcohol than matched controls. This may lead to heavy, and then problem, drinking. Men with family histories of problem drinking also typically experience a greater reduction in anxiety after drinking alcohol than the norm (Finn et al. 1992). Again, this is thought to reinforce drinking.

More biological studies have, in fact, implicated a number of genes in the process of addiction. These include genes for enzymes involved in alcohol metabolism (Whitfield 2005). One important genetic process involves the dopamine D2 receptor gene. This gene can take a number of forms: it is polymorphic. One variant of the D2 dopamine receptor gene, the DRD A1(+) allele, has been found to be more prevalent in individuals with a dependence on alcohol than those without such a dependence (Lawford et al. 1997). The gene may also influence the initiation and effect of a variety of drugs. Connor et al. (2005), for example, found that male adolescents with this allele tried alcohol and became intoxicated more often than those without it. In addition, they were more likely to develop a smoking habit and experience a marijuana 'high'.

Biological factors

The DRD A1(+) allele may impact through its affect on the dopamine receptors (Bowirrat and Oscar-Berman 2005). Consumption of alcohol triggers a cascade of chemical events resulting in the release of dopamine within the reward or 'pleasure centre' of the brain: a complex of structures that includes the basal ganglia, thalamus, amygdala, hypothalamus and nucleus accumbens. People with this gene may be more sensitive to the effects of alcohol than those without it (suggesting this may be an explanation of the findings of Finn et al. above). Thus, they may be encouraged to initiate alcohol and other drug use, because they find it easy to gain a 'high' from their alcohol consumption. This mechanism suggests that such individuals may need relatively little alcohol to provide an emotional reward, and therefore maintain their consumption. However, continued use of alcohol is thought to reduce the response of this reward system to other potential reinforcers, leading to a dependence on alcohol to maintain a desired mood state. In addition, other neurotransmitters may be involved in maintaining alcohol consumption. Alcohol also enhances the action of GABA within the hypothalamus and sympathetic nervous system (see Chapter 3), helping calm mood and behaviour. Over time, this results in a reduction in the natural production of GABA, leading to a dependence on alcohol to maintain desired emotional states. Abstinence results in sub-optimal levels of GABA, increases in anxiety and agitation, and the onset of physical withdrawal symptoms. These are relieved by continued drinking or, in time, the body's resumption of normal levels of GABA.

Socio-cultural factors

Alcohol is a socially sanctioned drug, and consumption is markedly influenced by social and environmental factors. Beginning to drink alcohol is seen as one of the transitions from childhood to adulthood, although this may happen relatively early in life: about one-third of British 13–14-year-olds report having been drunk on more than one occasion (Sutherland and Wilner 1998). The early consumption of alcohol by young people is associated with positive attitudes to alcohol use, some of which are linked to family and peer attitudes and behaviours, and may result from the positive images of consumption seen on television, in films, and so on (see Bennett and Murphy 1997). Social factors influence consumption once initiated. Round buying, for example, may increase consumption among young social drinkers, for whom alcohol is frequently linked to social and group activities. Life transitions, both good and bad, may also influence consumption: developing relationships and families, or getting and maintaining a job, may inhibit consumption. Adverse life-events may increase consumption, particularly among people who use alcohol as a means of coping with stress (Perreira and Sloan 2001).

Within countries, rates of drinking vary across cultural and social groups. Men are more likely to drink heavily than women. Blue-collar workers are more likely than white-collar workers to report problem drinking, as are workers with access to alcohol as part of their job. Binge drinking is most frequent among the young, male, lower-income and lower-educated groups (e.g. Hemmingsson et al. 1997). Levels of alcohol consumption may be particularly high in marginalized groups or groups under social pressure, such as the Native Americans in the USA (e.g. Bursac and Campbell 2003). Similarly, Latinas had a higher risk for alcohol use than their African- and Asian-American peers in a survey of alcohol consumption in the southern USA (Guiao and Thompson 2004). Not surprisingly, levels of alcohol consumption vary across countries also. The Japanese, for example, drink more alcohol than US or British people (Ueshima 2005).

Psychological factors

Behavioural explanations of alcohol consumption consider it to be the consequence of both operant and classical conditioning. Consumption is rewarded by both the pleasure associated with drinking, which may be physiological or social, or relief from stress. Once an individual has developed a dependence on alcohol, a further motivator to drink is the avoidance of withdrawal symptoms. Classical conditioning may occur as drinking becomes associated with particular cues or events, subsequent exposure to which may trigger episodes of drinking (e.g. Wilson 1988).

Cognitive theorists suggest that beliefs about alcohol, known as *addictive beliefs* (Beck et al. 1993), are important determinants of consumption at all stages in a drinking career. At the beginning of a history of alcohol use, positive beliefs such as 'It will be fun to get drunk' predominate. As the individual begins to rely on alcohol to counteract feelings of distress, relief-oriented thoughts ('I need a drink to get through the day') may predominate. Addictive beliefs are frequently accompanied by a wider set of negative core beliefs, including a negative view of oneself, one's circumstances and environment, which may contribute to depression or anxiety. Both addictive and negative beliefs may be triggered by external cues, including walking past a bar, or internal ones, such as adverse mood states. Toneatto (1999) identified a number of types of thoughts that trigger consumption and the expected impact that such consumption would have on long-term drug and alcohol users (see Table 15.2).

Interventions in excess alcohol consumption

Prevention: the socio-cultural approach

Approaches to preventing excess alcohol consumption have generally assumed that controls over drinking that affect the whole population will also impact on heavy or problem drinkers. As a result, preventive approaches have typically focused on all drinkers rather than just those who drink to excess (see also Chapter 4). These have generally attempted to change the context or rules surrounding consumption. Many have met with success. Drink–drive laws and related advertising, for example, have markedly decreased the number of alcohol-related accidents and appear to have made drink–driving much less acceptable than was previously the case (see Wagenaar et al. 1995). An apparent contrast to attempts to control drinking can be found in laws that have liberated the consumption of alcohol by extending the licensing hours. These do not seem to have resulted in increased consumption, and may have even decreased binge drinking, because the pressure to drink rapidly before closing time has been lessened (Bruce 1980).

Table 15.2 Type of thoughts leading to alcohol consumption and their impact

Cognitive state	Likelihood of consumption (%)	Expected consequence
Depression	74	Detachment
Stress	71	Reduction
Anxiety	67	Reduction
Grief	62	Detachment
Unpleasant thoughts	62	Detachment
Anger	51	Reduction
Unpleasant memories	50	Reduction
Boredom	49	Reduction
Pain	48	Intensification
Guilt	47	Detachment

Thinking about . . .

At the time of writing, a new UK law is enabling pubs and clubs to be open 24 hours a day, leading to fears that binge drinking and public disorder will rise to unprecedented levels – a fear expressed by, among others, the Royal College of Physicians. But is this really the case? Between 1980 and 2000, Australia increased the availability of alcohol, liberalized trading hours, and did not increase overall taxation on alcohol – changes associated with a *fall* in per-capita alcohol consumption of 24 per cent (Stockwell 2004). Over the same period in the UK, per-capita alcohol consumption increased by 31 per cent. Relatively subtle changes may reduce alcohol-related harm. Australia strengthened its drink–driving laws and their enforcement, with a linked fall in drink–driving related injuries and deaths. It also taxed low alcohol beers less than full strength beers. As a consequence, low alcohol beer now accounts for 40 per cent of all beer consumed in Australia.

So, availability of alcohol can increase, while its harmful effects on individuals and society can decrease. But are these effects specific to Australian culture? Or can drinking policies that enable wide access to alcohol accompany policies that reduce potential harm?

Alcoholism versus problem drinking

A sharp divide can be found between the beliefs that different practitioners hold about the nature and treatment of alcohol-associated problems, and the terminology they use. Some consider what they term 'alcoholism' to be a biological disease. Interventions based on this approach usually involve medical treatments or programmes of complete abstinence, such as that followed by Alcoholics Anonymous (AA). Others consider what they term 'problem drinking' to be the result of psychological and social factors, and argue that most people can learn to drink alcohol in moderation and appropriately. Interestingly, there is a substantial transatlantic split on this issue.

A majority of US practitioners subscribe to the medical, abstinence model; most Europeans subscribe to the psychosocial, controlled drinking model (Peele 1992). Advocates of the latter (e.g. Heather 1995) contend that many problem drinkers can moderate their consumption whereas others may refuse to consider abstinence. Attempts at abstinence by these people may result in more problems, not fewer. Trials that have offered dependent drinkers a choice between controlled drinking and abstinence (e.g. Booth et al. 1992) have resulted in similar gains in both conditions. The best treatment goal may therefore be the choice of the client, not the therapist.

Withdrawal

The initial treatment of people with alcohol problems may involve a period of withdrawal. This may take three to four days, and is usually aided by the use of sedatives such as diazepam (Valium) which moderate the severity of any withdrawal symptoms (Favre et al. 2005). Once they have withdrawn from alcohol, many people will receive one or more of the interventions described below.

Drug therapy

Antidipstrotrophics deter consumption by causing the drinker to feel ill if they consume alcohol while taking them. The most commonly used drug of this type is disulfiram (Antabuse). It prevents alcohol being broken down further than its intermediate metabolite acetaldehyde. This accumulates in the body and causes a number of symptoms, including flushing, headache, pounding in the head or chest, nausea and occasional vomiting, about 15–20 minutes after consumption of alcohol. Patients may be given a test reaction to alcohol to alert them to the consequences of consumption. The benefits of disulfiram depend on its regular consumption. Where this is enforced, it appears an effective barrier to consumption. It is less effective when taken voluntarily (Hughes and Cook 1997). Its use clearly follows a biological, abstinence model. However, some studies have evaluated the effectiveness of similar drugs in programmes that accept that participants may choose to drink on occasion. In these, it may be used as an occasional control to consumption, particularly when users feel they are losing control over their drinking (Sinclair 2001).

A second type of drug treatment for alcohol abuse involves the use of opioid agonists, such as naltrexone, which are thought to reduce cravings. Such programmes, of course, encounter the same problems as antabuse programmes: if people want to drink, they simply stop taking the medication. Accordingly, adherence to such programmes has been low. In an attempt to overcome this issue, Garbutt et al. (2005) gave long-lasting injections of naltrexone to people with alcohol dependence. Compared with placebo, 380 mg of long-acting naltrexone resulted in a 25 per cent decrease in heavy drinking days and 190 mg of naltrexone resulted in a 17 per cent decrease over a six-month period. A final drug type used to treat alcohol dependence involves drugs designed to reduce cravings through their action on GABA receptors. Boothby and Doering (2005) reviewed the evidence of the effectiveness of this type of drug, and found it to be of significant benefit. The percentage of patients who were completely abstinent when prescribed acamprosate throughout the different durations of the studies varied from 18 per cent to 61 per cent, compared with 4 per cent to 45 per cent with placebo

The 12-step approach

The 12-step approach is the treatment programme of AA. It is based on a belief that alcoholism is a physical, psychological and spiritual illness that cannot be cured, but can be controlled by total abstinence from alcohol. The organization provides a strong social support network that encourages emotional expression and the admission of failure. Attenders at group meetings are encouraged to accept that they are powerless to control their drinking, to cease their struggle and to allow a 'higher power' to take control (Gorski 1989).

The millions of attenders of AA meetings across the world attest to the potential benefits of this approach. More empirical data provide mixed support. In a meta-analysis of research prior to the mid-1990s, Kownacki and Shadish (1999) concluded that attendance at AA meetings resulted in minimal gains on measures of abstinence, and that some studies found it to be less effective than no treatment or alternative treatments. However, the particularly poor outcomes in their review were among people whose attendance at AA was compulsory. More positive results were reported by Timko et al. (2000), who compared outcomes on people who self-selected either into AA or a variety of formal treatment programmes including residential, psychological or psychiatric treatments. At one-year follow-up, 56 per cent of the participants in AA had a 'benign' drinking pattern in comparison with 33 per cent of those who received other formal interventions. At three-year follow-up, the figures were 64 and 43 per cent respectively. Note that while AA follows a model of abstinence, many of the people who engaged in this approach seemingly learned to drink within reasonable limits.

Cognitive behavioural approaches

A number of aversive approaches have been used in the treatment of alcohol-related problems, including presenting alcohol-related stimuli at the same time as mild electrical shocks or inducing feelings of suffocation by injection of succinylcholine. These have proven, at best, moderately effective in the short but not the long term, and are now considered ethically questionable. More recent cognitive behavioural programmes have involved training in social skills and strategies for preventing relapse (see Longabough and Morgenstern 2000). Social skills training involves teaching interpersonal and assertive skills to help participants cope more effectively with stressful situations, refuse drinks, and so on. In relapse prevention programmes, high-risk situations are identified, and the individual develops and rehearses strategies to help them cope with them should they arise. These may include specific strategies to challenge addictive beliefs and to cope with cravings to drink. These may be combined with drug therapies. Feeney et al. (2002), for example, reported abstinence rates of 14 per cent following a CBT relapse prevention programme, compared with one of 38 per cent in a CBT plus acamprosate in a group of patients considered to be at high risk of relapse.

Relapse is frequently associated with marital problems and prevented by strong marital cohesion. For this reason, some programmes involve the problem drinker's partner where this is possible. O'Farrell and Fals-Stewart (2000), for example, described an intervention intended to increase the communication and problem-solving skills of couples rather than just the individual. Both the problem drinker and their partner learned strategies to reduce consumption, including the partner changing behaviours that may trigger alcohol use, finding new ways to discuss drinking and situations involved with it, and new responses to their partner's drinking. A further strand of therapy focused on the type and quality of communication between the partners. In their review of the effectiveness of this approach, O'Farrell and Fals-Stewart (2000) concluded that it was consistently more effective than individual therapy on measures of alcohol consumption, abstinence, alcohol-related problems and the quality of marital relationships.

Brief therapies

Some problem drinkers may be helped by relatively brief interventions. Chick (1991), for example, considered that hospital patients may be particularly motivated to improve their general health, and screened medical patients for high levels of alcohol consumption. Those who reported alcohol-related problems were randomly allocated into either a single counselling session with a booklet detailing how to reduce consumption or no treatment. One year later, consumption was lower among those in the intervention group than among those who received no intervention. A similar opportunistic intervention was reported by Monti et al. (1999), who evaluated the effect of an intervention designed to enhance motivation to reduce consumption among adolescents treated in a casualty department following an alcohol-related incident. Those who received the intervention had a significantly lower incidence of drinking and driving, traffic violations, alcohol-related injuries and alcohol-related problems over the following year than those who received no intervention. A similar intervention provided by peers instead of health professionals has also proven of benefit (Bazargan-Hejazi et al. 2005).

The intervention used by Monti and Bazargan-Hejiza is known as motivational interviewing (Miller and Rollnick 2002). Its primary goal is to encourage individuals to explore both their positive and their negative beliefs about a particular behaviour or behavioural change. This process is intended to trigger a state of cognitive dissonance in which the individual actively considers two sets of opposing beliefs and attitudes towards a particular issue (in this case, the 'good' and 'not so good' things about drinking). According to cognitive dissonance theory, this is an aversive state and motivates cognitive work to reduce the discomfort. It may result in a rejection of the newly considered arguments, or the adoption of new beliefs or behaviours – in this case, a reduction in alcohol consumption. Summarizing the effectiveness of this intervention from their meta-analysis, Burke et al. (2003) found this approach resulted in a 56 per cent reduction in alcohol consumption.

An extended intervention based on increasing and maintaining motivation to change has proven effective in reducing consumption in problem drinkers. Sellman et al. (2001), for example, compared the effects of motivational therapy, non-directive reflective listening, and a no-treatment control among problem drinkers. The goal of therapy was controlled drinking, and the key outcome was the frequency of binge drinking. In the six months following the interventions, 43 per cent of people who received the motivational intervention had engaged in binge drinking, in comparison with over 63 per cent of those in the other conditions.

Project MATCH

Despite the differences in philosophy and strategies of the treatment approaches, their effectiveness appears to be very similar. The largest ever alcohol-treatment trial, involving over 1500 participants (Project MATCH Research Group 1998), found few differences in the effectiveness of a number of interventions, including motivational enhancement therapy, cognitive behavioural and 12-step approaches. By one-year follow-up, 35 per cent of all participants reported complete abstinence over the previous year; a further 25 per cent reported having not having drunk heavily on more than two consecutive days in this time, a measure considered to reflect some degree of control over their alcohol consumption. At one-year and three-year follow-ups, there were, again, no differences between the three intervention groups. The principal purpose of the study, however, was to determine which clients responded best to which treatments. Four such effects were found. People who entered treatment with a high level of state/trait anger fared best in motivational enhancement therapy through the three years of follow-up (Waldron et al. 2001). Those whose social support systems favoured continued drinking rather than abstinence, who had higher levels of dependence, and who had higher levels of mental health problems benefited most from the 12-step approach. People with lower levels of dependence fared better if they received cognitive behavioural therapy (Babor et al. 1999).

Heroin use

Opiates are a group of drugs derived from the opium poppy. The key derivatives, in order of strength and addictiveness, are opium, morphine and heroin. The most widely used form of the drug is heroin. Initially widely used as a sedative, the non-medical use of all opiates is now illegal across the world. Taking heroin results in profound feelings of warmth, relaxation and euphoria. Worries, fears and concerns are forgotten, and self-confidence increases. These effects last for between 4 and 6 hours, before the individual 'comes down' from the drug. Once dependent on the drug, withdrawal usually begins about 8 hours after an injection, and results in muscle pain, sweats, sneezes and uncontrollable yawning. Within 36 hours, the symptoms become increasingly severe, and include uncontrollable muscle twitching, cramps, chills, sweats, and a rise in heart rate. The person is unable to sleep, vomits and has diarrhoea. These symptoms typically last for about 72 hours, and then gradually reduce over a period of between 5 and 10 days.

For obvious reasons, it is difficult to estimate the use of heroin within the general population. However, a number of estimates have been made drawing on evidence from sources such as the number of people in treatment, police records, mortality data and/or AIDS/HIV data. These types of data led Kraus et al. (2003) to estimate the prevalence of drug injectors (usually opiates, but including amphetamine) within the populations of differing countries across Europe to lie somewhere between the extremes of 0.26 per cent of the population of Germany and 0.48 per cent of those in Luxembourg. Still in Europe, Bargagli et al. (2006) estimated mortality rates from drug overdoses and AIDS as a result of opiate use to be highest in Barcelona, with a rate of 10 deaths per 1000 person-years. Other countries, such as Italy, the UK and Austria had a rate of about 7 deaths per 1000 person-years.

In the 1960s to the early 1990s, heroin was taken predominantly through intravenous injection. Now it is more frequently smoked, a practice known as 'chasing the dragon'. In Dublin, for example, Smyth et al. (2000) reported a 330 per cent increase in the number of new attenders of drug clinics between 1991 and 1996. Over this time, the age of initiating heroin use fell, and users were more likely to smoke than inject it. Changing from being an injector to smoker of heroin is associated with an increased drug effect and perceived cost-effectiveness (Swift, Maher and Sunjic 1999). Chasers were more likely to be employed, younger, use fewer other drugs, and to be more educated and have a shorter history of use than people who injected. Cultural differences may also influence mode of consumption. Golub and Johnson (2005), for example, found that in New York, black and Hispanic men were more likely to smoke heroin, while white men continued to inject heroin over this period.

Most heroin users also use other drugs. Beswick et al. (2001) reported that 60 per cent of their sample of attenders at a London clinic also used crack cocaine, 58 per cent used alcohol, 11 per cent diazepam, 9 per cent methadone and 8 per cent used cocaine powder at the same time as taking heroin. Of note, are the findings of Degenhardt et al. (2005) who found that users may switch between quite different drugs such as heroin, metamphetamine and cocaine, depending on their relative availability and price.

Aetiology of heroin use

Genetic factors

Although environmental factors predominate in the development of drug addiction, there is evidence of a genetic vulnerability to drug abuse involving two pathways (Cadoret et al. 1995). The first involves a direct pathway of drug dependence. Cadoret and colleagues found that the adopted children of parents who evidenced alcohol abuse or dependence were three times more likely to develop drug dependence than those from non-alcohol-dependent parents, suggesting the potential of a gene for an 'addictive personality' rather than one for opiate addiction in particular. The second, indirect route identified by Cadoret involved genetic linkages of antisocial behaviour (see Chapter 11) that led to aggression, conduct disorder, antisocial personality and eventually drug or alcohol abuse. As with addiction to alcohol, the DRD2 dopamine gene may be involved in determining risk for opiate dependence, although the gene may work in different ways in different phenotypes: Xu et al. (2004) found that variants of the gene typically increased susceptibility to dependence in people of Chinese origin, but were associated with a low risk of dependence in Germans. Other genes may also be involved with opiate dependence, including genes involved with serotonin (Gerra et al. 2004) and endorphin activity (see below: Comings et al. 1999).

Biological factors

Just as with alcohol, the action of opiates results from their impact on dopamine systems within the 'pleasure centre'. A second mechanism through which they influence mood and well-being is through their chemical similarity to chemicals known as endorphins and enkephalins. These moderate pain and produce feelings of well-being, contributing, for example, to the 'runner's high' that can accompany intense prolonged physical exercise. Opiates bind to the same receptor sites as endorphins and enkephalins, resulting in a state of well-being, as well as having a sedating effect. Both chemicals are found throughout the brain, although there are high concentrations in the midbrain, hypothalamus and thalamus, as well as the spinal cord. Positron emission tomography (PET) scans of opiate receptors in the human brain show the highest concentrations in the thalamus which is involved in pain, intermediate concentrations in the basal ganglia, which play an important role in movement and emotions, and low levels in the visual cortex (see Lingford-Hughes 2005).

Socio-cultural factors

Only about 20 per cent of those who initiate drug use do so with the primary goal of pleasure seeking (Nutt and Law 2000). Other reasons include self-medication, social pressure and the search for 'meaning' or mystical experiences. Evidence of the use of heroin as a means of self-medication or as a means of reducing stress can be found in studies that show higher rates of heroin use in populations who live in stressful environments. Perhaps the most dramatic evidence of this is the estimated 40 per cent of American soldiers who used heroin during the Vietnam War, and the approximately 1 per cent who continued to use it when back in the USA (Grinspoon and Bakalar 1986). Further support for this hypothesis can be found in the high use of heroin and other drugs among people with conditions as varied as post-traumatic stress, eating disorders and schizophrenia (Najavitis et al. 1998).

A second route to the use of heroin is as a progression from the use of other drugs, as users seek a greater 'high' than or different experience from those already achieved. Use can escalate to abuse, and then to dependence, involving increased tolerance of the drug, compulsive drug taking and withdrawal symptoms if the drug is not taken regularly. Sharing needles is relatively common and may contain a social or ritual element. For many addicts, maintaining a drug habit can be expensive, and potentially beyond their financial resources, particularly where they find it difficult or choose not to hold down a job. As a result, use is often maintained by stealing: more than 95 per cent of American opiate-dependent individuals reported committing crimes to maintain their drug use (NIH Consensus Development Panel on Effective Treatment of Opiate Addiction 1998). Many users cannot maintain jobs, as much of their day is spent seeking and then taking drugs. The 'addiction career' often involves cycles of cessation and relapse, often over many years. Between one-quarter and one-third of users will die of a drug-related cause, generally an overdose. An example of this history is afforded by Dai, a 29-year-old brought up in an economically marginalized council estate in South Wales. Here is the story of his drug taking, its associated problems, and how it was at least partly maintained by the social world which he inhabited:

> Started smoking ciggies when I was 9 . . . bunk off school – hang around with me
> mates – some of the older kids – just hang around all day – no worries – just

wander the streets all day. Soon got into sniffing glue – did it for about a year, year and a half. Didn't start as a regular thing – every now and then – but did it most days after a while. Used to be one of us would have a bag and some glue. Gave us a buzz. Yeah! Move on to dope at about 12. Did it with my mates. Spend a day in someone's house shitless on dope. F . . . cking good! Still smoke. Mellows me out. But then went on to speed. Took it about when I was 12 and something. Only took it at weekends, washed down with lager. Billy whiz . . . keeps you going, going, going. Good for dancing . . . After a while, taking the stuff everyday – starts getting expensive, so start lifting things, nicking, TWOCing [taking without consent: stealing cars]. Problems with the police – in front of the bench a few times. Got a fine, so have to nick again! Parents found out once got to police. Went ballistic when they found out. First time they knew I was taking drugs. Beaten shitless by my father. Grounded – not that that did much good. Old man's a hypocrite anyway – drinks loads, but dead against drugs. Anyway, tried loads of other shit after that – LSD, tabs [benzodiazepines], Temazies, E's, uppers, downers. Sixteen. Stoned out of my mind on dope, one of my mates asked if I wanted some smack. So I said, 'Yeah!' Anything for a buzz. He injected me. That did it. What a rush! I felt I was superman! I could do anything. That was it. Hooked. Stopped taking speed – smack was it.

Left school at 16. Parents knew I taking smack. Took me to loads of docs, but didn't do anything. So, they washed their hands of me – didn't want to know – chucked me out. Crashed on my mates' floors for a while. Got a council house pretty quickly. Got chucked out pretty quickly too – didn't pay the rent! Not good at paying rent! Smack had me hooked. The more I used, the more money I needed. So, I got into breaking and entering – always getting caught. Fines, probation, then time in prison. But that didn't stop me taking the stuff. You can get anything you want inside if you know the right people. Went to prison for the first time just before my 18th birthday – four months for burglary.

Cut a long story short – been in and out of prison for the last 12 years. Had girlfriends. Lived with one woman for about three years. Got a daughter with her – see her sometimes, but not a lot. They don't come and see me when I'm inside . . . Smack has a hold on me and I can't let go. My mates all take the stuff. I don't know anyone that doesn't use. So, I've nothing else. Did give up once. Went on a programme in prison. Came out clean – stayed clean for about three months. They put me up in a hostel when I came out – so I could stay away from my mates . . . Stop using in the 'real world' . . . But then I had to leave as they didn't have money to keep me there. So, I went back to my old haunts. Soon back to jacking up . . .

Don't enjoy the dope now. I'm pissed with the routine – take drugs, steal, go to prison, take drugs . . . Don't get the buzz from using. I've got to take it so it doesn't do my head in. I'm trying to get out of it – stop using. I'm on methadone [see p. 407], so I can stop taking the stuff. But they don't give enough . . . still get withdrawals – heart pounding, sweats, cramps. So I'm still using – but less than I was – was using about three bags a day, now it's a bag, bag and a half. I'll try to get more methadone – try to keep off the smack altogether, but they don't like to give you too much.

Psychological factors

The psychological factors associated with opiate use are similar to those involved in alcohol use (discussed earlier in the chapter). That is, the pleasure of taking the drug establishes an operant conditioning process in which the individual is rewarded for taking the drug by the pleasant effects and reductions in tension associated with its use, and then the avoidance of withdrawal symptoms. Classical conditioning triggers cravings for heroin when a user encounters conditions similar to its previous use. These conditioned responses may be both powerful and sustained over time. Meyer (1995), for example, reported that the sight of a needle may decrease the severity of withdrawal symptoms while coming off heroin. Conversely, cues conditioned to withdrawal may trigger its symptoms, even years after heroin use has been stopped. Cognitive factors are also involved in expectancies of both pleasure and ultimately, fear of withdrawal.

Solomon's (1980) *opponent-process theory* suggested that the neurological mechanisms that result in pleasurable emotions have a rebound effect in which a drug-induced 'high' is inevitably followed by some negative after-effects (the opponent element), in which the individual feels worse than usual. As a result, they become increasingly motivated to avoid these negative consequences, and less so by the initial pleasure associated with the drug. There is certainly evidence that many drug users do become increasingly anxious and depressed over time (Roggla and Uhl 1995), although specific evidence of the neural mechanisms suggested by Solomon has not been systematically examined.

Treatment of heroin use

Harm minimization approaches: the socio-cultural approach

Harm minimization strategies do not attempt to 'treat' addiction. Instead, they reduce the harm associated with the continued use of drugs either by substituting the use of heroin with a safer oral medication, known as methadone, or reducing risk of infection by ensuring those who continue to inject do so using clean needles.

Methadone maintenance Methadone is an opiate agonist. Methadone replacement programmes provide opiate users with an orally taken drug that does not give them the high associated with opiate use, but does prevent withdrawal symptoms when opiates are not taken. Its use is intended to prevent the risks of needle sharing and overdose, and to prevent withdrawal when individuals initially seek help: a time that may be particularly chaotic in their lives. Methadone can be prescribed for periods of a year or more, during which time the recipient is expected to 'stabilize' their life and prepare for subsequent withdrawal from it. Users typically have to report to a drug centre on a daily basis – where they are given sufficient methadone to get them through to the next day, to try to maintain contact with support services and to stop them selling it on the black market – or, in the UK, a pharmacist or family doctor. About half of UK family doctors are providing methadone to opiate users at any one time (Strang et al. 2005).

This approach appears to be moderately successful. In the largest study of its use, the Drug Abuse Treatment Outcome Study (Hubbard et al. 1997) followed nearly 3000 people receiving outpatient methadone treatment. In the year following its prescription, the percentage of people to use heroin weekly or daily fell from 90 to 30 per cent. Only 17 per cent of those who remained in the programme for a year were still using heroin at follow-up. Reasons given for continued use of heroin included being maintained on too low a dose of methadone, the desire for the 'high' achieved with opiates, the strength of self-identity as an 'addict', and living with a partner or continued social relationships with people who took intravenous drugs (Avants et al. 1999).

Needle-exchange schemes Needle-exchange schemes exchange old for new needles and prevent the need for sharing, reducing risk of cross-infection of various blood-borne viruses including HIV and hepatitis. Some right-wing and church groups in the USA have condemned this approach, claiming that it maintains, or even encourages, the use of drugs. As a result, needle-exchange schemes are legal in some US states and illegal in others. A report by the North American Syringe Exchange Network (in Yoast et al. 2001), for example, found that of a sample of 100 US programmes, 52 were legal, 16 were illegal but 'tolerated', while 32 were 'underground'. Longitudinal studies suggest that where syringes cannot legally be obtained elsewhere, needle-exchange programmes are effective in reducing use of shared needles (Kerr et al. 2005). Most studies have also found lower rates of HIV infection among intravenous drug users who use needle-exchange schemes than among those who do not. The failure to find consistent gains in levels of HIV should, perhaps, be expected, as most people continue to share needles at a reduced rate and may still engage in other risky behaviours, such as unprotected sex.

One final and perhaps important study published since Gibson and colleagues' review (Taylor et al. 2001) reported the prevalence of shared needle use between 1990 and 1999 in Scotland. These data showed a reduction in the use of shared needles between 1990 and 1992 following the introduction of needle-exchange schemes, but then a gradual increase in sharing whether from a partner or 'casual acquaintance' in the following years despite their continued provision. These data mirror some of the changes in risk behaviours in other populations at risk for HIV, where initial changes towards safer behaviours have dwindled and more risky behaviours have returned over time. The reasons for this are unclear, but may relate to the relatively low profile given to HIV/AIDS awareness in the UK and increasing beliefs that AIDS can be 'cured'.

Withdrawal

Most of the interventions described below follow a period of withdrawal. This often involves levels of methadone being gradually reduced over a period of weeks, to minimize withdrawal symptoms. A shorter-term withdrawal involves rapid detoxification, with withdrawal symptoms controlled by other opiate agonists such as clonidine hydrochloride (Marsch et al. 2005). This reduces, but does not totally prevent, many of the symptoms of withdrawal. These strategies can be used in both in-patient and outpatient settings, and can achieve total withdrawal within three days.

Drug therapy

Longer-term use of drug therapy may involve the use of drugs that negate the effects of heroin. Naltrexone is an opiate antagonist that binds with opioid receptors in the brain and blocks the effect of opiate drugs. It is taken on a regular basis and prevents the 'high' associated with opiates if taken. As few as 3 per cent of people offered this form of intervention chose to take it up, and many fail to take the drug regularly. This may be the consequence of an inability to withdraw from opiates, fear of a new drug and residual dependence, or a lack of genuine motivation to remain drug-free (Tucker and Ritter 2000). Among highly motivated individuals who actually use naltrexone, outcomes are relatively good. It results in lower cravings for opiates, longer periods of abstinence, and greater improvements in psychosocial functioning than placebo. Despite these successes, many people will restart or continue using opiates following treatment. Abstinence rates as high as 64 per cent have been found in well-supported and 'high coping' individuals at 18-month follow-up, although rates between 31 and 53 per cent are more typical (Tucker and Ritter 2000). The effects of naltrexone may be added to by combining it with a benzodiazepine to reduce insomnia and 'excitability' that may accompany its use (Stella et al. 2005).

Psychological approaches

Operant programmes   Many people who take methadone also continue to use opiates (see the case of Dai, pp. 405–6). In an attempt to minimize this, Gruber et al. (2000) investigated whether providing extrinsic rewards to people attending methadone clinics could increase attendance and drug abstinence. Their incentives to attend counselling sessions included bus tokens and vouchers to be spent on activities or items agreed by their counsellor. As incentives for abstinence, participants received free weekend recreational activities, lunches, a modest financial sum per week in vouchers and rent payment. This approach was compared with a standard treatment approach in which clients were encouraged to attend routine methadone clinics but were not rewarded for doing so. One month after entry, 61 per cent of participants in this condition, compared with 17 per cent of those in the standard treatment, were enrolled in treatment; 50 per cent of participants compared with 21 per cent of controls had achieved 30 days of abstinence from heroin.

Cognitive behavioural therapy   Despite their effectiveness in the treatment of alcohol problems, there are relatively few studies of the effectiveness of cognitive behavioural programmes in injecting drug users – although several studies in other drug-dependent populations such as cocaine or amphetamine users suggest they would be of benefit (e.g. Baker et al. 2005). One of the few interventions to be reported (Woody et al. 1983), examined whether the addition of either supportive psycho-dynamic counselling or cognitive behavioural therapy enhanced the effectiveness of methadone maintenance and standard drug counselling. Psychodynamic counselling involved supportive techniques to foster a safe therapeutic environment in which the individual explored their relationship patterns and 'worked through' relationship themes. Special attention was given to themes that involved drug dependence, the role of drugs in relation to problem feelings and behaviours, and how these could be resolved without the use of drugs. Cognitive behavioural therapy followed the relapse prevention model described above in relation to alcohol. Standard drug counselling involved support, monitoring of drug usage and exploration of current problems. Both additional treatments added to the effect of counselling up to one-year follow-up on measures as diverse as employment status, legal problems, psychiatric symptoms and opiate-negative urine specimens. Neither was more effective than the other. Some years later, Scherbaum et al. (2005) compared group cognitive therapy with standard treatment and, although they found no immediate benefits, people who participated in the therapy were using fewer opiates than the standard treatment group six months following the intervention.

Couples therapy   Just as for alcohol problems, couples therapy may be more effective in the treatment of drug dependence than individual therapy. In their review of interventions, O'Farrell and Fals-Stewart (2000) reported that those people who received couples therapy had improved relationships and used fewer drugs, in both the short and the long term, than comparative groups in either no-treatment or individual therapy conditions. In addition, drop-out rates were significantly lower than for any other treatment approaches. This has important implications, as it means that more people received a beneficial 'level' of intervention, some of whom may have been 'less motivated' individuals who would have dropped out of other forms of intervention. That couples therapy still appears more effective than the other treatment approaches, while including a 'harder to treat' group of clients, reinforces its high success levels.

Pathological gambling

Most of us gamble at some time. However, for some, gambling becomes addictive and is as difficult to stop as the use of drugs. Although it is identified as an impulse disorder in DSM-IV-TR (APA 2000), pathological gambling is considered in the same behavioural terms as an addiction. Its diagnosis requires five or more of the following:

- a preoccupation with gambling
- a need to gamble with increasing amounts of money in order to achieve the desired excitement
- repeated, unsuccessful efforts to control, cut back or stop gambling
- its use as a way of escaping from problems or relieving **dysphoric** mood states
- a return to gambling following losses in the hope of 'getting even' ('chasing')
- lying to family members or others to conceal the extent of gambling
- committing illegal acts such as forgery or fraud to continue gambling
- jeopardizing or losing significant relationships as a result of gambling.

Pathological gambling is usually the end-point of a gradual shift through social, frequent, problem and finally pathological gambling. Each 'stage' involves a greater psychological and financial commitment to gambling, and an increase in associated problems. A survey commissioned by the British gambling charity GamCare reported that 0.8 per cent of British gamblers could be classified as 'problem gamblers': lower than the USA (1.1 per cent), Australia (2.3 per cent) and Spain (1.4 per cent).

Pathological gambling can result in the individual jeopardizing or losing a significant relationship or job. When they can no longer raise the money needed, they may turn to criminal activity to obtain money: an estimated 60 per cent of pathological gamblers have committed criminal offences in order to continue gambling (Blaszczynski 1995). It has been linked to antisocial, narcissistic and borderline personality disorders. In addition, up to 30 per cent of pathological gamblers may have alcohol-related problems. The relationship with alcohol is important, as some have taken it to suggest that both alcohol and gambling problems are indicative of a more general 'addictive' personality. About 20 per cent of individuals in treatment for pathological gambling are reported to have attempted suicide (APA 1994).

Aetiology of pathological gambling

Genetic factors

Some studies (e.g. Eisen et al. 1998–99) involving large numbers of twin pairs have found shared environmental and genetic factors to account for between 35 and 54 per cent of the vulnerability to pathological gambling, with much of the vulnerability thought to be accounted for by genetic factors. One potential genetic process is through the dopamine D2 receptor gene (Comings et al. 1996). A variant of the D2 dopamine receptor, D2A1, has been found to be more prevalent in individuals with pathological gambling than in normal populations (Potenza 2001: see also its relationship with alcohol and opiate dependence). Summarizing the evidence, Comings et al. (2001) reported that the DRD2, DRD4, DAT1, TPH, ADRA2C, NMDA1, and PS1 genes (moderating dopamine, serotonin and norepinephrine metabolism) were involved in moderating risk of pathological gambling – although the variance in behaviour explained by each gene was very low (less than 1 per cent).

Biological factors

One of the factors thought to be associated with gambling is the 'buzz' of winning or coming close to winning, which has been equated with the 'high' achieved through taking drugs. A number of neurotransmitters seem to mediate this response. Dopamine levels have been found to rise after a winning streak (Shinohara et al. 1999), with activation of the reward system common to other addictions. Raised levels of norepinephrine have also been found following episodes of gambling. These may impact on activity within both the brain and the sympathetic nervous system (see Chapter 3 and Research box 15). In social gamblers, these neurochemical processes typically occur while gambling. Among pathological gamblers, they occur while anticipating gambling or as a classically conditioned response to gambling-related stimuli (Sharpe et al. 1995). There is some evidence that endorphin levels may also rise during gambling, although more evidence is required to substantiate this finding (Shinohara et al. 1999). These effects are not trivial, and withdrawal from gambling may result in symptoms similar, or even more severe, to those experienced while coming off drugs.

Rosenthal and Lesieur (1992), for example, found that two-thirds of pathological gamblers reported at least one physical side-effect during withdrawal. These included insomnia, headaches, loss of appetite, physical weakness, heart racing, muscle aches, breathing difficulty, and chills, and were often more severe than those experienced by a comparison group reporting their experiences of withdrawal from drugs.

Research box 15

Meyer, G., Schwertfeger, J., Exton, M.S. et al. (2004) Neuroendocrine response to casino gambling in problem gamblers, *Psychoneuroendocrinology*, 29: 1272–80.

According to the authors, self-reports and observations of gamblers attending casinos indicate that gambling can directly affect physiological, emotional, and mental states. The monetary stakes, recognition of risk, and the hope of winnings produce stimulation, arousal, well-being and euphoria. To date, however, only a few studies have investigated the effect of gambling on physiological emotional states. Their study examined the effect of gambling on cardiovascular (heart rate) and neuroendocrine activity (cortisol – a stress hormone) in a real gambling situation.

Method

Participants
Fourteen regular blackjack players were approached in a casino and agreed to participate in the study. Two were subsequently excluded from analyses due to alcohol consumption, one had a viral infection, and one was taking blood pressure medication. As a consequence, a final group of 10 male gamblers (mean age 44.5 years) participated in the study.

Measures
Heart rate was continuously measured using a portable heart rate monitor. The ECG was transmitted from a chest patch to a receiver that was worn around the wrist in the mode of a watch. Saliva samples were collected for the detection of cortisol using a cotton wool swab placed in participants' mouths for 2 minutes. The swab was subsequently placed into a prepared tube and stored on ice until assessment of cortisol levels. The severity of pathological gambling was assessed using a 20-item questionnaire which assessed items including preoccupation with gambling, loss of control, escapism, financial indebtedness, 'chasing one's losses', illegal acts, and feelings of guilt.

Procedure
Each person participated in a gambling and a control session, with both sessions occurring in the same casino environment. In each condition they sat at a blackjack table and either participated in the game using their own money or played a game of cards without any monetary stakes for a period of two hours. In both conditions, salivary measures of cortisol were taken at baseline, after 30 and 60 minutes, and following the end of play. Heart rate was measured continuously, with data reported at the same times as the cortisol was measured.

Results

Figure 15.1 shows the heart rate during gambling and the control condition. Salivary cortisol was also elevated in the period of gambling compared with control conditions. Peak cortisol increase at 60 minutes was significantly higher than control levels. Although salivary cortisol levels dropped following completion of the gambling session, cortisol remained significantly elevated compared with levels at the end of play. Severity of pathological gambling was unrelated to the reactivity of heart rate during gambling.

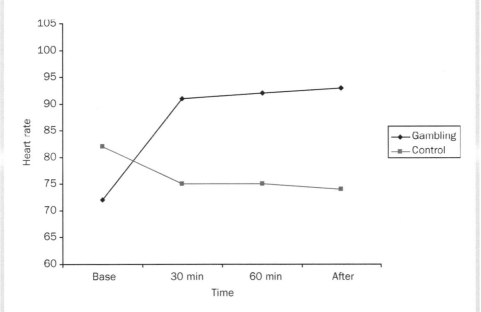

Figure 15.1 Heart rate during gambling and the control condition

Discussion

The degree of increased heart rate during gambling was lower than that associated with the acute stress of parachute jumping, but was comparable to that evoked by the stress of public speaking and mental arithmetic – but lasted much longer. In addition, and unlike these previous stressors, heart rate elevations continued following termination of gambling. Severity of pathological gambling was unrelated to the reactivity of heart rate during gambling.

The study provided the first demonstration that the arousal of gambling induces a secretion of salivary cortisol. This was lower than salivary cortisol responses to very brief, intense stressors. Instead, the cortisol profile was similar to that observed in acute stress situations that last between 1 and 2 hours.

The sympathetic (and unmeasured dopaminergic and endorphin activity) consequences of gambling may reinforce and encourage future gambling. However, the relevance of increased cortisol for the maintenance of gambling behaviour is unclear. Physiological responses to gambling enhance mood, and winning can produce a 'euphoric' state. Cortisol may contribute to such mood alterations because acute cortisol administration has been shown to enhance positive feelings – although longer-term secretion may be associated with lowering of mood.

Socio-cultural factors

In general, greater access to gambling opportunities seems to increase both social and problem gambling. Ladouceur et al. (1999), for example, found that as availability of gambling increased over time in a number of countries, so too did rates of pathological gambling. In Australia, the Productivity Commission (1999), however, found little difference in levels of gambling-related expenditure and problem gambling as a consequence of significant differences in access to gambling across various Australian states. The one exception to this was access to gaming machines. In this case, greater availability was associated with higher rates of problem gambling. These data led the Commission to suggest that if gaming machine availability were to increase in the states where access was restricted to the same level as the more liberal ones, there would be a 110 per cent increase in problem gamblers in those states. In the UK, despite some concerns, the introduction of a national lottery in 1994 did not result in widespread gambling problems. A 1998 survey by GamCare, for example, found that 65 per cent of the UK population had played the National Lottery in the previous year, a figure below the 90 per cent of adults in Sweden and New Zealand who played their national equivalent over the same period.

Once in a gambling context, a number of factors may influence the extent of gambling. Alcohol consumption, in particular, seems to increase gambling, particularly among 'pathological gamblers' (Ellery et al. 2005). Pols and Hawks (1991), for example, found that young game machine players persisted for twice as long when losing after drinking moderate amounts of alcohol than they did when sober. The increasing location of gaming machines in drinking areas suggests that some of those who drink regularly may also come to gamble regularly (Sharpe 2002). It is perhaps noteworthy that many regular casino gamblers drink less while gambling than they usually do: a finding that led Dickerson and Baron (2000) to challenge the notion that gambling and alcohol consumption share a common genetic risk.

Psychological factors

Impulsivity High levels of impulsivity in childhood, at its most extreme evident as childhood attention-deficit/hyperactivity disorder (ADHD: see Chapter 13), may be a risk factor for pathological gambling. Carlton and Manowicz (1994), for example, found that adult pathological gamblers reported a higher rate of ADHD as children than is found within the general population. Prospective longitudinal studies have supported this retrospective evidence. Vitaro et al. (1999), for example, investigated the predictive strength of four measures of impulsivity in 13–14-year-olds: teacher ratings, self-report and performance on a card-playing task and a 'delay in gratification task'. Gambling was subsequently measured at the age of 17 years. Among the factors that predicted gambling at this time were perseveration on the card-playing task and an inability to delay gratification. These findings were considered indicative of a tendency to respond excessively to positive outcomes, to require immediate reinforcement, and insensitivity to negative consequences: characteristics of the pathological gambler. Evidence that biological factors contribute both to gambling and impulsivity in adults was reported by Krueger, Schedlowski and Meyer (2005), who found that people who scored highly on a measure of impulsivity had significantly higher heart rate levels while gambling than those with low impulsivity. Higher impulsivity scores were also significantly correlated with the severity of gambling problems.

Learning history As with other addictions, operant and classical conditioning serve to maintain gambling behaviour. Early models of gambling assumed that gambling was essentially maintained by the intermittent reinforcement – both biological and economic – inherent in gambling. Losses would be sustained in the hope of later gains. Variable and intermittent reinforcement schedules lead to the rapid acquisition of behaviour and render it resistant to extinction. Sharpe (2002) suggested that while these undoubtedly contribute to high levels of social gambling, they do not fully explain pathological gambling, where consistent and significant losses do not result in a cessation of gambling. Sharpe suggested that large pay-outs, and in particular a 'big win' early in a gambling career, establish and sustain pathological gambling. These presumably distort expectations of the outcomes of gambling, and support losses in the expectation of future 'big wins'.

Cognitive processes Differing cognitive processes instigate and maintain gambling. Pro-gambling attitudes increase the likelihood of gambling, and may be a consequence of early exposure to family influences. Oei and Raylu (2004), for example, found that parents', and especially fathers', attitudes towards gambling were predictive of their children's beliefs and attitudes. Although pro-gambling attitudes appear to lead to participation in gambling activities, they do not sustain gambling once initiated (Sharpe 2002). Other forms of cognitive self-talk may be important at this time. Delfabbro and Winefield (1999), for example, found that 75 per cent of all game-related cognitions during gambling were irrational in nature and supportive of continued gambling. Such thoughts may stimulate impulsivity, discount losses and even lead the individual to feel that they have some degree of control over their fate. This type of self-talk may also sustain arousal while gambling: a number of studies (e.g. Sharpe et al. 1995) have found a relationship between the frequency of irrational verbalizations and arousal levels.

Negative emotions Low mood or anxiety also appear to be triggers to gambling among some pathological gamblers. Dickerson et al. (1996), for example, reported that 9 per cent of a sample of regular gamblers did so as an escape from feeling depressed; 30 per cent were more likely to gamble following a 'frustrating day'. Dysphoric mood before gambling may also result in more persistent gambling following losses. As a partial explanation for this phenomenon, Dickerson and Baron (2000) suggested that low mood may reduce perceptions of control over gambling, and hence reduce attempts to curtail the activity even when losing.

A biopsychosocial model of gambling

These various findings each contributed to Sharpe's (2002) biopsychosocial model of gambling. She suggested that this may involve three early risk factors:

- a biological vulnerability involving the dopaminergic and serotonergic systems
- family attitudes that support gambling
- high levels of impulsivity.

These factors may lead to a number of gambling experiences as a relatively young individual. In these, the individual becomes socialized into a gambling culture. A pattern of early wins may also reinforce gambling and distort beliefs about, and attitudes towards, it. More attention may be paid, for example, to success than failures. At the same time, the individual may become pleasantly physiologically aroused while gambling. All of these factors serve to maintain an interest. As a gambling career progresses, episodes may be triggered by hopes of avoiding stress, boredom or improving mood. Gambling is used to increase arousal and as a means of escape from reality. Once in the gambling situation, cognitive biases and the arousal experienced serve to maintain the behaviour, whether winning or losing.

Stop and think . . .

Gambling has never been easier. Internet gambling, in particular, allows the possibility of winning, or losing, significant amounts of money in the comfort of your own home. Mark Griffiths, a well-known UK gambling researcher identified a number of factors associated with Internet gambling that makes this potentially tempting and risky for people with gambling problems: accessibility, affordability, anonymity, convenience, escape immersion/dissociation, disinhibition, event frequency, asociability and interactivity (Griffiths 2003).

Given these risks, should there be controls over who can gamble on the Internet? If so, how should such controls be determined? Or should such gambling be open to all . . . and at their own risk?

Treatment of pathological gambling

Empirical evaluations of treatments for pathological gambling are still relatively rare, although what evidence there is, is encouraging (Pallesen et al. 2005). Self-help programmes such as the Gamblers Anonymous 12-step programme have achieved abstinence rates of about 8 per cent over a one-year period and 7 per cent over two years (Stewart and Brown 1988). More formal interventions have reported one-year abstinence rates as high as 55 per cent.

Behavioural approaches

One of the earliest treatment studies, reported by McConaghy et al. (1983), compared the effectiveness of aversion therapy and imaginal desensitization. Aversion therapy involved participants reading aloud words on a series of cards, some of which were related to gambling activities and some of which described alternative actions such as 'went straight home'. Each time they read out a gambling-related phrase they received a mild electric shock described as 'unpleasant but not emotionally upsetting' (McConaghy et al. 1983: 367) for two seconds. Imaginal desensitization involved participants imagining a variety of gambling-related scenarios at the same time as using relaxation procedures to reduce arousal. The latter approach proved the most effective on measures of gambling urge and behaviour over the year following treatment. Long-term follow-up, conducted between two and nine years after the end of therapy, found that 79 per cent of those who took part in the desensitization programme reported control over or having stopped gambling. Just over 50 per cent of the aversion therapy group reported the same outcomes (McConaghy et al. 1991).

Cognitive behavioural approaches

A small number of studies have reported positive results following cognitive behavioural procedures. Ladouceur et al. (2001), for example, randomly allocated pathological gamblers into either cognitive therapy or waiting list control group. The cognitive intervention had two elements. The first involved cognitive correction, in which participants' misconceptions on randomness were challenged. This involved both an educational component on the nature of randomness and the identification and challenge of erroneous cognitions made while gambling. This was achieved by tape-recording verbalizations ('. . . if I lose four times in a row, I will definitely win the next time . . .') made during a session of imaginal gambling followed by the therapist 'correcting' them within the therapy session. The second element involved training in relapse prevention. In this, participants identified high-risk situations and planned how to cope with them should they arise. The intervention was successful: 54 per cent of participants in the cognitive intervention improved by at least 50 per cent on a composite measure of recovery which included frequency of gambling and perceived control over gambling behaviour, compared with only 7 per cent of those in the control group. Furthermore, 85 per cent of participants in the treatment programme compared with only 14 per cent of those in the control group achieved 50 per cent improvements on at least three of the four measures. These gains were generally maintained at six-month, twelve-month and two-year follow-up (Ladouceur et al. 2003).

Pharmacological therapies

In one of the few evaluations of drug therapies in the treatment of pathological gambling, Hollander et al. (2000) evaluated the effectiveness of fluvoxamine, an SSRI, in a small study involving 15 people. They were first treated with a placebo drug before entering an eight-week period of active treatment. Only ten people completed the study, but the drug showed a significant benefit, with greater reductions in gambling and urges to gamble than in the placebo treatment phase. More trials are clearly needed before any strong conclusions about the effectiveness of drug therapies are required. These findings were supported by the findings of Grant et al. (2003) who found another SSRI, paroxetine, to be of benefit and Dannon et al. (2005) who found the effects of an SSRI to be comparable with those of naltrexone.

Chapter summary

1 Drug use is relatively common throughout most social groups, although some groups use more than others do.

2 Excess alcohol consumption results in a number of negative short-term social consequences, including risky or dangerous behaviours, and long-term health consequences, such as cirrhosis and Korsakoff's syndrome.

3 Genetic factors may influence risk for high levels of alcohol.

4 Alcohol influences mood through its impact on levels of GABA and dopamine.

5 Social factors, including ease of access, peer influence, cost and advertising, influence levels of consumption.

6 Psychological explanations of drinking include operant and classical conditioning experiences and cognitions that support consumption.

7 Legal and social interventions impact on drinking levels throughout the population.

8 Treatment of alcohol-dependent individuals usually begins with a period of withdrawal.

9 Antidipstrotrophics can help maintain abstinence in highly motivated groups or where its use is compulsory.

10 Both the 12-step model which advocates abstinence and cognitive behavioural interventions that can support abstinence or controlled drinking appear equally effective in maintaining abstinence or appropriate drinking levels.

11 Couples therapy is particularly effective for people with drinking problems.

12 Opiates exert their action through dopamine levels, endorphins and enkephalins.

13 Harm reduction strategies, including methadone maintenance and needle-exchange schemes, can be successful in reducing opiate-use-related harm.

14 As with alcohol, behavioural therapy and social approaches can be effective in the treatment of opiate dependence: couples therapy may be the most effective intervention where appropriate.

15 Gambling results in similar neurochemical changes to those associated with drug use.

16 The biopsychosocial model implicates biological, family, psychological and learning history factors in the aetiology of problem gambling.

17 Cognitive behavioural therapy, antidepressants and opiate antagonists may prove effective in reducing gambling-related problems.

For discussion

1 Why might the various approaches to the treatment of alcohol-related problems differ little in their effectiveness?

2 Switzerland legalized opiate use in 2004. What are the costs and benefits of this approach for the individual and society?

3 Many people receiving treatment for addictions continue to engage in their addiction. Is this an acceptable behaviour within therapy?

4 Should access to gaming machines be controlled?

Further reading

Ferri, M., Davoli, M. and Perucci, C.A. (2005) Heroin maintenance for chronic heroin dependents, *Cochrane Database of Systematic Reviews*, Part 2.

Heather, N. (1995) The great controlled drinking consensus: is it premature? *Addiction*, 90: 1160–3.

Petersen, T. and McBride, A. (2002) *Working with Substance Misusers: A Guide to Theory and Practice*. London: Routledge.

Sharpe, L. (2002) A reformulated cognitive behavioral model of problem gambling: a bio-psychosocial perspective, *Clinical Psychology Review*, 22: 1–25.

Toneatto, T. and Ladouceur, R. (2003) Treatment of pathological gambling: a critical review of the literature, *Psychology of Addictive Behavior*, 17: 284–92.

Glossary

Aetiology explanations of the causes of disease.

Agonist drug that increases the action of a neurotransmitter.

Agranulocytosis condition in which the bone marrow fails to produce enough white blood cells called neutrophils. Leaves the individual prone to infection.

Alexithymia a paucity of emotional experience and awareness, with an associated poverty of imagination and a tendency to focus upon the tangible and mundane.

Alogia poverty of speech; literally, 'no words'.

Alzheimer's disease the most common cause of dementia in old age.

Antagonist drug that inhibits the action of a neurotransmitter.

Anterograde amnesia lack of memory for events that occur after an event that causes amnesia.

Aphonia inability to speak.

Ataxia an incoordination and unsteadiness due to brain's failure to regulate posture and strength and direction of limb movement.

Avolition lack of volition, or voluntary motivation.

Behaviour therapy form of therapy that targets behavioural change by changing the triggers or consequences of behaviour using operant or classical conditioning-based interventions.

Blood-brain barrier protective barrier formed in blood vessels of the brain. Prevents some drugs from passing from the blood to the brain.

Catatonic behaviour behaviour found in one form of schizophrenia; includes posturing, or 'waxy flexibility', mutism and stupor.

Catharsis reliving past repressed emotions in order to come to terms with past conflicts.

Chromosome structures within a cell that contain genes.

Classical conditioning the learned association between two co-occurring stimuli, such that a similar response is evoked by either.

Client a term often used to denote an individual in therapy. In contrast to words such as patient or subject, it is used to indicate the helping, non-hierarchical nature of the therapeutic relationship between therapist and individual.

Clinical supervision discussion and feedback on therapy by peers or experts intended to improve therapeutic formulation and treatment.

Cognitive challenge the identification and disputation of maladaptive cognitions.

Cognitive schema a consistent set of beliefs that influence mood and behaviour.

Community Mental Health Team a multi-disciplinary team providing mental health care within the community. Usually includes psychiatrists, community psychiatric nurses, psychologists and other therapists.

Confabulate to make up 'facts', usually to hide confusion or poor memory.

Defence mechanism an unconscious mental act that prevents the individual from psychological harm.

Delusion a strongly held inappropriate belief; usually a belief that is normally considered impossible.

Depot injection injection of a slow-release drug that will provide a therapeutic dose for days or weeks.

Disorganized symptoms (of schizophrenia) include confused thinking and speech and behaviour that do not make sense.

DSM-IV-TR the *Diagnostic and Statistical Manual* (fourth edition with text revision: APA 2000) – US system of classification of mental health disorders.

Dysphoric unhappy, but not sufficiently so to warrant a diagnosis of depression.

Dyzygotic (DZ) twins non-identical twins.

Effect size provides a measure of the effect of an intervention; 0.2 is considered small, above 0.6 is a large effect, and between is moderate.

Ego according to Freud, the part of the personality that operates under the reality principle and works to maximize gratification within the constraints of the 'real world'.

Electroconvulsive therapy (ECT) treatment involving passing a brief electric current through the temporal lobe(s) as a treatment for depression and schizophrenia.

Executive function neurological coordination of a number of complex processes, including speech, motor coordination and behavioural planning.

Extrapyramidal symptoms symptoms that result from low levels of dopamine in the extrapyramidal regions of the brain, often as a result of long-term phenothiazine use. Include Parkinsonism and tardive dyskinesia.

Flattened mood lack of emotional response, either positive or negative, to events.

Functional dyspepsia chronic upper abdominal discomfort or pain unrelated to heartburn. Associated symptoms include nausea, vomiting, abdominal distension, bloating and anorexia. No obvious cause can be found.

Glucocorticoid a corticosteroid. Have anti-inflammatory and immunosuppressive effect.

Half-life the time required for half the quantity of a drug to be metabolized or eliminated by normal biological processes.

Hallucination the experience of touch, visions or sounds in the absence of external stimuli.

Heritability coefficient the degree to which individual differences are due to genetic factors.

Hydrocephalus retention of cerebrospinal fluid within the ventricles of the brain. The fluid is often under increased pressure and can compress and damage the brain.

Hyperalgesia abnormally increased pain sensation – a lowered pain threshold.

Hyperventilation short rapid breaths that lead to low levels of carbon dioxide in the blood and physical sensations including tingling in the arms, dizziness and feelings of an inability to breathe.

Hysterical disorder physical symptoms in the absence of physical pathology.

Id according to Freud, the personality component driven by the basic instincts of sex and aggression.

Ideas of reference the, inappropriate, belief that objects, events or people are of personal significance. For example, a person may think that a television programme he is watching is all about him. May reach sufficient intensity to constitute delusions.

Incidence the frequency with which new cases of a condition arise within the population.

Interpersonal psychotherapy a form of therapy focusing exclusively on changing interpersonal problems that contribute to mental health problems.

Learned helplessness a belief that one has no control over events; results in a cessation of attempts at control.

Lobotomy an early form of psychosurgery.

Major tranquillizers see **phenothiazines**.

MAOI (monoamine oxidase inhibitor) a form of antidepressant, whose action is on the norepinephrine system.

Mental Health Act Commission established by the British government to keep under review the operation of the UK Mental Health Act 1983 with respect to patients liable to be detained under the Act.

Meta-analysis a statistical method of combining the data from several studies using similar measures that allows a more powerful analysis of the effect of the intervention than that provided by single, relatively small studies.

Monozygotic (MZ) twins identical twins, with identical genetic structure.

Narcolepsy a disorder characterized by sudden and uncontrollable, though often brief, attacks of deep sleep.

Negative symptoms (of schizophrenia) include absence of activation, and include apathy, lack of motivation, or poverty of speech.

Neologism making up new words.

Neuroleptics a broad class of drugs used to treat psychotic condition such as schizophrenia; otherwise known as major tranquillizers or phenothiazines.

Neurotransmitter chemical involved in maintaining neuronal activity; transmits information across the synaptic cleft.

Operant (Skinnerian) conditioning manipulation of behaviour through the use of reinforcement and punishment schedules.

Perseveration inability to shift from a cognitive set, resulting in inappropriate repetitive behaviour, including speech.

Pharmacotherapy treatment with drugs.

Phenothiazines major tranquillizers used to treat schizophrenia, of which the best known is chlorpromazine; their action is usually on the dopaminergic system.

Placebo inactive treatments (either pharmacological or psychological) against which active treatment trials are often evaluated. These allow the assessment of the general effects of receiving some form of attention or 'treatment'. Differences in outcomes between placebo conditions and active interventions are considered to show the specific effects of the therapy against which it is compared.

Polygenic caused by multiple genes.

Positive symptoms (of schizophrenia) include hallucinations, delusions, disorganized speech or positive thought disorder.

Prevalence the frequency with which a particular condition is found within the population at any one time.

Primary care basic or general health care focused on the point at which a patient ideally first seeks assistance from the medical care system.

Psychoanalysis there are a number of different psychoanalytic therapies. Most share a number of therapeutic goals, including gaining insight into the nature of the original trauma and bringing troubling material to consciousness so the individual can cope with it without the use of ego defence mechanisms.

Psycho-educational programme a treatment usually combining elements of education about a problem or means of coping with it with cognitive behavioural strategies of change.

Psychomotor movements involving both mental and motor processes.

Psychosis includes a number of mental health conditions, such as schizophrenia, each of which have the common symptom of a loss of contact with reality.

Psychotherapist a generic term for someone who provides some form of therapy. In this book, it does not denote any particular therapeutic orientation, and may include therapists as diverse as cognitive and psychoanalytic in practice.

Psychotic the presence of a mental health condition, such as schizophrenia, of which the main symptom is a loss of contact with reality.

Psychotropic medication drugs used to treat mental health problems by their action on neurotransmitter levels.

Retrograde amnesia lack of memory for events that occurred before an event that causes amnesia.

Self-actualization described by the humanists as the experience of fulfilling one's potential for growth.

Self-instruction training developed by Meichenbaum, involves the use of coping self-statements at times of stress.

Spillover here, a failure to separate work and home life, such that each intrudes on the other.

SNRIs (serotonin/norepinephrine re-uptake inhibitors) antidepressants thought to inhibit neuronal uptake of serotonin, norepinephrine and dopamine in the central nervous system.

SSRIs (selective serotonin re-uptake inhibitors) a form of antidepressant, whose action is on the serotinergic system.

Stereotypic behaviours repetitive, non-spontaneous, apparently non-functional behaviours.

Stress management a specialist cognitive behavioural intervention focusing on teaching people to cope with stress; includes the usual elements of this approach, including relaxation, self-instruction and cognitive challenge.

Superego according to Freud, contains the individual's morals and societal values; the psychoanalytical equivalent of the conscience.

Transference the unconscious transfer of experience from one interpersonal context to another, i.e. the reliving of past interpersonal relationships in current situations, including therapies.

Tricyclic a form of antidepressant whose action is on the serotonin and norepinephrine systems.

Ventricle one of a system of four communicating cavities within the brain that are continuous with the central canal of the spinal cord.

Vicarious learning learning the outcomes of behaviour or situations from observation of others.

Waiting list control used in randomized controlled trial; provides a group whose treatment is delayed, so comparisons can be made between treatment and no-treatment conditions without withholding treatment to some people.

Waxy flexibility a condition found in schizophrenia in which individuals maintain the posture in which they are placed for prolonged periods of time.

References

Abela, J.R.Z. and D'Allesandro, D.U. (2002) Beck's cognitive theory of depression: the diathesis-stress and causal mediation components, *British Journal of Clinical Psychology*, 41, 111–128.

Abela, J.R.Z. and Seligman, M.E.P. (2000) The hopelessness theory of depression: a test of the diathesis-stress component in the interpersonal and achievement domains, *Cognitive Therapy and Research*, 23: 361–78.

Aberg Yngwe, M., Fritzell, J., Lundberg, O. et al. (2003) Exploring relative deprivation: is social comparison a mechanism in the relation between income and health?, *Social Science and Medicine*, 57: 1463–73.

Abiodun, O.A. (1995) Pathways to mental health care in Nigeria, *Psychiatric Services*, 46: 823–6.

Abraham, H.C. (1956) Therapeutic and psychological approach to cases of unconsummated marriage, *British Medical Journal*, 1: 837–9.

Abramson, L.Y., Alloy, L.B., Hankin, B.L. et al. (2002) Cognitive vulnerability–stress models of depression in a self-regulatory and psychobiological context, in I.H. Gotlib and C.L. Hammen (eds) *Handbook of Depression*. New York: Guilford.

Abramson, L.Y., Seligman, M.E. and Teasdale, J.D. (1978) Learned helplessness in humans: critique and reformulation, *Journal of Abnormal Psychology*, 87: 49–74.

Ackerman, K.D., Heyman, R., Rabin, B.S. et al. (2002) Stressful life events precede exacerbations of multiple sclerosis. *Psychosomatic Medicine*, 64: 916–20.

Adebowale. T.O. and Ogunlesi A.O. (1999) Beliefs and knowledge about aetiology of mental illness among Nigerian psychiatric patients and their relatives, *African Journal of Medicine and Medical Science*, 28: 35–41.

Agras, W.S., Rossiter, E.M. and Arnow, B. (1994) One-year follow-up of psychosocial and pharmacologic treatments for bulimia nervosa, *Journal of Clinical Psychiatry*, 55: 179–83.

Agras, W.S., Walsh, T., Fairburn, C.G. et al. (2000) A multicenter comparison of cognitive-behavioral therapy and interpersonal psychotherapy for bulimia nervosa, *Archives of General Psychiatry*, 57: 459–66.

Ahern, J., Galea, S., Resnick, H. et al. (2002) Television images and psychological symptoms after the September 11 terrorist attacks, *Psychiatry*, 65: 289–300.

Ahmed, S.M. (2001) Differing health and health-seeking behaviour: ethnic minorities of the Chittagong Hill Tracts, Bangladesh, *Asian Pacific Journal of Public Health*, 13: 100–8.

Allan, A., Roberts, M.C., Allan, M.M. et al. (2001) Intoxication, criminal offences and suicide attempts in a group of South African problem drinkers, *South African Medical Journal*, 91: 145–50.

Allen, M.G. (1976) Twin studies of affective illness, *Archives of General Psychiatry*, 33: 1476–8.

Allison, R.B. and Schwarz, T. (1980) *Minds in Many Pieces*. New York: Rawson Wade.

Alloy, L.B. and Abramson, L.Y. (1979) Judgement of contingency in depressed and non-depressed students: sadder but wiser?, *Journal of Experimental Psychology: General*, 108: 441–85.

Altmann, P., Cunningham, J., Dhanesha, U. et al. (1999) Disturbance of cerebral function in people exposed to drinking water contaminated with aluminium sulphate: retrospective study of the Camelford water incident, *British Medical Journal*, 319: 807–11.

American Psychiatric Association (APA) (1987) *Diagnostic and Statistical Manual of Mental Disorders*, 3rd edn, text revision. Washington, DC: APA.

American Psychiatric Association (APA) (1994) *Diagnostic and Statistical Manual of Mental Disorders*, 4th edn. Washington, DC: APA.

American Psychiatric Association (APA) (2000) *Diagnostic and Statistical Manual of Mental Disorders*, 4th edn, text revision (DSM-IV-TR) Washington, DC: APA.

Anderson, D.A. and Maloney, K.C. (2001) The efficacy of cognitive-behavioral therapy on the core symptoms of bulimia nervosa, *Clinical Psychology Review*, 21: 971–88.

Anderson, I.M. (1998) SSRIS versus tricyclic antidepressants in depressed inpatients: a meta-analysis of efficacy and tolerability, *Depression and Anxiety*, 7 (Suppl. 1): 11–17.

Anderson, I.M. (2000) Selective serotonin reuptake inhibitors versus tricyclic antidepressants: a meta-analysis of efficacy and tolerability, *Journal of Affective Disorders*, 58: 19–36.

Anderson, R.N. and Smith B.L. (2003) Deaths: leading causes for 2001, *National Vital Statistics Report*, 52: 1–86.

Andreasson, S., Allebeck, P. and Engstrom, A. (1987) Cannabis and schizophrenia: a longitudinal study of Swedish conscripts, *Lancet*, 2: 1483–6.

Andrews, B., Brewin C.R. and Rose, S. (2003) Gender, social support, and PTSD in victims of violent crime, *Journal of Traumatic Stress*, 16: 421–7.

Andrews, B., Brewin C.R., Rose, S. and Kirk M.P. (2000) Predicting PTSD symptoms in victims of violent crime: the role of shame, anger, and childhood abuse, *Journal of Abnormal Psychology*, 109: 69–73.

Andrews, G., Stewart, G., Allen, R. et al. (1990) The genetics of six neurotic disorders: a twin study, *Journal of Affective Disorders*, 19: 23–9.

Angst, J. (1999) The epidemiology of depressive disorders, *European Neuropharmacology* (Suppl.): 95–8.

Aouizerate, B., Pujol, H., Grabot, D. et al. (2003) Body dysmorphic disorder in a sample of cosmetic surgery applicants, *European Psychiatry*, 18: 365–8.

Appiah-Poku, J. Laugharne, R., Mensah, E. et al. (2004) Previous help sought by patients presenting to mental health services in Kumasi, Ghana, *Social Psychiatry and Psychiatric Epidemiology*, 39: 208–11.

Arntz, A., Klokman, J. and Sieswerda, S. (2005) An experimental test of the schema mode model of borderline personality disorder, *Journal of Behavior Therapy and Experimental Psychiatry*, 36: 226–39.

Aronson, K.J. (1997) Quality of life among persons with multiple sclerosis and their caregivers, *Neurology*, 48: 74–80.

Arreola, S.G., Neilands, T.B., Pollack, L.M. et al. (2005) Higher prevalence of childhood sexual abuse among Latino men who have sex with men than non-Latino men who have sex with men: data from the Urban Men's Health Study, *Child Abuse and Neglect*, 29: 285–90.

Asen, E. (2002) Outcome research in family therapy, *Advances in Psychiatric Treatment*, 8: 230–8.

Ataoglu, A., Ozcetin, A., Icmeli, C. et al. (2003) Paradoxical therapy in conversion reaction, *Journal of Korean Medical Science*, 18: 581–4.

Attia, E. and Schroeder, L. (2005) Pharmacologic treatment of anorexia nervosa: where do we go from here?, *International Journal of Eating Disorders*, 37 (Suppl.): S60–3.

Austen, B., Christodoulou, G. and Terry, J.E. (2002) Relation between cholesterol levels, statins and Alzheimer's disease in the human population, *Journal of Nutrition, Health and Aging*, 6: 377–82.

Avants, S.K., Margolin, A. and McKee, S. (1999) A path analysis of cognitive, affective, and behavioral predictors of treatment response in a methadone maintenance program, *Journal of Substance Abuse*, 11: 215–30.

Awad, A.D. and Vorungati, L.N. (1999) Quality of life and new antipsychotics in schizophrenia: are patients better off?, *International Journal of Social Psychiatry*, 45: 268–75.

Babor, T.F., Miller, W.R., DiClemente, C.C. and Longabaugh, R. (1999) A study to remember: Response of the Project MATCH Research Group, *Addiction*, 94: 66–9.

Bacaltchuk, J., Hay, P. and Trefiglio, R. (2002) Antidepressants versus psychological treatments and their combination for bulimia nervosa, *CochraneDatabase of Systematic Reviews*, Issue 1.

Bacaltchuk, J., Trefiglio, R., Lima, M.S. et al. (1999) Antidepressants versus psychotherapy for bulimia nervosa: a systematic review, *Journal of Clinical Pharmacy and Therapeutics*, 24: 23–31.

Bailey, A., Le Couteur, A., Gottesman, I. et al. (1995) Autism as a strongly genetic disorder: evidence from a British twin study, *Psychological Medicine*, 25: 63–77.

Baker, A., Lee, N.K. and Claire, M. (2005) Brief cognitive behavioural interventions for regular amphetamine users: a step in the right direction, *Addiction*, 100: 367–78.

Bakker, A., Van Dyck, R., Spinhoven, P. et al. (1999) Paroxetine, clomipramine, and cognitive therapy in the treatment of panic disorder, *Journal of Clinical Psychiatry*, 60: 831–8.

Ballenger, J.C. (1999) Current treatments of the anxiety disorders in adults, *Biological Psychology*, 46: 1579–94.

Ballenger, J.C. (2000) Panic disorder and agoraphobia, in M.G. Gelder, J.J. Lopez-Ibor Jr and N.C. Andreasen (eds) *New Oxford Textbook of Psychiatry*. Oxford: Oxford University Press.

Ballenger, J.C. (2004) Remission rates in patients with anxiety disorders treated with paroxetine, *Journal of Clinical Psychiatry*, 65: 1696–707.

Bancroft, J. (1999) Central inhibition of sexual response in the male: a theoretical perspective, *Neuroscience Biobehavioral Review*, 23: 763–84.

Bandelow, B., Krause, J., Wedekind, D. et al. (2005) Early traumatic life events, parental attitudes, family history, and birth risk factors in patients with borderline personality disorder and healthy controls, *Psychiatry Research*, 134: 169–79.

Bandura, A. (1977) Self-efficacy: toward a unifying theory of behavioural change, *Psychological Review*, 84: 191–215.

Banerjee, T. and Banerjee, G. (1995) Determinants of help-seeking behaviour in cases of epilepsy attending a teaching hospital in India: an indigenous explanatory model, *International Journal of Social Psychiatry*, 41: 217–30.

Barber, J.P. and Luborsky, L. (1991) A psychodynamic view of simple phobias and prescriptive matching: a commentary, *Psychotherapy*, 28: 469–72.

Barbaree, H.E. (1990) Stimulus control of sexual arousal, in W.L. Marshall, D.R. Laws and H.E. Barbaree (eds) *Handbook of Sexual Assault: Issues, Theories, and Treatment of the Offender*. New York: Plenum.

Barbaree, H.E. (1991) Denial and minimization among sex offenders: assessment and treatment outcome, *Forum on Corrections Research*, 3: 30–3.

Barbaree, H.E. and Marshall, W.L. (1989) Erectile responses among heterosexual child molesters, father–daughter incest offenders and matched nonoffenders: five distinct age preference profiles, *Canadian Journal of Behavioural Science*, 21: 70–82.

Barbaree, H.E. and Seto, M.C. (1997) Pedophila: assessment and treatment, in D.R. Laws and W. O'Donohue (eds) *Sexual Deviance: Theory, Assessment, and Treatment.* New York: Guilford.

Bargagli, A.M., Hickman, M., Davoli, M. et al. (2006) Drug-related mortality and its impact on adult mortality in eight European countries, *European Journal of Public Health,* 16: 198–202.

Barker, C., Pistrang, N., Shapiro, D.A. et al. (1993) You in Mind: a preventive mental health television series, *British Journal of Clinical Psychology,* 32: 281–93.

Barkley, A. (1997) Behavioral inhibition, sustained attention and executive functions: constructing a unifying theory of ADHD, *Psychological Bulletin,* 121: 65–94.

Barkley, R.A., Edwards, G., Laneri, M. et al. (2001) The efficacy of problem solving communication training alone, behavior management training alone, and their combination for parent–adolescent conflict in teenagers with ADHD and ODD, *Journal of Consulting and Clinical Psychology,* 69: 926–41.

Barlow, D.H., Bruce, T.J., Gregg, M.K. et al. (2000) Cognitive-behavioral therapy, imipramine, or their combination for panic disorder: a randomized controlled trial, *Journal of the American Medical Association,* 283: 2529–36.

Barlow, D.H., Reynolds, E.J. and Agras, W.S. (1973) Gender identity change in a transsexual, *Archives of General Psychiatry,* 29: 569–76.

Barr, L.C., Goodman, W.K. and Price, L.H. (1992) Acute exacerbation of body dysmorphic disorder during tryptophan depletion, *American Journal of Psychiatry,* 149: 1406–7.

Barsky, A.J. and Ahern, D.K. (2004) Cognitive behavior therapy for hypochondriasis: a randomized controlled trial, *Journal of the American Medical Association,* 291: 1464–70.

Barsky, A.J., Ahern, D.K., Bailey, E.D. et al. (2001) Hypochondriacal patients' appraisal of health and physical risks, *American Journal of Psychiatry,* 158: 783–787.

Barsky, A.J., Brener, J., Coeytaux, R.R. et al. (1995) Accurate awareness of heartbeat in hypochondriacal and non-hypochondriacal patients, *Psychosomatic Medicine,* 39: 489–97.

Barsky, A.J., Wool, C., Barnett, M.C. et al. (1994) Histories of childhood trauma in adult hypochondriacal patients, *American Journal of Psychiatry,* 151: 397–401.

Bass, C. and Murphy, M. (1995) Somatoform and personality disorders: syndromal co-morbidity and overlapping developmental pathways, *Journal of Psychosomatic Research,* 39: 405–27.

Bass, E. and Davis, L. (1988) *The Courage to Heal: A Guide for Women Survivors of Sexual Abuse.* New York: Harper and Row.

Basso, M.R., Nasrallah, H.A., Olson, S.C. et al. (1998) Neuropsychological correlates of negative, disorganized and psychotic symptoms in schizophrenia, *Schizophrenia Research,* 25: 99–111.

Bateson, G., Jackson, D., Haley, J. et al. (1956) Toward a theory of schizophrenia, *Behavioural Science,* 1: 251–64.

Battle, Y.L., Martin, B.C., Dorfman, J.H. et al. (1999) Seasonality and infectious disease in schizophrenia: the birth hypothesis revisited, *Journal of Psychiatric Research,* 33: 501–9.

Bazargan-Hejazi, S., Bing, E., Bazargan, M. et al. (2005) Evaluation of a brief intervention in an inner-city emergency department, *Annals of Emergency Medicine,* 46: 67–76.

Bebbington, P. and Ramana, R. (1995) The epidemiology of bipolar affective disorder, *Social Psychiatry and Psychiatric Epidemiology,* 30: 279–92.

Beck, A.T. (1977) *Cognitive Therapy of Depression.* New York: Guilford.

Beck, A.T. (1997) Cognitive therapy: reflections, in J.K. Zeig (ed.) *The Evolution of Psychotherapy: The Third Conference.* New York: Brunner/Mazel.

Beck, A.T., Freeman, A. and associates (1990) *Cognitive Therapy of Personality Disorders.* New York: Guilford.

Beck, A.T., Mendelson, M., Mock, J. et al. (1961) Inventory for measuring depression, *Archives of General Psychiatry*, 4: 561–71.

Beck, A.T., Rush, A.J., Shaw, B.F. and Emery, G. (1979) *Cognitive Therapy for Depression*. New York: Guilford.

Beck, A.T., Ward, C.H., Mendelson, M. et al. (1962) Reliability of psychiatric diagnoses. 2: A study of consistency of clinical judgements and ratings, *American Journal of Psychiatry*, 119: 351–7.

Beck, A.T., Wright, F.D., Newman, C.F. et al. (1993) *Cognitive Therapy of Substance Abuse*. New York: Guilford.

Beidel, D.C. and Turner, S.M. (1986) A critique of the theoretical bases of cognitive-behavioral theories and therapy, *Clinical Psychology Review*, 6: 177–97.

Benbadis, S.R., Allen Hauser, W. (2000) An estimate of the prevalence of psychogenic non-epileptic seizures, *Seizure*, 9: 280–1.

Bennett, P., Conway, M. and Clatworthy, J. (2001) Predicting post-traumatic symptoms in cardiac patients, *Heart and Lung*, 30: 458–65.

Bennett, P., Lowe, R. and Honey, K. (2002) Appraisals and emotions: a test of the consistency of reporting and their associations, *Cognition and Emotion*, 17: 511–20.

Bennett, P. and Murphy, S. (1997) *Psychology and Health Promotion*. Buckingham: Open University Press.

Bennett, P., Smith, C., Nugent, Z. et al. (1991) 'Pssst . . . the really useful guide to alcohol': evaluation of an alcohol education television series, *Health Education Research, Theory and Practice*, 6: 57–64.

Bennett, P., Williams, Y., Page, N., et al. (2001) Associations between organizational and incident factors and emotional distress in emergency ambulance personnel, *British Journal of Clinical Psychology*, 12: 215–26.

Ben-Shachar, D., Gazawi, H., Riboyad-Levin, J. et al. (1999) Chronic repetitive transcranial magnetic stimulation alters beta-adrenergic and 5-HT2 receptor characteristics in rat brain, *Brain Research*, 816: 78–83.

Bentall, R.P. (1993) Deconstructing the concept of 'schizophrenia', *Journal of Mental Health*, 2: 223–38.

Bentall, R.P., Corcoran, R., Howard, R. et al. (2001) Persecutory delusions: a review and theoretical integration, *Clinical Psychology Review*, 21: 1143–92.

Bentall, R.P. and Slade, P.D. (1985) Reality testing and auditory hallucinations, *British Journal of Clinical Psychology*, 24: 159–169.

Berlin, F.S. and Meinecke, C.F. (1981) Treatment of sex offenders with antiandrogenic medication: conceptualization, review of treatment modalities and preliminary findings, *American Journal of Psychiatry*, 138: 601–8.

Berretini, W.H. (2000) Susceptibility loci for bipolar disorder: overlap with inherited vulnerability to schizophrenia, *Biological Psychiatry*, 47: 245–51.

Berrios, G.E. and Quemada, J.I. (1990) Depressive illness in multiple sclerosis: clinical and theoretical aspects of the association, *British Journal of Psychiatry*, 156: 10–16.

Berrios, R.P. (1991) Delusions as 'wrong beliefs': a conceptual history, *British Journal of Psychiatry*, 159: 6–13.

Beswick, T., Best, D., Rees, S. et al. (2001) Multiple drug use: patterns and practices of heroin and crack use in a population of opiate addicts in treatment, *Drug and Alcohol Review*, 20: 201–4.

Bettelheim, B. (1967) *The Empty Fortress*. New York: Free Press.

Bettelheim, B. (1973) Bringing up children, *Ladies Home Journal*, 90: 28.

Beutler, L. and Consoli, A. (1993) Matching the therapist's interpersonal stance to clients' characteristics: contributions from systemic eclectic psychotherapy, *Psychotherapy: Theory, Research and Practice*, 30: 417–22.

Bezchlibuyle-Butler, K.Z. and Jeffries, J.J. (2003) *Clinical Handbook of Psychotropic Drugs*, 13th edn., Cambridge, MA: Hogrefe and Huber.

Bhatt, A., Tomenson, B. and Benjamin, S. (1989) Transcultural patterns of somatization in primary care: a preliminary report, *Journal of Psychosomatic Research*, 33: 671–80.

Biby, E.L. (1998) The relationship between body dysmorphic disorder and depression, self-esteem, somatization, and obsessive-compulsive disorder, *Journal of Clinical Psychology*, 54: 489–99.

Biederman, J., Petty, C., Faraone, S.V. et al. (2005) Childhood antecedents to panic disorder in referred and nonreferred adults, *Journal of Child and Adolescent Psychopharmacology*, 15: 549–61.

Biederman, J., Swanson, J.M., Wigal, S.B. et al. (2005) Efficacy and safety of modafinil film-coated tablets in children and adolescents with attention-deficit/hyperactivity disorder: results of a randomized, double-blind, placebo-controlled, flexible-dose study, *Pediatrics*, 116: 777–84.

Biondi, M. and Picardi, A. (2003) Increased probability of remaining in remission from panic disorder with agoraphobia after drug treatment in patients who received concurrent cognitive-behavioural therapy: a follow-up study, *Psychotherapy and Psychosomatics*, 72: 34–42.

Birbaumer, N., Veit, R., Lotze, M. et al. (2005) Deficient fear conditioning in psychopathy: a functional magnetic resonance imaging study, *Archives of General Psychiatry*, 62: 799–805.

Birch, H., Richardson, S.A., Baird, D. et al. (1970) *Mental Subnormality in the Community: A Clinical and Epidemiological Study*. Baltimore, MD: Williams and Wilkins.

Birchwood, M., Fowler, D. and Jackson, C. (eds) (2000) *Early Intervention in Psychosis*. London: Wiley.

Bird, C.E. and Rieker, P.P. (1999) Gender matters: an integrated model for understanding men's and women's health, *Social Science and Medicine*, 48: 745–55.

Birmingham, C.L., Su, J., Hlynsky, J.A. et al. (2005) The mortality rate from anorexia nervosa, *International Journal of Eating Disorders*, 38: 143–6.

Bjornstad, G. and Montgomery, P. (2005) Family therapy for attention-deficit disorder or attention-deficit/hyperactivity disorder in children and adolescents, *Cochrane Database of Systematic Reviews*, Issue 2.

Black, D.W., Noyes, R. Jr, Goldstein, R.B. et al. (1992) A family study of obsessive-compulsive disorder, *Archives of General Psychiatry*, 49: 362–8.

Blaszczynski, A. (1995) Criminal offences in pathological gamblers, *Psychiatry, Psychology and Law*, 1: 129–38.

Blazer, D.G., Hughes, D., George, L.K. et al. (1991) Generalized anxiety disorder, in L.N. Robins and D.A. Regier (eds) *Psychiatric Disorders in America: The Epidemiologic Catchment Area Study*. New York: Maxwell Macmillan International.

Blazer, R.C., Hughes, W.D. and George, L.K. (1987) Stressful life events and the onset of a generalized anxiety disorder, *American Journal of Psychiatry*, 114: 1178–83.

Bleathman, C. and Morton, I. (1992) Validation therapy: extracts from 20 groups with dementia sufferers, *Journal of Advanced Nursing*, 17: 658–66.

Blehar, M.C. and Rosenthal, N.E. (1989) Seasonal affective disorders and phototherapy, report of a National Institute of Mental Health-sponsored workshop, *Archives of General Psychiatry*, 46: 469–74.

Bleuler, E. (1908) Die Prognose der Dementia praecox – Schizophreniegruppe, *Präger Medicinische Wochenschrift*, 16: 321–5.

Bliss, E.L. (1986) *Multiple Personality, Allied Disorders and Hypnosis*. New York: Oxford University Press.

Blonigen, D.M., Hicks, B.M., Krueger, R.F. et al. (2005) Psychopathic personality traits:

heritability and genetic overlap with internalizing and externalizing psychopathology, *Psychological Medicine*, 35: 637–48.

Bohlmeijer, E., Valenkamp, M., Westerhof, G. et al. (2005) Creative reminiscence as an early intervention for depression: results of a pilot project, *Aging and Mental Health*, 9: 302–4.

Bohne, A., Keuthen, N.J., Wilhelm, S. et al. (2002) Prevalence of symptoms of body dysmorphic disorder and its correlates: a cross-cultural comparison, *Psychosomatics*, 43: 486–90.

Boon, S. and Draijer, N. (1993) Multiple personality disorder in The Netherlands: a clinical investigation of 71 patients, *American Journal of Psychiatry*, 150: 489–94.

Boone, M.L., McNeil, D.W., Masia, C.L. et al. (1999) Multimodal comparisons of social phobia subtypes and avoidant personality disorder, *Journal of Anxiety Disorders*, 13: 271–92.

Booth, P.G., Dale, B., Slade, P.D. et al. (1992) A follow-up study of problem drinkers offered a goal choice option, *Journal of Studies on Alcohol*, 53: 594–600.

Boothby, L.A. and Doering P.L. (2005) Acamprosate for the treatment of alcohol dependence, *Clinical Therapeutics*, 27: 695–714.

Borduin, C.M. (1999) Multisystemic treatment of criminality and violence in adolescents, *Journal of the Academy of Child and Adolescent Psychiatry*, 38: 242–9.

Borduin, C.M., Mann, B.J., Cone, L.T. et al. (1995) Multisystemic treatment of serious juvenile offenders: long-term prevention of criminality and violence, *Journal of Consulting and Clinical Psychology*, 63: 569–78.

Borkovec, T.D. and Costello, E. (1993) Efficacy of applied relaxation and cognitive behavioral therapy in the treatment of generalized anxiety disorder, *Journal of Consulting and Clinical Psychology*, 51: 611–19.

Boury, M., Treadwell, T. and Kumar, V.K. (2001) Integrating psychodrama cognitive therapy: an exploratory study, *International Journal of Action Methods*, 54: 13–28.

Bower, G.H. (1981) Mood and memory, *American Psychologist*, 36: 129–48.

Bowirrat, A. and Oscar-Berman, M. (2005) Relationship between dopaminergic neurotransmission, alcoholism, and Reward Deficiency syndrome, *American Journal of Medical Genetics. B: Neuropsychiatric Genetics*, 132: 29–37.

Boyle, M. (1990) Is schizophrenia what it was? A re-analysis of Kraepelin's and Bleuler's population, *Journal of the History of the Behavioral Sciences*, 26: 323–33.

Brain, K., Norman, P., Gray, J. et al. (2002) A randomized trial of specialist genetic assessment: psychological impact on women at different levels of familial breast cancer risk, *British Journal of Cancer*, 86: 233–8.

Brambilla, F., Bellodi, L., Arancio, C. et al. (2001) Central dopaminergic function in anorexia and bulimia nervosa: a psychoneuroendocrine approach, *Psychoneuroendocrinology*, 26: 293–409.

Bransford, J.D. and Stein, B.S. (1984) *The Ideal Problem Solver: A Guide for Improving Thinking, Learning, and Creativity*. New York: W.H. Freeman.

Brassington, J.C. and Marsh, N.V. (1999) Neuropsychological aspects of multiple sclerosis, *Neuropsychology Review*, 8: 43–77.

Brewin, C.R. (2001) A cognitive neuroscience account of posttraumatic stress disorder and its treatment, *Behaviour Research and Therapy*, 39: 373–93.

Brewin, C.R. and Andrews, B. (1998) Recovered memories of trauma: phenomenology and cognitive mechanisms, *Clinical Psychology Review*, 18: 949–70.

Bridges, K.W. and Goldberg, D.P. (1985) Somatic presentation of DSM-III psychiatric disorders in primary care, *Journal of Psychosomatic Research*, 29: 563–9.

Broadbent, D.E. (1971) *Decision and Stress*. London: Academic Press.

Bronisch, T. (1996) The relationship between suicidality and depression, *Archives of Suicide Research*, 2: 235–54.

Bronisch, T. and Wittchen, H.U. (1994) Suicidal ideation and suicide attempts: comorbidity with depression, anxiety disorders, and substance abuse disorder, *European Archives of Psychiatry and Clinical Neuroscience*, 244: 93–8.

Brooks, N., Campsie, L., Symington, C. et al. (1986) The five year outcome of severe blunt head injury: a relative's view, *Journal of Neurology, Neurosurgery, and Psychiatry*, 49: 764–70.

Brown, G.K., Newman, C.F., Charlesworth, S.E. et al. (2004) An open clinical trial of cognitive therapy for borderline personality disorder, *Journal of Personality Disorders*, 18: 257–71.

Brown, G.K., Ten Have, T., Henriques, G.R. et al. (2005) Cognitive therapy for the prevention of suicide attempts: a randomized controlled trial, *Journal of the American Medical Association*, 294: 563–70.

Brown, G.R. and Anderson, B. (1991) Psychiatric morbidity in adult clients with childhood histories of sexual and physical abuse, *American Journal of Psychiatry*, 148: 55–61.

Brown, G.W., Birley, J.L.T. and Wing, J.K. (1972) The influence of family life on the course of schizophrenic disorders: a relocation, *British Journal of Psychiatry*, 121: 241–58.

Brown, G.W. and Harris, T.O. (1978) *Social Origins of Depression: A Study of Psychiatric Disorder in Women*. London: Tavistock.

Brown, J.S.L., Cochrane, R. and Hancox, T. (2000) Large-scale health promotion stress workshops for the general public: a controlled evaluation, *Behavioural and Cognitive Psychotherapy*, 28: 139–51.

Brown, M. and Barraclough, B. (1997) Epidemiology of suicide pacts in England and Wales, 1988–92, *British Medical Journal*, 315: 286–7.

Bruce, D. (1980) Changes in Scottish drinking habits and behaviour following the extension of permitted evening opening hours, *Health Bulletin*, 38: 133–7.

Bruch, H. (1982) Anorexia nervosa: therapy and theory, *American Journal of Psychiatry*, 139: 1531–8.

Brüne, M. (2005) 'Theory of mind' in schizophrenia : a review of the literature, *Schizophrenia Bulletin*, 31: 21–42.

Bryant, M.J., Simons, A.D. and Thase, M.E. (1999) Therapist skill and patient variables in homework compliance: controlling an uncontrolled variable in cognitive therapy outcome research, *Cognitive Therapy and Research*, 23: 381–99.

Buccafusco, J.J. and Jackson, W.J. (1991) Beneficial effects of nicotine administered prior to a delayed matching-to-sample task in young and aged monkeys, *Neurobiology of Aging*, 12: 233–8.

Buhlmann, U., Etcoff, N.L. and Wilhelm, S. (2006) Emotion recognition bias for contempt and anger in body dysmorphic disorder, *Journal of Psychiatric Research*, 40: 105–11.

Bulik, C.M., Prescott, C.A. and Kendler, K.S. (2001) Features of childhood sexual abuse and the development of psychiatric and substance use disorders, *British Journal of Psychiatry*, 179: 444–9.

Bullough, V. and Weinberg, T. (1988) Women married to transvestites: problems and adjustments, *Journal of Psychology and Human Sexuality*, 1: 83–6.

Burgio, L., Engel, B.T., McCormick, K. et al. (1988) Behavioral treatment for urinary incontinence in elderly inpatients: initial attempts to modify prompting and toileting procedures, *Behavior Therapy*, 19: 345–57.

Burke, B.L., Arkowitz, H., Menchola, M. (2003) The efficacy of motivational interviewing: a meta-analysis of controlled clinical trials, *Journal of Consulting and Clinical Psychology*, 71: 843–61.

Bursac, Z. and Campbell, J.E. (2003) From risky behaviors to chronic outcomes: current status and Healthy People 2010 goals for American Indians in Oklahoma, *Journal of the Oklahoma State Medical Association*, 96: 569–73.

Butler, A.C., Chapman, J.E., Forman, E.M. et al. (2006) The empirical status of cognitive-behavioral therapy: a review of meta-analyses, *Clinical Psychology Review*, 26: 17–31.

Butler, G., Fennell, M., Robson, P. et al. (1991) A comparison of behaviour therapy and cognitive behavior therapy in the treatment of generalized anxiety disorder, *Journal of Consulting and Clinical Psychology*, 59: 167–75.

Button, T.M., Scourfield, J., Martin, N. et al. (2005) Family dysfunction interacts with genes in the causation of antisocial symptoms, *Behavioral Genetics*, 35: 115–20.

Byerly, M.J., Fisher, R., Carmody, T. and Rush, A.J. (2005) A trial of compliance therapy in outpatients with schizophrenia or schizoaffective disorder, *Journal of Clinical Psychiatry*, 66: 997–1001.

Cadoret, R.J. (1982) Genotype–environment interaction in antisocial behavior, *Psychological Medicine*, 12: 235–9.

Cadoret, R.J., Yates, G.A., Geyer, M.A. et al. (1995) Adoption study demonstrating two genetic pathways to drug abuse, *Archives of General Psychiatry*, 52: 45–52.

Calhoun, L.G. and Tedeschi, R.G. (1999) *Facilitating Posttraumatic Growth: A Clinician's Guide*, Mahwah, NJ: Lawrence Erlbaum Associates.

Campbell, M., Adams, P., Perry, R. et al. (1988) Tardive and withdrawal dyskinesias in autistic children: a prospective study, *Psychopharmacology Bulletin*, 24: 251–5.

Campbell, M., Anderson, L.T., Small, A.M. et al. (1993) Naltrexone in autistic children: behavioral symptoms and attentional learning, *Journal of the American Academy of Child and Adolescent Psychiatry*, 32: 1283–91.

Campion, J. and Bhugra, D. (1997) Experiences of religious healing in psychiatric patients in south India, *Social Psychiatry and Psychiatric Epidemiology*, 32: 215–21.

Carey, G. and Gottesman, I.I. (1981) Twin and family studies of anxiety, phobic and obsessive disorders, in D.F. Klein and J. Rabkin (eds) *Anxiety: New Research and Changing Concepts*. New York: Raven.

Carlton, P.L. and Manowicz, P. (1994) Factors determining the severity of pathological gambling in males, *Journal of Gambling Studies*, 10: 147–57.

Carr, A.T. (1974) Compulsive neurosis: a review of the literature, *Psychological Bulletin*, 81: 311–18.

Caspi, A., Moffitt, T.E., Cannon, M., et al. (2005) Moderation of the effect of adolescent-onset cannabis use on adult psychosis by a functional polymorphism in the catechol-O-methyltransferase gene: longitudinal evidence of a gene X environment interaction, *Biological Psychiatry*, 57: 1117–27.

Cassady, J.D., Kirschke, D.L., Jones, T.F. et al. (2005) Case series: outbreak of conversion disorder among Amish adolescent girls, *Journal of the American Academy of Child and Adolescent Psychiatry*, 44: 291–7.

Cassin, S.E. and von Ranson, K.M. (2005) Personality and eating disorders: a decade in review, *Eating and Weight Disorders*, 10: 98–106.

Castellanos, F.X., Giedd, J.N., Marsh, W.L. et al. (1996) Quantitative brain magnetic resonance imaging in attention-deficit hyperactivity disorder, *Archives of General Psychiatry*, 53: 607–16.

Castellanos, F.X., Xavier, L., Sharp, P.P. et al. (2002) Developmental trajectories of brain volume abnormalities in children and adolescents with attention-deficit/hyperactivity disorder, *Journal of the American Medical Association*, 288: 1740–8.

Channon, S., deSilva, P., Helmsley, D. et al. (1989) A controlled trial of cognitive behavioural and behavioural treatments of anorexia nervosa, *Behaviour Research and Therapy*, 27: 529–35.

Charlop-Christy, M.H. and Haymes, L.K. (1998) Using obsessions as reinforcers with and without mild reductive procedures to decrease inappropriate behaviors of children with autism, *Journal of Autism and Developmental Disorders*, 26: 527–46.

Chemtob, C., Roitblatt, H., Hamada, J. et al. (1988) A cognitive action theory of posttraumatic stress disorder, *Journal of Anxiety Disorders*, 2: 253–75.

Chen, D. (1995) Cultural and psychological influences on mental health issues for Chinese Americans, in L.L. Adler and R.R. Mukherji (eds) *Spirit versus Scalpel: Traditional Healing and Modern Psychotherapy*. Westport, CT: Bergin and Garvey.

Cherland, E. and Fitzpatrick, R. (1999) Psychotic side effects of psychostimulants: a 5-year review, *Canadian Journal of Psychiatry*, 44: 811–13.

Chiang, Y.L., Yeh, S.S., Hsiao, C.C. et al. (1999) Treatment of a transvestic fetishist with cognitive-behavioral therapy and supportive psychotherapy: case report, *Changgeng Yi Xue Za Zhi*, 22: 299–312.

Chick, J. (1991) Early intervention for hazardous drinking in the general hospital, *Alcohol and Alcoholism*, 1: 477–9.

Chorpita, B.F. and Barlow, D.H. (1998) The development of anxiety: the role of control in the early environment, *Psychological Bulletin*, 124: 3–21.

Chretien, R.D. and Persinger, M.A. (2000) 'Prefrontal deficits' discriminate young offenders from age-matched cohorts: juvenile delinquency as an expected feature of the normal distribution of prefrontal cerebral development, *Psychological Reports*, 87: 1196–202.

Christodoulou, C., Melville, P., Scherl, W.F. et al. (2005) Perceived cognitive dysfunction and observed neuropsychological performance: longitudinal relation in persons with multiple sclerosis, *Journal of the International Neuropsychological Society*, 11: 614–19.

Chugani, D.C. (2004) Serotonin in autism and pediatric epilepsies, *Mental Retardation and Developmental Disabilities Research Reviews*, 10: 112–16.

Clark, D.M. (1986) A cognitive approach to panic disorder, *Behaviour Research and Therapy*, 24: 461–70.

Clark, D.M., Salkovskis, P.M., Gelder, M. et al. (1988) Tests of a cognitive model of panic, in I. Hand and U. Wittchen (eds) *Panic and Phobias*, Vol. 2. Berlin: Springer Verlag.

Clark, D.M., Salkovskis, P.M., Hackmann, A. et al. (1994) A comparison of cognitive therapy, applied relaxation and imipramine in the treatment of panic disorder, *British Journal of Psychiatry*, 164: 759–69.

Clark, D.M., Salkovskis, P.M., Hackmann, A. et al. (1998) Two psychological treatments for hypochondriasis: a randomised controlled trial, *British Journal of Psychiatry*, 173: 218–25.

Clark, L.A., Watson, D. and Reynolds, S. (1995) Diagnosis and classification of psychopathology: challenges to the current system and future directions, *Annual Review of Psychology*, 46: 121–53.

Clarke, R. (2000) Perceptions of interethnic group racism predict increased vascular reactivity to a laboratory challenge in college women, *Annals of Behavioral Medicine*, 22: 214–22.

Clomipramine Collaborative Study Group (1991) Clomipramine in the treatment of patients with OCD, *Archives of General Psychiatry*, 48: 730–8.

Cloutier, S., Martin, S.L. and Poole, C. (2002) Sexual assault among North Carolina women: prevalence and health risk factors, *Journal of Epidemiology and Community Health*, 56: 265–71.

Coffey, M. (1999) Psychosis and medication: strategies for improving adherence, *British Journal of Nursing*, 8: 225–30.

Cohen, L.J., McGeoch, P.G., Gans, S.W. et al. (2002) Childhood sexual history of 20 male pedophiles vs. 24 male healthy control subjects, *Journal of Nervous and Mental Diseases*, 190: 757–66.

Cohen-Kettenis, P.T., Van Goozen, S.H., Doorn, C.D. et al. (1998) Cognitive ability and cerebral lateralisation in transsexuals, *Psychoneuroendocrinology*, 23: 631–41.

Cole, S.W., Kemeny, M.E., Taylor, S.E. and Visscher, B.R. (1996) Elevated physical health risk among gay men who conceal their homosexual identity, *Health Psychology*, 15: 243–51.

Collins, A.M. and Loftus, E.F. (1975) A spreading activation theory of semantic memory, *Psychological Review*, 82: 407–28.

Colom, F., Victa, E., Martinez-Aran, A. et al. (2003) A randomized trial on the efficacy of group psycho-education in the prophylaxis of recurrences in bipolar patients whose disease is in remission, *Archives of General Psychiatry*, 60: 402–7.

Comings, D.E., Blake, H., Dietz G. et al. (1999) The proenkephalin gene (PENK) and opioid dependence, *Neuroreport*, 10: 1133–5.

Comings, D.E., Gade-Andavolu, R., Gonzalez, N. et al. (2001) The additive effect of neurotransmitter genes in pathological gambling, *Clinical Genetics*, 60: 107–16.

Comings, D.E., Rosenthal, R.J., Lesieur, H.R. et al. (1996) A study of the dopamine D2 receptor gene in pathological gambling, *Pharmacogenetics*, 6: 223–34.

Commander, M.J., Odell, S.M., Surtees, P.G. et al. (2004) Care pathways for south Asian and white people with depressive and anxiety disorders in the community, *Social Psychiatry and Psychiatric Epidemiology*, 39: 259–64.

Compton, W.M., Helzer, J.E., Hwu, H. et al. (1991) New methods in crosscultural psychiatry: psychiatric illness in Taiwan and the United States, *American Journal of Psychiatry*, 148: 1697–704.

Conner, B.T., Noble, E.P., Berman, S.M. et al. (2005) DRD2 genotypes and substance use in adolescent children of alcoholics, *Drug and Alcohol Dependency*, 79: 379–87.

Coogan, P.F., Palmer, J.R., Strom, B.L. et al. (2005) Use of Selective Serotonin Reuptake Inhibitors and the risk of breast cancer, *American Journal of Epidemiology*, 162: 835–8.

Coolidge, F.L., Thede, L.L. and Young, S.E. (2002) The heritability of gender identity disorder in a child and adolescent twin sample, *Behavioral Genetics*, 32: 251–7.

Coons, P.M., Bowman, E.S. and Milstein, V. (1988) Multiple personality disorder: a clinical investigation of 50 cases, *Journal of Nervous and Mental Disease*, 176: 519–27.

Cooper, P.J. and Fairburn, C.G. (1983) Binge-eating and self-induced vomiting in the community, *British Journal of Psychiatry*, 142: 139–44.

Cornoldi, C., Marzocchi, G.M., Belotti, M. et al. (2001) Working memory interference control deficit in children referred by teachers for ADHD symptoms, *Neuropsychology, Development, and Cognition. Section C: Child Neuropsychology*, 7: 230–40.

Cororve, M.B. and Gleaves, D.H. (2001) Body dysmorphic disorder: a review of conceptualizations, assessment, and treatment strategies, *Clinical Psychology Review*, 6: 949–70.

Corrigan, P.W. (1991) Social skills training in adult psychiatric populations: a meta-analysis, *Journal of Behavior Therapy and Experimental Psychiatry*, 22: 203–10.

Corsico, A. and McGuffin, P. (2001) Psychiatric genetics: recent advances and clinical implications, *Epidemiologia e Psichiatria Sociale*, 10: 253–9.

Cory, F., Newman, L., Beck, R.L., et al. (2001) *Bipolar Disorder: A Cognitive Therapy Approach*. Washington, DC: American Psychological Association.

Costa, P.T. and McCrea, R.R. (1992) The five-factor model of personality and its relevance to personality disorders, *Journal of Personality Disorders*, 6: 343–59.

Costa, P.T. and McCrae, R.R. (1995) Domains and facets: hierarchical personality assessment using the Revised NEO Personality Inventory, *Journal of Personal Assessment*, 64: 21–50.

Costello, C. (1982) Fears and phobias in women: a community study, *Journal of Abnormal Psychology*, 91: 280–6.

Costello, E.J., Edelbrock, C.S. and Costello, A.J. (1985) Validity of the NIMH Diagnostic Interview Schedule for Children: a comparison between psychiatric and pediatric referrals, *Journal of Abnormal Child Psychology*, 13: 579–95.

Cottraux, J., Note, I., Yao, S.N. et al. (2001) A randomized controlled trial of cognitive therapy versus intensive behavior therapy in obsessive-compulsive disorder, *Psychotherapy and Psychosomatics*, 70: 288–97.

Cox, A., Rutter, M., Newman, S. et al. (1975) A comparative study of infantile autism and specific developmental language disorders. 2: Parental characteristics, *British Journal of Psychiatry*, 126: 146–59.

Cox, B.J., Kuch, K., Parker, J.D.A. et al. (1994) Alexithymia in somatoform disorder patients with chronic pain, *Journal of Psychosomatic Research*, 35: 523–7.

Craddock, N. and Jones, I. (1999) Genetics of bipolar disorder, *Journal of Medical Ethics*, 36: 585–94.

Craig, J.S., Hatton, C., Craig, F.B. et al. (2004) Persecutory beliefs, attributions and theory of mind: comparison of patients with paranoid delusions, Asperger's syndrome and healthy controls, *Schizophrenia Research*, 69: 29–33.

Craig, T.K., Bialas, I., Hodson, S. et al. (2004) Intergenerational transmission of somatization behaviour. 2: Observations of joint attention and bids for attention, *Psychological Medicine*, 34: 199–209.

Craig, T.K., Boardman, A.P., Mills, K. et al. (1993) The South London Somatization Study. I: Longitudinal course and the influence of early life experiences, *British Journal of Psychiatry*, 163: 579–88.

Craig, T.K., Cox, A.D. and Klein, K. (2002) Intergenerational transmission of somatization behaviour: a study of chronic somatizers and their children, *Psychological Medicine*, 32: 805–16.

Cranston-Cuebas, M.A. and Barlow, D.H. (1990) Cognitive and affective contributions to sexual functioning, *Annual Review of Sexual Research*, 1: 119–61.

Craven, J.L. and Rodin, G.M. (1987) Cyproheptadine dependence associated with an atypical somatoform disorder, *Canadian Journal of Psychiatry*, 32: 143–5.

Crawford, L.L., Holloway, K.S. and Domjan, M. (1993) The nature of sexual reinforcement, *Journal of Experimental Analysis of Behaviour*, 60: 55–66.

Creed, F. and Barsky, A. A (2004) Systematic review of the epidemiology of somatisation disorder and hypochondriasis, *Journal of Psychosomatic Research*, 56, 391–408.

Crimlisk, H.L., Bhatia, K., Cope, H., David, A. and Marsden, C.D., Ron M.A. (1998) Slater revisited: 6 year follow up study of patients with medically unexplained motor symptoms, *British Medical Journal*, 316: 582–6.

Crimlisk, H.L. and Ron, M.A. (1999) Conversion hysteria: history, diagnostic issues and clinical practice, in P. Halligan (ed.) *Conversion Hysteria: Towards a Cognitive Neuropsychological Account*. Hove: Psychology Press.

Crits-Cristoph, P., Cooper, A. and Luborsky, L. (1988) The accuracy of therapists' interpretations and the outcome of dynamic psychotherapy, *Journal of Consulting and Clinical Psychology*, 56: 490–5.

Cromarty, P. and Marks, I. (1995) Does rational role-play enhance the outcome of exposure therapy in dysmorphophobia? A case study, *British Journal of Psychiatry*, 167: 399–402.

Crowe, R. (1974) An adoption study of antisocial personality disorder, *Archives of General Psychiatry*, 31: 785–91.

Curran, H.V. (1991) Benzodiazepines, memory and mood: a review, *Psychopharmacology*, 105: 1–8.

Dahl, A.A. (1994) Heritability in personality disorders – an overview, *Clinical Genetics*, 46: 138–43.

Dalgleish, T., Rosen, K. and Marks, M. (1996) Rhythm and blues: the theory and treatment of seasonal affective disorder, *British Journal of Clinical Psychology*, 35: 163–82.

Dalos, N.P., Rabins, P.V., Brooks, B.R. et al. (1983) Disease activity and emotional state in multiple sclerosis, *Annals of Neurology*, 13: 573–7.

Dannon, P.N., Lowengrub, K., Musin, E. et al. (2005) Sustained-release bupropion versus naltrexone in the treatment of pathological gambling: a preliminary blind-rater study, *Journal of Clinical Psychopharmacology*, 25: 593–6.

Dare, C., Eisler, I., Russell, G. et al. (2001) Psychological therapies for adults with anorexia nervosa, *British Journal of Psychiatry*, 178: 216–21.

Davey, G.C.L. (1989) Dental phobias and anxieties: evidence for conditioning processes in the acquisition and modulation of a learned fear, *Behaviour Research Therapy*, 27: 51–8.

Davey, G.C.L. (1995) Rumination and enhancement of fear: some laboratory findings, *Behavioural and Cognitive Psychotherapy*, 23: 203–15.

Davey, G.C.L. (1997) A conditioning model of phobias, in G.C.L. Davey (ed.) *Phobias: A Handbook of Theory, Research and Treatment*. Chichester: Wiley.

Davey, G.C.L. (1999) A conditioning model of phobias, in G.C.L. Davey (ed.) *Phobias: A Handbook of Theory, Research, and Treatment*. Chichester: Wiley.

Davey, G.C.L., De Jong, P.J. and Tallis, F. (1993) UCS rehearsal in the aetiology of a variety of anxiety disorders: some case histories, *Behaviour Research and Therapy*, 31: 495–8.

Davey Smith, G., Dorling, D., Gordon, D. et al. (1999) The widening health gap: what are the solutions?, *Critical Public Health*, 9: 151–70.

Davidson, J.R.T. (2001) Pharmacotherapy of Generalised Anxiety Disorder, *Journal of Clinical Psychiatry*, 62 (Suppl. 11): 46–50.

Davidson, K. (2000) *Cognitive Therapy for Personality Disorders*. Oxford: Butterworth-Heinemann.

Davidson, P.R. and Parker, K.C.H. (2001) Eye movement desensitization and reprocessing (EMDR): a meta-analysis, *Journal of Consulting and Clinical Psychology*, 69: 305–16.

Day, J.C., Bentall, R.P., Roberts, C. et al. (2005) Attitudes toward antipsychotic medication: the impact of clinical variables and relationships with health professionals, *Archives of General Psychiatry*, 62: 717–24.

Degenhardt, L., Day, C., Dietze, P., Pointer, S., Conroy, E., Collins, L. and Hall, W. (2005) Effects of a sustained heroin shortage in three Australian States, *Addiction*, 100: 908–20.

De Jong, P., Muris, P., Ter Host, G. et al. (1995) Acquisition and maintenance of dental anxiety: the role of conditioning experiences and cognitive factors, *Behaviour Research and Therapy*, 33: 205–10.

De la Fuente, J.M. Goldman, S. Stanus, E. et al. (1997) Brain glucose metabolism in borderline personality disorder, *Journal of Psychiatric Research*, 31: 531–41.

Delfabbro, P.H. and Winefield, A.H. (1999) Poker machine gambling: an analysis of within session characteristics, *British Journal of Psychology*, 90: 425–32.

Deltito, J.A. and Stam, M. (1989) Psychopharmacological treatment of avoidant personality disorder, *Comprehensive Psychiatry*, 30: 498–504.

Demicheli, V., Jefferson, T., Rivetti, A. et al. (2005) Vaccines for measles, mumps and rubella in children, *Cochrane Database of Systematic Reviews*, Issue 5.

Demyttenaere, K., Van Ganse, E., Gregoirre, J. et al. (1998) Compliance in depressed patients treated with fluoxetine or amitriptyline. Belgian Compliance Study Group, *International Clinical Psychopharmacology*, 13: 11–17.

Department of Health and Human Services (1999) *Mental Health: Culture, Race and Ethnicity. A Supplement to Mental Health: A Report of the Surgeon General*. Washington, DC: US Public Health Service.

DeRubeis, R.J., Gelfand, L.A., Tang, T.Z. et al. (1999) Medications versus cognitive behavior therapy for severely depressed outpatients: mega-analysis of four randomized comparisons, *American Journal of Psychiatry*, 156: 1007–13.

Desai, N. (1999) Switching from depot antipsychotics to risperidone: results of a study of chronic schizophrenics, *Advances in Therapy*, 16: 78–88.

Devanand, D.P., Dwork, A.J., Hutchinson, E.R. et al. (1994) Does ECT alter brain structure?, *American Journal of Psychiatry*, 151: 957–70.

Devilly, G.J. and Spence, S.H. (1999) The relative efficacy and treatment distress of EMDR and a cognitive-behavior trauma treatment protocol in the amelioration of posttraumatic stress disorder, *Journal of Anxiety Disorders*, 13: 131–57.

Dhawan, S. and Marshall, W.L. (1996) Sexual abuse histories of sexual offenders, *Sexual Abuse: A Journal of Research and Treatment*, 8: 7–15.

Dickerson, M. and Baron, E. (2000) Contemporary issues and future directions for research into pathological gambling, *Addiction*, 95: 1145–59.

Dickerson, M.G., Baron, E., Hong, S-M. et al. (1996) Estimating the extent and degree of gambling related problems in the Australian population: a national survey, *Journal of Gambling Studies*, 12: 161–78.

Dobkin, B.H. (1996) *Neurologic Rehabilitation*. Philadelphia, PA: F.A. Davis.

Docter, R.F. and Prince, V. (1997) Transvestism: a survey of 1032 crossdressers, *Archives of Sexual Behavior*, 26: 589–605.

Dodge, K.A. and Frame, C.L. (1982) Social cognitive biases and deficits in aggressive boys, *Child Development*, 53: 620–35.

Dolan, M. (1994) Psychopathy – a neurobiological perspective, *British Journal of Psychiatry*, 165: 151–9.

Dollard, J. and Miller, N.E. (1950) *Personality and Psychotherapy*. New York: McGraw-Hill.

Donohoe, G., Owens, N., O'Donnell, C. et al. (2001) Predictors of compliance with neuroleptic medication among inpatients with schizophrenia: a discriminant function analysis, *European Psychiatry*, 16: 293–8.

Driessen, M., Herrmann, J., Stahl, K. et al. (2000) Magnetic resonance imaging volumes of the hippocampus and the amygdala in women with borderline personality disorder and early traumatization, *Archives of General Psychiatry*, 57: 1115–22.

Drury, V., Birchwood, M. and Cochrane, R. (2000) Cognitive therapy and recovery from acute psychosis: a controlled trial. 3: Five-year follow-up, *British Journal of Psychiatry*, 177: 8–14.

Duddu, V., Isaac, M.K. and Chaturvedi, S.K. (2003) Alexithymia in somatoform and depressive disorders, *Journal of Psychosomatic Research*, 54: 435–8.

Dugas, M.J., Marchand, A., Ladouceur, R. et al. (2005) Further validation of a cognitive-behavioral model of generalized anxiety disorder: diagnostic and symptom specificity, *Journal of Anxiety Disorders*, 19: 329–43.

Dumais A., Lesage A.D., Alda M. et al. (2005) Risk factors for suicide completion in major depression: a case-control study of impulsive and aggressive behaviors in men, *American Journal of Psychiatry*, 162: 2116–24.

Duncan, G.E., Sheitman, B.B. and Lieberman, J.A. (1999) An integrated view of pathophysiological models of schizophrenia, *Brain Research Reviews*, 29: 250–64.

Durham, R.C., Murphy, T., Allan, T. et al. (1994) Cognitive therapy, analytic psychotherapy and anxiety management training for generalised anxiety disorder, *British Journal of Psychiatry*, 16: 315–23.

Durkheim, E. ([1897] 1951) *Suicide*. New York: Free Press.

Dyer, C. (1997) High court detains girl with anorexia, *British Medical Journal*, 314: 845.

Eagles, J.M., Wileman, S.M., Cameron, I.M. et al. (1999) Seasonal affective disorder among primary care attenders and a community sample in Aberdeen, *British Journal of Psychiatry*, 175: 472–5.

Eamon, M.K. and Mulder, C. (2005) Predicting antisocial behavior among Latino young adolescents: an ecological systems analysis, *American Journal of Orthopsychiatry*, 75: 117–27.

Eaton, W.W., Kramer, M., Anthony, J.C. et al. (1989) The incidence of specific DIS/DSM-III mental disorders: data from the NIMH Epidemiologic Catchment Area Program, *Acta Psychiatrica Scandinavica*, 79: 163–78.

Ebert, A. and Dyck, M.J. (2004) The experience of mental death: the core feature of complex posttraumatic stress disorder, *Clinical Psychology Review*, 24: 617–35.

Eddy, J.M. and Chamberlain, P. (2000) Family management and deviant peer associations as mediators of the impact of treatment condition on youth antisocial behavior, *Journal of Consulting and Clinical Psychology*, 68: 857–63.

Edwards, G., Anderson, P., Babor, T.F. et al. (1994) *Alcohol Policy and the Public Good.* Oxford: Oxford University Press.

Ehlers, A., Mayou, R.A. and Bryant, B. (1998) Psychological predictors of chronic post-traumatic stress disorder after motor vehicle accidents, *Journal of Abnormal Psychology*, 107: 508–19.

Ehrhardt, A. and Money, J. (1967) Progestin-induced hermaphroditism: IQ and psychosexual identity in a study of ten girls, *Journal of Sex Research*, 3: 83–100.

Eisen, S.A., Lin, N., Lyons, M.J. et al. (1998–99) Familial influences on gambling behavior: an analysis of 3,359 twin pairs, *Addiction*, 93: 1375–84.

Eisler, I., Dare, C., Hodes, M. et al. (2000) Family therapy for adolescent anorexia nervosa: the results of a controlled comparison of two family interventions, *Journal of Child Psychology and Psychiatry*, 41: 727–36.

Elkin, I., Shea, T., Watkins, J.T. et al. (1989) National Institute of Mental Health Treatment of Depression Collaborative Research Program: general effectiveness of treatments, *Archives of General Psychiatry*, 46: 971–82.

Elkins, G., Rajab, M.H. and Marcus, J. (2005) Complementary and alternative medicine use by psychiatric inpatients, *Psychological Reports*, 96: 163–6.

Ellery, M., Stewart, S.H. and Loba, P. (2005) Alcohol's effects on video lottery terminal (VLT) play among probable pathological and non-pathological gamblers, *Journal of Gambling Studies*, 21: 299–324.

Elliott, M. (2000) Gender differences in the causes of depression, *Women and Health*, 33: 163–77.

Ellis, A. (1977) The basic clinical theory of rational-emotive therapy, in A. Ellis and R. Grieger (eds) *Handbook of Rational-Emotive Therapy.* New York: Springer.

Elzinga, B.M., Phaf, R.H., Ardon, A.M. et al. (2003) Directed forgetting between, but not within, dissociative personality states, *Journal of Abnormal Psychology*, 112: 237–43.

Emerson, E. (1998) Working with people with challenging behaviour, in E. Emerson, C. Hatton, J. Bromley et al. (eds) *Clinical Psychology and People with Intellectual Disabilities.* Chichester: Wiley.

Emerson, E., Hatton, C., Felce, D. et al. (2001) *Learning Disabilities: The Fundamental Facts.* London: Mental Health Foundation.

Engel, S.M., Berkowitz, G.S., Wolff, M.S. et al. (2005) Psychological trauma associated with the World Trade Center attacks and its effect on pregnancy outcome, *Paediatric and Perinatal Epidemiology*, 19: 334–41.

Epstein, J., Wiseman, C.V., Sunday, S.R. et al. (2001) Neurocognitive evidence favors 'top down' over 'bottom up' mechanisms in the pathogenesis of body size distortions in anorexia nervosa, *Eating and Weight Disorders*, 6: 140–7.

Eriksen, H., Hellesnes, B., Staff, P. et al. (2004) Are subjective health complaints a result of modern civilisation?, *International Journal of Behavioral Medicine*, 11: 122–5.

Erikson, E. (1980) *Growth and Crisis of the Healthy Personality: Identity and the Life Cycle.* New York: W.W. Norton.

Evans, E., Kupfer, D.J., Perel, J.M. et al. (1992) Three-year outcomes for maintenance therapies in recurrent depression, *Archives of General Psychiatry*, 47: 1093–9.

Fahlen, T. (1995) Personality traits in social phobia. II: Changes during drug treatment, *Journal of Clinical Psychiatry*, 56: 569–73.

Fairburn, C.G. (1997) Eating disorders, in D.M. Clark and C.G. Fairburn (eds) *Science and Practice of Cognitive Behaviour Therapy.* Oxford: Oxford University Press.

Fairburn, C.G. and Beglin, S.J. (1994) Assessment of eating disorders: interview or self-report questionnaire?, *International Journal of Eating Disorders*, 16: 363–70.

Fairburn, C.G., Jones, R., Peveler, R.C. et al. (1993) Psychotherapy and bulimia nervosa: the longer-term effects of interpersonal psychotherapy, behaviour therapy and cognitive behaviour therapy, *Archives of General Psychiatry*, 50: 419–28.

Fairburn, C.G., Norman, P.A. and Welch, S.L. (1995) A prospective study of outcome in bulimia nervosa and the long-term effects of three psychological treatments, *Archives of General Psychiatry*, 52: 304–12.

Fallon, B.A., Qureshi, A.I., Schneier, F.R. et al. (2003) An open trial of fluvoxamine for hypochondriasis, *Psychosomatics*, 44: 298–303.

Fallon, B.A., Schneier, F.R., Marshall, R. et al. (1996) The pharmacotherapy of hypochondriasis, *Psychopharmacology Bulletin*, 32: 607–11.

Falloon, I.R., Boyd, J.L., McGill, C.W. et al. (1982) Family management in the prevention of exacerbations of schizophrenia: a controlled study, *New England Journal of Medicine*, 306: 1437–40.

Faraone, S.V., Biederman, J., Spencer, T. et al. (2005) Efficacy of atomoxetine in adult attention-deficit/hyperactivity disorder: a drug-placebo response curve analysis, *Behavioral and Brain Functions*, 1: 16–20.

Faravelli, C., Salvatori, S., Galassi, F. et al. (1997) Epidemiology of somatoform disorders: a community survey in Florence, *Social Psychiatry and Psychiatric Epidemiology*, 32: 24–9.

Farber, S. (1990) Institutional mental health and social control: the ravages of epistemological hubris, *Journal of Mind and Behavior*, 11: 285–300.

Farrell, J.M. and Shaw, I.A. (1994) Emotional awareness training: a prerequisite to effective cognitive-behavioral treatment of borderline personality disorder, *Cognitive and Behavioral Practice*, 1: 71–91.

Farrington, D.P. (2000) Psychosocial predictors of adult antisocial personality and adult convictions, *Behavioral Sciences and the Law*, 18: 605–22.

Farris, B. and Stancliffe, R.J. (2001) The co-worker training model: outcomes of an open employment pilot project, *Journal of Intellectual and Developmental Disability*, 26: 143–59.

Favre, J.D., Allain, H., Aubin, H.J. et al. (2005) Double-blind study of cyamemazine and diazepam in the alcohol withdrawal syndrome, *Human Psychopharmacology*, 20: 511–19.

Feeney, G.F., Young, R.M. et al. (2002) Cognitive behavioural therapy combined with the relapse-prevention medication acamprosate: are short-term treatment outcomes for alcohol dependence improved?, *Australian and New Zealand Journal of Psychiatry*, 36: 622–8.

Feil, N. (1990) Validation therapy helps staff reach confused patients, *Nursing*, 16: 33–4.

Feingold, B.F. (1979) *The Feingold Cookbook for Hyperactive Children*. New York: Random House.

Feinstein, A., Ron, M. and Thompson, A. (1993) A serial study of psychometric and magnetic resonance imaging changes in multiple sclerosis, *Brain*, 116: 569–602.

Feiring, C., Taska, L. and Lewis, M. (2002) Adjustment following sexual abuse discovery: the role of shame and attributional style, *Developmental Psychology*, 38:79–92.

Feldman-Summers, S. and Pope, K.S. (1994) The experience of 'forgetting' childhood abuse: a national survey of psychologists, *Journal of Consulting and Clinical Psychology*, 62: 636–9.

Felner, R.D., Brand, S., Adan, A.M. et al. (1993) Restructuring the ecology of the school as an approach to prevention during school transitions: longitudinal follow-ups and extensions of the School Transitional Environment Project (STEP), *Prevention in Human Services*, 10: 103–9.

Fenoglio, C., Galimberti, D. and Ban, M. (2005) SELPLG and SELP single-nucleotide polymorphisms in multiple sclerosis, *Neuroscience Letters*, Oct. 25.

Ferguson, C.P., La Via, M.C., Crossan, P.J. et al. (1999) Are serotonin selective reuptake inhibitors effective in underweight anorexia nervosa?, *International Journal of Eating Disorders*, 25: 7–11.

Fergusson, D., Doucette, S., Glass, K.C. et al. (2005) Association between suicide attempts and selective serotonin reuptake inhibitors: systematic review of randomised controlled trials, *British Medical Journal*, 330: 396–9.

Fergusson, D.M. and Horwood, L.J. (1995) Predictive validity of categorically and dimensionally scored measures of disruptive childhood behaviors, *Journal of the American Academy of Child and Adolescent Psychiatry*, 34: 477–85.

Ferrie, J.E., Martikainen, P., Shipley, M.J. et al. (2001) Employment status and health after privatisation in white collar civil servants: prospective cohort study, *British Medical Journal*, 322: 647–51.

Fielding, J.E. and Piserchia, P.V. (1989) Frequency of worksite health promotion activities, *American Journal of Public Health*, 79: 16–20.

Fink, D. and Golinkoff, M. (1990) Multiple personality disorder, borderline personality disorder, and schizophrenia: a comparative study of clinical features, *Dissociation*, 3: 127–34.

Fink, P., Hansen, M.S. and Oxhoj, M-L. (2004) The prevalence of somatoform disorders among internal medical inpatients, *Journal of Psychosomatic Research*, 56, 413–18.

Fink, P., Ornbol, E., Toft, T. et al. (2004) A new, empirically established hypochondriasis diagnosis, *American Journal of Psychiatry*, 161: 1680–91.

Finkelhor, D. (1984) *Child Sexual Abuse: New Theory and Research*. New York: Free Press.

Finn, P.R., Earleywine, M. and Pihl, R.O. (1992) Sensation seeking, stress reactivity, and alcohol dampening discriminate the density of a family history of alcoholism, *Alcoholism: Clinical and Experimental Research*, 16: 585–90.

Fishbain, D.A. and Aldrich, T.E. (1985) Suicide pacts: international comparisons, *Journal of Clinical Psychiatry*, 46: 11–15.

Foa, E.B. and Kozak, M.J. (1986) Emotional processing of fear: exposure to corrective information, *Psychological Bulletin*, 99: 20–35.

Foa, E.B., Liebowitz, M.R., Kozak, M.J. et al. (2005) Randomized, placebo-controlled trial of exposure and ritual prevention, clomipramine, and their combination in the treatment of obsessive-compulsive disorder, *American Journal of Psychiatry*, 162: 151–61.

Foa, E.B., Rothbaum, B.O., Riggs, D.S. et al. (1991) Treatment of posttraumatic stress disorder in rape victims: a comparison between cognitive and behavioral procedures and counselling, *Journal of Consulting and Clinical Psychology*, 59: 715–23.

Foa, E.B., Steketee, G. and Rothbaum, B.O. (1989) Behavioral/cognitive conceptualizations of post-traumatic stress disorder, *Behavior Therapy*, 20: 155–76.

Forette, F. and Rockwood, K. (1999) Therapeutic intervention in dementia, in G.K. Wilcock, R.S. Bucks and K. Rockwood (eds) *Diagnosis and Management of Dementia: A Manual for Memory Disorders Teams*. Oxford: Oxford University Press.

Forsythe, A.J.M. (1996) Places and patterns of drug use in the Scottish dance scene, *Addiction*, 91: 511–21.

Fox, J.C., Blank, M., Berman, J. et al. (1999) Mental disorders and help seeking in a rural impoverished population, *International Journal of Psychiatry in Medicine*, 29: 181–95.

Fox, J.W. (1990) Social class, mental illness, and social mobility: the social selection-drift hypothesis for serious mental illness, *Journal of Health and Social Behavior*, 31: 344–53.

Frank, J.D. (1961) *Persuasion and Healing: A Comparative Study of Psychotherapy*. Baltimore, MD: Johns Hopkins University Press.

Fraser, G.A. (1992) Multiple personality disorder, *British Journal of Psychiatry*, 161: 416–17.

Freedy, J.R., Resnick, H.S., and Kilpatrick, D.G. (1992) Conceptual framework for evaluating disaster impact: implications for clinical intervention, in L.S. Austin (ed.) *Responding to*

Disaster: A Guide for Mental Health Professionals. Washington, DC: American Psychiatric Press.

Freeman, C. (1995) *The ECT Handbook.* London: Royal College of Psychiatrists.

Freeman, C.P.L., Trimble, M.R., Deakin, J.F.W. et al. (1994) Fluvoxamine versus clomipramine in the treatment of obsessive-compulsive disorder: a multicenter, randomized, double-blind, parallel group comparison, *Journal of Clinical Psychiatry*, 55: 301–5.

Freud, S. (1900) *The Interpretation of Dreams.* New York: Wiley.

Freud, S. (1906) Analysis of a phobia in a five-year-old boy, in J. Strachey (ed. and trans.). *Standard Edition of Complete Psychological Works*, Vol. 10. London: Hogarth Press, pp. 5–149.

Freud, S. (1922) *Introductory Lectures on Psychoanalysis.* London: George Allen and Unwin.

Freud, S. ([1917] 1957) Mourning and melancholia, in J. Strachey (ed. and trans.) *The Standard Edition of Complete Psychological Works*, Vol. 14. London: Hogarth Press.

Freud, S. ([1920] 1990) *Beyond the Pleasure Principle.* New York: W.W. Norton.

Freud, S. and Breur, J. (2004) *Studies in Hysteria.* New York: Penguin.

Freyd, J.J. (1996) *Betrayal Trauma: The Logic of Forgetting Childhood Abuse.* Cambridge, MA: Harvard University Press.

Friedberg, J. (1977) Shock treatment, brain damage, and memory loss: a neurological perspective, *American Journal of Psychiatry*, 13: 1010–14.

Frith, C.D. and Corcoran, R. (1996) Exploring 'theory of mind' in people with schizophrenia, *Psychological Medicine*, 26: 521–30.

Fromm-Reichman, F. (1948) Notes on the development of treatment of schizophrenia by psycho-analytic psychotherapy, *Psychiatry*, 11: 263–73.

Frost, A. (2004) Therapeutic engagement styles of child sexual offenders in a group treatment program: a grounded theory study, *Sexual Abuse*, 16: 191–208.

Fryers, T., Melzer, D., Jenkins, R. et al. (2005) The distribution of the common mental disorders: social inequalities in Europe. *Clinical Practice and Epidemiology in Mental Health*, 1: 14.

Fukunishi, I. (1997) Alexithymic characteristics of bulimia nervosa in diabetes mellitus with end-stage renal disease, *Psychological Reports*, 81: 627–33.

Fukunishi, I., Sasaki, K., Chisima, Y. et al. (1996) Emotional disturbances in trauma patients during the rehabilitation phase: studies of post-traumatic stress disorder and alexithymia, *General Hospital Psychiatry*, 18: 121–7.

Gada, M.T. (1982) A cross-cultural study of symptomatology of depression: eastern versus western patients, *International Journal of Social Psychology*, 28: 195–202.

Gaebel, W., Janner, M., Frommann, N. et al. (2002) First vs multiple episode schizophrenia: two-year outcome of intermittent and maintenance medication strategies, *Schizophrenia Research*, 53: 145–59.

Gagné, G.G., Furman, M.J., Carpenter, L.L. et al. (2000) Efficacy of continuation ECT and antidepressant drugs compared to long-term anti-depressants alone in depressed patients, *American Journal of Psychiatry*, 157: 1960–9.

Galea, S., Vlahov, D., Resnick, H. et al. (2003) Trends of probable post-traumatic stress disorder in New York City after the September 11 terrorist attacks, *American Journal of Epidemiology*, 158: 514–24.

Gallagher-Thompson, D. and Steffen, A.M. (1994) Comparative effects of cognitive-behavioral and brief psychodynamic psychotherapies for depressed family caregivers, *Journal of Consulting and Clinical Psychology*, 62: 543–9.

Garbutt, J.C., Kranzler, H.R., O'Malley S.S. et al. (2005) Efficacy and tolerability of long-acting injectable naltrexone for alcohol dependence: a randomized controlled trial, *Journal of the American Medical Association*, 293: 1617–25.

Garner, D.M. and Bemis, K.M. (1985) Cognitive therapy for anorexia nervosa, in D.M. Garner and P.E. Garfinkel (eds) *Handbook of Psychotherapy for Anorexia Nervosa and Bulimia.* New York: Guilford.

Geddes, J.R., Verdoux, H., Takei, N. et al. (1999) Schizophrenia and complications of pregnancy and labor: an individual patient data meta-analysis, *Schizophrenia Bulletin,* 25: 413–23.

Gena, A., Couloura, S., Kymissis, E. (2005) Modifying the affective behavior of preschoolers with autism using in-vivo or video modeling and reinforcement contingencies, *Journal of Autism and Developmental Disorders,* 35: 1–12.

Geoffrey, C. (1991) A Prozac backlash, *Newsweek,* 1 April, p. 64.

Gerra, G., Garofano, L., Santoro, G. et al. (2004) Association between low-activity serotonin transporter genotype and heroin dependence: behavioral and personality correlates, *American Journal of Medical Genetics. B: Neuropsychiatric Genetics,* 126: 37–42.

Gibson, D.R., Flynn, N.M. and Perales, D. (2001) Effectiveness of syringe exchange programs in reducing HIV risk behavior and HIV seroconversion among injecting drug users, *AIDS,* 15: 1329–41.

Gillespie, K., Duffy, M., Hackmann, A. et al. (2002) Community based cognitive therapy in the treatment of post-traumatic stress disorder following the Omagh bomb, *Behaviour Research and Therapy,* 40: 345–57.

Gillespie, N.A., Zhu, G., Heath, A.C. et al. (2000) The genetic aetiology of somatic distress, *Psychological Medicine,* 30: 1051–61.

Gizatullin, R., Zaboli, G., Jonsson, E.G. et al. (2006) Haplotype analysis reveals tryptophan hydroxylase (TPH) 1 gene variants associated with major depression, *Biological Psychiatry,* 59: 295–300.

Gladue, B.A. (1985) Neuroendocrine response to estrogen and sexual orientation, *Science,* 230: 961.

Gleaves, D.H. (1996) The sociocognitive model of dissociative identity disorder: a reexamination of the evidence, *Psychological Bulletin,* 120: 42–59.

Gleaves, D.H., May, M.C. and Cardena, E. (2001) An examination of the diagnostic validity of dissociative identity disorder, *Clinical Psychology Review,* 21: 577–608.

Glickman, G., Byrne, B., Pineda, C. et al. (2006) Light therapy for seasonal affective disorder with blue narrow-band light-emitting diodes (LEDs), *Biological Psychiatry,* 59: 502–7.

Goddard, A.W., Mason, G.F., Almai, A. et al. (2001) Reductions in occipital cortex GABA levels in panic disorder detected with ^{1}H-magnetic resonance spectroscopy, *Archives of General Psychiatry,* 58: 556–61.

Goldbloom, D.S., Hicks, L.K. and Garfinkel, P.E. (1990) Platelet serotonin uptake in bulimia nervosa, *Biological Psychiatry,* 28: 644–7.

Golding, L., Emerson, E. and Thornton, A. (2005) An evaluation of specialized community-based residential supports for people with challenging behaviour, *Journal of Intellectual Disability,* 9: 145–54.

Goldman, A. and Carroll, J.L. (1990) Educational intervention as an adjunct to treatment of erectile dysfunction in older couples, *Journal of Sexual and Marital Therapy,* 16: 127–41.

Goldstein, F.C., McKendall, R.R. and Haut, M.W. (1992) Gist recall in multiple sclerosis, *Archives of Neurology,* 49: 1060–4.

Goldstein, I., Lue, T.F., Padma-Nathan, H. et al. (1998) Oral sildenafil in the treatment of erectile dysfunction: Sildenafil Study Group, *New England Journal of Medicine,* 338: 1397–404.

Golub, A. and Johnson, B.D. (2005) The new heroin users among Manhattan arrestees: variations by race/ethnicity and mode of consumption, *Journal of Psychoactive Drugs,* 37: 51–61.

Gomez-Perez, J.C., Marks, I.M. and Gutierrez-Fisac, J.L. (1994) Dysmorphophobia: clinical features and outcome with behavior therapy, *European Psychiatry*, 9: 229–35.

Goodman, G.S., Ghetti, S., Quas, J.A. et al. (2003) A prospective study of memory for abuse: new findings relevant to the repressed memory debate, *Psychological Science*, 14: 113–18.

Goodman, R. and Stevenson, J. (1989) A twin study of hyperactivity – II: the etiological role of genes, family relationships, and perinatal adversity, *Journal of Child Psychology and Psychiatry*, 30: 691–709.

Goodyear-Smith, F.A., Laidlaw, T.M. and Large, R.G. (1997) Memory recovery and repression: what is the evidence?, *Health Care Analysis*, 5: 99–111.

Gordon, C.T., State, R.C., Nelson, J.E. et al. (1993) A double-blind comparison of clomipramine, desipramine, and placebo in the treatment of autistic disorder, *Archives of General Psychiatry*, 50: 441–7.

Gorski, T.T. (1989) *Understanding the Twelve Steps*. New York: Prentice Hall/Parkside.

Goudriaan, A.E., Oosterlaan, J., de Beurs, E. et al. (2004) Pathological gambling: a comprehensive review of biobehavioral findings, *Neuroscience and Biobehavioral Review*, 28: 123–41.

Gould, R.A., Otto, M.W. and Pollack, M.H. (1995) A meta-analysis of treatment outcome for panic disorder, *Clinical Psychology Review*, 15: 819–44.

Goyer, P., Andreason, P.J., Semple, W.E. et al. (1994) Positron-emission tomography and personality disorders, *Neuropsychopharmacology*, 10: 21–8.

Grant, B.F., Hasin, D.S., Stinson, F.S. et al. (2005) Prevalence, correlates, co-morbidity, and comparative disability of DSM-IV generalized anxiety disorder in the USA: results from the National Epidemiologic Survey on Alcohol and Related Conditions, *Psychological Medicine*, 35: 1747–59.

Grant, B.F., Stinson, F.S., Hasin, D.S. et al. (2005) Prevalence, correlates, and comorbidity of bipolar I disorder and axis I and II disorders: results from the National Epidemiologic Survey on Alcohol and Related Conditions, *Journal of Clinical Psychiatry*, 66: 1205–15.

Grant, J.E., Kim, S.W. and Potenza, M.N. (2003) Paroxetine treatment of pathological gambling: a multi-centre randomized controlled trial, *International Clinical Psychopharmacology*, 18: 243–9.

Gray, J.A. (1983) A theory of anxiety: the role of the limbic system, *Encephale*, 9 (Suppl. 2): 161B–6B.

Gray, N.S., Brown, A.S., MacCulloch, M.J. et al. (2005) Implicit test of the associations between children and sex in pedophiles, *Journal Abnormal Psychology*, 114: 104–8.

Green, R. (1987) *The 'Sissy Boy Syndrome' and the Development of Homosexuality*. New Haven, CT: Yale University Press.

Green, R. and Blanchard, R. (1995) Gender identity disorders, in H.I. Kaplan and B.J. Sadock (eds) *Comprehensive Textbook of Psychiatry*. Baltimore, MD: Williams and Wilkins.

Greenberg, D.M., Bradford, J. and Curry, S. (1993) A comparison of sexual victimizations in the childhoods of pedophiles and hebephiles, *Journal of Forensic Sciences*, 38: 432–6.

Greenberg, P. and Kusche, C. (1998) Preventive intervention for school-age deaf children: the PATHS curriculum, *Journal of Deaf Studies and Deaf Education*, 3: 49–63.

Gresham, F.M. and MacMillan, D.L. (1998) Early intervention project: can its claims be substantiated and its effects replicated?, *Journal of Autism and Developmental Disorders*, 28: 5–13.

Griffiths, M. (2003) Internet gambling: issues, concerns, and recommendations, *Cyber Psychology and Behavior*, 6: 557–68.

Grinspoon, L. and Bakalar, J.B. (1986) Can drugs be used to enhance the psychotherapeutic process, *American Journal of Psychotherapy*, 40: 393–404.

Gruber, K., Chutuape, M.A. and Stitzer, M.L. (2000) Reinforcement-based intensive outpatient treatment for inner city opiate abusers: a short-term evaluation, *Drug and Alcohol Dependence*, 57: 211–23.

Gude, T. and Vaglum, P. (2001) One-year follow-up of patients with cluster C personality disorders: a prospective study comparing patients with 'pure' and comorbid conditions within cluster C, and 'pure' C with 'pure' cluster A or B conditions, *Journal of Personality Disorders*, 15: 216–28.

Guiao, I.Z. and Thompson, E.A. (2004) Ethnicity and problem behaviors among adolescent females in the United States, *Health Care for Women International*, 25: 296–310.

Gunnell, D., Magnusson, P.K. and Rasmussen, F. (2005) Low intelligence test scores in 18 year old men and risk of suicide: cohort study, *British Medical Journal*, 30: 67.

Gunnell, D., Saperia, J. and Ashby, D. (2005) Selective serotonin reuptake inhibitors (SSRIs) and suicide in adults: meta-analysis of drug company data from placebo controlled, randomized controlled trials submitted to the MHRA's safety review, *British Medical Journal*, 330: 385–90.

Gupta, M.A. and Johnson, A.M. (2000) Nonweight-related body image concerns among female eating-disordered patients and nonclinical controls: some preliminary observations, *International Journal of Eating Disorders*, 27: 304–9.

Gureje, O., Acha, R.A. and Odejide, O.A. (1995) Pathways to psychiatric care in Ibadan, Nigeria, *Tropical and Geographical Medicine*, 47: 125–9.

Gurvits, I.G., Koenigsberg, H.W. and Siever, L.J. (2000) Neurotransmitter dysfunction in patients with borderline personality disorder, *Psychiatric Clinics of North America*, 23: 27–40.

Guscott, R. and Taylor, L. (1994) Lithium prophylaxis in recurrent affective illness: efficacy, effectiveness and efficiency, *British Journal of Psychiatry*, 164: 741–6.

Guthrie, E. (1996) Psychotherapy for somatisation disorders, *Current Opinion in Psychiatry*, 9: 182–7.

Haaga, D.A. and Beck, A.T. (1995) Perspectives on depressive realism: implications for cognitive theory of depression, *Behaviour Research and Therapy*, 33: 41–8.

Haasen, C., Prinzleve, M., Zurhold, H., et al. (2004) Cocaine use in Europe – a multi-centre study: methodology and prevalence estimates, *European Addiction Research*, 10: 139–46.

Haddock, G., Slade, P.D., Bentall, R.P. et al. (1998) A comparison of the long-term effectiveness of distraction and focusing in the treatment of auditory hallucinations, *British Journal of Medical Psychology*, 71: 339–49.

Haenen, M-A., de Jong, P.J., Schmidt, A.J.M. et al. (2000) Hypochondriacs' estimation of negative outcomes: domain-specificity and responsiveness to reassuring and alarming information, *Behaviour Research and Therapy*, 38: 819–33.

Haenen, M-A., Schmidt, A.J., Schoenmakers, M. et al. (1997) Tactual sensitivity in hypochondriasis, *Psychotherapy and Psychosomatics*, 66: 128–32.

Haines, J.L. and Pericak-Vance, M.A. (1999) Genetics of multiple sclerosis, *Current Directions in Autoimmunology*, 1: 273–88.

Hall, G.C.N. (1995) Sexual offender recidivism revisited: a meta-analysis of recent treatment studies, *Journal of Consulting and Clinical Psychology*, 63: 802–9.

Halliburton, M. (2005) 'Just some spirits': the erosion of spirit possession and the rise of 'tension' in South India, *Medical Anthropology*, 24: 111–44.

Halligan, P.W., Athwal, B.S., Oakley, D.A. et al. (2000) Imaging hypnotic paralysis: implications for conversion hysteria, *Lancet*, 355: 986–7.

Hanson, R.K. and Slater, S. (1988) Sexual victimization in the history of child sexual abusers: a review, *Annals of Sex Research*, 1: 485–99.

Haraldsen, I.R., Opjordsmoen, S., Egeland, T. et al. (2003) Sex-sensitive cognitive performance in untreated patients with early onset gender identity disorder, *Psychoneuroendocrinology*, 28: 906–15.

Hardy, G., Aldridge, J., Davidson, C. et al. (1999) Therapist responsiveness to client attachment styles and issues observed in client-identified significant events in psychodynamic-interpersonal psychotherapy, *Psychotherapy Research*, 9: 36–53.

Hare, R.D. (1991) *The Hare Psychopathy Checklist-Revised (PCL-R)*. Toronto: Multi-Health Systems.

Hare, R.D., Clark, D., Grann, M. et al. (2000) Psychopathy and the predictive utility of the PCL-R: an international perspective, *Behavioural Sciences and the Law*, 18: 623–45.

Harris, J.K., Godfrey, H.P., Partridge, F.M. et al. (2001) Caregiver depression following traumatic brain injury (TBI): a consequence of adverse effects on family members?, *Brain Injury*, 15: 223–38.

Harris, M.B., Deary, I.J. and Wilson, J.A. (1996) Life events and difficulties in relation to the onset of globus pharynges, *Journal of Psychosomatic Research*, 40: 603–15.

Harrow, M., Grossman, L.S., Jobe, T.H. and Herbener, E.S. (2005) Do patients with schizophrenia ever show periods of recovery? A 15-year multi-follow-up study, *Schizophrenia Bulletin*, 31:723–34.

Haworth-Hoeppner, S. (2000) The critical shapes of body image: the role of culture and family in the production of eating disorders, *Journal of Marriage and the Family*, 62: 212–27.

Hawton, K. (1997) Attempted suicide, in D.M. Clark and C.G. Fairburn (eds) *Science and Practice of Cognitive Behaviour Therapy*. Oxford: Oxford University Press.

Hawton, K., Catalan, J. and Fagg, J. (1992) Sex therapy for erectile dysfunction: characteristics of couples, treatment outcome and prognostic factors, *Archives of Sexual Behavior*, 21: 161–75.

Hawton, K., Catalan, J., Martin, P. et al. (1986) Long-term outcome of sex therapy, *Behaviour Research and Therapy*, 24: 665–75.

Hayward, P. and Wardle, J. (1999) The use of medication in the treatment of phobias, in G.C.L. Davey (ed.) *Phobias: A Handbook of Theory, Research, and Treatment*. Chichester: Wiley.

Heather, N. (1995) The great controlled drinking consensus: is it premature?, *Addiction*, 90: 1160–3.

Hedden, T. and Gabrieli, J.D. (2005) Healthy and pathological processes in adult development: new evidence from neuroimaging of the aging brain, *Current Opinion in Neurology*, 18: 740–7.

Heiman, J.R. and LoPiccolo, J. (1988) *Becoming Orgasmic*. London: Piatkus.

Hellawell, S.J. and Brewin C.R. (2002) A comparison of flashbacks and ordinary autobiographical memories of trauma: cognitive resources and behavioural observations, *Behaviour Research and Therapy*, 40: 1143–56.

Hellawell, S.J. and Brewin, C.R. (2004) A comparison of flashbacks and ordinary autobiographical memories of trauma: content and language, *Behaviour Research and Therapy*, 42: 1–12.

Hellstrom, K., Fellenius, J. and Öst, L-G. (1996) One versus five sessions of applied tension in the treatment of blood phobia, *Behaviour Research and Therapy*, 34: 101–12.

Hemsley, D.R. (1996) Schizophrenia: a cognitive model and its implications for psychological intervention, *Behavior Modification*, 20: 139–69.

Hemsley, D.R. (1998) The disruption of the 'sense of self' in schizophrenia: potential links with disturbances of information processing, *British Journal of Medical Psychology*, 71: 115–24.

Hemsley, D.R. (2005) The development of a cognitive model of schizophrenia: placing it in context, *Neuroscience and Biobehavioral Reviews*, 29: 977–88.

Hemsley, D.R. and Murray, R.M. (2000) Commentary: psychological and social treatments for schizophrenia: not just old remedies in new bottles, *Schizophrenia Bulletin*, 26: 145–51.

Hemmingsson, T., Lundberg, I., Romelsjo, A. et al. (1997) Alcoholism in social classes and occupations in Sweden, *International Journal of Epidemiology*, 26: 584–91.

Hendin, H. (1992) The psychodynamics of suicide, *International Review of Psychiatry*, 4: 157–67.

Henggeler, S.W., Melton, G.B. and Smith, L.A. (1992) Family preservation using multisystemic therapy: an effective alternative to incarcerating serious juvenile offenders, *Journal of Consulting and Clinical Psychology*, 60: 953–61.

Henningsen, P., Zimmerman, T. and Sattel, H. (2003) Medically unexplained physical symptoms, anxiety, and depression: a meta-analysis, *Psychosomatic Medicine*, 65: 528–33.

Henquet. C., Murray. R., Linszen. D. et al. (2005) The Environment and schizophrenia: The role of cannabis use, *Schizophrenia Bulletin*, 31: 608–12.

Henry, D.B., Tolan, P.H. and Gorman-Smith, D. (2001) Longitudinal family and peer group effects on violence and nonviolent delinquency, *Journal of Clinical Child Psychology*, 30: 172–86.

Hepp, U., Kraemer, B., Schnyder, U. et al. (2005) Psychiatric comorbidity in gender identity disorder, *Journal of Psychosomatic Research*, 58: 259–61.

Hermann, B.P. and Chabria, S. (1980) Interictal psycho-pathology in patients with ictal fear, *Archives of Neurology*, 37: 667–8.

Herz, M.I. and Melville, C. (1980) Relapse in schizophrenia, *American Journal of Psychiatry*, 137: 801–5.

Hettema, J.M., Neale, M.C. and Kendler, K.S. (2001a) A review and meta-analysis of the genetic epidemiology of anxiety disorders, *American Journal of Psychiatry*, 158: 1568–78.

Hettema, J.M., Prescott, C.A. and Kendler, K.S. (2001b) A population-based twin study of generalized anxiety disorder in men and women, *Journal of Nervous and Mental Disorders*, 189: 413–20.

Hettema, J.M., Prescott, C.A., Myers, J.M. et al. (2005) The structure of genetic and environmental risk factors for anxiety disorders in men and women, *Archives of General Psychiatry*, 62: 182–9.

Heumann, K.A. and Morey, L.C. (1990) Reliability of categorical and dimensional judgements of personality disorders, *American Journal of Psychiatry*, 147: 498–500.

Hibell, B., Andersson, B., Bjarnasson, T. et al. (1997) *The 1995 ESPAD Report: Alcohol and Other Drug Use Among Students in 26 European Countries*. Stockholm: Council of Europe Pompidou Group.

Hill, C.E., Nutt-Williams, E., Heaton, K.J. et al. (1996) Therapist retrospective recall of impasses in long-term psychotherapy: a qualitative analysis, *Journal of Counseling Psychology*, 43: 207–17.

Hill, P. (1998) Attention deficit hyperactivity disorder, *Archives of Diseases of Childhood*, 79: 381–5.

Hiller, W., Leibbrand, R., Rief, W. et al. (2002) Predictors of course and outcome in hypochondriasis after cognitive-behavioral treatment, *Psychotherapy and Psychosomatics*, 71: 318–25.

Hinney, A., Fridel, A., Remschmidt, H. et al. (2004) Genetic risk factors in eating disorders, *American Journal of Pharmacogenomics*, 4: 209–23.

Hirschfeld, R.M.A. (1999) Efficacy of SSRIs and newer antidepressants in severe depression: comparison with TCAs, *Journal of Clinical Psychiatry*, 60: 326–35.

Ho, B.C., Alicata D., Mola C. and Andreasen, N.C. (2005) Hippocampus volume and treatment delays in first-episode schizophrenia, *American Journal of Psychiatry*, 162: 1527–9.

Hobfoll, S.E. (1989) Conservation of resources: a new attempt at conceptualising stress, *American Psychologist*, 44: 513–24.

Hoffman, R.E., Rapaport, J., Mazure, C.M. et al. (1999) Selective speech perception alterations in schizophrenic patients reporting hallucinated 'voices', *American Journal of Psychiatry*, 156: 393–9.

Holden, U.P. and Woods, R.T. (1995) *Positive Approaches to Dementia Care*. Edinburgh: Churchill Livingstone.

Holen-Hoeksema, S. (1990) *Sex Difference in Depression*. Stanford, CA: Stanford University Press.

Hollander, E., DeCaria, C.M., Finkell, J.N. et al. (2000) A randomized double blind fluvoxamine/placebo crossover trial in pathologic gambling, *Biological Psychiatry*, 47: 813–17.

Hollon, S.D., DcRubeis, R.J., Shelton, R.C. et al. (2005) Prevention of relapse following cognitive therapy vs medications in moderate to severe depression, *Archives of General Psychiatry*, 62: 417–22.

Holmes, S. (2000) Treatment of male sexual dysfunction, *British Medical Bulletin*, 56: 798–808.

Honda, H., Shimizu, Y., Rutter, M. (2005) No effect of MMR withdrawal on the incidence of autism: a total population study, *Journal of Child Psychology and Psychiatry*, 46: 72–9.

Honig, A., Romme, M.A., Ensink, B.J. et al. (1998) Auditory hallucinations: a comparison between patients and nonpatients, *Journal of Nervous and Mental Disease*, 186: 646–51.

Horn, W.F., Ialongo, N.S., Pascoe, J.M. et al. (1991) Additive effects of psychostimulants, parent training, and self-control therapy with ADHD children, *Journal of the American Academy of Child and Adolescent Psychiatry*, 30: 233–40.

Horowitz, M.J. (1986) Stress-response syndromes: a review of posttraumatic and adjustment disorders, *Hospital and Community Psychiatry*, 37: 241–9.

House, J.S., Kessler, R., Herzog, A.R. et al. (1991) Social stratification, age, and health, in K.W. Scheie, D. Blazer and J.S. House (eds) *Aging, Health Behaviours, and Health Outcomes*. Hillsdale, NJ: Erlbaum.

Hoven, C.W., Duarte, C.S., Lucas, C.P. et al. (2005) Psychopathology among New York City public school children 6 months after September 11, *Archives of General Psychiatry*, 62: 545–52.

Huang, T.L., Zandi, P.P., Tucker, K.L. et al. (2005) Benefits of fatty fish on dementia risk are stronger for those without APOE epsilon4, *Neurology*, 65: 1409–14.

Hubbard, R.L., Craddock, S.G., Flynn, P.M. et al. (1997) Overview of 1-year follow-up outcomes in the Drug Abuse Treatment Outcome Study (DATOS), *Psychological Addiction and Behavior*, 4: 1303–10.

Huber, S.J., Bornstein, R.A., Rammohan, K.W. et al. (1992) Magnetic resonance imaging and correlates of neuropsychological impairment in multiple sclerosis, *Journal of Neuropsychiatry and Clinical Neurosciences*, 4: 152–8.

Hughes, J.C. and Cook, C. (1997) The efficacy of disulfram – a review of outcome studies, *Addictions*, 92: 381–96.

Hunter, E. (1997) Memory loss for childhood sexual abuse: distinguishing between encoding and retrieval factors, in D. Read and D.S. Lindsay (eds) *Recollections of Trauma: Scientific Research and Clinical Practice*. New York: Plenum.

Hunter, L.C., O'Hare, A., Herron, W.J. et al. (2003) Opioid peptides and dipeptidyl peptidase in autism, *Developmental Medicine and Child Neurology*, 45: 121–8.

Huntjens, R.J., Postma, A., Woertman, L. et al. (2005) Procedural memory in dissociative identity disorder: when can inter-identity amnesia be truly established?, *Consciousness and Cognition*, 14: 377–89.

Hyman, I.E., Husband, T.H. and Billings, F.J. (1995) False memories of childhood experiences, *Applied Cognitive Psychology*, 9: 181–97.

International Molecular Genetic Study of Autism Consortium (1998) A full genome screen for autism with evidence for linkage to a region on chromosome 7q, *Human Molecular Genetics*, 7: 571–8.

Intrator, J., Hare, R., Strizke, P. et al. (1997) A brain imaging (single photon emission computerized tomography) study of semantic and affective processing in psychopaths, *Biological Psychiatry*, 42: 96–103.

Ishihara, K. and Sasa, M. (1999) Mechanism underlying the therapeutic effects of electroconvulsive therapy (ECT) on depression, *Japanese Journal of Pharmacology*, 80: 185–9.

Jacobson, N.S. and Hollon, S.D. (1996) Cognitive-behavior therapy versus pharmacotherapy: now that the jury's returned its verdict, it's time to present the rest of the evidence, *Journal of Consulting and Clinical Psychology*, 64: 74–80.

Jaffe, S.R., Moffitt, T.E., Caspi, A. et al. (2002) Differences in early childhood risk factors for juvenile-onset and adult-onset depression, *Archives of General Psychiatry*, 59: 215–22.

Jakes, S., Rhodes, J. and Turner, T. (1999) Effectiveness of cognitive therapy for delusions in routine clinical practice, *British Journal of Psychiatry*, 175: 331–5.

Jansen, A., Van den Hout, M.A. and Griez, E. (1989) Does bingeing restore bulimic's alleged 5-HT deficiency?, *Behaviour Research and Therapy*, 27: 555–60.

Janssen, P.L. (1985) Psychodynamic study of male potency disorders: an overview, *Psychotherapy and Psychosomatics*, 44: 6–17.

Jenike, M.A. (1998) Neurosurgical treatment of obsessive-compulsive disorder, *British Medical Journal*, 163 (Suppl. 35): 75–90.

Jenike, M.A., Ballantine, H.T., Martuza, R.L. et al. (1991) Cingulotomy for refractory obsessive-compulsive disorder: a long-term follow-up of 33 patients, *Archives of General Psychiatry*, 48: 548–55.

Jenkins, R., Bebbington, P., Brugha, T.S. et al. (1998) British psychiatric morbidity survey, *British Journal of Psychiatry*, 173: 4–7.

Jenkins, R.L., Lewis, G., Bebbington, P. et al. (1997) The National Psychiatric Morbidity Surveys of Great Britain: initial findings from the household survey, *Psychology and Medicine*, 27: 775–89.

Jennett, B. (1996) Epidemiology of head injury, *International Journal of Neurology, Neurosurgery and Psychiatry*, 60: 362–9.

Jennett, B., Snoek, F.J. and Bond, M.R. (1981) Disability after severe head injury: observations on the use of the Glasgow Outcome Scale, *Journal of Neurology, Neurosurgery and Psychiatry*, 44: 285–93.

Jensen, P.S., Arnold, L.E., Richters, J.E. et al. (1999) A 14-month randomized clinical trial of treatment strategies for attention-deficit/hyperactivity disorder, *Archives of General Psychiatry*, 56: 1073–86.

Jick, S.S., Dean, A.D. and Jick, H. (1995) Antidepressants and suicide, *British Medical Journal*, 310: 215–18.

Jimerson, D.C., Herzog, D.B. and Brotman, A.W. (1993) Pharmacologic approaches in the treatment of eating disorders, *Harvard Review of Psychiatry*, 1: 82–93.

Jimerson, D.C., Lesem, M.D., Kaye, W.H. et al. (1992) Low serotonin and dopamine metabolite concentrations in cerebrospinal fluid from bulimic patients with frequent bulimic episodes, *Archives of General Psychiatry*, 49: 132–8.

Johnston, M., Earll, L., Giles, M. et al. (1999) Mood as a predictor of disability and survival in patients newly diagnosed with ALS/MND, *British Journal of Health Psychology*, 4: 127–36.

Johnstone, L. (2000) *Users and Abusers of Psychiatry: A Critical Look at Psychiatric Practice*. London: Routledge.

Jones, C., Cormac, I., Mota, J. et al. (2000) Cognitive behaviour therapy for schizophrenia (Cochrane Review), *The Cochrane Library*, Issue 3. Oxford: Update Software.

Jones, M.P., Schettler, A., Olden, K. et al. (2004) Alexithymia and somatosensory amplification in functional dyspepsia, *Psychosomatics*, 45: 508–16.

Jones, P. and Cannon, M. (1998) The new epidemiology of schizophrenia, *Psychiatric Clinics of North America*, 21: 1–25.

Joseph, S., Dalgleish, T., Thrasher, S. et al. (1996) Crisis support following the Herald of Free Enterprise disaster: a longitudinal perspective, *Journal of Traumatic Stress*, 9: 833–45.

Joseph, S., Williams, R. and Yule, W. (1995) Psychosocial perspectives on posttraumatic stress, *Clinical Psychology Review*, 15: 515–44.

Jovev, M. and Jackson H.J. (2004) Early maladaptive schemas in personality disordered individuals, *Journal of Personality Disorders*, 18: 467–78.

Jung, C.G. ([1912] 1956) *Symbols of Transformation*. New York: Bollingen, no. 5. (Original edition published in 1912 as *The Psychology of the Unconscious*.)

Kabat-Zinn, J., Massion, A.O., Kristeller, J. et al. (1992) Effectiveness of a meditation-based stress reduction program in the treatment of anxiety disorders, *American Journal of Psychiatry*, 149: 936–43.

Kalyna, Z., Bezchlibnyk-Butler, J. and Jeffries, J. (eds) (2003) *Clinical Handbook of Psychotropic Drugs*. Cambridge, MA: Hogrefe and Huber.

Kamann, M.P. and Wong, B.Y. (1993) Inducing adaptive coping self-statements in children with learning disabilities through self-instruction training, *Journal of Learning Disabilities*, 26: 630–8.

Kamphuis, J.H., Emmelkamp, P.M. and Bartak, A. (2003) Individual differences in post-traumatic stress following post-intimate stalking: stalking severity and psychosocial variables, *British Journal of Clinical Psychology*, 42: 145–56.

Kanno, M., Matsumoto, M., Togashi, H. et al. (2003) Effects of repetitive transcranial magnetic stimulation on behavioral and neurochemical changes in rats during an elevated plus-maze test, *Journal of Neurological Sciences*, 211: 5–14.

Karasz, A. (2005) Cultural differences in conceptual models of depression, *Social Science and Medicine*, 60: 1625–35.

Karno, M., Golding, J.M., Sorensen, S.B. et al. (1988) The epidemiology of OCD in five US communities, *Archives of General Psychiatry*, 45: 1094–9.

Kashala, E., Tylleskar, T., Elgen, I. et al. (2005) Attention deficit and hyperactivity disorder among school children in Kinshasa, Democratic Republic of Congo, *African Health Sciences*, 5: 172–81.

Kasper, S. and Resinger, E. (2001) Panic disorder: the place of benzodiazepines and selective serotonin reuptake inhibitors, *European Neuropsychopharmacology*, 11: 307–21.

Katan, M. (1953) Mania and the pleasure principle, in P. Greenacre (ed.) *Affective Disorders*. New York: International University Press.

Kawachi, I. and Berkman, L.F. (2001) Social ties and mental health, *Journal of Urban Health*, 78: 458–67.

Kaye, W.H. (1997) Anorexia nervosa, obsessional behaviour, and serotonin, *Psychopharmacology Bulletin*, 33: 335–44.

Kaye, W.H., Frank, G.K., Bailer, U.F. et al. (2005) Serotonin alterations in anorexia and bulimia nervosa: insights from imaging studies, *Physiology and Behavior*, 85: 73–81.

Kaye, W.H., Frank, G.K. and McConaha, C. (1999) Altered dopamine activity after recovery from restricting-type anorexia nervosa, *Neuropsychopharmacology*, 21: 503–6.

Kaye, W.H., Gwirtsman, H.E., Brewerton, T.D. et al. (1988) Bingeing behaviour and plasma amino acids: a possible involvement of brain serotonin in bulimia nervosa, *Psychiatry Research*, 23: 31–43.

Kaye, W.H., Gwirtsman, H.E., Brewerton, T.D. et al. (1991) Altered serotonin activity in anorexia nervosa after long-term weight restoration. Does elevated cerebrospinal fluid 5-hydroxyindoleacetic acid level correlate with rigid and obsessive behaviour?, *Archives of General Psychiatry*, 48: 556–62.

Kaye, W.H., Klump, K.L., Frank, G.K. et al. (2001a) Anorexia and bulimia nervosa, *Annual Review of Medicine*, 51: 299–313.

Kaye, W.H., Nagata, T., Weltzin, T.E. et al. (2001b) Double-blind placebo-controlled administration of fluoxetine in restricting- and restricting-purging-type anorexia nervosa, *Biological Psychiatry*, 49: 644–52.

Kaye, W.H. and Weltzin, T.E. (1991) Serotonin activity in anorexia and bulimia nervosa: relationship to the modulation of feeding and mood, *Journal of Clinical Psychiatry*, 52 (Suppl.): 41–8.

Keane, T.M., Fairbank, J.A., Caddell, J.M. et al. (1989) Implosive (flooding) therapy reduces the symptoms of PTSD in Vietnam combat veterans, *Behavior Therapy*, 20: 245–60.

Keel, P.K., Klump, K.L., Miller, K.B. et al. (2005) Shared transmission of eating disorders and anxiety disorders, *International Journal of Eating Disorders*, 38: 99–105.

Keesey, R.E. (1986) Set-point theory of obesity, in K.D. Brownell and J.P. Foreyt (eds) *Handbook of Eating Disorders*. New York: Basic Books.

Keesey, R.E. and Corbett, S.W. (1984) Metabolic defense of the body weight set-point, *Research Publications: Association of Research in Nervous and Mental Disease*, 62: 87–96.

Keller, M.B., Klerman, G.L., Lavori, P.W. et al. (1984) Long-term outcome of episodes of major depression: clinical and public health significance, *Journal of the American Medical Association*, 252: 788–92.

Kellett, S. (2005) The treatment of dissociative identity disorder with cognitive analytic therapy: experimental evidence of sudden gains, *Journal of Trauma and Dissociation*, 6: 55–81.

Kelly, K.A. (1993) Multiple personality disorders: treatment coordination in a partial hospital setting, *Bulletin of the Menninger Clinic*, 57: 390–8.

Kemp, R., Kirov, G., Everitt, B, et al (1998) Randomised controlled trial of compliance therapy: 18-month follow-up, *British Journal of Psychiatry*, 172: 413–19.

Kendler, K.S., Jacobson, K.C., Myers, J. et al. (2002) Sex differences in genetic and environmental risk factors for irrational fears and phobias, *Psychological Medicine*, 32: 209–17.

Kendler, K.S., MacLean, C., Neale, M. et al. (1991) The genetic epidemiology of bulimia nervosa, *American Journal of Psychiatry*, 148: 1627–37.

Kendler, K.S., Neale, M.C., Kessler, R.C. et al. (1993) Panic disorder in women: a population-based twin study, *Psychological Medicine*, 40: 397–406.

Kent, G. (1997) Dental phobias, in G.C.L. Davey (ed.) *Phobias: A Handbook of Theory, Research, and Treatment*. Chichester: Wiley.

Kenworthy, T., Adams, C.E., Bilby, C. et al. (2004) Psychological interventions for those who have sexually offended or are at risk of offending, *Cochrane Database of Systematic Reviews*, Issue 1.

Kernberg, O.F. (1985) *Borderline Conditions and Pathological Narcissism*. Northvale, NJ: Jason Aronson.

Kerns, A., Eso, K., Thomson, J. et al. (1999) Investigation of a direct intervention for improving attention in young children with ADHD, *Developmental Neuropsychology*, 16: 273–95.

Kerr, T., Tyndall, M., Li, K. et al. (2005) Safer injection facility use and syringe sharing in injection drug users, *Lancet*, 366: 316–18.

Kessler, R.C., McGonagle, K.A., Zhao, S. et al (1994) Lifetime and 12-month prevalence of DSM-III-R psychiatric disorders in the United States. Results from the National Comorbidity Survey, *Archives of General Psychiatry*, 51: 8–19.

Kessler, R.C., Sonnega, A., Bromet, E. et al. (1995) Posttraumatic stress disorder in the national comorbidity survey, *Archives of General Psychiatry*, 52: 1048–60.

Kety, S.S., Rosenthal, D., Wender, P.H. et al. (1975) Mental illness in the biological and adoptive families of adopted individuals who become schizophrenic: a preliminary report based on psychiatric interviews, in R.R. Fieve, D. Rosenthal and H. Brill (eds) *Genetic Research in Psychiatry*. Baltimore, MD: Johns Hopkins University Press.

Kiehl, K.A., Smith, A.M., Hare, R.D. et al. (2001) Limbic abnormalities in affective processing by criminal psychopaths as revealed by functional magnetic resonance imaging, *Biological Psychiatry*, 50: 677–84.

Kilic, C., Rezaki, M., Ustun, T.B. et al. (1994) Pathways to psychiatric care in Ankara, *Social Psychiatry and Psychiatric Epidemiology*, 29: 131–6.

Kinderman, P., Prince, S., Waller, G. et al. (2003) Self-discrepancies, attentional bias and persecutory delusions, *British Journal of Clinical Psychology*, 42: 1–12.

Kirkpatrick, D.R. (1984) Age, gender, and patterns of common intense fears among adults, *Behaviour Research and Therapy*, 22: 141–50.

Kirmayer, L.J. (1991) The place of culture in psychiatric nosology: taijin kyofusho and DSM-III-R, *The Journal of Nervous and Mental Disease*, 179: 19–28.

Kirmayer, L.J., Groleau, D., Looper, K.J. et al. (2004) Explaining medically unexplained symptoms, *Canadian Journal of Psychiatry*, 49: 663–72.

Kirmayer, L.J., Robbins, J.M. and Paris, J. (1994) Somatoform disorders: personality and social matrix of somatic disorder, *Journal of Abnormal Psychology*, 103: 125–36.

Klein, M. (1927) The psychological principles of infant analysis, *International Journal of Psychoanalysis*, 8: 25–37.

Kleindienst, N., Engel, R.R. and Greil, W. (2005) Psychosocial and demographic factors associated with response to prophylactic lithium: a systematic review for bipolar disorders, *Psychological Medicine*, 35: 1685–94.

Kleinman, A.M. (1977) Depression, somatization and the 'new cross-cultural psychiatry', *Social Science and Medicine*, 11: 3–10.

Kleinman, A. (1988) *Rethinking Psychiatry*. New York: Macmillan.

Kluft, R.P. (1994) Multiple personality disorder: observations on the etiology, natural history, recognition, and resolution of a long-neglected condition, in R. Klein and B.K. Doane (eds) *Psychological Concepts and Dissociative Disorders*. Hillsdale, NJ: Erlbaum.

Kluft, R.P. (1999) An overview of the psychotherapy of dissociative identity disorder, *American Journal of Psychotherapy*, 53: 289–319.

Klump, K.L., Miller, K.B., Keel, P.K. et al. (2001) Genetic and environmental influences on anorexia nervosa syndromes in a population-based twin sample, *Psychological Medicine*, 31: 737–40.

Knight, B.G., Lutzsky, S.M. and Macofsky-Urban, F. (1992) A meta-analytic review of interventions for care-giver distress: recommendations for future research, *Gerontologist*, 33: 475–8.

Knivsberg, A.M., Reichelt, K.L., Høien, T. et al. (1998) Parents' observations after one year of dietary intervention for children with autistic syndromes, *Psychobiology of Autism: Current Research and Practice*, 13–24.

Koegel, R.L., O'Dell, M.C. and Dunlap, G. (1988) Producing speech use in nonverbal autistic children by reinforcing attempts, *Journal of Autism and Developmental Disorders*, 18: 525–38.

Koegel, R.L., Koegel, L.K. and McNerney, E.K. (2001) Pivotal areas in intervention for autism, *Journal of Clinical Child Psychology*, 30: 19–32.

Korten, A.E., Jorm, A.F., Henderson, A.S. et al. (1993) Assessing the risk of Alzheimer's disease in first-degree relatives of Alzheimer's disease cases, *Psychological Medicine*, 23: 915–23.

Kovach, C. (1990) Promise and problems in reminiscence research, *Journal of Gerontological Nursing*, 16: 10–14.

Kownacki, R.J. and Shadish, W.R. (1999) Does Alcoholics Anonymous work? The results from a meta-analysis of controlled experiments, *Substance Use and Misuse*, 34: 1897–916.

Kraepelin, E. ([1883] 1981) *Clinical Psychiatry* (trans. A.R. Diefendorf). Delmar, NY: Scholar's Facsimiles and Reprints.

Kraus, L., Augustan, R., Frischer, M. et al. (2003) Estimating prevalence of problem drug use at national level in countries of the European Union and Norway, *Addiction*, 98: 471–85.

Kringlen, E. (1993) Genes and environment in mental illness: perspectives and ideas for future research, *Acta Psychiatrica Scandinavica*, 370: 79–84.

Kroenke, K. and Price, R.K. (1993) Symptoms in the community: prevalence, classification, and psychiatric comorbidity, *Archives Internal Medicine*, 153: 2474–80

Krueger, T.H., Schedlowski, M. and Meyer, G. (2005) Cortisol and heart rate measures during casino gambling in relation to impulsivity, *Neuropsychobiology*, 52: 206–11.

Kruijver, F.P., Zhou, J.N., Pool, C.W. et al. (2000) Male-to-female transsexuals have female neuron numbers in a limbic nucleus, *Journal of Clinical Endocrinology and Metabolism*, 85: 2034–41.

Krupp, L.B., Christodoulou, C., Melville, P. et al. (2004) Donepezil improved memory in multiple sclerosis in a randomized clinical trial, *Neurology*, 63: 1579–85.

Kua, E.H., Chew, P.H. and Ko, S.M. (1993) Spirit possession and healing among Chinese psychiatric patients, *Acta Psychiatrica Scandinavica*, 88: 447–50.

Kulka, R.A., Schlenger, W.E., Fairbank, J.A. et al. (1990) *Trauma and the Vietnam War Generation: Report of Findings from the National Vietnam Veterans Readjustment Study*. New York: Brunner/Mazel.

Kwon, P. and Laurenceau, J-P. (2002) A longitudinal study of the hopelessness theory of depression: testing the diathesis-stress model within a differential reactivity and exposure framework, *Journal of Clinical Psychology*, 58: 1305–21.

Laakso, M.P., Vaurio, O., Koivisto, E. et al. (2001) Psychopathy and the posterior hippocampus, *Behavioural Brain Research*, 118: 187–93.

Lackner, J.M., Gudleski, G.D. and Blanchard, E.B. (2004) Beyond abuse: the association among parenting style, abdominal pain, and somatization in IBS patients, *Behaviour Research and Therapy*, 42: 41–56.

Ladouceur, R., Jacques, C., Ferland, F. et al. (1999) Prevalence of problem gambling: a replication study 7 years later, *Canadian Journal of Psychiatry*, 44: 802–4.

Ladouceur, R., Sylvain, C., Boutin, C. et al. (2001) Cognitive treatment of pathological gambling, *Journal of Nervous and Mental Disease*, 189: 774–80.

Ladouceur, R., Sylvain, C., Boutin, C. et al. (2003) Group therapy for pathological gamblers: a cognitive approach, *Behavioural Research and Therapy*, 41: 87–96.

Lai, C.K., Chi, I. and Kayser-Jones, J. (2004) A randomized controlled trial of a specific reminiscence approach to promote the well-being of nursing home residents with dementia, *International Psychogeriatrics*, 16: 33–49.

Lai, D.W. (2004) Impact of culture on depressive symptoms of elderly Chinese immigrants, *Canadian Journal of Psychiatry*, 49: 820–7.

Lam, D.H., Watkins, E.R., Hayward, P. et al. (2003) A randomized controlled study of cognitive therapy for relapse prevention for bipolar affective disorder, *Archives of General Psychiatry*, 60: 145–52.

Langstrom, N. and Zucker, K.J. (2005) Transvestic fetishism in the general population: prevalence and correlates, *Journal of Sexual and Marital Therapy*, 31: 87–95.

Larcombe, N.A. and Wilson, P.H. (1984) An evaluation of cognitive-behaviour therapy for depression in patients with multiple sclerosis, *British Journal of Psychiatry*, 145: 366–71.

Latimer, P.R. (1981) Irritable bowel syndrome: a behavioral model, *Behaviour Research and Therapy*, 19: 475–83.

Laumann, E.O., Paik, A. and Rosen, R. (1999) Sexual dysfunction in the United States: prevalence and predictors, *Journal of the American Medical Association*, 21: 537–44.

Lawford, B.R., Young, R., Rowell, J.A. et al. (1997) D2 dopamine receptor A1 allele with alcoholism: medical severity of alcoholism and type of controls, *Biological Psychiatry*, 41: 386–93.

Laws, D.R. and Marshall, W.L. (1991) Masturbatory reconditioning with sexual deviates: an evaluative review, *Advances in Behavior Research and Therapy*, 13: 13–25.

Lechtenberg, R. (1988) *Multiple Sclerosis Fact Book*. Philadelphia, PA: F.A. Davis.

Leff, J., Sartorius, N., Jablensky, A. et al. (1992) The International Pilot Study of Schizophrenia: five-year follow-up findings, *Psychological Medicine*, 22: 131–45.

Leff, J. and Vaughn, C. (1985) *Expressed Emotions in Families: Its Significance for Mental Illness*. New York: Guilford.

Lengua, L.J., Long, A.C., Smith, K.I. et al. (2005) Pre-attack symptomatology and temperament as predictors of children's responses to the September 11 terrorist attacks, *Journal of Child Psychology and Psychiatry*, 46: 631–45.

Lenox, R.H., McNamara, R.F., Papke, R.L. et al. (1998) Neurobiology of lithium: an update, *Journal of Clinical Psychiatry*, 59 (Suppl. 6): 37–47.

Leskin, G.A., Kaloupek, D.G. and Keane, T.M. (1998) Treatment for traumatic memories: review and recommendations, *Clinical Psychology Review*, 18: 983–1002.

Letonoff, E.J., Williams, T.R., Sidhu, K.S. (2002) Hysterical paralysis: a report of three cases and a review of the literature, *Spine*, 27: E441–5.

Levin, H.S. (1993) Neurobehavioral sequelae of closed head injury, in P.R. Cooper (ed.) *Head Injury*. Baltimore, MD: Williams and Wilkins.

Levinson, D.F. (2005) The genetics of depression: a review, *Biological Psychiatry*, in press.

Lewinsohn, P.M. (1988) A prospective study of risk factors for unipolar depression, *Journal of Abnormal Psychology*, 97: 251–84.

Lewinsohn, P.M., Youngren, M.A. and Grosscup, S.J. (1979) Reinforcement and depression, in A. Depue (ed.) *The Psychobiology of the Depressive Disorders*. New York: Academic Press.

Lewy, A.J., Bauer, V.K. and Cutler, N.L. (1998) Morning vs evening light treatment of patients with winter depression, *Archives of General Psychiatry*, 55: 890–6.

Ley, P. (1997) Compliance among patients, in A. Baum, S. Newman, J. Weinman et al. (eds) *Cambridge Handbook of Psychology, Health and Medicine*. Cambridge: Cambridge University Press.

Liau, A.K., Barriga, A.Q. and Gibbs, J.C. (1998) Relations between self-serving cognitive distortions and overt vs. covert antisocial behavior in adolescents, *Aggressive Behavior*, 24: 335–46.

Lidbeck, J. (2003) Group therapy for somatization disorders in primary care: maintenance of treatment goals of short cognitive-behavioural treatment one-and-a-half-year follow-up, *Acta Psychiatrica Scandinavica*, 107: 449–56.

Liddle, P., Carpenter, W.T. and Crow, T. (1994) Syndromes of schizophrenia: classic literature, *British Journal of Psychiatry*, 165: 721–7.

Lieberman, J.A., Kinon, B.J. and Loebel, A.D. (1990) Dopaminergic mechanisms in idiopathic and drug-induced psychoses, *Schizophrenia Bulletin*, 16: 97–109.

Lilienfeld, S.O., Lynn, S.J., Kirsch, I. et al. (1999) Dissociative identity disorder and the sociocognitive model: recalling the lessons of the past, *Psychological Bulletin*, 125: 507–23.

Lin, K.M., Inui, T.S., Kleinman, A.M. et al. (1982) Sociocultural determinants of the help-seeking behavior of patients with mental illness, *Journal of Nervous and Mental Disorders*, 170: 78–85.

Lindauer, R.J., Vlieger, E.J., Jalink, M., et al. (2005) Effects of psychotherapy on hippocampal volume in out-patients with post-traumatic stress disorder: a MRI investigation, *Psychological Medicine*, 35: 1421–31.

Linde, K. and Mulrow, C.D. (2002) St John's wort for depression, *Cochrane Database of Systematic Reviews*, Issue 1.

Lindsay, S. and Jackson, C. (1993) Fear of routine dental treatment in adults: its nature and management, *Psychology and Health*, 8: 135–53.

Linehan, M.M., Heard, H.L. and Armstrong, H.E. (1993) Naturalistic follow-up of a behavioral treatment for chronically parasuicidal borderline patients, *Archives of General Psychiatry*, 50: 971–4.

Lingford-Hughes, A. (2005) Human brain imaging and substance abuse, *Current Opinion in Pharmacology*, 5: 42–6.

Lingjaerde, O., Ahlfors, U.G., Bech, P. et al. (1987) The UKU side effect rating scale: a new comprehensive rating scale for psychotropic drugs and a cross-sectional study of side effects in neuroleptic-treated patients, *Acta Psychiatrica Scandinavica*, 334: 1–100.

Lipinski, J.F., Mallya, G., Zimmerman, P. et al. (1989) Fluoxetine-induced akathisia: clinical and theoretical implications, *Journal of Clinical Psychiatry*, 59: 339–42.

Lipsanen, T., Saarijarvi, S. and Lauerma, H. (2004) Exploring the relations between depression, somatization, dissociation and alexithymia – overlapping or independent constructs?, *Psychopathology*, 37: 200–6.

Lipton, A.A. and Simon, F.S. (1985) Psychiatric diagnosis in a state hospital: Manhattan state revisited, *Hospital and Community Psychiatry*, 36: 368–73.

Lisanby, S.H., Maddox, J.H., Prudic, J. et al. (2000) The effects of electroconvulsive therapy on memory of autobiographical and public events, *Archives of General Psychiatry*, 57: 581–90.

Lloyd, G.G. and Lishman, W.A. (1975) Effect of depression on the speed of recall of pleasant and unpleasant experiences, *Psychological Medicine*, 5: 173–80.

Loebel, J.P., Loebel, J.S., Dager, S.R. et al. (1991) Anticipation of nursing home placement may be a precipitant of suicide among the elderly, *Journal of the American Geriatric Society*, 39: 407–8.

Loewe, B., Zipfel, S., Buchholz, C. et al. (2001) Long-term outcome of anorexia nervosa in a prospective 21-year follow-up study, *Psychological Medicine*, 31: 881–90.

Loftus, E.F. and Coan, D. (1998) The construction of childhood memories, in D. Peters (ed.) *The Child Witness in Context: Cognitive, Social, and Legal Perspectives*. New York: Kluwer.

Loftus, E.F. and Ketcham, K. (1994) *The Myth of Repressed Memory*. New York: St Martin's Press.

Longabaugh, R. and Morgenstern, J. (2000) Cognitive-behavioral coping skills therapy for alcohol dependence: current status and future directions, *Alcohol Research and Health*, 23: 78–87.

Lopez, V.A. and Emmer, E.T. (2002) Influences of beliefs and values on male adolescents' decision to commit violent offenses, *Psychology of Men and Masculinity*, 3: 28–40.

Loranger, A.W., Sartorius, N., Andreoli, A. et al. (1994) The International Personality Disorders Examination: the World Health Organisation/Alcohol, Drug Abuse and Mental Health Administration international study of personality disorders, *Archives of General Psychiatry*, 51: 215–23.

Lovaas, O.I. (1987) Behavioral treatment and normal educational and intellectual functioning in young autistic children, *Journal of Consulting and Clinical Psychology*, 55: 3–9.

Lucock, M.P., Morley, S., White, C. et al. (1997) Responses of consecutive patients to reassurance after gastroscopy: results of self-administered questionnaire survey, *British Medical Journal*, 315: 572–5.

Lundberg, U., de Chateau, P., Weinberg, J. et al. (1981) Catecholamine and cortisol excretion patterns in three-year-old children and their parents, *Journal of Human Stress*, 7: 3–11.

Lyon, H.M., Startup, M. and Bentall, R.P. (1999) Social cognition and the manic defense: attributions, selective attention, and self-schema in bipolar affective disorder, *Journal of Abnormal Psychology*, 108: 273–82.

Lynam, D.R., Caspi, A., Moffitt, T.E. et al. (2005) Adolescent psychopathy and the big five: results from two samples, *Journal of Abnormal Child Psychology*, 33: 431–43.

Lyon-Caen, O., Jouvent, R., Hauser, S. et al. (1986) Cognitive function in recent onset demyelinating diseases, *Archives of Neurology*, 43: 1138–41.

McBride, P.A., Anderson, G.M. and Shapiro, T. (1996) Autism research: bringing together approaches to pull apart the disorder, *Archives of General Psychiatry*, 53: 980–3.

McCabe, R., Leudar, I. and Antaki, C. (2004) Do people with schizophrenia display theory of mind deficits in clinical interactions?, *Psychological Medicine*, 34: 401–12.

McCall, W.V. (2001) Electroconvulsive therapy in the era of modern psychopharmacology, *International Journal of Neuropsychopharmacology*, 4: 315–24.

McClure, G.M. (2000) Changes in suicide in England and Wales, 1960–1997, *British Journal of Psychiatry*, 176: 64–7.

McConaghy, N., Armstrong, M.S., Blaszczynski, A. et al. (1983) Controlled comparison of aversive therapy and imaginal desensitization in compulsive gambling, *British Journal of Psychiatry*, 142: 366–72.

McConaghy, N., Blaszczynski, A. and Frankova, A. (1991) Comparison of imaginal desensitization with other behavioural treatments of pathological gambling: a two to nine year follow-up, *British Journal of Psychiatry*, 159: 390–3.

McDougle, C.J., Naylor, S.T., Volkmar, F.R. et al. (1994) A double-blind, placebo-controlled investigation of fluvoxamine in adults with autism, *Society for Neuroscience Abstracts*, 20: 396.

McDowell, I. (2001) Alzheimer's disease: insights from epidemiology, *Aging*, 13: 143–62.

McGhie, A. and Chapman, J. (1961) Disorders of attention and perception in early schizophrenia, *British Journal of Medical Psychology*, 34: 103–16.

McGorry, P.D., Yung, A.R., Phillips, L.J. et al. (2002) Randomized controlled trial of interventions designed to reduce the risk of progression to first-episode psychosis in a clinical sample with subthreshold symptoms, *Archives of General Psychiatry*, 59: 921–8.

McGuffin, P., Katz, R., Watkins, S. et al. (1996) A hospital-based twin register of the heritability of DSM-IV unipolar depression, *Archives of General Psychiatry*, 53: 129–36.

McGuire, P.K. Silbersweig, D.A. Wright, I. et al. (1996) The neural correlates of inner speech and auditory verbal imagery in schizophrenia: relationship to auditory verbal hallucinations, *British Journal of Psychiatry*, 169: 148–59.

McIntosh, V.W., Jordan, J., Carter, F.A. et al. (2005) Three psychotherapies for anorexia nervosa: a randomized, controlled trial, *American Journal of Psychiatry*, 162: 741–7.

McKay, D., Todaro, J., Neziroglu, F. et al. (1997) Body dysmorphic disorder: a preliminary evaluation of treatment and maintenance using exposure with response prevention, *Behaviour Research and Therapy*, 35: 67–70.

McKenzie, S.J., Williamson, D.A. and Cubic, B.A. (1993) Stable and reactive body image disturbances in bulimia nervosa, *Behavior Therapy*, 24: 195–207.

McLean, P.D., Whittal, M.L., Thordarson, D.S. et al. (2001) Cognitive versus behavior therapy in the group treatment of obsessive-compulsive disorder, *Journal of Consulting and Clinical Psychology*, 69: 205–14.

McMahon, A. and Rhudick, P. (1964) Reminiscing, *Archives of General Psychiatry*, 10: 292–8.

Madden, P.A.F., Heath, A.C., Rosenthal, N.E. et al. (1996) Seasonal changes in mood and behavior: the role of genetic factors, *Archives of General Psychiatry*, 53: 47–55.

Maes, S., Verhoeven, C., Kittel, F. et al. (1998) Effects of the Brabantia-project, a Dutch wellness-health programme at the worksite, *American Journal of Public Health*, 88: 1037–41.

Maffei, C., Fossati, A., Agostini, I., Barraco, A. et al. (1997) Interrater reliability and internal consistency of the Structured Clinical Interview for Axis II personality disorders (SCID-II), version 2, *Journal of Personality Disorders*, 11: 279–84.

Magnusson, A. and Partonen, T. (2005) The diagnosis, symptomatology, and epidemiology of seasonal affective disorder, *CNS Spectrum*, 10: 625–34.

Mahmood, T. and Silverstone, T. (2001) Serotonin and bipolar disorder, *Journal of Affective Disorders*, 66: 1–11.

Malizia, A.L. (2000) Neurosurgery for psychiatric disorders, in M.G. Gelder, J.J. Lopez-Ibor Jr and N.C. Andreasen (eds) *New Oxford Textbook of Psychiatry*. Oxford: Oxford University Press.

Malizia, A.L. and Bridges, P.K. (1991) The management of treatment resistant affective disorders: clinical perspectives, *Journal of Psychopharmacology*, 6: 145–55, 172–5.

Mannuzza, S. and Klein, R.G. (2000) Long-term prognosis in attention-deficit/hyperactivity disorder, *Child and Adolescent Psychiatric Clinics of North America*, 9: 711–26.

Marjoram, D., Tansley, H. Miller, P. et al. (2005) A Theory of Mind investigation into the appreciation of visual jokes in schizophrenia, *BMC Psychiatry*, 5: 12–20.

Marks, I. (1977) Phobias and obsessions: clinical phenomena in search of laboratory models, in J.D. Maser and M.E.P. Seligman (eds) *Psychopathology: Experimental Models*. San Francisco: Freeman.

Marks, I., Gelder, M. and Bancroft, J. (1970) Sexual deviants two years after electric shock aversion, *British Journal of Psychiatry*, 117: 173–85.

Marks, I., Green, R. and Mataix-Cols, D. (2000) Adult gender identity disorder can remit, *Comprehensive Psychiatry*, 41: 273–5.

Marks, I., Lovell, K., Noshirvani, H. et al. (1996) Treatment of post-traumatic stress disorder by exposure and/or cognition restructuring, *Archives of General Psychiatry*, 55: 317–25.

Marmar, C.R. (1991) Brief dynamic psychotherapy for post-traumatic stress disorder, *Psychiatric Annals*, 21: 405–14.

Marmot, M.G., Smith, G.D., Stansfeld, S. et al. (1991) Health inequalities among British civil servants: the Whitehall II study, *Lancet*, 337: 1387–93.

Maron, E. and Shlik, J. (2005) Serotonin function in panic disorder: important, but why? *Neuropsychopharmacology*, Aug. 31.

Marques, J.K., Nelson, C., Alaarcon, J-M. and Day, D.M. (2000) Preventing relapse in sex offenders: what we learned from SOTEP's experimental treatment program, in D.R. Laws, S.M. Hudson and T. Ward (eds) *Remaking Relapse Prevention with Sex Offenders: A Sourcebook*. Thousand Oaks, CA: Sage.

Marsch, L.A., Bickel, W.K., Badger, G.J. et al. (2005) Comparison of pharmacological treatments for opioid-dependent adolescents: a randomized controlled trial, *Archives of General Psychiatry*, 62: 1157–64.

Marshall, J.C., Halligan, P.W., Fink, G.R., et al. (1997) The functional anatomy of a hysterical paralysis, *Cognition*, 64: B1–8.

Marshall, W.L. (1994) Treatment effects on denial and minimization in incarcerated sex offenders, *Behaviour Research and Therapy*, 32: 559–64.

Maslow, A.H. (1970) *Motivation and Personality*, New York: Harper and Row.

Masters, W.H. and Johnson, V.E. (1970) *Human Sexual Inadequacy*. Boston, MA: Little, Brown.

Matano, R.A., Futa, K.T., Wanat, S.F. et al. (2000) The Employee Stress and Alcohol Project: the development of a computer-based alcohol abuse prevention program for employees, *Journal of Behavioral Health Service Research*, 27: 152–65.

Mayou, R., Bryant, B. and Ehlers, A. (2001) Prediction of psychological outcomes one year after a motor vehicle accident, *American Journal of Psychiatry*, 158: 1231–8.

Meehl, P.E. (1990) Towards an integrated theory of schizotaxia, schizotypy, and schizophrenia, *Journal of Personality Disorders*, 4: 1–99.

Meichenbaum, D. (1985) *Stress Inoculation Training*. New York: Pergamon.

Meltzer, H.Y. (1998) Suicide in schizophrenia: risk factors and clozapine treatment, *Archives of General Psychiatry*, 52: 200–2.

Menzies, R.G. and Clarke, J.C. (1995) The etiology of phobias: a non-associative account, *Clinical Psychology Review*, 15: 23–48.

Merckelbach, H. and de Jong, P.J. (1999) Evolutionary models of phobias. In G.C.L. Davey (ed.) *Phobias: A Handbook of Theory, Research, and Treatment*. Chichester: Wiley.

Merckelbach, H., Devilly, G.J. and Rassin, E. (2002) Alters in dissociative identity disorder: metaphors or genuine entities?, *Clinical Psychology Review*, 22: 481–97.

Merskey, H. (1992) The manufacture of personalities: the production of multiple personality disorder, *British Journal of Psychiatry*, 160: 327–40.

Meyer, R.E. (1995) Biology of psychoactive substance dependence disorders: opiates, cocaine, ethanol, in A.F. Schatzberg and C.B. Nemeroff (eds) *The American Psychiatric Press Handbook of Psychopharmacology*. Washington, DC: American Psychiatric Press.

Meyer-Bahlung, H. (1979) Sex hormones and female homosexuality: a critical examination, *Archives of Sexual Behavior*, 8: 101–19.

Mihailides, S., Devilly, G.J. and Ward, T. (2004) Implicit cognitive distortions and sexual offending, *Sexual Abuse: A Journal of Research and Treatment*, 16: 333–50.

Miklowitz, D.J. (2004) The role of family systems in severe and recurrent psychiatric disorders: a developmental psychopathology view, *Developmental Psychopathology*, 16: 667–88.

Miklowitz, D.J., Simponeau, T.L., George, E.L. et al. (2003) Family-focused treatment of bipolar disorder: 1-year effects of a psychoeducational program in conjunction with pharmacotherapy, *Biological Psychiatry*, 48: 582–92.

Miles, C., Green, R., Sanders, G. et al. (1998) Estrogen and memory in a transsexual population, *Hormones and Behavior*, 34: 199–208.

Miller, E. (1999) Conversion hysteria: is it a viable concept?, in P. Halligan (ed.) *Conversion Hysteria: Towards a Neuropsychological Account*. Hove: Psychology Press.

Miller, W.R. and Rollnick, S. (2002) *Motivational Interviewing*, 2nd edn. New York: Guilford.

Millward, C., Ferriter, M., Calver, S. et al. (2004) Gluten- and casein-free diets for autistic spectrum disorder, *Cochrane Database of Systematic Reviews*, Issue 2.

Minden, S.L. and Schiffer, R.B. (1990) Affective disorders in multiple sclerosis: review and recommendations for clinical research, *Archives of Neurology*, 47: 98–104.

Minuchin, S. (1974) *Families and Family Therapy*. London: Tavistock.

Minuchin, S., Rosman, B. and Baker, L. (1978) *Psychosomatic Families: Anorexia Nervosa in Context*. Cambridge, MA: Harvard University Press.

Miranda, J. and Gross, J.J. (1997) Cognitive vulnerability depression, and the mood-state dependent hypothesis: is it out of sight out of mind?, *Cognition and Emotion*, 11: 585–605.

Modestin, J. (1992) Multiple personality disorder in Switzerland, *American Journal of Psychiatry*, 149: 88–92.

Modestin, J., Furrer, R. and Malti, T. (2005) Different traumatic experiences are associated with different pathologies, *Psychiatry Quarterly*, 76: 19–32.

Moene, F.C., Spinhoven, P., Hoogduin, K.A. and Van Dyck, R. (2003) A randomized controlled clinical trial of a hypnosis-based treatment for patients with conversion disorder, motor type, *International Journal of Clinical and Experimental Hypnosis*, 51: 29–50.

Mohr, D.C. and Goodkin, D.E. (1999) Treatment of depression in multiple sclerosis: review and meta-analysis, *Clinical Psychology: Science and Practice*, 6: 1–9.

Mohr, D.C., Goodkin, D.E., Bacchetti, P. et al. (2000a) Psychological stress and the subsequent appearance of new brain MRI lesions in MS, *Neurology*, 55: 55–61.

Mohr, D.C., Likosky, W., Bertagnolli, A. et al. (2000b) Telephone-administered cognitive-behavioral therapy for the treatment of depressive symptoms in multiple sclerosis, *Journal of Consulting and Clinical Psychology*, 68: 356–61.

Mondraty, N., Birmingham, C.L., Touyz, S. et al. (2005) Randomized controlled trial of olanzapine in the treatment of cognitions in anorexia nervosa, *Australasian Psychiatry: Bulletin of Royal Australian and New Zealand College of Psychiatrists*, 13: 72–5.

Montgomery, S.A., Dufour, H., Brion, S. et al. (1993) Guidelines for treatment of depressive illness with antidepressants, *Journal of Psychopharmacology*, 7: 19–23.

Monti, P.M., Colby, S.M., Barnett, N.P. et al. (1999) Brief intervention for harm reduction with alcohol-positive older adolescents in a hospital emergency department, *Journal of Consulting and Clinical Psychology*, 67: 989–94.

Moore, M.L., Eichner, S.F., Jones, J.R. (2004) Treating functional impairment of autism with selective serotonin-reuptake inhibitors, *Annals of Pharmacotherapy*, 38: 1515–19.

Moos, R.H., Cronkite, R.C. and Moos, B.S. (1998) Family and extrafamily resources and the 10-year course of treated depression, *Journal of Abnormal Psychology*, 107: 450–60.

Morton, J., Andrews, B., Bekerian, D. et al. (1995) *Recovered Memories*. Leiccster: British Psychological Society.

Morey, L.C. (1988) Personality disorders in DSM-III and DSM-IIIR: convergence, coverage, and internal consistency, *American Journal of Psychiatry*, 145: 573–7.

Morimoto, T., Hashimoto, K., Yasumatsu, H. et al. (2002) Neuropharmacological profile of a novel potential atypical antipsychotic drug Y-931 (8-fluoro-12-(4-methylpiperazin-1-yl)-6H-[1]benzothieno[2,3-b][1,5] benzodiazepine maleate), *Neuropsychopharmacology*, 26: 456–67.

Mottronb, J.R.L., Friesenc, C.K. et al. (2005) Eyes are special but not for everyone: the case of autism, *Cognitive Brain Research*, 24; 715–18.

Mowrer, O.H. (1947) On the dual nature of learning: a reinterpretation of 'conditioning' and 'problem-solving', *Harvard Education Review*, 17: 102–48.

Muhle, R., Trentacoste, S.V. and Rapin, I. (2004) The genetics of autism, *Pediatrics*, 113: 472–86.

Murphy, K. and Barkley, R.A. (1996) Attention deficit hyperactivity disorder adults: comorbidities and adaptive impairments, *Comprehensive Psychiatry*, 37: 393–401.

Murphy, P.M., Cramer, D. and Lillie, F.J. (1984) The relationship between curative factors perceived by patients in their psychotherapy and treatment outcome: an exploratory study, *British Journal of Medical Psychology*, 57: 187–92.

Murray, E.J. and Foote, F. (1979) The origins of fear of snakes, *Behaviour Research and Therapy*, 17: 489–93.

Murray, J.B. (2000) Psychological profiles of pedophiles and child molesters, *Journal of Psychology*, 134: 211–24.

Myers, E.D. and Branthwaite, A. (1992) Out-patient compliance with antidepressant medication, *British Journal of Psychiatry*, 160: 83–6.

Najavitis, L.M., Gastfriend, D.R., Barber, J.P. et al. (1998) Cocaine dependence with and without PTSD among subjects in the National Institute on Drug Abuse collaboration cocaine treatment study, *American Journal of Psychiatry*, 155: 214–19.

Nakao, M., Myers, P., Fricchione, G. et al. (2001) Somatization and symptom reduction through a behavioral medicine intervention in a mind/body medicine clinic, *Behavioral Medicine*, 26: 169–76.

Naranjo, C.A. and Bremner, K.E. (1993) Behavioural correlates of alcohol intoxication, *Addiction*, 88: 25–35.

National Institutes of Health (1985) Electroconvulsive therapy, *NIH Consensus Statement Online*, 5: 1–23.

Nazroo, J.Y. (1998) *Genetic, Cultural or Socio-economic Vulnerability? Explaining Ethnic Inequalities in Health*. Oxford: Blackwell.

Neal, M. and Briggs, M. (2003) Validation therapy for dementia, *Cochrane Database of Systematic Reviews*, Issue 3.

Neisser, U. and Harsch, N. (1992) Phantom flashbulbs: false recollections of hearing the news about Challenger, in E. Winograd and U. Neisser (eds) *Affect and Accuracy in Recall: Studies in Flashbulb Memories.* Cambridge: Cambridge University Press.

Neitzert, C.S., Davis, C. and Kennedy, S.H. (1997) Personality factors related to the prevalence of somatic symptoms and medical complaints in a healthy student population, *British Journal of Medical Psychology*, 70: 93–101.

Neumeister, A., Praschak-Rieder, N., Hesselmann, B. et al. (1997) Rapid tryptophan depletion in drug-free depressed patients with seasonal affective disorder, *American Journal of Psychiatry*, 154: 1153–5.

New, A.S., Buchsbaum, M.S., Hazlett, E.A. et al. (2004) Fluoxetine increases relative metabolic rate in prefrontal cortex in impulsive aggression, *Psychopharmacology (Berl)*, 176: 451–8.

New, A.S., Hazlett, E.A., Buchsbaum, M.S. et al. (2003) m-CPP PET and impulsive aggression in borderline personality disorder, *Biological Psychiatry*, 53: S104.

Newcomb, M.D. (1985) The role of perceived relative parent personality in the development of heterosexuals, homosexuals, and transvestites, *Archives of Sexual Behavior*, 14: 147–64.

Nevonen, L. and Broberg, A.G. (2005) A comparison of sequenced individual and group psychotherapy for patients with bulimia nervosa, *International Journal of Eating Disorders*, Oct. 17.

Neziroglu, F., McKay, D., Todaro, J. et al. (1996) Effect of cognitive behavior therapy on persons with body dysmorphic disorder and comorbid axis II diagnoses, *Behavior Therapy*, 27: 67–77.

Nickell, A.D., Waudby, C.J. and Trull, T.J. (2002) Attachment, parental bonding and borderline personality disorder features in young adults, *Journal of Personality Disorders*, 16: 148–59.

Nigg, J.T. and Goldsmith, H.H. (1994) Genetics of personality disorders: perspectives from personality and psychopathology research, *Psychological Bulletin*, 115: 346–80.

NIH Consensus Development Panel on Effective Treatment of Opiate Addiction (1998) Effective medical treatment of opiate addiction, *Journal of the American Medical Association*, 280: 1936–43.

NIH Consensus Development Panel on Rehabilitation of Persons with Traumatic Brain Injury (1999) Rehabilitation of persons with traumatic brain injury, *Journal of the American Medical Association*, 282: 974–83.

Nock, M.K. and Kazdin, A.E. (2005) Randomized controlled trial of a brief intervention for increasing participation in parent management training, *Journal of Consulting and Clinical Psychology*, 73: 872–9.

Nordahl, H.M. and Nysaeter, T.E. (2005) Schema therapy for patients with borderline personality disorder: a single case series, *Journal of Behavior Therapy and Experimental Psychiatry*, 36: 254–64.

Nordahl, H.M. and Stiles, T.C. (1997) Perceptions of parental bonding in patients with various personality disorders, lifetime depressive disorders, and healthy controls, *Journal of Personality Disorders*, 11: 391–402.

Noyes, R., Happel, R., Muller, B. et al. (1998) Fluvoxamine for somatoform disorders: an open trial, *General Hospital Psychiatry*, 20: 339–44.

Noyes, R., Langbehn, D.R., Happel, R.L. et al. (2001) Personality dysfunction among somatizing patients, *Psychosomatics*, 42: 320–9.

Noyes, R., Stuart, S.P., Langbehn, D.R. et al. (2003) Test of an interpersonal model of hypochondriasis, *Psychosomatic Medicine*, 65: 292–300.

Nugent, A.C., Milham, M.P., Bain, E.E. et al. (2006) Cortical abnormalities in bipolar disorder investigated with MRI and voxel-based morphometry, *Neuroimage*, 30: 485–97.

Nutt, D.J. and Law, F.D. (2000) Pharmacological and psychological aspects of drugs of abuse, in M.G. Gelder, J.J. Lopez-Ibor Jr and N.C. Andreasen (eds) *New Oxford Textbook of Psychiatry*. Oxford: Oxford University Press.

Oakley, D.A. (1999) Hypnosis and conversion hysteria: a unifying model, in P. Halligan and A.S. David (eds) *Conversion Hysteria: Towards a Neuropsychological Account*. Hove: Psychology Press.

O'Connor, T.G., Deater-Deckard, K., Fulker, D. et al. (1998) Genotype–environment correlations in late childhood and early adolescence: antisocial behavioral problems and coercive parenting, *Developmental Psychology*, 34: 970–81.

Oda, A.M.G., Banzato, M. and Delgalarrondo, P. (2005) Some origins of cross-cultural psychiatry, *History of Psychiatry*, 16: 155–69.

Oei, T.P. and Raylu, N. (2004) Familial influence on offspring gambling: a cognitive mechanism for transmission of gambling behavior in families, *Psychological Medicine*, 34: 1279–88.

O'Farrell, T.J. and Fals-Stewart, W. (2000) Behavioral couples therapy for alcoholism and drug abuse, *Journal of Drug Abuse Treatment*, 18: 51–4.

Öhman, A. (1986) Face the beast and fear the face: animal and social fears as the prototypes for evolutionary analyses of emotion, *Psychophysiology*, 23: 123–45.

Oke, S. and Kanigsberg, E. (1991) Occupational therapy in the treatment of individuals with multiple personality disorder, *Canadian Journal of Occupational Therapy*, 58: 234–40.

Oldenburg, B. and Harris, D. (1996) The workplace as a setting for promoting health and preventing disease, *Homeostasis in Health and Disease*, 37: 226–32.

Onder, G., Zanetti, O., Giacobini, E. et al. (2005) Reality orientation therapy combined with cholinesterase inhibitors in Alzheimer's disease: randomised controlled trial, *British Journal of Psychiatry*, 187: 450–5.

Ono, Y., Yoshimura, K., Sueoka, R. et al. (1996) Avoidant personality and taijin kyoufu: sociocultural implications of the WHO/ADAMHA International Study of Personality Disorders in Japan, *Acta Psychiatrica Scandinavica*, 93: 172–6.

Oosthuizen, P.P. and Castle, D. (1998) Body dysmorphic disorder – a distinct entity? *South African Medical Journal*, 88: 766–9.

Oosthuizen, P., Lambert, T. and Castle, D.J. (1998) Dysmorphic concern: prevalence and associations with clinical variables, *Australian and New Zealand Journal of Psychiatry*, 32: 129–32.

Oppenheimer, R., Howells, K., Palmer, R.L. et al. (1985) Adverse sexual experience in childhood and clinical eating disorders: a preliminary description, *Journal of Psychiatric Research*, 19: 357–61.

Osman, S., Cooper, M., Hackmann, A. and Veale, D. (2004) Spontaneously occurring images and early memories in people with body dysmorphic disorder, *Memory*, 12: 428–36.

Öst, L-G. (1987) Age of onset of different phobias, *Journal of Abnormal Psychology*, 96: 223–9.

Öst, L-G. (1996) One-session group treatment of spider phobia, *Behaviour Research and Therapy*, 34: 707–15.

Öst, L-G., Salkovskis, P.M. and Hellström, K. (1991) One-session therapist-directed exposure vs. self-exposure in the treatment of spider phobia, *Behavior Therapy*, 22: 407–22.

Ovesey, L. and Person, E. (1973) Gender identity and sexual pathology in men: a psychodynamic analysis of heterosexuality, transsexualism, and transvestism, *Journal of the American Academy of Psychoanalysis*, 1: 53–72.

Owen, M., Liddell, M. and McGuffin, P. (1994) Alzheimer's disease, *British Medical Journal*, 308: 672–3.

Pallesen, S., Mitsem, M., Kvale, G. et al. (2005) Outcome of psychological treatments of pathological gambling: a review and meta-analysis, *Addiction*, 100: 1412–22.

Palumbo, R., Fontanillas, L., Salmaggi, A. et al. (1998) Stressful life events and multiple sclerosis: a retrospective study, *Italian Journal of Neurological Sciences*, 19: 259–60.

Pantelis, C., Yucel, M., Wood, S.J. et al. (2005) Structural brain imaging evidence for multiple pathological processes at different stages of brain development in schizophrenia, *Schizophrenia Bulletin*, 31: 672–96.

Papageorgiou, C. and Wells, A. (1998) Effects of attention training on hypochondriasis: a brief case series, *Psychological Medicine*, 28: 193–200.

Paris, J. (1991) Personality disorders, parasuicide, and culture, *Transcultural Psychiatric Research*, 28: 25–39.

Paris, J. (1996) Antisocial personality disorder: a biopsychosocial model, *Canadian Journal of Psychiatry*, 41: 75–80.

Paris, J. and Zweig-Frank, H. (2001) A 27-year follow-up of patients with borderline personality disorder, *Comprehensive Psychiatry*, 42: 482–7.

Park, N.W., Proulx, G.B. and Towers, W.M. (1999) Evaluation of the Attention Process Training programme, *Neuropsychological Rehabilitation*, 9: 135–54.

Parker, G. (1981) Parental representations of patients with anxiety neurosis, *Acta Psychiatrica Scandinavica*, 63: 33–6.

Parker, G. and Lawton, D. (1990) *Further Analysis of the 1985 General Household Survey Data on Informal Care. Report 1: A Typology of Caring*, Working Paper DHSS 716, 12.90. York: Social Policy Research Unit, University of York.

Parker, G. and Lipscombe, P. (1980) The relevance of early parental experiences to adult dependency, hypochondriasis and utilization of primary physicians, *British Journal of Medical Psychology*, 53: 355–63.

Parker, G., Roy, K., Wilhelm, K. et al. (1999) An exploration of links between early parenting experiences and personality disorder type and disordered personality functioning, *Journal of Personality Disorders*, 13: 361–74.

Parnas, J., Cannon, T., Schulsinger, F. and Mednick, S.A. (1995) Early predictors of onset and course of schizophrenia: results from the Copenhagen High-Risk Study, in H. Häfner and W.F. Gattaz (eds) *Search for the Causes of Schizophrenia*, Vol. 3. Berlin: Springer Verlag.

Parnas, J., Licht, D and Bovet, P. (2005) Cluster A personality disorders: a review, in M. Maj, H.S. Akiskal, J.E. Mezzich and A. Okasha (eds) *Personality Disorders*. Chichester: Wiley.

Partonen, T. and Lonnqvist, J. (1998) Seasonal affective disorder, *Lancet*, 352: 1369–74.

Patel, V., Musara, T., Butau, T. et al. (1995) Concepts of mental illness and medical pluralism in Harare, *Psychological Medicine*, 25: 485–93.

Pato, M.T., Zohar-Kadouch, R., Zohar, J. et al. (1988) Return of symptoms after discontinuation of clomipramine in patients with obsessive-compulsive disorder, *American Journal of Psychiatry*, 145: 1521–5.

Pavlov, I.P. ([1927] 1960) *Conditioned Reflexes* (ed. and trans. G.V. Anrep). New York: Dover.

Paykel, E.S. (1994) Life events, social support and depression, *Acta Psychiatrica Scandinavica*, 377: 50–8.

Paykel, E.S., Brugha, T. and Fryers, T. (2005) Size and burden of depressive disorders in Europe, *European Neuropsychopharmacology*, 15: 411–23.

Peele, S. (1992) Alcoholism, politics, and bureaucracy: the consensus against controlled-drinking therapy in America, *Addictive Behaviors*, 17: 49–62.

Pehek, E.A., Nocjar, C., Roth, B.L. et al. (2006) Evidence for the preferential involvement of 5-HT2A serotonin receptors in stress- and drug-induced dopamine release in the rat medial prefrontal cortex, *Neuropsychopharmacology*, 31: 265–77.

Pelham, W.E., Carlson, C., Sams, S.E. et al. (1993) Separate and combined effects of methylphenidate and behavior modification on boys with attention deficit/hyperactivity in the classroom, *Journal of Consulting and Clinical Psychology*, 61: 506–15.

Peralta, V. and Cuesta, M.J. (1992) Influence of cannabis abuse on schizophrenic psychopathology, *Acta Psychiatrica Scandinavica*, 85: 127–30.

Perkin, G.D. (1989) An analysis of 7936 successive new outpatient referrals, *Journal of Neurology, Neurosurgery and Psychiatry*, 52: 44–78.

Perkins, S., Schmidt, U., Eisler, I. et al. (2005) Why do adolescents with bulimia nervosa choose not to involve their parents in treatment?, *European Child and Adolescent Psychiatry*, 14: 376–85.

Perkonigg, A., Kessler, R.C. and Wittchen, H-U. (2000) Traumatic events and post-traumatic stress disorder in the community: prevalence, risk factors and comorbidity, *Acta Psychiatrica Scandinavica*, 101: 46–59.

Perreira, K.M. and Sloan, F. (2001) Life events and alcohol consumption among mature adults: a longitudinal analysis, *Journal of Studies on Alcohol*, 62: 501–8.

Perry, A., Tarrier, N., Morris, R. et al. (1999) Randomised controlled trial of efficacy of teaching patients with bipolar disorder to identify early symptoms of relapse and obtain treatment, *British Medical Journal*, 318: 149–53.

Perugi, G., Akiskal, H.S., Giannotti, D. et al. (1997) Gender-related differences in body dysmorphic disorder (dysmorphophobia), *Journal of Nervous and Mental Disease*, 185: 578–82.

Petersen, R.C., Thomas, R.G., Grundman, M. et al. (2005) Alzheimer's Disease Cooperative Study Group. Vitamin E and donepezil for the treatment of mild cognitive impairment, *New England Journal of Medicine*, 352: 2379–88.

Pharoah, F.M., Mari, J.J. and Streiner, D. (2000) Family intervention for schizophrenia (Cochrane Review), *The Cochrane Library*, Issue 4. Oxford: Update Software.

Phillips, K.A. (1991) Body dysmorphic disorder: the distress of imagined ugliness, *American Journal of Psychiatry*, 148: 1138–49.

Phillips, K.A. (1996a) *The Broken Mirror*. New York: Oxford University Press.

Phillips, K.A. (1996b) Pharmacologic treatment of body dysmorphic disorder, *Psychopharmacology Bulletin*, 32: 597–605.

Phillips, K.A. (2004) Psychosis in body dysmorphic disorder, *Journal of Psychiatric Research*, 38: 63–72.

Phillips, K.A., Albertini, R.S. and Rasmussen, S.A. (2002) A randomized placebo-controlled trial of fluoxetine in body dysmorphic disorder, *Archives of General Psychiatry*, 59: 381–8.

Phillips, K.A., Albertini, R.S., Siniscalchi, J.M. et al. (2001) Effectiveness of pharmacotherapy for body dysmorphic disorder: a chart-review study, *Journal of Clinical Psychology*, 62: 721–7.

Phillips, K.A. and Diaz, S.F. (1997) Gender differences in body dysmorphic disorder, *Journal of Mental Disease*, 9, 570–7.

Phillips, K.A., McElroy, S.L., Keck, P.E. et al. (1993) Body dysmorphic disorder: 30 cases of imagined ugliness, *American Journal of Psychiatry*, 150, 302–8.

Phillips, K.A. and Rasmussen, S.A. (2004) Change in psychosocial functioning and quality of life of patients with body dysmorphic disorder treated with fluoxetine: a placebo-controlled study, *Psychosomatics*, 45: 438–44.

Piaget, J. (1954) *The Child's Construction of Reality*. London: Routledge and Kegan Paul.

Pike, K.M. (1998) Long-term course of anorexia nervosa: response, relapse, remission, and recovery, *Clinical Psychology Review*, 18: 447–75.

Pike, K.M., Walsh, B.T., Vitousek, K. et al. (2003) Cognitive behaviour therapy in the post hospitalisation treatment of anorexia nervosa, *American Journal of Psychiatry*, 160: 2046–9.

Pike, M.J. and Rodin, J. (1991) Mothers, daughters, and disordered eating, *Journal of Abnormal Psychology*, 100: 198–204.

Pinkston, E.M., Linsk, N.L. and Young, R.N. (1988) Home-based behavioural family therapy treatment of the impaired elderly, *Behavior Therapy*, 19: 331–44.

Piotrkowski, C.S. and Brannen, S.J. (2002) Exposure, threat appraisal, and lost confidence as predictors of PTSD symptoms following September 11, 2001, *American Journal of Orthopsychiatry*, 72: 476–85.

Piper, A. and Merskey, H. (2004) The persistence of folly: a critical examination of dissociative identity disorder. Part I. The excesses of an improbable concept, *Canadian Journal of Psychiatry*, 49: 592–600.

Piper, W.E., Joyce, A.S., McCallum, M. et al. (1993) Concentration and correspondence of transference interpretations in short-term psychotherapy, *Journal of Consulting and Clinical Psychology*, 61: 586–95.

Piper, W.E., Ogrodniczuk, J.S., Joyce, A.S. et al. (1999b) Prediction of dropping out in time-limited, interpretive individual psychotherapy, *Psychotherapy*, 36: 114–22.

Pithers, W.D. (1990) Relapse prevention with sexual aggressors: a method for maintaining therapeutic gain and enhancing external supervision, in W.L. Marshall, D.R. Laws and H.E. Barbaree (eds) *Handbook of Sexual Assault: Issues, Theories, and Treatment of the Offender*. New York: Plenum.

Pjerk, E., Winkler, D. and Kasper, S. (2005) Pharmacotherapy of seasonal affective disorder. *CNS Spectrums*, 10: 664–69.

Pjerk, E., Winkler, D., Statsny, J. et al. (2004) Bright light therapy in seasonal affective disorder – does it suffice?, *European Neuropsychopharmacology*, 14: 347–51.

Pols, R. and Hawks, D. (1991) *Is There a Safe Level of Daily Consumption of Alcohol for Men and Women?* Canberra: Australian Government Publishing Service.

Pope, K.S. and Feldman-Summers, S. (1992) National survey of psychologists' sexual and physical abuse history and their evaluation of training and competence in these areas, *Professional Psychology: Research and Practice*, 23: 353–61.

Potenza, M.N. (2001) The neurobiology of pathological gambling, *Seminars in Clinical Neuropsychiatry*, 6: 217–26.

Poulton, R. and Menzies, R.G. (2002) Fears born and bred: toward a more inclusive theory of fear acquisition, *Behaviour Research and Therapy*, 40: 197–208.

Powell, G.E. and Lindsay, S.J.E. (1994) *The Handbook of Clinical Adult Psychology*. London: Routledge.

Power, K.G., Simpson, R.J., Swanson, V. et al. (1990) A controlled study of cognitive behavior therapy, diazepam, and placebo in the management of generalised anxiety, *Behavioural Psychotherapy*, 17: 10–14.

Prescott, C.A. and Kendler, K.S. (1999) Genetic and environmental contributions to alcohol abuse and dependence in a population-based sample of male twins, *American Journal of Psychiatry*, 156: 34–40.

Price, V.A. (1982) *Type A Behavior Pattern: A Model for Research and Practice*. New York: Academic Press.

Productivity Commission (1999) *Australia's Gambling Industries: Inquiry Report*. Melbourne: Productivity Commission.

Project MATCH Research Group (1998) Matching alcoholism treatments to client heterogeneity: project MATCH three-year drinking outcomes, *Alcoholism: Clinical and Experimental Research*, 22: 1300–11.

Putnam, F.W. (1997) *Dissociation in Children and Adolescents*. New York: Guilford.

Quinsey, V.I., Harris, G.T. and Rice, M.E. (1995) Actuarial prediction of sexual recidivism, *Journal of Interpersonal Violence*, 10: 85–105.

Rachman, S. (2003) *The Treatment of Obsessions*. Oxford: Oxford University Press.

Rachman, S.J. and de Silva, P. (1978) Abnormal and normal obsessions, *Behaviour Research and Therapy*, 16: 233–8.

Raine, A., Lencz, T., Bihrle, S. et al. (2000) Reduced prefrontal gray matter volume and reduced autonomic activity in antisocial personality disorder, *Archives of General Psychiatry*, 57: 119–27.

Raine, A., Reynolds, C. and Venables, P.H. (1998) Fearlessness, stimulation seeking, and large body size at 3 years as early predispositions to childhood aggression at age 11 years, *Archives of General Psychiatry*, 55: 745–51.

Rajagopal, S. (2004) Suicide pacts and the internet, *British Medical Journal*, 329: 1298–9.

Ralevski, E., Sanislow, C.A. and Grilo, C.M. (2005) Avoidant personality disorder and social phobia: distinct enough to be separate disorders?, *Acta Psychiatrica Scandinavica*, 112: 208–14.

Ralph, D. and McNicholas, T. (2000) UK management guidelines for erectile dysfunction, *British Medical Journal*, 321: 499–503.

Rampello, L., Nicoletti, F. and Nicoletti, F. (2000) Dopamine and depression: therapeutic implications, *CNS Drugs*, 13: 35–45.

Ramsay, M. (2001) Genetic susceptibility for panic and phobic disorders, *Trends in Molecular Medicine*, 7: 539.

Rapee, R., Mattick, R. and Murrell, E. (1986) Cognitive mediation of anxiety and panic: a cognitive account, *Journal of Behavior Therapy and Experimental Psychiatry*, 17: 245–53.

Raskin, M., Peeke, H.Y., Dickman, W. et al. (1982) Panic and generalized anxiety disorders. Developmental antecedents and precipitants, *Archives of General Psychiatry*, 39: 687–9.

Razali, M.S. (1995) Psychiatrists and folk healers in Malaysia, *World Health Forum*, 16: 56–8.

Razali, S.M., Khan, U.A. and Hasanah, C.I. (1996) Belief in supernatural causes of mental illness among Malay patients: impact on treatment, *Acta Psychiatrica Scandinavica*, 94: 229–33.

Razali, S.M. and Najib, MA. (2000) Help-seeking pathways among Malay psychiatric patients, *International Journal of Social Psychiatry*, 46, 281–9.

Rea, M., Tompson, M., Miklowitz, D. et al. (2003) Family-focused treatment versus individual treatment for bipolar disorder: results of a randomized clinical trial, *Journal of Consulting and Clinical Psychology*, 71: 482–92.

Reed, G.F. (1985) *Obsessional Experience and Compulsive Behaviour*. London: Academic Press.

Reeve, W. and Ivison, D. (1985) Use of environmental manipulation and classroom and modified informal reality orientation with institutionalized, confused elderly patients, *Age and Ageing*, 14: 119–21.

Regier, D.A., Rae, D.S., Narrow, W.E. et al. (1998) Prevalence of anxiety disorders and their comorbidity with mood and addictive disorders, *British Journal of Psychiatry*, 173 (Suppl. 34): 24–6.

Reichelt, K.L., Knivsberg, A.M, Lind, G. et al. (1991) Probable etiology and possible treatment of childhood autism, *Brain Dysfunction*, 4: 308–19.

Reid, W.H. and Gacono, C. (2000) Treatment of antisocial personality, psychopathy, and other characterologic antisocial syndromes, *Behavioral Science and Law*, 18: 647–62.

Reimherr, F.W., Wender, P.H., Wood, D.R. et al. (1987) An open trial of L-tyrosine in the treatment of attention deficit disorder, residual type, *American Journal of Psychiatry*, 144: 1071–3.

Rekers, G.A. and Lovaas, O.I. (1974) Behavioral treatment of deviant sex role behaviours in a male child, *Journal of Applied Behavioral Analysis*, 7: 173–90.

Remafedi, G., French, S., Story, M. et al. (1998) The relationship between suicide risk and sexual orientation: results of a population-based study, *American Journal of Public Health*, 88: 57–60.

Research Units on Pediatric Psychopharmacology Autism Network (2005) Risperidone treatment of autistic disorder: longer-term benefits and blinded discontinuation after 6 months, *American Journal of Psychiatry*, 162: 1361–9.

Revill, S. and Blunden, R. (1977) *Home Training of Pre-school Children with Developmental*

Delay: Report of the Development and Evaluation of the Portage Service in South Glamorgan. Cardiff: Mental Handicap in Wales Applied Research Unit.

Rey, J.M., Walter, G., Plapp, J.M. et al. (2000) Family environment in attention deficit hyperactivity, oppositional defiant and conduct disorders, *Australia and New Zealand Journal of Psychiatry*, 34: 453–7.

Ricca, V., Nacmias, B., Cellini, E. et al. (2002) 5-HT2A receptor gene polymorphism and eating disorders, *Neuroscience Letters*, 323: 105–8.

Rice, M.E., Harris, G.T. and Cormier, C.A. (1992) An evaluation of a maximum security therapeutic community for psychopaths and other mentally disordered offenders, *Law and Human Behavior*, 16: 399–412.

Rice, M.E., Quinsey, V.L. and Harris, G.T. (1991) Sexual recidivism among child molesters released from a maximum security psychiatric institution, *Journal of Consulting and Clinical Psychology*, 59: 381–6.

Rief, W., Hiller, W. and Margraf, J. (1998) Cognitive aspects of hypochondriasis and the somatization syndrome, *Journal of Abnormal Psychology*, 107: 587–95.

Rief, W., Pilger, F., Ihle, D. et al. (2004) Psychobiological aspects of somatoform disorders: contributions of monoaminergic transmitter systems, *Neuropsychobiology*, 49: 24–9.

Rieker, P.P. and Bird, C.E. (2000) Sociological explanations of gender differences in mental and physical health, in C.E. Bird, P. Conrad and A.M. Fremont (eds) *Handbook of Medical Sociology*. Upper Saddle River, NJ: Prentice Hall.

Riley, D.E. (2002) Reversible transvestic fetishism in a man with Parkinson's disease treated with selegiline, *Clinical Neuropharmacology*, 25: 234–7.

Rinne, T., Van den Brink, W., Wouters, L. et al. (2002) SSRI treatment of borderline personality disorder: a randomized, placebo-controlled clinical trial for female patients with borderline personality disorder, *American Journal of Psychiatry*, 159: 2048–54.

Ritsher, J.E.B., Warner, V., Johnson, J.G. et al. (2001) Inter-generation longitudinal study of social class and depression: a test of social causation and social selection models, *British Journal of Psychiatry*, 178 (Suppl. 40): S84–S90.

Roberts, J.S. (2000) Schizophrenia epigenesis?, *Theoretical Medicine and Bioethics*, 21: 191–215.

Robin, A.L., Siegel, P.T. and Moye, A. (1995) Family therapy versus individual therapy for anorexia: impact on family conflict, *International Journal of Eating Disorders*, 17: 313–22.

Robins, L.N., Helzer, J.E., Croughan, J. et al. (1981) National Institute of Mental Health Diagnostic Interview Schedule: its history, characteristics, and validity, *Archives of General Psychiatry*, 38: 381–9.

Roca, W., Cha, R. and Waring, S. (1998) Incidence of dementia and Alzheimer's disease: a reanalysis of data from Rochester, Minnesota, 1975–1984, *American Journal of Epidemiology*, 48: 51–2.

Rocca, P., Fonzo, V., Scotta, M. et al. (1997) Paroxetine efficacy in the treatment of generalized anxiety disorder, *Acta Psychiatrica Scandinavica*, 95: 444–50.

Rocca, P., Marchiaro, L, Cocuzza, E. et al. (2002) Treatment of borderline personality disorder with risperidone, *Journal of Clinical Psychiatry*, 63: 241–4.

Rocchi, A., Pellegrini, S. and Siciliano, G. (2003) Causative and susceptibility genes for Alzheimer's disease: a review, *Brain Research Bulletin*, 61: 1–24.

Roeleveld, N., Zielhuis, G.A. and Gabreels, F. (1997) The prevalence of mental retardation: a critical review of recent literature, *Developmental Medicine and Child Neurology*, 39: 125–32.

Roelofs, K., Spinhoven, P., Sandijck, P. et al. (2005) The impact of early trauma and recent life-events on symptom severity in patients with conversion disorder, *Journal of Nervous and Mental Disease*, 193: 508–14.

Rogers, C.R. (1961) *On Becoming a Person*. Boston, MA: Houghton Mifflin.

Rogers, S.L., Farlow, M.R., Doody, R.S. et al. (1998) A 24-week, double-blind, placebo-controlled trial of donepezil in patients with Alzheimer's disease, *Neurology*, 50: 136–45.

Roggla, H. and Uhl, A. (1995) Depression and relapses in treated alcoholics, *International Journal of Addictions*, 30: 337–49.

Romme, M.A. and Escher, A.D. (1989) Hearing voices, *Schizophrenia Bulletin*, 15: 209–16.

Rooney, B., McClelland, L., Crisp, A.H. et al. (1995) The incidence and prevalence of anorexia nervosa in three suburban health districts in south west London, U.K., *International Journal of Eating Disorders*, 18: 299–307.

Rosati, G. (2001) The prevalence of multiple sclerosis in the world: an update, *Neurological Sciences*, 22: 117–39.

Rose, S., Bisson, J. and Wessely, W. (2002) Psychological debriefing for preventing post traumatic stress disorder (PTSD), *Cochrane Database of Systematic Reviews*, Issue 1.

Rose, S., Lewontin, R.C. and Kamin, L.J. (1984) *Not in Our Genes: Biology, Ideology, and Human Nature*. New York: Penguin.

Rosen, J.C. (1996) Body dysmorphic disorder: assessment and treatment, in J.K. Thompson (ed.) *Body Image, Eating Disorders, and Obesity*. Washington, DC: American Psychological Association.

Rosen, J.C. and Ramirez, E. (1998) A comparison of eating disorders and body dysmorphic disorder on body image and psychological adjustment, *Journal of Psychosomatic Research*, 44: 441–9.

Rosen, J.C., Reiter, J. and Orosan, P. (1995) Cognitive-behavioral body image therapy for body dysmorphic disorder, *Journal of Consulting and Clinical Psychology*, 63: 263–9.

Rosen, R. and Garety, P. (2005) Predicting recovery from schizophrenia: a retrospective comparison of characteristics at onset of people with single and multiple episodes, *Schizophrenia Bulletin*, 31: 735–50.

Rosen, R.C. (2001) Psychogenic erectile dysfunction: classification and management, *Urologic Clinics of North America*, 28: 269–78.

Rosenhan, D.L. (1973) On being sane in insane places, *Science*, 179: 250–8.

Rosenthal, N.E., Sack, D.A., Gillin, J.C. et al. (1984) Seasonal affective disorder: a description of the syndrome and preliminary findings with light therapy, *Archives of General Psychiatry*, 41: 72–80.

Rosenthal, R. and Lesieur, H. (1992) Self-reported withdrawal symptoms and pathological gambling, *American Journal of Addiction*, 1: 150–4.

Ross, C.A., Miller, S.D., Reagor, P. et al. (1991) Structured interview data on 102 cases of multiple personality disorder from four centres, *American Journal of Psychiatry*, 147: 596–600.

Ross, C.A. and Norton, R. (1989) Effects of hypnosis on the features of multiple personality disorder, *American Journal of Clinical Hypnosis*, 32: 99–106.

Ross, C.A., Norton, R. and Wozney, K. (1989) Multiple personality disorder: an analysis of 236 cases, *Canadian Journal of Psychiatry*, 34: 97–101.

Rossel, R. (1998) Multiplicity: the challenges of finding place in experience, *Journal of Constructivist Psychology*, 11: 221–40.

Rossell, S.L. and Boundy, C.L. (2005) Are auditory-verbal hallucinations associated with auditory affective processing deficits?, *Schizophrenia Research*, 78: 95–106.

Roth, A. and Fonagy, P. (1998) *What Works for Whom? A Critical Review of Psychotherapy Research*. New York: Guilford.

Rothschild, A.J. and Locke, C.A. (1991) Reexposure to fluoxetine after serious suicide attempts by three patients: the role of akathisia, *Journal of Clinical Psychiatry*, 12: 491–3.

Royal College of Psychiatrists (RCP) (1986) *Alcohol: Our Favourite Drug*. London: RCP.

Roy-Byrne, P.P., Craske, M.G., Stein, M.B. et al. (2005) Randomized effectiveness trial of cognitive-behavioral therapy and medication for primary care panic disorder, *Archives of General Psychiatry*, 62: 290–8.

Ruberman, W., Weinblatt, E., Goldberg, J.D. et al. (1984) Psychosocial influences on mortality after myocardial infarction, *New England Journal of Medicine*, 311: 552–9.

Rubinstein, S. and Caballero, B. (2000) Is Miss America an undernourished role model?, *Journal of the American Medical Association*, 283: 1569.

Rudd, M.D. (2000) The suicidal mode: a cognitive-behavioral model of suicidality, *Suicide and Life Threatening Behavior*, 30: 18–33.

Rush, A.J., Weissenburger, J. and Eaves, G. (1986) Do thinking patterns predict depressive symptoms, *Cognitive Therapy and Research*, 10: 225–35.

Russell, G.F.M., Szmukler, G.I., Dare, C. et al. (1987) An evaluation of family therapy in anorexia nervosa and bulimia nervosa, *Archives of General Psychiatry*, 44: 1047–56.

Russell, V.A., Sagvolden T. and Johansen E.B. (2005) Animal models of attention-deficit hyperactivity disorder, *Behavioral and Brain Functions*, 1: 9.

Russon, L. and Alison, D. (1998) Palliative care does not mean giving up, *British Medical Journal*, 317: 195–7.

Ryle, A. (1975) *Cognitive Analytic Therapy: Developments in Theory and Practice*. Chichester: Wiley.

Sadnovick, A.D., Eisen, K., Paty, D.W. et al. (1991) Cause of death in patients attending multiple sclerosis clinics, *Neurology*, 41: 1193–6.

Sagvolden, T., Johansen, E.B., Aase, H. et al. (2005) A dynamic developmental theory of attention-deficit/hyperactivity disorder (ADHD) predominantly hyperactive and combined subtypes, *Behavioral and Brain Sciences*, 28: 397–68.

Salekin, R.T. (2002) Psychopathy and therapeutic pessimism: clinical lore or clinical reality?, *Clinical Psychology Review*, 22: 79–112.

Salkovskis, P. and Kirk, J. (1997) Obsessive-compulsive disorder, in D.M. Clark and C.G. Fairburn (eds) *Science and Practice of Cognitive Behaviour Therapy*. Oxford: Oxford University Press.

Salkovskis, P.M., Atha, C. and Storer, D. (1990) Cognitive-behavioural problem-solving in the treatment of patients who repeatedly attempt suicide: a controlled trial, *British Journal of Psychiatry*, 157: 871–6.

Sandberg, S. (2005) The biopsychosocial context of ADHD, *The Behavioral and Brain Sciences*, 28: 441–2.

Sar, V., Akyuz, G., Kundakci, T. et al. (2004) Childhood trauma, dissociation, and psychiatric comorbidity in patients with conversion disorder, *American Journal of Psychiatry*, 161: 2271–6.

Sarti, P. and Cournos, F. (1990) Medication and psychotherapy in the treatment of chronic schizophrenia, *Psychiatric Clinics of North America*, 13: 215–28.

Sassi, R.B., Stanley, J.A., Axelson, D. et al. (2005) Reduced NAA levels in the dorsolateral prefrontal cortex of young bipolar patients, *American Journal of Psychiatry*, 162: 2109–15.

Satel, S.L. and Edell, W.S. (1991) Cocaine-induced paranoia and psychosis proneness, *American Journal of Psychiatry*, 141: 1708–11.

Satz, P., Zaucha, K., Forney, D.L. et al. (1998) Neuropsychological, psychosocial, and vocational correlates of the Glasgow Outcome Scale at 6 months postinjury: a study of moderate to severe traumatic brain injury patients, *Brain Injury*, 12: 555–67.

Scheib, J.E., Gangestad, S.W. and Thornhill, R. (1999) Facial attractiveness, symmetry and cues to good genes, *Proceedings of the Royal Society of London*, 266: 1913–17.

Schell, T.L., Marshall, G.N. and Jaycox, L.H. (2004) All symptoms are not created equal: the prominent role of hyperarousal in the natural course of posttraumatic psychological distress, *Journal of Abnormal Psychology*, 113: 189–97.

Schenk, D., Barbour, R., Dunn, W. et al. (1999) Immunization with amyloidbeta attenuates Alzheimer-disease-like pathology in the PDAPP mouse, *Nature*, 400: 173–7.

Scherbaum, N., Kluwig, J., Specka, M. et al. (2005) Group psychotherapy for opiate addicts in methadone maintenance treatment – a controlled trial, *European Addiction Research*, 11: 163–71.

Schneider A.J., Mataix-Cols D., Marks I.M. et al. (2005) Internet-guided self-help with or without exposure therapy for phobic and panic disorders, *Psychotherapy and Psychosomatics*, 74: 154–64.

Schotte, D.E. and Clum, G.A. (1987) Problem-solving skills in suicidal psychiatric patients, *Journal of Consulting and Clinical Psychology*, 55: 49–54.

Schubert, D.S. and Foliart, R.H. (1993) Increased depression in multiple sclerosis patients: a meta-analysis, *Psychosomatics*, 34: 124–30.

Schuckit, M.A., Tsuang, J.W., Anthenelli, R.M. et al. (1996) Alcohol challenges in young men from alcoholic pedigrees and control families: a report from the COGA project, *Journal of Studies in Alcohol*, 57: 368–77.

Schultz, T., Passmore, J.L. and Yoder, C.Y. (2003) Emotional closeness with perpetrators and amnesia for child sexual abuse, *Journal of Child Sexual Abuse*, 12: 67–88.

Schulze-Rauschenbach, S.C., Harms, U., Schlaepfer, T.E. et al. (2005) Distinctive neurocognitive effects of repetitive transcranial magnetic stimulation and electroconvulsive therapy in major depression, *British Journal of Psychiatry*, 186: 410–16.

Schwartz, C.E., Foley, F.W., Rao, S.M. et al. (1999) Stress and course of disease in multiple sclerosis, *Behavioral Medicine*, 25: 110–16

Schwartz, D.M. and Thompson, M.G. (1981) Do anorexics get well? Current research and future needs, *American Journal of Psychiatry*, 138: 319–23.

Schwarz, T. (1981) *The Hillside Strangler: A Murderer's Mind*. New York: New American Library.

Schwitzer, A.M., Rodriguez, L.E., Thomas, C. et al. (2001) The eating disorders NOS diagnostic profile among college women, *Journal of the American College of Health*, 49: 157–66.

Scott, J. (2001) Cognitive-behavioral management of patients with bipolar disorder who relapse while on lithium prophylaxis, *Journal of Clinical Psychiatry*, 62: 556–9.

Scott, J., Garland, A. and Moorhead, S. (2001) A pilot study of cognitive therapy in bipolar disorders, *Psychological Medicine*, 31: 459–67.

Scott, J., Stanton, B., Garland, A. et al. (2000) Cognitive vulnerability in patients with bipolar disorder, *Psychoogical Medicine*, 30: 467–72.

Secker, J. (1998) Current conceptualisations of mental health and mental health promotion, *Health Education Research Theory and Practice*, 13: 57–66.

Seedat, S. and Stein, M.B. (2004) Double-blind, placebo-controlled assessment of combined clonazepam with paroxetine compared with paroxetine monotherapy for generalized social anxiety disorder, *Journal of Clinical Psychiatry*, 65: 244–8.

Sel, R. (1997) Dissociation as complex adaptation, *Medical Hypothesis*, 48: 2205–8.

Seligman, M.E.P. (1970) On the generality of the laws of learning, *Psychological Review*, 77: 406–18.

Seligman, M.E.P. (1971) Phobias and preparedness, *Behavior Therapy*, 2: 307–20.

Seligman, M.E.P. (1975) *Helplessness*. San Francisco, CA: Freeman.

Sellman, J.D., Sullivan, P.F., Dore, G.M. et al. (2001) A randomized controlled trial of motivational enhancement therapy (MET) for mild to moderate alcohol dependence, *Journal of Studies in Alcohol*, 62: 389–96.

Semrud-Clikeman, M., Nielsen, K.H., Clinton, A. et al. (1999) An intervention approach for the children with teacher- and parent-identified attentional difficulties, *Journal of Learning Disabilities*, 32: 581–90.

Seto, M.C. and Barbaree, H.E. (1999) Psychopathy, treatment behavior, and sex offender recidivism, *Journal of Interpersonal Violence*, 14: 1235–48.

Seto, M.C., Harris, G.T., Rice, M.E. et al. (2004) The screening scale for pedophilic interests predicts recidivism among adult sex offenders with child victims, *Archives of Sexual Behaviour*, 33: 455–66.

Shadish, W.R., Montgomery, L.M., Wilson, P. et al. (1993) Effects of family and marital psychotherapies: a meta-analysis. *Journal of Consulting and Clinical Psychology*, 61: 992–1002.

Shapiro, D.A. and Shapiro, D. (1983) Comparative therapy outcome research: methodological implications of meta-analysis, *Journal of Consulting and Clinical Psychology*, 45: 543–51.

Shapiro, F. (1995) *Eye Movement Desensitisation and Reprocessing: Basic Principles*. New York: Guilford.

Sharafi, M. (2005) Comparison of classical and clozapine treatment on schizophrenia using Positive and Negative Syndrome Scale of Schizophrenia (PANSS) and SPECT Imaging, *International Journal of Medical Science*, 2: 79–86.

Sharpe, L. (2002) A reformulated cognitive-behavioral model of problem gambling: a bio-psychosocial perspective, *Clinical Psychology Review*, 22: 1–25.

Sharpe, L., Tarrier, N., Schotte, D. et al. (1995) The role of autonomic arousal in problem gambling, *Addiction*, 90: 1529–40.

Shea, M.T., Elkin, I., Imber, S.D. et al. (1992) Course of depressive symptoms over follow-up: findings from the National Institute of Mental Health Treatment of Depression Collaborative Research Program, *Archives of General Psychiatry*, 49: 782–7.

Shea, S.C. (1998) *Psychiatric Interviewing: The Art of Understanding*, 2nd edn. Philadelphia, PA: Saunders.

Sheard, M.H. (1971) Effect of lithium on human aggression, *Nature*, 230: 113–14.

Sheikh, S. and Furnham, A. (2000) A cross-cultural study of mental health beliefs and attitudes towards seeking professional help, *Social Psychiatry and Psychiatric Epidemiology*, 35: 326–34.

Sher, L. (2001) Genetic studies of seasonal affective disorder and seasonality, *Comprehensive Psychiatry*, 42: 105–10.

Sherer, M., Madison, C.F. and Hannay, H.J. (2000) A review of outcome after moderate and severe closed head injury with an introduction to life care planning, *Journal of Head Trauma and Rehabilitation*, 15: 767–82.

Sherman, J.J., LeResche, L., Huggins, K.H. et al. (2004) The relationship of somatization and depression to experimental pain response in women with temporomandibular disorders, *Psychosomatic Medicine*, 66: 852–60.

Shimizu, E., Hashimoto, K., Koizumi, H. et al. (2005) No association of the brain-derived neurotrophic factor (BDNF) gene polymorphisms with panic disorder, *Progress in Neuro-Psychopharmacology and Biological Psychiatry*, 29: 708–12.

Shinohara, K., Yanagisawa, A., Kagota, Y. et al. (1999) Physiological changes in Pachinko players: beta-endorphin, catecholamines, immune system substances and heart rate, *Applied Human Science*, 18: 37–42.

Siegert, R.J. and Abernethy, D.A. (2005) Depression in multiple sclerosis: a review, *Journal of Neurology Neurosurgery and Psychiatry*, 76: 469–75.

Simeon, D., Greenberg, J., Nelson, D. et al. (2005) Dissociation and posttraumatic stress 1 year after the World Trade Center disaster: follow-up of a longitudinal survey, *Journal of Clinical Psychiatry*, 66: 231–7.

Simon, R. (1995) Gender, multiple roles, role meanings, and mental health, *Journal of Health and Social Behavior*, 36: 182–94.

Sinclair, J.D. (2001) Evidence about the use of naltrexone and for different ways of using it in the treatment of alcoholism, *Alcohol and Alcoholism*, 36: 2–10.

Singh, S.P. and Lee, A.S. (1997) Conversion disorders in Nottingham: alive, but not kicking, *Journal of Psychosomatic Research*, 43: 425–30.

Sinha, S., Anderson, J., John, V. et al. (2000) Recent advances in the understanding of the processing of APP to beta amyloid peptide, *Annals of the New York Academy of Science*, 920: 206–8.

Sinnakaruppan, I. and Williams, D.M. (2001) Head injury and family carers: a critical appraisal of case management programmes in the community, *Brain Injury*, 15: 653–72.

Sir, A., D'Souza, R.F., Uguz, S. et al. (2005) Randomized trial of sertraline versus venlafaxine XR in major depression: efficacy and discontinuation symptoms, *Journal of Clinical Psychiatry*, 66: 1312–20.

Sirey, J.A., Bruce, M.L., Alexopoulos, G.S. et al. (2001) Stigma as a barrier to recovery: perceived stigma and patient-rated severity of illness as predictors of antidepressant drug adherence, *Psychiatric Services*, 52: 1615–20.

Sivberg, B. (2002) Family system and coping behaviors: a comparison between parents of children with autistic spectrum disorders and parents with non-autistic children, *Autism*, 6: 397–409.

Skinner, B.F. (1953) *Science and Human Behavior*. New York: Macmillan.

Skre, I., Onstad., S, Torgersen, S. et al. (2000) The heritability of common phobic fear: a twin study of a clinical sample, *Journal of Anxiety Disorders*, 14: 549–62.

Skrzypek, S., Wehmeier, P.M. and Remschmidt, H. (2001) Body image assessment using body size estimation in recent studies on anorexia nervosa: a brief review, *European Child and Adolescent Psychiatry* 10: 215–21.

Slade, P. and Brodie, D. (1994) Body-image distortion and eating disorder: a reconceptualization based on the recent literature, *European Eating Disorders Review*, 2: 32–46.

Smith, A.J., Brown, R.T., Bunke, V. et al. (2002) Psychosocial adjustment and peer competence of siblings of children with attention-deficit/hyperactivity disorder, *Journal of Attention Disorder*, 5: 165–77.

Smith, C.A. and Lazarus, R.S. (1993) Appraisal components, core relational themes and the emotions, *Cognition and Emotion*, 7: 233–96.

Smith, M.L. and Glass, G.V. (1977) Meta-analysis of psychotherapy outcome studies, *American Psychologist*, 32: 752–60.

Smith, M.L., Glass, G.V. and Miller, T.I. (1980) *The Benefits of Psychotherapy*. Baltimore, MD: Johns Hopkins University Press.

Smith, T., Buch, G.A. and Gamby, T.E. (2000) Parent-directed, intensive early intervention for children with pervasive developmental disorder, *Research in Developmental Disabilities*, 21: 297–309.

Smith, Y.L.S., Van Goozen, S.H.M. and Cohen-Kettenis, P.T. (2001) Adolescents with gender identity disorder who were accepted or rejects for sex reassignment surgery: a prospective follow-up study, *Journal of the Academy of Child and Adolescent Psychiatry*, 40: 472–81.

Smyth, B.P., O'Brien, M. and Barry, J. (2000) Trends in treated opiate misuse in Dublin: the emergence of chasing the dragon, *Addiction*, 95: 1217–23.

Sobanski, E. and Schmidt, M.H. (2000) 'Everybody looks at my pubic bone': a case report of an adolescent patient with body dysmorphic disorder, *Acta Psychiatrica Scandinavica*, 101: 80–2.

Sobczak, S., Riedel, W.J., Booij, I. et al. (2002) Cognition following acute tryptophan depletion: difference between first-degree relatives of bipolar disorder patients and matched healthy control volunteers, *Psychological Medicine*, 32: 503–15.

Sohlberg, M.M. and Mateer, C.A. (1989) Training use of compensatory memory books: a three-stage behavioural approach, *Journal of Clinical and Experimental Neuropsychology*, 11: 871–91.

Sohlberg, M.M. and Mateer, C.A. (2001) Improving attention and managing attentional problems: adapting rehabilitation techniques to adults with ADD, *Annals of the New York Academy of Sciences*, 931: 359–75.

Soloff, P.H., Anselm, G., Nathan, R.S. et al. (1986) Paradoxical effect of amitriptyline on borderline patients, *American Journal of Psychiatry*, 143: 1603–5.

Soloff, P.H., Cornelius, J.R., George, A. et al. (1993) Efficacy of phenelzine and haloperidol in borderline personality disorder, *Archives of General Psychiatry*, 50: 377–85.

Solomon, R.L. (1980) The opponent-process theory of acquired motivation: the costs of pleasure and the benefits of pain, *American Psychologist*, 35: 691–712.

Sotgiu, S., Pugliatti, M., Fois, M.L. et al. (2004) Genes, environment, and susceptibility to multiple sclerosis, *Neurobiology of Disease*, 17: 131–43.

Spanos, N.P. (1994) Multiple identity enactments and multiple personality disorder: a socio-cognitive perspective, *Psychological Bulletin*, 116: 143–65.

Spanos, N.P., Weekes, J.R. and Bertrand, L.D. (1985) Multiple personality: a social psychological perspective, *Journal of Abnormal Psychology*, 94: 362–76.

Sparks, D.L., Sabbagh, M.N., Connor, D.J. et al. (2005) Atorvastatin for the treatment of mild to moderate Alzheimer disease: preliminary results, *Archives of Neurology*, 62: 753–7.

Spencer, T., Heiligenstein, J.H., Biederman, J. et al. (2002) Results from 2 proof-of-concept, placebo-controlled studies of atomoxetine in children with attention-deficit/hyperactivity disorder, *Journal of Clinical Psychiatry*, 63: 1140–7.

Spector, A, Thorgrimsen, L, Woods, B. et al. (2003) Efficacy of an evidence-based cognitive stimulation therapy programme for people with dementia: randomised controlled trial, *British Journal of Psychiatry*, 83: 248–54.

Spiegel, D. (1993) Multiple post-traumatic personality disorder, in R.P. Kluft and C.G. Fine (eds) *Clinical Perspectives on Multiple Personality Disorder*. Washington, DC: American Psychiatric Press.

Spiegel, D. (1999) Commentary: deconstructing self-destruction, *Psychiatry*, 62: 329–30.

Spiegel, D.A. and Barlow, D.H. (2000) Generalized anxiety disorders, in M.G. Gelder, J.J. López-Ibor Jr. and N.C. Andreasen (eds) *New Oxford Textbook of Psychiatry*. Oxford: Oxford University Press.

Spiegel, D.A., Bruce, T.J., Gregg, S.F. et al. (1994) Does cognitive behaviour therapy assist slow-taper alprazolam discontinuation in panic disorder?, *American Journal of Psychiatry*, 151: 876–81.

Squire, L.R. and Slater, P.C. (1983) Electroconvulsive therapy and complaints of memory dysfunction: a prospective three-year follow-up, *British Journal of Psychiatry*, 142: 1–8.

Squires-Wheeler, E., Friedman, D., Skodol, A.E. and Erlenmeyer-Kimling, L. (1993) A longitudinal study relating P3 amplitude to schizophrenia spectrum disorders and to global personality functioning, *Biological Psychiatry*, 33: 774–85.

Stahl, S.M., Grady, M.M. et al. (2005) SNRIs: their pharmacology, clinical efficacy, and tolerability in comparison with other classes of antidepressants, *CNS Spectrum*, 10: 732–47.

Stanton, M.D. and Shadish, W.R. (1997) Outcome, attrition, and family-couples treatment for drug abuse: a meta-analysis and review of the controlled, comparative studies, *Psychological Bulletin*, 122: 170–91.

Startup, M., Jackson, M.C., Evans, K.E. and Bendix, S. (2005) North Wales randomized controlled trial of cognitive behaviour therapy for acute schizophrenia spectrum disorders: two-year follow-up and economic evaluation, *Psychological Medicine*, 35: 1307–16.

Steege, M.W., Wacker, D.P., Cigrand, K.C. et al. (1990) Use of negative reinforcement in the treatment of self-injurious behavior, *Journal of Applied Behavior Analysis*, 23: 459–67.

Steiger, H., Gauvin, L., Engelberg, M.J. et al. (2005) Mood- and restraint-based antecedents to binge episodes in bulimia nervosa: possible influences of the serotonin system, *Psychological Medicine*, 35: 1553–62.

Stein, D.J., Zungu-Dirwayi, N., Van der Linden, G.J.H. et al. (2002) Pharmacotherapy for Posttraumatic Stress Disorder, *Cochrane Database of Systematic Reviews*, Issue 1.

Stein, K.F. and Corte, C. (2003) Reconceptualizing causative factors and intervention strategies in the eating disorders: a shift from body image to self-concept impairments, *Archives of Psychiatric Nursing*, 17: 57–66.

Steinberg, M., Cichetti, D., Buchanan, J. et al. (1993) Clinical assessment of dissociative symptoms and disorders: the Structured Clinical Interview for DSM-III dissociative disorders (SCID-D), *Dissociation*, 6: 3–15.

Steiner, H., Smith, C., Rosenkranz, R.T. et al. (1991) The early care and feeding of anorexics, *Child Psychiatry and Human Development*, 21: 163–7.

Steinhausen, H.C. and Glanville, K. (1983) Follow-up studies of anorexia nervosa: a review of research findings, *Psychological Medicine*, 13: 239–49.

Stella, L., D'Ambra, C., Mazzeo, F. et al. (2005) Naltrexone plus benzodiazepine aids abstinence in opioid-dependent patients, *Life Sciences*, 77: 2717–22.

Steptoe, A. and Noll, A. (1997) The perception of bodily sensations, with special reference to hypochondriasis, *Behaviour Research and Therapy*, 35: 901–10.

Sterling, R.C., Gottheil, E., Weinstein, S.P. et al. (2001) The effect of therapist/patient race- and sex-matching in individual treatment, *Addiction*, 96: 1015–22.

Stewart, R.M. and Brown, R.I. (1988) An outcome study of Gamblers Anonymous, *British Journal of Psychiatry*, 152: 284–8.

Stewart, S.M., Kennard, B.D., Lee, P.W. et al. (2005) Hopelessness and suicidal ideation among adolescents in two cultures, *Journal of Child Psychology and Psychiatry*, 46: 364–72.

Stockwell, T. (2004) Australian alcohol policy and the public interest: a brief report card, *Drug and Alcohol Review*, 23: 377–9.

Stoller, R.J. (1968) *Sex and Gender*. Vol. 1. *The Development of Masculinity and Femininity*. New York: Jason Aronson.

Strang, J., Sheridan, J., Hunt, C. et al. (2005) The prescribing of methadone and other opioids to addicts: national survey of GPs in England and Wales, *British Journal of General Practice*, 55: 444–51.

Strange, P.G. (1992) *Brain Biochemistry and Brain Disorders*. New York: Oxford University Press.

Strickland, B.R. (1992) Women and depression, *Current Directions in Psychological Science*, 1: 132–5.

Striegal-Moore, R.H. and Smolak, L. (2000) The influence of ethnicity on eating disorders in women, in R.M. Esler and M. Hersen (eds) *Handbook of Gender, Culture, and Health*. Mahwah, NJ: Erlbaum.

Struewing, J.P. and Gray, G.C. (1990) An epidemic of respiratory complaints exacerbated by mass psychogenic illness in a military recruit population, *American Journal of Epidemiology*, 132: 1120–9.

Stuart, S. and Noyes, R. (1999) Attachment and interpersonal communication in somatization, *Psychosomatics*, 40: 34–43.

Sukhodolsky, D.G. and Ruchkin, V.V. (2004) Association of normative beliefs and anger with aggression and antisocial behavior in Russian male juvenile offenders and high school students, *Journal of Abnormal Child Psychology*, 32: 225–36.

Sullivan, H.S. (1953) *The Interpersonal Theory of Psychiatry*. New York: Norton.

Sumaya, I., Rienzi, B.M., Deegan II, J.F. et al. (2001) Bright light treatment decreases depression in institutionalized older adults: a placebo-controlled crossover study, *Journal of Gerontology*, 56A: M356–M360.

Sundet, J.M., Skre, I., Okkenhaug, J.J. et al. (2003) Genetic and environmental causes of the interrelationships between self-reported fears: a study of a non-clinical sample of Norwegian identical twins and their families, *Scandinavian Journal of Psychology*, 44: 97–106.

Suppes, T., Baldessarini, R.J., Faedda, G.L. et al. (1991) Risk of recurrence following discontinuation of lithium treatment in bipolar disorder, *Archives of General Psychiatry*, 48: 1082–8.

Surtees, P.G., Wainwright, N.W., Willis-Owen, S.A. et al. (2006) Social adversity, the serotonin transporter (5-HTTLPR) polymorphism and major depressive disorder, *Biological Psychiatry*, 58: 451–6.

Sutherland, I. and Wilner, P. (1998) Patterns of alcohol, cigarette and illicit drug use in English adolescents, *Addiction*, 93: 1199–208.

Svartberg, M., Stiles, T.C. and Seltzer, M.H. (2004) Randomized, controlled trial of the effectiveness of short-term dynamic psychotherapy and cognitive therapy for cluster C personality disorders, *American Journal of Psychiatry*, 161: 810–17.

Swanson, M.C., Bland, R.C. and Newman, S.C. (1994) Antisocial personality disorders, *Acta Psychiatrica Scandinavica*, Suppl. 37: 63–70.

Swift, W., Maher, L. and Sunjic, S. (1999) Transitions between routes of heroin administration: a study of Caucasian and Indochinese heroin users in south-western Sydney, Australia, *Addiction*, 94: 71–82.

Szasz, T.S. (1971) From the slaughterhouse to the madhouse, *Psychotherapy Theory Research and Practice*, 8: 64–7.

Takei, N., Van Os, J. and Murray, R.M. (1995) Maternal exposure to influenza and risk of schizophrenia: a 22-year study from the Netherlands, *Journal of Psychiatric Research*, 29: 435–45.

Tallmadge, J. and Barkley, R.A. (1983) The interactions of hyperactive and normal boys with their fathers and mothers, *Journal of Abnormal Child Psychology*, 11: 565–79.

Tamam, L. and Ozpoyraz, N. (2002) Selective serotonin reuptake inhibitor discontinuation syndrome: a review, *Advances in Therapy*, 19: 17–26.

Tan, E., Marks, I.M. and Marset, P. (1971) Bimedial leucotomy in obsessive compulsive neurosis: a controlled serial inquiry, *British Journal of Psychiatry*, 118: 155–64.

Tandon, R. and Fleischhacker, W.W. (2005) Comparative efficacy of antipsychotics in the treatment of schizophrenia: a critical assessment, *Schizophrenia Research*, 79: 145–55.

Tang, T.Z. and DeRubeis, R. (1999) Sudden gains and critical sessions in cognitive–behavioral therapy for depression, *Journal of Consulting and Clinical Psychology*, 67: 1–11.

Tarrier, N., Kinney, C., McCarthy, E. et al. (2000) Two-year follow-up of cognitive–behavioral therapy and supportive counseling in the treatment of persistent symptoms in chronic schizophrenia, *Journal of Consulting and Clinical Psychology*, 68: 917–22.

Taylor, A., Goldberg, D., Hutchinson, S. et al. (2001) High risk injecting behaviour among injectors from Glasgow: cross-sectional community-wide surveys 1990–1999, *Journal of Epidemiology and Community Health*, 55: 766–7.

Taylor, B., Miller, E., Farringdon, C.P. et al. (1999) MMR vaccine and autism: no epidemiological evidence of a causal association, *Lancet*, 353: 2026–9.

Taylor, S., Thordarson, D.S., Maxfield, L. et al. (2003) Comparative efficacy, speed, and adverse effects of three PTSD treatments: exposure therapy, EMDR, and relaxation training, *Journal of Consulting and Clinical Psychology*, 71: 330–8.

Teasdale, J.D. (1993) Emotion and two kinds of meaning: cognitive therapy and applied cognitive science, *Behaviour Research and Therapy*, 31: 339–54.

Teasdale, W. and Engberg, A.W. (2001) Suicide after traumatic brain injury: a population study, *Journal of Neurology, Neurosurgery and Psychiatry*, 71: 436–40.

Telch, M.J., Jacquin, K., Smits, J.A. et al. (2003) Emotional responding to hyperventilation as a predictor of agoraphobia status among individuals suffering from panic disorder, *Journal of Behavior Therapy and Experimental Psychiatry*, 34: 161–70.

Terman, M. (1988) On the question of mechanism in phototherapy for seasonal affective disorder: considerations of clinical efficacy and epidemiology, *Journal of Biological Rhythms*, 3: 155–72.

Terman, M., Terman, J.S., Quitkin, F.M. et al. (1989) Light therapy for seasonal affective disorder: a review of efficacy, *Neuropsychopharmacology*, 2: 1–22.

Terr, L.C. (1991) *Unchained Memories*. New York: Basic Books.

Thapar, A., O'Donovan, M. and Owen, M.J. (2005) The genetics of attention deficit hyperactivity disorder, *Human Molecular Genetics*, 14 (Suppl. 2): R275–82.

Tharyan, P. (2002) Electroconvulsive therapy for schizophrenia, *Cochrane Database of Systematic Reviews*, Issue 1.

Tharyan, P. and Adams, C.E. (2005) Electroconvulsive therapy for schizophrenia, *Cochrane Database of Systematic Reviews*, Issue 2.

Thase, M.E. (2005) Bipolar depression: issues in diagnosis and treatment, *Harvard Review of Psychiatry*, 13: 257–71.

Thompson, C., Raheja, S.K. and King, E.A. (1995) A follow-up study of seasonal affective disorder, *British Journal of Psychiatry*, 167: 380–4.

Tienari, P., Wynne, L.C., Moring, J. et al. (2000) Finnish adoptive family study: sample selection and adoptee DSM-III-R diagnoses, *Acta Psychiatrica Scandinavica*, 101: 433–43.

Timko, C., Moos, R.H., Finney, J.W. et al. (2000) Long-term outcomes of alcohol use disorders: comparing untreated individuals with those in Alcoholics Anonymous and formal treatment, *Journal of Studies in Alcohol*, 61: 529–40.

Toneatto, T. (1999) Metacognition and substance use, *Addictive Behaviors*, 24: 167–74.

Toneatto, T. and Ladouceur, R. (2003) Treatment of pathological gambling: a critical review of the literature, *Psychology of Addictive Behavior*, 17: 284–92.

Torgersen, S. (1983) Genetic factors in anxiety disorders, *Archives of General Psychiatry*, 40: 1085–90.

Torgersen, S., Kringlen, E. and Cramer, V. (2001) The prevalence of personality disorders in a community sample, *Archives of General Psychiatry*, 58: 590–6.

Torgersen, S., Lygren, S., Oien, P.A. et al. (2000) A twin study of personality disorders, *Comprehensive Psychiatry*, 41: 416–25.

Torrey, E.F., Miller, J., Rawlings, R. et al. (1997) Seasonality of births in schizophrenia and bipolar disorders: a review of the literature, *Schizophrenia Research*, 28: 1–38.

Touchette, P.E., McDonald, R.F. and Langer, S.N. (1985) A scatter plot for identifying stimulus control of problem behavior, *Journal of Applied Behavior Analysis*, 18: 343–51.

Treasure, J., Todd, G., Brolly, M. et al. (1995) A pilot study of a randomised trial of cognitive analytical therapy vs educational behavioural therapy for adult anorexia nervosa, *Behaviour Research and Therapy*, 33: 363–7.

Treasure, T. (2001) *The Mental Health Act and Eating Disorders*. Institute of Psychiatry, Division of Psychological Medicine, Eating Disorders Research Unit. (www.iop.kcl.ac.uk)

Tremlett, H.L., Luscombe, D.K. and Wiles, C.M. et al. (2001) Prescribing for multiple sclerosis patients in general practice: a case-control study, *Journal of Clinical Pharmacy and Therapeutics*, 26: 437–44.

Troisi, A., Massaroni, P. and Cuzzolaro, M. (2005) Early separation anxiety and adult attachment style in women with eating disorders, *British Journal of Clinical Psychology*, 44: 89–97.

Truax, C.B. (1966) Reinforcement and nonreinforcement in Rogerian psychotherapy, *Journal of Abnormal Psychology*, 71: 1–9.

Trull, T.J. (2005) A dimensional view challenging DSM, *Journal of Personality Disorders*, 19: 262–82.

Tsai, Y.F., Yeh, S.H. and Tsai, H.H. (2005) Prevalence and risk factors for depressive symptoms among community-dwelling elders in Taiwan, *International Journal of Geriatric Psychiatry*, 20: 1097–102.

Tsuang, M.T. (2000) Schizophrenia: genes and environment, *Biological Psychiatry*, 47: 210–20.

Tsuang, M.T., Simpson, S.J.C. and Fleming, J.A. (1986) Diagnostic criteria for subtyping schizoaffective disorder, in A. Marneros and M.T. Tsuang (eds) *Schizoaffective Disorder*. Berlin: Springer-Verlag.

Tucker, T.K. and Ritter, A. (2000) Naltrexone in the treatment of heroin dependence: a literature review, *Drug and Alcohol Review*, 19: 73–82.

Turner, R.J., Lloyd, D.A. and Roszell, P. (1999) Personal resources and the social distribution of depression, *American Journal of Community Psychology*, 27: 643–72.

Turner, R.M. (1989) Case study evaluations of a bio-cognitive-behavioral approach for the treatment of borderline personality disorder, *Behavior Therapy*, 20: 477–89.

Tyrer, P. (2002) Practice guideline for the treatment of borderline personality disorder: a bridge too far, *Journal of Personality Disorders*, 16: 113–18.

Tyrer, P., Seivewright, N., Ferguson, B., Murphy, S. and Johnson, A.L. (1993) The Nottingham study of neurotic disorder: effect of personality status on response to drug treatment, cognitive therapy and self-help over two years, *British Journal of Psychiatry*, 162: 219–26.

Ueshima, H. (2005) Do the Japanese drink less alcohol than other peoples? The finding from INTERMAP, *Nihon Arukoru Yakubutsu Igakkai Zasshi*, 40: 27–33.

Uhlmann, V., Martin, C.M., Sheils, O. et al. (2001) Potential viral pathogenic mechanism for new variant inflammatory bowel disease, *Journal of Clinical Pathology: Molecular Pathology*, 55: 1–6.

Ulbrich, P.M., Warheit, G.J. and Zimmerman, R.S. (1989) Race, socio-economic status, and psychological distress: an examination of differential vulnerability, *Journal of Health and Social Behavior*, 30: 131–46.

Ullrich, S., Borkenau, P. and Marneros, A. (2001) Personality disorders in offenders: categorical versus dimensional approaches, *Journal of Personality Disorders*, 15: 442–9.

US Department of Health and Human Services (1999) *Mental Health: A Report of the Surgeon General. Mental Health: Culture, Race, Ethnicity – Supplement*. Washington, DC: Office of the Surgeon General, SAMHSA.

Van den Bosch, L.M., Koeter, M.W., Stijnen, T. et al. (2005) Sustained efficacy of dialectical behaviour therapy for borderline personality disorder, *Behaviour Research and Therapy*, 43: 1231–41.

Van der Sande, R., Buskens, E., Allart, E. et al. (1997) Psychosocial intervention following suicide attempt: a systematic review of treatment interventions, *Acta Psychiatrica Scandinavica*, 96: 43–50.

Van Elst, L.T., Hesslinger, B. Thiel, T. et al. (2003) Frontolimbic brain abnormalities in patients with borderline personality disorder: a volumetric MRI study, *Biological Psychiatry*, 54: 163–71.

Van Goozen, S.H.M., Cohen-Kettenis, P.T., Gooren, L.J.G. et al. (1995) Gender differences in behaviour: activating effects of cross-sex hormones, *Psychoneuroendocrinology*, 20: 343–63.

Van Oppen, P., de Haan, E., Van Balkom, A.J. et al. (1995) Cognitive therapy and exposure in vivo in the treatment of obsessive-compulsive disorder, *Behaviour Research and Therapy*, 33: 379–90.

Van Os, J. and Selten, J.P. (1998) Prenatal exposure to maternal stress and subsequent schizophrenia: the May 1940 invasion of The Netherlands, *British Journal of Psychiatry*, 172: 324–6.

Van Trotsenburg, A.S., Vulsma, T. et al. (2005) The effect of thyroxine treatment started in the neonatal period on development and growth of two-year-old Down syndrome children: a randomized clinical trial,. *Journal of Clinical Endocrinology and Metabolism*, 90: 3304–11.

Vaughn, C.E. and Leff, J.P. (1976) The influence of family and social factors on the course of psychiatric patients, *British Journal of Psychiatry*, 129: 125–37.

Veale, D., Gournay, K., Dryden, W., Boocock, A., Shah, F., Wilson, R. and Walburn, J. (1996) Body dysmorphic disorder: a cognitive behavioural model and pilot randomised controlled trial, *Behaviour Research and Therapy*, 9: 717–29.

Vernberg, E.M., Jacobs, A.K. and Hershberger, S.L. (1999) Peer victimization and attitudes about violence during early adolescence, *Journal of Clinical Child Psychology*, 28: 386–95.

Viken, R.J., Treat, T.A., Nosofsky, R.M. et al. (2002) Modeling individual differences in perceptual and attentional processes related to bulimic symptoms, *Journal of Abnormal Psychology*, 111: 598–609.

Visschedijk, M.A., Collette, E.H. and Polman, C.H. (2004) Development of a cognitive behavioral group intervention programme for patients with multiple sclerosis: an exploratory study, *Psychological Reports*, 95: 735–46.

Vitaro, F., Arseneault, L. and Tremblay, R.E. (1999) Impulsivity predicts problem gambling in low SES adolescent males, *Addiction*, 94: 565–75.

Wagenaar, A.C., Zobeck, T.S., Williams, G.D. et al. (1995) Methods used in studies of drink-drive control efforts: a meta-analysis of the literature from 1960 to 1991, *Accident Analysis Review*, 27: 307–16.

Wahlberg, K-E., Jackson, D., Haley, H. et al. (2000a) Gene environment interaction in vulnerability to schizophrenia: findings from the Finnish Adoptive Family Study of Schizophrenia, *American Journal of Psychiatry*, 154: 355–62.

Wahlberg, K.E., Wynne, L.C., Oja, H. et al. (2000b) Thought disorder index of Finnish adoptees and communication deviance of their adoptive parents, *Psychological Medicine*, 30: 127–36.

Wagner, A., Greer, P., Bailer, U.F. et al. (2006) Normal brain tissue volumes after long-term recovery in anorexia and bulimia nervosa, *Biological Psychiatry*, 59: 291–3.

Wakefield, A.J., Murch, S.H., Anthony, A. et al. (1998) Ileal-lymphoid-nodular hyperplasia, non-specific colitis, and pervasive developmental disorder in children, *Lancet*, 351: 637–41.

Wald, J., Taylor, S. and Scamvougeras, A. (2004) Cognitive behavioural and neuropsychiatric treatment of post-traumatic conversion disorder: a case study, *Cognitive and Behavior Therapy*, 33: 12–20.

Waldron, H.B., Miller, W.R., and Tonigan, J.S. (2001) Client anger as a predictor of differential response to treatment, in R. Longabaugh and P.W. Wirtz (eds) *Project MATCH Hypotheses: Results and Causal Chain Analyses*. Project MATCH Monograph Series, Vol. 8. Bethesda, MD: National Institute on Alcohol Abuse and Alcoholism.

Walker, E.F. and Diforio, D. (1997) Schizophrenia: a neural diathesis-stress model, *Psychological Review*, 4: 667–85.

Walsh, B.T., Agras, W.S., Devlin, M.J. et al. (2000) Fluoxetine for bulimia nervosa following poor response to psychotherapy, *American Journal of Psychiatry*, 157: 1332–4.

Walsh, B.T., Fairburn, C.G., Mickley, D. et al. (2004) Treatment of bulimia nervosa in a primary care setting, *American Journal of Psychiatry*, 161: 556–61.

Walshe, D.G., Lewis, E.J., Kim, S.I. et al. (2003) Exploring the use of computer games and virtual reality in exposure therapy for fear of driving following a motor vehicle accident, *Cyberpsychology and Behavior*, 6: 329–34.

Walters, E.E. and Kendler, K.S. (1995) Anorexia nervosa and anorexic-like syndromes in a population-based female twin sample, *American Journal of Psychiatry*, 152: 64–71.

Ward, A., Ramsay, R., Turnbull, S. et al. (2001) Attachment in anorexia nervosa: a transgenerational perspective, *British Journal of Medical Psychology*, 74: 497–505.

Ward, E. and Ogden, J. (1994) Experiencing vaginismus: sufferers' beliefs about causes and effects, *Sexual and Marital Therapy*, 9: 33–45.

Ward, T., Hudson, S.M. and Marshall, W.L. (1996) Attachment style in sex offenders: a preliminary study, *Journal of Sex Research*, 33: 17–26.

Wardle, J. and Marsland, L. (1990) Adolescent concerns about weight and eating: a social-developmental perspective, *Journal of Psychosomatic Research*, 34: 377–91.

Warman, D.M., Grant, P., Sullivan, K. et al. (2005) Individual and group cognitive-behavioral therapy for psychotic disorders: a pilot investigation, *Journal of Psychiatric Practice*, 11: 27–34.

Warwick, H.M. and Salkovskis, P.M. (1990) Hypochondriasis, *Behaviour Research and Therapy*, 28: 105–17.

Warwick Daw, E., Payami, H., Nemens, E.J. et al. (2000) The number of trait loci in late-onset Alzheimer disease, *American Journal of Human Genetics*, 66: 196–204.

Watson, D. and Pennebaker, J.W. (1989) Health complaints, stress, and distress: exploring the central role of negative affectivity, *Psychological Review*, 96: 234–54.

Watson, J.B. and Rayner, R. (1920) Conditioned emotional reaction, *Journal of Experimental Psychology*, 3: 1–14.

Watzlawick, P., Weakland, J.H. and Fisch, R. (1974) *Change: Principles of Problem Formulation and Problem Resolution*. New York: W.W. Norton.

Weich, S., Sloggett, A. and Lewis, G. (1998) Social roles and gender difference in the prevalence of common mental disorders, *British Journal of Psychiatry*, 173: 489–93.

Weiner, H.L., Lemere, C.A., Maron, R. et al. (2000) Nasal administration of amyloid-beta peptide decreases cerebral amyloid burden in a mouse model of Alzheimer's disease, *Annals of Neurology*, 48: 567–79.

Wells, A. (1995) Meta-cognition and worry: a cognitive model of generalized anxiety disorder, *Behavioural and Cognitive Psychotherapy*, 23: 301–20.

Wells, A. (2000) *Emotional Disorders and Metacognition: Innovative Cognitive Therapy*. Chichester: Wiley.

Wells, A. and Sembi, S. (2004) Metacognitive therapy for PTSD: a preliminary investigation of a new brief treatment, *Journal of Behavior Therapy*, 35: 307–18.

Weltzin, T.E., Fernstrom, M.H., Fernstrom. J.D. et al. (1995) Acute tryptophan depletion and increased food intake and irritability in bulimia nervosa, *American Journal of Psychiatry*, 152: 1668–71.

Wender, P.H., Kety, S.S., Rosenthal, D. et al. (1986) Psychiatric disorders in the biological and adoptive families of adopted individuals with affective disorders, *Archives of General Psychiatry*, 43: 923–9.

Wender, P.H., Wolf, L.E. and Wasserstein, J. (2001) Adults with ADHD: an overview, *Annals of the New York Academy of Science*, 931: 1–16.

Wessels, C., Van Kradenberg, J., Mbanga, I. et al. (1999) Television as a medium for psycho-education in South Africa: analysis of calls to a mental health information centre after screening of a TV series on psychiatric disorders, *Central African Journal of Medicine*, 45: 1–3.

Wessex Institute for Health Research and Development (WIHRD) (1998) *Surgical Gender Reassignment for Male to Female Transsexual People*, Development and Evaluation Committee Report. Southampton: WIHRD.

Westra, H.A. and Stewart, S.H. (1998) Cognitive behavioural therapy and pharmacotherapy: complementary or contradictory approaches to the treatment of anxiety?, *Clinical Psychology Review*, 18: 307–40.

Whalen, C.K., Henker, B. and Hinshaw, S.P. (1985) Cognitive-behavioral therapies for hyperactive children: premises, problems, and prospects, *Journal of Abnormal Child Psychology*, 13: 391–409.

Whitaker-Azmitia, P.M. (2005) Behavioral and cellular consequences of increasing serotonergic activity during brain development: a role in autism?, *International Journal of Developmental Neuroscience*, 23: 75–83.

Whitehouse, P.J., Struble, R.G., Clark, A.W. et al. (1982) Alzheimer disease: plagues, tangles, and the basal forebrain, *Annals of Neurology*, 12: 494.

Whitfield, J.B. (2005) Alcohol and gene interactions, *Clinical Chemistry and Laboratory Medicine*, 43: 480–7.

Whittal, M.L. and Zaretsky, A. (1996) Cognitive-behavioral strategies for the treatment of eating disorders, in M.H. Pollack, M.W. Otto and J.F. Rosenbaum (eds) *Challenges in Clinical Practice: Pharmacologic and Psychosocial Strategies*. New York: Guilford.

Wicki, W., Angst, J. and Merikangas, K.R. (1992) The Zurich Study, XIV: epidemiology of seasonal depression, *European Archives of Psychiatry and Clinical Neuroscience*, 241: 301–6.

Widiger, T.A. and Corbitt, E.M. (1995) Antisocial personality disorder, in W.J. Livesley (ed.) *The DSM-IV Personality Disorders: Diagnosis and Treatment of Mental Disorders*. New York: Guilford.

Widiger, T.A. and Costa, P.T. Jr (1994) Personality and personality disorders, *Journal of Abnormal Psychology*, 95: 43–51.

Widiger, T.A., Frances, A. and Trull, T.J. (1987) A psychometric analysis of the social interpersonal and cognitive perceptual items for the schizotypal personality disorder, *Archives of General Psychiatry*, 44: 786–95.

Wiersma, D., Nienhuis, F.J., Slooff, C.J. et al. (1998) Natural course of schizophrenic disorders: a 15-year following of a Dutch incidence cohort, *Schizophrenia Bulletin*, 24: 75–85.

Wileman, S.M., Eagles, J.M., Andrew, J.E. et al. (2001) Light therapy for seasonal affective disorder in primary care, *British Journal of Psychiatry*, 178: 311–16.

Wilhelm, K., Boyce, P. and Brownhill, S. (2004) The relationship between interpersonal sensitivity, anxiety disorders and major depression, *Journal of Affective Disorders*, 79: 33–41.

Wilk, A.I., Jensen, N.M. and Havighurst, T.C. (1997) Meta-analysis of randomized control trials addressing brief interventions in heavy alcohol drinkers, *Journal of General Internal Medicine*, 12: 274–83.

Wilkinson, M. (1992) Income distribution and life expectancy, *British Medical Journal*, 304. 165–8.

Willemsen-Swinkels, S.H., Buitlaar, J.K., Nijhof, G.J. et al. (1995) Failure of naltrexone hydrochloride to reduce self-injurious and autistic behavior in mentally retarded adults: double-blind placebo-controlled studies, *Archives of General Psychiatry*, 52: 766–73.

Williams, D.R. (1999) Race, socioeconomic status, and health: the added effects of racism and discrimination, *Annals of the New York Academy of Science*, 896: 173–88.

Williams, G-J., Power, K.G., Millar, H.R. et al. (1993) Comparison of eating disorders and other dietary/weight groups on measures of perceived control, assertiveness, self-esteem, and self-directed hostility, *International Journal of Eating Disorders*, 4: 7–32.

Wilsnack, S.C., Wonderlich, S.A., Kristjanson, A.F., et al. (2002) Self-reports of forgetting and remembering childhood sexual abuse in a nationally representative sample of US women, *Child Abuse and Neglect*, 26: 139–47.

Wilson, B. (1989) Models of cognitive rehabilitation, in R.L. Wood and P.G. Eames (eds) *Models of Brain Injury Rehabilitation*. Baltimore, MD: Johns Hopkins University Press.

Wilson, B.A., Emslie, H.C., Quirk, K. et al. (2001) Reducing everyday memory and planning problems by means of a paging system: a randomised control crossover study, *Journal of Neurology, Neurosurgery and Psychiatry*, 70: 477–82.

Wilson, G.T. (1988) Alcohol use and abuse: a social learning analysis, in C.D. Chaudron and D.A. Wilkinson (eds) *Theories on Alcoholism*. Toronto: Addiction Research Foundation.

Wilson, G.T. (1996) Treatment of bulimia nervosa: when CBT fails, *Behaviour Research and Therapy*, 34: 197–212.

Winters, K.C. and Neale, J.M. (1985) Mania and low self-esteem, *Journal of Abnormal Psychology*, 94: 282–90.

Wiser, S. and Goldfried, M.R. (1998) Therapist interventions and client emotional experiencing in expert psychodynamic-interpersonal and cognitive-behavioral therapies, *Journal of Consulting and Clinical Psychology*, 66: 634–40.

Wittchen, H.U. and Essau, C.A. (1993) Epidemiology of panic disorder: progress and unresolved issues, *Journal of Psychiatric Research*, 27 (Suppl. 1): 47–68.

Wolfensberger, W. (1972) *The Principle of Normalization in Human Services*. Toronto: National Institutes of Mental Retardation.

Wolfensberger, W. (1983) Social role valorization: a proposed new term for the principle of normalization, *Mental Retardation*, 21: 234–9.

Wolfersdorf, M. (1995) Depression and suicidal behaviour: psychopathological differences between suicidal and non-suicidal depressive patients, *Archives of Suicide Research*, 1: 273–88.

Wolpe, J. (1982) *The Practice of Behavior Therapy*, 3rd edn. New York: Pergamon.

Wong, S. and Hare, R.D. (2002) *Program Guidelines for the Institutional Treatment of Violent Psychopathic Offenders*. Toronto: Multi-Health Systems.

Wood, S.J., Yucel, M., Velakoulis, D., Phillips, L.J., Yung, A.R., Brewer, W., McGorry P.D. and Pantelis C. (2005) Hippocampal and anterior cingulate morphology in subjects at ultra-high-risk for psychosis: the role of family history of psychotic illness, *Schizophrenia Research*, 75: 295–301.

Woods, R. and Bird, M. (1999) Non-pharmacological approaches to treatment, in G.K. Wilcock, R.S. Bucks and K. Rockwood (eds) *Diagnosis and Management of Dementia: A Manual for Memory Disorders Teams*. Oxford: Oxford University Press.

Woods, R. and Roth, A. (1996) Effectiveness of psychological therapy with older people, in A. Roth and P. Fonagy, *What Works for Whom? A Critical Review of Psychotherapy Research*. New York: Guilford.

Woody, G.E., Luborsky, L., McLellan, A.T. et al. (1983) Psychotherapy for opiate addicts. Does it help?, *Archives of General Psychiatry*, 40: 639–45.

World Health Organization (1979) *Schizophrenia: An International Follow-up Study*. Chichester: Wiley.

World Health Organization (WHO) (1992) *Tenth Revision of the International Classification of Diseases*. Geneva: WHO.

World Health Organization (WHO) (1996) *Ottawa Charter for Health Promotion*. Geneva: WHO.

Wurtman, R.J. and Wurtman, J.J. (1986) Carbohydrate craving, obesity, and brain serotonin, *Appetite*, 7 (Suppl.): 99–103.

Xu, K., Lichtermann, D., Lipsky, R.H. et al. (2004) Association of specific haplotypes of D2 dopamine receptor gene with vulnerability to heroin dependence in 2 distinct populations, *Archives of General Psychiatry*, 61: 597–606.

Yale, R. (1995) *Developing Support Groups for Individuals with Early Stage Alzheimer's Disease: Planning, Implementation and Evaluation*. Baltimore, MD: Health Profession Press.

Yalom, I.D., Green, R. and Fisk, N. (1973) Prenatal exposure to female hormones: effect on psychosocial development in boys, *Archives of General Psychiatry*, 28: 554–61.

Yang, C.F., Gray, P. and Pope, H.G. Jr. (2005) Male body image in Taiwan versus the West: Yanggang Zhiqi meets the Adonis complex, *American Journal of Psychiatry*, 162: 263–9.

Yang, L.H., Phillips M.R., Licht D.M. et al. (2004) Causal attributions about schizophrenia in families in China: expressed emotion and patient relapse, *Journal of Abnormal Psychology*, 113: 592–602.

Yerevanian, B.I., Koek, R.J., Feusner, J.D. et al. (2004) Antidepressants and suicidal behaviour in unipolar depression, *Acta Psychiatrica Scandinavica*, 110: 452–8.

Yoast, R., Williams, M.A., Deitchman, S.D. et al. (2001) Report of the Council on Scientific Affairs: methadone maintenance and needle-exchange programs to reduce the medical and public health consequences of drug abuse, *Journal of Addictive Diseases*, 20: 15–40.

Yonkers, K.A., Dyck, I.R., Warshaw, M. et al. (2000) Factors predicting the clinical course of generalised anxiety disorder, *British Journal of Psychiatry*, 176: 544–9.

Young, J.E. (1999) *Cognitive Therapy for Personality Disorders: A Schema-Focused Approach.* Professional Resource Exchange Inc.

Young, J.E. and Lindemann, M.D. (1992) An integrative schema-focused model for personality disorders, *Journal of Cognitive Psychotherapy*, 6: 11–23.

Zanarini, M.C., Frankenburg, F.R., Hennen, J. et al. (2005) The McLean Study of Adult Development (MSAD): overview and implications of the first six years of prospective follow-up, *Journal of Personality Disorders*, 19: 505–23.

Zangen, A. and Hyodo, K. (2002) Transcranial magnetic stimulation induces increases in extracellular levels of dopamine and glutamate in the nucleus accumbens, *NeuroReport*, 13: 2401–5.

Zarros A.C., Kalopita K.S. and Tsakiris S.T. (2005) Serotoninergic impairment and aggressive behavior in Alzheimer's disease, *Acta Neurobiologiae Experimentalis*, 65: 277–86.

Zerbe, K.J. (2001) The crucial role of psychodynamic understanding in the treatment of eating disorders, *Psychiatric Clinics of North America*, 24: 305–13.

Zhou, J-N., Hofman, M.A. and Black, K. (1995) A sex difference in the human brain and its relation to transsexuality, *Nature*, 378: 68–70.

Zilbergeld, B. (1992) *The New Male Sexuality.* New York: Bantam.

Zimmerman, J. and Grosz, H.J. (1966) 'Visual' performance of a functionally blind person, *Behaviour Research and Therapy*, 4: 119–34.

Zimmerman, M. (1994) *Diagnosing Personality Disorders: A Review of the Scientific Evidence.* New York: The Lindemith Center.

Zola, S.M. (1998) Memory, amnesia, and the issue of recovered memory: neurobiological aspects, *Clinical Psychology Review*, 18: 915–32.

Zucker, K.J. and Bradley, S.J. (1995) *Gender Identity Disorder and Psychosexual Problems in Children and Adolescents.* New York: Guilford.

Zucker, K.J., Green, R., Garofano, C. et al. (1994) Prenatal gender preference of mothers of feminine and masculine boys: relation to sibling sex composition and birth order, *Journal of Abnormal Child Psychology*, 22: 1–13.

Zweig-Frank, H. and Paris, J. (2002) Predictors of outcome in a 27-year follow-up of patients with borderline personality disorder, *Comprehensive Psychiatry*, 43: 103–7.

Index

Sir, A., 71
Sirey, J.A., 78
situationally accessible memories (SAMs), 239, 240
Skinner, B.F., 36, 37
Skre, I., 182
Skrzypek, S., 327
Slade, P., 157, 327, 340
slow release (depot) injections, 78, 162
Smith, A.J., 361
Smith, B.L., 216
Smith, M.L., 59
Smith, T., 356
Smith, Y.L.S., 286
SNRIs, 70, 71, 212
Sobczak, S., 227
social causation, 93, 94, 152
social drift, 24, 93, 94, 152
social groups, 5, 86, 97, 108, 167, 230, 324, 397, 418
social interaction, 37, 52, 348, 349, 354, 356, 368, 375, 377, 389
social isolation, 94, 291, 350
social learning theory, 41, 42
social role valorization, 345, 368
social skills, 275, 284, 307, 312, 347, 365, 366, 401
social stress, 24, 95, 97, 100, 172, 186, 207
social support, 26, 94, 143, 162, 182, 207, 229, 236, 241, 242, 291, 298, 307, 313, 346, 401, 403
social workers, 8
socio-cultural, 3, 18, 23, 27, 128, 172, 207, 219, 230, 297, 306–7, 324, 325, 339, 397, 398, 405, 407, 424
socioeconomic, 23, 24, 26, 86, 93–97, 104, 108, 128, 152, 172, 173, 206, 225, 234, 319, 324, 343
Socratic method, 48
Sohlberg, M.M., 367, 382, 383
Soloff, P.H., 302
Solomon, R.L., 407
somatogenic approach, 6
somatization, 12, 138
somatization disorder, 113–119, 121, 138, 139
  aetiology, 116–118
  treatment, 119
somatize, 98, 115, 117, 118
somatoform disorder, 113–140

Sotgiu, S., 385
Spanos, N.P., 252–258, 261
Sparks, D.L., 375
special schools, 345, 346
spectating, 263, 286
Spector, A, 376
Spence, S.H., 245
Spencer, T., 363
Spiegel, D., 172, 193, 258, 259
splitting, 34, 197, 253, 297
Squire, L.R., 81
SSRIs (selective serotonin reuptake inhibitors), 67, 70, 71, 73, 74, 76, 78, 119, 123, 126, 130, 138, 139, 177, 186, 192, 193, 201, 212, 213, 223, 224, 245, 302, 315, 335, 339, 340, 355, 417
St John's wort, 213, 231
Stahl, S.M., 71
Startup, M., 166, 232
starvation, 318–320, 327, 330, 339
Steege, M.W., 349
Steiger, H., 323, 326
Stein, B.S., 382
Stein, D. J., 245
Stein, K.F., 325
Stein, M.B., 193
Steinberg, M., 254
Steiner, H., 328
Stella, L., 409
Steptoe, A., 122
stereotatic subcaudate cingulotomy, 82, 202
stereotypic behaviours, 355
Stewart, R.M., 416
Stewart, S.H., 193
Stewart, S.M., 217
Stoller, R.J., 279
Strang, J., 407
Strange, P.G., 76
strategic family therapy, *see* family therapy
stress inoculation training, 51
stress management, 106, 107, 124, 165–166
Strickland, B.R., 96
Striegal-Moore, R.H., 324
structural family therapy, 87, 88, 108, 333
Struewing, J.P., 133
Stuart, S., 121
subcaudate tractotomy, 82, 83, 202
sublimation, 32